Getting Started with Microsoft System Center Operations Manager

A beginner's guide to help you design, deploy and administer your System Center Operations Manager 2016 and 2012 R2 environments

Kevin Greene

[PACKT] enterprise
PUBLISHING
professional expertise distilled

BIRMINGHAM - MUMBAI

Getting Started with Microsoft System Center Operations Manager

First published: June 2016

Production reference: 1240616

Published by Packt Publishing Ltd.
Livery Place
35 Livery Street
Birmingham B3 2PB, UK.

ISBN 978-1-78528-974-3

www.packtpub.com

Credits

Author
Kevin Greene

Reviewers
Abhilash V Menon
Randall Smith
Sridhar Vishwanatham

Commissioning Editor
Amarabha Banerjee

Acquisition Editor
Vinay Argekar

Content Development Editor
Mamata Walkar

Technical Editor
Nirant Carvalho

Copy Editor
Sneha Singh

Project Coordinator
Kinjal Bari

Proofreader
Safis Editing

Indexer
Hemangini Bari

Graphics
Kirk D'Penha

Production Coordinator
Shantanu N. Zagade

Cover Work
Shantanu N. Zagade

About the Author

Kevin Greene is a Microsoft MVP in the Cloud and Datacenter Management space and has been working in the IT industry since 1999. He is employed as a Cloud Technologies Consultant at Ergo in Dublin, Ireland; in this role, he works with clients to deliver enterprise grade solutions using System Center, Windows Server, and Azure.

On the Microsoft certification track since the nostalgic days of Windows NT 4.0, he holds qualifications that include MCSE, MCSA, MCITP, MCP, and MCTS. Kevin is an active participant in the System Center and Cloud OS community through his blog at http://kevingreeneitblog.blogspot.com and he can also be found hanging around Twitter as @kgreeneit.

A regular speaker at local and international events, he has also co-authored a number of books including *Mastering System Center 2012 – Operations Manager* (Sybex, 2012) and *Mastering Windows Server 2012 R2* (Sybex, 2013).

Kevin lives in Sallins, Co. Kildare, Ireland with his wife, Laura, and his two sons, Matthew and Dylan. When he's not working on his laptop, he spends his free time with his family and supporting Manchester United. He also holds a second-degree black belt in freestyle kickboxing and although he is not as involved in the sport as he used to be, he's still an avid follower of the martial arts.

About the Reviewers

Abhilash V Menon was born in a beautiful village called Puthuvely in Kerala, India. From childhood, he was curious about everything came into his way. He was crazy about exploring them until he could solve the puzzle. One day, a desktop computer came into his way. He started exploring it as usual. He noticed that whenever he put a piece of puzzle in its place, there are hundreds of other new pieces popping up around him. He is still putting them together, every day, hoping one day he could design a piece by himself.

He wanted to become a programmer when he was doing his graduation, but when he saw the industry closely, that changed his mind.

He realized that spending entire life in doing programming in a certain language is not what he likes. He wanted to learn something new, and entirely different every day. So he elected Infrastructure Monitoring as his career, as there is a wide opportunity to learn both latest and oldest technologies every day.

He enjoys sharing knowledge a lot. He believes that hiding knowledge is a crime. He learns new things till late night and share them to his friends and colleagues in the day time.

He had worked on a number of leading infrastructure monitoring tools like Microsoft SCOM, BMC Proactive Net, CA Spectrum, HP OpenView and Nagios. Now he is a Senior SCOM Engineer and Management Pack Developer at Datacom New Zealand. He could literally monitor anything from the status of your server to the brightness of your bedroom lamp through SCOM! He introduced a term called SCOMification which he defines as "The process of discovering and monitoring a mission critical real world business scenario in Microsoft SCOM.

In such a way that it can be discovered automatically, monitored flexibly, notified to different technical towers, presented to different business level people in different format which make sense to them, and the data could be stored in data warehouse for historical analysis and business intelligence."

He recently started a blog for upcoming SCOMifiers, which is intended to help them SCOMify anything they want for FREE.

You can access the blog at `http://scomifyit.com`.

You can read more about him at `http://abhie.me` or contact him directly through his email `abhie@abhie.me`.

I would like to thank my beautiful wife, Asha Puthusseril and our little bundle of joy Advik Menon, for their endless motivation and support.

I would also like to thank my parents Viswanadhan and Usha, brother Akhilesh Menon, my uncle Biju and my mentor Ajish Kumar Sir, for making me like this.

Finally I would like to thank You for buying this book and making our effort worthy.

Randall Smith is a Sr. Systems Administrator for Adams State University. He has been administering Windows, Linux, and BSD systems since 1999.

Randall has been active in helping other SysAdmins solve problems and making their jobs easier though his blog, IRC, and social media. He has presented at the Colorado Higher Ed Computing Organization and Educause conferences, on topics such as Linux KVM, and the Ceph storage system.

www.PacktPub.com

eBooks, discount offers, and more

Did you know that Packt offers eBook versions of every book published, with PDF and ePub files available? You can upgrade to the eBook version at www.PacktPub.com and as a print book customer, you are entitled to a discount on the eBook copy. Get in touch with us at customercare@packtpub.com for more details.

At www.PacktPub.com, you can also read a collection of free technical articles, sign up for a range of free newsletters and receive exclusive discounts and offers on Packt books and eBooks.

https://www2.packtpub.com/books/subscription/packtlib

Do you need instant solutions to your IT questions? PacktLib is Packt's online digital book library. Here, you can search, access, and read Packt's entire library of books.

Why subscribe?

- Fully searchable across every book published by Packt
- Copy and paste, print, and bookmark content
- On demand and accessible via a web browser

Instant updates on new Packt books

Get notified! Find out when new books are published by following @PacktEnterprise on Twitter or the *Packt Enterprise* Facebook page.

Table of Contents

Preface

System Center Operations Manager (OpsMgr) is Microsoft's flagship solution for monitoring private, public, and hybrid cloud environments. Its a best-of-breed monitoring tool for Microsoft operating system and application workloads; it also has the ability to monitor datacenter hardware components, such as servers, network devices, SAN's, UPS's, and even air-conditioning units, along with a wide range of cross-platform UNIX and Linux operating systems.

Without a proper understanding of how all these monitoring capabilities can come together centrally within OpsMgr, you will find administering it becomes a complex challenge. The aim of this book is to address that challenge and break down the barriers of complexity to help you get up and running with your monitoring scenarios within a relatively short space of time.

What this book covers

Chapter 1, *Introduction to System Center Operations Manager*, aims to provide an overview of the System Center suite of datacenter management components, including an introduction to OpsMgr and its core features.

Chapter 2, *Installing System Center Operations Manager*, covers the design and deployment of your first OpsMgr management group.

Chapter 3, *Exploring the Consoles*, walks you through the various views and settings that can be found across the different workspaces in both the Operations console and the Web console.

Chapter 4, *Deploying Agents*, focuses on deploying and managing Windows agents in single or multiple management groups. This chapter also demonstrates how to deploy cross-platform agents to your UNIX/Linux computers.

Chapter 5, Working with Management Packs, includes an overview of what a management pack is, some tips on where to download them from as well as walk-through's to show you how to import, export, and manage them.

Chapter 6, Managing Network Devices, provides information about the out-of-box network monitoring capability of OpsMgr, which can use SNMP or ICMP communications to monitor your network devices.

Chapter 7, Configuring Service Models with Distributed Applications, takes an often under-utilized feature of OpsMgr and provides step-by-step information to help you create models of your IT services for maximum monitoring visibility.

Chapter 8, Alert Tuning the Easy Way, presents process-driven methods and real-world tips to ensure excessive alert noise is kept to a minimum and your alert views stay manageable.

Chapter 9, Visualizing Your IT with Dashboards, shows how to configure and populate built-in dashboard templates with the various widgets on offer as well as introducing you to some hidden dashboard treasures that will maximize the visibility of the IT services monitored within your organization.

Chapter 10, Creating Alert Subscriptions and Reports, covers the creation of alert notification channels, subscribers, and custom subscriptions. In this chapter, we also dive into the powerful reporting feature of OpsMgr to help you create and customize the type of reports that your senior-level IT managers and teams request on a regular basis.

Chapter 11, Backing Up, Maintenance and Troubleshooting, focuses on backing up and optimizing your OpsMgr environment. You will also discover how to work with Maintenance Mode, deploy update rollups, and troubleshoot common OpsMgr issues.

What you need for this book

To complete all the exercises in this book, it's preferable to have access to four servers (virtual or physical) along with downloaded copies of the latest supported media versions of OpsMgr and SQL.

The four servers will be configured using the step-by-step examples discussed in *Chapter 2, Installing System Center Operations Manager* and will end up with the following roles:

- **Server 1**: SQL Server hosting the OpsMgr databases and Reporting Server role

- **Server 2**: OpsMgr RMS Emulator, Web and Operations console roles

- **Server 3**: OpsMgr Secondary Management Server and Operations console roles

- **Server 4**: OpsMgr Gateway Server role

If you're working through this book with limited server resources at your disposal, then for testing purposes, feel free to co-locate the roles from **Servers 1 - 3** on a single server and then deploy the Gateway Server role on a second server.

Who this book is for

The target audience for this book is the IT Pro or System Administrator who wants to deploy and use System Center Operations Manager but has no previous knowledge of the product.

As a Getting Started book, our primary objective is to equip you with the knowledge you need to feel comfortable when working with common monitoring scenarios in OpsMgr. With this in mind, deep-diving into less-common OpsMgr features such as Audit Collection Services (ACS), Agentless Exception Monitoring (AEM) and Application Performance Monitoring (APM) has been intentionally omitted.

Conventions

In this book, you will find a number of text styles that distinguish between different kinds of information. Here are some examples of these styles and an explanation of their meaning.

Code words in text, database table names, folder names, filenames, file extensions, pathnames, dummy URLs, user input, and Twitter handles are shown as follows: "Copy the `MOMCertImport.exe` utility to a location on your C drive."

A block of code is set as follows:

```
Import-Module ServerManager
Add-WindowsFeature Web-Server,NET-Framework-Core,NET-HTTP-
Activation,NET-WCF-HTTP-Activation45,Web-Mgmt-Console,Web-Net-Ext,Web-
Net-Ext45,Web-Static-Content,Web-Default-Doc,Web-Dir-Browsing,Web-
Http-Errors,Web-Http-Logging,Web-Request-Monitor,Web-Filtering,Web-
Stat-Compression,Web-ISAPI-Ext,Web-ISAPI-Filter,Web-Metabase,Web-Asp-
Net,Web-Windows-Auth,Windows-Identity-Foundation -restart
```

When we wish to draw your attention to a particular part of a code block, the relevant lines or items are set in bold:

```
Param([string]$subscription)
Import-Module OperationsManager
Get-SCOMNotificationSubscription | where {$_.displayname -like
$subscription} | Disable-SCOMNotificationSubscription
```

New terms and **important words** are shown in bold. Words that you see on the screen, for example, in menus or dialog boxes, appear in the text like this: "The last thing you need to do now is to enable the **Server Proxy** setting on the new Gateway server."

Warnings or important notes appear in a box like this.

Tips and tricks appear like this.

Reader feedback

Feedback from our readers is always welcome. Let us know what you think about this book—what you liked or disliked. Reader feedback is important for us as it helps us develop titles that you will really get the most out of.

To send us general feedback, simply e-mail feedback@packtpub.com, and mention the book's title in the subject of your message.

If there is a topic that you have expertise in and you are interested in either writing or contributing to a book, see our author guide at www.packtpub.com/authors.

Customer support

Now that you are the proud owner of a Packt book, we have a number of things to help you to get the most from your purchase.

Errata

Although we have taken every care to ensure the accuracy of our content, mistakes do happen. If you find a mistake in one of our books—maybe a mistake in the text or the code—we would be grateful if you could report this to us. By doing so, you can save other readers from frustration and help us improve subsequent versions of this book. If you find any errata, please report them by visiting http://www.packtpub. com/submit-errata, selecting your book, clicking on the **Errata Submission Form** link, and entering the details of your errata. Once your errata are verified, your submission will be accepted and the errata will be uploaded to our website or added to any list of existing errata under the Errata section of that title.

To view the previously submitted errata, go to https://www.packtpub.com/books/ content/support and enter the name of the book in the search field. The required information will appear under the **Errata** section.

Piracy

Piracy of copyrighted material on the Internet is an ongoing problem across all media. At Packt, we take the protection of our copyright and licenses very seriously. If you come across any illegal copies of our works in any form on the Internet, please provide us with the location address or website name immediately so that we can pursue a remedy.

Please contact us at copyright@packtpub.com with a link to the suspected pirated material.

We appreciate your help in protecting our authors and our ability to bring you valuable content.

Questions

If you have a problem with any aspect of this book, you can contact us at questions@packtpub.com, and we will do our best to address the problem.

1

Introduction to System Center Operations Manager

Thank you for purchasing this book and we hope that it will help you through your journey of getting started with System Center Operations Manager. In this chapter, we will give you an overview of System Center and introduce you to Operations Manager, its capabilities and the minimum system requirements that you need to have in place before you begin deployment.

The following topics will be covered in this chapter:

- Overview of System Center
- Introduction to Operations Manager
- IT as a Service
- Operations Manager core features
- Minimum installation requirements

System Center overview

System Center is a suite of enterprise cloud and datacenter management tools from Microsoft, developed and structured on the **Microsoft Operations Framework (MOF)** and **IT Infrastructure Library (ITIL)** framework. The concept behind MOF and ITIL is to deliver IT service excellence for your organization through a process-driven guidance and team structure. You can learn more about MOF by referring to `http://tinyurl.com/mofintro` and for ITIL you can refer to `http://tinyurl.com/itilintro`.

The goal of System Center is to help deliver centralized monitoring and management of your applications, virtual environments, physical environments, and cloud-based workloads.

Operations Manager is one of the most popular components of System Center and before we dive into that, let's take a look at some of the other components in the suite:

- **Virtual Machine Manager**: This is used for the centralized management of your physical and virtual IT infrastructure. Although it was primarily designed for Microsoft Hyper-V, it can also manage VMware ESX hosts and their associated virtual machines. Using the library feature, you can create virtual machines and service templates to support the fast provisioning of resources in the datacenter.

- **Data Protection Manager**: Used for backing up and recovering your data, this is a best of breed tool for protecting Microsoft workloads such as SQL, Exchange, SharePoint, and Hyper-V. It also has native site-to-site replication and cloud backup options for disaster recovery scenarios.

- **Configuration Manager**: This is a unified infrastructure that provides a central console from which to push out updates, deploy applications and operating system packages, and even manage your anti-virus. You can use this to ensure that the corporate compliance and control of servers, PCs and mobile devices is maintained.

- **Service Manager**: This is deployed as a platform to manage your corporate ITIL-based processes and to ensure that an acceptable standard of IT compliance is achieved. Manage incident and problem resolution, change control and configuration management through the use of a central **configuration management database (CMDB)**.

- **Orchestrator**: Through the use of workflows to automate tasks, you can use this tool to manage any manual tasks that you or your IT team need to carry out on a regular basis, such as new employee account creation, virtual machine provisioning, and alert remediation. Orchestrator is also at the heart of the integration story of the other System Center suite components.

A few years back, in early 2012, Microsoft announced a major change in how they licensed and supported System Center. This new change meant that customers could no longer license an individual component from the System Center suite (there were eight components to choose from at the time); instead, the license model changed to view the whole of System Center as a single product. The thinking behind this shift wasn't to simply make more money from a higher license cost but to position System Center as a fully integrated cloud and datacenter management solution, where each of its components can be interconnected to deliver an enterprise-grade IT Service Management offering.

Introducing Operations Manager

Now that you have an understanding of the other key components of System Center, it's time to introduce you to **Operations Manager (OpsMgr)** — the core monitoring solution from Microsoft for over a decade. OpsMgr built its reputation in infrastructure monitoring of Microsoft workloads before expanding its capabilities to cover cross-platform monitoring of Unix/Linux distributions. The first OpsMgr 2012 release branched out to include monitoring of physical network devices as well as cloud and fabric environments, through its integration with Virtual Machine Manager and Microsoft Azure.

On top of all this, Microsoft has given us the opportunity to truly deliver full 360 degree monitoring of our applications by modeling them as IT services in OpsMgr and gaining code-level visibility with **Application Performance Monitoring** (APM). With OpsMgr 2012 R2 and the release of OpsMgr 2016, we get deep integration into Microsoft's cloud-based **Operations Management Suite** (OMS) - which gives us enhanced capabilities for log analytics, alert remediation and best practice recommendations.

If you have a requirement to report back to senior management in your organization on how available your IT services are, then OpsMgr has that covered too. **Service Level Agreements (SLAs)** can be tracked and reported on easily to determine the overall level of SLA compliance.

> With everything that OpsMgr can do, if you find yourself constantly troubleshooting issues in your environment or not knowing where to start looking when a problem arises, then this will be a formidable tool to add to your box of tricks.

IT as a Service explained

Here's a scenario that might sound familiar, it's Friday afternoon (because these things always seem to happen before you clock off for the weekend), an end-user in your organization notifies you of an outage to an application and it's the first time you've heard of the incident.

Suddenly, you find yourself scrambling to find a solution to the application outage by trawling through the many e-mail alerts that your monitoring tool has kindly filled your inbox with and you're not even sure where to begin. Then your boss starts demanding to know when exactly everything will be back up and running again.

Finally, it's close to midnight and everyone's gone home except you. You've eliminated most of the noisy alerts in your inbox and narrowed the problem down to a bunch of alerts referring to network connectivity. Eventually, you find the network cable that the new junior admin earlier mistakenly disconnected from one of the many switches you manage in the datacenter! Once the cable is plugged back in, everything comes back online and you get to start your weekend.

This is a classic example of reactive monitoring—wherein, even though you had a monitoring tool in place, due to the constant stream of alerts you've been receiving, you missed the alert about the cable being disconnected and only reacted after the end-user logged an application outage incident. Even if you had picked up the network connectivity alert, there's still a good chance that you don't understand the overall impact of it on the business and it might not even be considered to be a valid reason for end-users complaining about their application outages.

What you really need in this situation is a monitoring solution that can bring all of the related components of an application together in the form of an IT service to help reduce your **Mean Time to Resolution (MTTR)**, which translates to you resolving incidents quicker and keeping your end-users happy.

This is where OpsMgr comes in very useful. With OpsMgr, you can create comprehensive maps of your IT services based on your IT service catalog. With your IT services mapped out, you can then begin to understand all the components that make up each service.

If we apply this strategy to our example scenario, the next time someone disconnects a network cable, red lights will start to appear on a dashboard monitoring the IT service. It then becomes very easy to quickly identify the root cause of the outage. In *Figure 1.1*, you can see an example of an IT service modeled in OpsMgr that has been affected by someone disconnecting a cable from a network device.

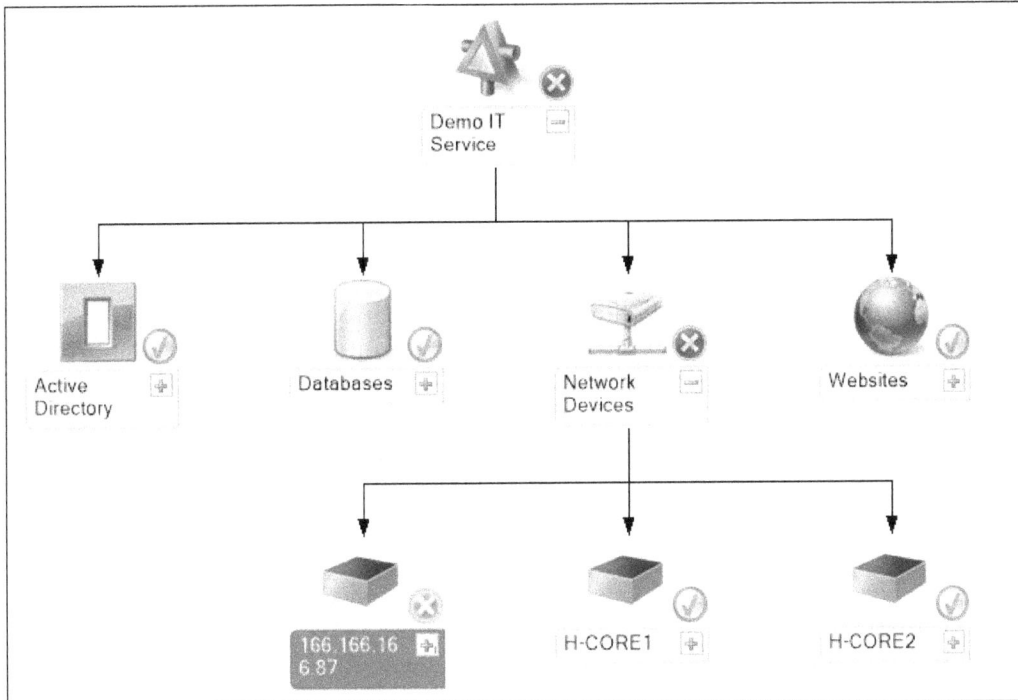

Figure 1.1: The Operations Console

Adopting a similar monitoring strategy will enable you to focus on the IT services that run your business from a holistic management perspective, instead of on an individual component-by-component basis. This model is defined as **IT as a Service (ITaaS)**.

> Using ITaaS you can manage your services in the same way that your end-users consume them—essentially viewing each complex IT service as a single entity with a green, amber, or red health state, similar to a traffic light status!

As you progress through this book, you will learn more about how to use the ITaaS model. This will not only help you reduce the amount of time you spend trying to identify the root cause of problems, but it will facilitate you to move closer to delivering a proactive monitoring approach for all your IT services and one where you can catch possible incidents before they become bigger problems.

Operations Manager core features

In this section, we will cover some of the most common features used in OpsMgr. It's important that you have a high-level understanding of these features before installing OpsMgr. This will assist you during the planning and design phase of your deployment.

Management group

Created during the initial installation of OpsMgr, a management group is a unique logical administrative unit that defines the security boundaries of your monitoring environment.

When choosing a management group name, you must ensure that the name is unique within your Active Directory forest and also understand that whatever name you choose, it's case sensitive. It's also recommended that you refrain from using any unsupported special characters in the name and stick with letters and numbers.

You can have multiple management groups running concurrently in the same domain without a problem (this is useful for pre-production and production environments) and all configuration changes and customizations that you make will be contained inside each unique group.

Operational database

A SQL database that forms the central component of every Management Group, the Operational database installs with a default name of `OperationsManager`. It contains all your OpsMgr customizations along with configuration and monitoring data for all managed objects. A dedicated Operational database is required for every OpsMgr management group you deploy.

Data is retained in the Operational database by default for seven days - think of this as OpsMgr's short-term memory store. This retention period can be modified for different types of datasets by configuring database grooming within the Operations console.

Data Warehouse database

The data warehouse is a SQL database that can be either dedicated or shared by an OpsMgr management group. This database has a default installation name of `OperationsManagerDW`.

All historical alerting and monitoring data is stored here and with retention period of up to four-hundred days, this can be considered OpsMgr's long-term memory store. Having the ability to retain data for such a long period means OpsMgr can use the data warehouse to generate rich reports that will help you to better understand the availability and performance of your IT services.

RMS Emulator

Installed by default onto the first management server that you deploy, the **Root Management Server (RMS)** Emulator exists to support backward compatibility with legacy OpsMgr management packs that specifically target the RMS role. If there are no legacy management packs that contain rules targeted at the RMS role, then essentially, the RMS Emulator is not required and all management servers are considered equal.

In early releases of OpsMgr, the RMS role was arguably the most important role within the management group and unless you deployed Failover Clustering across two servers, it was also a single-point of failure. Since OpsMgr 2012, the single-point of failure RMS role was removed and out-of-box high availability was made possible using a new feature called **Resource Pools**. These pools are a collection of management servers that distribute the workload and ensure that monitoring continues in the event of a management server failing.

> Using the Operations Manager Shell (which is the PowerShell module that gets deployed during the installation of OpsMgr), you can easily move the RMS Emulator role between management servers using the following line of code:
>
> ```
> Get-SCOMManagementServer -Name "opsmgr1.yourdomain.com"
>  | Set-SCOMRMSEmulator
> ```

Management Server

The Management Server role is responsible for managing and communicating with agents, maintaining management group configuration, communicating with the OpsMgr SQL databases, and facilitating console connections.

After installation of this role, you will find five new Windows services installed on your server. Out of the five services, three are configured with a service start up type of **Automatic** and two of them are set to **Disabled**.

These management server services and their startup types are detailed in the following table:

Service name	Startup type	Description
Microsoft Monitoring Agent	Automatic	• Monitors the health of your computers. • Responsible for executing modules called workflows to support different monitoring scenarios. • Listens on TCP port 5723. • Also known as the 'HealthService'.
System Center Data Access	Automatic	• This runs on all management servers. • Handles communications with the OpsMgr consoles and Report servers. • It reads and writes data to the OpsMgr databases on behalf of workflows running on agents and gateway servers. • It listens on TCP port 5724. • It's also known as the 'SDK' service.
System Center Management Configuration	Automatic	• This runs on all management servers. • It monitors configuration changes within the management group and passes any updated changes to agents. • It's also known as the 'Configuration' service.
Microsoft Monitoring Agent Audit Forwarding	Disabled	• This is installed on all management servers, gateway servers and agents but disabled by default. • It's used with the **Audit Collection Services (ACS)** feature of OpsMgr. • It sends security event logs to an ACS collector server.
Microsoft Monitoring Agent APM	Disabled	• This is installed on all management servers, gateway servers and agents but is disabled by default. • It's used with the **Application Performance Monitoring (APM)** feature of OpsMgr to monitor code-level health of .NET applications.

Reporting Server

The OpsMgr Reporting Server role integrates with **SQL Server Reporting Services (SSRS)** and gives you the ability to generate and schedule reports from an intuitive user interface inside the Operations Console. You can choose from ready-made reports that come bundled with the various management packs you deploy or you can generate your own custom reports using some of the generic templates on offer.

Good reporting enables you to visualize the monitoring data generated from your IT infrastructure and provide exactly the kind of high-level information that senior management teams request on a regular basis. You also have the option to e-mail reports on a specific schedule or simply export them into various easy-to-read formats, such as Word, Excel, PDF, CSV, and TIFF to name a few.

Gateway Server

The primary role of a Gateway Server is to act as a go-between for monitored agents that are located in untrusted domains and networks - DMZ's are a great example of where to use this role in your environment.

When located in an untrusted domain, a Gateway Server must use certificates to authenticate with the main OpsMgr environment. It communicates with management servers over TCP port 5723 and cannot connect directly to the OpsMgr databases.

A Gateway Server also acts as a data compressor and can be used to compress monitoring traffic from agents to the management servers by up to 50% in certain scenarios.

Agents

The OpsMgr agent is used for server and client monitoring of Windows and Unix/Linux operating systems. A push installation can be initiated from management servers and gateway servers to make the deployment nice and easy. It can also be deployed manually or added into computer images and packaged as an application for deployment with a tool such as System Center Configuration Manager.

On a Windows computer, after the agent has been installed, three new windows services are created. These new services and their startup types are detailed in the following table:

Service Name	Startup Type	Description
Microsoft Monitoring Agent	Automatic	• Monitors the health of your computers • Responsible for executing workflow modules and scripts to support different monitoring scenarios • Listens on TCP port 5723 • Also known as the 'HealthService'
Microsoft Monitoring Agent Audit Forwarding	Disabled	• Installed on all management servers, gateway servers and agents but is disabled by default • Used with the **Audit Collection Services (ACS)** feature of OpsMgr • Sends security event logs to an ACS collector server
Microsoft Monitoring Agent APM	Disabled	• Installed on all management servers, gateway servers and agents but is disabled by default • Used with the **Application Performance Monitoring (APM)** feature of OpsMgr to monitor code-level health of .NET applications

The agent's job is to communicate with management and gateway servers, discover objects, execute workflows, and run diagnostic tasks on monitored computers.

If you have deployed multiple management groups, the OpsMgr agent can perform a feature called 'multi-homing' whereby it can communicate with up to four different management groups at any given time. This feature will be discussed in more detail in *Chapter 4, Deploying Agents*.

Consoles

There are a number of consoles that you can interact with when you are working with OpsMgr. The most common one is the **Operations Console**, which is essentially the main console that you will use when administering OpsMgr. In *Figure 1.2*, you can see the Operations Console in action monitoring some Windows computers.

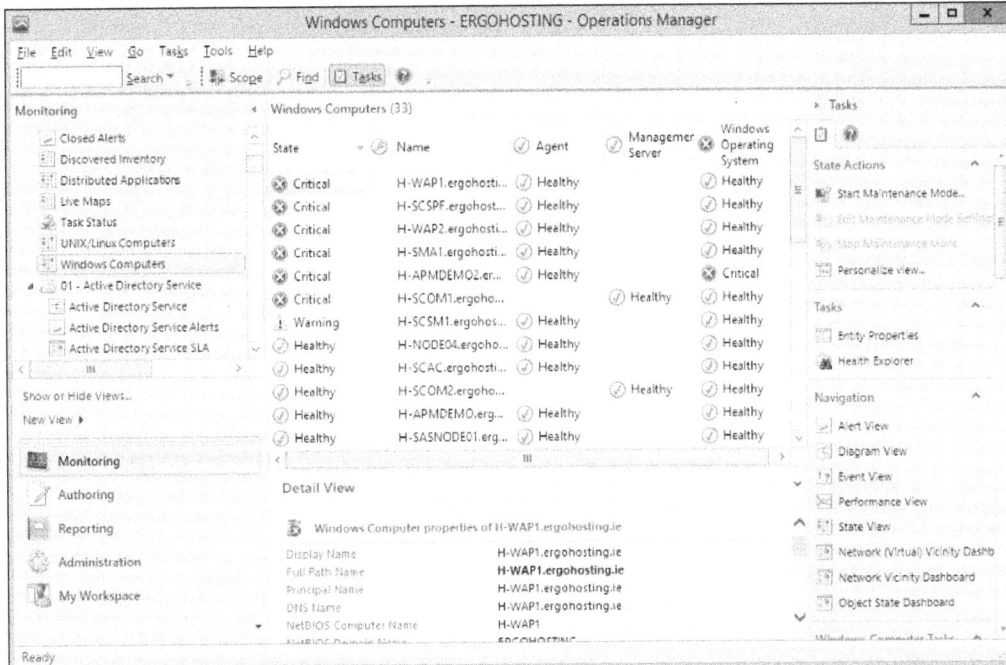

Figure 1.2: The Operations Console

During installation, you can choose to deploy the **Web Console**, which is a lighter and scaled-down version of the Operations Console. This console will be deployed as an IIS website on whichever server you choose to run it from. Although you can't perform any administration or reporting tasks here, the Web Console is useful if you want to give your OpsMgr users read-only access to the monitored environment.

> The maximum recommended number of concurrent Operational Console connections per management server is limited to 50. If you go over this number, then you will encounter performance issues. The Web Console however, has no limit to the number of concurrent connections you can make.

When you deploy the Web Console role with the installation wizard, you get an automatic installation of the **Application Advisor** and **Application Diagnostics** consoles - both of which are used in conjunction with the APM feature for code-level monitoring of your applications.

Management packs

If you want to get any monitoring value at all from OpsMgr, then you are going to need to install some management packs. These are small files based on XML that can be imported into OpsMgr and which hold information about how to monitor a specific application or hardware product set.

Management packs can contain some or all of the following objects:

- Class definitions
- Discoveries
- Monitors
- Rules
- Views
- Knowledge
- Reports
- Templates

In *Chapter 5, Working with Management Packs*, you will learn much more about management packs and how to use them to get the most out of your OpsMgr deployment.

Application Performance Monitoring

Another optional and very useful feature of OpsMgr is **Application Performance Monitoring (APM)**. When configured, this gives IT Operations teams the ability to help troubleshoot problems inside applications at the code-level, similar to the world of a Developer. This synergy has become known as 'DevOps', and it's something that has gained a lot of traction in the last few years.

A real benefit of deploying APM in OpsMgr is that, not only do you get to dive deep into your .NET and Java application code; you can also see the health of the underlying infrastructure that runs those applications.

Network device monitoring

If you're going to monitor the full breadth of your IT services, then you will no doubt want to include network device monitoring in your designs. With a choice of ICMP or SNMP (v1/v2c/v3) monitoring, you can take advantage of the built-in Network Node and Vicinity dashboards to give you rich visualizations on the health of your network infrastructure. *Chapter 6, Managing Network Devices,* will get you up and running with this feature in no time.

Audit Collection Services

Audit Collection Services (ACS) is an optional feature used to collect security event logs from monitored systems and bring them together in a central SQL database for auditing and compliance purposes. ACS uses its own SQL database (named `OpsMgrAC` by default), which is kept completely separate from the `OperationsManager` and `OperationsManagerDW` databases.

To enable ACS, you must deploy a management server and configure it as an ACS Collector. The ACS Collector then receives and processes the audited security event logs from targeted computers and passes that information into the `OpsMgrAC` database.

Specific computers running the OpsMgr agent can be targeted with ACS audit policies to enable them as an ACS Forwarder. When Windows computers are enabled as ACS Forwarders, the Microsoft Monitoring Agent Audit Forwarding service is started on those computers and configured with an 'Automatic' start up state. When this service is running, the ACS audit policies are applied and security events will be sent to the ACS Collector for auditing.

Agentless Exception Monitoring

Agentless Exception Monitoring (AEM) is an optional feature that centralizes the collection of hardware, operating system, and application crash information from selected computers. If you're familiar with the old 'Dr. Watson Debugger for Windows' tool that collects data from your computer when it crashes, then AEM is a centralized version of this which feeds the crash data into OpsMgr.

Minimum installation requirements

When the time comes to perform your first installation of OpsMgr, it's important to understand all of the minimum requirements that must be in place before you begin.

OpsMgr Sizing Helper tool

The OpsMgr Sizing Helper tool is an interactive Excel document designed to assist you with planning and sizing your deployments. As shown in *Figure 1.2*, you can choose from a number of different configuration scenarios and all you need to have is a rough idea of what it is that you actually need to monitor.

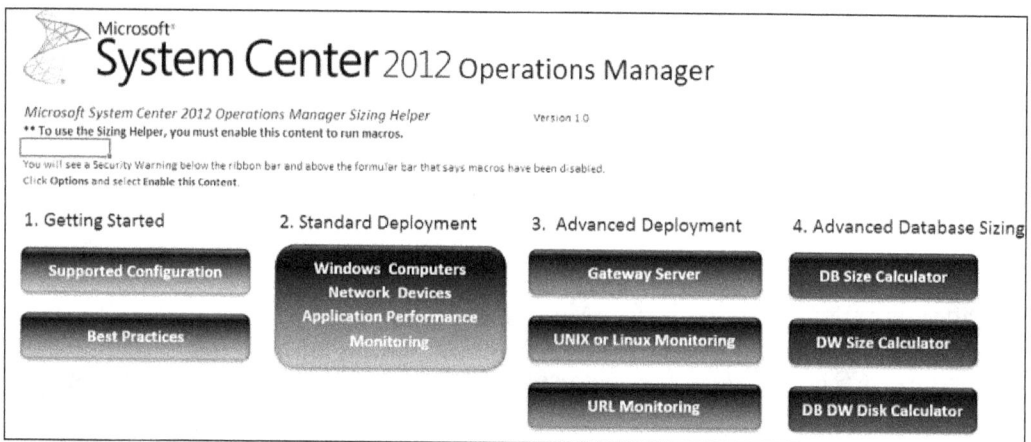

Figure 1.3: OpsMgr Sizing Helper Tool

This should be the go-to tool that you use prior to every OpsMgr deployment that you do. Although the information it feeds back to you is to be used purely as a guide, it goes a long way to ensure that your designs are aligned as close to best-practice recommendations as possible. You can download the tool from `http://tinyurl.com/opsmgrsizing`.

Virtualization support

All OpsMgr features are fully supported by Microsoft to run in a virtual environment that meets the minimum requirements outlined in the OpsMgr Sizing Helper tool. Purely for performance reasons, Microsoft recommends running the OpsMgr SQL databases on physical disks rather than on virtual disks but this is only a recommendation and there is no issue if you want to deploy the databases in a virtual environment, assuming of course, that you have configured the underlying storage where your virtual disks are located according to best practice recommendations for SQL workloads.

You also have the option of running some or your entire OpsMgr environment on **Microsoft Azure** for the following three recommended scenarios:

- You run OpsMgr on a Microsoft Azure virtual machine and use it to monitor other Microsoft Azure virtual machines
- You run OpsMgr on a Microsoft Azure virtual machine and use it to monitor instances that are not running on Microsoft Azure
- You run OpsMgr on-premises and use it to monitor Microsoft Azure virtual machines

Database requirements

If you're running OpsMgr 2012 R2, then the following versions of SQL Server are supported to host the databases:

- SQL Server 2014 SP1, Standard and Enterprise
- SQL Server 2014, Standard and Enterprise
- SQL Server 2012 SP2, Standard and Enterprise
- SQL Server 2012 SP1, Standard and Enterprise
- SQL Server 2012, Standard and Enterprise
- SQL Server 2008 R2 SP2, Standard and Datacenter
- SQL Server 2008 R2 SP1, Standard and Datacenter

If you're running OpsMgr 2016, then your SQL choice is slightly more limited:

- SQL Server 2016, Standard and Enterprise
- SQL Server 2014 SP1, Standard and Enterprise
- SQL Server 2014, Standard and Enterprise
- SQL Server 2012 SP2, Standard and Enterprise

Operating system requirements

The following operating systems are supported to run OpsMgr 2012 R2:

- Windows Server 2012 R2, Standard and Datacenter
- Windows Server 2012, Standard and Datacenter
- Windows Server 2008 R2 SP2
- Windows Server 2008 R2 SP1

OpsMgr 2016 can be deployed on these operating systems:

- Windows Server 2016, Standard and Datacenter
- Windows Server 2012 R2, Standard and Datacenter

Web console requirements

If you deploy the OpsMgr 2012 R2 Web Console role, the following Internet Explorer and Silverlight versions are supported:

- Internet Explorer 8 and higher
- Silverlight 5

The OpsMgr 2016 Web Console has the following requirements:

- Internet Explorer 11 and higher
- Silverlight 5

Firewall requirements

In the following table, we can see the TCP port numbers and outgoing directions that the various OpsMgr features require. This information can be useful when configuring communication across firewalls in your organization.

From feature	TCP port number and direction	To feature
Management server	1433→	Operational database
Management server	1433→	Data Warehouse database
Management server	5723,5724→	Management server
Reporting server	5723,5724→	Management server
Reporting server	1433→	Data Warehouse database
Gateway server	5723→	Management server
Operations console	5724→	Management server
Operations console (Reports)	80, 443→	SQL Reporting services
Web Console browser	51908→	Web Console server
Windows agent	5723→	Management server
Management server	135→	Windows agent (RPC for push install)
Management server	445→	Windows agent (SMB for push install)
Management server	139→	Windows agent (RPC for push repair)
Management server	1270→	UNIX/Linux agent
Management server	22→	UNIX/Linux agent (Remote management)
Connector framework source	51905→	Management server
Connected management server (Local)	5724→	Connected management server (Remote)
AEM data from client	51906→	Management server AEM file share
ACS collector	1433→	ACS database
ACS forwarder	51909→	Management Server ACS collector

Although the majority of firewall ports required for OpsMgr are TCP-based, the following table lists the UDP port numbers and the direction they should be enabled for:

From feature	UDP port number and direction	To feature
Management server	137→	Windows agent (push install)
Management server	138→	Windows agent (push install)
Management server	445→	Windows agent (push install)
Management server	1434→	Operational database
Management server	1434→	Data Warehouse database
SNMP network device	161→	Management server
Management server	161→	SNMP network device
SNMP network device	162→	Management server
Management server	162→	SNMP network device

Windows agent requirements

If you need to deploy an OpsMgr 2012 R2 agent to your Windows estate for monitoring, then the following is a list of supported server and client operating systems:

- Windows Server 2016
- Windows Server 2012 R2, Windows Server 2012
- Microsoft Hyper-V Server 2012 R2
- Windows 2008 Server R2, Windows 2008 Server R2 SP1, Windows 2008 Server SP2
- Windows Server 2003 SP2
- Windows 10
- Windows 8.1, Windows 8
- Windows 7
- Windows 7 Embedded
- Windows Vista SP2

- Windows XP Pro SP3, SP2
- Windows XP Embedded

For OpsMgr 2016 agents, the following Windows server and client operating systems are supported:

- Windows Server 2016
- Windows Server 2012 R2, Windows Server 2012
- Microsoft Hyper-V Server 2012 R2
- Windows 2008 Server R2, Windows 2008 Server R2 SP1, Windows 2008 Server SP2
- Windows Server 2003 SP2
- Windows 10
- Windows 8.1, Windows 8
- Windows 7
- Windows 7 Embedded
- Windows Vista SP2

UNIX/Linux agent requirements

A wide range of cross-platform operating systems are supported and the following list details the versions you can monitor with both OpsMgr 2012 R2 and OpsMgr 2016:

- HP-UX 11i V3/V2 (PA-RISC and Itanium)
- Oracle Solaris 11/10 (SPARC and x86)
- Oracle Solaris 9 (SPARC)
- Oracle Linux 7 (x64)
- Oracle Linux 6/5 (x86/x64)
- Red Hat Enterprise Linux 7 (x64)
- Red Hat Enterprise Linux 6/5/4 (x86/x64)
- SUSE Linux Enterprise Server 12 (x64)
- SUSE Linux Enterprise Server 11/10 (x86/x64)
- SUSE Linux Enterprise Server 9 (x86)
- IBM AIX 7.1/6.1/5.3 (POWER)
- CentOS 7 (x64)

- CentOS 6/5 (x86/x64)
- Debian 7/6/5 (x86/x64)
- Ubuntu Server 14.04/12.04/10.04 (x86/x64)

Summary

In this chapter, we first learned about the System Center suite and its associated components before diving into an introduction about Operations Manager and its core features. After that, we discussed ITaaS using a real-world example to help you understand what it is.

At the end of the chapter, we introduced the OpsMgr Sizing Helper tool and provided you with information about the supported operating systems that you can run OpsMgr and its associated features on.

In the next chapter, we will show you some examples to help with the design and planning of your deployments before diving into installing OpsMgr for the first time.

2
Installing System Center Operations Manager

Building on the knowledge gained in *Chapter 1, Introduction to System Center Operations Manager*, you should now have an understanding of the core components of **Operations Manager** (**OpsMgr**) and its minimum installation requirements. In this chapter, we will walk you through designing and then deploying a new OpsMgr environment.

The following topics will be covered in this chapter:

- Designing an Operations Manager environment
- Creating service accounts
- Configuring prerequisites
- Installing Management servers
- Installing the Reporting Server
- Deploying the Web console
- Installing a Gateway server

Designing the environment

Before you dive in and begin installing OpsMgr, its best practice to take a step back and think about how you will design the environment. A good design takes into account the overall monitoring requirements of the business, the physical and logical locations of the infrastructure to be monitored and any existing monitoring applications that are currently in place.

Involving members of each business unit/department in the organization is paramount to delivering a monitoring solution that works for everybody and can deliver real benefits and time-saving back to the business.

Here's some advice to get you started with your initial OpsMgr designs:

- **Don't run before you can walk**: A full enterprise deployment of OpsMgr can be very complex and could span across many geographical locations monitoring thousands of computers and network devices. For this reason, it's recommended to start small and approach your design in different phases. Postpone deployment of advanced features such as **Audit Collection Services (ACS)** and **Application Performance Monitoring (APM)** until you first get comfortable working with the basic monitoring that OpsMgr has to offer.

- **Understand your goals**: When creating your design, be totally focused on what it is that you expect to achieve by the end of your first deployment phase. If you're an IT administrator looking to deploy OpsMgr into your organization, then document everything that you and (more importantly) your boss would like to achieve by the end of the project. If you're an IT consultant deploying OpsMgr for your customer, ensure you have agreed on a statement of work that clearly specifies each task that will be carried out as part of the design.

- **Stick to the game plan**: When sizing the infrastructure that will run your OpsMgr deployment, avoid using the 'finger in the air' estimation method when deciding things like memory, CPU and database size allocations. Instead, use the OpsMgr Sizing Tool (`http://tinyurl.com/opsmgrsizing`), official documentation and the best practice recommendations available to you within this book.

Design examples

In the consulting world (depending on customer requirements), the design for each OpsMgr deployment varies from one instance to the other. There are however, several general designs that share the same characteristics, which can always be applied as a design foundation to get you started.

The following designs are some of the most common examples of how to deploy OpsMgr and each one assumes that there is already a working Active Directory domain and DNS environment configured and available.

Single server design

This is the most basic OpsMgr design and one that should only be used as a lab or testing environment. With no focus on performance or high-availability, this design enables you to get up and running quickly by co-locating the SQL and OpsMgr roles onto a single physical or virtual computer.

Although this design should satisfy the majority of basic testing scenarios, it's worth remembering here that you cannot install the OpsMgr Gateway server role onto a server that is already designated as a Management server. If testing the Gateway role is required, you will need to deploy an additional server to host it.

There is no scenario in the OpsMgr Sizing Helper Tool to give you guidance on disk, CPU and memory allocations for a single server design so ensure that you have enough resources on your test computer to run all roles at an acceptable speed.

Figure 2.1 shows what a single server OpsMgr design would look like.

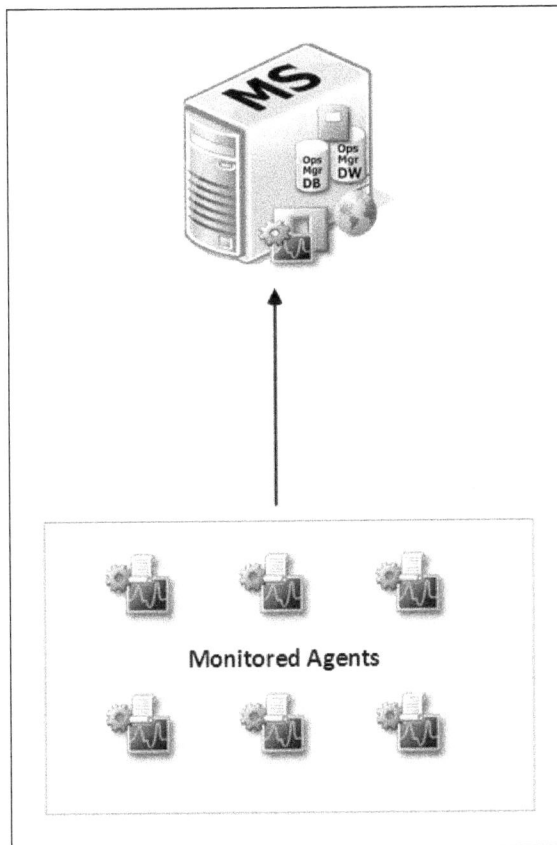

Figure 2.1: Single server design

Small distributed server design

The smallest OpsMgr design recommended for a production environment separates the SQL and OpsMgr roles across two different computers. This design is ideal for small-sized production environments and can be deployed relatively quickly - however, it has limited scalability and no high-availability. If either computer is unavailable, then monitoring will not work.

Figure 2.2 shows how this small distributed server design would look.

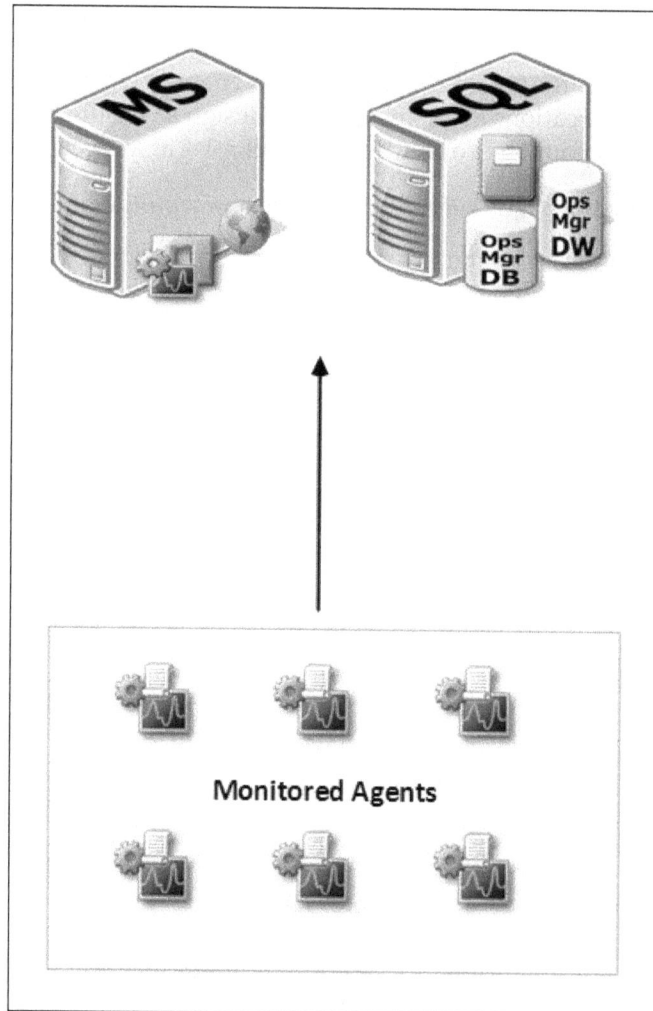

Figure 2.2: Small distributed server design

Using the OpsMgr Sizing Helper Tool to scope this design for monitoring up to approximately 100 servers in a small organization, it's recommended to configure the memory and CPU on your management server as shown in the following table:

Component	Description
Server role	Management server, Web console
Memory	8GB
CPU	4 Cores

For the SQL server, you can configure it as shown in this table:

Component	Description
Server role	SQL Operational database, Operational Data Warehouse, Reporting server
Memory	16GB
CPU	4 Cores

The OpsMgr Sizing Helper Tool also gives us the following recommendations for sizing our SQL databases:

Component	Description
Number of monitored servers	100
Operational database data retention	7 days
Operational database size	2.5GB
Operational Data Warehouse data retention	365 days
Operational Data Warehouse size	71GB

Medium distributed server design

Expanding on the small distributed server design, this one adds high availability and better performance by adding an additional Management server and further separating the SQL and OpsMgr roles onto different server computers.

When you get to this type of design, you're beginning to build for scale and although all of the OpsMgr roles are fully supported to run within a virtual environment, it's a good time to start seriously thinking about the underlying hardware that the SQL databases are sitting on. It's not uncommon to deploy the SQL components of this design on physical hardware to ensure that the best possible performance gains are achieved and for designs where the SQL components are running on virtual machines, high-end disk storage for the database and log volumes is always a good recommendation.

By deploying two Management servers in this design, we can take advantage of the built-in high availability **Resource Pools** feature of OpsMgr. We can also ensure that our monitored agents are divided equally between each server - providing a basic form of load balancing.

In *Figure 2.3*, we can see how the SQL and OpsMgr roles are deployed in a medium distributed server design.

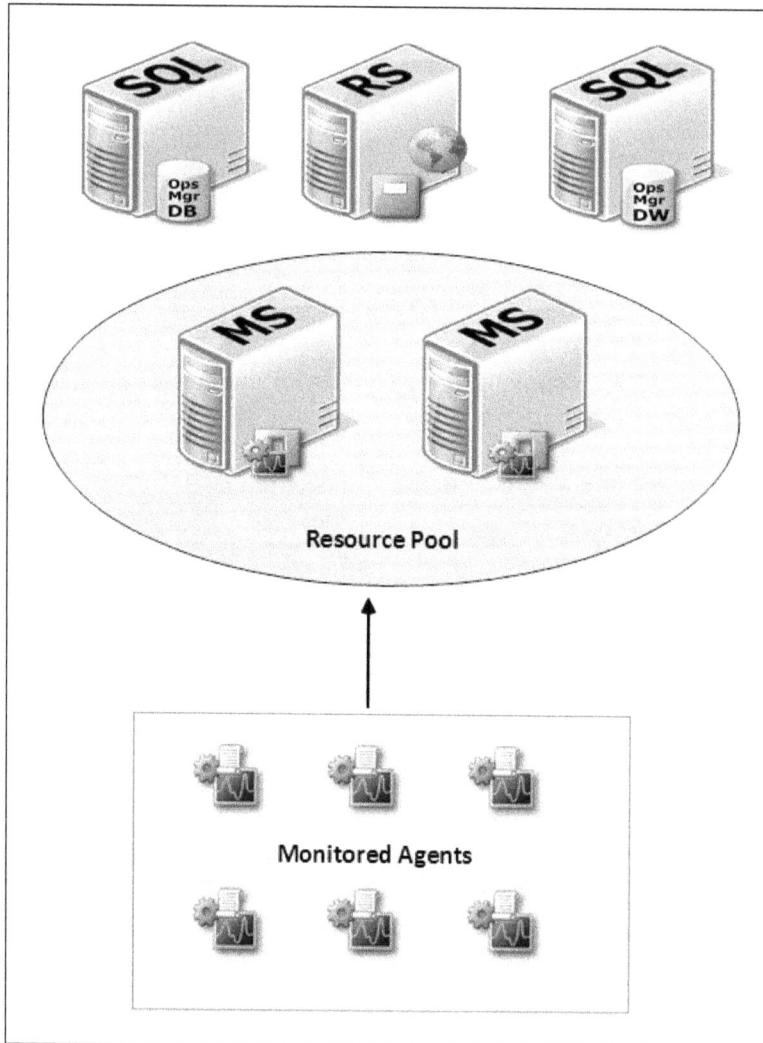

Figure 2.3: Medium distributed server design

Again using the OpsMgr Sizing Helper Tool, we scope this design to monitor approximately 500 servers. The following table shows the recommended configuration results for our two Management servers:

Component	Description
Server role	Management servers (x2)
Memory	8GB
CPU	4 Cores

For the SQL server hosting the Operational database, you can configure it as shown in this table:

Component	Description
Server role	SQL Operational database
Memory	16GB
CPU	4 Cores

The SQL server hosting the Operational Data Warehouse, configure it as shown in this table:

Component	Description
Server role	SQL Operational Data Warehouse
Memory	16GB
CPU	4 Cores

For the server hosting the SQL Reporting and Web console roles, configure it as shown in this table:

Component	Description
Server role	SQL Reporting server, Web console server
Memory	8GB
CPU	4 Cores

The OpsMgr Sizing Helper Tool also gives us the following recommendations for sizing our SQL databases with this design:

Component	Description
Number of monitored servers	500
Operational database data retention	7 days
Operational database Size	12GB
Operational Data Warehouse data retention	365 days
Operational Data Warehouse size	356GB

Large distributed server design

Very similar to the medium distributed server design, here we add an additional Management server and also a Gateway server to provide monitoring for a number of agents in an untrusted domain. The additional Management server will be used to support traffic coming from the Gateway server. The other two Management servers provide a layer of high-availability and load balancing for the main bulk of monitored agents in the trusted domain.

The Gateway server will be a member server of the untrusted domain and will authenticate back to the main OpsMgr environment using PKI certificates. The untrusted domain could be located in the same datacenter as the domain that OpsMgr resides in or it could even be located in a different country. Either way, this is where the Gateway server role becomes very useful when you need to extend the reach of your monitoring scope.

Figure 2.4 shows how we would design an OpsMgr environment for this type of scenario.

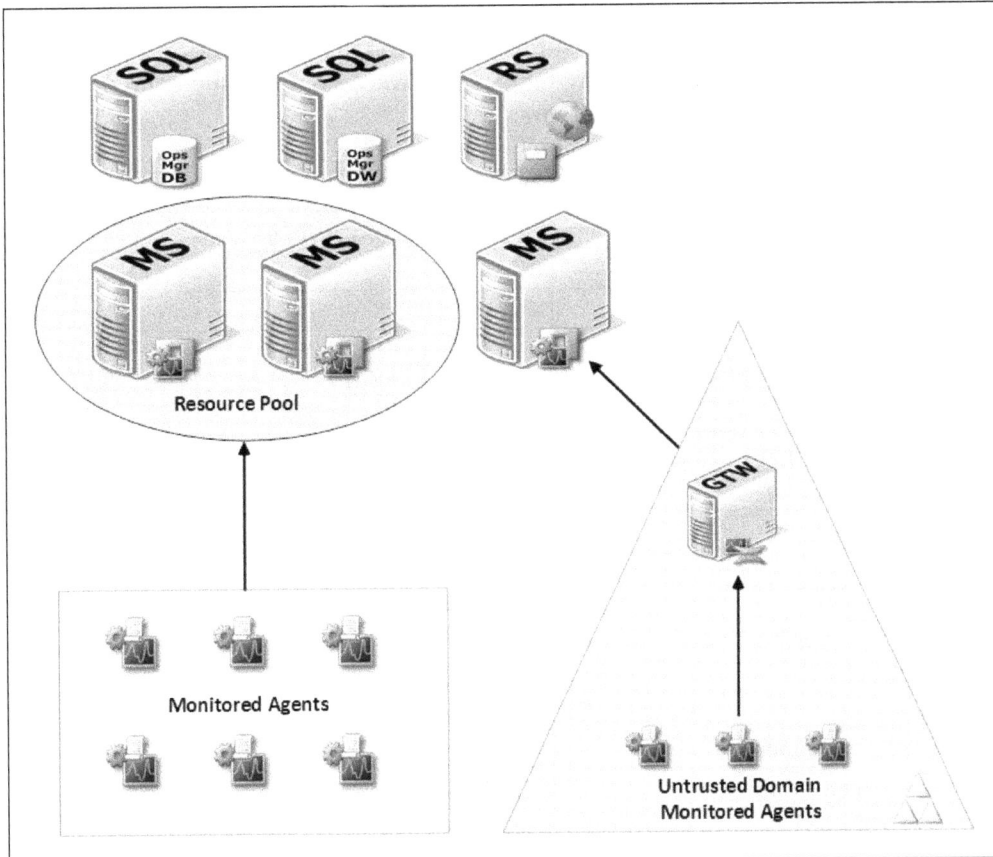

Figure 2.4: Large distributed server design

A design like this is very flexible and can be easily upgraded to comply with any high availability requirements your organization might have. You can do this by first adding some additional SQL servers to the back-end and deploying them in a clustered or mirrored configuration to keep the databases online in the event of a failure. For the untrusted domain, you can add another Gateway server and configure failover on the agents to communicate with the second one in the event of an outage or maintenance on the primary Gateway. It would also be advisable to deploy another Management server to act as a Gateway failover.

This time using the OpsMgr Sizing Helper Tool, we will scope our design to monitor approximately 2000 servers spread across the main production domain and untrusted domain. The following table shows the recommended configuration results for our three Management servers:

Component	Description
Server role	Management servers (x3)
Memory	8GB
CPU	4 Cores

The additional Gateway server will be configured like this:

Component	Description
Server role	Gateway server
Memory	8GB
CPU	4 Cores

For the SQL server hosting the Operational database, you can configure it as shown in this table:

Component	Description
Server role	SQL Operational database
Memory	16GB
CPU	4 Cores

The SQL server hosting the Operational Data Warehouse, configure it as shown in this table:

Component	Description
Server role	SQL Operational Data Warehouse
Memory	16GB
CPU	4 Cores

For the server hosting the SQL Reporting and Web console roles, configure it as shown in this table:

Component	Description
Server role	SQL Reporting server, Web console server
Memory	8GB
CPU	4 Cores

The OpsMgr Sizing Helper Tool also gives us the following recommendations for sizing our SQL databases:

Component	Description
Number of monitored servers	2000
Operational Database data retention	7 days
Operational database Size	48GB
Operational Data Warehouse data retention	365 days
Operational Data Warehouse size	1.5TB

As you can see from the database sizing requirements here, in large enterprise environments, the OpsMgr databases can potentially expand to a huge scale and it's paramount that the underlying SQL server disk configurations are built to handle the heavy traffic that passes through these databases.

Creating the service accounts

When you've decided on the design that best suits your needs, you can begin preparing the environment for the installation of OpsMgr. The first thing to do is to understand the service accounts that will be used and then go ahead and create them in the Active Directory environment.

The following table details the four accounts requested during installation and also gives a suggested name for each.

Account	Suggested Name	Description
Management server action account	`opsmgr_action`	• Used for collecting data from providers and running responses on monitored computers across the network. • This account should be configured as a standard domain user account in Active Directory. • Should not be granted domain administrative privileges.
System Center Configuration service and System Center Data Access service account	`opsmgr_sdk`	• Used to update and read information in the Operational database • Can be configured as either Local System or as a domain account. • If the Operational database is hosted on a remote SQL computer that is not a management server, then a domain account must be used.
Data Reader account	`opsmgr_dataread`	• Required when you are installing the Reporting server role and is used to run queries against the Operations Manager reporting data warehouse. • Should be configured as a domain user account. • Needs to have SQL Server logon rights and Management server logon rights.
Data Writer account	`opsmgr_datawrite`	• Used to write data from the Management server to the Data Warehouse and reads data from the Operational database. • Should be configured as a domain user account. • Assigned write permissions on the Data Warehouse database and read permissions on the Operational database. • Needs to have SQL Server logon rights and logon rights for the computers hosting both the Operational database and the Data Warehouse.

Be mindful of any Active Directory group policies configured in your environment that dictate how frequently your user account passwords need to be changed. In most cases, the domain user service accounts used by OpsMgr should be configured with the *Password never expires* option. If security policy dictates that all accounts must change their password periodically, then you will need to manage this change in OpsMgr each time.

Creating an OpsMgr security group

After you've created the four service accounts, it's useful to create a new Active Directory security group named something similar to `OpsMgr_AdminGroup` and then add the OpsMgr service accounts to it. This group will become a member of the Local Administrators group on each OpsMgr Management server you deploy.

An optional service account that you could create for your OpsMgr deployments is a user account with domain administrative permissions (call it `opsmgr_admin` for example). This account can then be used to install SQL and OpsMgr with elevated rights and would save you from possibly having to make some database changes post-installation.

Tips for deploying SQL

Before you can install OpsMgr, you need to deploy a SQL environment to host the databases. A full installation of SQL is relatively straight-forward and you can refer to `http://tinyurl.com/sqlinstall` for a step-by-step walkthrough of SQL 2014 (the steps in this link are also applicable for SQL 2012 R2 and SQL 2016).

There are however, a few pointers that you need to take into account when deploying SQL with OpsMgr and this section will help you avoid some of the common pitfalls that people encounter.

SQL features and collation setting

During the installation of SQL, you will be asked to choose the features that you want installed into your new instance. A database requirement of OpsMgr is that the **Full-Text and Semantic Extractions for Search** feature shown in *Figure 2.5* is selected and this is something that a lot of people miss when deploying OpsMgr for the first time.

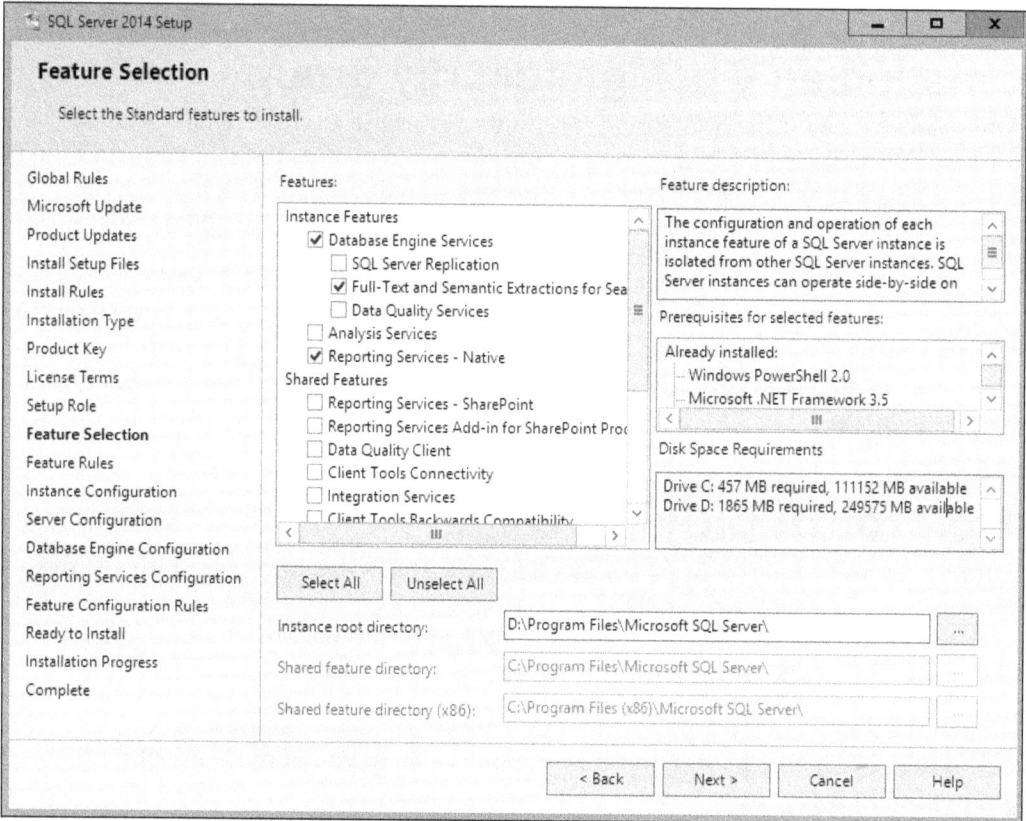

Figure 2.5: Choosing the Full Text Search feature

> When selecting features for a new SQL instance, make sure to select the **Management Tools – Complete** feature as this will add the SQL Management Studio interface. This graphical tool greatly simplifies SQL administration.

Further on through the SQL installation wizard and at the **Server Configuration** dialog box, change the SQL Server Agent service startup type to **Automatic** (the default setting here is **Manual**). If you don't make this change now, the OpsMgr prerequisite checker will pick up on it later and you will need to revisit this step.

Staying at the **Server Configuration** dialog box and clicking on the **Collation** tab, you will be presented with an option for the database engine SQL Collation setting as shown in *Figure 2.6*.

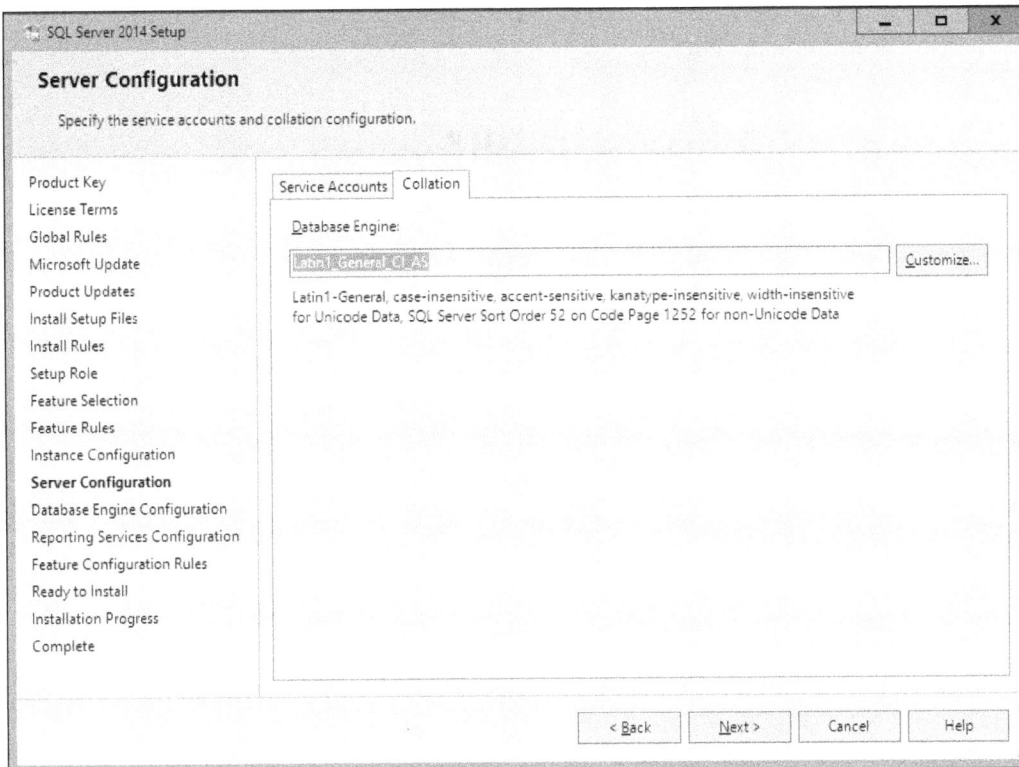

Figure 2.6: Configuring SQL collation

Now, depending on the version of OpsMgr that you are planning to install, this collation setting could become very important. For example, prior to OpsMgr 2012 R2, there were very specific SQL collation settings that needed to be applied depending on the language locale of the system and type of data that you store in the databases.

If you are working through the steps in this book to help you deploy an older version of OpsMgr, then we highly recommend you first read through this post from Microsoft - `http://tinyurl.com/sysctrcollation` and then configure your SQL collation accordingly.

For OpsMgr 2012 R2 and higher, the requirement for changing your SQL collation setting on English systems has been removed and there's no need to change it from the default setting.

SQL Server authentication mode

During the SQL installation wizard and at the **Database Engine Configuration** dialog box, you will be prompted to specify an **Authentication Mode** setting. For OpsMgr, it is recommended to configure this setting using the **Windows authentication mode** option.

SQL Server administrators

Also at the **Database Engine Configuration** dialog box, you will be prompted to specify your SQL Server administrators for the instance. If you've already created the OpsMgr service accounts and added them to the security group as suggested earlier in this chapter, then you can specify that the security group is a SQL Server administrator as shown in *Figure 2.7*.

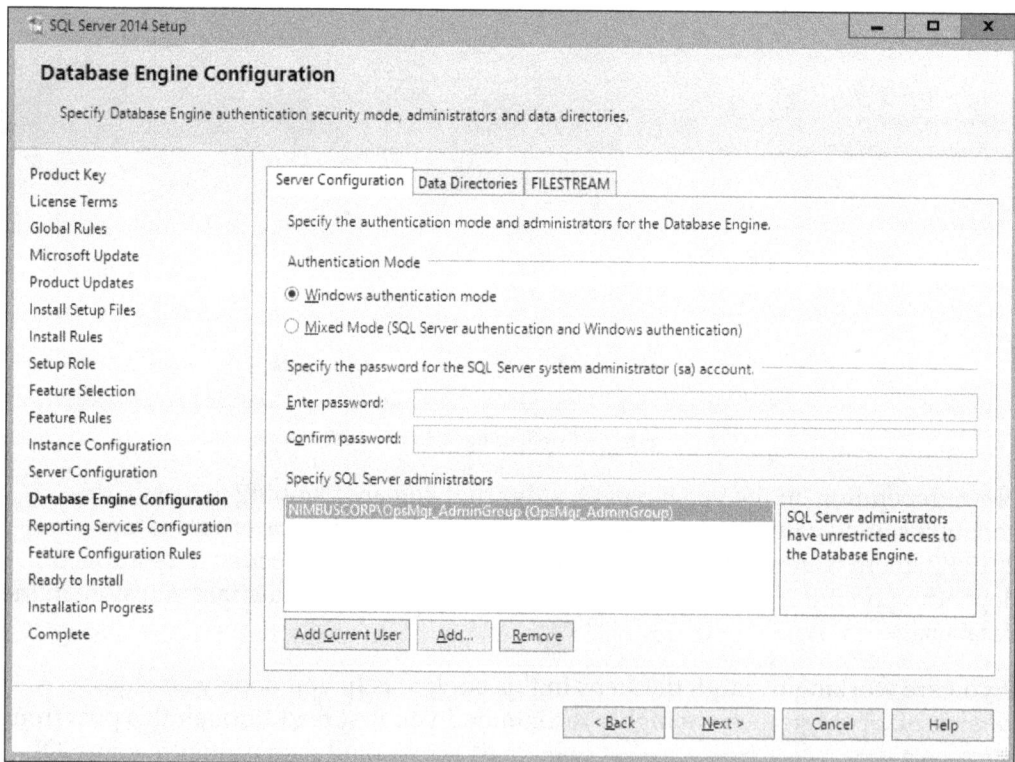

Figure 2.7: Adding SQL administrators

The benefit of adding the security group that contains your OpsMgr service accounts here is that all of the relevant permissions are now in place for the OpsMgr installation to do its job.

Configuring SQL memory allocation

Any time you deploy an instance of SQL, it is best practice to assign a designated amount of memory to that particular instance. The reason for this is that by default, the SQL installation wizard configures the new SQL instance to use up all of the available memory on your server – leaving nothing for the operating system!

This clearly isn't an optimal configuration and over a short period of time, if left as it is, your SQL Server will slowly grind to a halt as the operating system doesn't have the memory resources it needs to support itself.

Changing this setting is easy when you use the SQL Server Management Studio and connect to the SQL instance that hosts your OpsMgr databases. When the instance opens, you can view its properties by right-clicking on the instance name and selecting the **Properties** option as shown in *Figure 2.8*.

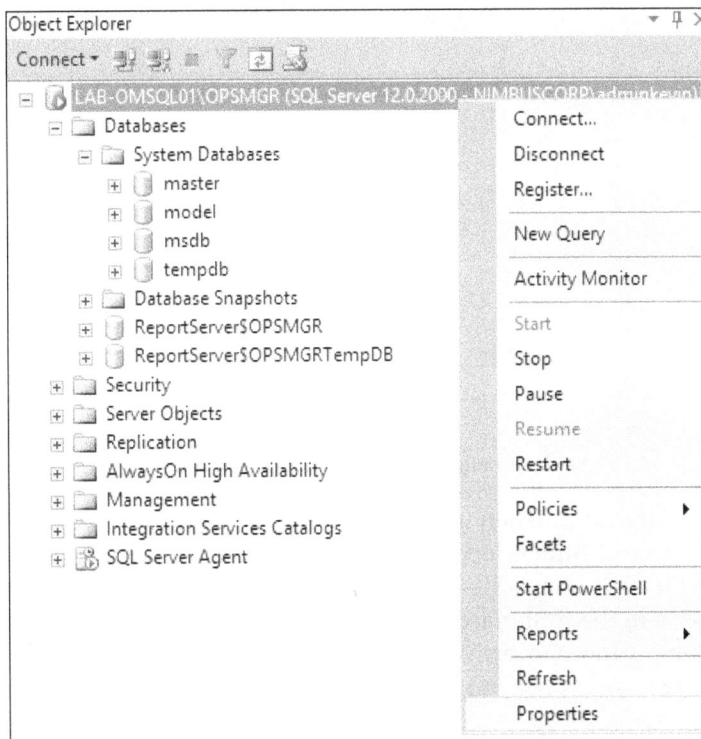

Figure 2.8: Access the SQL instance properties

Inside the **Server Properties** dialog box, click on the **Memory** page from the navigation menu on the left, then input the amount of memory that you wish to allocate to this SQL instance. You can see from *Figure 2.9* that we've allocated a total of 8192 MB (or 8GB) of memory to this instance.

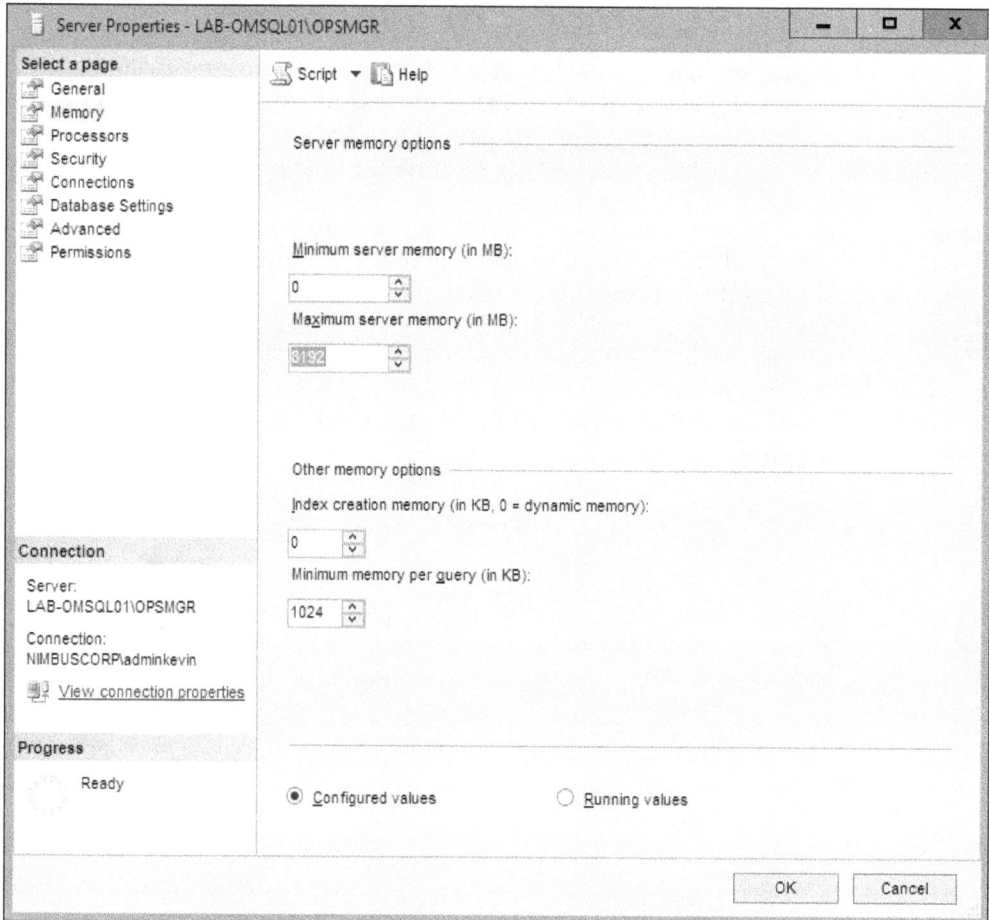

Figure 2.9: Configuring SQL Maximum Server Memory

As a general rule of thumb when trying to work out how much memory you should allocate, it's recommended that you leave anywhere between 2GB and 5GB for the operating system – depending on how much physical memory you have to work with in the first place. Check out this post from System Center MVP Stefan Roth for more information on performance tuning for your SQL Server - http://tinyurl.com/sqlperftuning

There are many other options – including High Availability - you can apply to the SQL infrastructure that will be responsible for running your OpsMgr environment and if you want to learn more, then you can download an excellent free whitepaper from System Center MVP Paul Keely at `http://tinyurl.com/sysctrsql`.

Configuring the prerequisites

With SQL deployed and optimized, it's now time to install the prerequisite software that must be in place prior to deploying OpsMgr. Both the Management server and the reporting server roles don't have any special software requirements to consider apart from the initial operating system and version of SQL that they're installed on.

If you are installing the Operations console or Web console however, then here's what you need to have in place for each:

Operations console prerequisites

The Operations console has a dependency on the **Microsoft Report Viewer 2012 Runtime** package and you can download it from here:

`http://www.microsoft.com/en-us/download/details.aspx?id=35747`.

As the Report Viewer 2012 Runtime package has in itself a dependency on the **Microsoft System CLR Types for SQL Server 2012**, this then becomes an indirect dependency for the Operations console too. You can download the System CLR Types for SQL Server 2012 as part of the **SQL Server 2012 Feature Pack** from here:

`http://www.microsoft.com/en-us/download/details.aspx?id=29065`.

Web console prerequisites

Now, if you thought preparing your server for the Operations console was easy, then the Web console takes things to a whole new level!

Here's what's required:

- Microsoft System CLR Types for SQL Server 2012
- Microsoft Report Viewer 2012 Runtime
- IIS Web Server Role
- Static Content
- Default Document

- Directory Browsing
- HTTP Errors
- HTTP Logging
- Request Monitor
- Request Filtering
- Static Content Compression
- Web Server (IIS) Support
- IIS 6 Metabase Compatibility
- ASP.NET (both the 2.0 and 4.0 versions of ASP.NET are required.)
- Windows Authentication

Using the download links from the Operations console prerequisite checker (which runs during initial installation), you can get the Microsoft System CLR Types and Report Viewer installed. The rest of the list is made up of Windows Server features that don't need to be downloaded, but will still need to be installed - either one by one through the GUI-based Server Manager interface or all together using PowerShell.

If you're using PowerShell to deploy these features, the following commands will get them installed:

```
Import-Module ServerManager
Add-WindowsFeature Web-Server,NET-Framework-Core,NET-HTTP-
Activation,NET-WCF-HTTP-Activation45,Web-Mgmt-console,Web-Net-Ext,Web-
Net-Ext45,Web-Static-Content,Web-Default-Doc,Web-Dir-Browsing,Web-
Http-Errors,Web-Http-Logging,Web-Request-Monitor,Web-Filtering,Web-
Stat-Compression,Web-ISAPI-Ext,Web-ISAPI-Filter,Web-Metabase,Web-Asp-
Net,Web-Windows-Auth,Windows-Identity-Foundation -restart
```

> To make things nice and easy for you, here's a link for a PowerShell script I've created that will automatically download and install all prerequisite software for the OpsMgr web console role: `http://tinyurl.com/scomprereq/`

Granting Local Administrator rights

Next, you need to logon to each server that you will deploy OpsMgr to with an account that has administrative rights on the local server and add the domain security group that we created earlier (we named it Opsmgr_AdminGroup) to the local **Administrators** group as shown in *Figure 2.10*.

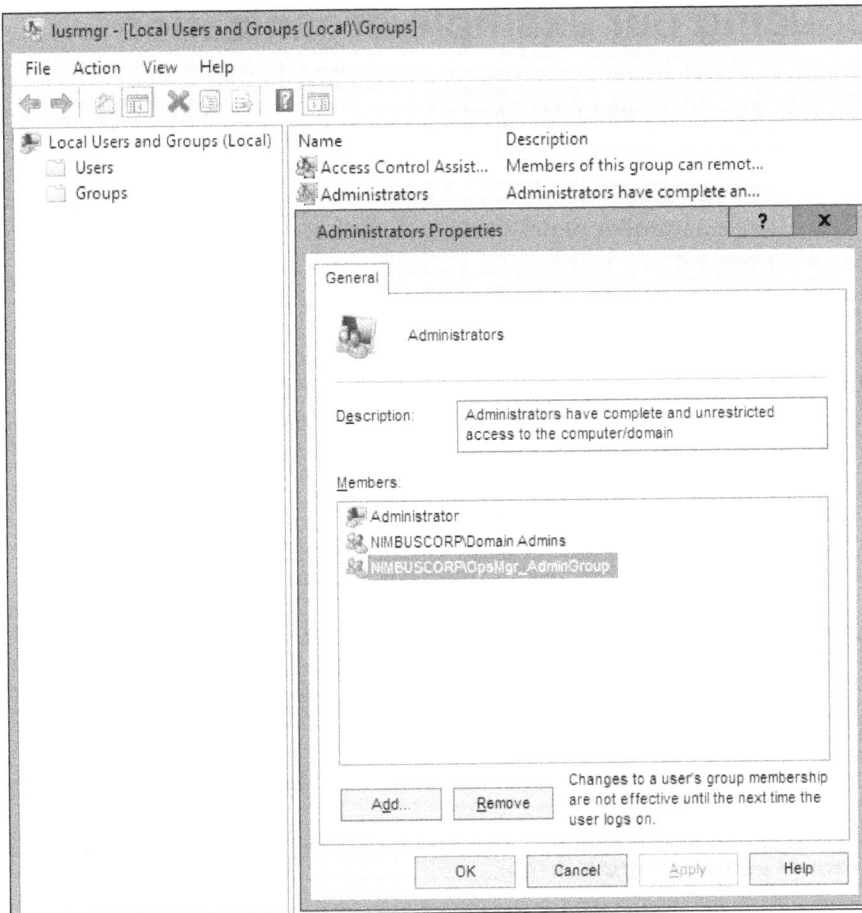

Figure 2.10: The Local Administrators group

Installing your first Management server

Now you're ready to install your first OpsMgr Management server and at this point, you should have decided on the type of OpsMgr design that you wish to deploy along with having the service accounts, SQL and prerequisite software all in place.

If you haven't done so already, you can download a fully functional 180-day evaluation version of the OpsMgr software from here: `http://tinyurl.com/sysctreval`. This evaluation can be easily upgraded to a licensed version with a valid license key that can be obtained when you purchase System Center for your organization.

Introducing our example organization

For the purpose of this book, we have created a fictional organization called Nimbus Corporation who is running an Active Directory domain named `NimbusCorp.com`.

They have a need to use OpsMgr to monitor an IT infrastructure made up of a mix of Microsoft Windows and UNIX/Linux computers spread across multiple domains and DMZ's. There's a number of network devices that need to be monitored and a business requirement to represent their IT service catalog through dashboard visualizations has become a top priority for senior management too.

For this deployment, we will use the 'Small Distributed Server' design as a starting foundation and we will customize the design by adding a secondary Management server for agent failover as well as a Gateway server to support untrusted domain monitoring.

> It is important to note that this fictional deployment has been created to ensure that everyone reading this book can use it to easily walk through the various tasks required for getting a basic OpsMgr deployment up and running. Depending on the complexity and IT policies of the organization you will be deploying into, your own production build of OpsMgr could look different to the examples in this book.

The following steps will walk you through installing the first Management server:

1. From the OpsMgr installation media, right-click on `setup.exe` and choose **Run as administrator** to begin.

2. When the splash screen opens, choose whether or not you wish to download the latest updates to the setup program, then click on **Install**.

3. In the **Select Features to Install** dialog box, choose the **Management server** and **Operations console** options, as shown in *Figure 2.11*, then click **Next** to continue.

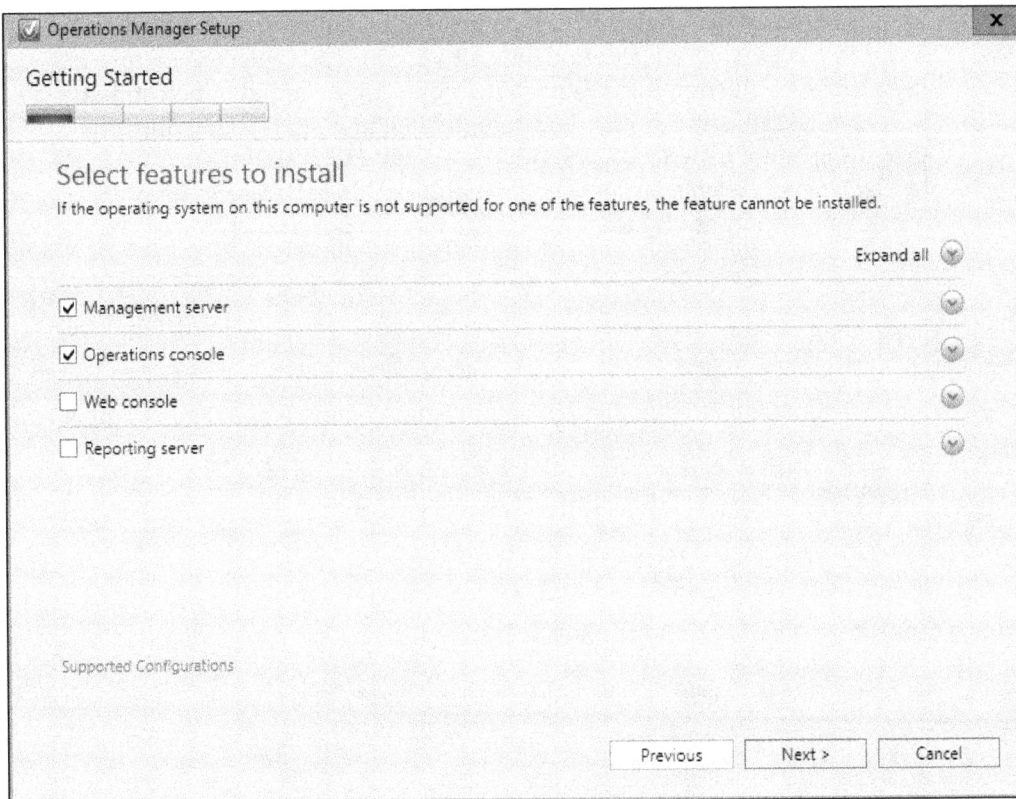

Figure 2.11: Choosing your OpsMgr features

4. Choose a location (or leave the default as it is) for the OpsMgr installation files, then click on **Next** to move on.

5. In the **Prerequisites** dialog box, the OpsMgr installation wizard runs a script to ensure that all prerequisite software for each selected feature has been installed. If something is missing, you will see a dialog box similar to *Figure 2.12* informing you the prerequisites that are missing and also providing some instructions on how to obtain and install them. Please refer to *Configuring the prerequisites* section earlier in this chapter to help you quickly resolve these issues.

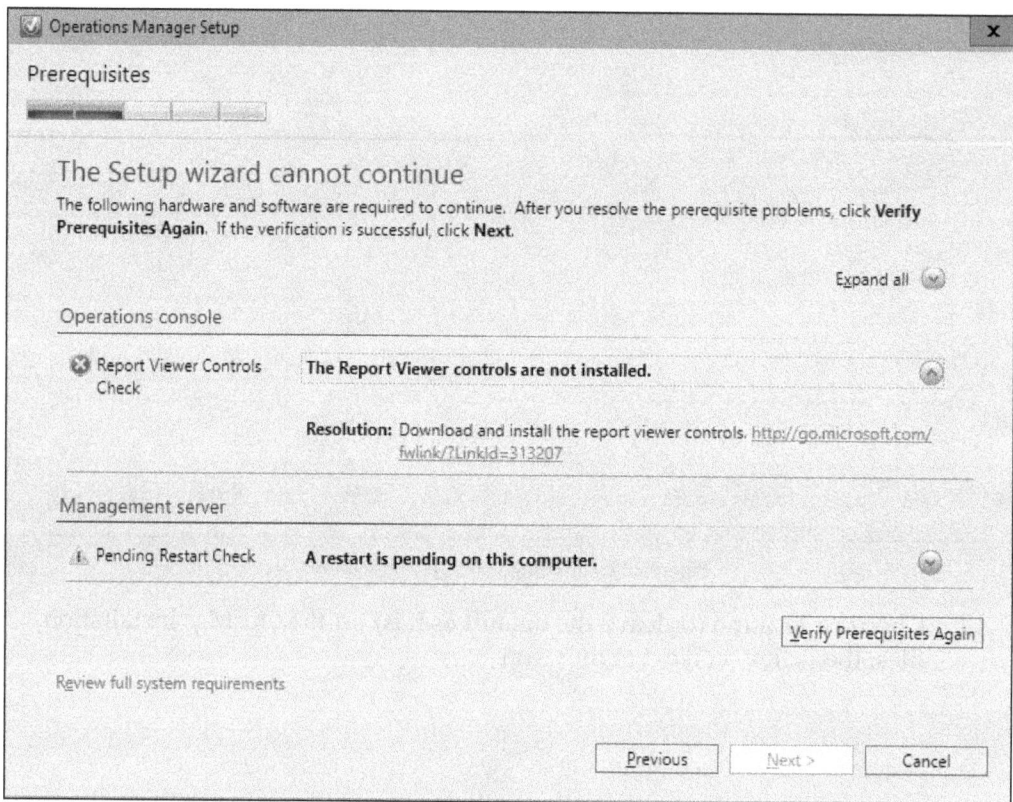

Figure 2.12: OpsMgr prerequisite check

6. When the prerequisite check has passed, you then move on to the **Configuration** dialog box where you need to either specify that this will be the first Management server in a new management group, or if it will simply be an additional Management server in an existing management group. As this is our first Management server, we will choose that option and will enter a Management Group name of NIMBUSMG1 here.

> Be careful when selecting a new Management Group name here as it is case-sensitive, does not support the following special characters: ( ) ^ ~ : ; . ! ? " , ' ` @ # % \ / * + = $ | & [ ] <> {} and can't contain a leading or trailing space. We recommend keeping it short and simple in an alpha-numeric format where possible. Also, this name cannot be changed later without reinstalling the entire management group so choose wisely!

7. Accept the license terms and click on **Next** to continue.

8. Configure the location, size and SQL port of your Operational database in this next dialog box - making sure that you specify it in the `server name\ instance name` format as shown in *Figure 2.13*. It's recommended to leave the name of this database as its default **OperationsManager**.

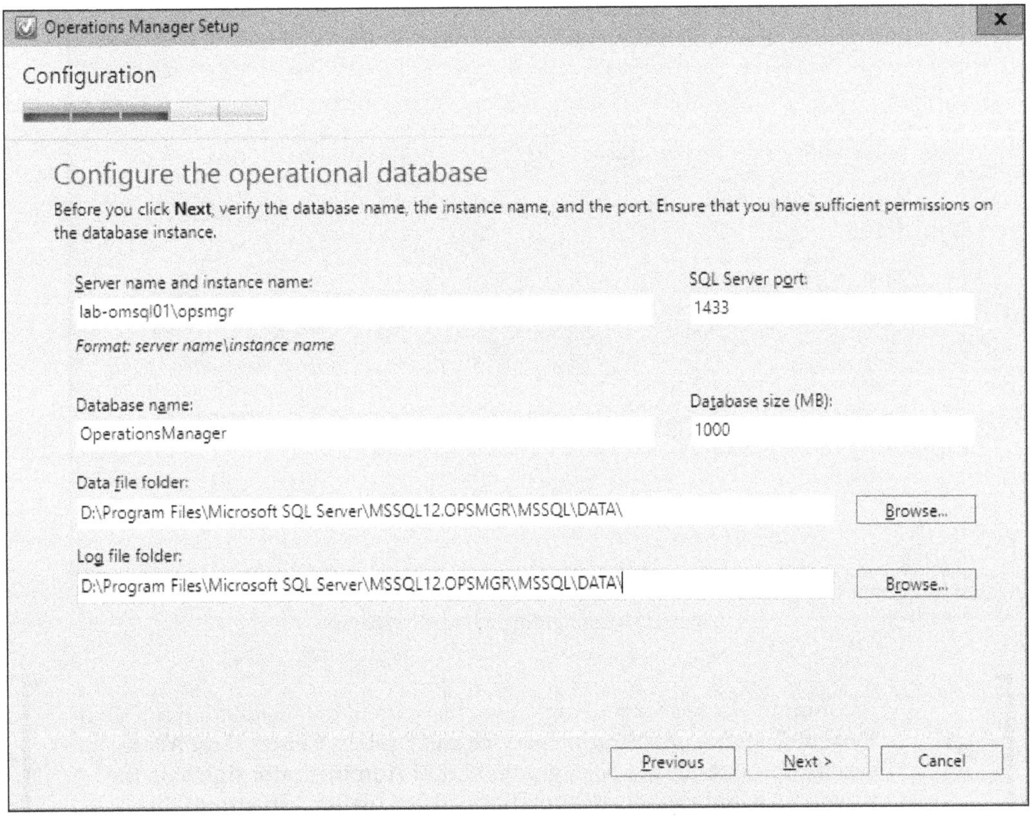

Figure 2.13: Configuring the Operational database

9. Configure the data warehouse database using the same methods from the previous step and ensure that you have used the OpsMgr Sizing Helper Tool to size the database appropriately. Click on **Next** when you're ready to move on.

10. The **Configure Operations Manager Accounts** dialog box is often the point where a lot of first-time OpsMgr installations fail or are configured incorrectly. Unless you are deploying a 'Single Server' design whereby your SQL is installed on the same server as OpsMgr, then you must configure your service accounts as shown in *Figure 2.14* (pay particular attention here to how we've configured **System Center Configuration service and System Center Data Access service** account with the **Domain Account** option).

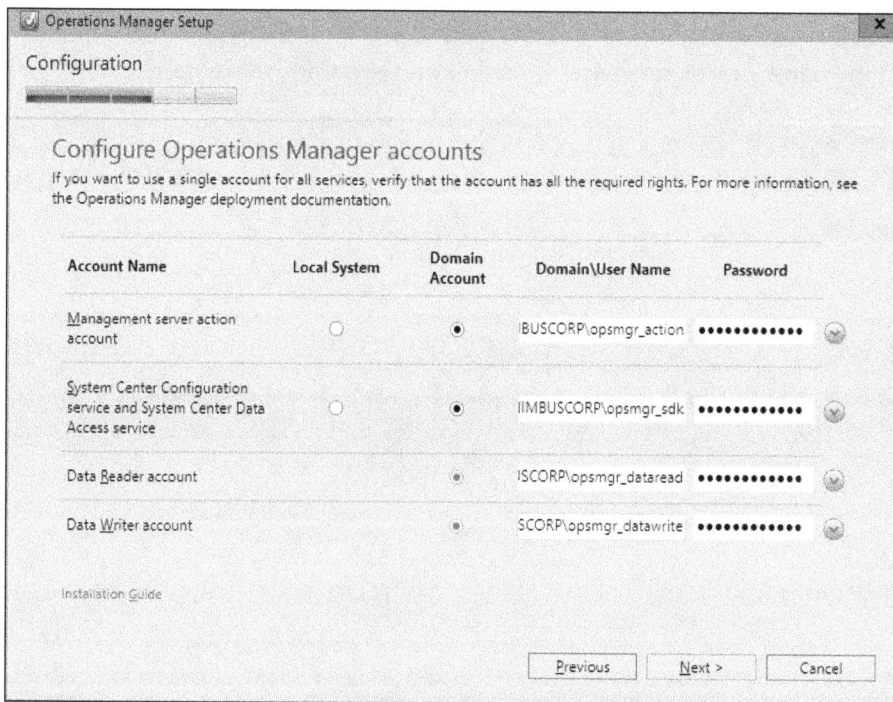

Figure 2.14: Configuring the service accounts

A common blocker for moving on at this point of the installation is if your **System Center Configuration service and System Center Data Access service** account has not been granted Local Administrator rights on the server. To avoid this, ensure you have added the security group that contains your OpsMgr service accounts to the **Administrators** group on the local server.

11. Click through to the **Microsoft Update** dialog box and choose whether or not you'd like to use Microsoft Update to deliver automatic OpsMgr updates (we'll choose the **No** option here as we will deploy OpsMgr updates manually at a later stage), then click on **Next** to continue.

12. Finally, review everything that you have entered at the **Installation Summary** dialog box and then hit **Install** to begin the OpsMgr installation.

13. When the installation process is finished, you should see the **Setup is Complete** dialog box as shown in *Figure 2.15*. No need to worry about the **Management server** warning text, this is simply stating that you need to update the license key and we'll perform this action in the next step. Also, uncheck the **Start the Operations console when the wizard closes** option as we need to give OpsMgr a few minutes to automatically close some alerts in the console that would have been generated as a part of the normal installation process. Click on the **Close** button to exit the wizard.

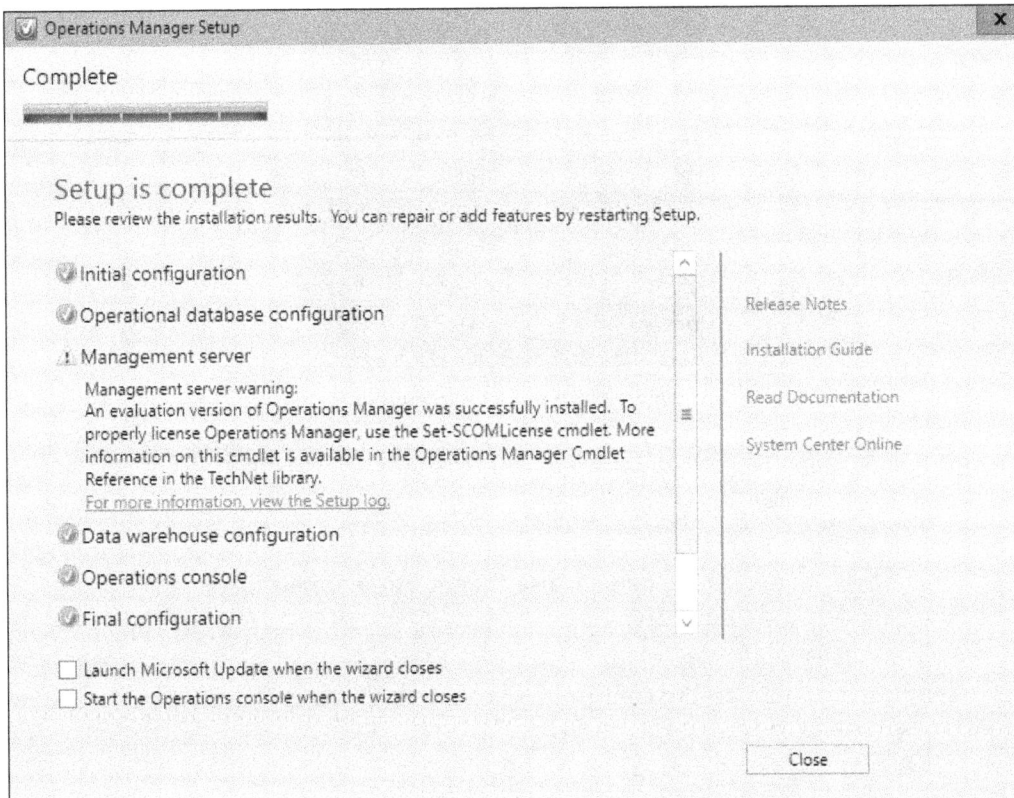

Figure 2.15: Successful installation

14. When the wizard closes, similar to *Figure 2.16*, you will notice two new entries in your Start Menu – one for opening the **Operational Console** and the other for opening the Operations Manager PowerShell module. We'll use this module to update the OpsMgr license key.

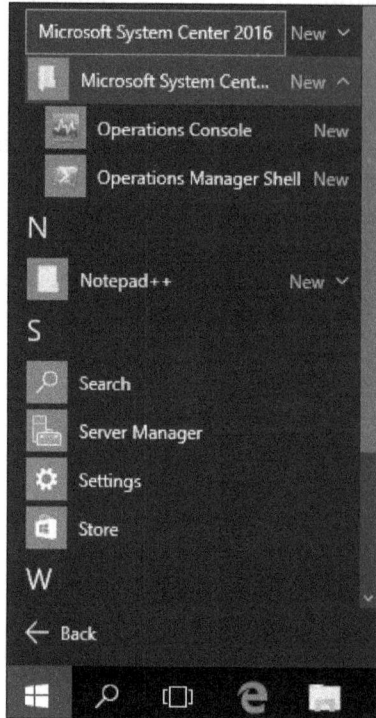

Figure 2.16: New OpsMgr shortcuts

15. Launch the Operations Manager Shell, and type the following (replacing the XXXX characters with your own license key):

```
Set-SCOMLicense -ProductID XXXXX-XXXXX-XXXXX-XXXXX-XXXXX
```

16. Choose **Y** to accept the new license change and then hit *Enter*.

17. Restart the server to update the new license key information and when it comes back online, open the Operations Manager Shell again and type the following command to confirm the license has been applied:

```
Get-SCOMManagementGroup | ft skuforlicense, version,
timeofexpiration -a
```

18. If the license has been applied successfully, the **SkuForLicense** entry should change to **Retail** (as opposed to Eval) and this then completes your first management server deployment.

> After the first Management server has been installed and using the SQL Management Studio, open up the instance that hosts the new OpsMgr databases, right-click on each database and check the domain account that has been assigned as the database owner. This owner will be defined as the account that you used to install your first OpsMgr Management server and if you have any strict password reset policies applied (or if this account is a temporary account that will soon be disabled once OpsMgr has been deployed), then it's recommended to change the owner of the databases to an appropriate user account.

Installing additional Management servers

The process for installing an additional Management server is very similar to deploying the first one in a management group. To complete these steps, you will need to have a second virtual or physical computer running a supported server operating system version available.

Here's what you need to do:

1. On your second server, browse to the OpsMgr installation media location, right-click on `setup.exe` and choose **Run as administrator** to begin.

2. From the splash screen that opens up, choose whether or not you wish to download the latest updates to the setup program and then click on **Install**.

3. In the Select Features to Install dialog box, choose the **Management server** and **Operations console** options, as shown earlier in *Figure 2.11* and then click on **Next** to continue.

4. Choose a location for the OpsMgr installation files and then click on **Next**.

5. Let the prerequisites check complete and click on **Next** to move on.

6. In the **Specify an Installation Option** dialog box, choose the **Add a Management server to an existing Management Group** option as shown in *Figure 2.17*, then click on **Next**.

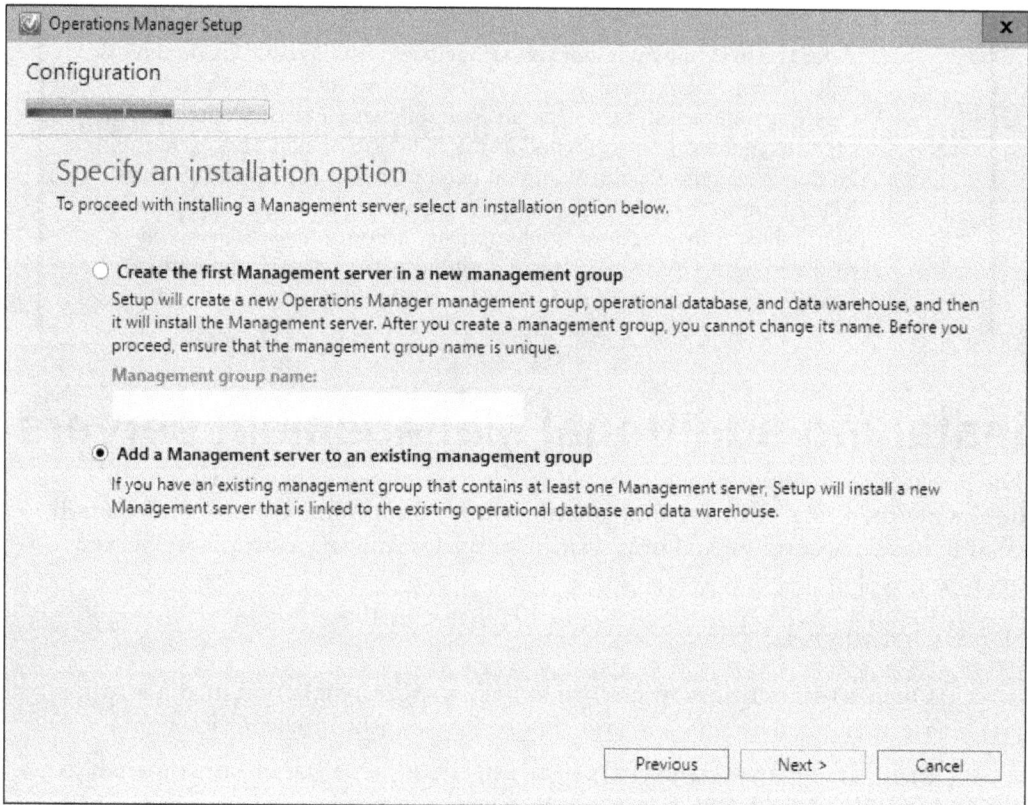

Figure 2.17: Adding a new Management server

7. Accept the license terms at the next dialog box and then click on **Next** to continue.

8. Input the server name, instance name (in the format of `server name\instance name`) and SQL port to identify where your Operational database is located and then choose the **OperationsManager** database name from the drop-down menu. Click on **Next** to continue.

9. In the Configure Operations Manager Accounts dialog box, change **System Center Configuration service and System Center Data Access service** account option to a **Domain Account**, then input your OpsMgr service account info as shown in *Figure 2.18*. Click on **Next** to move on.

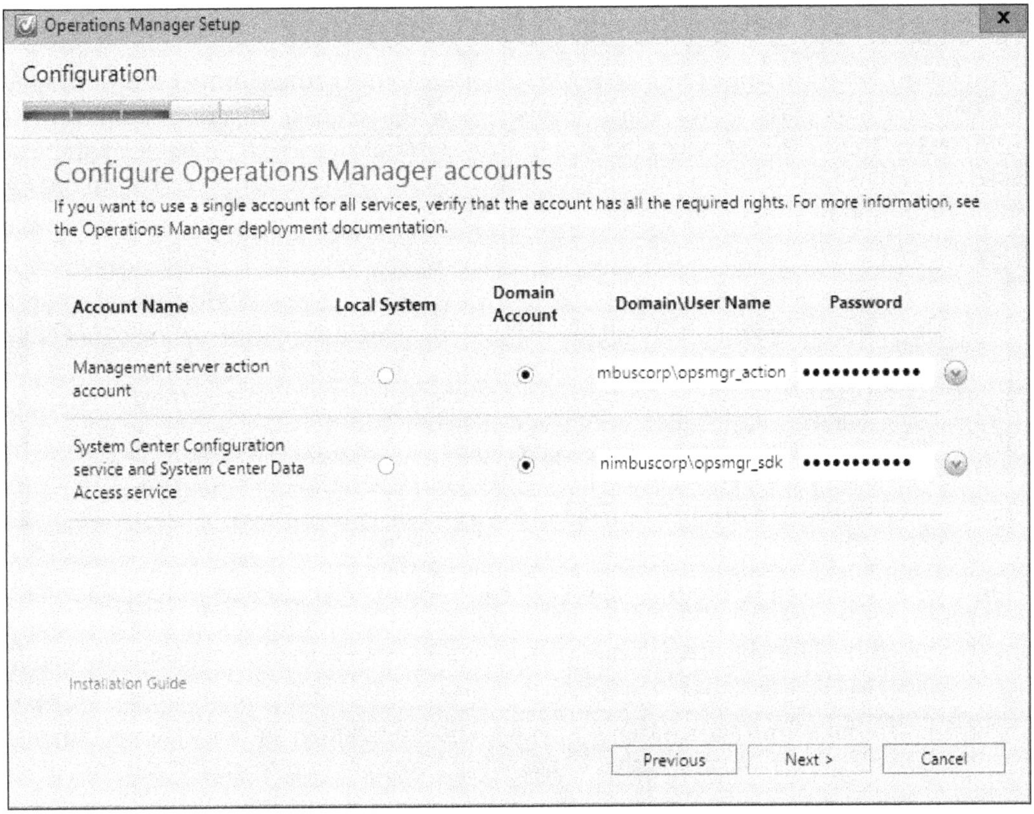

Figure 2.18: Configuring OpsMgr accounts

> If you see an error message stating **One or more accounts provided could not be validated**. Please provide valid user names and passwords here and then assuming you have actually typed in the correct user name and password, the most likely reason for this error is that you forgot to add the OpsMgr_AdminGroup to the 'Administrators' group on the local server. The reason for this is that the OpsMgr_SDK account must be a Local Administrator on the computer for the installation to validate.

10. Click through to the **Microsoft Update** dialog box and choose whether or not you'd like to use Microsoft Update to deliver automatic OpsMgr updates, then click on **Next** to continue.

11. Finally, review everything that you have entered at the **Installation Summary** dialog box and hit **Install** to begin the Management server installation. When the process is complete your additional Management server is ready to go.

Installing the Reporting server

With your Management servers installed, we need to now concentrate on installing the OpsMgr Reporting server role. For this, you will need to have a server running SQL **Server Reporting Services (SSRS)** in Native Mode. This SSRS instance will be used exclusively by OpsMgr and cannot be shared with any other products due to the security model it operates within.

> Prior to installing the OpsMgr Reporting Server role, the SSRS instance should be pre-configured in **Native Mode**. This is the default option selected for you when you deploy SSRS on the same server as the Database Engine Services feature and the SQL installation wizard will automatically configure SSRS in Native Mode for you. If you chose to not install SSRS on the same server as the Database Engine Services instance, then you will need to use the SQL Reporting Services Configuration Manager to manually configure the server for Native Mode.

Here's what you need to do to get the OpsMgr Reporting server role deployed:

1. From the OpsMgr installation media, right-click on `setup.exe` and choose 'Run as administrator' to begin.

2. From the splash screen that opens up, choose whether or not you wish to download the latest updates to the setup program and then click on **Install**.

3. In the **Select Features to Install** dialog box, choose the **Reporting server** option then click on **Next** to continue.

4. Let the prerequisites check complete and click on **Next** to continue.

5. Accept the license terms at the next dialog box and then click on **Next**.

6. Specify the name of the first management server that you installed into your Management Group as shown in *Figure 2.19* and click on **Next** to move on.

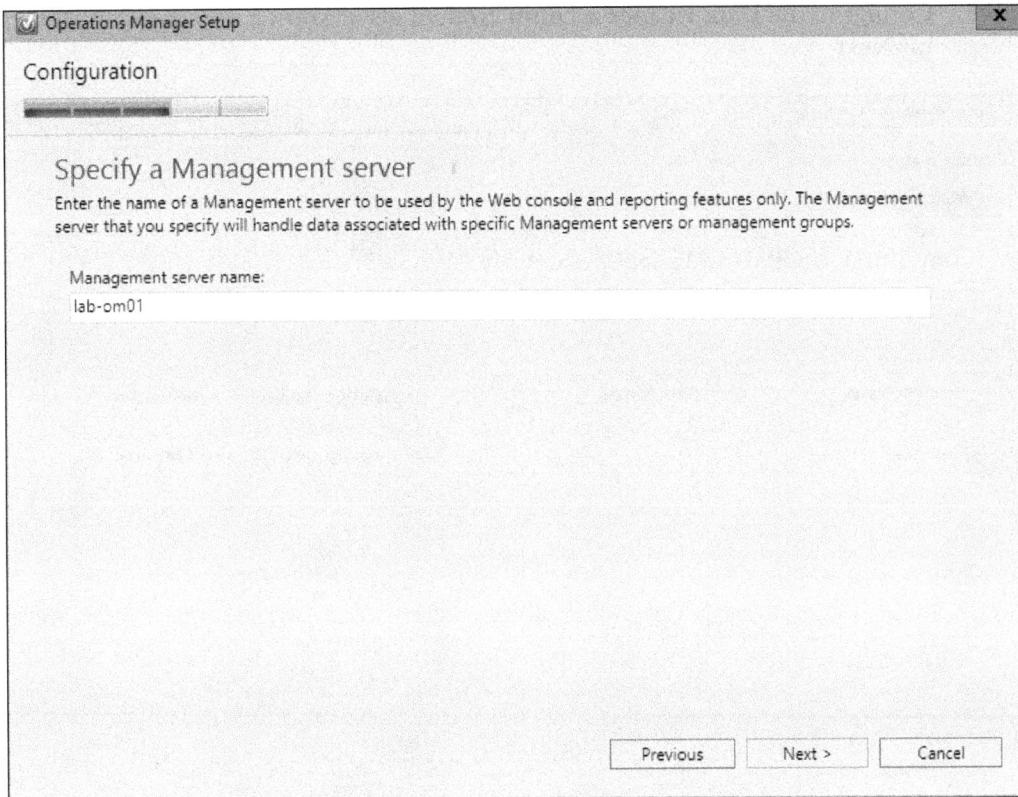

Figure 2.19: Specifying a Management server for the Reporting role

7. In the next dialog box, choose the name of the SQL Server instance that you wish to host SSRS on, then click on **Next**.

8. Configure the **Data Reader account** credentials as shown in *Figure 2.20*, then hit **Next**.

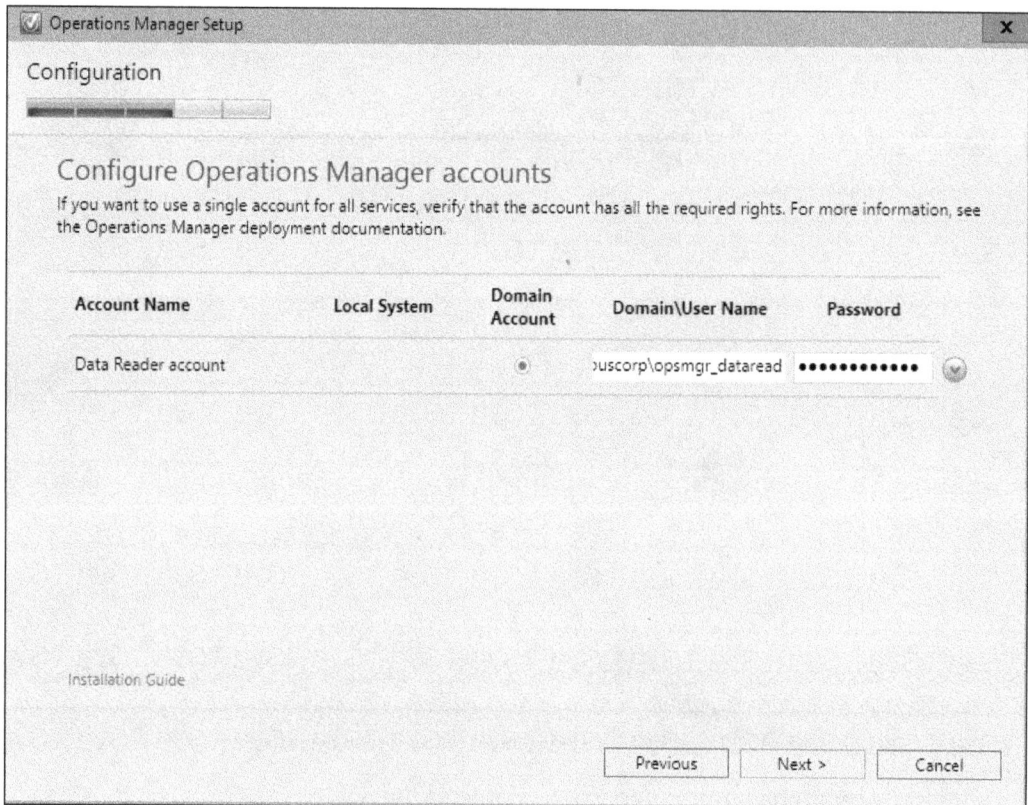

Figure 2.20: Configuring the Data Reader account

9. Click through to the **Microsoft Update** dialog box and choose whether or not you'd like to use Microsoft Update to deliver automatic OpsMgr updates, then click on **Next** to continue.

10. Finally, review everything that you have entered at the **Installation Summary** dialog box and hit **Install** to begin the Reporting server installation.

11. When the process has completed, you can confirm your Reporting Server is working by launching the Operations console and confirming the **Reporting** tab is present in the navigation bar. After a few minutes, similar to *Figure 2.21*, you should see reports populating in the relevant folders. Be aware that it can sometimes take up to 30 minutes for this process to occur after the Reporting role has been deployed.

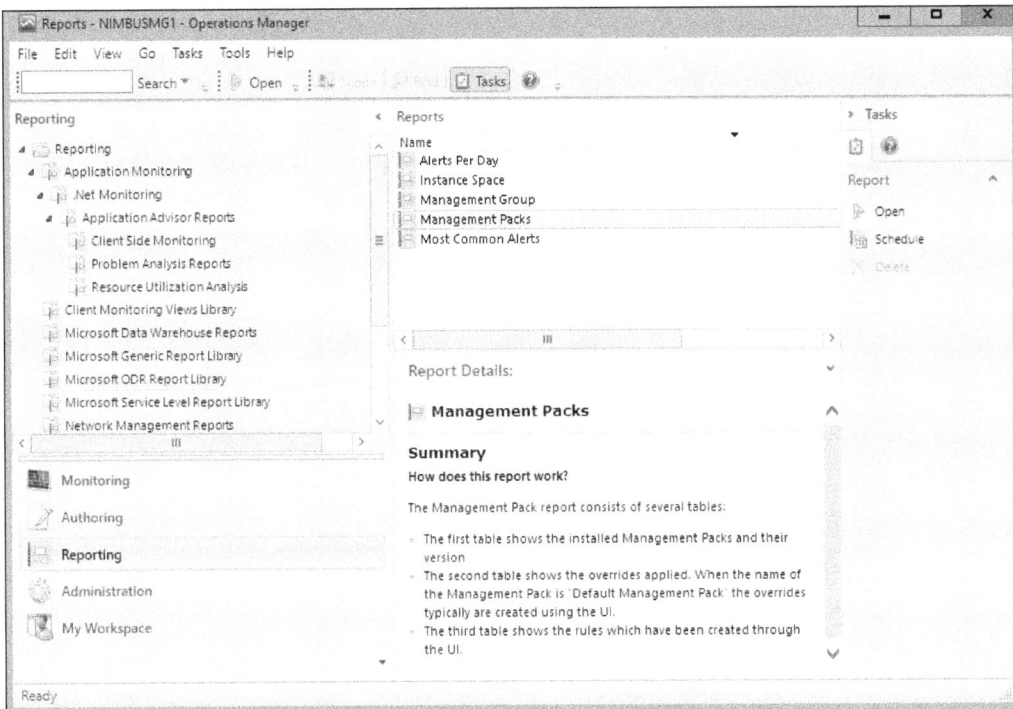

Figure 2.21: Confirming the Reporting Role

12. Double-click on one of the reports from the Microsoft ODR Report Library and a new report should generate automatically. This confirms the Reporting server role is functioning properly.

Deploying the Web console

Depending on the design you have chosen for your OpsMgr deployment, you might decide to run the Web console role on one of your existing Management servers or instead, you could just choose to deploy it on a separate server. Either way, the following steps will walk you through the installation process:

1. From the OpsMgr installation media, right-click on `setup.exe` and choose **Run as administrator** to begin.

2. From the splash screen that opens up, choose whether or not you wish to download the latest updates to the setup program and then click on **Install**.

3. In the **Select Features to Install** dialog box, choose the **Web console** option and then click on **Next** to continue.

4. If the prerequisite check fails, download and run the prerequisite script from `http://tinyurl.com/scomprereq` to ensure everything has been configured correctly and then hit **Next** to move on.

5. Specify the IIS website that you wish to deploy the Web console into. *Figure 2.22* shows the default setting of the **Default Web Site** offered and you can also optionally choose to **Enable SSL** here for more secure communications (this option requires an SSL certificate to be assigned in IIS). Click on **Next** to continue.

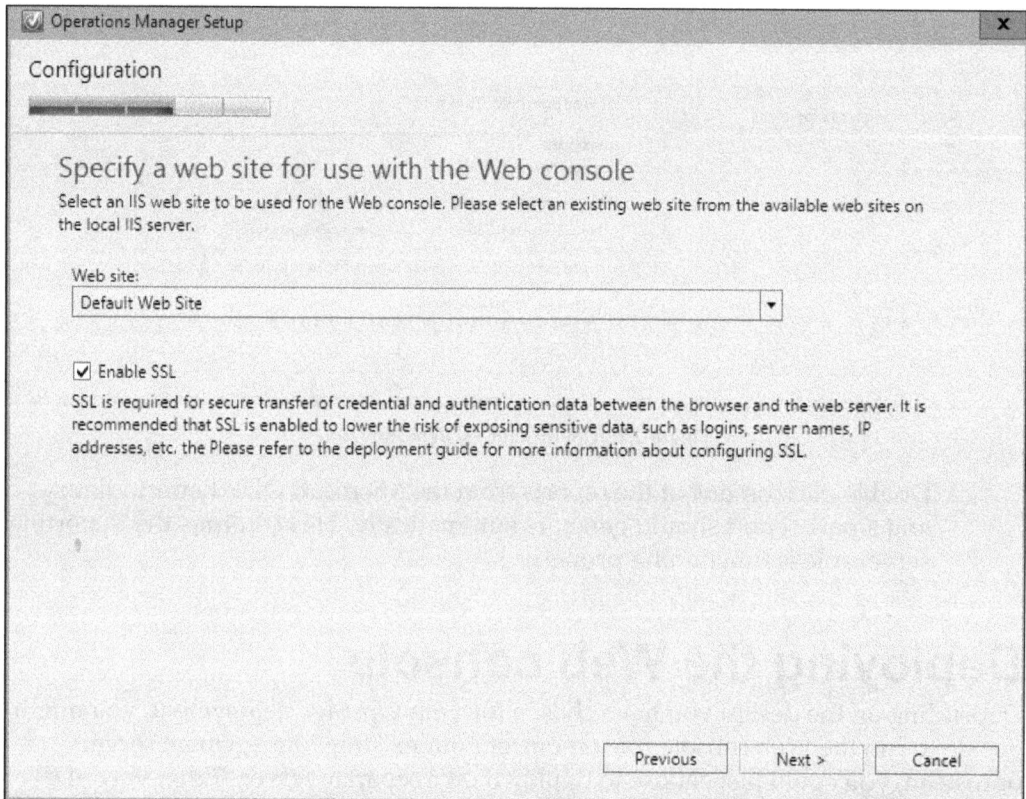

Operations Manager Setup   **x**

Configuration

Specify a web site for use with the Web console

Select an IIS web site to be used for the Web console. Please select an existing web site from the available web sites on the local IIS server.

Web site:

Default Web Site   ▼

☑ Enable SSL

SSL is required for secure transfer of credential and authentication data between the browser and the web server. It is recommended that SSL is enabled to lower the risk of exposing sensitive data, such as logins, server names, IP addresses, etc. the Please refer to the deployment guide for more information about configuring SSL.

Previous   Next >   Cancel

Figure 2.22: Choosing the website and SSL setting

6. At the **Select an Authentication Mode** for use with the Web console dialog box, choose from either **Mixed Authentication** (used for Intranet scenarios) or **Network Authentication** (used when accessing the web console externally over the Internet). Click on **Next** to move on.

7. Click through to the **Microsoft Update** dialog box and choose whether or not you'd like to use Microsoft Update to deliver automatic OpsMgr updates, then click on **Next** to continue.

8. From the **Installation Summary** dialog box shown in *Figure 2.23*, you can see that three different website addresses will be created. The **OperationsManager** website address will become your Web console and the **AppDiagnostics** and **AppAdvisor** addresses are used for the **Application Performance Monitoring (APM)** functionality of OpsMgr. Confirm you are happy to proceed and then click on **Install** to deploy the Web console.

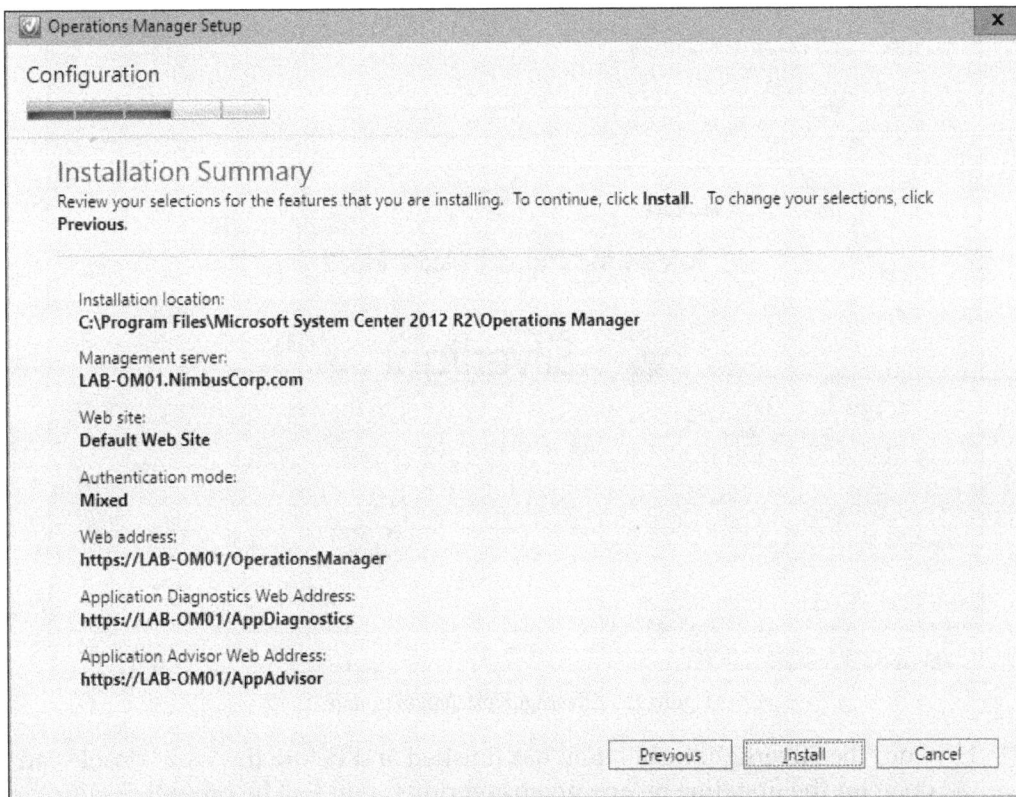

Figure 2.23: Web console installation summary

9. When you see the **Setup is Complete** dialog box, click on the **Close** button to finish the process.

10. To test that the website has installed correctly, open Internet Explorer and browse to the address of the Web console (we're using SSL so our URL is `https://lab-om01/operationsmanager` but if you're not using SSL, then your address should start with `http://` instead). The first time you access the Web console from a computer you will be prompted to install the latest version of Microsoft Silverlight as shown in *Figure 2.24*. Select the **Click Now to Install** button to download the latest version and follow the on-screen prompts to finish the Silverlight installation.

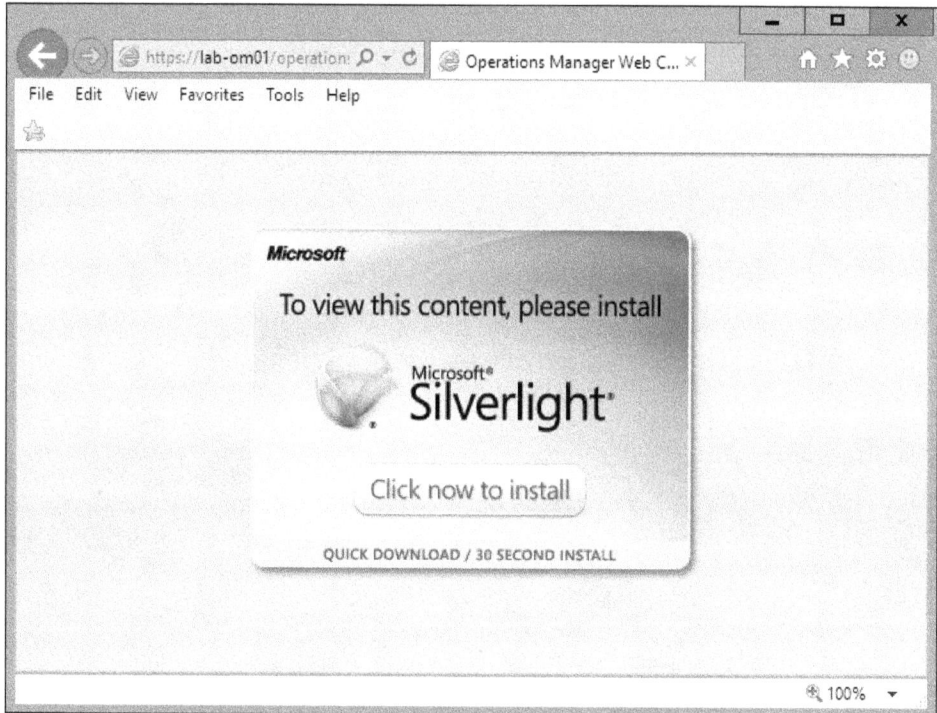

Figure 2.24: Silverlight installation prompt

11. Once the Silverlight installation has finished and before the Web console can open for the first time on any given computer, you will be presented with the Web console **Configuration Required** dialog box shown in *Figure 2.25*. Just click on the **Configure** button to download the updated Silverlight file from the web console to your computer.

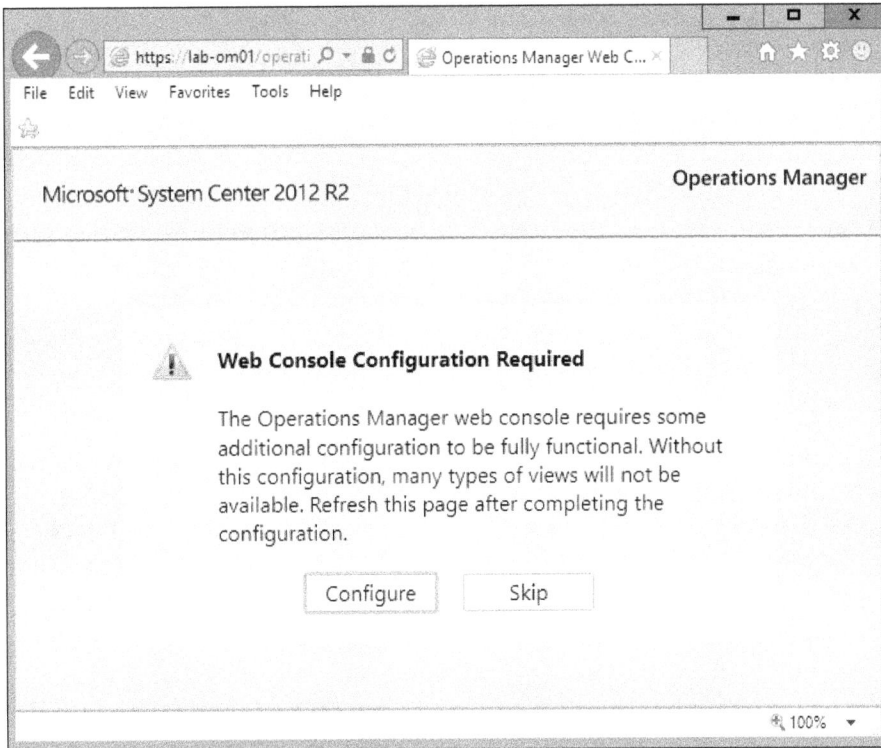

Figure 2.25: Silverlight Web console configuration options

12. When configuration is complete, you will see the following message - **The Operations Manager web console was successfully configured on this computer**. Now hit *F5* on your keyboard to refresh the page and the OpsMgr Web console should now open successfully.

Deploying a Gateway server

The final role that we need to install is the OpsMgr Gateway server. This role enables OpsMgr agent communication across different security boundaries – such as DMZ and untrusted Active Directory domains. The Gateway server can also be used to compress agent traffic across slow WAN links inside a Management Group domain.

In our example for this book, the Gateway server is a member of an untrusted Active Directory domain and we will need to utilize a **public key infrastructure (PKI)** for certificate-based authentication back into the OpsMgr Management Group.

Here's what we need before we begin:

- A **certificate authority (CA)** configured in the same domain as the OpsMgr Management Group.

- The **fully qualified domain name (FQDN)** of the OpsMgr Management server that the Gateway server will connect to.

- The `Microsoft.EnterpriseManagement.GatewayApprovalTool.exe` and its associated configuration file from the OpsMgr installation media.

- The `MOMCertImport.exe` tool from the OpsMgr installation media.

Now let's get started with the installation. Follow these steps to deploy your first Gateway server:

1. Logon to a Management server with an account that has administrative permissions and browse to the location where you have the OpsMgr installation media (we'll use `lab-om01.nimbuscorp.com` here but change this to whatever management server you want your new Gateway server to report into).

2. Copy both the `Microsoft.EnterpriseManagement.GatewayApprovalTool.exe` and `Microsoft.EnterpriseManagement.GatewayApprovalTool.exe.config` files from the `\SupportTools\AMD64` folder on the OpsMgr installation media to the OpsMgr program files `\Server` folder on your Management server.

> Depending on the version of OpsMgr you're deploying, the `\Server` folder is typically located at either `"%ProgramFiles%\System Center 2012 R2\Operations Manager\Server"` or `"%ProgramFiles%\Microsoft System Center 2016\Operations Manager\Server"`.

3. Now open a command prompt with administrative permissions on the Management server and change directory to the `\Server` folder location that you've just copied these files to.

4. In this example, we will approve a new Gateway server with an FQDN of `lab-omgw01.unifiedcommunications.ie` and configure it to report to `lab-om01.nimbuscorp.com`. From the command prompt, type the following to approve the new Gateway server:

```
Microsoft.EnterpriseManagement.GatewayApprovalTool.exe /
ManagementServerName=lab-om01.nimbuscorp.com /GatewayName=lab-
omgw01.unifiedcommunications.ie /Action=Create
```

5. In *Figure 2.26*, we can see the Gateway approval process completed successfully and we are ready to install the Gateway server role onto our prospective server.

Figure 2.26: Successful Gateway server approval

6. Now, logon to the server that you wish to install the Gateway server role to and browse to the location of the OpsMgr installation media.

7. From the OpsMgr installation media, right-click on `setup.exe` and choose **Run as administrator** to begin.

8. In the Optional Installations section of the splash screen (shown in *Figure 2.27*), click on the **Gateway management server** link to start the wizard.

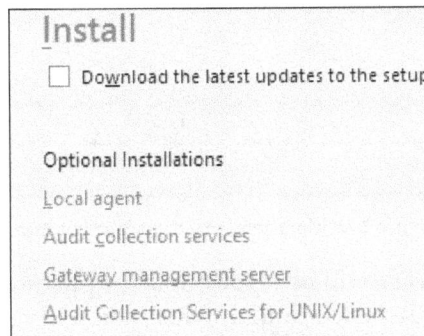

Figure 2.27: Gateway server installation link

9. At the welcome screen for the Gateway server setup wizard, click on **Next** to continue, then click to agree the license terms and move on.

10. Choose the folder location that you wish to install the Gateway server role to and then click on **Next**.

11. In the **Management Group Configuration** dialog box, input the **Management Group Name** (don't forget that this is case-sensitive) and the FQDN of the **Management Server** that you want the Gateway server to report to (always check the FQDN of your servers from the **System Properties** view on the server itself). *Figure 2.28* shows an example of how to complete this dialog box. Click on **Next** to continue.

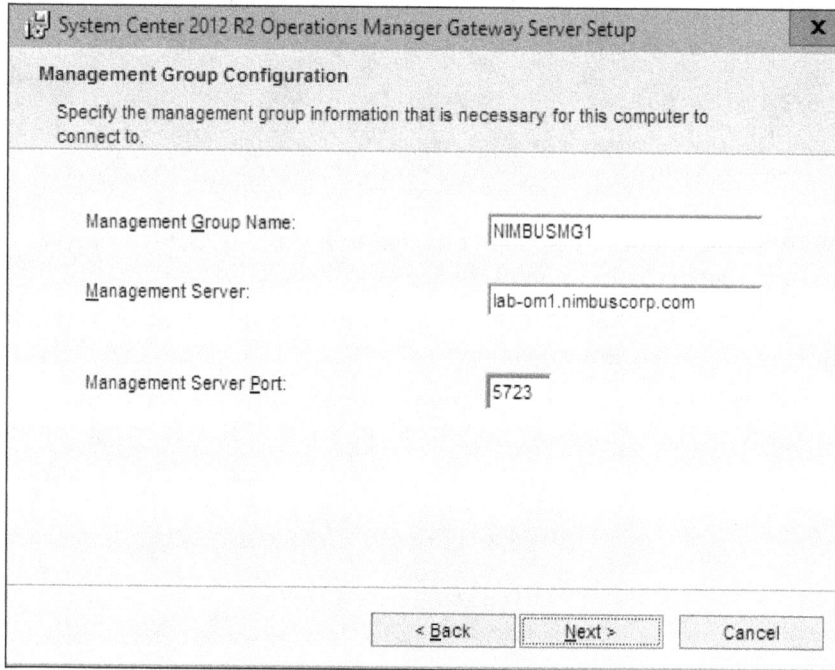

Figure 2.28: Management Group Configuration

12. If this Gateway server will be responsible for pushing out agents to computers in the untrusted domain, then you will need to configure an administrative domain user account for the **Gateway Action Account** as shown in *Figure 2.29*. Click **Next** when you're ready to move on.

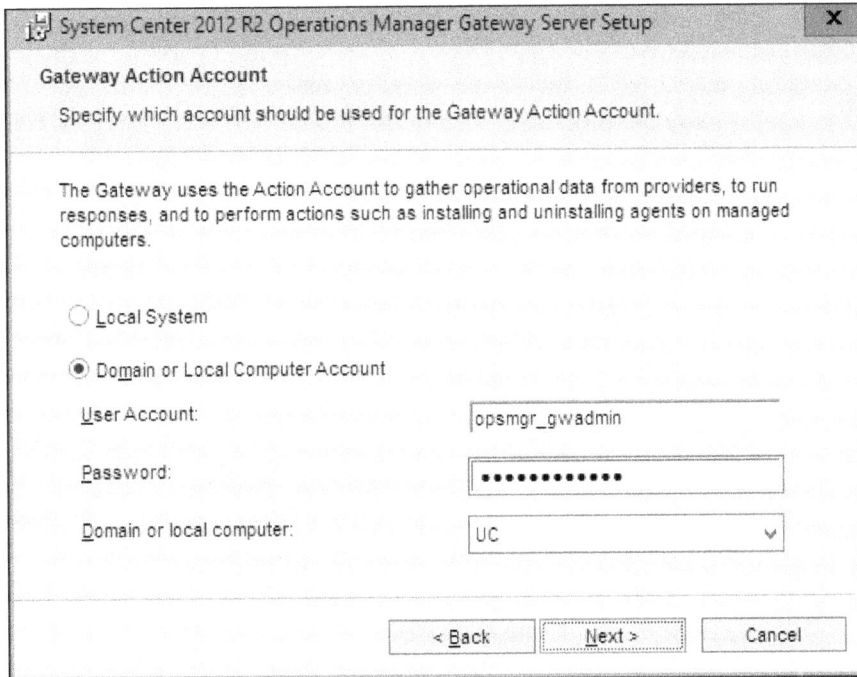

Figure 2.29: Configuring the Gateway Action Account

13. Choose if you want to use Microsoft Update to automatically update your Gateway server, then at the **Ready to Install** dialog box, confirm your settings and hit the **Install** button.

14. When the wizard completes successfully, click on the **Finish** button to close.

15. Now, assuming you are deploying your Gateway server into an untrusted domain or DMZ scenario, you will need to walk through a process on your Gateway server of requesting a certificate from a Certificate Authority and installing that certificate into the 'Local Computer' store.

> If you haven't carried out this task before or you aren't too comfortable working with certificates, then take a look at this blog series I wrote a while back for a complete walkthrough - http://tinyurl.com/scomprivcerts. Although this series was written originally on Windows Server 2008 R2, it's still valid for Windows Server 2012 R2 and higher.

16. We'll take the certificate authentication process up again here at the point in the blog series where we need to use the MOMCertImport.exe utility.

17. With the new certificate now imported into the `Local Computer\Personal` certificate store, we now need to open up a command prompt with elevated permissions on the Gateway server and change directory to `\Support Tools\AMD64` on the OpsMgr installation media where `MOMCertImport.exe` is located.

18. As shown in *Figure 2.30*, add the `/subjectname` switch to the end of the `MOMCertImport.exe` utility and specify the full subject name of your imported certificate exactly as it is displayed in the `Local Computer\ Personal\Certificates` store. Your command should look something similar to the following example: `MOMCertImport.exe /subjectname lab-gw01.unifiedcommunications.ie`.

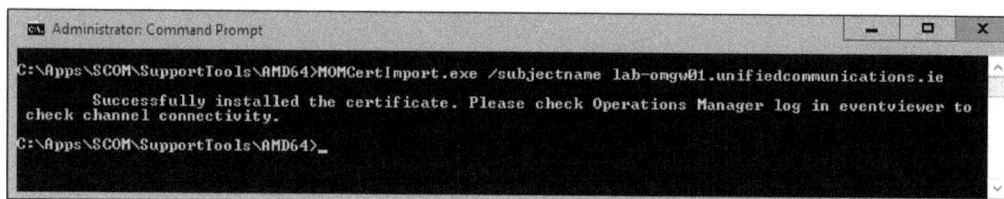

Figure 2.30: Importing the Gateway server certificate

19. After a short while, you should then see your new Gateway server lighting up in the **Administration | Device Management | Management servers** section of the Operations console with a healthy status as shown in *Figure 2.31*.

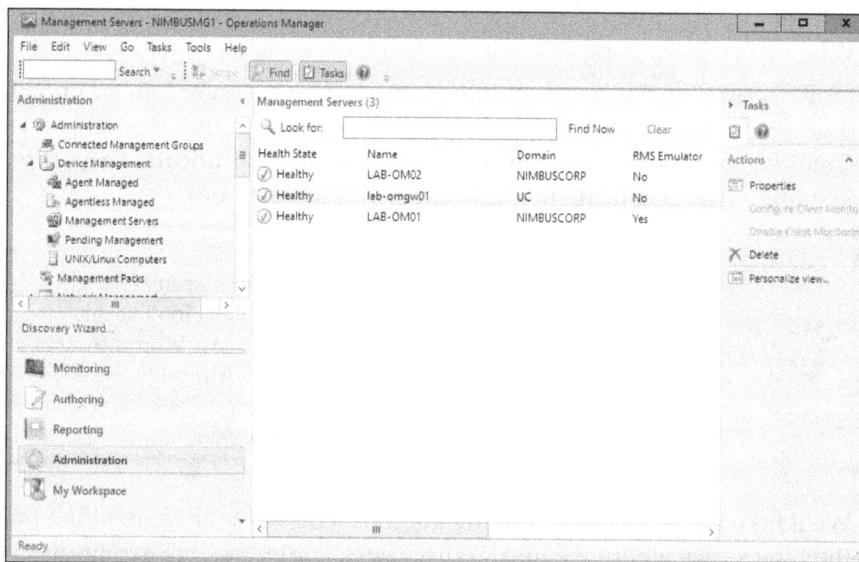

Figure 2.31: Successful untrusted domain Gateway server installation

20. The last thing you need to do now is to enable the **Server Proxy** setting on the new Gateway server. You can do this by first browsing to the Management Servers view in the Administration workspace of the Operations console and double-clicking on the Gateway server object. From there, select the **Security** tab and then enable the **Allow this server to act as a proxy and discover managed objects on other computers** check box shown in *Figure 2.32*.

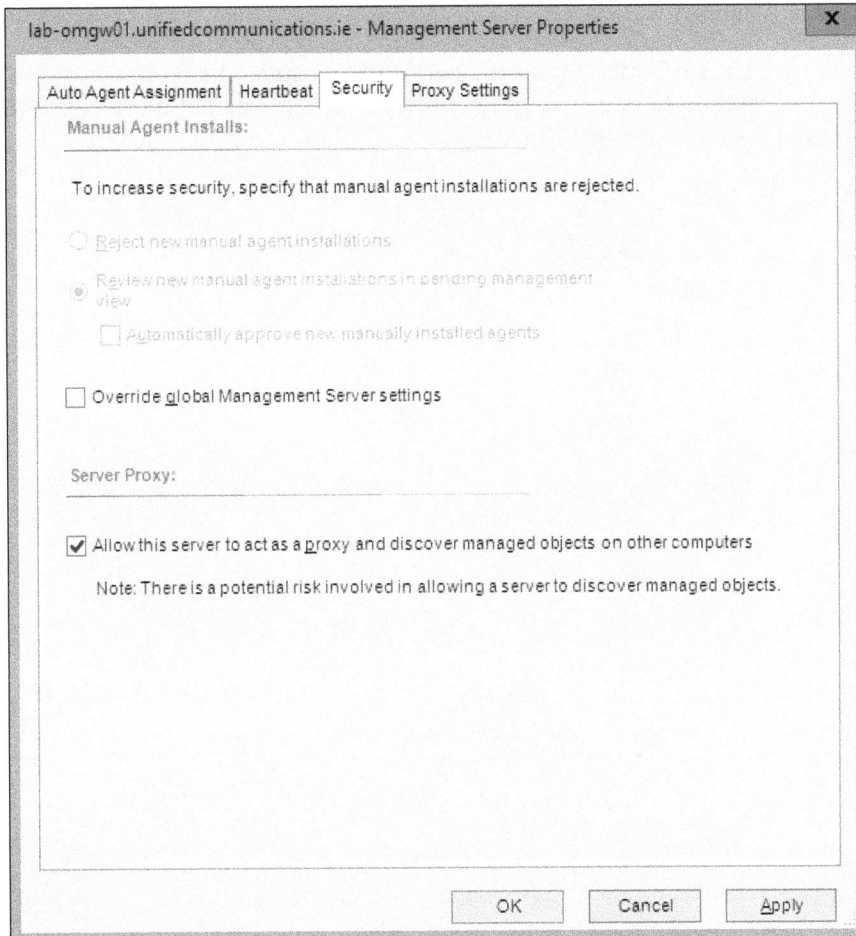

Figure 2.32: Enabling Server Proxy on the Gateway server

Summary

In this chapter, you learned about some of the different designs that can be used as a foundation for deploying OpsMgr. We also discussed the service account and software requirements for a new OpsMgr installation as well as some tips on SQL configuration to ensure everything runs smoothly during the deployment. Finally, we walked you through installing Management servers, Reporting servers, consoles and Gateway servers.

In the next chapter, we'll dive into the Operations console and Web console to help you better understand how to navigate around OpsMgr and get more comfortable with the various views and tasks on offer.

3
Exploring the Consoles

At this point, you should have your OpsMgr environment up and running and ready for a test drive. If you don't have this ready just yet, we suggest you take a read over *Chapter 2, Installing System Center Operations Manager* before you attempt to work through any of the examples here.

In this chapter, you will learn about the Operations console and its associated 'little brother' — the Web console. These consoles are essential tools that help you and your operators navigate around OpsMgr and they're the first place you visit when you want to make any customizations or troubleshoot problems.

Here's what we'll cover in this chapter:

- Overview of the Operations console
- Navigating the workspaces
- Working with different views
- Configuring global settings
- Introduction to the Web console

Operations console overview

The central hub of administration in OpsMgr, the Operations console is where you will find yourself frequenting when you need to interact with your monitored environment.

Although most commonly installed onto Management servers, it's a best practice recommendation to run the Operations console completely separate on either a standalone server or a client workstation. The reason for this is that you want to ensure that your Management servers can utilize all their resources for the day-to-day running of OpsMgr.

In large enterprise deployments, a dedicated server running a version of Windows Server Remote Desktop Services is usually deployed to run the Operations console and operators can use an RDP session to logon with their individual user accounts and use it to manage OpsMgr.

A more familiar scenario for Operations console deployments is to install it onto a workstation running a supported Windows client operating system and this is how we will roll it out for our fictional organization 'Nimbus Corporation'.

The minimum requirements for installing the Operations console onto a Windows client operating system are shown in the following table:

Requirement	Description
Operating system	Must be Windows 7, Windows 8, Windows 8.1 or Windows 10.
Processor architecture	Can be x64 or x86 for a client computer.
Disk space	System drive requires at least 512 MB free hard disk space.
File system	System drive must be formatted with the NTFS file system.
Windows PowerShell	Windows PowerShell version 2.0. Windows PowerShell version 3.0 is required to use Windows PowerShell cmdlets for administration of UNIX and Linux computers.
Windows Installer	At least Windows Installer 3.1.
.NET Framework	.NET Framework 4 or .NET Framework 4.5 / 4.5.1 is required.
Additional software dependencies	• Microsoft Report Viewer 2012 Runtime • Microsoft System CLR Types for SQL Server 2012

Deploying the console

The following steps will walk you through installing the Operations console on a Windows 10 client computer:

1. From the OpsMgr installation media, right-click on `setup.exe` and choose **Run as administrator** to begin.

2. From the splash screen that opens up, choose whether or not you wish to download the latest updates to the setup program and then click on **Install**.

3. In the **Select Features to Install** dialog box, choose the Operations console option as shown in *Figure 3.1*, then click on **Next** to continue.

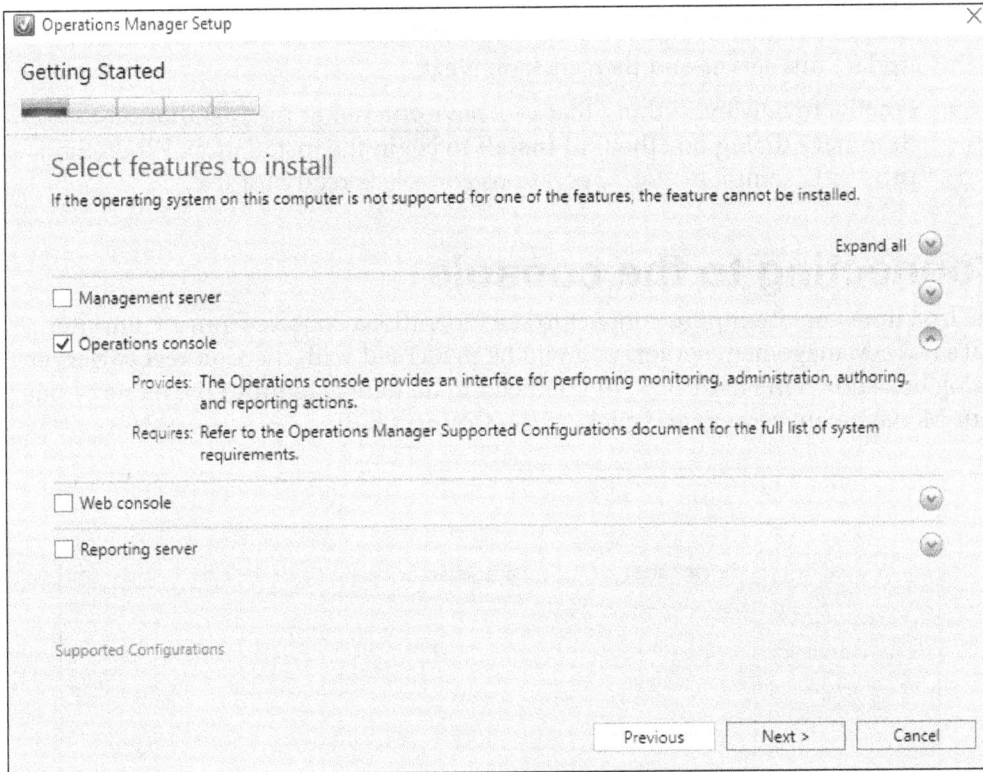

Figure 3.1: Installing the Operations console

4. Choose a location (or leave the default as it is) for the OpsMgr installation files at the next dialog box, then click on **Next** to move on.

5. In the **Prerequisites** dialog box, the OpsMgr installation wizard runs a script to ensure that the **Report Viewer Controls** package and its dependencies have been installed. If these are missing, you will be presented with a dialog box with some instructions on how to obtain and install them. Please refer to the *Configuring the prerequisites* section of *Chapter 2, Installing System Center Operations Manager* to help you quickly resolve any errors here in relation to the Operations console prerequisites.

6. When you're ready and if applicable, click on the **Verify Prerequisites Again** button and you should now have the option to continue with the setup. Accept the license terms at the next dialog box and then click on **Next** to continue.

7. In the **Help Improve Operations Manager** dialog box choose if you want to anonymously send data to Microsoft to help them improve customer experience and future OpsMgr updates. Click on **Next** to move on.

8. Decide whether or not you would like Microsoft Update to automatically update this server and then click on **Next**.

9. Finally, review everything that you have entered at the **Installation Summary** dialog box then hit **Install** to begin the installation. When the process is complete your Operations console is ready for use.

Connecting to the console

The first time you attempt to connect to the Operations console from a computer that's not a Management server, you will be presented with the **Connect to Server** dialog box shown in *Figure 3.2*. All you need to do here is to input the name of one of your Management servers and click on the **Connect** button.

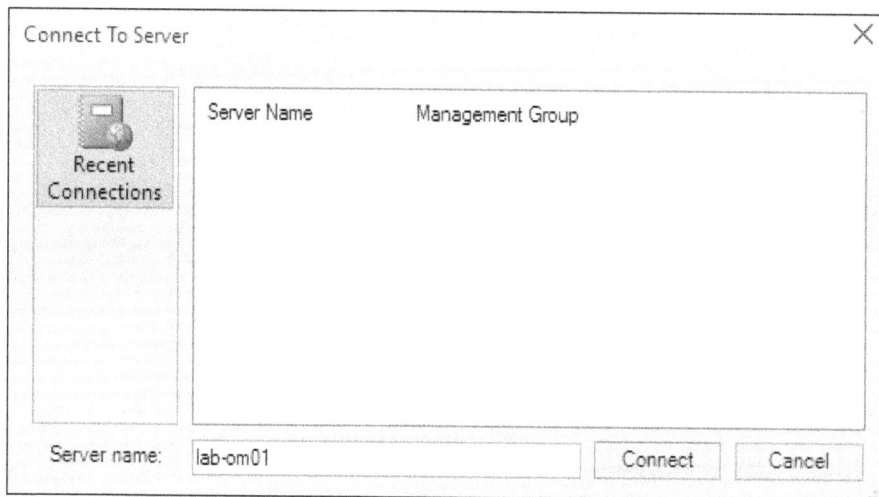

Figure 3.2: Connecting to the Operations console

The next time you open the Operations console from the same computer, the Management server name that you last connected to is remembered and you won't need to input it again. If you need to change the Management server you connect to, from the console at any point, then you can use the **Connect** option from the **Tools** menu that will open the **Connect to the Server** dialog box again.

Although there's no hard limit to the number of Operations consoles that you can deploy in your environment, due to the additional load each open console connection puts on the Management servers, it's generally accepted that you should plan for no more than 50 simultaneous console connections within a single Management Group at any one time.

The Monitoring Overview page

The fact that you can see the **Monitoring Overview** page, shown in *Figure 3.3*, when you open the Operations console, means that you have already carried out a basic health check of your OpsMgr environment. At least one Management server, the Operational database and your console need to be functional for the Monitoring Overview page to open in the first place.

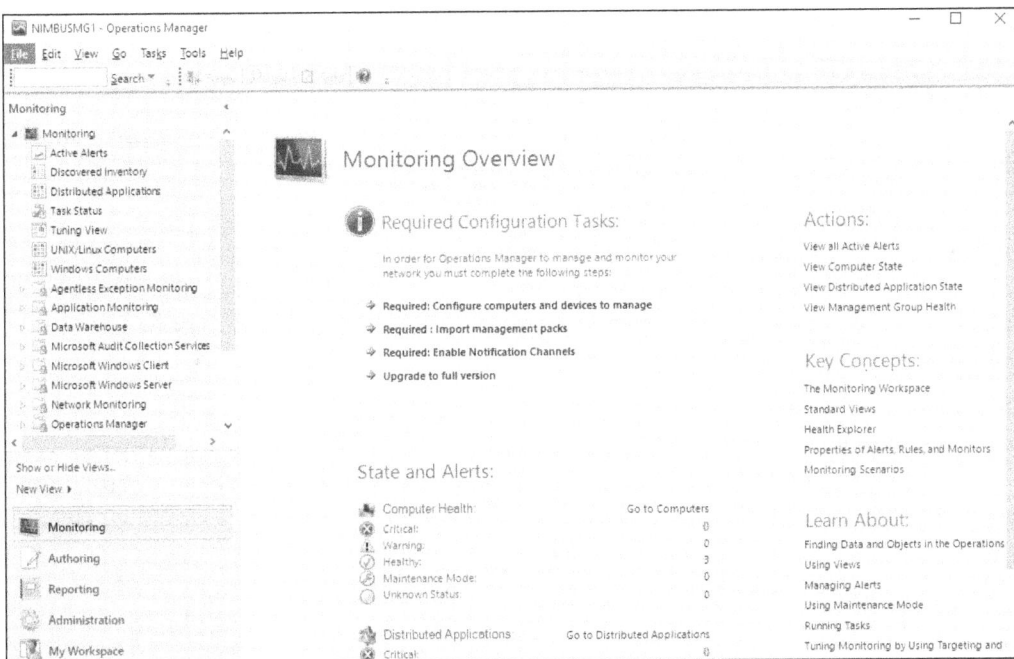

Figure 3.3: Monitoring Overview page

This page is the default view and first one you will see each time you connect to OpsMgr using the Operations console. It can be extremely useful if you've just installed OpsMgr and if you look at the **Required Configuration Tasks** section, you can see there are some highlighted steps you need to carry out next to get up and running.

The **State and Alerts** section gives you a quick run-down of the overall health of your computers and distributed applications and the **Actions** section will give you access to some common OpsMgr views.

Nearly everything on the Monitoring Overview page is a link that can be clicked on as a shortcut to run wizards, show views, read the built-in help or even open a web page to learn more information.

> If you're logged into the Operations console and need to quickly identify the name of the Management Group you are connected to, take a look at the bar across the top of the page and you'll see the management group name listed there.

Navigating the workspaces

Down the bottom-left side of the page you will notice the navigation pane, more commonly known as the *Wunderbar*. This term came about during the original design for Microsoft's Outlook 2003 email application when a large number of German speakers were working on the design team and it was seen as a snappy name with fun connotations (Wonder).

People in Microsoft liked the Wunderbar design so much at the time that a decision was made to use it for other products, such as Microsoft Exchange and System Center. This meant that users had a more familiar **user interface** (**UI**) and navigation experience across a multitude of core products from Microsoft – making the learning curve all the easier to get to grips with.

In OpsMgr, the Wunderbar comprises five buttons that serve as links to help you move around the following five workspaces:

- **Monitoring**: This workspace contains a collection of different views that give you the ability to see things like alerting, health status, diagrams or performance data of your monitored objects.

- **Authoring**: This is where a lot of your customizations in OpsMgr will occur. Here, you can create new rules, monitors, groups, custom tasks and service models along with synthetic transactions that allow you to monitor services, process and even website URL connectivity.

- **Reporting**: An intuitive UI that sits on top of SQL Server Reporting Services, it's here where you can see all the reports that are available in OpsMgr. Using existing report templates, you can configure new custom reports in this workspace as well as creating schedules for common reports to be distributed to your teams. We discuss reporting in more detail in *Chapter 10, Creating Alert Subscriptions and Reports.*

> You won't see the Reporting workspace appearing in the Wunderbar until the OpsMgr Reporting role has been deployed into your Management Group.

- **Administration**: This workspace is where you go when you want to manage and deploy new agents for Windows and UNIX/Linux computers along with providing you with an administration interface for the out-of-box network monitoring feature OpsMgr has to offer. You will also visit here to create alert notifications, manage your management packs, configure role-based access and modify global management group settings.

- **My Workspace**: A personalized area where users can create a customized console view of the monitored services, computers and alerts that they have responsibility for. The views created in this workspace are only visible to the user that created them.

Exploring the Monitoring workspace

The Monitoring workspace is where both OpsMgr administrators and operators will find themselves spending a lot of time analyzing and working with alerts, dashboards and views. When you click on the **Monitoring** button in the Wunderbar for the first time, you'll be presented with a number of different views and folders as shown in *Figure 3.4*.

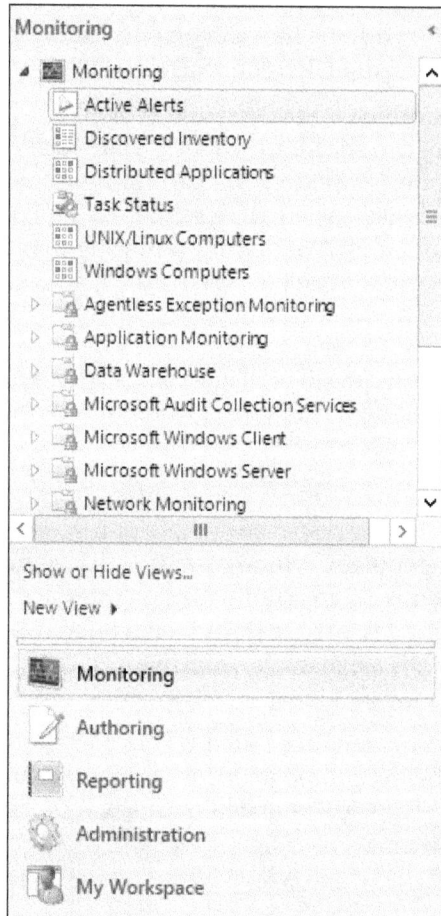

Figure 3.4: Monitoring workspace views and folders

Directly under the root of the Monitoring workspace, you can see six default views that are generally referred to as **Global Views** and these are listed as follows:

- **Active Alerts**: This view shows all current alerts with any resolution states that have not yet been configured with a resolution state of 'Closed'. Although this is a useful view to have, in larger environments, the sheer volume of active alerts in this view could become difficult to determine exactly what's happening when there is a problem and which systems are being affected.

> We recommend complementing the Active Alerts view with additional and more granular alert views that display specific resolution states, such as 'New', 'Acknowledged', or 'Assigned to Engineering'. We will discuss how to create new alert views in the *Working with Views* section of this chapter.

- **Discovered Inventory**: Every object that gets discovered when a management pack is imported can be found using scoped targeting within this view. This view comes in handy when for whatever reason, you have difficulty locating a monitored object through its vendor-built management pack views. You can simply select a target class from a management pack and the Discovered Inventory view will show you all of the discovered objects under that class.

- **Distributed Applications**: This view is where the health state of all your IT Service models can be viewed in the form of OpsMgr distributed applications. Using distributed applications, you can bring all the monitored components of an IT service together into a centralized and easy-to-manage single entity. You'll learn much more about these in *Chapter 7, Configuring Service Models with Distributed Applications*, and when you're comfortable working with them, you can use this view as a launch pad to navigate to other types of views that relate to your distributed applications.

- **Task Status**: Used for when you are running tasks in OpsMgr and want to get an update of their status. Here you can revisit the results of tasks that you have run in the past, or view those that don't return results directly to the screen immediately after you initiate them.

- **UNIX/Linux Computers**: Here you will find the health state of all your cross-platform UNIX and Linux systems that are being monitored by OpsMgr.

- **Windows Computers**: Here you will find the health state of all your Microsoft Windows computers that are being monitored by OpsMgr.

Understanding folders

Folders are used to store views and other customizations in OpsMgr and the majority of folders visible in the Monitoring workspace represent installed management packs.

A properly organized OpsMgr deployment will have views stored in folders, which in turn are stored within management packs. Think similar to how Active Directory **organizational units (OU's)** are deployed to deliver structure to the overall infrastructure; this is essentially the same concept.

Folders with a small padlock icon tell us that they are stored in a sealed management pack and folders with no padlock icon are stored in unsealed management packs. The contents of a folder stored in a sealed management pack cannot be modified however, folders stored in unsealed management packs can be modified as required. In *Chapter 5*, *Working with Management Packs*, we discuss management packs in much more detail.

Working with Views

As you navigate your way around the Monitoring workspace, you will encounter eight different view types from which you can consume monitoring data about your environment. The majority of these view types simply represent different ways to display data in the consoles based on queries to the OpsMgr databases.

In the following sections, we will explain each view type shown in *Figure 3.5* and give you a walkthrough on how to create new views within the Monitoring workspace.

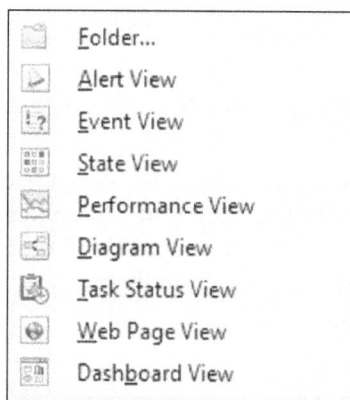

Figure 3.5: Different OpsMgr view types

Alert View

These types of views display alerts that have been generated based on different rules and monitors, which are defined in the management packs. You can find your first example of one of these views in the form of the 'Active Alerts' default Global View that we discussed earlier.

An alert view can be scoped with a very granular level of criteria to ensure that you only see the specific types of alerts within the view that you need.

One of the first custom alert views that I always create in new OpsMgr environments is the 'Closed Alerts' view. Strangely enough, Microsoft didn't give us a pre-built view that showed us all alerts with a resolution state of 'Closed' and having this simple view can really help you troubleshoot problems as you can quickly build a picture of recently closed historical alerts.

Here's how you can create an alert view that shows only Closed Alerts:

1. In the Monitoring workspace, right-click on the location that you wish to create your new view (as we want our view to sit alongside the default Global Views, we'll choose the Monitoring icon at the top of the tree), click on **New**, then click on **Alert View** as shown in *Figure 3.6*.

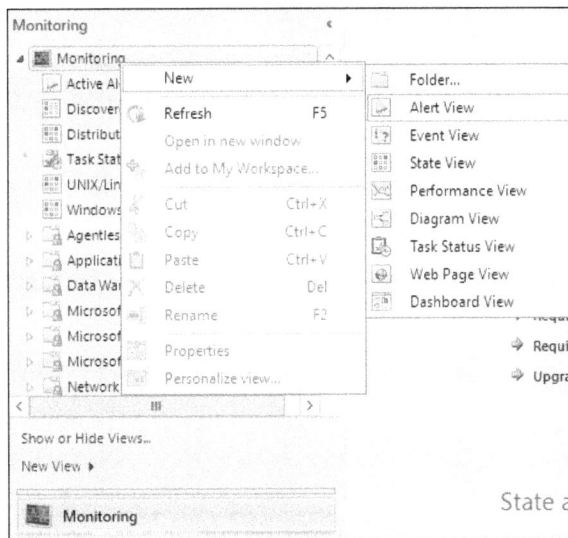

Figure 3.6: Creating a new Alert View

2. In the **Name** field, type a name to identify the view – we'll use 'Closed Alerts' as an example. Optionally, you can type a description of the view into the **Description** field.

3. On the **Criteria** tab, define the parameters of your alert view:

   ○ On the **Show Data Related To** box, click on the ellipsis **(...)** button and select the alert data type that you wish to target. We'll leave this as the default **Object** target option.

   ○ In the **Show Data Contained In A Specific Group** box, select the group that you want to filter the alert data to. In this example, the **(All)** groups option is fine.

   ○ In the **Select Conditions** area, select the check boxes for the alert criteria that you wish to show in the view. Here, we'll choose the **with specific resolution state** option.

   ○ In the **Criteria Description** box, click on the underlined words to edit the alert criteria that you wish to show in the view. In our example, we will click on on the **specific** criteria link.

   ○ Now choose the criteria that you wish to apply to this alert view, then click on **OK**. In our example shown in *Figure 3.7*, we've chosen a specific resolution state of **Closed (255)** for our alerts.

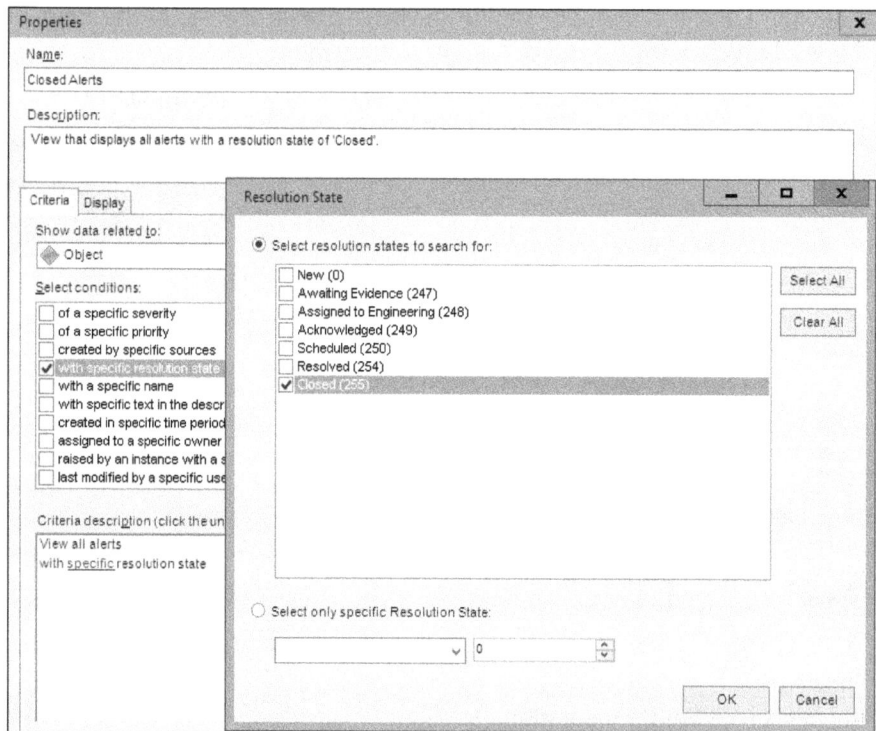

Figure 3.7: Choosing alert view criteria

4. Now click on the **Display** tab and choose which columns to display and your preferred sort and group order. We'll add an additional column here for **Repeat Count** and we'll change the **Group items by** option to **Descending** as shown in *Figure 3.8*.

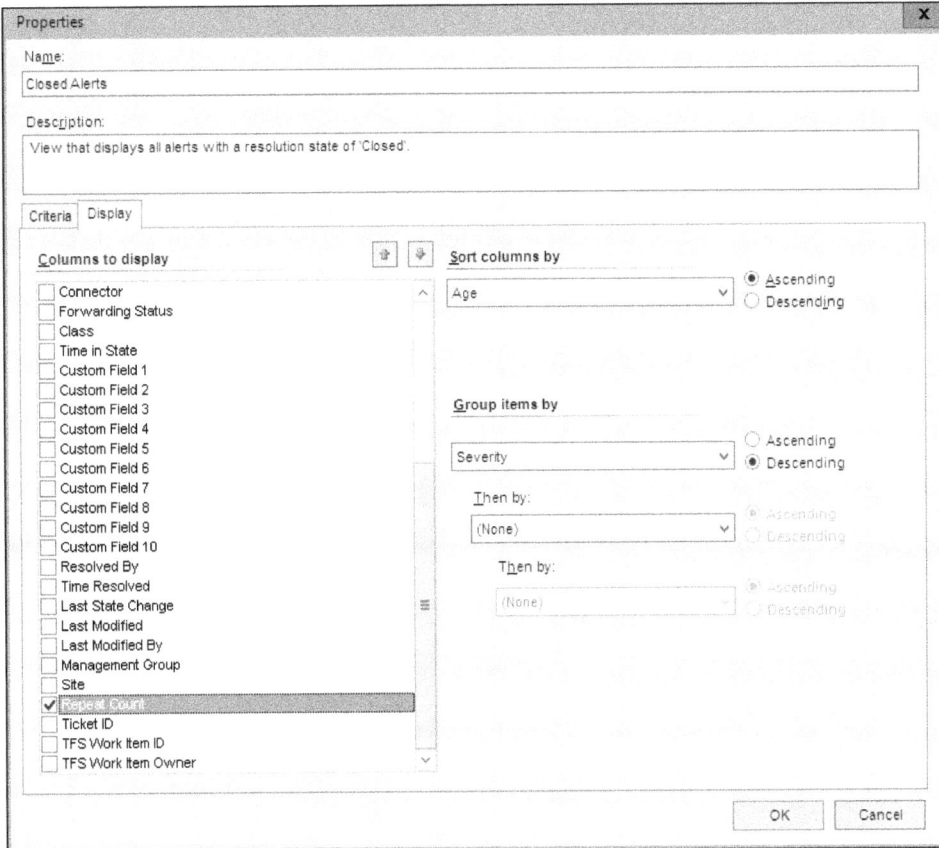

Figure 3.8: Modifying the display options

5. Click on **OK** to close the Alert View properties page and this will then create the new Alert View in the console for you.

When creating your alert views, pay particular attention to the **Display** tab where you have the option to show the **Repeat Count** column. This column is not enabled in any alert view by default and it's a great way of quickly identifying the rules that are generating noisy alerts within the Management Group.

Event View

The Event View shows specific event data that is stored in the Operational database. Similar to the Alert View, you can scope this view to display specific types of events so that you can target your troubleshooting efforts in a more concise fashion.

To create a new event view, follow these steps:

1. In the Monitoring workspace, right-click on the location that you wish to create your new view (as we want our view to sit alongside the default Global Views, we'll choose the Monitoring icon at the top of the tree), click on **New**, then click on **Event View**.

2. In the **Name** field, type a name to identify the view – we'll use 'NIMBUSMG1 Events' as an example. Optionally, you can type a description of the view into the **Description** field.

3. On the **Criteria** tab, define the parameters of your event view:

    ° On the **Show Data Related To box**, click on the ellipsis (**...**) button and select the alert data type that you wish to target. We'll leave this as the default **Object** target.

    ° In the **Show Data Contained In A Specific Group** box, select the group that you want to filter the event data to. In this example, the **(All)** groups option is fine.

    ° In the **Select Conditions** area, select the check boxes for the event data criteria that you wish to show in the view.

    ° In the **Criteria Description** box, click on the underlined words to edit the event criteria that you wish to show in the view.

    ° Now choose the criteria that you wish to apply to this event view, then click on **OK**.

4. Click on the **Display** tab and choose the columns to display and your preferred sort and group order. We'll add an additional column here for **Rule Name**.

5. Click on **OK** to close the dialog box and create your new Event View similar to *Figure 3.9*.

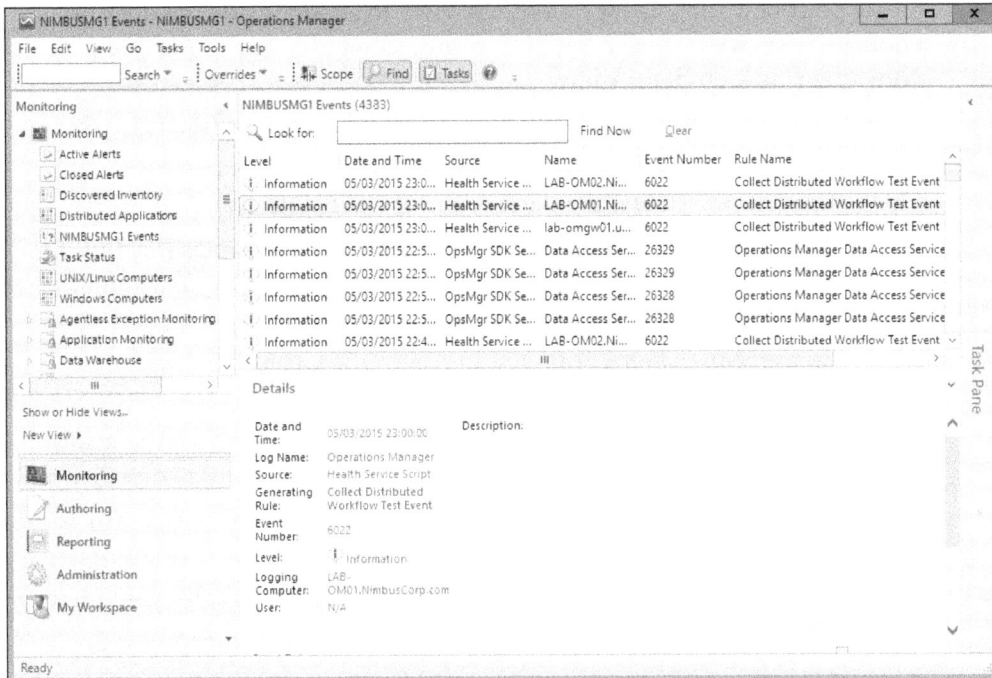

Figure 3.9: Custom Event View

State View

One of the most used views in OpsMgr, the state view will show you a 'traffic-light' type view for the health state of your monitored objects. In the default Global View list, the Distributed Applications, UNIX/Linux Computers and Windows Computers views are all examples of different use cases for state views.

When we model our IT services as Distributed Applications, we can use a state view to display even the most complex of services as a single 'Green, Yellow or Red' health state entity and from there, we can select the service and pivot to another view, which can help you quickly identify the root cause of a problem.

Here's what you need to do to create a new custom state view:

1. In the Monitoring workspace, right-click on the location that you wish to create your new view (as we want our view to sit alongside the default Global Views, we'll choose the Monitoring icon at the top of the tree), click on **New**, then click on **State View**.

2. In the Name field, type a name to identify the view and optionally, you can type a description of the view into the Description field.

3. On the Criteria tab, define the parameters of your state view:

   ° On the Show Data Related To box, click on the ellipsis **(...)** button and select the alert data type that you wish to target. This time, we're going to change this option to target the **Windows Server** class.

   ° In the Show Data Contained In A Specific Group box, select the group that you want to filter the health state data to.

   ° In the Select Conditions area, select the check boxes for the health state criteria that you wish to show in the view.

   ° In the Criteria Description box, click on any underlined words to edit the criteria that you wish to show in the view.

   ° Now choose the criteria that you want to apply to this event view, then click on **OK**.

4. Click on the **Display** tab and choose the columns to display and your preferred sort and group order. We'll add some additional columns here to help us identify the IP address and number of logical processors it has.

> Although OpsMgr isn't typically an asset management or inventory tool, it does contain an abundance of information about the computers and network devices it monitors. Through state views, we can add in extra columns to display information such as IP addresses, CPU, Memory, and Active Directory location to name a few. Your choice of columns containing this useful information is dependent on the management packs that have been deployed into the Management Group.

5. Click on **OK** to close the dialog box and create your new State View similar to *Figure 3.10*.

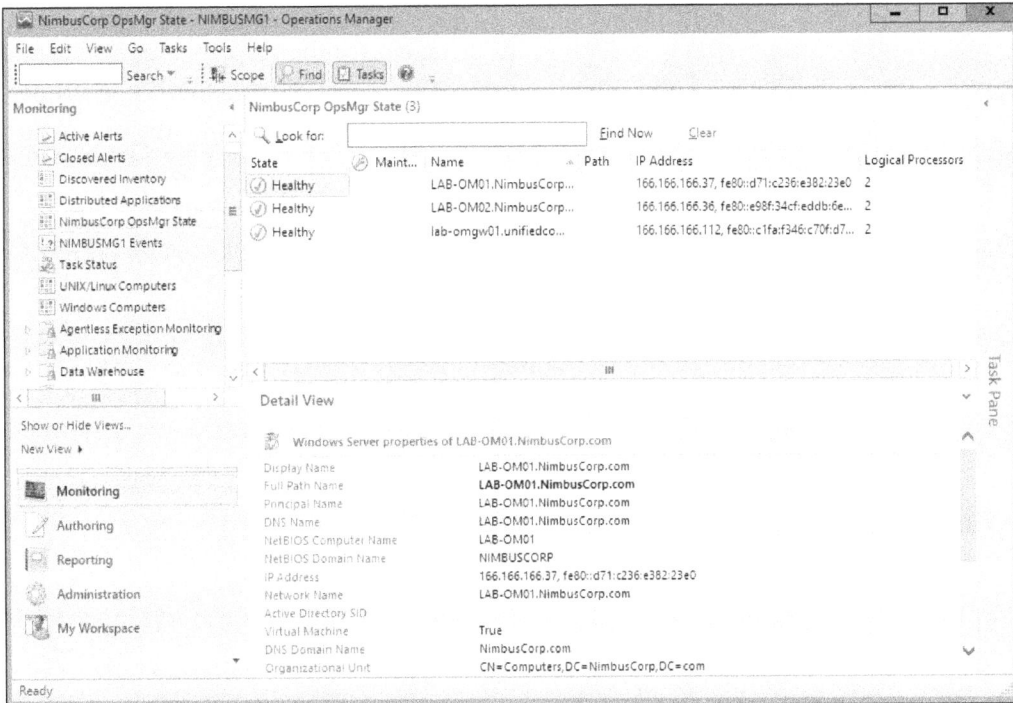

Figure 3.10: Displaying health and additional information with state views

Performance View

The Performance view can be used to display performance counter data that has been collected from specific monitored systems or groups. The view can be controlled so that only performance data from a specific target is displayed, or you can display the same performance object and counter for the entire set of monitored objects in the management group. Think of this view as a centralized version of the old **PerfMon** tool that was built into Windows computers – only this is far more flexible and much better!

To create a new custom performance view, here's what you need to do:

1. In the **Monitoring** workspace, right-click on the location that you wish to create your new view (as we want our view to sit alongside the default Global Views, we'll choose the Monitoring icon at the top of the tree), click on **New**, then click on **Performance View**.

2. In the **Name** field, type a name to identify the view and optionally, you can type a description of the view into the Description field.

3. On the **Criteria** tab, define the parameters of your performance view:

   ○ On the **Show Data Related To** box, click on the ellipsis (**...**) button and select the alert data type that you wish to target. We'll change this to target the **Health Service** class.

   ○ In the **Show Data Contained In A Specific Group** box, select the group that you want to filter the health state data to or leave the **(All)** groups option as it is.

   ○ In the **Select Conditions** area, select the check boxes for the performance criteria conditions that you want to show in the view (or leave them unchecked to be presented with everything).

   ○ In the **Criteria Description** box, click on any underlined words to edit the performance criteria that you wish to show in the view.

   ○ Now choose the criteria that you wish to apply to this performance view, then click on **OK**.

4. Clicking the **Display** tab here, you will notice that this view looks different to previous views that we've configured:

   ○ In the Date and Time section, select the number of minutes, hours, or days to return performance data from.

   ○ In the **Chart** section, select the drop-down menu to format the data as a line or spline graph, then provide further formatting by selecting the **Enable 3D** and **Point Labels** check boxes if appropriate for your view.

   ○ The **X Axis** and **Y Axis** areas allow you to further define how the view will be formatted by giving you the option to show the axis details, as well as gridlines and colors to define the gradations.

   ○ Click on the **Change** buttons on each of the axis sections to define the color for each axis, and then click on **OK** to close and create the view.

5. In *Figure 3.11*, we can see our new performance view that we've targeted at the Health Service class. In this view, we can select the same performance counter on multiple servers to build a comparison over time on how they stack up against each other.

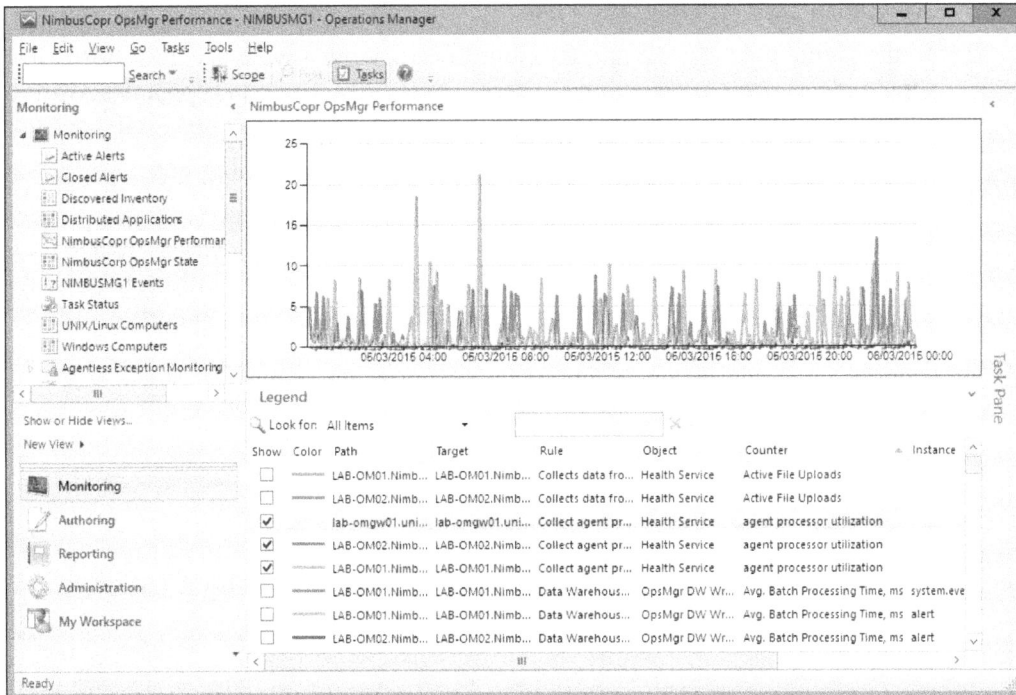

Figure 3.11: Viewing performance counters for multiple servers

Diagram View

A personal favorite of mine, the diagram view presents a graphical representation of managed objects and their relationships to one another. Using a diagram view in conjunction with a distributed application model, you can view a map of all the components that make up any given IT service.

This means that you can click right through the different tiers of an IT service to show the various health states of each component from the top-level service itself, down to something like a fan, network interface, a power supply unit on an individual server, or a network device. In *Chapter 7, Configuring Service Models with Distributed Applications*, we will discuss this topic in more detail.

Here's what's required to create a new diagram view:

1. In the **Monitoring** workspace, right-click on the location that you wish to create your new view (as we want our view to sit alongside the default Global Views, we'll choose the Monitoring icon at the top of the tree), click on **New**, then click on **Diagram View**.

2. In the Name field, type a name to identify the view – we'll use 'Nimbus Corp OpsMgr Diagram' as an example here. Optionally, you can type a description of the view into the Description field.

3. Click on the **Browse** button to open the **Object Search** dialog box.

4. From the **Look For** drop-down menu, choose the **Service** class (we've picked this for our example, but feel free to experiment with other classes to see how they're represented as a diagram view), then hit the **Search** button to display all available services in your Management Group as shown in *Figure 3.12*.

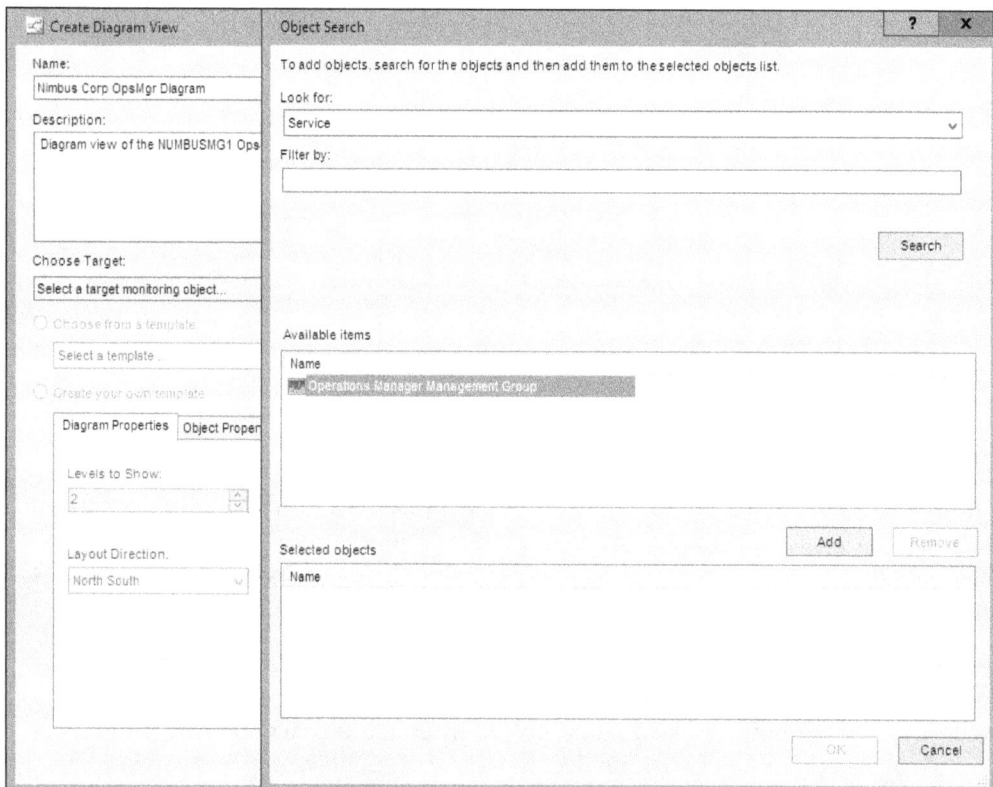

Figure 3.12: Choosing a diagram view target

5. Select the target you wish to create a diagram view of from the **Available Items** section (we've chosen the **Operations Manager Management Group** service), click on the **Add** button, then hit **OK** to return to the **Create Diagram View** dialog box.

6. Now you need to choose a template from which you can build your diagram view. In this example, we will customize a new template by selecting the **Create your own template** option from the **Create Diagram View** dialog box.

> If the specific target you have chosen is associated with an existing diagram view template, then you can click on the **Choose from a Template** drop-down menu and pick the pre-built diagram view template.

7. Define the parameters of your diagram view using the following tabs:

   ° In the **Diagram Properties** tab, use the **Levels to Show** section and choose how many levels deep that you want your diagram view to open with by default. If you're using this to display an IT service modeled as a distributed application, then two or three levels are common settings to choose here. You can also use the **Layout Direction** option to decide which direction the diagram view maps out to – North South, South North, East West and West East are your choices here.

   ° In the **Object Properties** tab, choose the **Containment Style** (box or non-box) and also the maximum number of **Nodes Per Row** for your diagram view. Depending on what your diagram view is based on, either leave the settings at their defaults or just experiment with them on a view-by-view basis.

   ° In the **Line Properties** tab, you can modify the **Containment Line** and **Non Containment Line** style and width to make each diagram view more appealing or relevant.

   ° From the **Virtual Groups** tab you can choose whether or not you wish to **Virtually Group** the number of child components of your service. The default option for a custom diagram view is set to **Do not virtually group** and this is normally a recommended setting as it enables you to quickly see all of the child components inside each tier of any given diagram view.

> System Center MVP Cameron Fuller has written an excellent blog
> post on this topic that explains everything you need to know about
> OpsMgr virtual grouping with diagram views. Check it out at
> `http://tinyurl.com/opsmgrvirtualgrouping`

8. When you're finished configuring how the diagram view will look, click on
    the **Create** button to close the dialog box and create your new view. *Figure
    3.13* shows our example diagram view where we've expanded the OpsMgr
    Management Group down to its database tier.

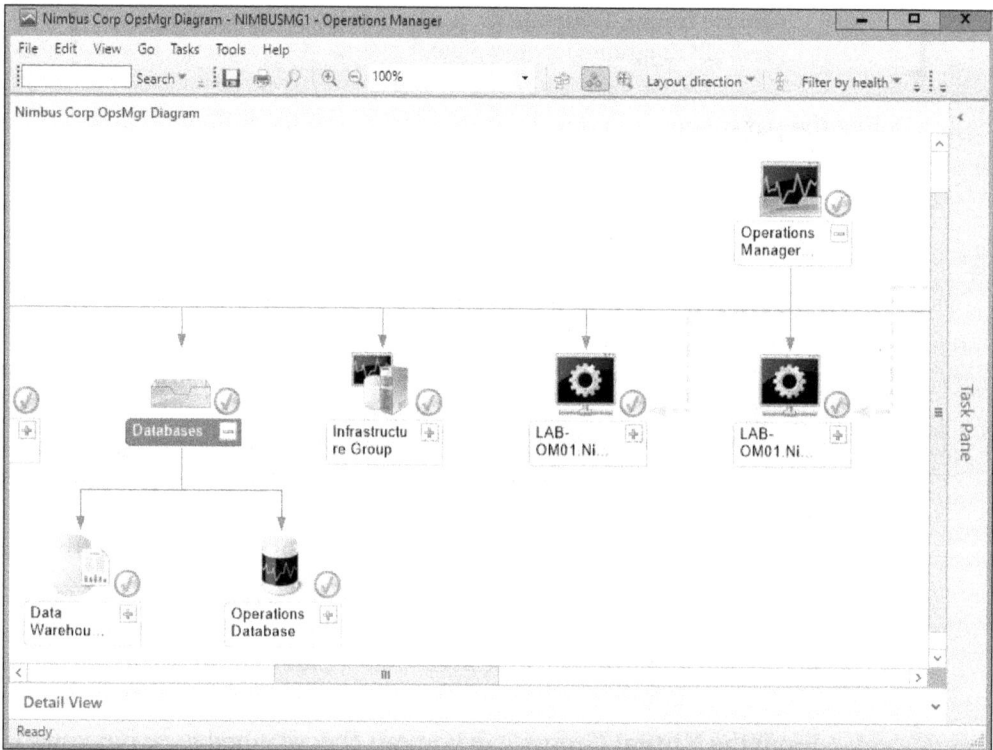

Figure 3.13: Diagram view of OpsMgr Management Group

Task Status View

When you run a task to perform a particular action in OpsMgr, a dialog box appears to show you the progress and output of the task. If the task is going to take a while to run or if you have other troubleshooting to carry out while waiting on the task to complete, then you're going to need somewhere to go to check the status information on those tasks.

This is where the Task Status view comes in useful. You can scope this view to display status information for specific tasks, tasks with a specific output, tasks submitted by a specific person or even tasks that are running during certain time periods.

Here's what you need to do to create a new Task Status view:

1. In the Monitoring workspace, right-click on the location that you wish to create your new view (as we want our view to sit alongside the default Global Views, we'll choose the Monitoring icon at the top of the tree), click on **New**, then click on **Task Status View**.

2. In the Name field, type a name to identify the view – we'll use 'Nimbus Corp OpsMgr Tasks Status' as an example. Optionally, you can type a description of the view into the Description field.

3. On the Criteria tab, define the parameters of your task status view:

   ° On the **Show Data Related To** box, click on the ellipsis (**...**) button and select the alert data type that you wish to target. We'll leave this as the default **Object** target.

   ° In the **Show Data Contained In A Specific Group** box, select the group that you want to filter the event data to. In this example, the **(All)** groups option is fine.

   ° In the **Select Conditions** area, select the check boxes for the event data criteria that you wish to show in the view.

   ° In the **Criteria Description** box, click on the underlined words to edit the task status criteria that you wish to show in the view.

   ° Now choose the criteria that you wish to apply to this task status view, then click on **OK**.

4. Click on the Display tab and choose which columns to display and your preferred sort and group order. We'll add an additional column here for 'Task Description'.

5. Click on **OK** to close the dialog box and create your new Task Status View similar to *Figure 3.14*.

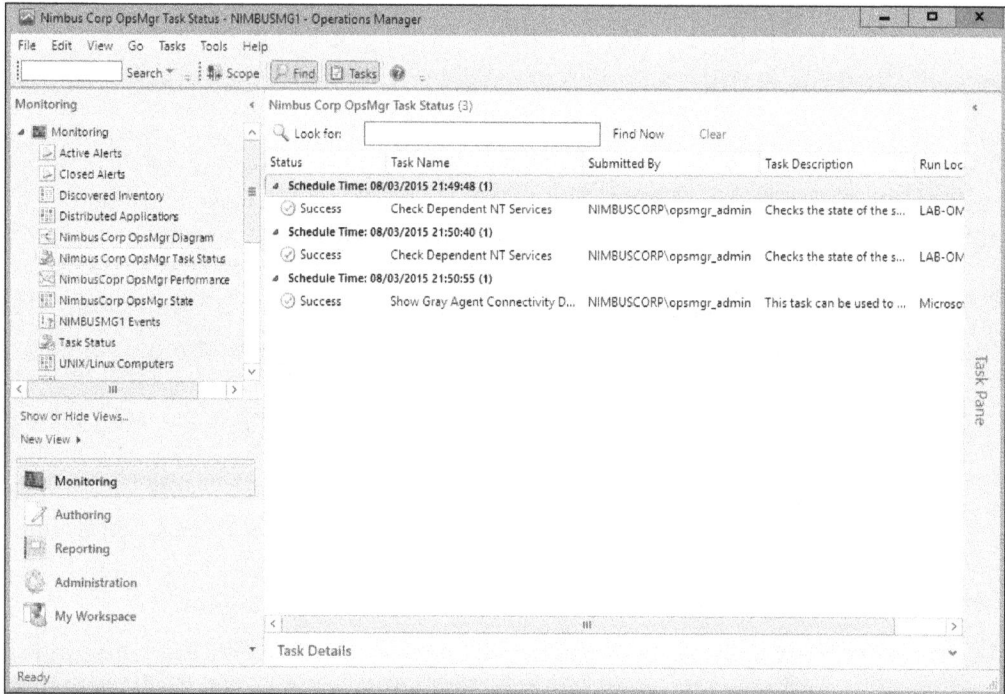

Figure 3.14: Viewing the status of tasks

Web Page View

A much simpler concept than other OpsMgr views, this view gives you the ability to launch a new web browser window from within the Operations console. Why would you want to do this? Well, let's say you wanted to give your operators the option to launch an external knowledgebase that was hosted on the Internet or even an internal website , such as an intranet or third-party management portal, then the **Web Page View** will give you a flexible way to meet these requirements.

To create a new Web Page View, here's what you need to do:

1. In the Monitoring workspace, right-click on the location that you wish to create your new view (as we want our view to sit alongside the default Global Views, we'll choose the Monitoring icon at the top of the tree), click on **New**, then click on **Web Page View**.

2. In the Name field, type a name to identify the view – we'll use 'Nimbus Corp Web Page' as an example. Optionally, you can type a description of the view into the Description field.

3. Now input the full web page address into the **Target Website** field, then click on **OK** to create the view.

Dashboard View

Over the past number of years, Microsoft has increased their focus on providing rich out-of-box visualizations through the use of dashboards and widgets in OpsMgr. The Dashboard View is essentially a visualization framework that comprises a number of layouts and templates that enable you to consolidate your monitoring data and views into an easy-to-consume format.

When you create a dashboard layout it will be empty and you will need to populate it with widgets, which are plug-ins that look and feel very similar to the standard views that we've been working with up to this point. The information in this section will serve as an initial introduction for the content in *Chapter 9, Visualizing Your IT with Dashboards*– where we dive much deeper into these concepts.

Here's what you need to do to first create an empty dashboard layout:

1. In the Monitoring workspace, right-click on the location that you wish to create your new view (as we want our view to sit alongside the default Global Views, we'll choose the Monitoring icon at the top of the tree), click on **New**, then click on **Dashboard View**.

2. Choose a dashboard layout style from the **Select a dashboard layout or widget template** dialog box. We'll choose the **Grid Layout** as shown in *Figure 3.15*. Click on **Next** to continue.

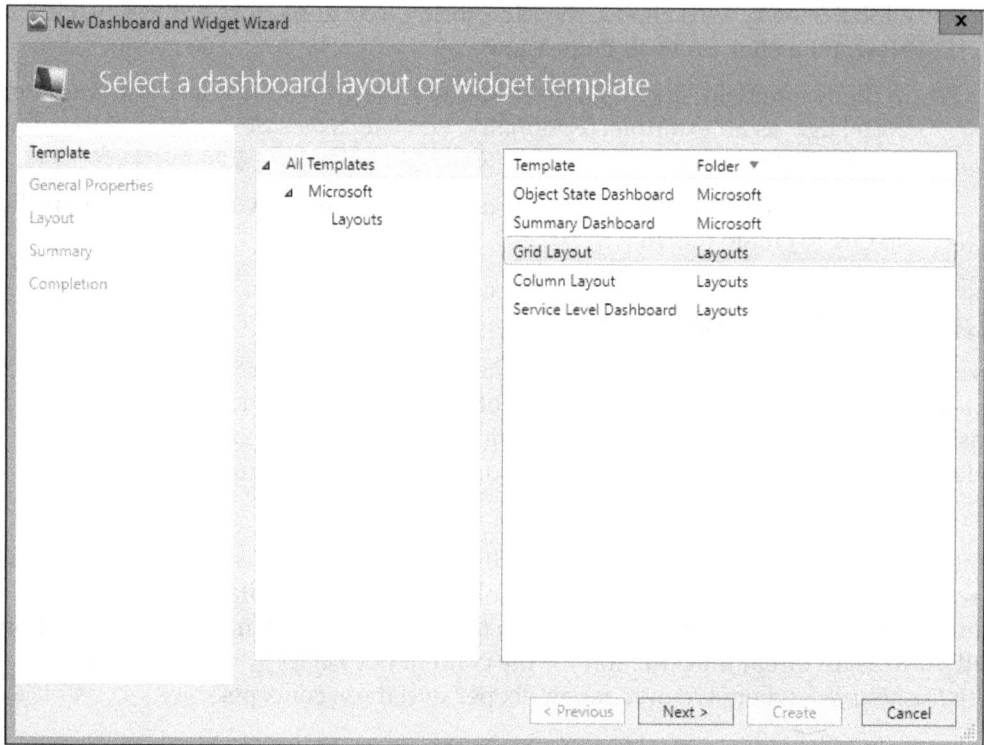

Figure 3.15: Choosing a dashboard layout

3. In the Name field, type a name to identify the view – we'll use 'Nimbus Corp OpsMgr Dashboard' as an example. Optionally, you can type a description of the view into the Description field.

4. In the **Specify the layout of the dashboard** dialog box, select the number of cells that you wish to have in your dashboard (each cell will contain its own view and be aware that the more cells you choose for your dashboard, the more real-estate you'll need on your screen to view everything together). In our example, we'll keep things simple and choose **4 Cells** as shown in *Figure 3.16*. Click on **Next** to move on when you're ready.

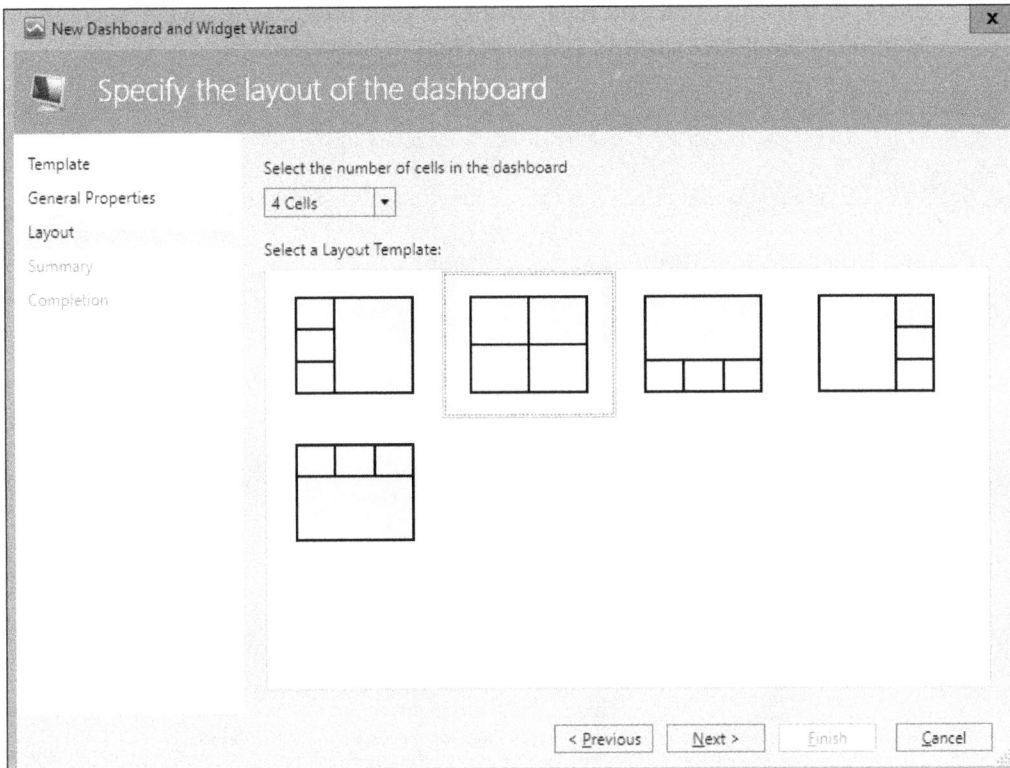

Figure 3.16: Specifying the number of cells in the dashboard

5. Confirm your settings at the **Summary** dialog box and then hit the **Create** button to create the new dashboard layout. Click on the **Close** button to complete the wizard.

Now that you have your dashboard layout created, the following steps will walk you through adding a new state widget to your dashboard layout:

1. From the dashboard layout that you created in the previous steps, you will see that each cell in the dashboard has a link titled **Click to add widget...** and when you click on one of these links, you'll be presented with the **New Dashboard and Widget Wizard** shown in *Figure 3.17*. Here you can choose the type of widget that you wish to add to your dashboard – we'll select the **State Widget** as an example. Click on **Next** to move on.

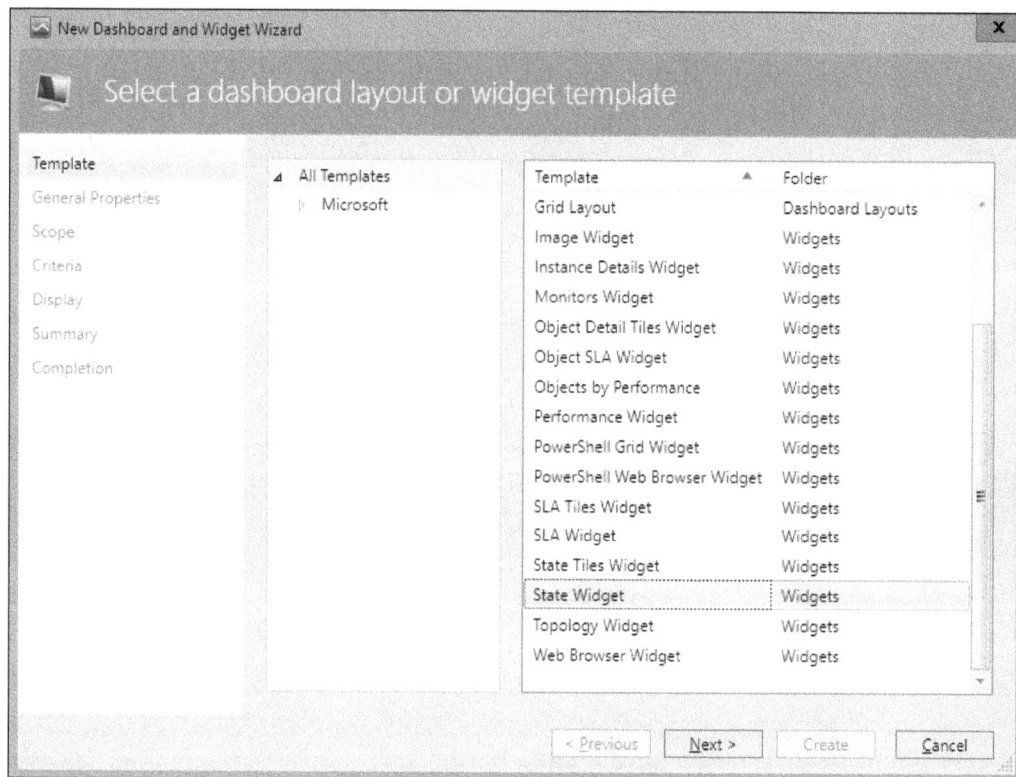

Figure 3.17: Choosing your dashboard widgets

2. In the Name field, type a name to identify the widget – we'll use 'Management Servers Health State' as an example. Optionally, you can type a description of the view into the Description field. Click on **Next** to continue.

3. In the **Specify the Scope** dialog box, click on the **Add** button and from the **Add Groups or Objects** dialog box, choose the group or object that you wish to view the health state of (we'll pick the Operations Manager Management servers group here), then click on the **OK** button.

4. Back at the Specify the Scope dialog box, select a class to scope the members of your chosen group or just leave this as its default **Object** setting. Click on **Next** to move on.

5. From the **Specify the Criteria** dialog box, decide if you wish to scope the types of health state that the dashboard widget will display or just leave the default settings as they are to display all health states. Click on **Next** to continue.

6. Similar to when we created an Alert View earlier, choose the columns to display along with your preferred sorting and grouping settings, then click on **Next**.

7. Hit the **Create** button from the Summary dialog box, then the **Close** button to complete the wizard and create your first OpsMgr dashboard widget.

You can repeat these steps for each additional widget in your dashboard layout until you have it fully populated similar to *Figure 3.18*, where we've configured a State Widget, an Alert Widget, an Objects by Performance Widget and an Instance Details Widget.

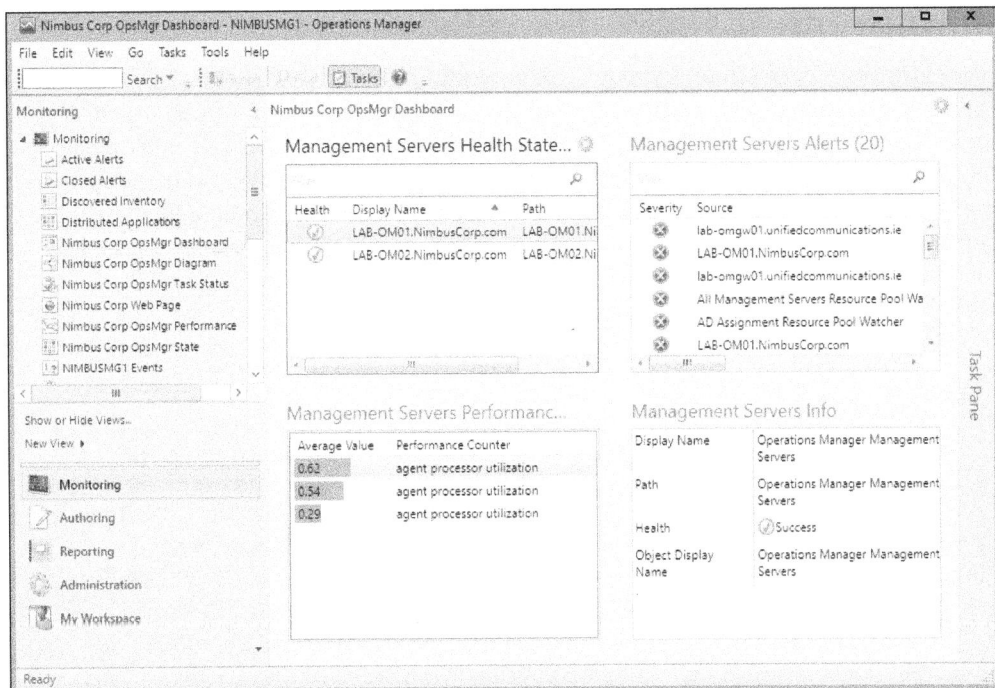

Figure 3.18: Fully populated four-cell dashboard view layout

Exploring the Authoring workspace

While the Monitoring workspace is where you analyse and work with the different views and alerts that OpsMgr has to offer, it's the Authoring workspace that you will frequent when you want to start customizing things. Here you can create new monitors, rules, groups, distributed applications and synthetic transactions to name but a few.

This is the workspace in OpsMgr that scares people the most due to the misconception that you need a developer-type background to work your way around it but thankfully, the folks in Microsoft have made things a lot easier than that for us!

Within the Authoring workspace we have four sections to get familiar with and this chapter will serve as an introductory primer for when we interact with some of those sections in more detail later in the book.

The four sections within the Authoring workspace are:

Management Pack Templates

This section is where you can create a new management pack from a pre-defined template with minimum fuss. Using the Add Monitoring Wizard, you can create monitors, rules and classes to target custom object types for each different scenario that you might have. These templates can help you build **synthetic transactions** that emulate the performance and availability of ports, databases, processes, websites and even bespoke Windows services.

When you initially deploy OpsMgr, you are presented with nine different templates to work with and these are listed in the following table:

Template Name	Description
.NET Application Performance Monitoring	Part of the **Application Performance Monitoring (APM)** capability of OpsMgr, this template monitors ASP.NET and **Windows Communication Foundation (WCF)** applications from a server-side and client-side perspective.
OLE DB Data Source	Use this template to create a synthetic transaction to monitor the availability and performance of a specific database. You input a connection string to execute test queries from one or more designated OpsMgr agents – known as 'Watcher Nodes'.

Template Name	Description
Process Monitoring	Monitor the availability, performance and number of occurrences of a particular 'wanted' process on a monitored computer or verify that an 'unwanted' process (such as a virus) is not running.
TCP Port	Another synthetic transaction template, this monitors the availability of an application that is listening on a specific TCP port. This is a great way to monitor devices and applications that you can't get an agent installed onto, but the ones that can be connected to through a particular port. You can perform TCP Port tests from one or more monitored Watcher Nodes.
UNIX/Linux Log File Monitoring	Monitors a UNIX or Linux log file for a specific log entry. It can be targeted at a specific computer or at a group of computers.
UNIX/Linux Process Monitoring	Allows you to monitor whether or not a particular process installed on a UNIX or Linux computer is running.
Web Application Availability Monitoring	Create availability monitoring tests for one or more web application URLs and run these monitoring tests from internal locations by default. This template can be extended to use external locations by signing up to System Center **Global Service Monitor** (GSM) and attaching your GSM account to OpsMgr.
Web Application Transaction Monitoring	Here you can perform basic availability and performance monitoring of web applications as well as having the option to record a web browser session to emulate end-user experience.
Windows Service	Use this template to monitor the availability and performance of a specific service running on one or more Windows-based computers. This is often required when monitoring a bespoke line-of-business application where no vendor management pack exists. You can check if the service is running or have an alert fire when it uses up too much CPU or memory on the monitored computer.

In *Chapter 7, Configuring Service Models with Distributed Applications*, we will walk you through creating synthetic transactions using some of the templates mentioned here.

Distributed Applications

The best way to get the most out of your OpsMgr deployment is to map out your monitored environment into individual IT services and the Distributed Applications section of the Authoring workspace is where you'll go to create those service maps.

When you create distributed applications to represent your IT services, you will invoke the **Distributed Application Designer** by either clicking on the **New Distributed Application** link from the Authoring workspace or by right-clicking on the **Create a New Distributed Application** option from the resulting context menu as shown in *Figure 3.19*.

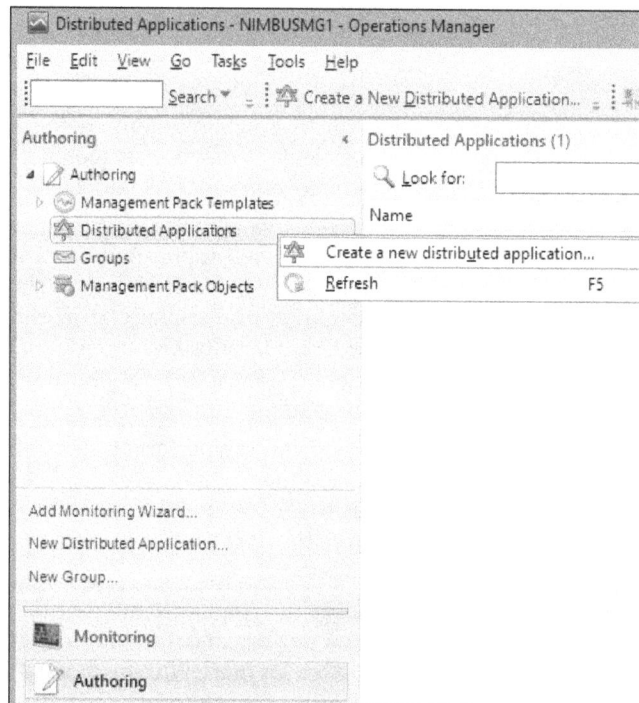

Figure 3.19: Invoking the Distributed Application Designer

When the **Create a Distributed Application** dialog box opens, you will be presented with a choice of **Distributed Application Templates** to work with.

These templates are defined as:

- **.NET 3-Tier Application**: Containing presentation, business, and data tiers, this template can be used to monitor .NET web applications
- **Line of Business Web Application**: Useful for monitoring applications containing websites and databases
- **Messaging**: This template contains components that are common to messaging services, such as Microsoft Exchange
- **Blank (Advanced)**: This is the only template that has no pre-built component groups deployed and it's recommended to choose this when you are designing your distributed application from the ground up

We'll revisit this topic later in *Chapter 7, Configuring Service Models with Distributed Applications*, and dig much deeper into creating Distributed Applications for our IT services.

Groups

When you need to target (or even disable) monitoring for a collective number of objects, then it makes sense to create a group for those objects and this is the section where you need to go to manage groups in OpsMgr.

A group can also be used to scope views, configure reports and assist with alert tuning. You can automatically populate a group based on specific properties of monitored objects or you can explicitly add specific objects as you wish.

To create a new group, follow these steps:

1. In the Authoring workspace, right-click on **Groups** and choose the **Create a New Group** option (or just click on the **New Groups** shortcut above the Wunderbar) to open the wizard.

2. In the **General Properties** dialog box, type a name and description for the group then either create a new management pack or choose an existing management pack to store the new group in. Click on **Next** to continue.

3. In the **Explicit Members** dialog box, you can optionally choose whether or not you wish to explicitly add objects to the group. In our example, we will add some Windows Server objects to our group as shown in *Figure 3.20*. Click on **Next** when you're ready to move on.

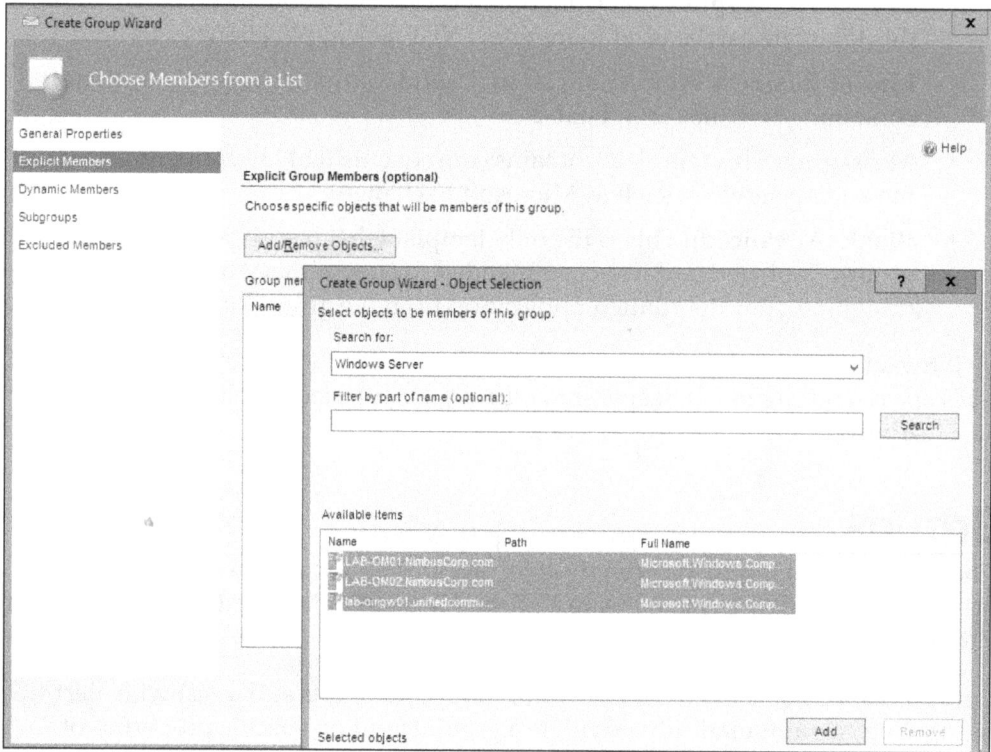

Figure 3.20: Explicitly adding group members

4. For the **Dynamic Members** dialog box you can again optionally decide whether or not to specify dynamic inclusion rules to add all objects with common shared attributes to the group. We'll leave this section empty for our example here. Click on **Next** to move on.

5. The **Subgroups** dialog box gives you the option to choose existing subgroups to add to this new group. In our example, we'll leave this blank for now and click on **Next**.

6. The final **Excluded Members** dialog box allows you to specify objects that will not be included as group members. Think of this as a reverse option to Step 3 where we explicitly added members to the group. Again we'll leave this blank for our example. When you're ready, click on the **Create** button to create the group.

> If required, an OpsMgr group can be configured to contain a combination of both explicit and dynamic members.

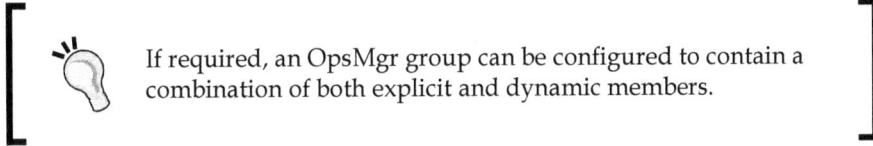

To view the members of your newly created group, right-click on the new group from the Groups section of the Authoring workspace and click on **View Group Members** as shown in *Figure 3.21*.

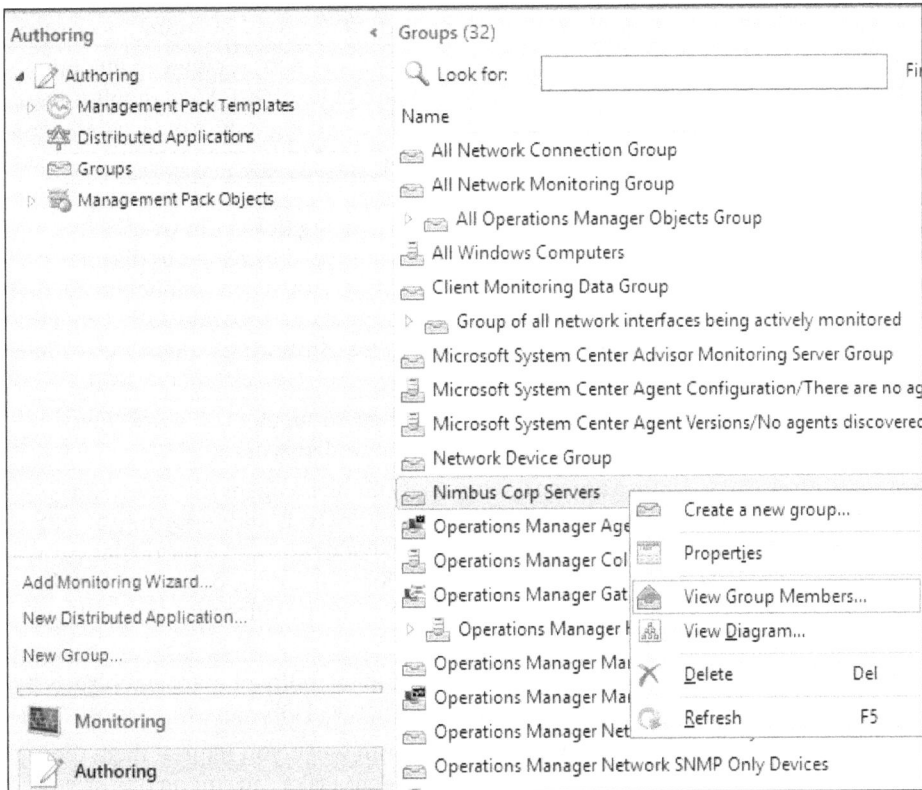

Figure 3.21: Viewing group members

Management Pack Objects

The final section within the Authoring workspace is Management Pack Objects. This is where you will go to manage and maintain the management pack elements listed in the following table:

Element Name	Description
Attributes	An attribute is defined as a property of a class in a management pack. Custom attributes can be added to collect additional information about managed objects, which can then be used to support group membership or accessed by monitors or rules.
Monitors	These are essentially workflows that run on an agent and determine the current health of an object. Each monitor uses a particular data source the event log, performance data, or a script to collect its information. Alerts generated by monitors are referred to as '**stateful**'.
Object Discoveries	Used to view and manage existing object discoveries in management packs. Overrides can be created to disable or modify the frequency that they run at. You cannot create new object discoveries here though and a separate authoring tool, such as Visual Studio with the Authoring Extensions installed is required for this.
Overrides	Overrides are used to change parameters on workflows including monitors, rules, and discoveries.
Rules	Rules are workflows that run on an agent that create an alert, collect information for analysis and reporting, or run a command on a schedule. Each rule uses a particular data source - the event log, performance data, or a script to collect its information. Alerts generated by rules are referred to as '**stateless**'.
Service Level Tracking	Here you can compare the availability of managed objects by creating and editing Service Level Objectives.
Tasks	Tasks are workflows that run when you request them through the Operations console. **Agent tasks** can run on one or more agent computers and **console tasks** run on the Operations console workstation.
Views	This management pack element simply shows all existing configured views that are available for each target class. Views are created and modified in the **Monitoring** workspace and you cannot create or modify them here.

In *Chapter 5, Working with Management Packs*, we will come back to these elements again as we begin to deploy new management packs into OpsMgr.

Introduction to the Reporting workspace

The Reporting workspace is a central location for you to work with all the reports that are available in OpsMgr and it only appears alongside the other workspaces after you install the Reporting Server role.

From here you can configure, run and schedule reports that have been exposed through the various management packs deployed in your OpsMgr environment.

There's also the Microsoft Generic Report Library shown in *Figure 3.22*, which contains generic reports, such as **Availability**, **Configuration Changes**, and **Most Common Alerts** to help you easily build customized reports as you need.

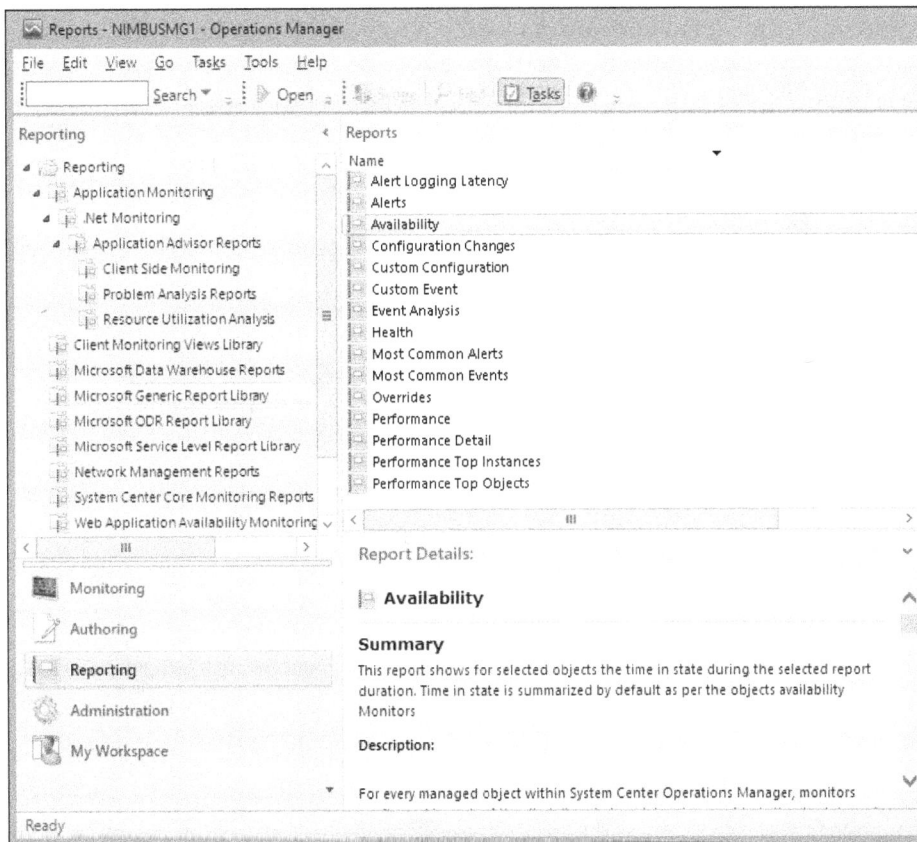

Figure 3.22: Generic Report Librar

In *Chapter 10, Creating Alert Subscriptions and Reports*, we will explore this workspace in much more detail as we create and schedule new reports.

Exploring the Administration workspace

This workspace is where most of your OpsMgr administrative tasks will take place. Here you can deploy and manage agents, install or remove management packs, configure network device monitoring, schedule alert notifications, configure role-based access control and define management group global settings.

> You will only be presented with the Administration workspace when the user account you are running the console with is a member of the 'Operations Manager Administrators' user role.

As shown in *Figure 3.23*, when you click on the root-level **Administration** link within the workspace, you will be presented with the **Administration Overview** page, which is not too dissimilar from the **Monitoring Overview** page that we discussed at the beginning of the chapter.

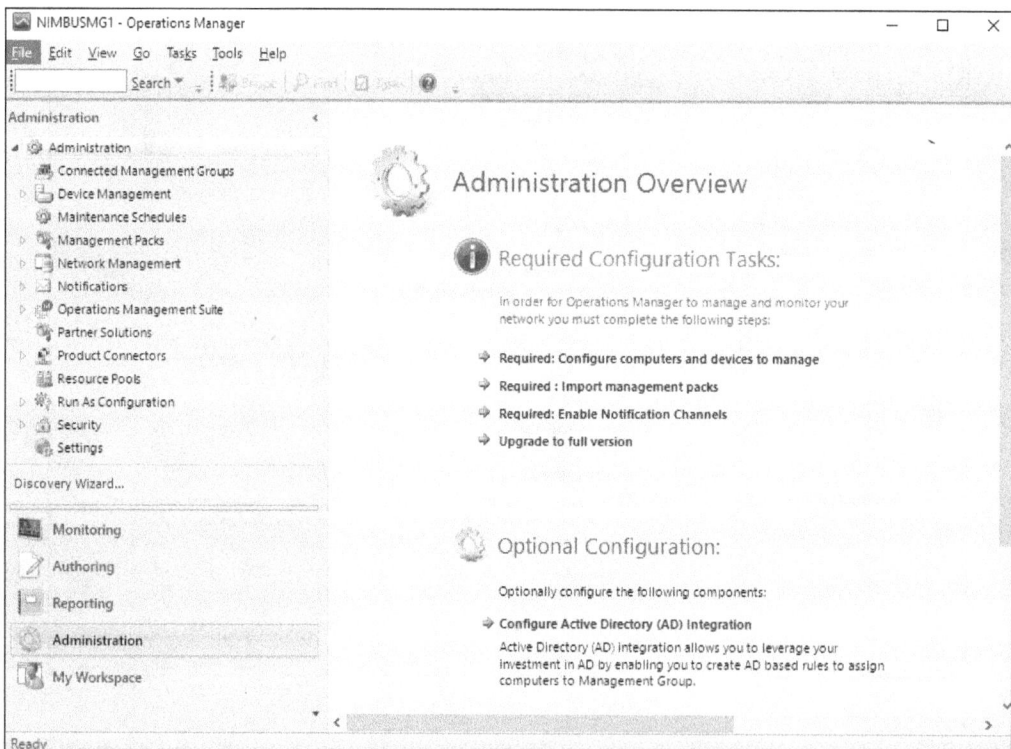

Figure 3.23: Administration Overview page

The Administration Overview page gives you some quick shortcuts to incomplete administration tasks in OpsMgr, such as configuring agents, importing management packs, creating notification channels, and upgrading your license version. You can also optionally choose to configure Active Directory integration to help automatically deploy OpsMgr to computers within the domain.

The navigation pane on the left of the Administration workspace contains eleven options and the following sections explain what each one can do.

Connected Management Groups

If you have deployed multiple OpsMgr Management Groups, then this is where you can connect them to one another to enable forwarding of alerts and other monitoring data.

Right-clicking on **Connected Management Groups** and choosing the **Add Management Group** option from the context menu will present you with the **Add Management Group** dialog box shown in *Figure 3.24*.

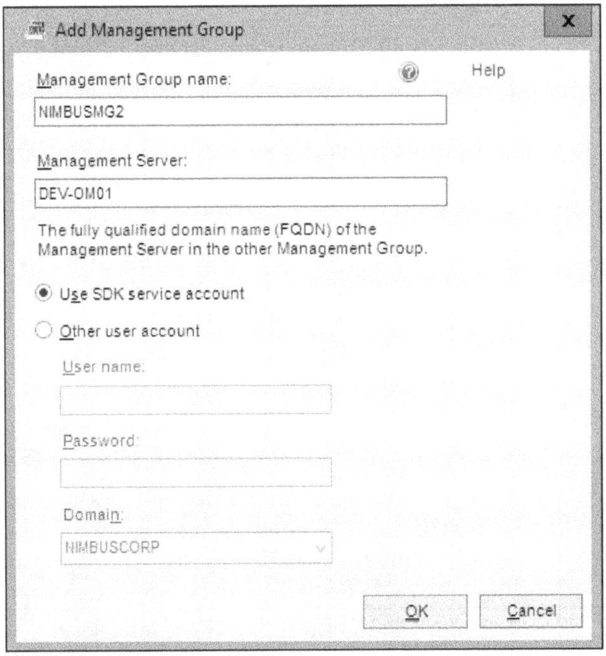

Figure 3.24: Connecting other Management Groups

Here you need to add the name of the other Management Group along with a Management Server name and SDK or other user account to complete the connection.

Device Management

You can use this section to perform configuration of specific management servers, agent-managed Windows computers, agentless-managed computers, UNIX servers, and Linux servers. The following table details each item in Device Management:

Item Name	Usage
Agent Managed	• Shows all Windows computers with installed OpsMgr agents. • Ability to change the primary management server. • Repair or uninstall an agent. • Option to override the management group agent heartbeat settings on a specific agent. • Option to configure an agent-managed computer as a proxy for agentless-managed computers.
Agentless Managed	• Displays all agentless managed computers. • Ability to change or delete the proxy agent for a particular agentless computer.
Management Servers	• Shows all Management servers and Gateway servers. • Here you can override the management group heartbeat failure setting and configure the number of missed heartbeats that a management server allows for an agent before it changes the state of the respective computer to critical. • Ability to override the Management Group Manual Agent Installs setting and configure a management server to reject or put manually installed agents into pending management. • You can configure a management server here as a proxy for agentless-managed computers. • If you are using an Internet Proxy Server, then you can configure those settings for a management server here.
Pending Management	• If you have enabled the **Review new manual agent installations in pending management view** option, then any manually installed agents will appear here awaiting approval before they can become monitored.
UNIX/Linux Servers	• Shows all monitored UNIX/Linux servers within the Management Group. • Ability to repair or uninstall the UNIX/Linux agent from a computer.

Management Packs

Here you can view and manage a list of all the management packs that have been imported into your Management Group – including the ones that were installed by default as part of the initial OpsMgr installation.

You can create new management packs here as well as exporting and deleting existing ones from the Management Group and there's useful Download/Import options to help you quickly get access to new management packs through the Microsoft Management Pack Catalog service. If you've deployed OpsMgr 2016, then you have some additional options in this section that can help you with alert tuning and management pack recommendations.

In *Chapter 5, Working with Management Packs*, we'll take these options for a test drive and discuss the recommended method of deploying management packs.

Network Management

This section is where you will manage and discover network devices that are to be monitored by OpsMgr. The following table describes the three options that are available to you here:

Option Name	Usage
Discovery Rules	Ability to create a network discovery rule to bring your network devices under monitoring control using either ICMP or SNMP.
Network Devices	Displays all network devices being monitored by OpsMgr.
Network Devices Pending Management	Any network devices that are in a pending management state will be listed here.

Chapter 6, Managing Network Devices will walk you through this section in much more detail.

Notifications

In the Notifications section, you can configure a number of different notification channels upon which to get your OpsMgr alerts. You can also administer subscribers and subscriptions for specific alerts based on scoped criteria.

The following table describes the options that are available to you here:

Option Name	Usage
Channels	Choose from SMTP (Email), Instant Message (IM), Text Message (SMS) or even a custom Command channel to deliver alerts.
Subscribers	Configure the subscribers that will receive alert notifications from OpsMgr and define which notification channel they will use.
Subscriptions	Create alert subscriptions based on scoped criteria to ensure that the correct alerts are delivered to the correct people.

In *Chapter 10, Creating Alert Subscriptions and Reports* we discuss this topic in greater detail.

Operations Management Suite

In this section of the Administration workspace, you have an option to connect your on-premise OpsMgr environment to Microsoft's cloud-based **Operations Management Suite (OMS)** as an attached service. OMS (shown in *Figure 3.25*) is an IT management solution that delivers cloud-based versions of scenarios similar to what we can currently deliver with on-premise System Center.

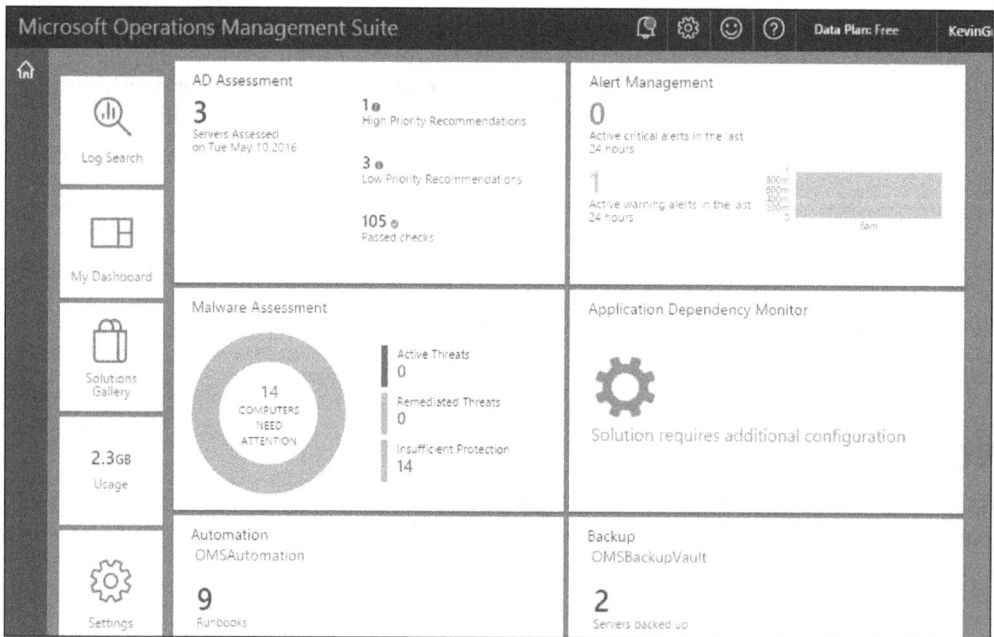

Figure 3.25: The OMS portal

Some examples of the management capabilities you can enable with OMS focus on Log Analytics, Alerting, Backup, Recovery, Automation, Security and Compliance to name just a few.

> You can sign up for a free OMS account at the official website (https://www.microsoft.com/oms) and if you want a comprehensive deep dive of what it can do, then download this excellent free ebook that was authored by some well-known MVP's and Microsoft guru's here: - http://tinyurl.com/omsebook

The OMS connection option in the Administration workspace enables OMS to collect data from your OpsMgr agents and then gives you the ability to perform deep and super-fast log analytics using the full computing power behind Microsoft's public cloud services. You can also use this connection to view your OpsMgr alerts within the OMS **Alert Management** solution as shown in *Figure 3.26*.

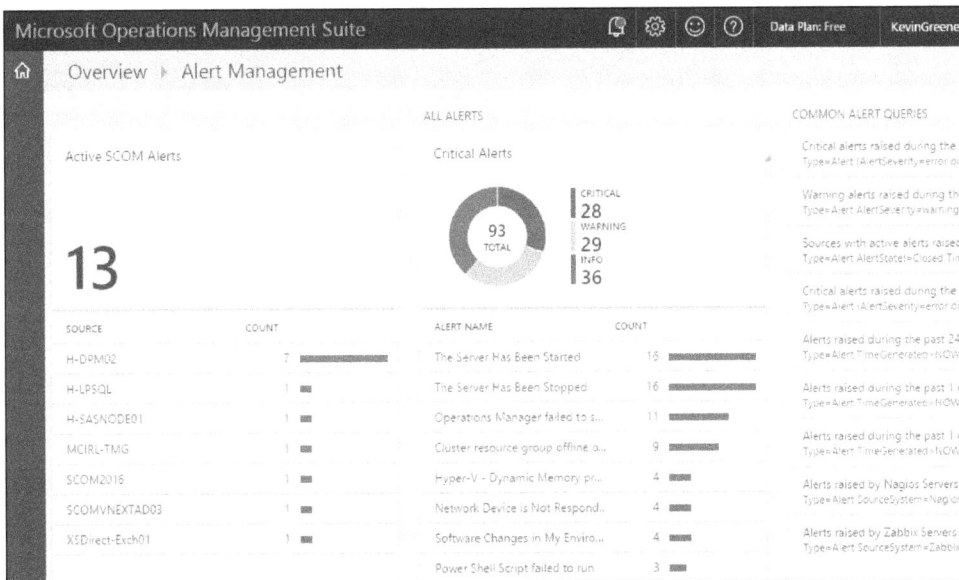

Figure 3.26: Alert Management in OMS

If you've signed up to OMS and would like to get your OpsMgr agents connected, then follow these steps in the OpsMgr console to get up and running (an internet connection is required on the computer hosting the console):

1. In the Administration workspace, expand **Operations Management Suite**, click on **Connection**, and then click on the **Register to Operations Management Suite** option as shown in *Figure 3.27*.

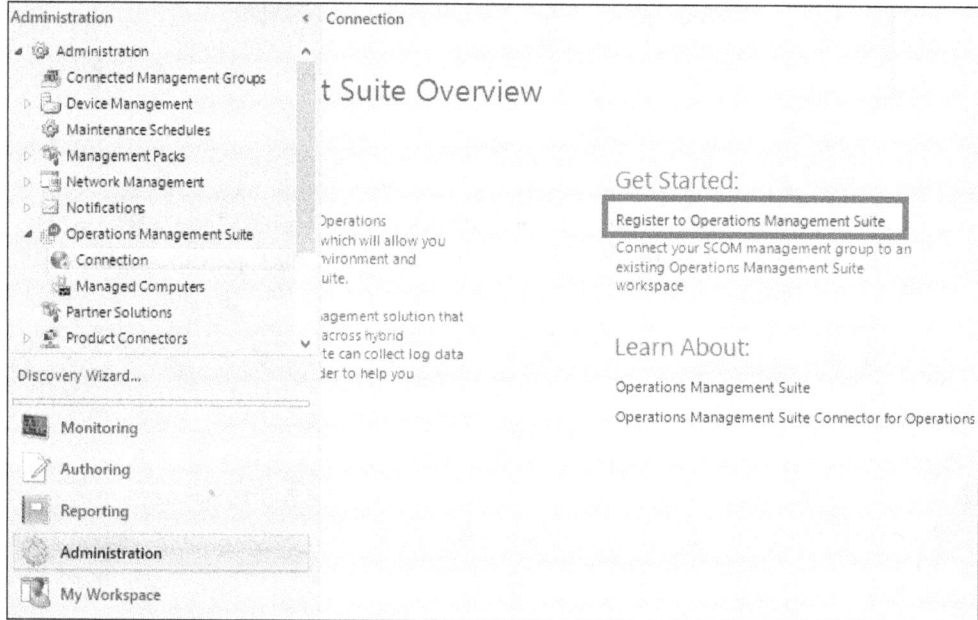

Figure 3.27: Alert Management in OMS

2. From the **Sign In** dialog box, enter the Microsoft account credentials that you use to connect to your OMS workspace and click on **Next** to continue.

> If you encounter an error when attempting to sign in to OMS through the OpsMgr console, then you might need to make some changes to your Internet Explorer security settings. System Center MVP Adin Ermie has put together a handy blog post that walks you through solving some of these OMS connectivity issues: http://tinyurl.com/omsconnectivity

3. In the next dialog box (shown in *Figure 3.28*), choose the OMS workspace that you want to connect your OpsMgr environment to and click on **Next**.

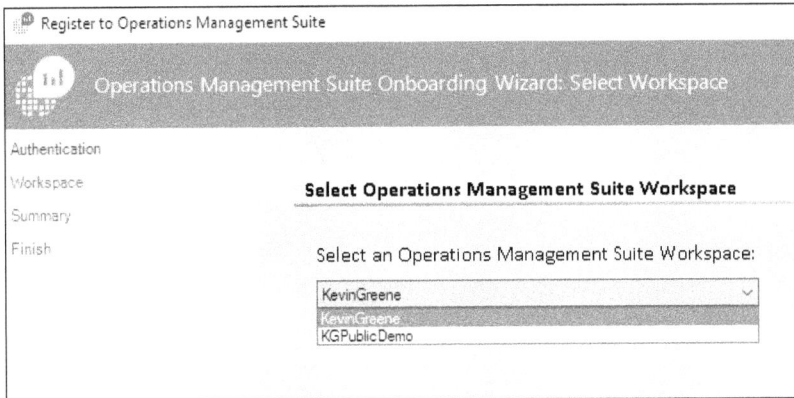

Figure 3.28: Choosing an OMS workspace

4. Confirm your settings in the final dialog box and then click on **Create**. When the connection to OMS has been created, hit the **Close** button to complete the wizard.

5. Back at the **Connection** area in the console, click on the **Add a Computer/ Group** action link shown in *Figure 3.29*.

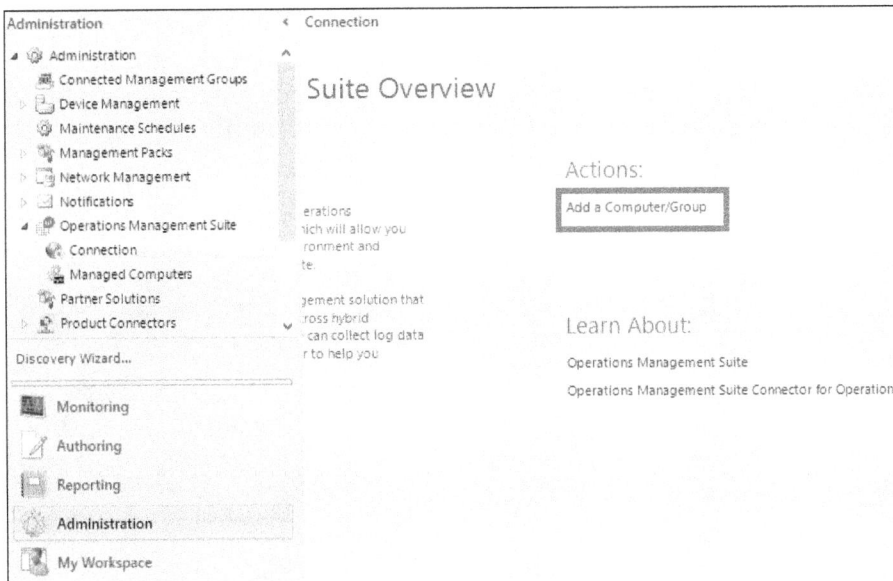

Figure 3.29: Adding a monitored computer to OMS

6. From the Computer Search dialog box shown in *Figure 3.30*, select a Windows computer from the **Available items** section, click on the **Add** button and then hit **OK**.

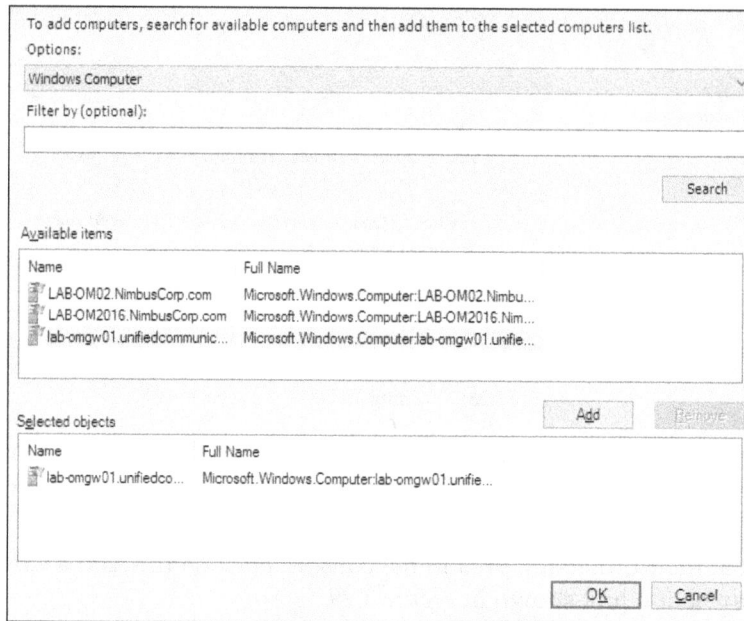

Figure 3.30: Selecting computers to add

7. To confirm the connection has been configured correctly, view the **Connected Sources** screen in the **Settings** section of OMS and you should see the name of your management group listed similar to *Figure 3.31*.

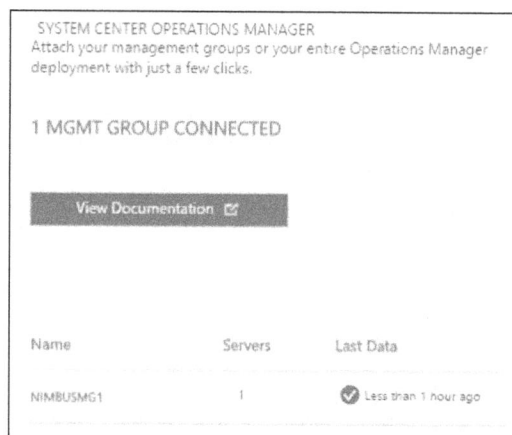

Figure 3.31: Confirming the OMS connection

Partner Solutions

The Partner Solutions area of the Administration workspace gives you an integrated overview of OpsMgr solutions from preferred partners endorsed by Microsoft. Vendors, such as NiCE, Comtrade, OpsLogix, and Silect were amongst the first to be listed here and for each vendor, you can get a description, version number and download link for the solution they are offering.

Product Connectors

Product connectors are used to synchronize and integrate OpsMgr data with other management systems. The following three internal connectors are installed by default:

- Network Monitoring Internal Connector
- SMASH Discovery Internal Connector
- Operations Manager Internal Connector

Resource Pools

This section in the Administration workspace is where you can manage a relatively new concept to OpsMgr called **Resource Pools**. These were introduced to provide scalability and built-in redundancy for Management Group operations – particularly when monitoring UNIX and Linux computers or Network devices.

A resource pool is a collection of management servers that distribute work amongst themselves and take over work from a failed member. They ensure the continuity of monitoring by providing multiple management servers that can take on monitoring workflows if one of the management servers becomes unavailable.

When you deploy OpsMgr, three resource pools are configured by default and all OpsMgr Management servers are automatically assigned as members of these pools.

These are described in the following table:

Option Name	Description
AD Assignment Resource Pool	Works with the Active Directory integration assignment for automatic OpsMgr agent deployment.
All Management Servers Resource Pool	Performs functions, such as health aggregation, availability, database grooming, and group calculation.
Notifications Resource Pool	Used for managing alert notifications.

Run As Configuration

The Run As Configuration section lists the accounts and profiles that OpsMgr uses to manage access to your IT environment. There are three default areas here:

Accounts

This is where Run As accounts are stored. Run As accounts are named sets of credentials that are presented by Run As profiles for authentication when monitors, rules or tasks are run. A Run As account may be used by one or more Run As profiles and there are eight different types of Run As account to choose from (depending on the monitoring requirement).

The following table lists the different Run As account types and what they do:

Account Type	Description
Windows	Requires standard Windows credentials.
Community String	Used for SNMP version 1 or SNMP version 2 monitoring.
Basic Authentication	Basic web authentication credentials.
Simple Authentication	Generic username and password credentials.
Digest Authentication	Digest web authentication.
Binary Authentication	User-defined binary authentication through the use of a binary account file.
Action Account	Must be configured using Windows credentials and is restricted to working with just the Action Account Run As profile.
SNMPv3 Account	Used for SNMP version 3 network monitoring credentials.

Profiles

Run As profiles allow monitors, rules and tasks to run as an account that has the required permissions to successfully monitor resources that have been locked down for security purposes. Active Directory and SQL are good examples of resources that require monitoring but will be locked down to just a specific group of administrators due to the sensitive data they hold.

We use these profiles to assign our preferred Run As accounts to our relevant monitored resources. In *Chapter 5, Working with Management Packs*, we will configure some Run As accounts and profiles to give you a good understanding of how they work.

UNIX/Linux Accounts

This section gives us the opportunity to specify Run As account credentials for monitoring UNIX and Linux computers. The credentials we enter here can be configured as a Monitoring account or as an Agent Maintenance account and we can then assign the Run As account to the relevant Run As profile as needed.

Security

The Security section of the Administration workspace is where you get to configure your **role-based access control (RBAC)** for OpsMgr. With RBAC, you can scope OpsMgr access for users or groups within your organization to eight pre-existing user roles or you can simply create your own custom user roles to deliver maximum flexibility and control.

The following table details the eight default user roles in OpsMgr:

User Role	Description
Administrator	• Full administration rights to OpsMgr. • Must contain one or more global groups.
Advanced Operator	• The Advanced Operator profile includes a set of privileges designed for users that need access to limited tweaking of monitoring configuration in addition to the Operators privileges. • A role based on the Advanced Operators profile grants members the ability to override the configuration of rules and monitors for specific targets or groups of targets within the configured scope.
Application Monitoring Operator	• The Application Monitoring Operator profile includes a set of privileges designed for users that need access to the APM Application Diagnostics Web console. • A user role based on the Application Monitoring Operator profile grants members the ability to see the Application Monitoring events in Application Diagnostics Web console.

User Role	Description
Author	• The Author profile includes a set of privileges designed for authoring of monitoring configuration. • A role based on the Authors profile grants members the ability to create, edit and delete monitoring configuration (tasks, rules, monitors and views) within the configured scope.
Operator	• The Operator profile includes a set of privileges designed for users that need access to Alerts, Views and Tasks. • A role based on the Operators profile grants members the ability to interact with Alerts, execute Tasks and access Views according to their configured scope.
Read-Only Operator	• The Read-Only Operator profile includes a set of privileges designed for users that need read-only access to Alerts and Views. • A role based on the Read-Only Operators profile grants members the ability to view Alerts, and access Views according to their configured scope.
Report Operator	• The Report Operator profile includes a set of privileges designed for users that need access to Reports. • A role based on the Report Operators profile grants members the ability to view reports according to their configured scope.
Report Security Administrator	• The Report Security Administrator profile includes a set of privileges designed to enable the integration of SQL Server Reporting Services security with Operations Manager.

Creating a New User Role

Due to limitations on how you can customize the default User Roles, it's recommended to create your own User Roles and to then scope each of those roles exactly as you require them.

Here's what you need to do to create a new custom User Role:

1. In the Administration workspace, right-click on **User Roles**, then click on **New User Role** and choose the type of user role that you wish to create as shown in *Figure 3.32* (we'll select the **Operator** role for our example).

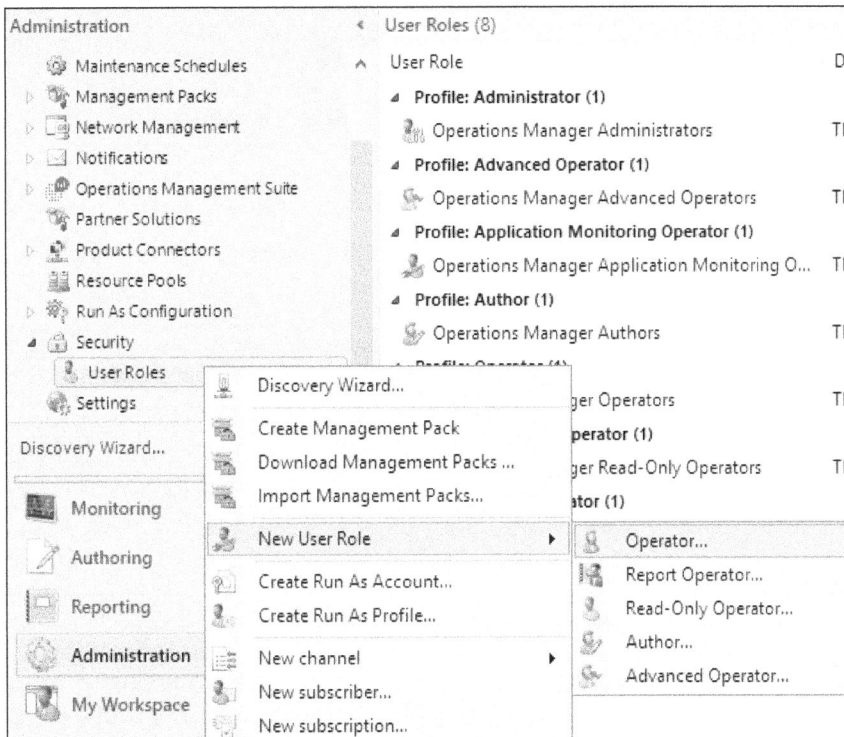

Figure 3.32: Creating a new user role

2. In the **User role name** field, type a name to identify the new user role – we'll use 'Nimbus Corp Operators' in our example. As shown in *Figure 3.33*, click on the **Add** button and specify the security group (or user account) that you wish to scope this role to. Type a description into the **Description** field and then click on **Next** to continue.

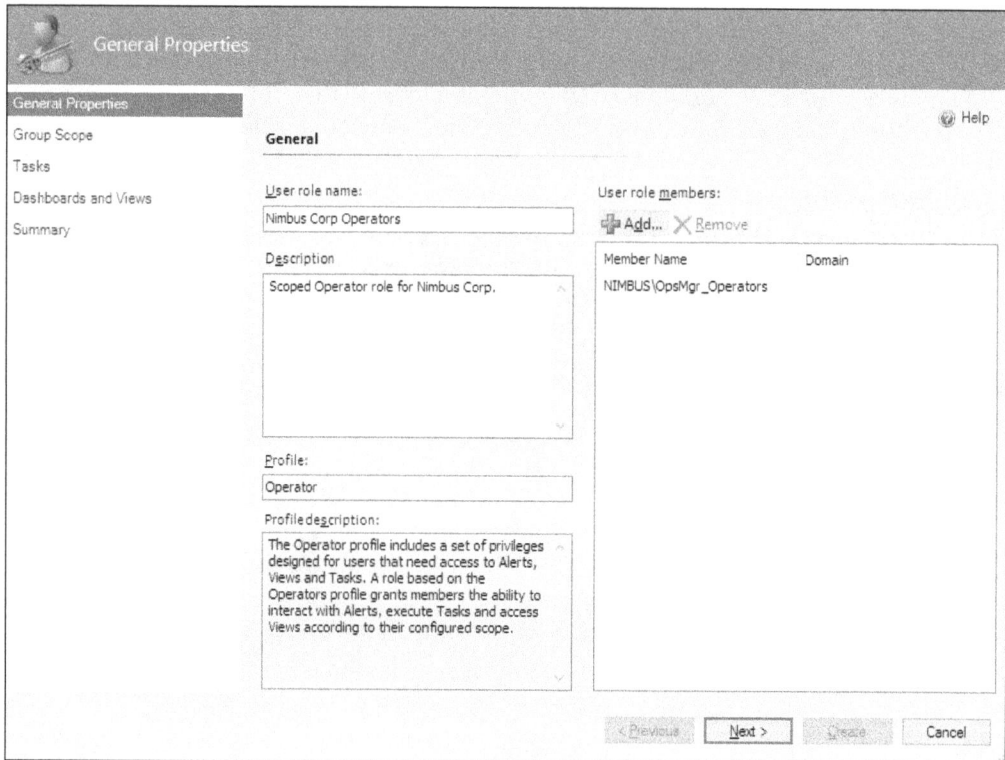

Figure 3.33: Adding user role members

3. In the **Group Scope** dialog box, you can see that all groups have been approved by default. Choose to leave this setting as it is or scope the groups that you want to approve and then click on **Next**.

4. From the **Tasks** dialog box, you can decide which tasks users are allowed to run when they're logged onto the console. This can be useful if you don't want users to have the option of restarting services or enabling/disabling monitoring for certain components. Choose the tasks you want to approve for this user role or leave all tasks automatically approved and then click on **Next** to move on.

5. The **Dashboards and Views** dialog box defines the views that users can see within the Monitoring workspace. In *Figure 3.34*, you can see that we have approved only the custom views that we configured earlier for this user role. Make your own choices here and then hit **Next** to continue.

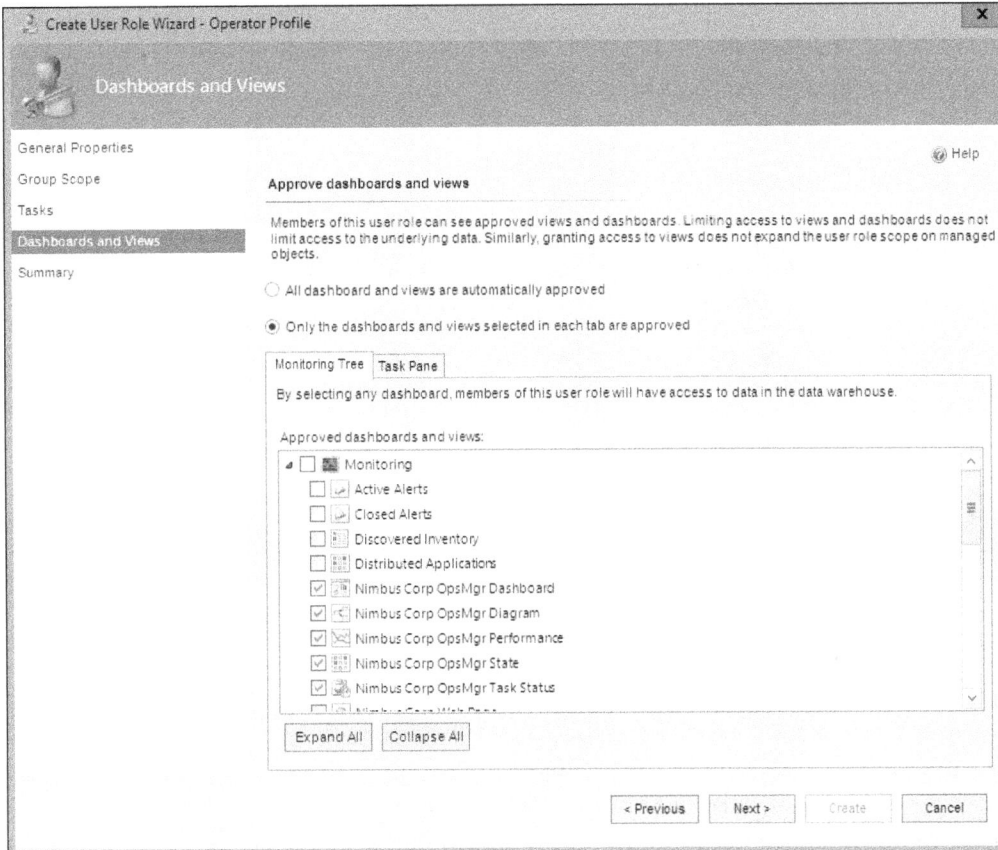

Figure 3.34: Approving dashboards and views

6. The Summary dialog box gives you the opportunity to review the parameters of the new user role that you have just specified and when you've confirmed they are correct, click on the **Create** button to create the new role.

Settings

This section is where you go when you want to configure the Global Management Group settings and it's divided up into three areas – **Agent, General** and **Server** as shown in *Figure 3.35*.

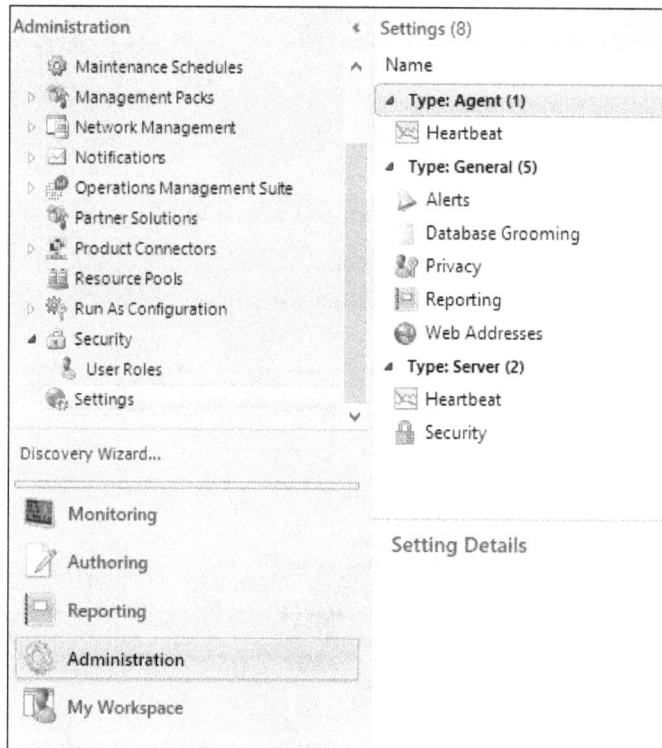

Figure 3.35: Global Management Group settings

Here's an explanation of the settings in each area:

Agent: Heartbeat

Agents generate a heartbeat at specific intervals to ensure they are operating correctly and this setting configures the global heartbeat interval. The default value here is 60 seconds and depending on your environment, you may want to change this to a higher or lower value.

General: Alerts

The Alerts setting enables you to create or modify **Alert Resolution States** and manage **Automatic Alert Resolution** times.

For the alert resolution states, you can create up to 254 custom states and these are very useful when tuning and working with alerts. As we learned earlier in *Working with Views*, an alert resolution state can be assigned to an alert view to scope specific alerts to categories, such as New, Closed, Escalated, Ticket Logged, and so on.

The automatic alert resolution setting determines how long OpsMgr waits before automatically resolving active alerts. The default options here are to resolve all active alerts with a resolution state of 'New' after 30 days and to resolve all active alerts where the alert source is now healthy after 7 days.

General: Database Grooming

This setting configures how long different types of data should be retained in the database and removes unnecessary data after a set period of time. *Figure 3.36* shows all records are configured to be purged after 7 days – with **Performance signature** data the only exception with a value of 2 days.

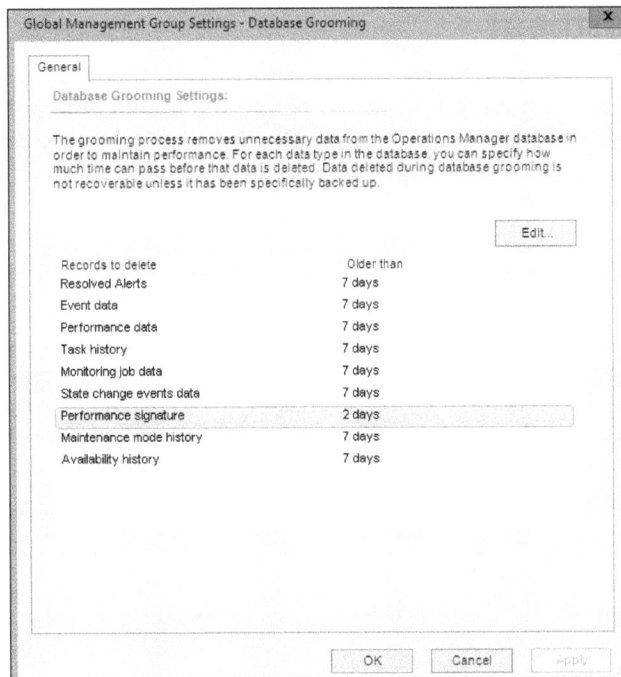

Figure 3.36: Database grooming settings

General: Privacy

The Privacy setting allows you to enable and configure settings for the Customer Experience Improvement Program, Operational Data Reporting, Error Reporting and Error Transmission Reporting. If configured, these will forward anonymous data to Microsoft to help them improve the overall quality of OpsMgr for future updates and releases.

General: Reporting

With this setting, you can view and modify the URL path for your SQL Reporting Server instance. It's best to leave this setting as it is unless you reconfigure your Reporting Server or you wish to move the URL over to an SSL connection.

General: Web Addresses

Here you can view and modify web addresses for the OpsMgr Web console and an online company knowledge portal. If you have deployed the OpsMgr Web console, then this section will automatically get populated and it will also appear in alert notifications as a link for recipients to follow for further information.

Server: Heartbeat

Moving onto the Server settings now, the heartbeat option enables us to configure the number of missed heartbeats before the management server pings the agent-managed computer. The default value for consecutive missed heartbeats is 3 and depending on your environment, you may want to modify this value higher or lower.

> The *Server Heartbeat* setting uses the *Agent Heartbeat* setting to determine how long it will be before you get an alert informing you an agent is unreachable. For example, if the Agent Heartbeat setting is configured with an interval value of 60 seconds and the Server Heartbeat is configured to fire an alert after 3 missed consecutive heartbeats, then it will be 180 seconds (or 3 minutes) before you know about that agent going offline.

Server: Security

Another setting to take note of, this one specifies how the management server should deal with manually installed agents. By default, this setting is configured to **Reject new manual installations** and if you're not aware of this, when you go to deploy agents at a later stage and for whatever reason need to manually install one, this setting will just reject the agent without any obvious indication.

For that reason, we recommend configuring this setting as shown in *Figure 3.37* to place all new manual agent installations into the Pending Management view.

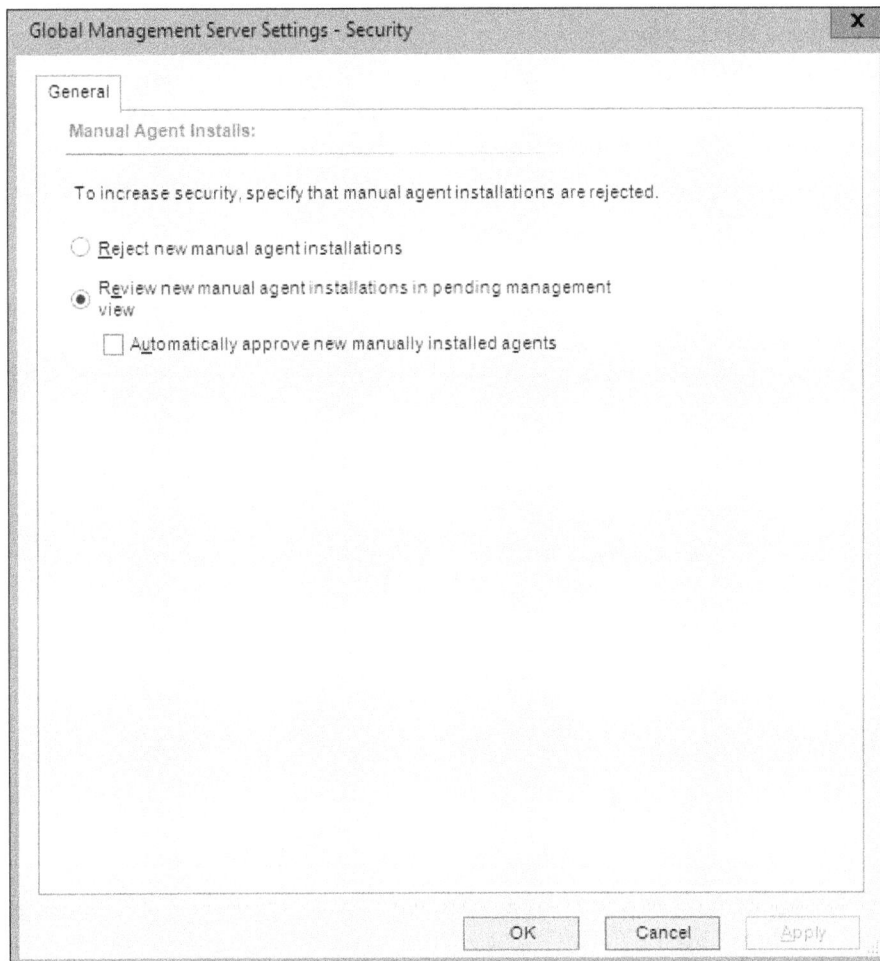

Figure 3.37: Enabling manual agent installation reviews

Getting personal with My Workspace

The final workspace in the Operations console that you need to get familiar with is My Workspace. Here, you (or your OpsMgr operators) get your own private space to customize and save commonly used views and searches.

Views created and saved in My Workspace will follow the operator from console to console and are even accessible through the Web console. There are two sections of note here:

Favorite Views

A cool feature of My Workspace is that you can right-click on any view from the Monitoring Workspace and choose the **Add to My Workspace** option to save the view as a Favorite View similar to *Figure 3.38*.

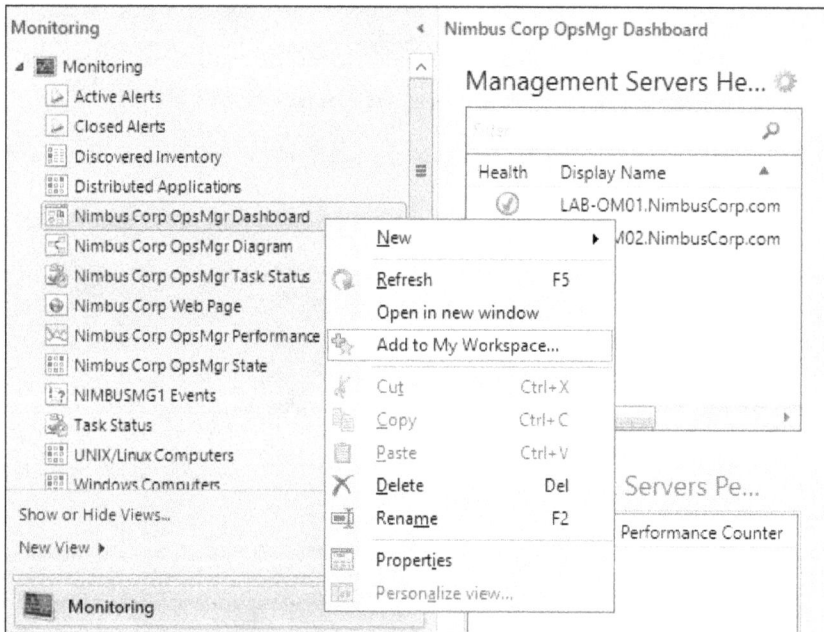

Figure 3.38: Adding Favorite View to My Workspace

You can also create new views by right-clicking on Favorite Views and selecting the **New** option to bring up the familiar list of default OpsMgr views to choose from. Any new views that you create inside your own My Workspace will be available only to you so you can create whatever types of views you wish without having the worry of cluttering up the production Operations console.

Saved Searches

The Saved Searches section becomes very useful when you find yourself running a specific search criterion from within the console on a regular basis. Here you can save those searches for quick access in My Workspace.

All you need to do to get started is first click on the Saved Searches link from the navigation pane on the left, then click on the **Create new search** option from the **Tasks** pane on the right-side of My Workspace. This opens the **Advanced Search** dialog box where you can click on the drop-down menu to choose specific object types to search for, before then providing search criteria similar to what we've entered in *Figure 3.39*.

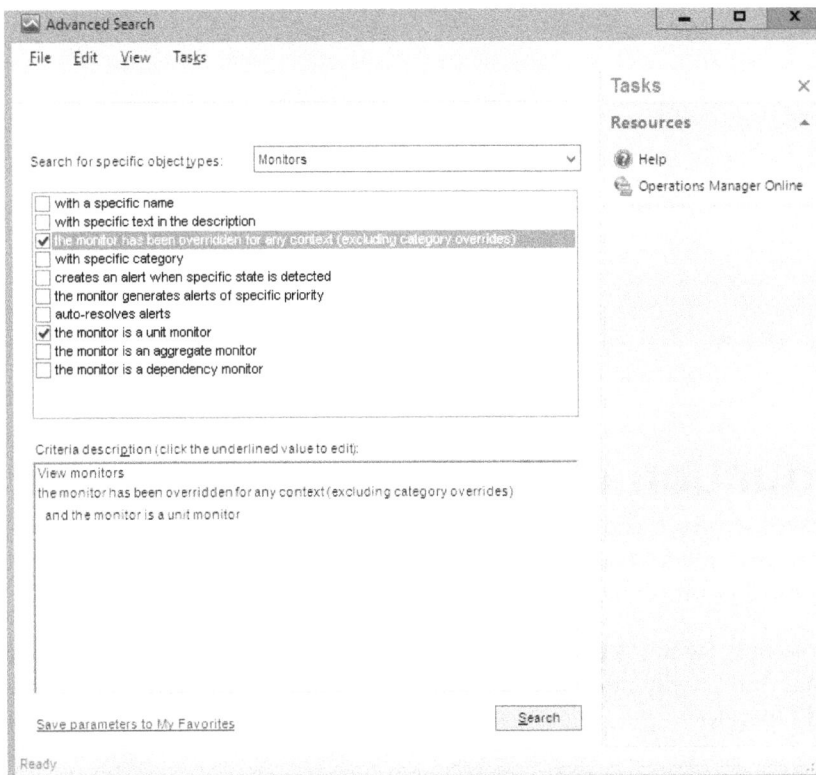

Figure 3.39: Creating a custom Saved Search

When you have specified the relevant criteria for your search, click on the **Save parameters to My Favorites** link, then give the search a new name and click on the **Search** button to run the search and also save it in My Workspace.

Your final My Workspace area including favourite views and saved searches should look something similar to ours in *Figure 3.40*.

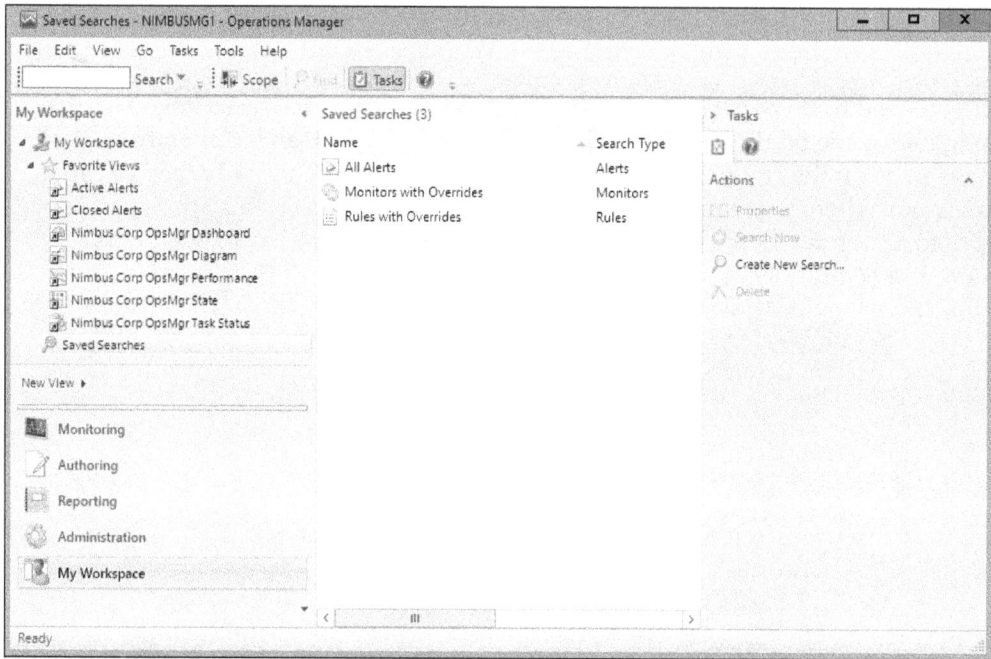

Figure 3.40: Favorite views and saved searches in My Workspace

Introduction to the Web console

Now that we've introduced you to the Operations console and its associated workspaces, it's time to discuss the Web console. Think of this console as the 'Lite' version of the Operations console.

This console only includes the Monitoring and My Workspace views and is targeted at users that don't really need to interact with OpsMgr as an Administrator or Advanced Operator.

In *Figure 3.41* you can see that even though we're logged on with an OpsMgr Administrator account, our options are limited - due to the Web console not having access to the Authoring, Reporting and Administration workspaces.

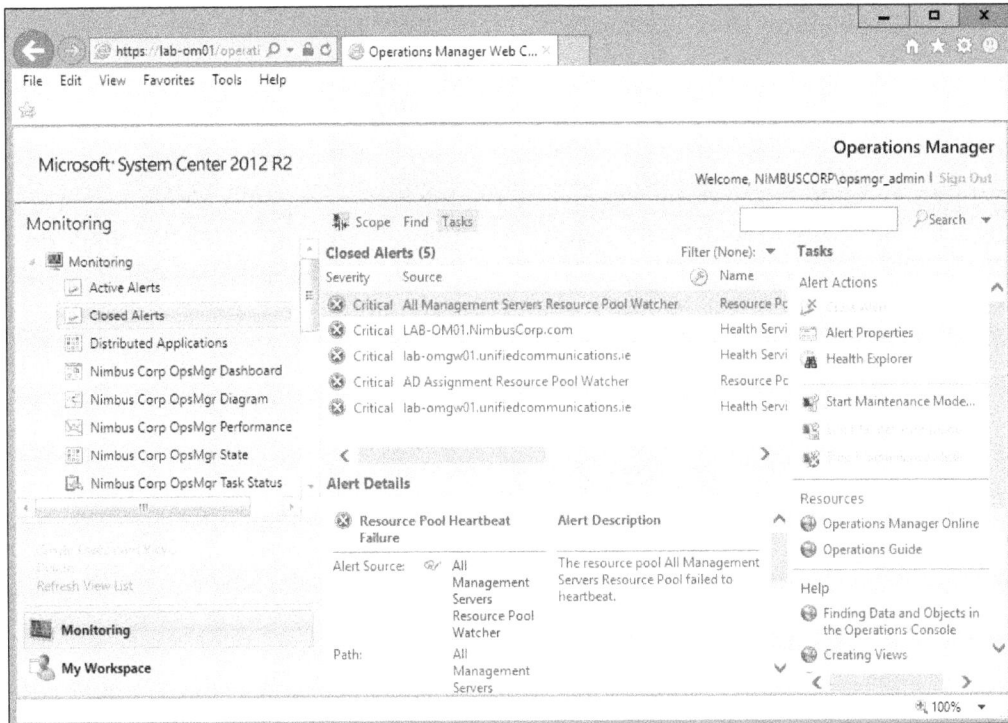

Figure 3.41: OpsMgr Web console

Although limited, the Web console can still prove useful for providing users with an overview of the monitoring environment without the need to install the full Operations console. With a few tweaks, it can be configured to display OpsMgr dashboards on a wall mounted monitor in a service desk or network operations center.

If you'd like to display the OpsMgr Web console on a monitor as a first-glance view of monitored objects, then you will need to change the default session timeout value from 30 minutes to save you having to keep re-inputting credentials when it automatically logs out.

You can learn more about changing the auto timeout value in this blog post by System Center MVP Cameron Fuller: `http://tinyurl.com/opsmgrwebtimeout`

Summary

In this chapter, we explored each of the workspaces within the Operations console and you learned how to create views, groups and user roles. You should also now feel comfortable connecting your OpsMgr environment to an OMS workspace.

Towards the end of the chapter we discussed the various global management group settings in the Operations console before giving you an introduction to the scaled-down Web console and its capabilities.

In the next chapter, we'll show you how to deploy and manage Windows agents and you'll find out how to connect those agents to multiple OpsMgr management groups. You will also learn how to deploy cross-platform monitoring by installing an agent to Linux.

4
Deploying Agents

Now that we have explored the consoles and also understand how to navigate around OpsMgr, it's time to deploy some agents.

In this chapter, we will first learn about the differences between agent-based and agentless monitoring. Then we will discuss specific requirements and different methods available for deploying agents to Microsoft Windows platforms. Once we have grasped the concept of deploying agents, we'll see how we can 'multihome' them to work with multiple OpsMgr management groups.

We will end the chapter by walking you through deploying agents to cross-platform UNIX/Linux environments.

Here's a high-level breakdown of what we'll cover in this chapter:

- Agent-based and agentless monitoring
- Deploying Microsoft Windows agents
- Different agent installation methods
- Working with multiple management groups
- Deploying UNIX/Linux agents

Agent-based monitoring

The **Agent Managed** section within the Administration workspace is where you can see a list of all Windows computers in the Management Group that have the OpsMgr agent installed. The agent is essentially a software component called the Microsoft Monitoring **Agent** that runs locally as a Windows service on each monitored computer.

Commonly referred to as the **HealthService**, the agent communicates with management servers to receive configuration data, perform tasks, and deliver monitoring information in a timely manner.

Most management packs will only work with agent-based monitoring and it is best practice to always deploy an agent when possible.

Agentless monitoring

With agentless monitoring, a management server, or another computer with the OpsMgr agent installed acts as a proxy agent for the agentless device to deliver monitoring data back into the Operations console.

The most common use of agentless monitoring that you'll come across in OpsMgr is where you monitor Microsoft Windows servers that are configured in a cluster and the cluster nodes act as a proxy agent for the virtual cluster object.

For example, let's say you create a Hyper-V Failover cluster with two servers named Node1 and Node2. When you run through the Failover Cluster wizard to initially create the new cluster, you'll be prompted for a virtual cluster name and IP address, which you can name Cluster1. Now, when you deploy the OpsMgr agent to both Node1 and Node2 and enable the Agent Proxy setting on each node, the virtual cluster object for Cluster1 will show up automatically in the **Agentless Managed** section of the Administration workspace.

In *Figure 4.1*, you can see an example of some agentless managed virtual cluster objects that have appeared in my console as a result of this scenario.

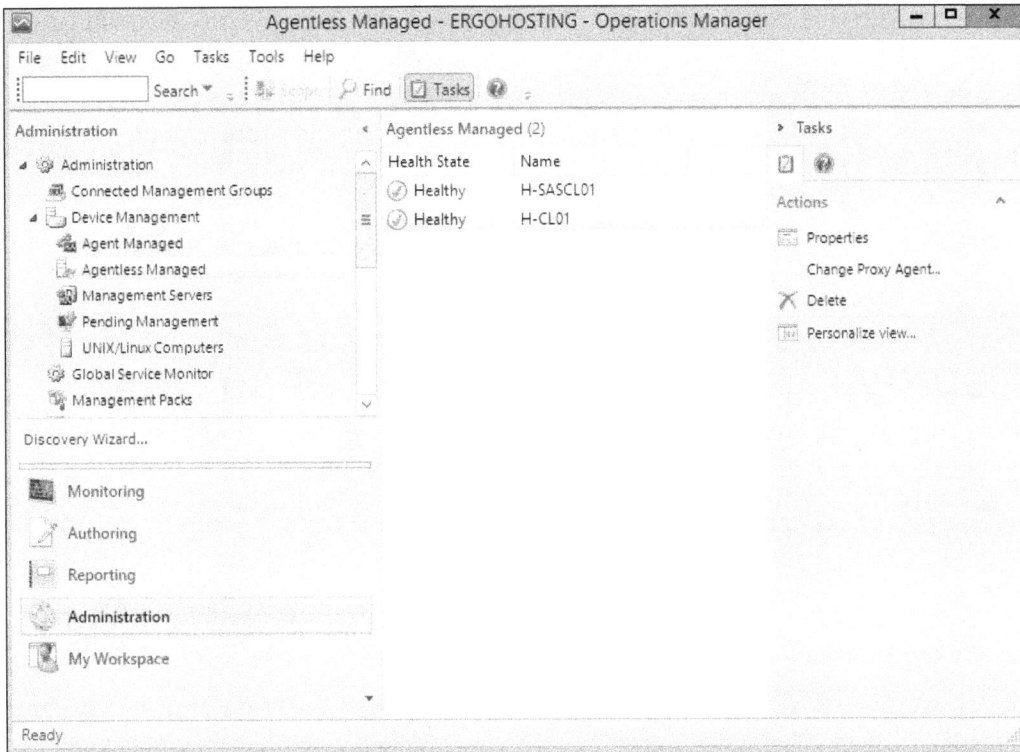

Figure 4.1: Agentless monitoring

The assigned proxy agent for an agentless managed object can be modified by clicking on the **Change Proxy Agent** option from the **Tasks** pane within the **Agentless Managed** view.

The following limitations are applicable when using agentless monitoring in OpsMgr:

- The Management servers only support up to 10 agentless managed objects
- A maximum of 60 agentless managed objects are supported in a single Management Group

- Monitoring between the agentless managed object and the proxy agent takes place over **Remote Procedure Call** (**RPC**) and therefore cannot be separated by a firewall

- The action account of the proxy agent performing monitoring of the agentless managed object must be granted Local Administrator permissions on the object

- Most management packs don't support agentless monitoring and instead require an agent to be deployed

Deploying Microsoft Windows agents

The majority of IT environments out there tend to have more Microsoft applications and operating systems deployed than any other vendor and for this reason; understanding how to deploy the OpsMgr agent to monitor Microsoft Windows computers has become an essential skill to learn.

Thankfully, as OpsMgr is a Microsoft product, the agent is designed for easy deployment and monitoring of pretty much everything Microsoft support. All you need to do is to ensure that the relevant prerequisites are in place and decide on your preferred deployment method.

Windows agent requirements

In the *Minimum installation requirements* section of *Chapter 1, Introduction to System Center Operations Manager*, we listed the supported Microsoft Windows operating systems that you can deploy the OpsMgr agent to. On the server side, you can monitor computers running on Windows Server 2003 SP2 right the way through to Windows Server 2016.

The following table lists the specific firewall ports you need to be aware of for OpsMgr Windows agent deployment:

Name	Port	Description
Microsoft Monitoring Agent (`HealthService.exe`)	TCP 5723	OpsMgr Windows agent communication.
RPC Endpoint Mapper	TCP 135	Required for OpsMgr agent push installations from the console.
NetBIOS Name Service	UDP 137	Required for OpsMgr agent push installations from the console.

Name	Port	Description
NetBIOS Datagram Service	UDP 138	Required for OpsMgr agent push installations from the console.
Server Message Block (SMB)	TCP/UDP 445	Required for OpsMgr agent push installations from the console.
NetBIOS Session Service	TCP 139	Required for OpsMgr agent push repair from the console.

The **RPC Endpoint Mapper**, **NetBIOS** and **SMB** ports are used when carrying out push installations, repairs, or upgrades of agents and in low-privilege security environments; they can be disabled outside of these operations. The Microsoft Monitoring Agent (TCP 5723) on the other hand, is used exclusively for communication between the OpsMgr management server and agent and this port always needs to be open.

> Be careful of the environments where both the Windows Firewall inside the operating system and an external hardware firewall are configured to filter traffic. In this scenario, you will need to ensure that the required ports are configured on both firewall solutions to allow agent deployment and management.

Using the console to deploy agents

When you have the relevant prerequisites in place, you can move onto deploying Windows agents using the OpsMgr console. This is the easiest method for deploying Windows agents, and the following steps walk you through how to do it:

1. From the **Administration** workspace in the OpsMgr console, expand **Device Management**, right-click on **Agent Managed** and then click on **Discovery Wizard**, as shown in *Figure 4.2* (you can also choose to just click the **Discovery Wizard...** link located above the Wunderbar).

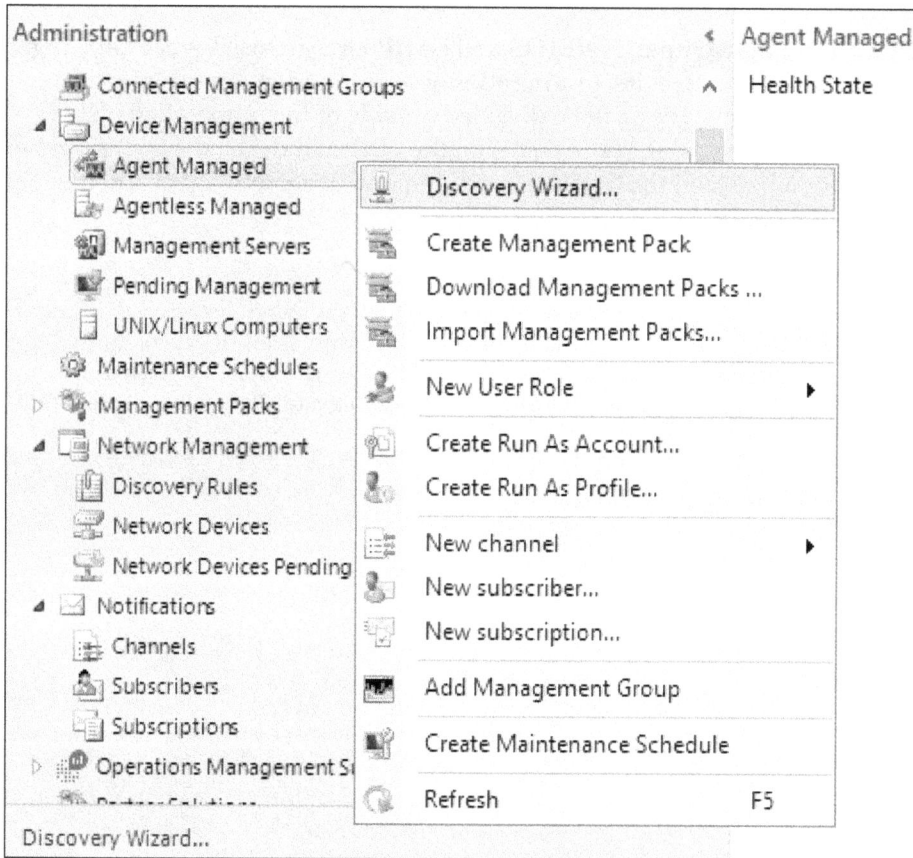

Figure 4.2: Running the Discovery Wizard

2. From the **What would you like to manage?** dialog box, select **Windows Computers** as the type of device to discover and then click on **Next**.

3. The **Automatic Computer Discovery** option from the next dialog box enables you to discover computers for agent deployment by automatically scanning all Windows computers in the Active Directory domain that the management server is a member of. This can be useful for smaller organizations where you need to carry out mass-deployment of agents. In most cases however, you will choose the **Advanced Discovery** option shown in *Figure 4.3*.

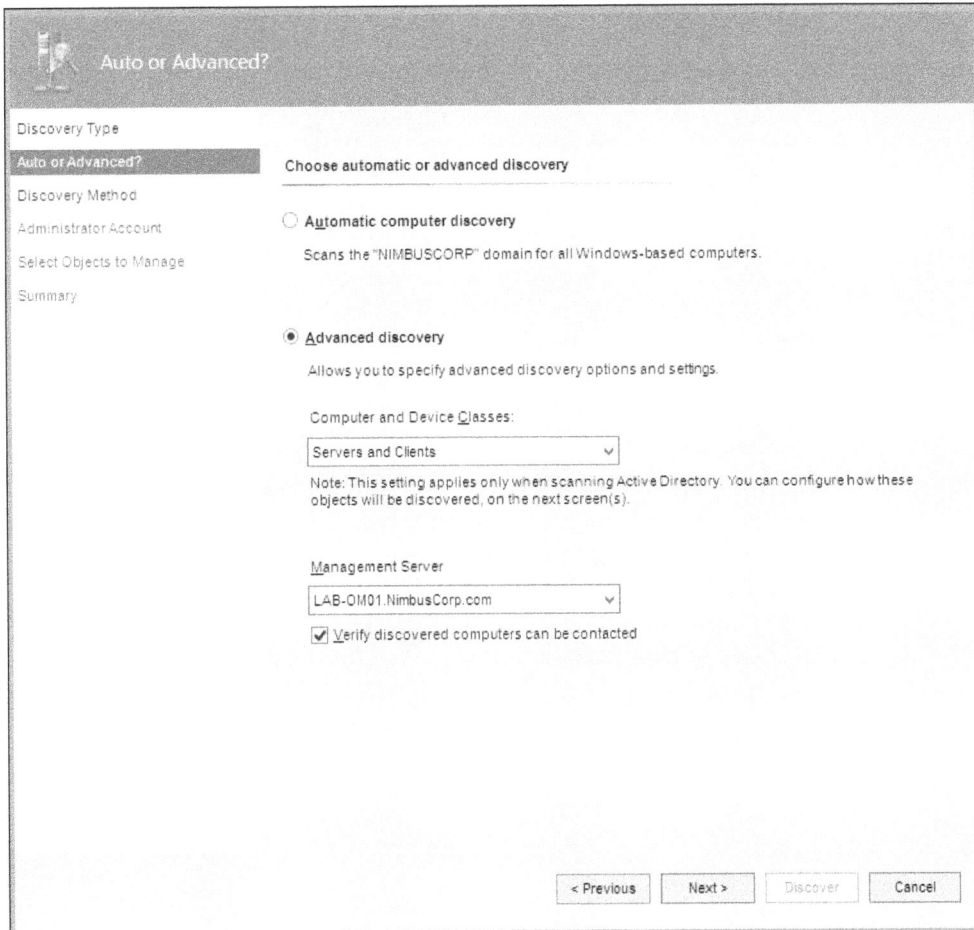

Figure 4.3: Choosing the discovery type

    ○   The **Computer and Device Classes** option here gives you the opportunity to filter the discovery to Servers and Clients, Servers Only or Clients Only. In our example, we will leave the default setting of **Servers and Clients** here. It's recommended to avoid using the Servers Only option here as this can slow down your discoveries due to each machine having to apply a filter to verify its type.

    ○   In the **Management Server** section, choose the management server that the agents will communicate with and click on the **Verify discovered computers can be contacted** option. Choosing this option can increase your deployment success rate as it will discover only computers that can be communicated with over the network. Click on **Next** to move on when you're ready.

4.   At the **Discovery Method** dialog box you have two more options:

    ○   The **Scan Active Directory** option lets you configure advanced LDAP queries to search domains for computers based on certain criteria. This can be useful for example, if you wanted to search for all domain controllers or even all computers with names beginning with certain characters. You can also choose from some pre-selected fields here by selecting the **Field** drop-down menu from the **Advanced** tab.

    ○   With the **Browse for, or type-in computer names** option, you can browse Active Directory or simply type computer names into the empty field and separate them with a semi-colon, comma or a new line. If you have a text file with a list of computer names, you can copy/paste them into here too. *Figure 4.4* shows where we can use the **Browse** button to search for all computers with a name that begins with **LAB**.

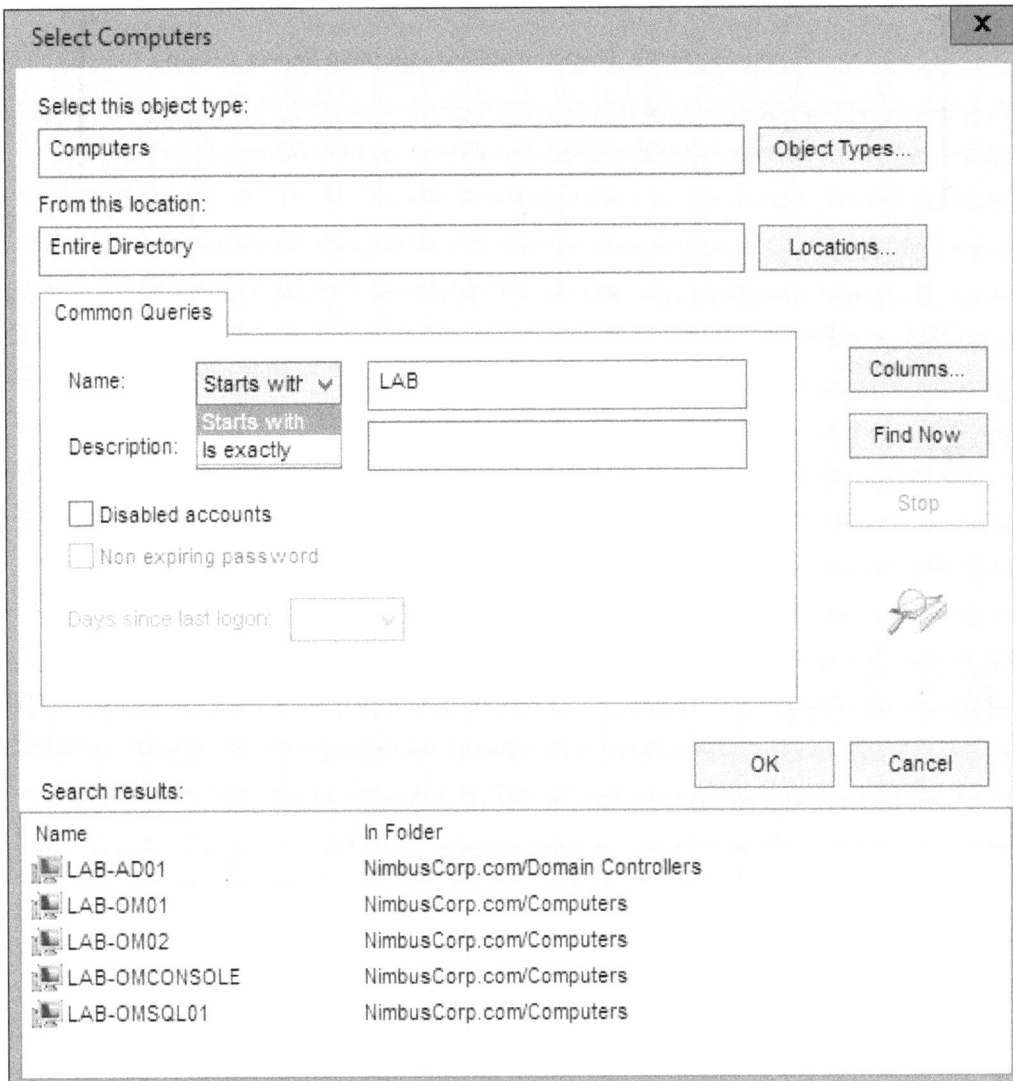

Figure 4.4: Using Active Directory to discover computers

5. When you've made your selections of computer names to discover, click on **Next** to continue.

6. The **Administrator Account** dialog box is where you specify the user account that will be used to install the OpsMgr agent onto the discovered computers. Choose the **Other user account** option and enter the username and password of an account that has Local Administrator rights on the computers you want to scan. Click on the **Discover** button when you're ready to continue.

> If you choose the **Use selected Management Server Action Account** option here, then you need to ensure that the OpsMgr Action account that you specified during installation has Local Administrator permissions on each of the discovered servers you wish to deploy the agent to.

7. When the discovery process finishes, you should be presented with a list of the computers that you can deploy the OpsMgr agent onto. Any systems that already have an agent installed or that you don't have permissions on won't be displayed in the **Select the devices you want to manage** section shown in *Figure 4.5*.

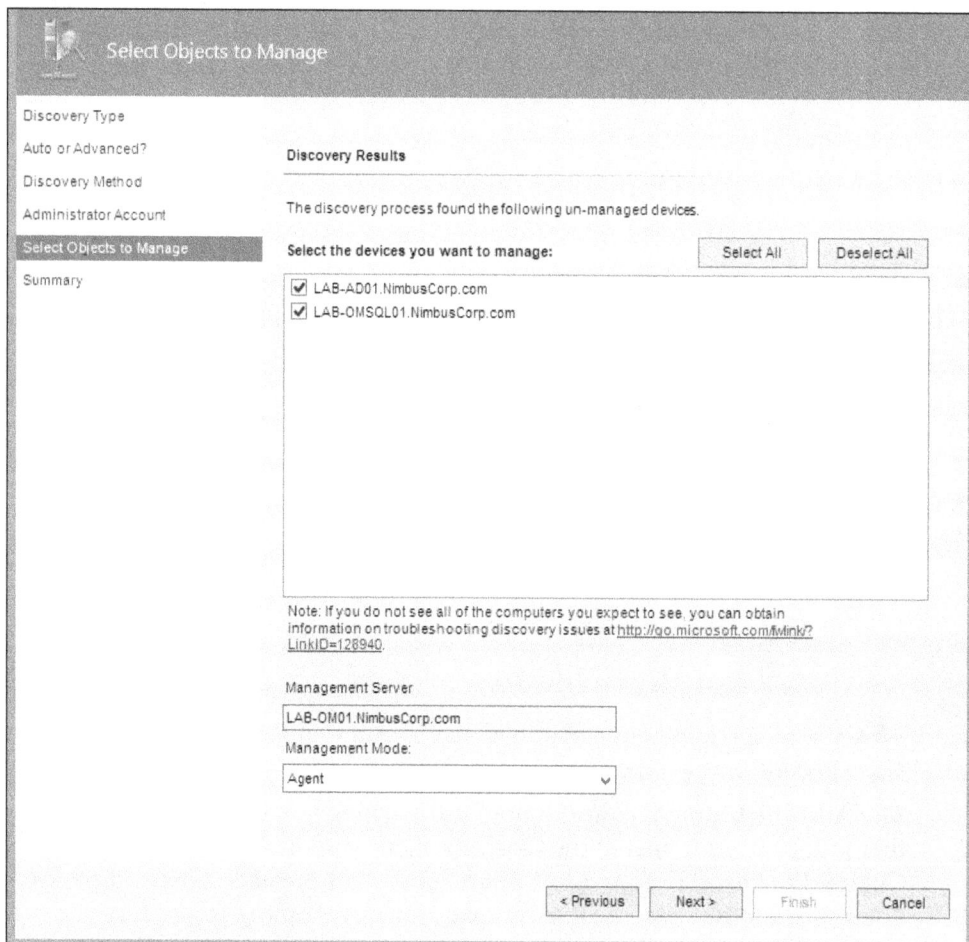

Figure 4.5: Selecting discovered computers for agent deployment

8. Leave the **Management Mode** setting as the default **Agent** and then click on **Next** to continue.

9. The final **Summary** dialog box enables you to choose the agent installation directory on the target computers along with the option of selecting the Agent Action Account that the agent will run under. We'll leave the **Agent Action Account** set to the default **Local System** option.

> It's a best practice recommendation to leave the Agent Action Account setting as the default **Local System.** Changing this to another account could stop certain management packs from working correctly on that agent.

10. Click on **Finish** to close the wizard and deploy your agents.

11. You can see the progress and overall status of your agent deployments in the **Agent Management Task Status** dialog box shown in *Figure 4.6*.

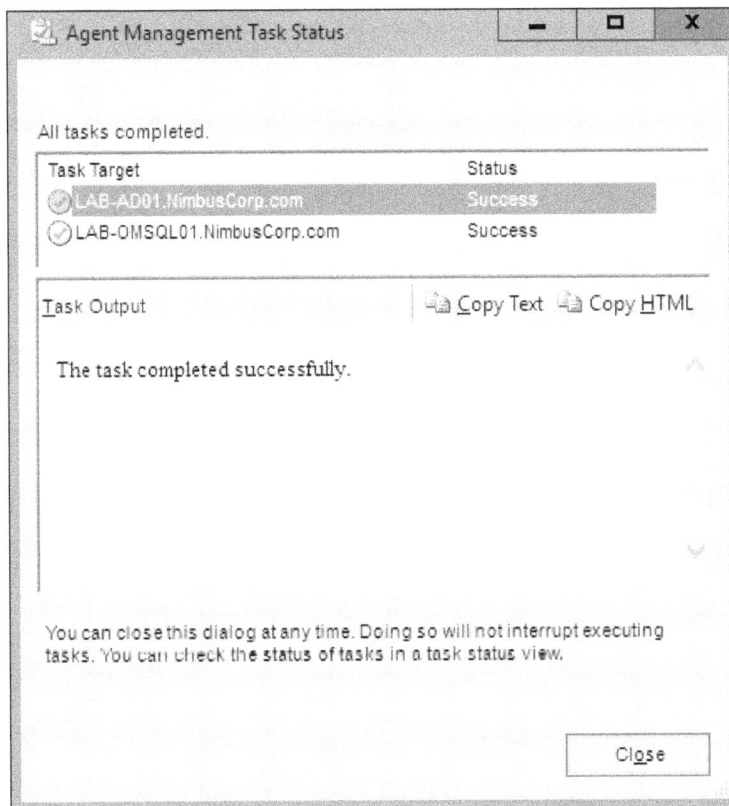

Figure 4.6: Successful push installation of agents from the console

> If you run into any problems with the Windows agent installation process, check out this useful troubleshooting article from Microsoft: http://support.microsoft.com/en-ie/kb/2566152.

Using a Gateway Server to deploy untrusted agents

In *Deploying a Gateway server* in *Chapter 2, Installing System Center Operations Manager* we walked you through the process of deploying an OpsMgr Gateway server into an untrusted domain. We will use this Gateway server as an example here to show you how to perform a push-deployment of agents into your untrusted domains and DMZ's.

Even though the Gateway Server is located in a different untrusted domain, we will use the OpsMgr console running on a computer in our trusted domain to deploy agents that will be managed by the Gateway Server.

1. From the Administration workspace in the OpsMgr console, expand **Device Management** and click on the **Management Servers** view to ensure you can see the Gateway Server located in the untrusted domain and confirm that it has a healthy state.

2. Now right-click on the **Management Servers** view and click on **Discovery Wizard**, as shown earlier in *Figure 4.2*.

3. From the **What would you like to manage?** dialog box, select **Windows Computers** as the type of device to discover and then click on **Next**.

4. Click on the **Advanced discovery** option from the next dialog box, leave the **Servers and Clients** option as it is and choose your Gateway Server located in the untrusted domain from the drop-down list in the **Management Server** section as shown in *Figure 4.7*. Click on **Next** to move on.

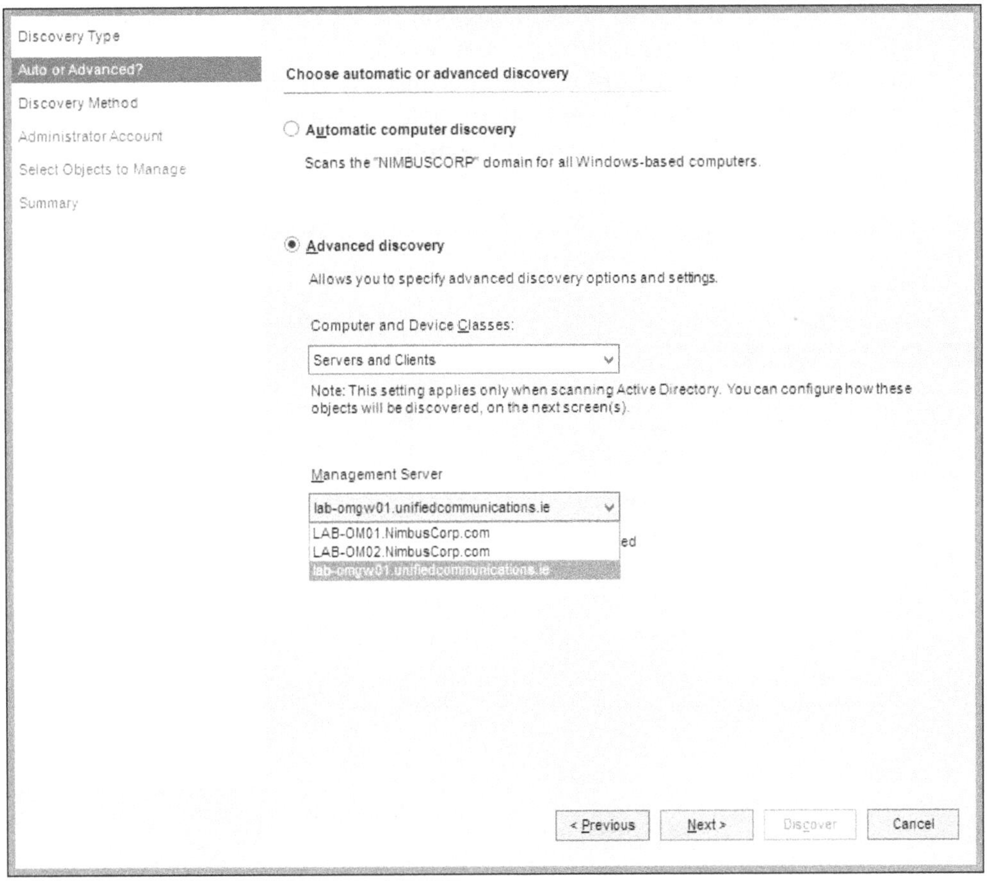

Figure 4.7: Selecting the Gateway Server for agent management

5. Click on the **Browse for, or type-in computer names** option and in the empty field, type the name of the server located in the untrusted domain or DMZ that you wish to deploy the agent to. Click on **Next** to move on.

> If the wizard cannot resolve the name of servers in your untrusted domain or DMZ and then you'll need to create an entry in your local hosts file or DNS server.

6. At the **Administrator Account** dialog box, select the **Other user account** option and type the username and password for an account in the untrusted domain that has local administrator permissions on the computer you wish to deploy the agent to. At the **Domain** field, instead of clicking on the drop-down menu, type the full name of the untrusted domain as shown in *Figure 4.8*.

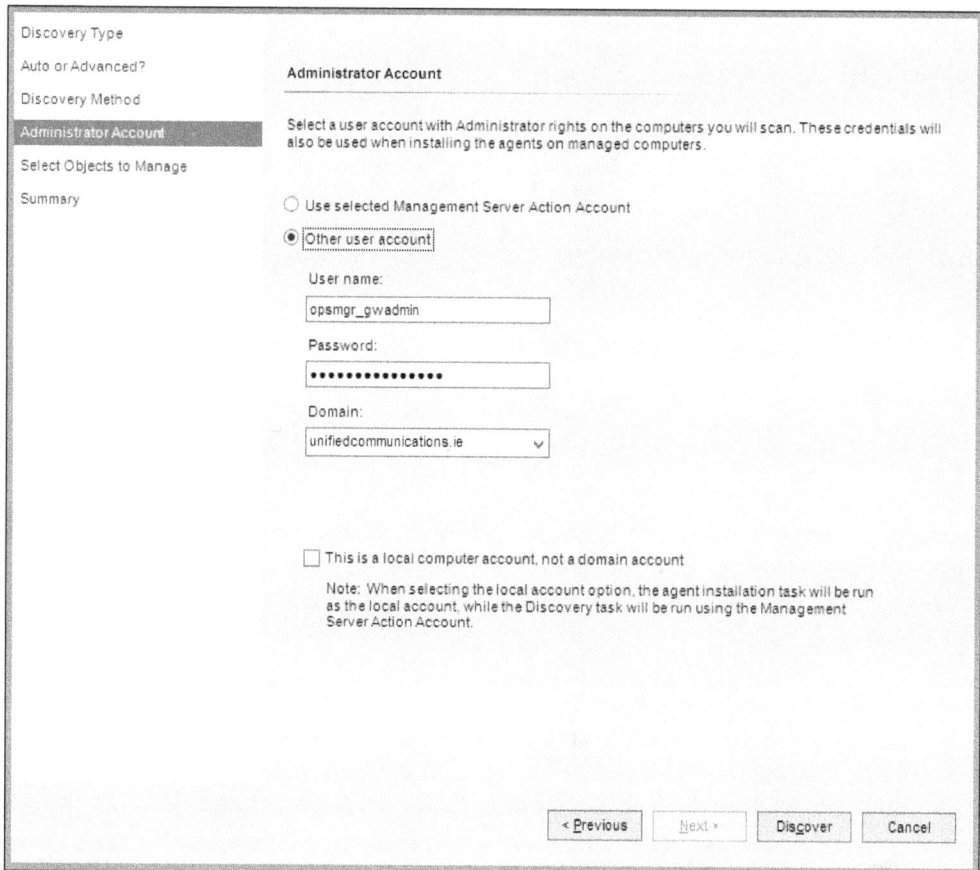

Figure 4.8: Specifying credentials for the untrusted domain

7. Click on the **Discover** button when you're ready to move on and then confirm **Yes** for the resulting warning that pops up with a message stating that the credentials can't be verified.

8. At the **Discovery Results** dialog box, select the discovered untrusted domain computer, ensure the Gateway Server is configured as the management server it will report to and then hit **Next** to continue.

9. Confirm the agent installation directory at the **Summary** dialog box, choose the **Agent Action Account** (we'll leave this set to the **Local System** option) and click on **Finish** to deploy the agent.

10. After a few minutes, you should have confirmation from the **Agent Management Task Status** dialog box that the untrusted domain agent deployment was successful. If you browse back to the **Agent Managed** view, you can then see the new untrusted domain agent being managed by your Gateway Server as shown in *Figure 4.9*.

Health State	FQDN	Name	Domain	Version	Action Account
Agent Managed (3)					
Look for:		Find Now	Clear		
Primary Management Server: LAB-OM01.NimbusCorp.com (2)					
⊘ Healthy	LAB-AD01.NimbusCorp.com	LAB-AD01	NIMBUSCORP	7.2.10126.0	SYSTEM
⊘ Healthy	LAB-OMSQL01.NimbusCorp....	LAB-OMSQL01	NIMBUSCORP	7.2.10126.0	SYSTEM
Primary Management Server: lab-omgw01.unifiedcommunications.ie (1)					
⊘ Healthy	IIS-LAB.unifiedcommunicatio...	IIS-LAB	UC	7.2.10126.0	SYSTEM

Figure 4.9: Confirming Gateway Server deployed agents

Manual agent deployment

From time-to-time and for whatever reason, you'll find that performing a push-installation of the OpsMgr agent from a Management or Gateway server isn't possible and a manual agent deployment is your only option.

> Before you deploy any agents manually, you will need to confirm that the **Server: Security** global setting is configured within the Administration workspace to allow new manual agent installations. This setting was discussed in the *Exploring the Administration workspace* section of *Chapter 3, Exploring the Consoles*. If this setting is left at the default option of '**Reject new manual agent installations**', then your manual agent deployment will fail. It's recommended to configure this setting with the '**Review new manual agent installations in pending management view**' option so you can choose the manually installed agents that are approved for management.

Here's what you need to do to deploy the agent manually:

1. Logon to the computer that you wish to install the OpsMgr agent to. From the OpsMgr installation media, right-click on `setup.exe` and choose **Run as administrator** to begin.

2. At the **Optional Installations** section shown in *Figure 4.10*, click on the **Local agent** server link to start the wizard.

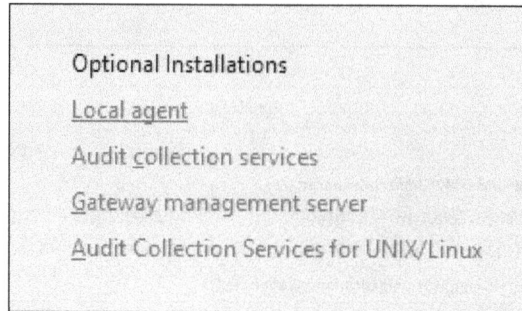

> Optional Installations
>
> Local agent
>
> Audit collection services
>
> Gateway management server
>
> Audit Collection Services for UNIX/Linux

Figure 4.10: Manually installing an agent from the OpsMgr media

If you want to avoid having to copy the entire OpsMgr installation media over to each server you wish to manually deploy the agent to, then you can just copy the \ Agent directory from the media and use the `MOMAgent.msi` installer to launch the setup wizard instead.

3. At the welcome screen for the **Microsoft Monitoring Agent Setup** wizard, click on **Next** to move on, and then hit **I Agree** to accept the software license and continue on.

4. The **Destination Folder** dialog box gives you the opportunity to choose where the agent is installed to and you can also click on the **Disk Usage** button here to check disk capacity on the volume you've specified. Click on **Next** to continue.

5. The **Agent Setup Options** dialog box is shown in *Figure 4.11* and this is where you can specify whether or not the agent will be connected to Microsoft's **Operations Management Suite** (**OMS**) along with confirming that you want to connect it to an OpsMgr Management Group. Choose **Connect the agent to System Center Operations Manager**, and then click on **Next**.

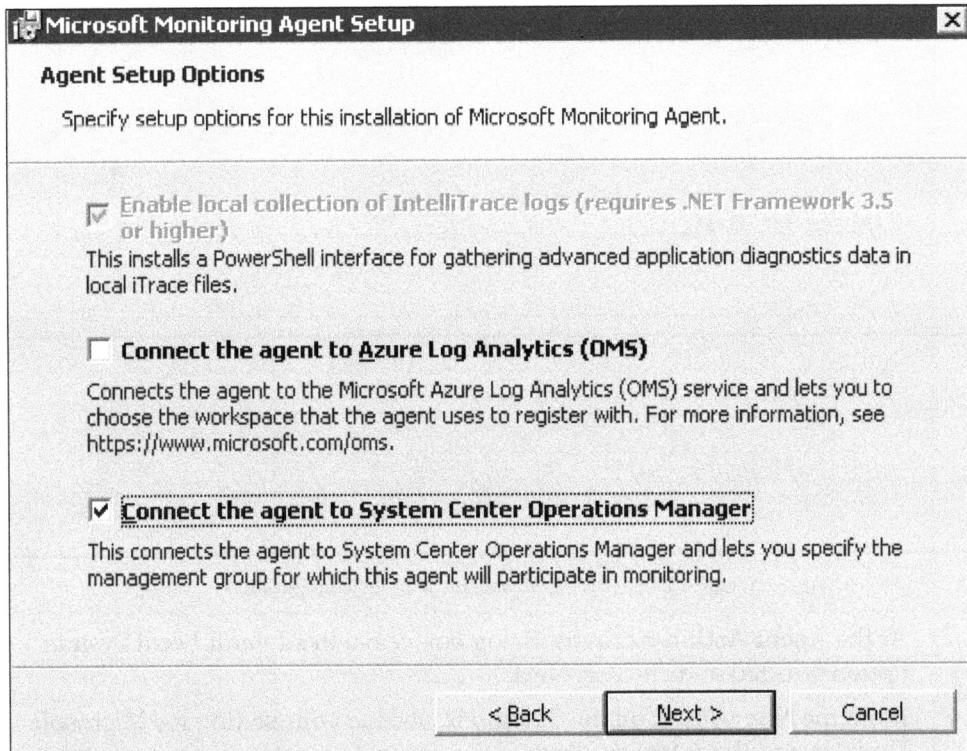

Figure 4.11: Manually configuring the agent setup options

6. As shown in *Figure 4.12*, at the **Management Group Configuration** dialog box, type the Management Group name (remember this is case sensitive), your management server name and the port that the agent will communicate over (TCP **5723** is the default port here). Click on **Next** to move on.

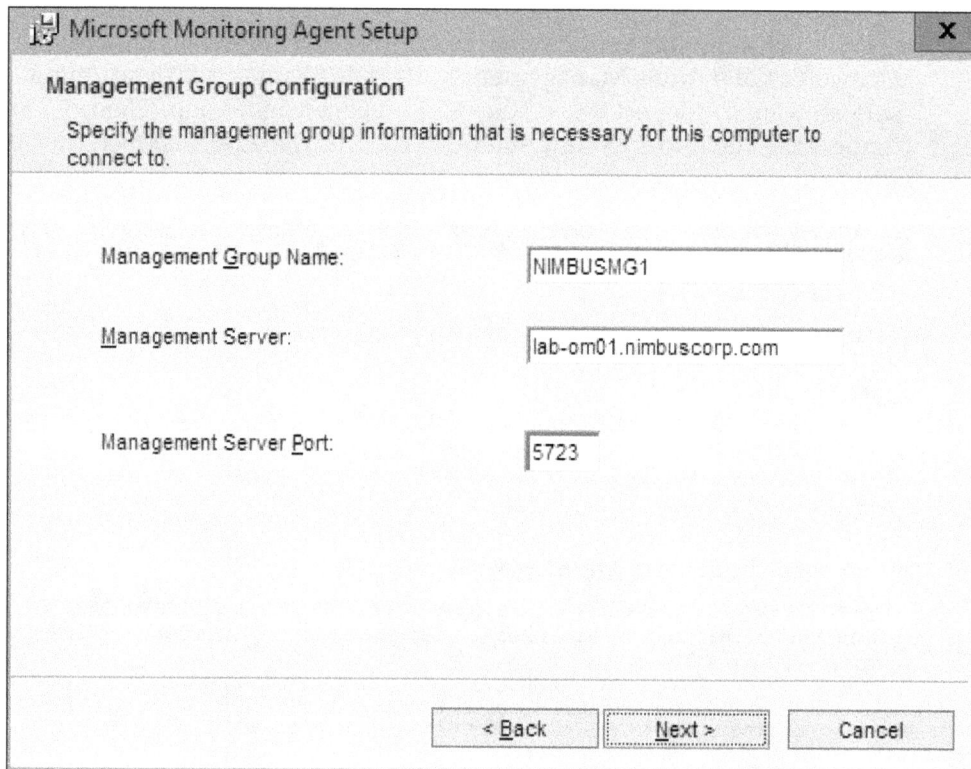

Figure 4.12: Specifying Management Group configuration

7. At the **Agent Action Account** dialog box, leave the default Local System option selected and click on **Next**.

8. From the **Microsoft Update** dialog box, choose your setting for Microsoft Updates and then click on **Next**.

9. At the **Ready to Install** dialog box, confirm all your choices are correct and that you haven't made any typing mistakes with the Management Group or Management Server names and then hit **Install** to begin the manual agent installation.

10. When the installation is complete, click on **Finish** to close the Setup wizard and then, back in the console, browse to the **Pending Management** view within the Administration workspace and check for agents that are awaiting approval. As shown in *Figure 4.13*, right-click on the manually installed agent and select **Approve** to enable management.

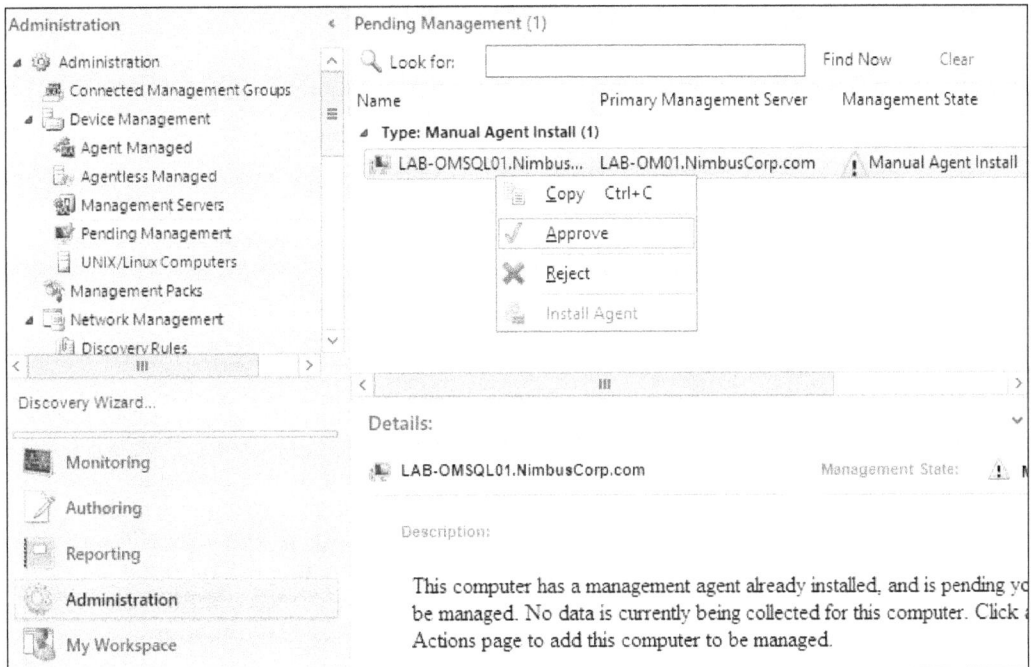

Figure 4.13: Approving manually installed agents

11. When you click back to the Agent Managed view, you can see the new manually installed agent alongside the other Windows agents in the Management Group but there's one small difference. As you can see from *Figure 4.14*, the manually installed agent has a **Remotely Manageable** setting of **No**, meaning we don't have the option to use the console to change the management server it's managed by or the ability to push new agent updates out to it. This setting is configured to **No** by design for all manually installed agents and if you want to change it, you can do so by following the instructions in the following post from Microsoft's Kevin Holman: `http://tinyurl.com/opsmgragentmanaged`.

Agent Managed (3)					
Look for:			Find Now	Clear	
Health State	FQDN ▲	Domain	Version	Remotely Manageable	Action Account
⊿ **Primary Management Server: LAB-OM01.NimbusCorp.com (2)**					
⊘ Healthy	LAB-AD01.NimbusCorp.com	NIMBUSCORP	7.2.10126.0	Yes	SYSTEM
⊘ Healthy	LAB-OMSQL01.NimbusCorp....	NIMBUSCORP	7.2.10126.0	No	SYSTEM
⊿ **Primary Management Server: lab-omgw01.unifiedcommunications.ie (1)**					
⊘ Healthy	IIS-LAB.unifiedcommunicatio...	UC	7.2.10126.0	Yes	SYSTEM

Figure 4.14: Viewing manually installed agents from the console

> If you need to manually deploy agents to untrusted domains or DMZ's, then similar to configuring the Gateway Server role, you will need to use certificate-based authentication between the untrusted agent and the Management Group. You can get a full walkthrough on how to configure your agents using an internal **Public Key Infrastructure** (**PKI**) from the following blog post: `http://tinyurl.com/opsmgrinternalcerts` or if you are using external public certificates, have a read through `http://tinyurl.com/opsmgrexternalcerts`

Active Directory Integration

The Active Directory Integration feature of OpsMgr allows you to use Active Directory to automatically assign agent-managed computers to management groups. This feature can be used for agents that have been deployed using methods other than the push-install from the console, such as manually installed or as part of an image-based deployment using a product like System Center Configuration Manager.

Active Directory Integration involves creating a container within the Active Directory infrastructure using the `MOMAdmin.exe` tool located on the OpsMgr installation media and also within the `\Server` folder of the OpsMgr install location. You can then create rules to dictate which agents communicate with specific Management Groups for Active Directory Integration using the **Auto Agent Assignment** tab in the properties of your management server, as shown in *Figure 4.15*.

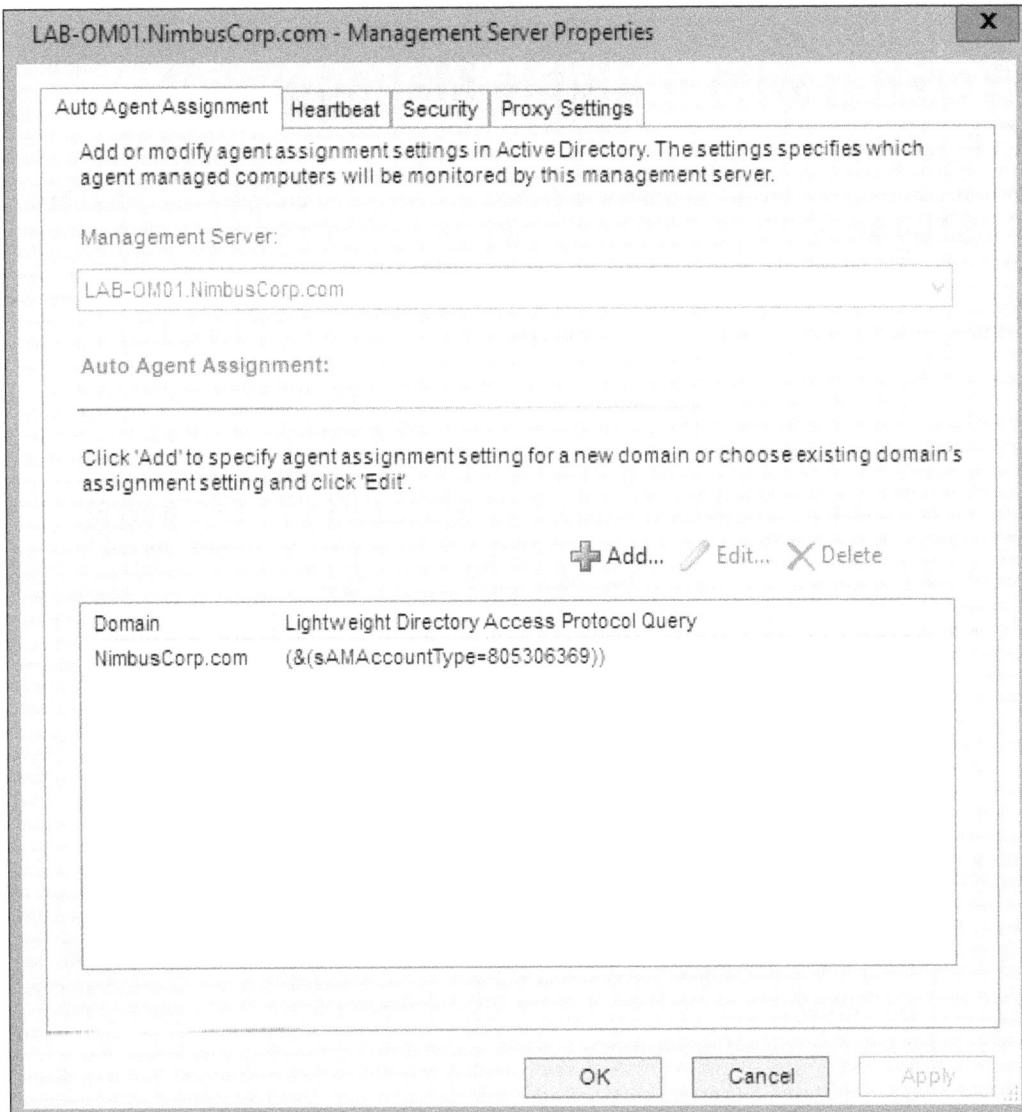

LAB-OM01.NimbusCorp.com - Management Server Properties   **X**

| Auto Agent Assignment | Heartbeat | Security | Proxy Settings |

Add or modify agent assignment settings in Active Directory. The settings specifies which agent managed computers will be monitored by this management server.

Management Server:

LAB-OM01.NimbusCorp.com

Auto Agent Assignment:

Click 'Add' to specify agent assignment setting for a new domain or choose existing domain's assignment setting and click 'Edit'.

                             ➕ Add...   ✎ Edit...   ✖ Delete

Domain	Lightweight Directory Access Protocol Query
NimbusCorp.com	(&(sAMAccountType=805306369))

OK   Cancel   Apply

Figure 4.15: Configuring rules for Active Directory Integration

Although not a very common deployment scenario, you can learn about some of the pros and cons of Active Directory Integration from the following post by Jonathan Almquist: `http://tinyurl.com/opsmgradintegration`.

Should you wish to learn more about Active Directory Integration (including a step-by-step guide on configuring it), you can do so from `https://technet.microsoft.com/en-us/library/hh212829.aspx`.

Working with multiple Management Groups

When you use the console to deploy a Windows agent, it's configured to report to a single Management Group. The OpsMgr agent however, has the very useful option of being able to report to up to four different management groups – depending on your requirements. This capability is referred to as **Multihoming** and means that the OpsMgr agent only needs to be installed once on each monitored computer.

When its multihomed, the agent processes rules and configuration information for each Management Group independently ensuring there's no conflict between monitoring environments.

There are a number of different scenarios where you could have more than one Management Group that you want your agents to report to. Here are some of the more common scenarios for multiple Management Groups:

- **Pre-production testing**: This is a recommended scenario and is quite common in organizations that wish to test new management packs, either the ones developed in-house or simply updated ones released by a particular vendor. In this case, a Management Group would be created (probably using a single-server design) specifically for the pre-production environment where all testing is carried out.

- **Support group separation**: In this scenario, an organization might have a requirement to separate monitoring across multiple OpsMgr environments. It could be that the Infrastructure team want to monitor the infrastructure from one Management Group and the Applications team prefer to monitor their applications from their own Management Group.

- **Migrating from older versions of OpsMgr**: Although some older versions of OpsMgr can perform an 'in-place' upgrade to a newer version, it can be cumbersome and most likely at some point during the upgrade, monitoring might be unavailable. For this reason, deploying a new Management Group with the later version of OpsMgr and having the agents report to both the old and new environments is the most common scenario for multihoming agents. This provides an option of keeping the monitoring environment up and running whilst migrating to the newer version.

Configuring multihoming

You can configure OpsMgr multihoming either through the console as a push installation or manually by using the Microsoft Monitoring Agent applet located in Control Panel.

Push installation method

The push installation method from the console is the quickest and most flexible way to multihome your agents and here's a high-level overview of what you need to do:

1. Push-install the agent from a console in your first Management Group using the steps outlined in the *Using the Console to Deploy Agents* section of this chapter.

2. Log on to a console in your other management group(s) with an account that has Local Administrator permissions on the agents that you wish to multihome.

3. Perform a push-install of the agent from this console in your other management group using the same steps that you followed when deploying the first Management Group agent. This action doesn't install a new instance of the OpsMgr agent, instead it automatically multihomes the agent to the new Management Group name as shown in *Figure 4.16*.

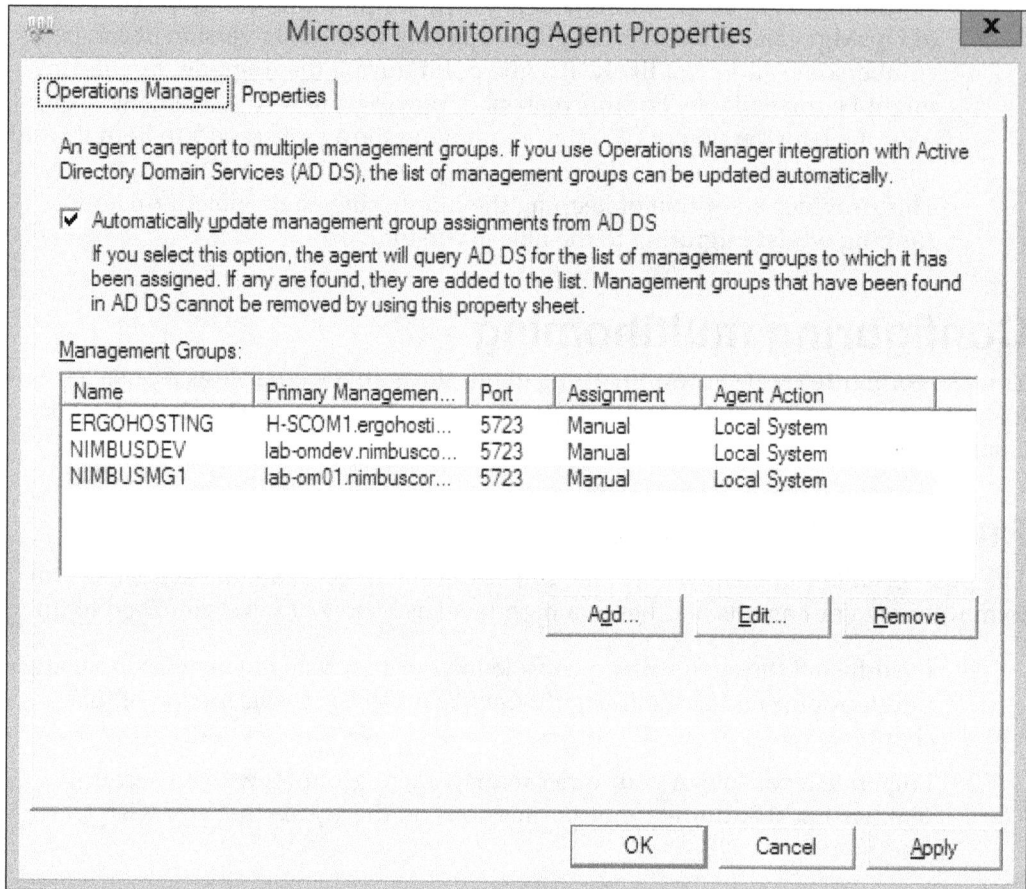

Figure 4.16: A multihomed agent reporting to three different Management Groups

Manual configuration method

If you want to manually configure multihoming, follow these steps:

1. Logon to a computer with the OpsMgr agent already installed, open Control Panel and click on the **Microsoft Monitoring Agent** applet shown in *Figure 4.17*.

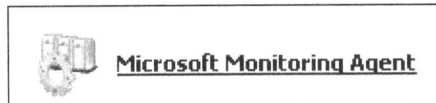

Figure 4.17: The Microsoft Monitoring Agent applet

2. At the **Operations Manager** tab of the **Microsoft Monitoring Agent Properties** dialog box, click on the **Add** button to add a new Management Group.

3. From the dialog box shown in *Figure 4.18*, enter the new **Management Group Configuration** information and **Agent Action Account** details, and then hit **OK** to continue.

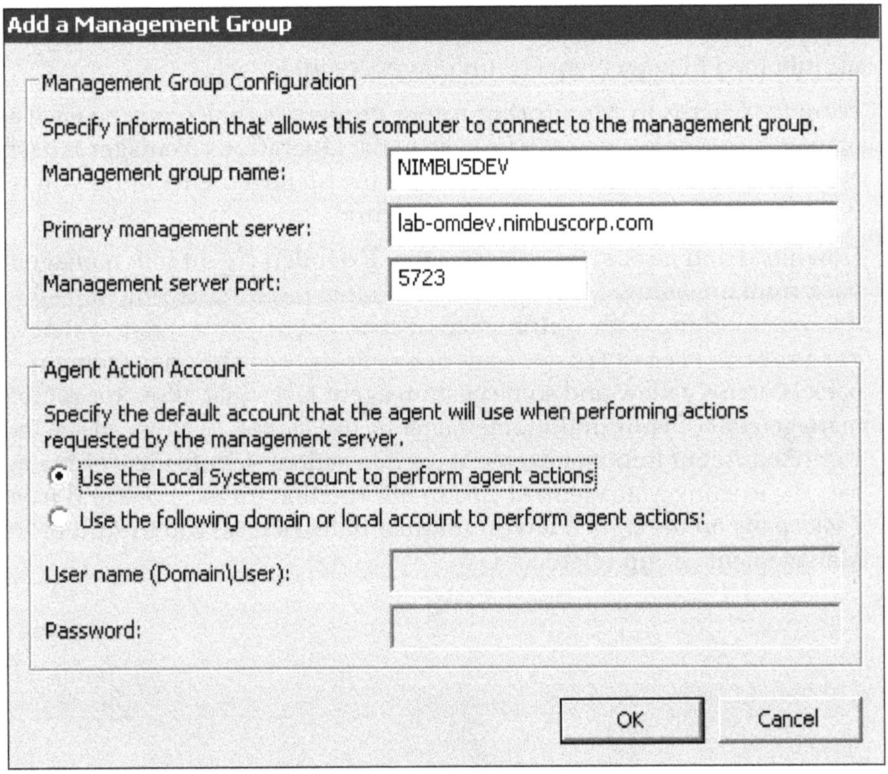

Figure 4.18: Manually multihoming an agent

4. Back at the **Microsoft Monitoring Agent Properties** dialog box, click on the **OK** button to add the new Management Group configuration. This will then close the dialog box and restart the **Monitoring Service** on the agent to save the settings.

Removing multihoming

If you need to remove a Management Group reference from an agent, then you have a few options:

- You can use the OpsMgr console that is part of the Management Group you wish to remove and simply perform an **Uninstall** from the **Agent Managed** view. This method will remove the configuration of the Management Group that you are performing the Uninstall action from and will leave any other multihomed Management Group references intact.

- From the **Microsoft Monitoring Agent Properties** dialog box on each agent managed computer, you can browse to the **Operations Manager** tab (shown earlier in *Figure 4.16*), select the name of the Management Group you wish to delete, and then click on the **Remove** button.

- Download and import the excellent free Extended Agent Info management pack from my fellow MVP Jose Fehse (a must have management pack if you're working with multihomed agents) `http://overcast.fehse.ca/2012/11/scom-2012-extended-agent-info/`. This management pack contains a view and some custom agent tasks that allow for remote management of your multihomed agents. In *Figure 4.19*, you can see the Extended Agent Info management pack in action. A state view of my agents lists the existing Management Group information for each one and from the Tasks pane on the right; I have a number of tasks I can run to Add or Remove Management Group references.

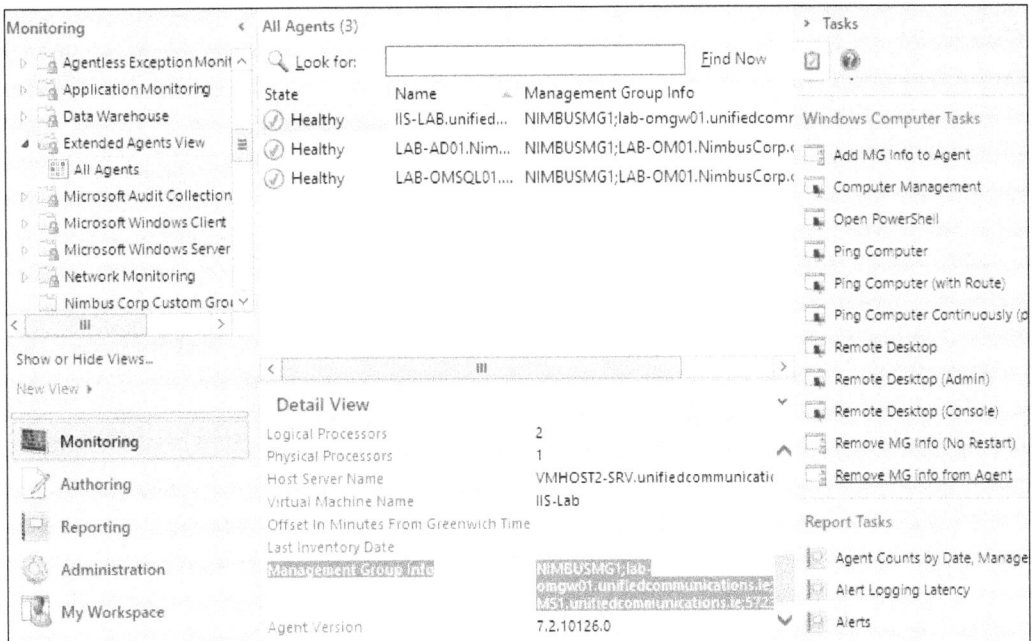

Figure 4.19: The Extended Agent Info management pack

Agent management

When you've deployed your Windows agents, you'll want to know how to manage them and in this section we will discuss the agent management options available to you from within the Administration workspace of the console.

Agent actions explained

From the **Device Management | Agent Managed** view shown in *Figure 4.20*, when you click on an agent, you can see that the **Actions** pane on the right presents you with five actions to help you manage the agent.

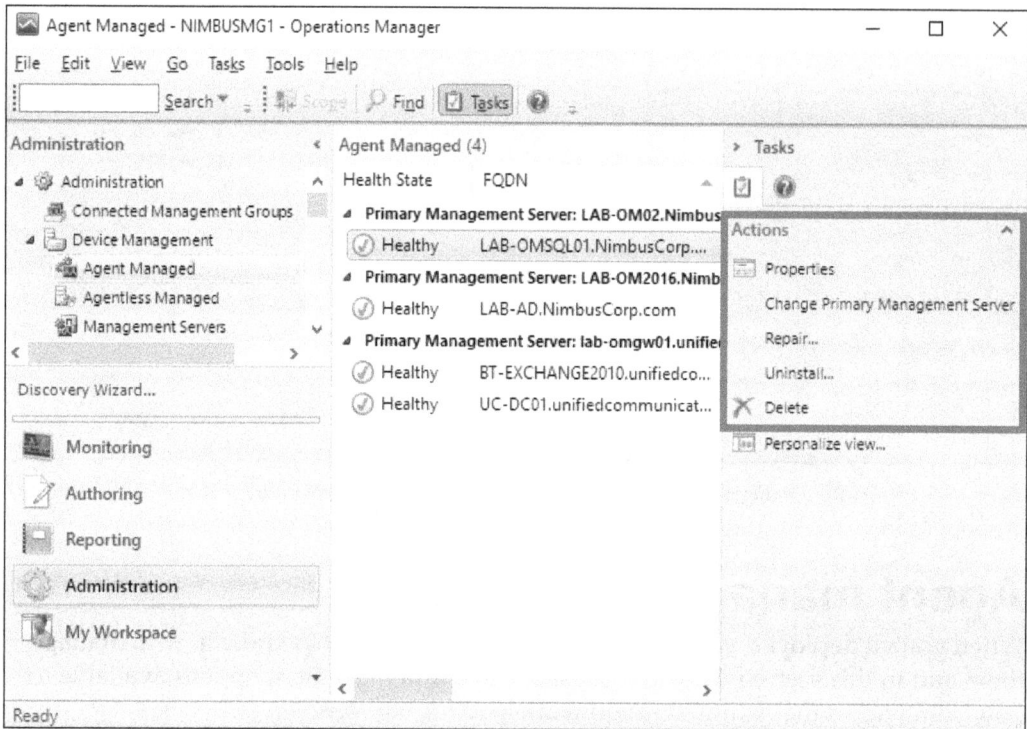

Figure 4.20: Viewing the actions for managing agents

These five agent management actions are explained as follows:

Properties

When you click on the **Properties** agent management action you are presented with two tabs – **Heartbeat** and **Security**.

The **Heartbeat** tab is where you see the heartbeat interval that has been configured for all agents by the **Agent: Heartbeat** global setting found in the **Settings** area of the Administration workspace. As you can see from *Figure 4.21*, this option is grayed out but you can change the heartbeat setting for an individual agent by clicking on the **Override global agent settings** option.

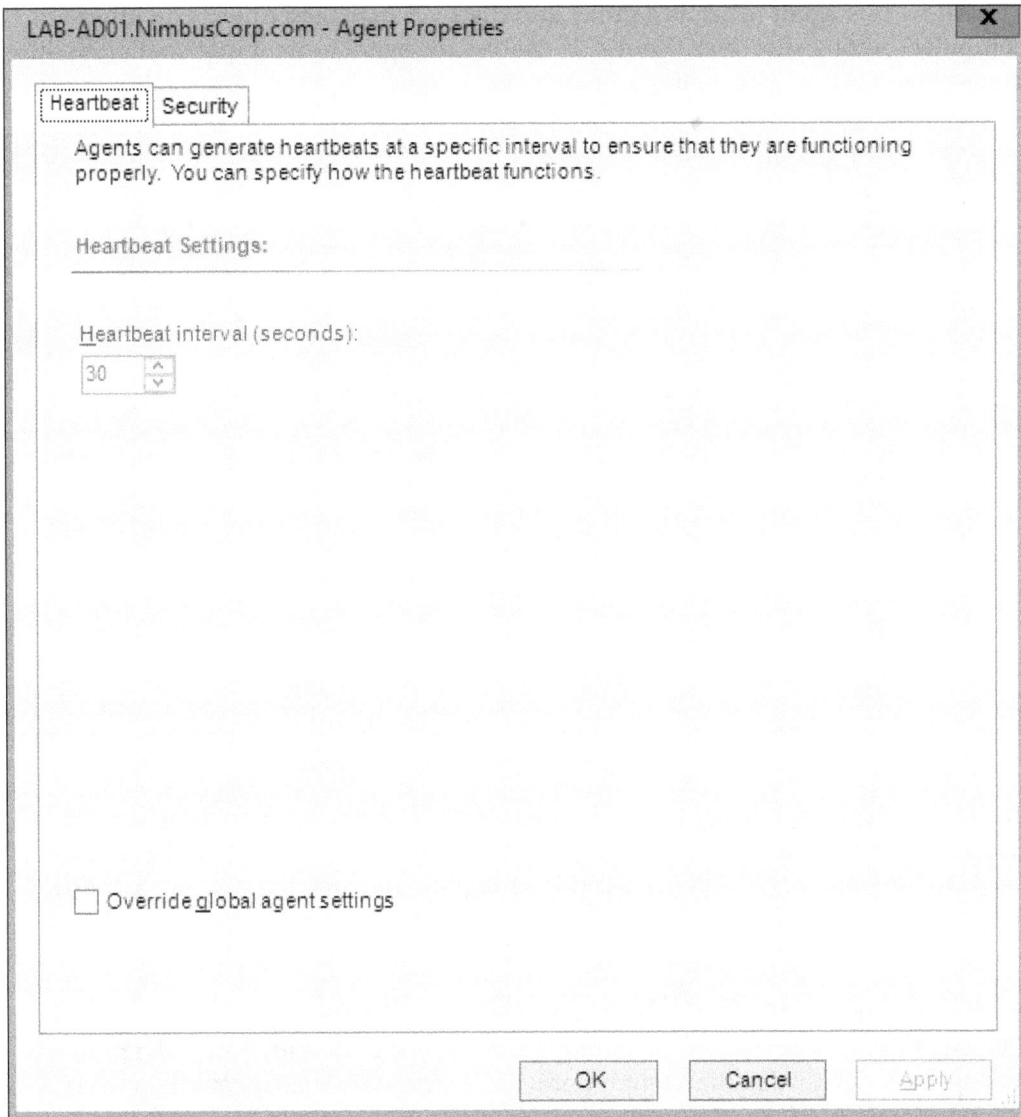

Figure 4.21: Managing the agent heartbeat setting

Clicking on the **Security** tab of the **Agent Properties** dialog box will enable you to configure the **Agent Proxy** setting.

The **Allow this agent to act as a proxy and discover managed objects on other computers** setting shown in *Figure 4.22* enables the agent to send information to the management server on behalf of unmanaged systems.

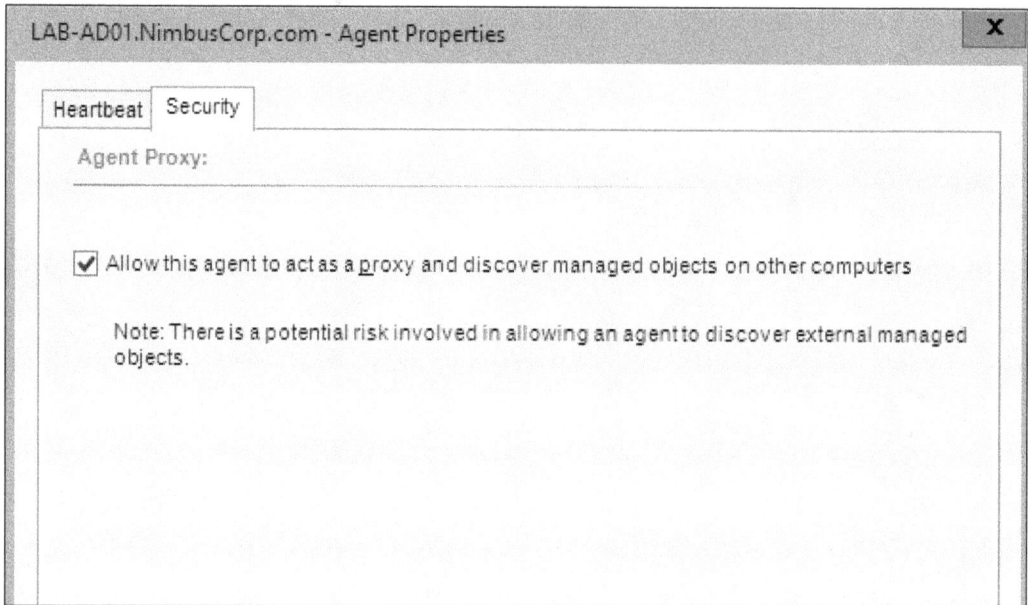

Figure 4.22: Configuring the Agent Proxy setting

While the note in this dialog box states this setting could potentially be a security risk, nearly every management pack guide that you read specifies that this setting needs to be enabled. We will discuss this setting in more detail in *Chapter 5, Working with Management Packs.*

Change primary management server

Clicking this agent management setting gives you the option to change the primary management server that the agent reports to. The primary management server is responsible for notifying the agent of any configuration changes and from time to time, you might need to change this setting for scenarios, such as load balancing agents or even adding new management servers.

In *Figure 4.23*, you can see that we have two management servers and a gateway server to choose from for our agents and we can also get a handy overview of the number of agents currently reporting to each one.

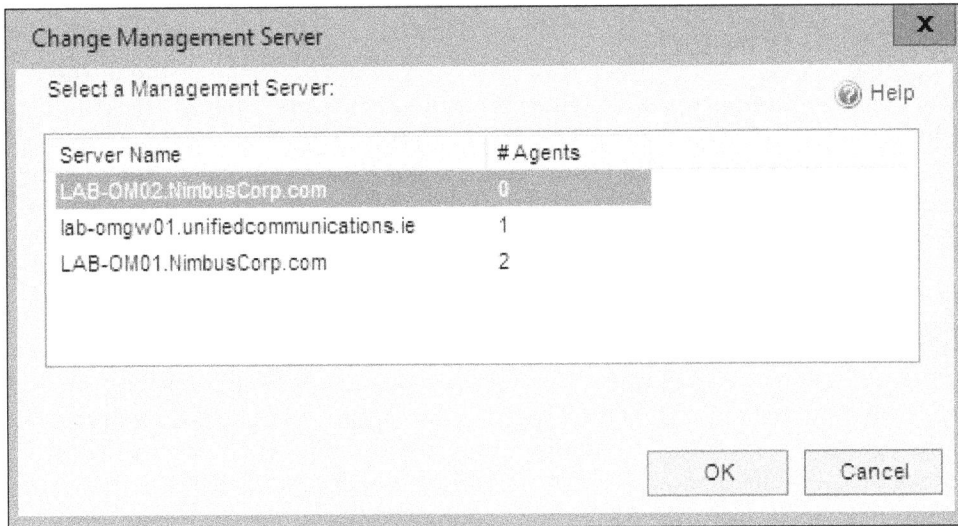

Figure 4.23: Choosing a management server for your agents

Repair

This option does exactly what is says on the tin—an action to repair the agent installation. When choosing this option, you will need to provide an account with Local Administrator permissions on the agent that is being repaired so as to ensure the process can complete successfully.

Uninstall

Another pretty self-explanatory agent management action, the Uninstall option will remove the OpsMgr agent from any computers you run this against. When the agent is uninstalled, its reference in the OpsMgr database is also removed.

It goes without saying that the agent needs to be online and contactable for it to be uninstalled with this action and if the computer is unavailable, this action will fail. You will need to provide credentials for an account with Local Administrator permissions on the agent to carry out this action.

Delete

In the scenario, where a computer with the OpsMgr agent is uncontactable and never to be powered on again, the Uninstall action is useless. This is where the Delete action comes in handy and when you run this against an agent, you will be prompted to confirm that you are happy to delete the monitoring agent for the selected computers. Confirming this will forcibly remove the agent reference from the OpsMgr database.

Opening agent views

Another way of accessing the agent management actions is to right-click on an agent to open up the context menu. From there, you can select the **Open** option and then pivot to a specific view type as shown in *Figure 4.24*. These view types were explained in detail in the *Working with Views* section of *Chapter 3, Exploring the Consoles*.

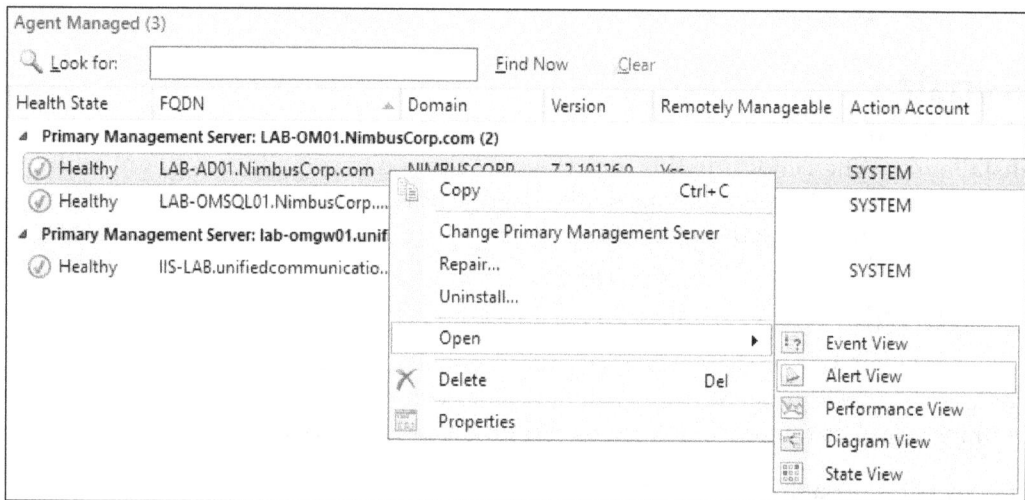

Figure 4.24: Accessing different view types from the agent managed context menu

Deploying UNIX/Linux agents

In today's world of heterogeneous IT environments, UNIX and Linux computers are widespread and OpsMgr wouldn't be much of a monitoring tool if it couldn't deploy an agent to these types of cross-platform operating systems.

The following sections detail the requirements for deploying the OpsMgr agent to UNIX/Linux computers and will walk you through using the console to push an agent out to an instance of Ubuntu Server.

UNIX/Linux agent requirements

In the *Minimum installation requirements* section of *Chapter 1, Introduction to System Center Operations Manager* we listed the supported UNIX/Linux operating systems that you can deploy the OpsMgr agent to and the following table lists the specific firewall ports you need to take into account:

Name	Port	Description
UNIX/Linux Agent	TCP 1270	Required for OpsMgr agent communications.
Secure Shell (SSH)	TCP 22	Required for OpsMgr agent push installations and maintenance from the console.

To ensure a successful deployment of your UNIX/Linux agents, you will need to be aware of the following:

- The cross-platform UNIX/Linux management packs found in the \ `ManagementPacks` folder of the OpsMgr installation media must be imported into OpsMgr before you deploy agents. Updated versions of these management packs can be downloaded from the Microsoft download center (`http://tinyurl.com/opsmgrxplatmps`) and you will learn how to import and manage them using the walkthrough's in *Chapter 5, Working with Management Packs*.

- A resource pool containing the management servers that UNIX/Linux agents will target is recommended to be created in the **Resource Pools** section of the Administration workspace.

- If you intend on having more than one management server in your resource pool to provide high-availability for UNIX/Linux agent monitoring, then you will need to configure your cross-platform certificates using the `scxcertconfig.exe` utility as detailed in the following article `https://technet.microsoft.com/en-us/library/hh287152.aspx`

- Although you can monitor UNIX/Linux computers using only an IP address, it's easier to identify the servers you're monitoring if you can resolve the hostname of the UNIX/Linux server to its IP address from the OpsMgr management servers. Use DNS or the local hosts file on the management servers to configure name resolution.

- You will need credentials for an account with su or sudo elevation permissions on the UNIX/Linux servers to create and configure the Run As accounts and profiles for monitoring and maintenance.

> You can get more information on creating and configuring Run
> As accounts and profiles for UNIX/Linux from the following
> article https://technet.microsoft.com/en-us/library/
> hh212926.aspx.

Creating a resource pool

In most environments, it's a good idea to always try and keep monitoring of your
UNIX/Linux agents separate to your Windows agents and network devices through
the use of resource pools in OpsMgr.

Creating a resource pool through the console is a quick and easy process and here's
all you need to do:

1. At the **Administration** workspace in the OpsMgr console, browse to the
    Resource Pools section and click on **Create Resource Pool** from the **Actions**
    pane on the right as shown in *Figure 4.25*.

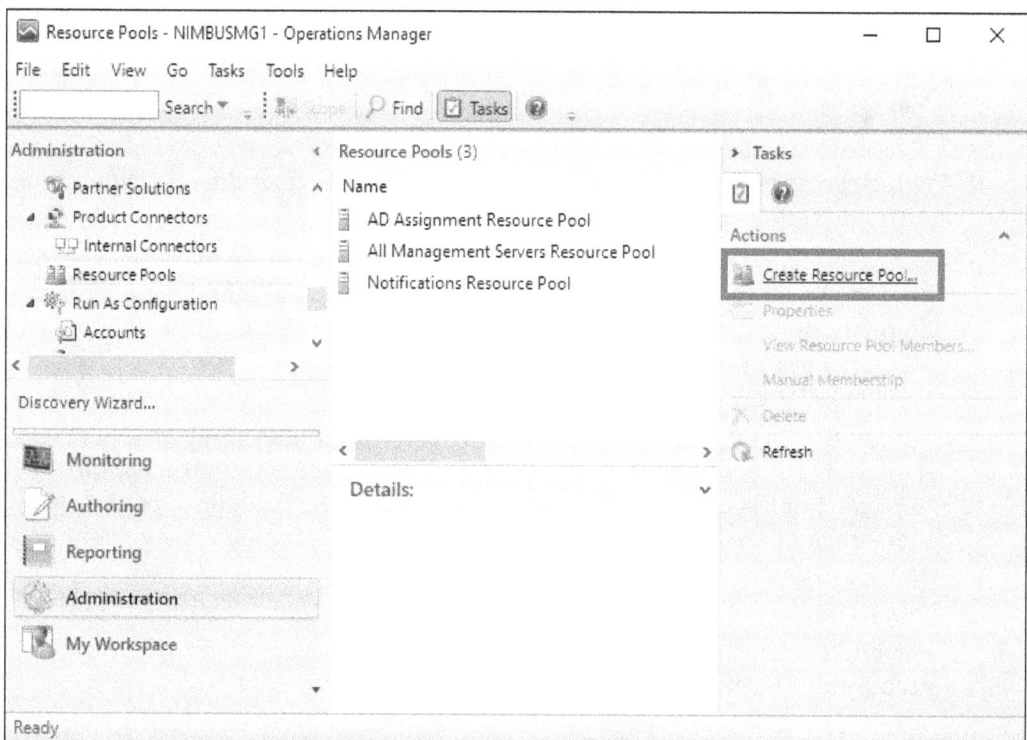

Figure 4.25: Creating a new resource pool

2. When the **Create a Resource Pool Wizard** (shown in *Figure 4.26*) opens, type a name and description for the resource pool, and then click on **Next** to move on.

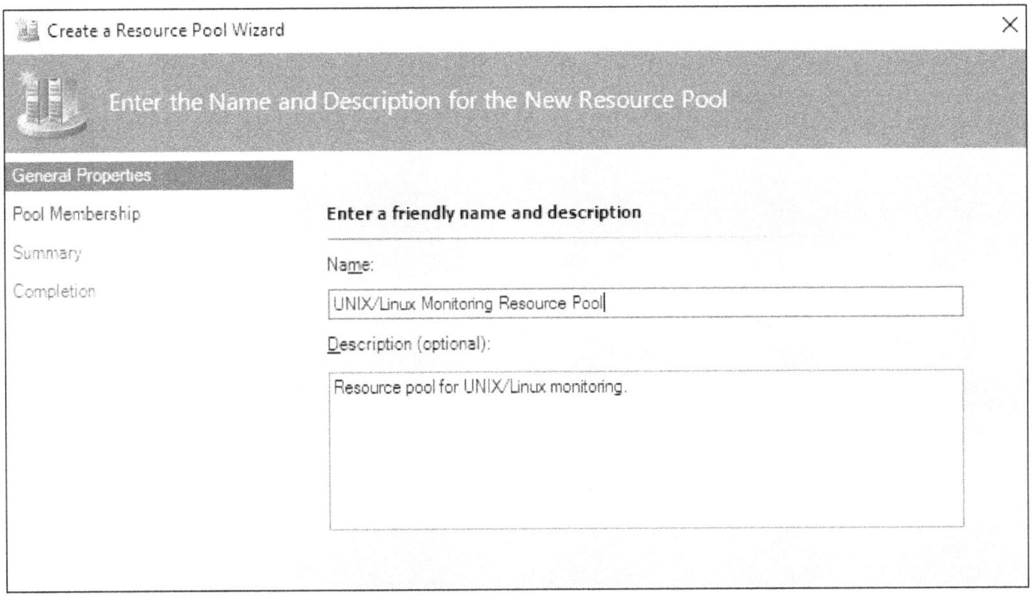

Figure 4.26: Naming the resource pool

3. At the **Resource pool members** dialog box, click on the **Add** button to open the **Member Selection** dialog box shown in *Figure 4.27*. From there, click on the **Search** button to show a list of all available items and then select the ones you wish to add to the pool and hit the **Add** button to confirm. Click on **OK** to close the dialog box.

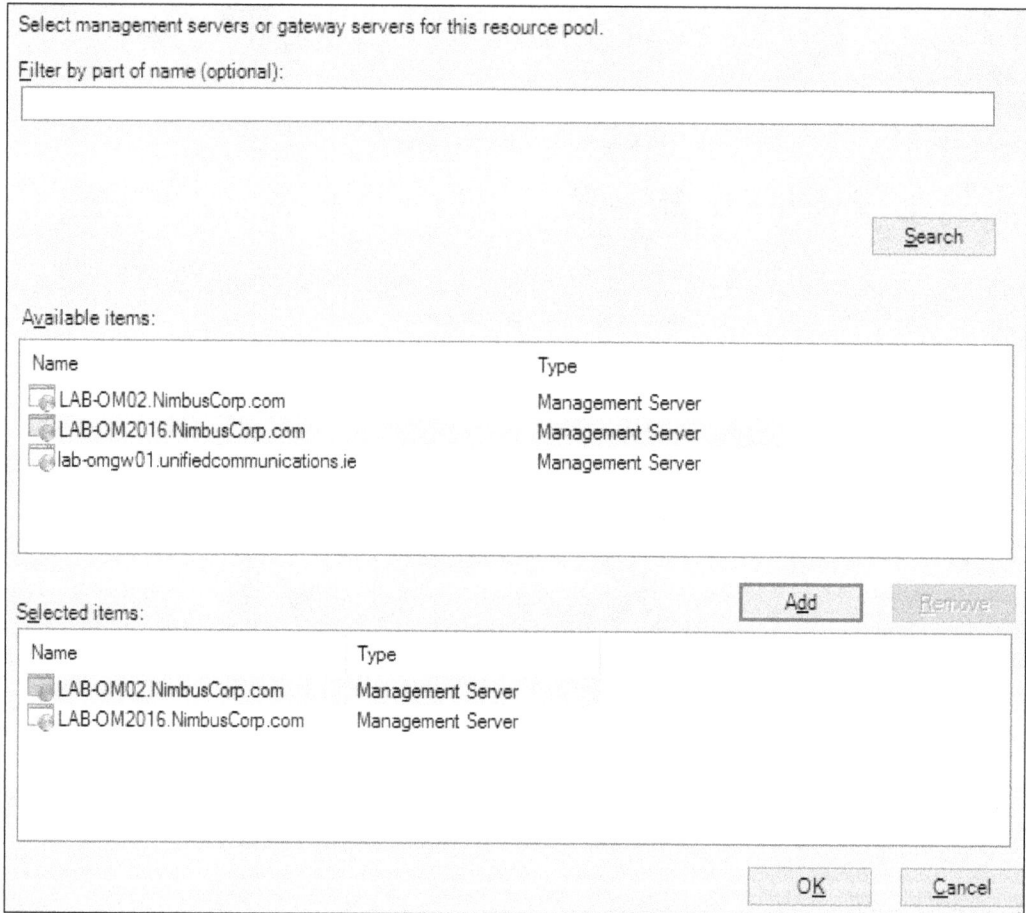

Figure 4.27: Adding members to the resource pool

4. Back at the **Resource pool members** dialog box shown in *Figure 4.28*, confirm you're happy with the servers that are to be added and then click on **Next**.

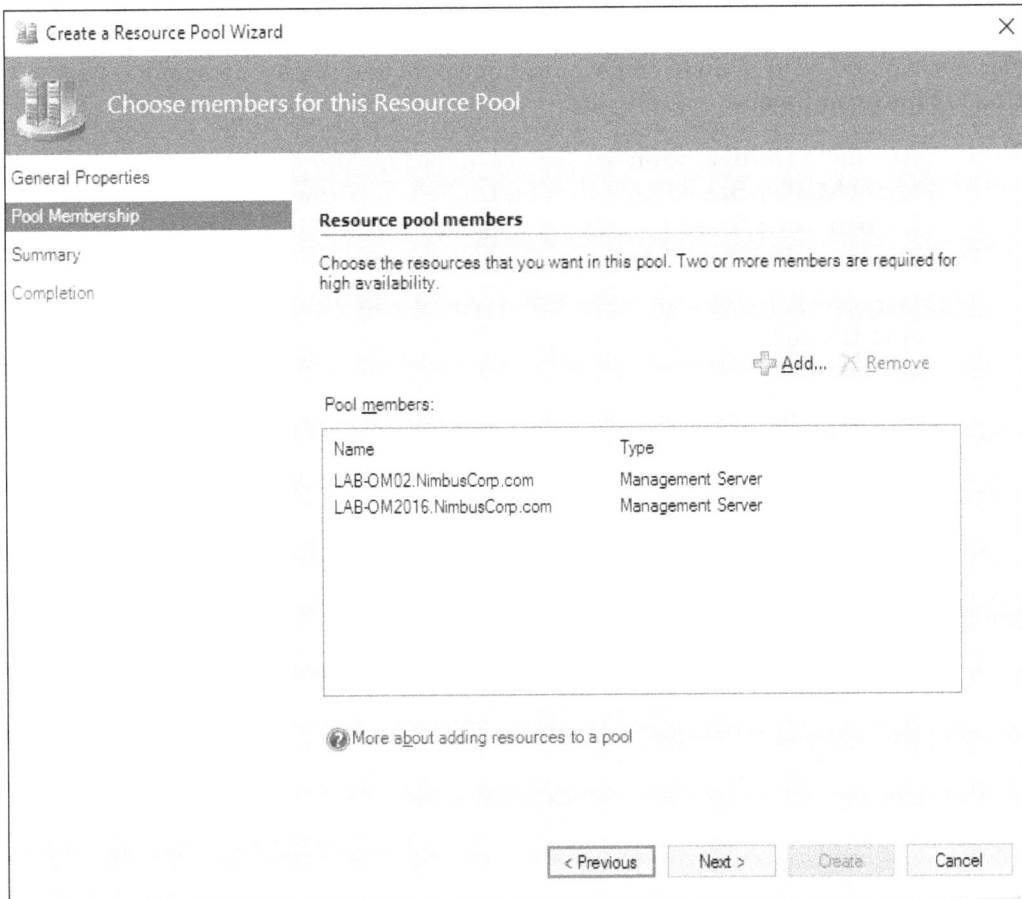

Figure 4.28: Confirming the pool members

5. Click on **Create** at the **Summary** dialog box and then hit **Close** to exit the wizard.

Deployment process

When you've confirmed the agent requirements have all been met, the process for deploying UNIX/Linux agents is quite similar to deploying Windows agents.

Here's what you need to do to create a resource pool and deploy an agent to your UNIX/Linux computers:

1. From the **Administration** workspace in the OpsMgr console, expand **Device Management**, right-click on **UNIX/Linux computers**, and then click on **Discovery Wizard** (you can also choose to just click on the **Discovery Wizard...** link located above the Wunderbar).

2. As shown in *Figure 4.29*, at the **What would you like to manage?** dialog box, select **UNIX/Linux Computers** as the type of device to discover and then click on **Next**.

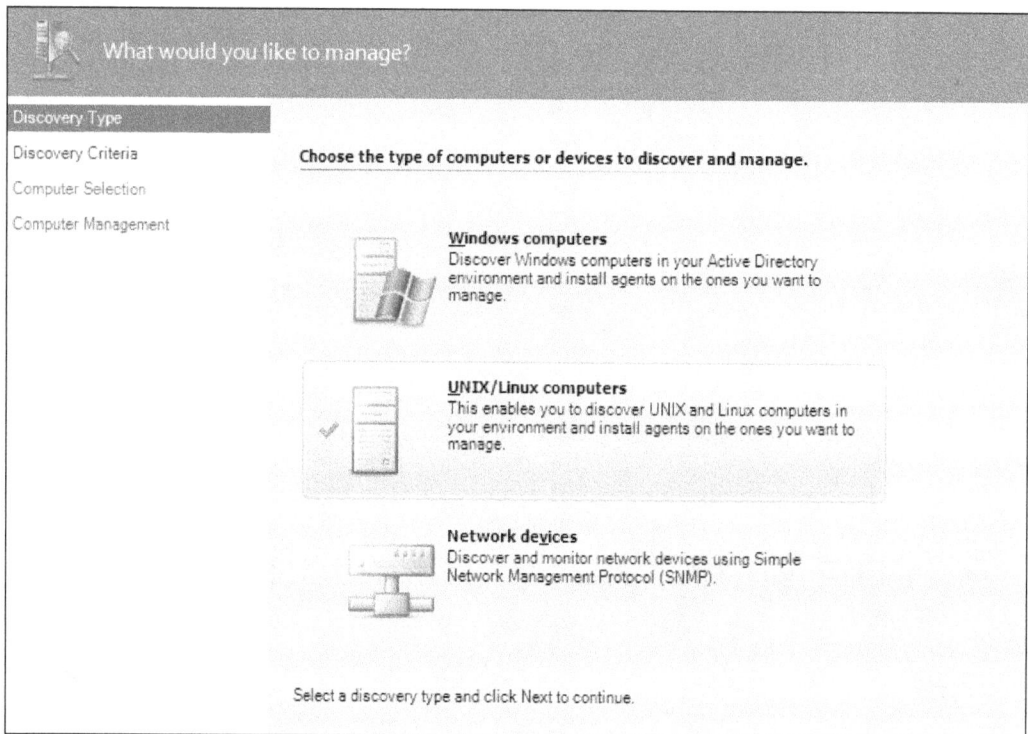

Figure 4.29: Selecting the UNIX/Linux computers option

3. At the **Discovery Criteria** dialog box, choose the resource pool from the drop-down menu that you created for UNIX/Linux monitoring and then click on the **Add** button to define a discovery scope as shown in *Figure 4.30*:

- ° For the **Discovery Scope** section, type the name or IP address of the UNIX/Linux server that you wish to monitor and confirm the SSH Port (the default SSH Port setting here is **22**).

- ° The **Discovery Type** section allows you to choose from **All Computers** (default setting) or **Only computers with an installed agent and signed certificate**. The latter option here comes in handy when working with manually deployed UNIX/Linux agents.

- ° At the **Credentials** section, assuming you have pre-configured your UNIX/Linux Run As credentials as per the agent requirements, select the **Use Run As Credentials** option or click on the **Set Credentials** button to specify the type of credential that you wish to use.

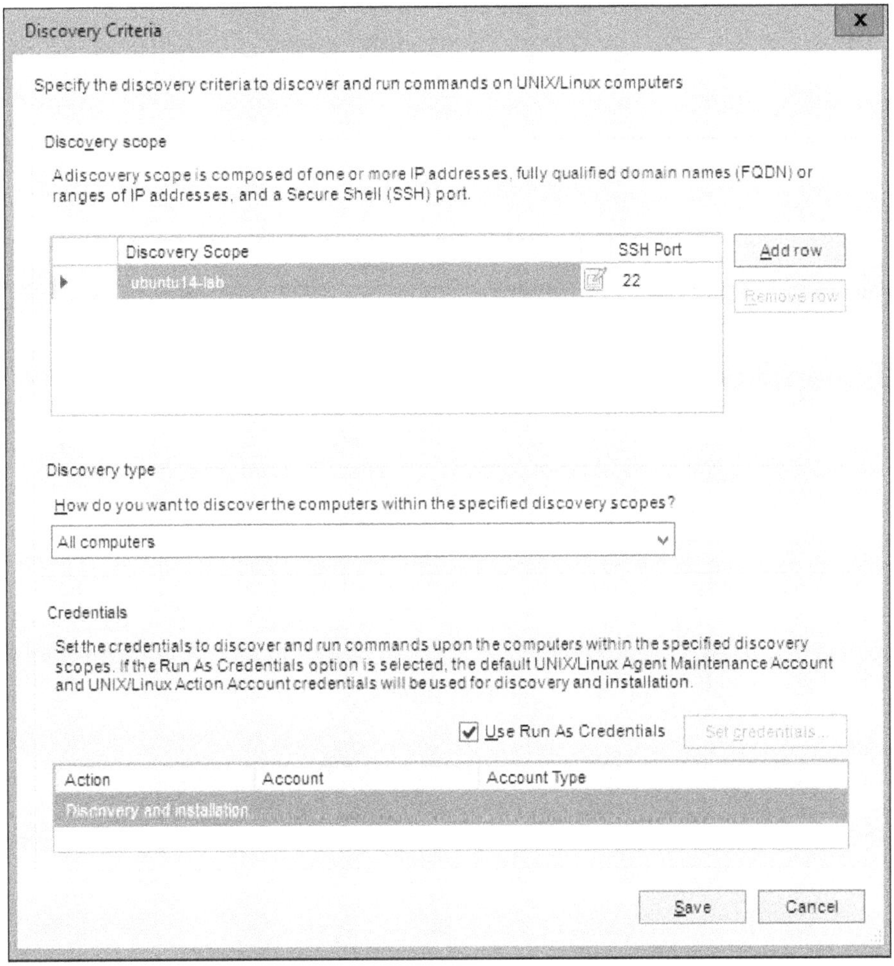

Figure 4.30: Discovering UNIX/Linux computers

4. When you've made your choices, click on **Save** and then hit the **Discover** button to begin the discovery. After a few moments and if everything has been configured correctly, you should see the name of your UNIX/Linux computer displayed in the **Manageable Computers** tab of the **Discovery results** section as shown in *Figure 4.31*.

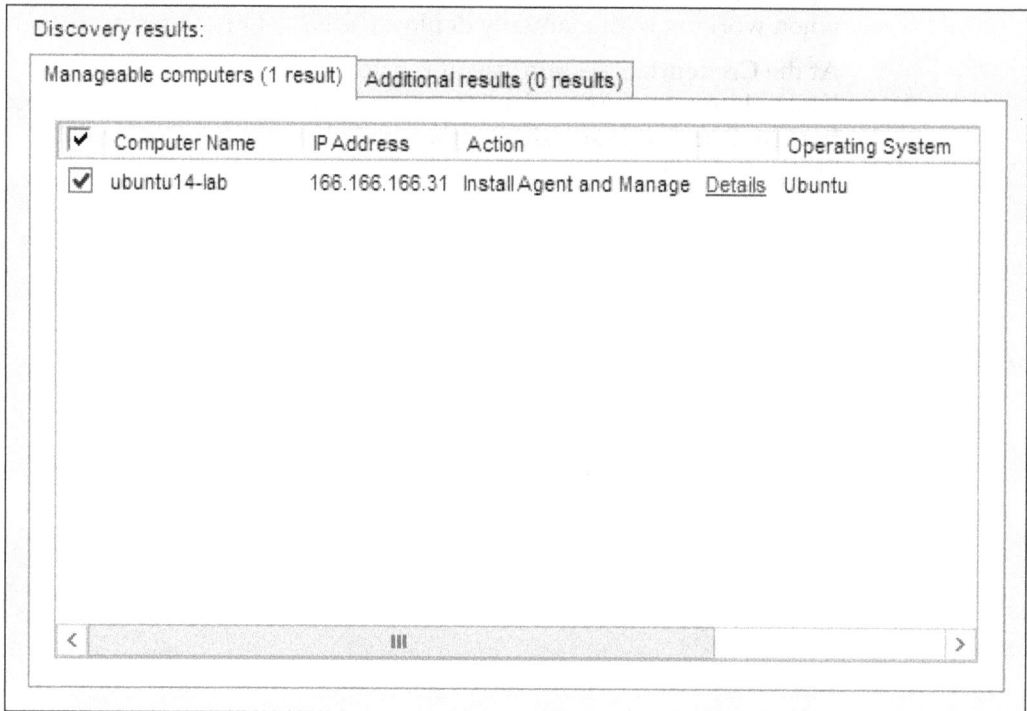

Figure 4.31: Discovering a UNIX/Linux computer

5. Select the check box beside the computer name and then click on the **Manage** button to deploy the agent. A status of **Successful** (similar to the one shown in *Figure 4.32*) indicates the agent has been deployed and you can then click on **Done** to close the wizard and complete the process.

Deployment and Management Complete

Please review the agent deployment results below. On computers where the deployment was not successful, it might be necessary to install the appropriate agent manually.

Deployment results:

Computer Name	Status		Operating System	Version	Architecture
ubuntu14-lab	Successful	Details	Ubuntu	14.04	x86_64

Figure 4.32: Successful deployment of the UNIX/Linux agent

For more information on deploying UNIX/Linux agents with OpsMgr, check out this blog post from Microsoft's Kevin Holman `http://tinyurl.com/opsmgrxplatagents`.

Summary

In this chapter, you learnt the difference between agent-based and agentless monitoring. We then deployed some Microsoft Windows agents and explored different agent installation methods. We discussed how to multihome agents with up to four different Management Groups and then ended the chapter with a walkthrough on deploying agents to UNIX/Linux computers.

In the next chapter, you will learn about Management Packs and their importance within the OpsMgr environment along with gaining an understanding of how to find, import and manage them.

5
Working with Management Packs

With agents already deployed, let's now discuss management packs — the secret sauce of OpsMgr. Management packs tell the agents what to monitor and dictate how they should react when certain criteria and thresholds have been met.

This chapter begins with an overview of different management pack types and then explores the contents of a typical management pack. You will learn how to find and download new management packs and also how to import them into your OpsMgr environment. We will also discuss how to export management packs as well as show you some PowerShell tricks to help you manage them in bulk.

Towards the end of the chapter, we will discuss some of the options available for authoring management packs.

Here's a breakdown of what we'll cover in this chapter:

- Management packs overview
- What's inside a management pack?
- Finding management packs
- Importing and exporting management packs
- Managing management packs
- Authoring tools

Management packs overview

Management packs give us a deep-dive ability to monitor things such as operating systems, applications, hardware components, websites, and cloud-based workloads to name just a few.

Containing workload-specific discoveries, monitors, rules, tasks, and reports, a management pack removes the need for IT administrators and service owners to get around a table and try to brainstorm (or guess) what might possibly go wrong with whatever it is that they want to monitor! Instead, a management pack will enable you to monitor everything you need as soon as it's deployed to a computer installed with an OpsMgr agent.

For all the comprehensive monitoring power that a management pack delivers, under the hood it's just a simple **Extensible Markup Language** (**XML**) file. By standardizing XML for their management pack format, Microsoft has ensured that anyone with even a basic knowledge of working with XML files has the ability to understand how to edit and search their contents.

Don't worry though, if you've never worked with XML files before, most of the management pack administration tasks that you need to carry out while getting started with OpsMgr can be delivered through the user-friendly interface of the console.

> Although every management pack is different (depending on what they monitor), they're all based on the same schema and can be easily transferred between your OpsMgr management groups.

The really cool thing about monitoring using management packs is that they are typically authored by the vendor of the product that you wish to monitor. For example, the management packs to monitor Windows Server, Exchange Server, or SQL are authored by Microsoft. Similarly, if you wanted to monitor Dell or HP hardware, those vendors have written specific management packs to light up all of their best practice recommendations for monitoring.

In *Figure 5.1* you can see some of the high-level components that make up a management pack.

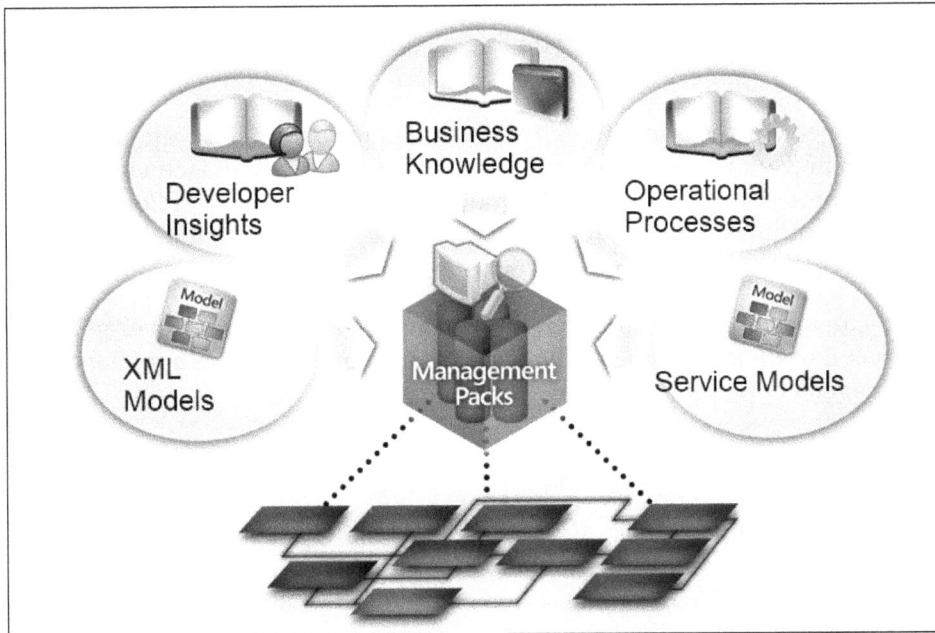

Figure 5.1: Management pack components

Of course, Microsoft and third-party vendors aren't the only people authoring management packs. There is a large (and very helpful) community in the OpsMgr space that works tirelessly to author new management packs so as to fill any gaps that vendor-specific management packs don't meet; in most cases, these community written management packs are available for free!

There are two different types of management packs that you will come across in OpsMgr — **sealed** and **unsealed**.

Sealed management packs

Although written in XML, a sealed management pack is identified by its file-type extension of **.MP** and this is the most common management pack type that you will encounter – particularly when you download management packs authored by Microsoft or other vendors.

Sealed management packs are digitally signed by the vendor and configured as read-only to prevent modification. The reason for making a management pack read-only isn't to protect the vendor's intellectual property (a one-liner of PowerShell can unseal them easily), but instead it's to ensure that the management pack 'does exactly what it says on the tin' every time it gets installed into any OpsMgr environment.

Sealing the management pack also gives the vendor version control over new upgrades and enables them to use the sealed management pack as a reference for other management packs.

Unsealed management packs

An unsealed management pack is identified by its file-type extension of **.XML**. It can deliver the same monitoring capabilities as a sealed management pack but isn't digitally signed, is read-write enabled and can be used to store additional elements such as rules, monitors, overrides, views and tasks.

The author of an unsealed management pack doesn't care too much about version control or over-the-top upgrades and these are a common format when downloading from the general OpsMgr community.

As you will learn in the *Importing management packs* section later, its best practice to create an unsealed management pack to store overrides for each sealed management pack that you have in your environment.

From the **Management Packs** section within the **Administration** workspace in the OpsMgr console, you can use the **Sealed** column view to identify which installed management packs are sealed or unsealed, as shown in *Figure 5.2*.

Management Packs (289)			
🔍 Look for:		Find Now	Clear
Name		▲ Version	Sealed
📦 Microsoft Audit Collection Services		7.1.10226.0	Yes
📦 Microsoft Data Warehouse Reports		7.1.10226.0	Yes
📦 Microsoft Exchange Server 2013 Monitoring		15.0.665.19	Yes
📦 Microsoft Exchange Server 2013 Overrides		1.0.0.0	
📦 Microsoft Exchange Server 2013 Reports		15.0.665.19	Yes
📦 Microsoft Exchange Server 2013 Visualization Library		1.1.121.91	Yes
📦 Microsoft Generic Report Library		7.1.10226.0	Yes
📦 Microsoft ODR Report Library		7.1.10226.0	Yes
📦 Microsoft Office 365		7.0.5115.0	Yes
📦 Microsoft Operational Insights Configuration Assessment		7.0.9802.0	Yes
📦 Microsoft Service Level Report Library		7.1.10226.0	Yes
📦 Microsoft Service Management Automation Overrides		1.0.0.0	

Figure 5.2: Identifying sealed and unsealed management packs

You can also quickly identify the management pack type by its associated icon within the console – sealed management packs have a padlock icon and unsealed management packs have a toolbox icon beside their name.

> A further extension to the familiar sealed and unsealed management packs in OpsMgr is the **Management Pack Bundle** (**MPB**). With a file-type of .MPB, a management pack bundle can contain resources such as images, reports, SQL scripts and assemblies. It's essentially an MSI file with the .MPB extension and is an easy way for management pack authors to 'bundle' a number of associated components together for monitoring in OpsMgr.

What's inside a management pack?

Now that you have an understanding of the different types of management packs that OpsMgr uses, it's time to take a look under the hood and discuss the contents of a management pack. Depending on what the management pack was authored for, you will find one or more of these elements inside.

Classes (Object types)

Also referred to as object types, classes represent a kind (or type) of object in OpsMgr and every object is basically a single unit of a class that can be monitored. Examples of an object could be a computer, a network device, a logical disk or a power supply. It could also be an Active Directory domain, an application or an installation of SQL.

Each object in OpsMgr has its own class and that object is an instance that shares a common set of properties with other objects that are all part of a particular class.

Think of it like this, you're monitoring the c:\ logical disk on a Windows Server 2012 computer. The logical disk is seen as an object in OpsMgr. As that logical disk runs on Windows Server 2012, it automatically becomes an instance of the Windows Server 2012 Logical Disk class, which represents all logical disks that run on any deployment of Windows Server 2012.

In *Figure 5.3* you can see the **Windows Server 2012 Logical Disk** class represented in the **Discovered Inventory** view from the **Administration** workspace. This view shows all of the monitored objects of that particular class.

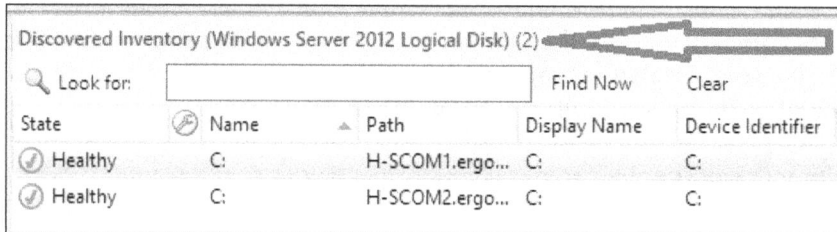

Figure 5.3: Viewing objects of a class

Relationships

Different classes can be associated with one another through defined **relationships**. There are three different relationship types that you will encounter in OpsMgr and the following sections describe each one:

Hosting relationship

In a hosting relationship, one class is hosted by another class and if you remove the management pack that contains the parent hosting class, then the child class is removed too. We'll use the Logical Disk class as good example of this relationship type. As the Logical Disk class (child) is hosted by the Windows Computer class (parent), it should make sense that if you remove an instance of Windows Computer from your management group, all associated logical disk instances hosted on that computer will also be removed.

Containment relationship

This relationship type is relatively straightforward and means that although one class has a relationship with another class; neither class has an explicit requirement for the other one. This is less restrictive than the hosting relationship as it means that one object can contain multiple objects and that object can also be contained by multiple other objects. Use cases for these relationships are typically used for health rollups and group memberships.

Reference relationship

The reference relationship is defined by the fact that the parent and child classes have no dependency on each other but still reference each other for aggregated health rollup monitoring. An example of this would be in a scenario where you have a database referencing another database for replication to support disaster recovery. Here, each database has no explicit dependency on the other and both are still discovered separately.

Discoveries

If you want to monitor your objects, then you first need to discover them with OpsMgr. When you deploy a management pack that has been authored to monitor a particular application or piece of infrastructure, you'll find that **discoveries** have been built into the management pack to query the agent or network device about the objects that it has to monitor.

Discoveries make the life of an OpsMgr administrator much easier as they remove the guess-work and potential for mistakes when new objects need to be brought under monitoring. Along with discovering completely new classes to be monitored, you can also use discoveries to add new instances of existing classes as well as to ensure old instances of existing classes no longer used are deleted.

Different management packs will have different schedules defined for their discoveries to run and some discoveries might only run once a day, where others could run every couple of hours by default.

As an example of how discoveries work, consider a scenario where you deploy the OpsMgr agent out to a large number of new servers and you have previously imported the Windows Server and SQL management packs into your management group. After a scheduled period of time, discoveries will fire on those agents and you will then see the Windows Server management pack views light up with logical disks, network connections and performance metrics for every agent. When the discoveries from the SQL management pack run, OpsMgr will automatically discover all of the databases and other SQL components that are present on any of the agents you've deployed.

It's easy to see from this example how discoveries can save you a lot of time and with them, the administration hassle of having to manually discover each object on each agent across your organization should be a thing of the past.

Monitors

Often referred to as stateful, monitors are responsible for setting the health state of objects in OpsMgr based on specific conditions that determine either two (Healthy or Critical) or three (Healthy, Warning or Critical) health states. Whichever health state is determined, the monitor can only ever be in a single health state at any given time.

An object in OpsMgr may have more than one monitor checking criteria against it to determine its overall health state and you can use monitors to optionally create alerts when objects are in a warning or critical state. The key thing with alerts generated by monitors is that when the specific criteria that originally fired the alert is no longer met, then the monitor will automatically close the alert and reset the state back to healthy.

There are three different types of monitors to choose from (depending on your requirements):

Unit monitors

The most common type of monitor you will come across, a unit monitor has responsibility for monitoring different aspects of the health of managed objects in OpsMgr. This type of monitor can be configured to use scripts, SNMP and WMI queries, to check performance counters or watch for any events that might indicate an error.

Consider that a unit monitor is a child and its health will be rolled up to its parent, which is an aggregate rollup monitor.

Dependency rollup monitors

This type of monitor rolls up health between different classes in OpsMgr. The benefit of dependency rollup monitors is that built-in algorithms determine the health of an object based on the collective health of other objects. It comes in useful when using distributed applications and inter-related application components to monitor IT services. Some of the algorithms that you can choose with dependency rollup monitors are:

- Worst state of any member
- Worst state of specified percentage of members in good health state
- Best state of any member

As an example, consider that you've created a distributed application model for the Active Directory service within your organization. Within that model, you've specified that all the **flexible single master operation** (**FSMO**) role servers are located in one component group named 'FSMO' and all other domain controllers are located within the 'DCs' component group.

In this instance, you'd want your dependency rollup monitors to be configured with the **Worst state of any member** algorithm on the 'FSMO' component group (as you'd expect to be alerted immediately if any FSMO role holders had an issue) and the 'DCs' group could be configured with the **Worst state of the specified percentage of members in good health state** option (as you could take a hit on a certain percentage of DC's going down before the actual service was affected). *Figure 5.4* shows an example of a dependency rollup monitor configured this way.

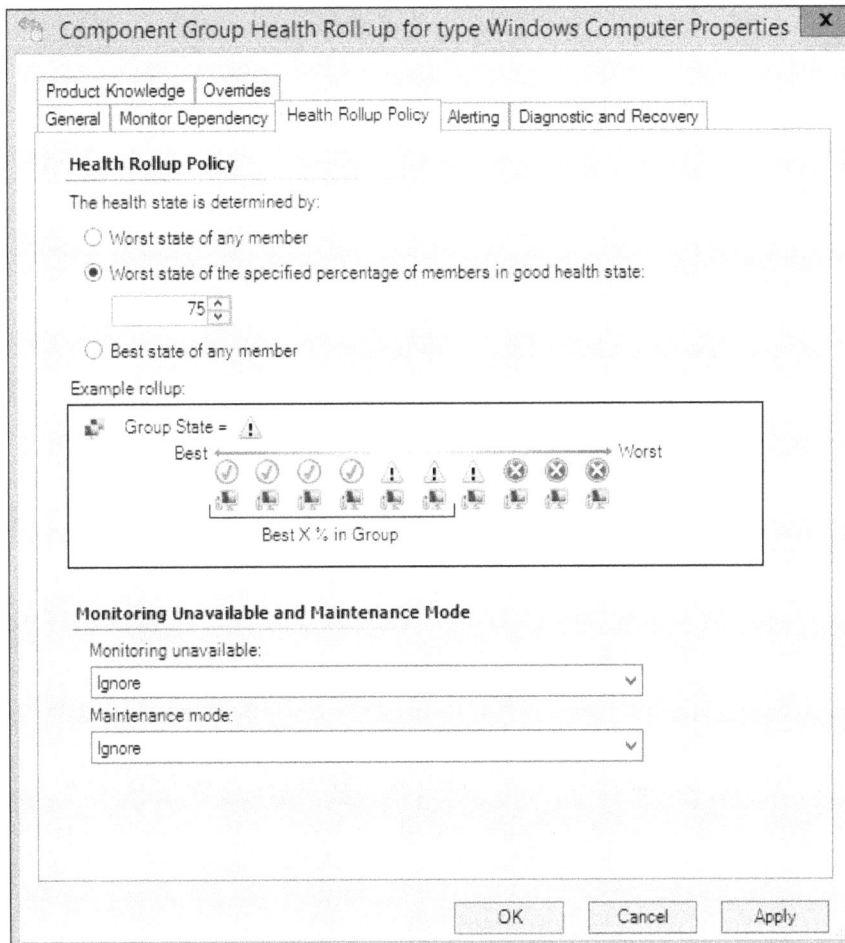

Figure 5.4: Dependency rollup monitor

Aggregate rollup monitors

An aggregate rollup monitor will combine health states from its child dependency and unit monitors. Its health state is determined by using the logical algorithm options of **Worst state of any member** and **Best state of any member** as shown in *Figure 5.5*.

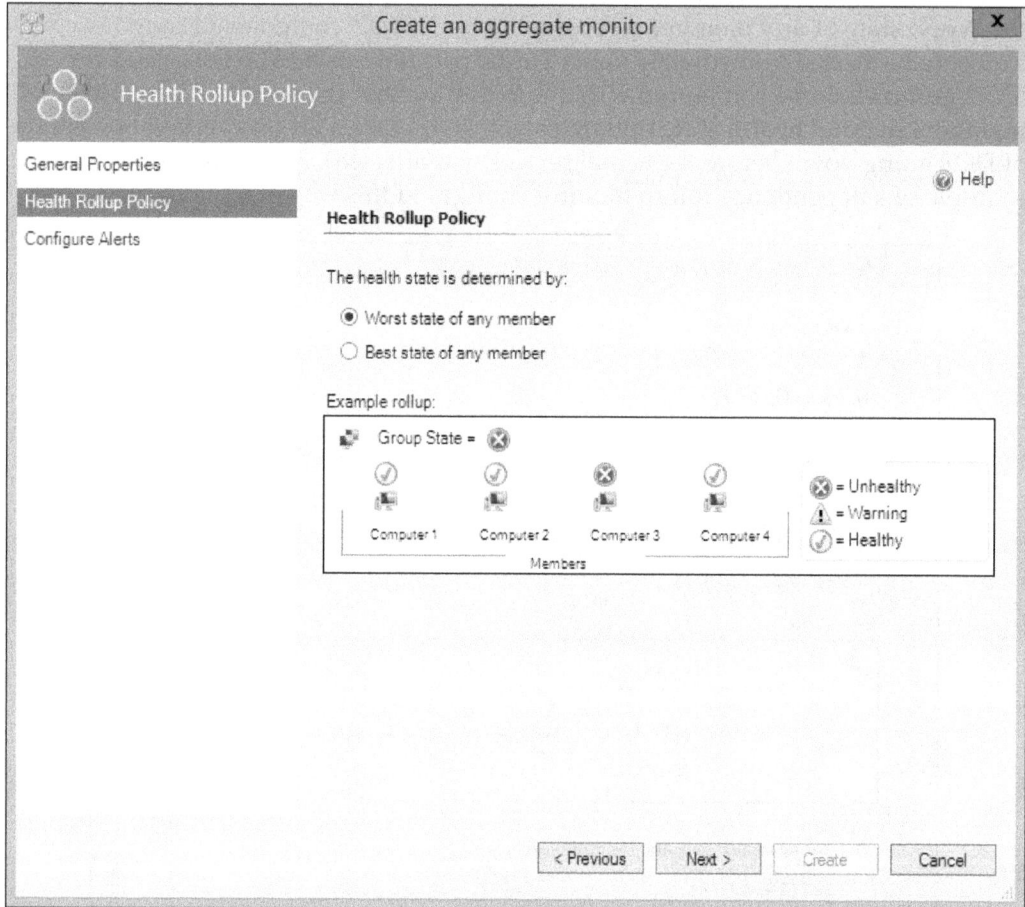

Figure 5.5: Aggregate monitor health rollup policy

In our earlier example about the distributed application for your organizations Active Directory service, an aggregate rollup monitor would sit at the very top of the service model where it determines the overall aggregated health state of the service.

Rules

If monitors are referred to as stateful, then rules can be considered stateless as they have no power to affect the availability and health state of an object. They're primarily used to collect data for alerting and reporting, based on how an object is functioning. Where a monitor might use a performance counter to set the health state of a particular object, a rule might access the same performance counter to store metrics for later reporting and analysis.

Don't be fooled into thinking however, that rules are basic and don't have too much value when compared to monitors. When I speak with customers and they ask me is there any way that we can use OpsMgr to monitor a specific application within their datacenter when there's no obvious vendor management pack available for it, then rules are the first thing that comes to mind for me to get the job done. By creating some custom rules to collect information from log files and performance counters, we can bring tangible alerts and information about the application into the console and forwarded to the relevant application owners for visibility.

Figure 5.6 shows an example of some of the different types of rules that you can create with OpsMgr.

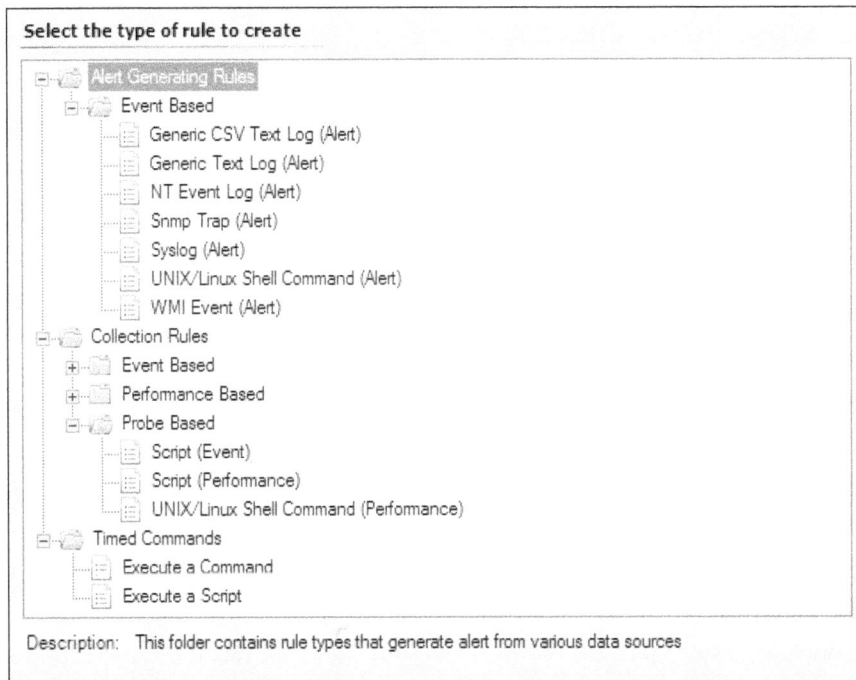

Figure 5.6: Rule types

Views

A well written management pack should always contain some views to help visualize and interact with the managed objects that it needs to monitor.

You can create and modify views from within the Monitoring workspace and the *Working with Views* section in *Chapter 3, Exploring the Consoles* discusses in detail, the various view options that you can include in a management pack.

Tasks

Tasks are useful actions that can be run on demand by a user or automatically as a workflow attached to a specific monitor. These are the four types of tasks that you will encounter in OpsMgr:

Console tasks

These tasks run on the computer where you've deployed the Operations Console to. If the task is responsible for running an application, then that application must be installed on the same computer. An example of a custom console task that I normally use in deployments is my **Google It!** task shown in *Figure 5.7*.

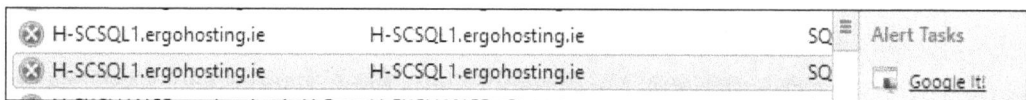

Figure 5.7: Custom console task

This task becomes available every time someone clicks on an alert from the console. When the user clicks on the task, it opens up a web browser (Internet Explorer in this case) and then appends the display name of the alert into a Google search to assist the user with alert tuning. For this task to work, the computer that the console is installed on needs to have the specified web browser application installed on it and the task will run under the same security context as the logged on user.

In *Chapter 8, Alert Tuning the Easy Way*, we discuss how to create and use this task along with some additional custom tasks to simplify alert tuning in your environment.

Agent tasks

As the name suggests, agent tasks run on a computer that has the OpsMgr agent installed. These tasks can be configured in the format of a script or an executable application and are a good way of performing specific actions on the agent-managed computer or even for retrieving information about its configuration.

An example of an agent task is the **DCDIAG** task that becomes available when you click on a domain controller being monitored using the Active Directory management pack. Running this particular task gives the same results as running the built-in DCDIAG task locally on a computer with Active Directory deployed.

In *Figure 5.8* you can see the output of the **DCDIAG** task running from the console and targeted at a monitored domain controller.

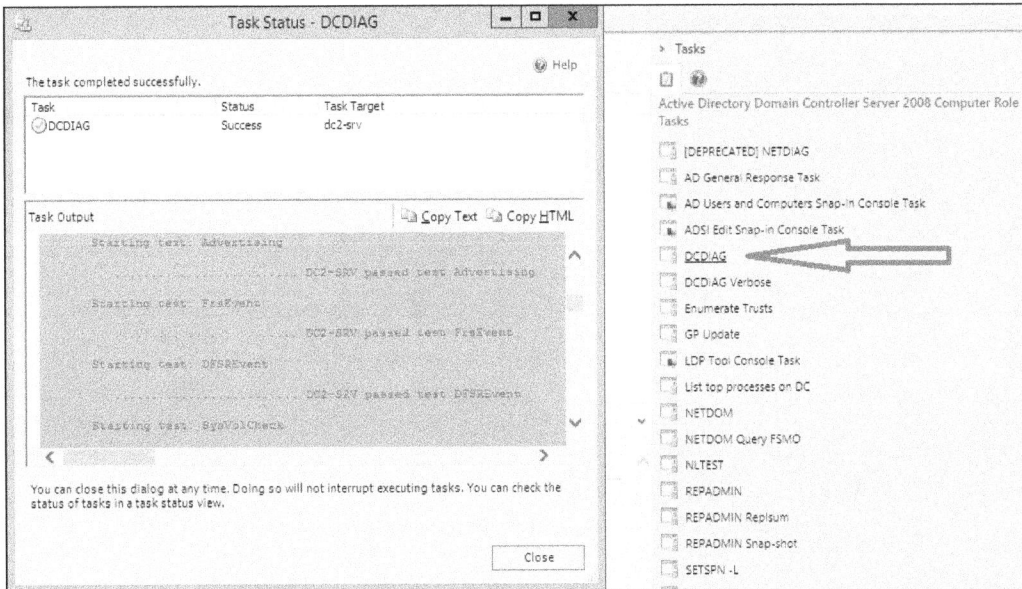

Figure 5.8: DCDIAG agent task

You should also notice in the figure, that the icon for an agent task is different to a console task, which has an image of a console instead of a computer in it.

Diagnostic tasks

A diagnostic task is different to console and agent tasks as it is typically initiated when a specific monitor fires an alert or changes its health state. The 'Health Service Heartbeat Failure' monitor in the System Center Core Monitoring management pack is a perfect example of when to use a diagnostic task.

This monitor checks the availability of the System Center Management Health Service (agent) on each monitored computer and if it detects a heartbeat failure of the agent not reporting back to the management group, it changes the monitor health state to critical. When this occurs, two diagnostic tasks are run automatically – one to ping the computer on heartbeat failure, the other to check if the Health Service is running. These diagnostic tasks are shown in *Figure 5.9*.

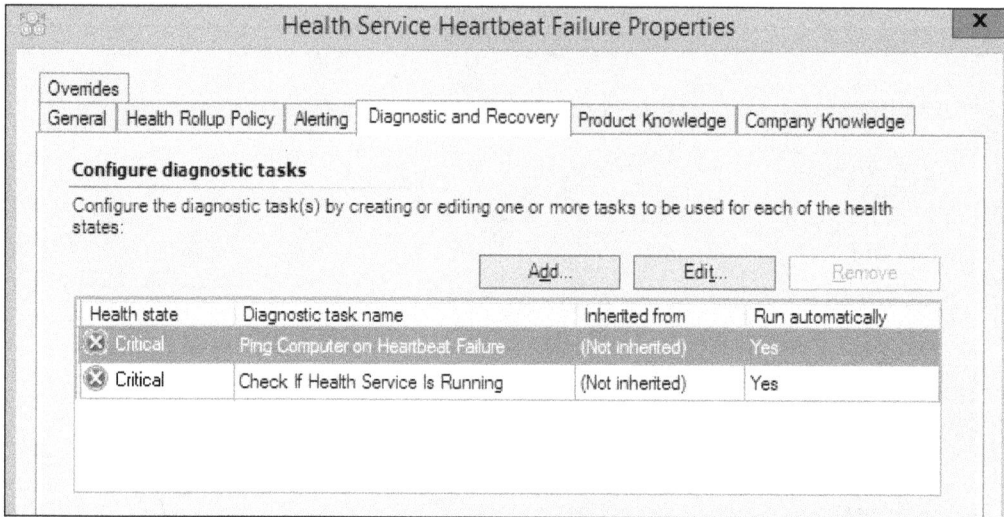

Figure 5.9: Diagnostic tasks run automatically from a monitor

Recovery tasks

Similar to diagnostic tasks, a recovery task can be automatically initiated by a monitor. Using the 'Health Service Heartbeat Failure' monitor as an example again, when the monitor changes its health state to critical and after the diagnostic tasks have failed to resolve the issue, a recovery task kicks in to enable the 'Computer Not Reachable' monitor – informing the administrator that there might be a more serious issue with the computer than just the agent service being stopped.

Figure 5.10 shows this recovery task attached to the 'Health Service Heartbeat Failure' monitor.

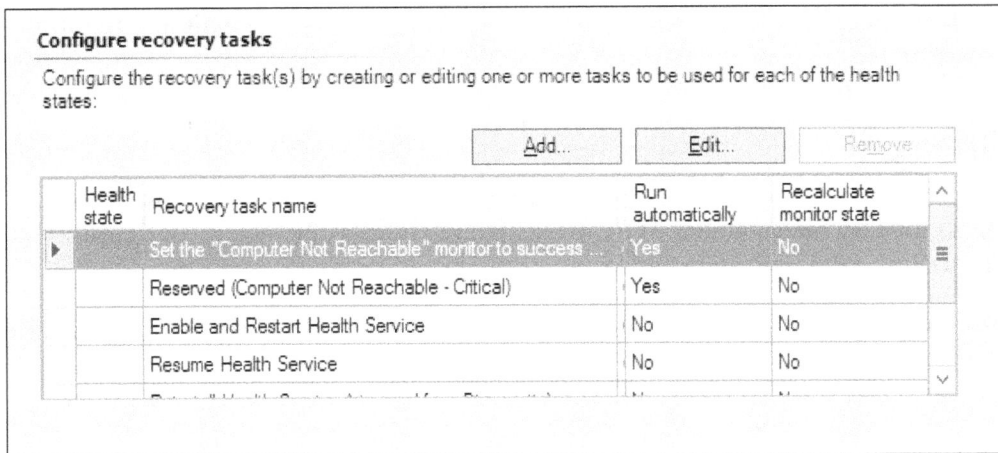

Configure recovery tasks

Configure the recovery task(s) by creating or editing one or more tasks to be used for each of the health states:

	Health state	Recovery task name	Run automatically	Recalculate monitor state	
▶		Set the "Computer Not Reachable" monitor to success ...	Yes	No	
		Reserved (Computer Not Reachable - Critical)	Yes	No	
		Enable and Restart Health Service	No	No	
		Resume Health Service	No	No	

Figure 5.10: Recovery task attached to a monitor

Reports

Another common element that you will find in a management pack is a report. As you deploy management packs from various vendors and community resources, you'll see new reports appear in the **Reports** workspace within the OpsMgr console.

As an example, *Figure 5.11* shows all of the reports that you get when you deploy the Microsoft Exchange Server 2013 management pack.

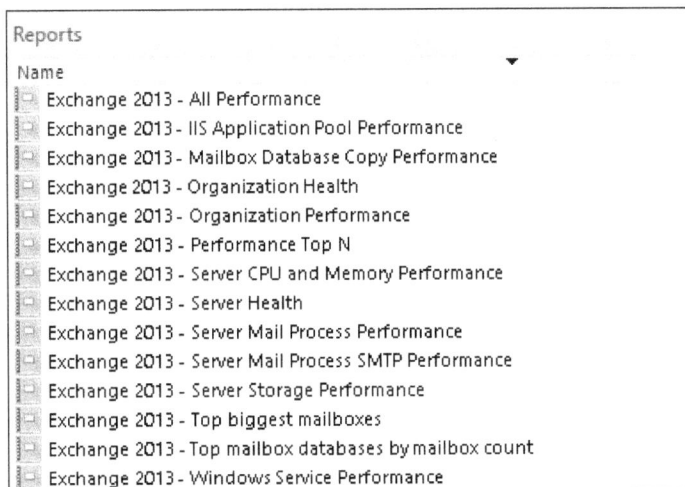

Reports

Name

Exchange 2013 - All Performance
Exchange 2013 - IIS Application Pool Performance
Exchange 2013 - Mailbox Database Copy Performance
Exchange 2013 - Organization Health
Exchange 2013 - Organization Performance
Exchange 2013 - Performance Top N
Exchange 2013 - Server CPU and Memory Performance
Exchange 2013 - Server Health
Exchange 2013 - Server Mail Process Performance
Exchange 2013 - Server Mail Process SMTP Performance
Exchange 2013 - Server Storage Performance
Exchange 2013 - Top biggest mailboxes
Exchange 2013 - Top mailbox databases by mailbox count
Exchange 2013 - Windows Service Performance

Figure 5.11: Pre-built reports from the Exchange Server 2013 management pack

Having access to prebuilt report templates specific to the application or hardware that the management pack is configured to monitor can make your job easier by quickly delivering rich information about historical outages or performance problems. In *Chapter 10, Creating Alert Subscriptions and Reports* we discuss reporting in more detail.

Groups

In OpsMgr, groups stored in management packs are used to organize discovered objects for easy management. We can use them to help scope views, configure reports and assist with alert tuning.

You can view all of your groups from within the **Authoring** workspace of the OpsMgr console as shown in *Figure 5.12*.

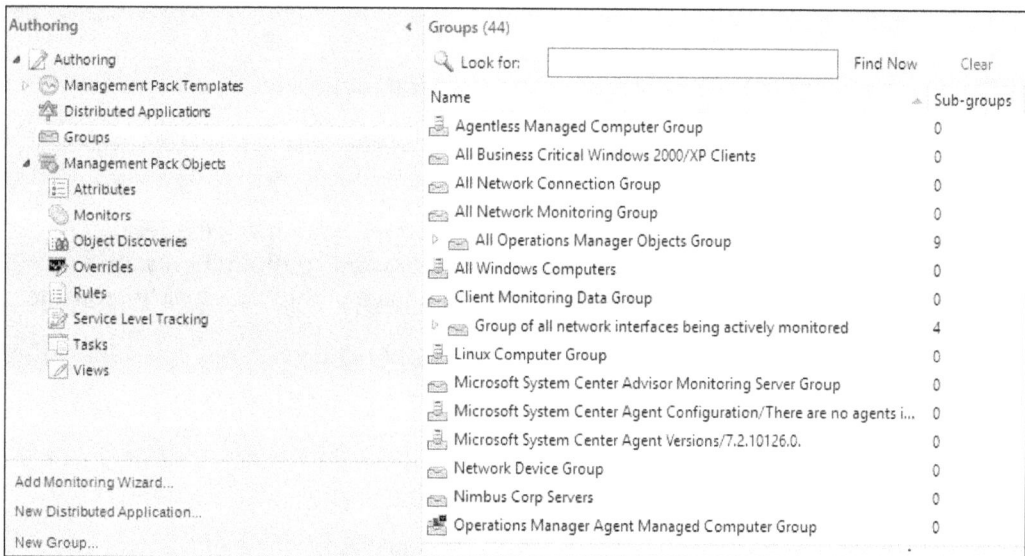

Authoring	Groups (44)	
▲ Authoring	Look for:	Find Now Clear
▷ Management Pack Templates	Name	Sub-groups
Distributed Applications	Agentless Managed Computer Group	0
Groups	All Business Critical Windows 2000/XP Clients	0
▲ Management Pack Objects	All Network Connection Group	0
Attributes	All Network Monitoring Group	0
Monitors	▷ All Operations Manager Objects Group	9
Object Discoveries	All Windows Computers	0
Overrides	Client Monitoring Data Group	0
Rules	▷ Group of all network interfaces being actively monitored	4
Service Level Tracking	Linux Computer Group	0
Tasks	Microsoft System Center Advisor Monitoring Server Group	0
Views	Microsoft System Center Agent Configuration/There are no agents i...	0
	Microsoft System Center Agent Versions/7.2.10126.0.	0
Add Monitoring Wizard...	Network Device Group	0
New Distributed Application...	Nimbus Corp Servers	0
New Group...	Operations Manager Agent Managed Computer Group	0

Figure 5.12: Viewing groups in OpsMgr

The *Exploring the Authoring workspace* section of *Chapter 3, Exploring the Consoles* walks you through how to create a new group and store it in a management pack.

Finding management packs

Up to this point we've given you an overview of what a management pack is and we took a quick look under the hood to understand the elements they can contain. In this section we'll give you some options and tips on where best to track down the management packs that you need for your environment.

Although they all share the same file types (.mp, .xml), the configuration of each management pack is unique and you need to understand what exactly the management pack can and cannot monitor by default. To help you gain a better understanding of what a management pack can do, most vendors and community authors provide an associated guide (user manual) and it's imperative that you have access to this guide when you locate and download the management pack.

To find management packs, you could just use your favorite Internet search engine and trawl through endless links to locate the latest version of the particular management pack you're looking for, or you could use one of the following methods to reduce your search time considerably:

MP Wiki

Given the fact that the majority of management packs you're likely to deploy are from Microsoft, it goes without saying that they should make things easy for you to get access to them! Thankfully, the **Microsoft Management Packs Wiki** (or **MP Wiki** as it's more commonly known) is the 'go to' place for locating Microsoft management packs.

Published initially by Microsoft's Daniel Savage (System Center Program Manager) and containing download links and version information for nearly two hundred Microsoft management packs, the MP Wiki is updated on a regular basis by members of System Center community. In fact, when a new management pack is added to the Microsoft download site, the Wiki is typically updated to reflect the new management pack within a matter of hours!

You can access the MP Wiki from the following URL:

```
http://tinyurl.com/opsmgrmpwiki
```

Figure 5.13 shows some management packs that are listed along with their version and release date in the MP Wiki:

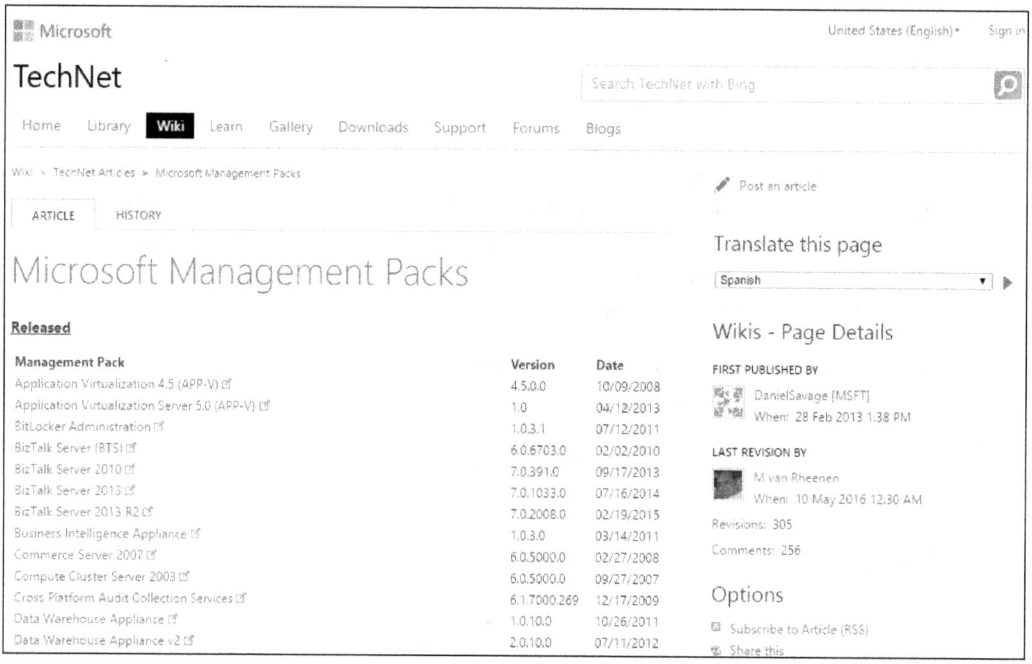

Figure 5.13: The OpsMgr MP Wiki

Clicking on a link from within the MP Wiki will direct you to the exact location on the Microsoft Download Center site where you can download the management pack (as shown in *Figure 5.14*).

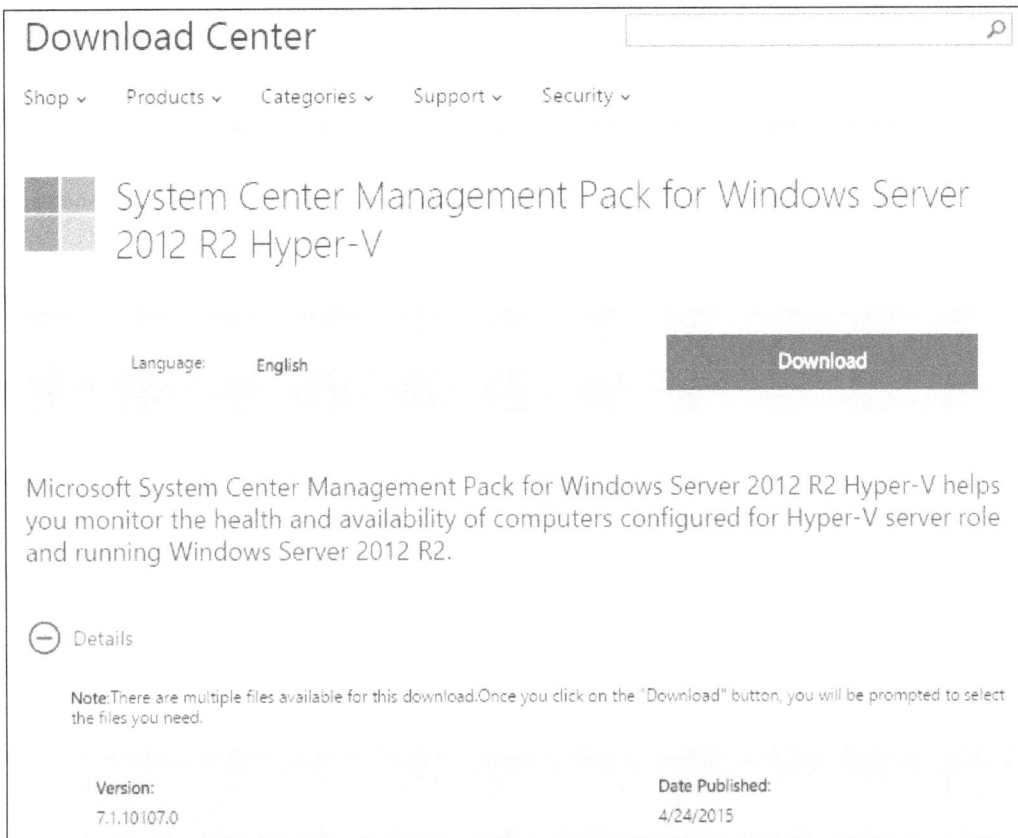

Figure 5.14: Downloading a management pack

When you hit the **Download** button, as shown in *Figure 5.15*, you will be presented with options to download the management pack (often as a packaged .msi file), the management pack guide, and other language versions of the management pack should you require them.

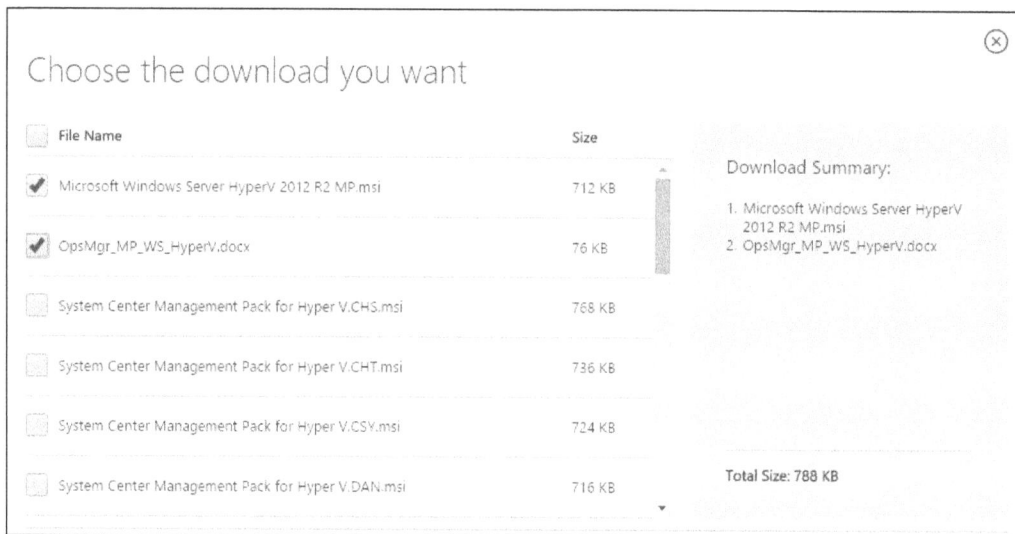

Figure 5.15: Selecting the management pack and guide for download

As you can see, using the MP Wiki to quickly locate and download Microsoft management packs and their associated management pack guides will save you a lot of time.

> If you're looking for a quick method of downloading all Microsoft management packs and their associated guides from the MP Wiki, then you need to look no further than the excellent **Get-All-SCOM-MPs** PowerShell script that was written by three fellow System Center MVP's — Stanislav Zhelyazkov, Damian Flynn, and Cameron Fuller.
>
> This script grabs the names and links for all management packs listed on the MP Wiki, and then downloads them to a location of your choice. You can download this script at the following link: http://tinyurl.com/opsmgrmpscript

OpsMgr MP Catalog

An alternative method of locating and downloading Microsoft management packs is the built-in catalog accessed through the Operations console. There are some pros and cons to using this method however and we'll discuss these points as we walk through the download process.

These steps will show you how to download management packs using the MP catalog:

1. In the **Administration** workspace, right-click on **Management Packs**, then click on the **Download Management Packs** option from the resultant menu.

2. From the **Select Management Packs** dialog box, choose a location on your computer to store the downloaded management packs, then click on the **Add** button to connect to the **Management Pack Catalog Web Service** (we're assuming you have an Internet connection on the computer that you are running this from).

3. The **Select Management Packs from Catalog** dialog box presents the following four options to search the online Microsoft Management Pack Catalog:

    ° All management packs in the catalog
    ° Updates available for installed management packs
    ° All management packs released within last 3 months
    ° All management packs released within last 6 months

> Choosing the **Updates available for installed management packs** option here is a handy method of quickly identifying the Microsoft management packs that have been installed and are now out of date. I use this option regularly when performing OpsMgr health checks for customers.

4. Choose the **All management packs in the catalog** option and hit the **Search** button to search the catalog contents. You will then be presented with a list of all Microsoft management packs the catalog knows about as shown in *Figure 5.16.*

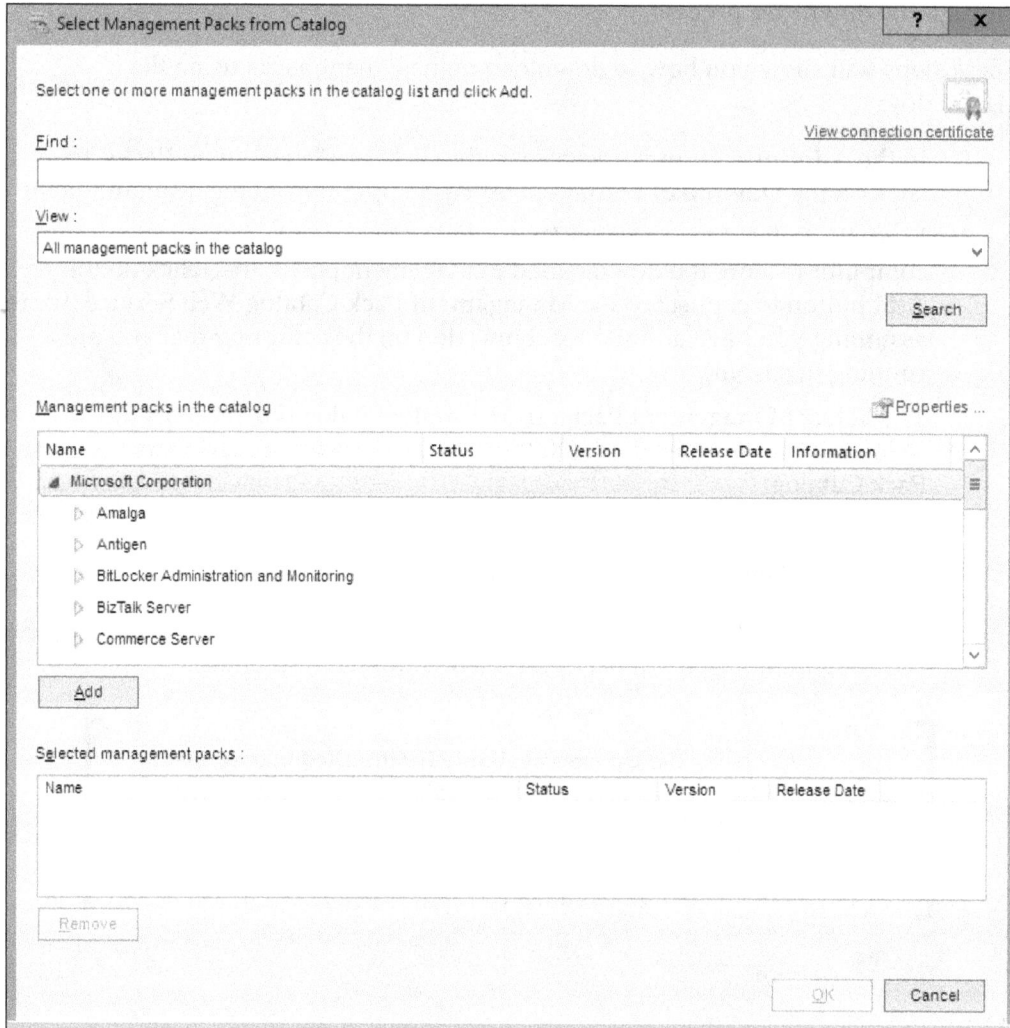

Figure 5.16: Searching the online OpsMgr MP Catalog

> A downside to using the built-in OpsMgr MP Catalog is that when you search for all management packs in the catalog, it doesn't contain the most up-to-date versions for every Microsoft management pack available. This of course, is a fail on Microsoft's part and at the time of writing, they are actively working on bringing the catalog contents more in line with the download center.

5. From the **Management Packs in the Catalog** section, scroll down and expand **Windows Server**, expand **Core OS** and use the **Add** button to add management packs relevant to your OS as shown in *Figure 5.17*. Click **OK** when you're ready to move on.

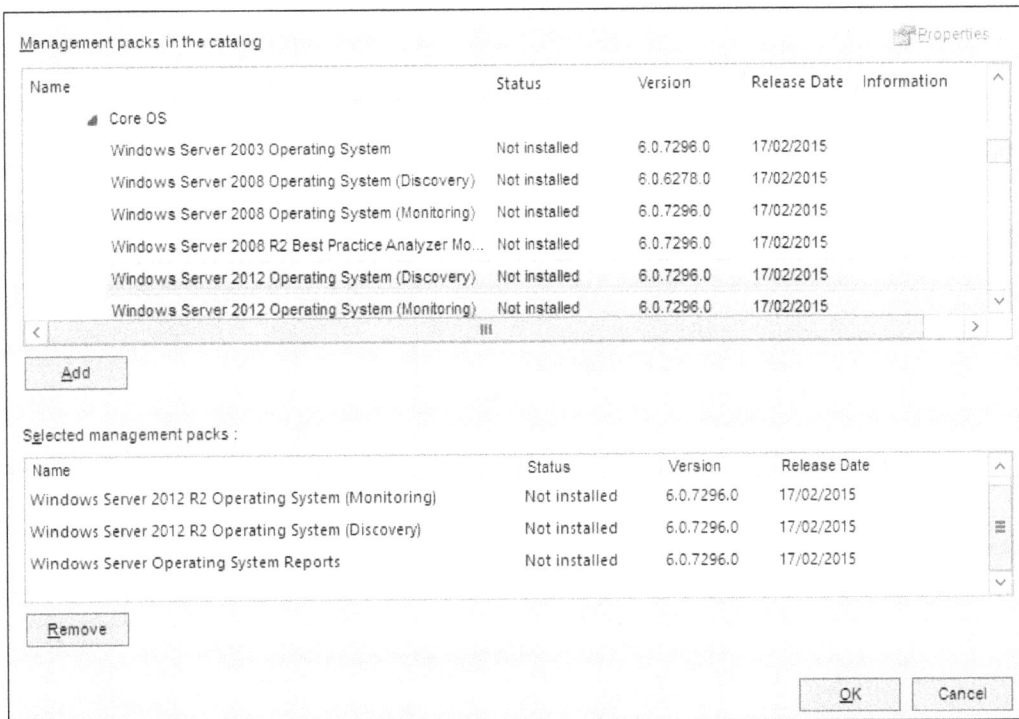

Management packs in the catalog   Properties

Name	Status	Version	Release Date	Information
▲ Core OS				
Windows Server 2003 Operating System	Not installed	6.0.7296.0	17/02/2015	
Windows Server 2008 Operating System (Discovery)	Not installed	6.0.6278.0	17/02/2015	
Windows Server 2008 Operating System (Monitoring)	Not installed	6.0.7296.0	17/02/2015	
Windows Server 2008 R2 Best Practice Analyzer Mo...	Not installed	6.0.7296.0	17/02/2015	
Windows Server 2012 Operating System (Discovery)	Not installed	6.0.7296.0	17/02/2015	
Windows Server 2012 Operating System (Monitoring)	Not installed	6.0.7296.0	17/02/2015	

[Add]

Selected management packs :

Name	Status	Version	Release Date
Windows Server 2012 R2 Operating System (Monitoring)	Not installed	6.0.7296.0	17/02/2015
Windows Server 2012 R2 Operating System (Discovery)	Not installed	6.0.7296.0	17/02/2015
Windows Server Operating System Reports	Not installed	6.0.7296.0	17/02/2015

[Remove]

[OK] [Cancel]

Figure 5.17: Choosing management packs from the catalog

> If you want more detailed information about a listed management
> pack in the catalog, simply double-click on the management pack
> name to be presented with three tabs – **General**, **Knowledge**
> and **Dependencies**. The General tab gives you a high-level
> overview, the Knowledge tab provides a detailed summary of
> the management pack and the Dependencies tab shows you any
> dependent management packs that need to be in place before
> importing this one.

6. Back at the **Select Management Packs** dialog box, when you've added your
   selections to the **Download List**, click on the **Download** button to begin
   downloading the management packs to your chosen location and hit **Close**
   when the download is complete.

7. Now, when you browse to the download location, you can see the newly
   downloaded management packs with a .mp extension, as shown in *Figure
   5.18*.

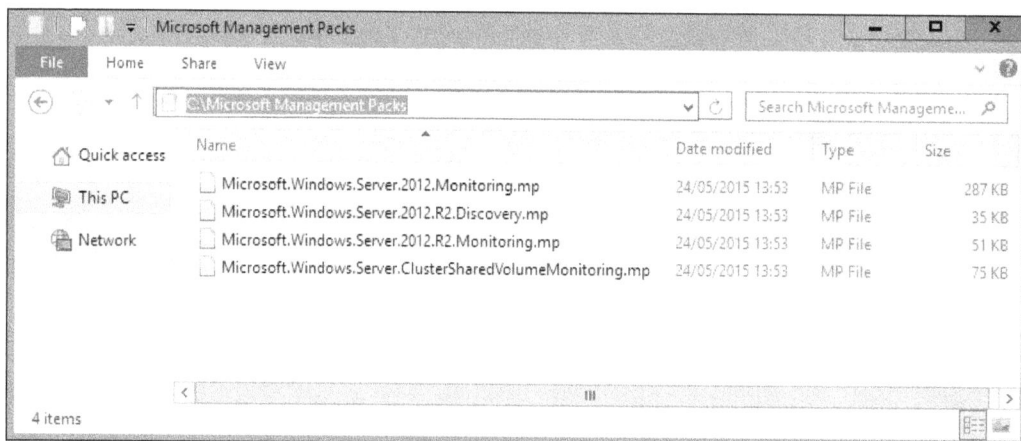

Figure 5.18: Downloaded management packs

Downloading management pack guides from the catalog

When we compare the management pack download experience between the MP
Wiki and the OpsMgr MP Catalog, the first obvious difference is that there's no clear
option to download the management pack guides for each management pack from
within the Catalog.

As we've mentioned earlier, these guides should be compulsory reading before importing any management packs into OpsMgr and I'll show you a lesser known trick to get download access to these guides from within the MP Catalog:

1. Open the MP Catalog, select a download folder location, click on the **Add** button to open the **Select Management Packs** from **Catalog** dialog box again and choose a search option – we'll use the **All management packs in the catalog** option in this example.

2. Browse to the parent management pack description in the list – we'll choose **Core OS** here as that's the parent description of all Windows Server management packs – but don't expand the selection.

3. To the right of the parent description, you'll notice four columns – **Status, Version, Release Date** and **Information**. Move your mouse pointer over to the **Information** column as indicated in *Figure 5.19* and you'll notice the pointer changes to a hand icon – indicating a hidden URL download link.

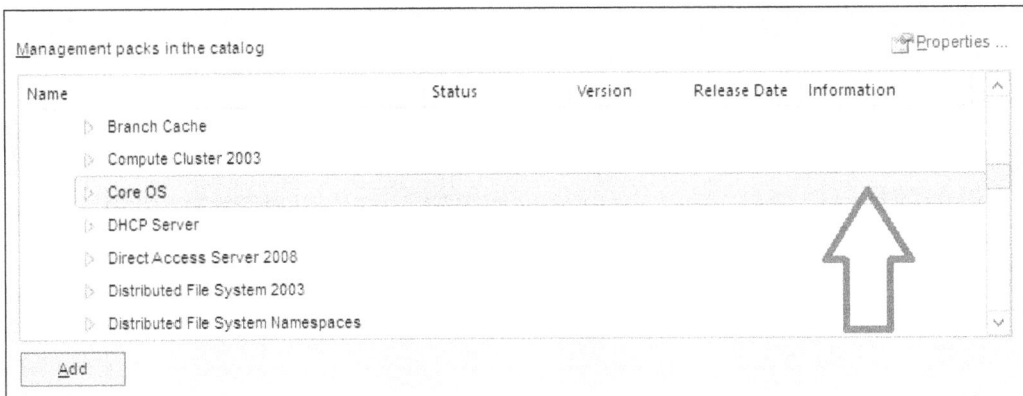

Figure 5.19: Access the hidden management pack guide download link

4. Click on the hidden link embedded in the empty space of the Information column and your web browser will start up and give you some options to open or save the management pack guide as shown in *Figure 5.20.*

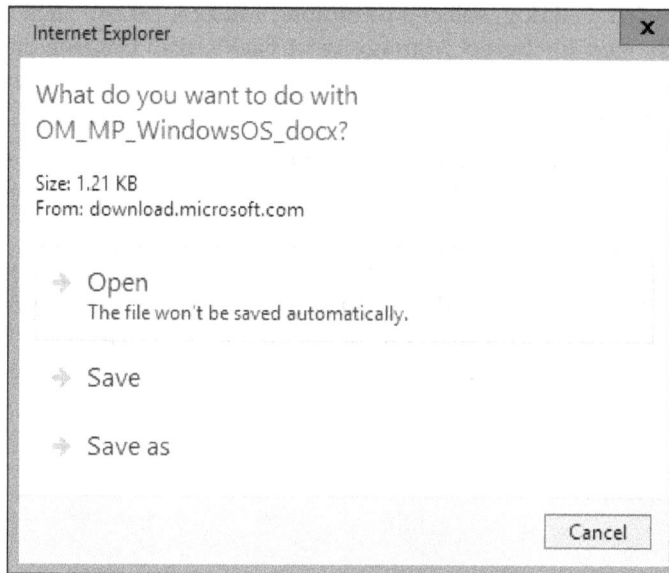

Figure 5.20: Downloading the management pack guide from the catalog

You can repeat this process for each management pack that you download; however, be aware that some legacy management packs might not have an associated management pack guide available and there's also a chance that the hidden download links might not give you access to the latest versions.

Updates and Recommendations

If you're using OpsMgr 2016, then you'll notice the **Updates and Recommendations** feature shown in *Figure 5.21*, which is located under the **Management Packs** area in the **Administration** workspace.

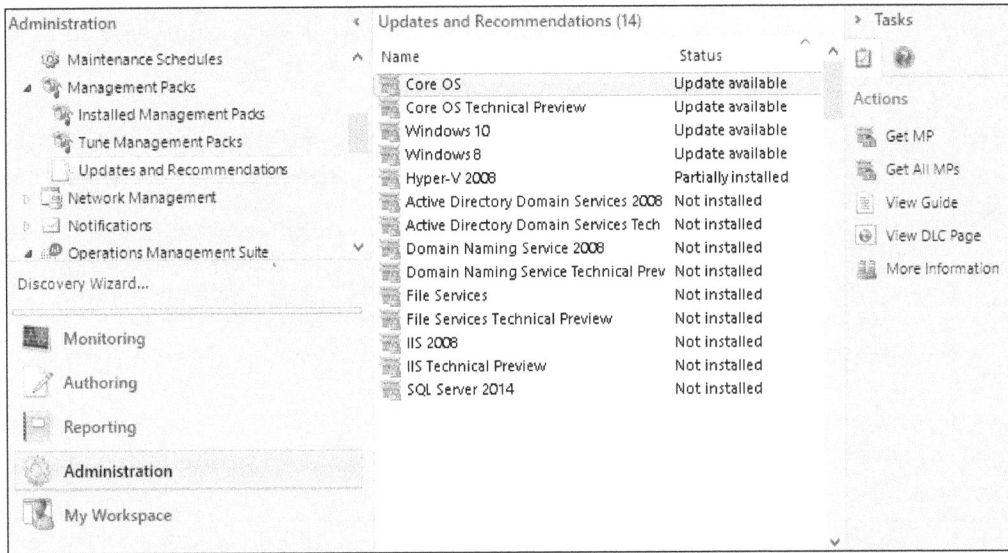

Figure 5.21: Updates and Recommendations feature

This feature scans the servers you have brought into OpsMgr and then makes recommendations about management packs that can help you monitor new Microsoft workloads on those servers that you currently don't have visibility on. This is also a handy place to go when you want to quickly see which updates are available for the management packs you've already imported.

The following five actions are available from the Tasks pane:

Get MP action

Selecting a management pack from the list and clicking on the **Get MP** action from the **Actions** pane connects to the Management Pack Catalog Service and offers you the selected management packs for download and import as shown in *Figure 5.22.*

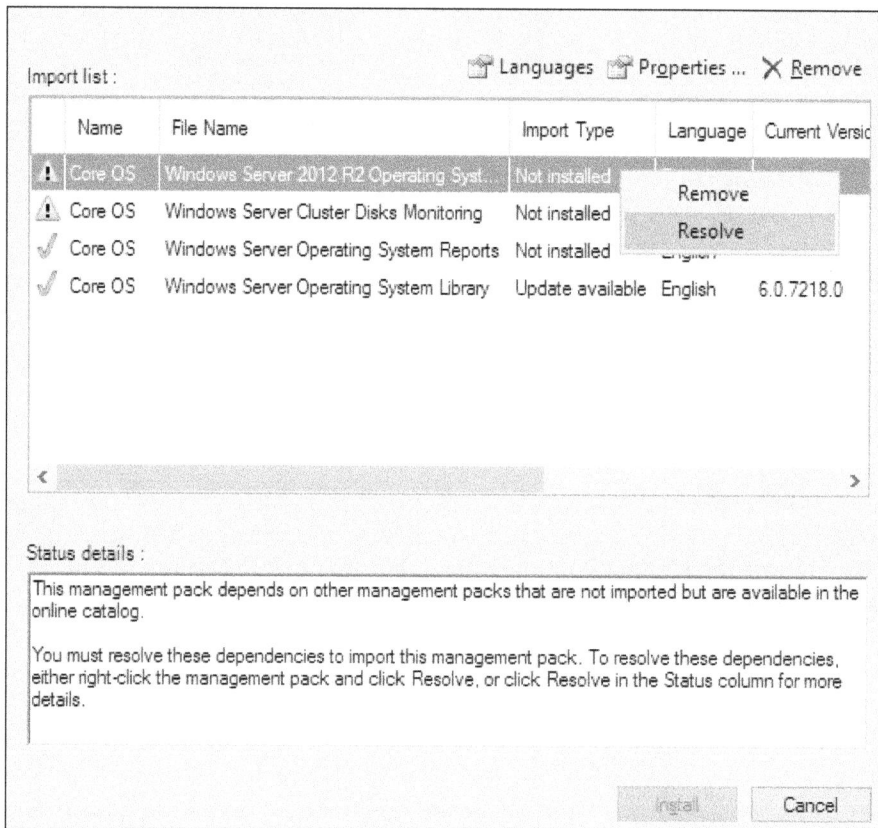

Figure 5.22: The GetMP action

From here you can right-click on any management packs that you want to remove or resolve their dependencies for along with having the option to click on the **Languages** button and choose a language version to import (English is always selected by default). You can also click on the **Properties** button here to view some basic information about the management pack and its dependencies.

Get All MPs action

Clicking on the **Get All MPs** action will launch the Management Pack Catalog Service with all of the recommended management packs added to the import list and ready for installation. Similar to the Get MP action, you can remove management packs, view their properties and resolve any dependencies they might have but you don't have an option to select a language version here.

View Guide action

When you select a management pack from the list and click on the **View Guide** action, your web browser will open and the relevant management pack guide will automatically download for you from the Microsoft download center. This is a quick way of gaining an understanding of what the management pack can offer and how it needs to be configured before you import it into OpsMgr.

View DLC Page action

Selecting a management pack from the list of recommendations and clicking on the **View DLC Page** action will automatically launch your web browser and connect to the Download Center page associated to the management pack you've selected. From there, you can get more information about the management pack along with the option to manually download the guide, installer and other language versions.

More Information action

Use the **More Information** action to get additional information about why a management pack recommendation was made. Clicking on this link from any recommendations in the list that have a status of **Not Installed** will show you a list of computers where the workload to be monitored was discovered.

For example, if I select the Active Directory Domain Services management pack from my list of recommendations and click on this action, in *Figure 5.23* you can see that the agent I've deployed to my domain controller is the one running the discovered workload that needs to be monitored.

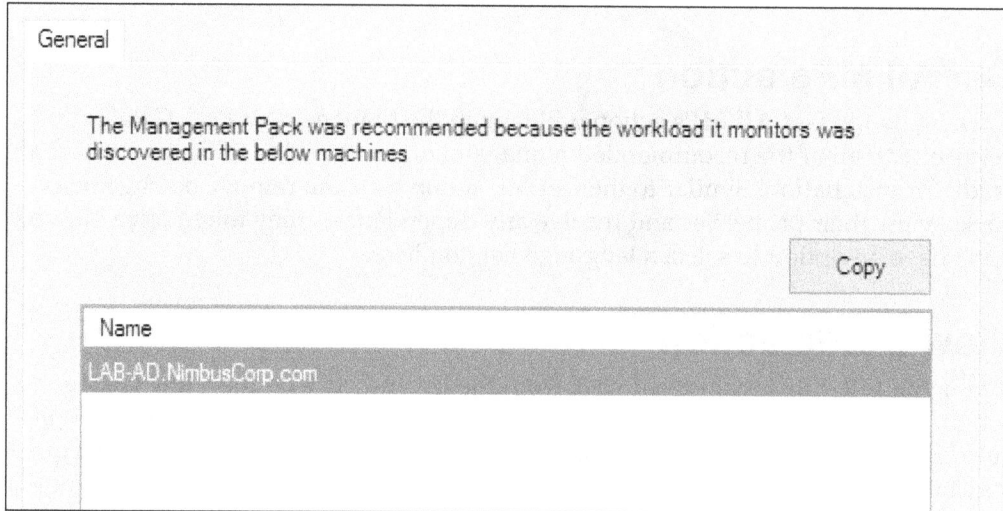

Figure 5.23: The More Information action

Locating non-Microsoft management packs

Using either the MP Wiki or the built-in OpsMgr MP Catalog, you can only download Microsoft management packs. To ensure you can monitor your entire IT estate, you'll obviously need to make use of other third party vendor and community authored management packs.

Traditionally, the process for locating these types of management packs would go something like this–go directly to the vendor's website, waste time searching through endless broken links and forum replies, find an out-of-date version of the management pack, start again, locate the correct version of the management pack, and finally download it!

Thankfully though, the OpsMgr community has come up with a number of solutions to help you track down those hard-to-find non-Microsoft management packs in a similar format to the MP Wiki.

The 'Unofficial' System Center catalog

An online resource that I've been using for a number of years now to track non-Microsoft management packs, the 'Unofficial' System Center Catalog is a simple but effective blog site that was put together by a member of the System Center community. It provides a consolidated list of non-Microsoft management packs organized by technology, vendor and cost as shown in *Figure 5.24*.

Technology	Developed by (w/Link)	Cost
Hardware		
Fujitsu Primergy	Fujitsu	Free
Unisys	Unisys	Free (logon required)
Dell PowerEdge / PowerVault, DRAC and CMC	Dell	Free
HP ProLiant	HP	Free
HP ProLiant (SNMP-based, for ESX hosts for example)	Community	Free
HP ProLiant (advanced capabilities, plus support for servers running Linux and VMware)	HP	Comes with HP Insight Control for System Center
IBM System x Servers, Flex System x Servers, System x iDataPlex, blades servers and BladeCenter Chassis	IBM	Free

Figure 5.24: The 'Unofficial' System Center Catalog

It's been a while since this catalog was last updated, but the majority of the links are still valid and if nothing else, it's a great starting point to finding those third-party vendor management packs.

You can access the Unofficial System Center Catalog from `http://tinyurl.com/opsmgrunofficialcatalog`.

With community maintained blog posts such as this, there's always a slight chance that the page can be taken down or become inaccessible for whatever reason.

As it'd be a shame to lose all those handy links to vendor management packs, it's a good idea to save the catalog web page as a locally stored web archive or full HTML page (any web browser can provide this functionality using the **Save As** option from the **File** menu). With an offline copy of the catalog page stored on your computer, you'll always have quick access to the download links for these management packs.

SystemCenterCentral.com

A well known and very popular resource, System Center Central (http://www.systemcentercentral.com/) is a community-based forum with an oasis of valuable knowledge on OpsMgr and other System Center products.

This is definitely the place to go when you want to get access to an abundance of free community management packs, the majority of which have been authored by some of the best contributors the System Center community has to offer – an example of some of these are shown in *Figure 5.25*.

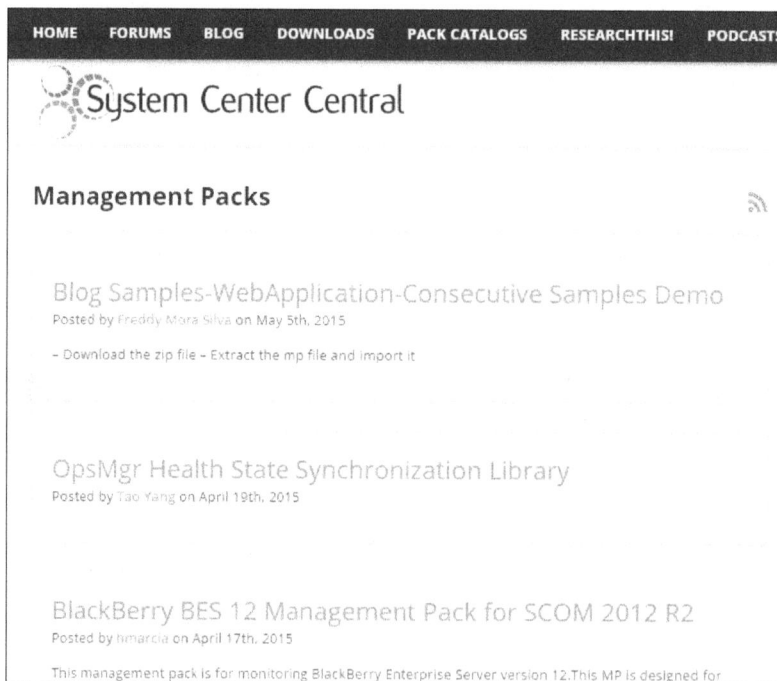

Figure 5.25: Community management packs on SystemCenterCentral.com

SystemCenterCore.com

Another excellent community resource, System Center Core (`http://systemcentercore.com/`) is a relatively recent project that really goes the extra mile. This site contains one of the most comprehensive technical documentation libraries of management packs for both Operations Manager and Service Manager.

In *Figure 5.26* you can see the homepage of this site where all of the latest Microsoft, third party vendor and community management packs (literally hundreds of them) are listed alongside the elements within each management pack, links to the guides and release notes for each.

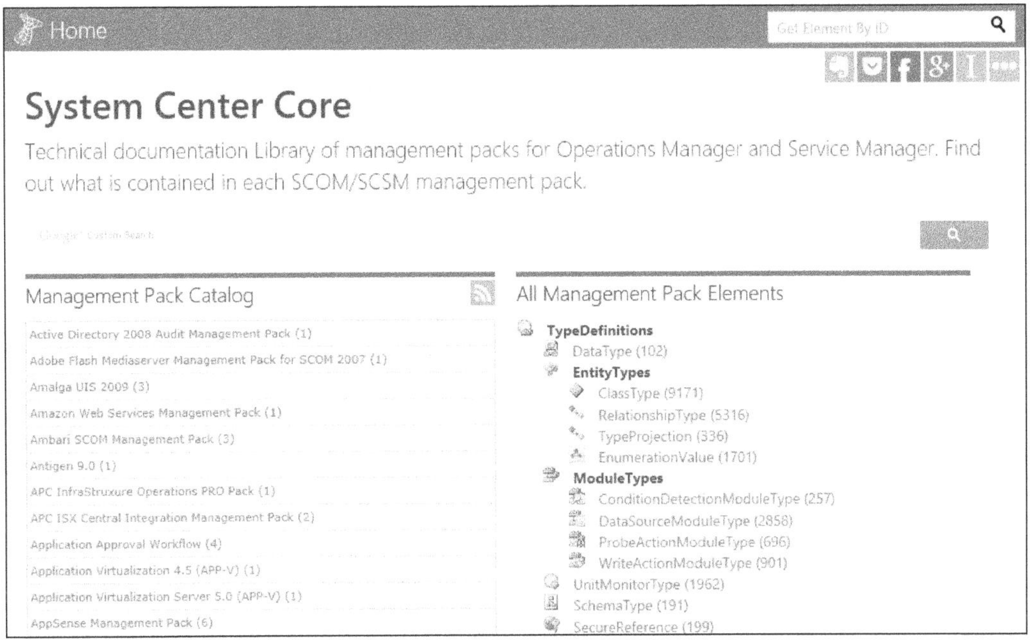

Figure 5.26: A combined management pack catalog on SystemCenterCore.com

Importing management packs

Once you've tracked down the management packs to monitor your environment with, you'll want to import them into OpsMgr, but before that – do you remember we mentioned the importance of reading the management pack guides first?

When you're working with a new management pack for the first time, think of the phrase **R.T.F.M.**, which of course stands for **Read the Friendly Manual**!

If you don't take the time to read through the management pack guide first and familiarize yourself with how to configure it to monitor your applications or devices, then you've already started off on the wrong foot. You see, although the process of installing a management pack into OpsMgr is nearly identical for every management pack out there, you'll soon find that most management packs are then configured differently when it comes to discoveries and out-of-box capabilities.

If you've been consecutively working through the activities in each chapter of this book, then up to this point, the only management packs you will have deployed are the ones that came bundled with the original installation.

For the next exercise, make sure to download the Windows Server Operating System and Active Directory management packs from the MP Wiki to a location on your management server (for example, "`C:\MPs`") and read through the management pack guides in preparation for deploying your first management pack.

Extracting the files

Most vendor management packs will come packaged as an **.MSI** file that needs to be extracted to a local folder location so we can gain access to the **.MP** files we need.

1. Browse to the location on your OpsMgr server that you've downloaded the management packs to, locate the **.MSI** file for the first one that you wish to import and double-click on it to begin.

2. Accept the license agreement, and then click on **Next** to bring you to the **Select Installation Folder** dialog box. Here you can choose the folder location to extract the **.MP** management pack files to. As you can see in *Figure 5.27*, the default parent folder location is "`C:\Program Files (x86)\ System Center Management Packs\`" – make a note of this location as you'll be coming back to it a little later.

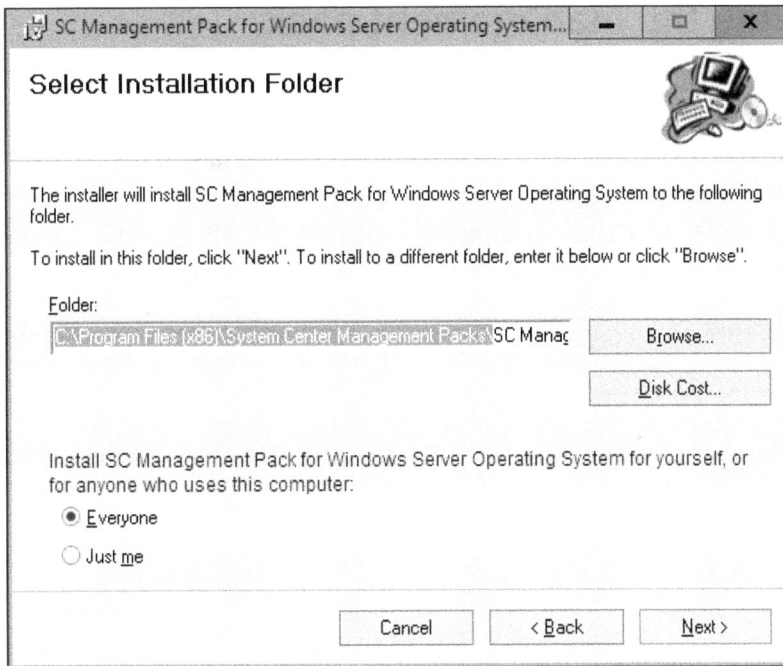

Figure 5.27: Choosing a location for your extracted management pack files

3. Click on **Next**, then at the **Confirm Installation** dialog box, hit the **Install** button to extract the management packs to your chosen folder location.

It's a really good idea to think about having a central storage location that contains all of your downloaded and extracted OpsMgr management packs. This can act as an organized library for old and new management packs and each management pack guide too. I've lost track of the amount of times that I've had to revert back to my own library – either to reference a management pack guide or to even roll back to an earlier version of a management pack due to a bug or missing functionality in a newer version.

Deploying the management pack

When you've extracted the management pack, follow these steps to get it deployed:

1. In the **Administration** workspace of the **Operations Console**, right-click on Management Packs, then click on the **Import Management Packs** option from the resultant menu.

2. From the **Select Management Packs** dialog box, click on the **Add** button, then choose the **Add from disk** option as shown in *Figure 5.28*.

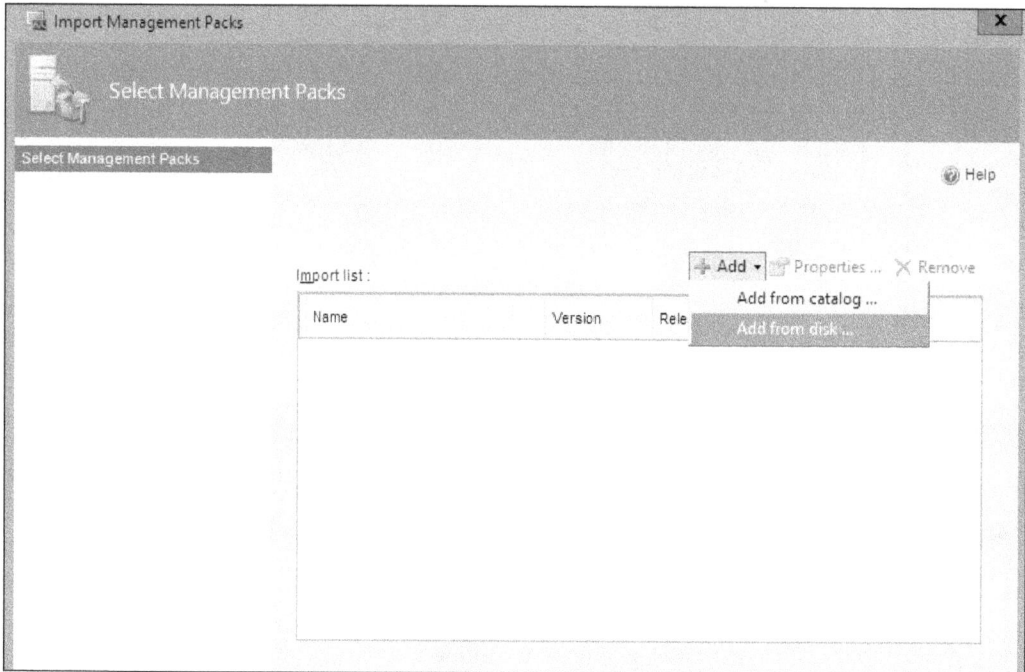

Figure 5.28: Importing a management pack from disk

3. At the Online Catalog Connection dialog box you can choose whether or not to search the online catalog for any missing dependencies that might be needed. We'll choose **No** here for now.

4. Now browse to the location where you extracted the **.MSI** file to earlier, remember the default location is "C:\Program Files (x86)\System Center Management Packs\".

5. As shown in *Figure 5.29*, select the management pack files that you want to import into OpsMgr, then click on the **Open** button to continue.

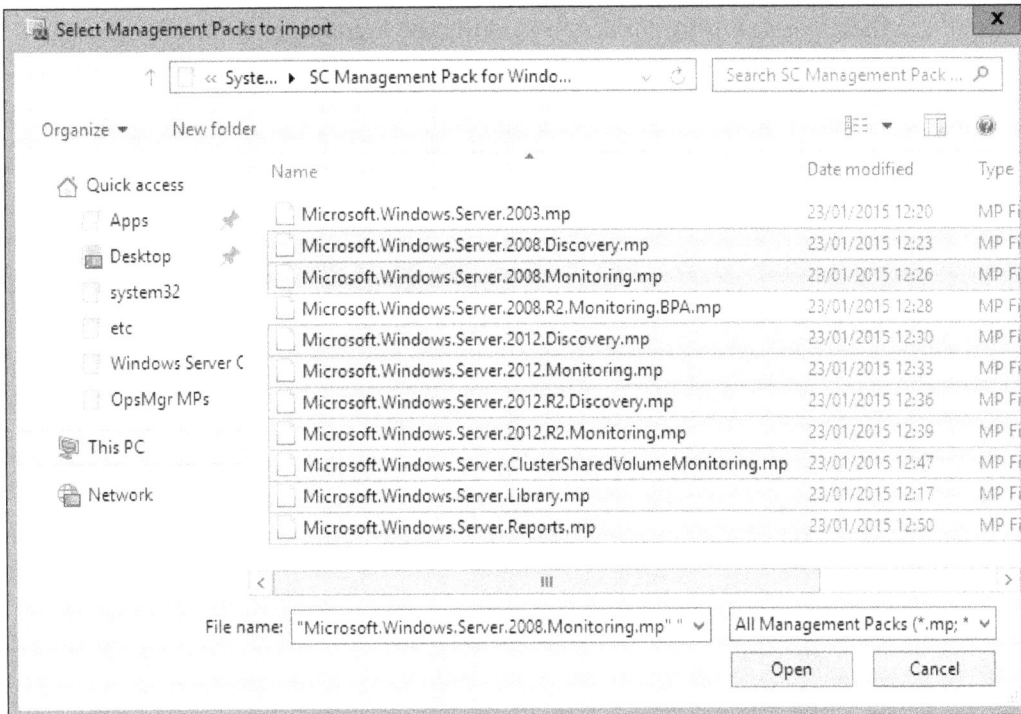

Figure 5.29: Choosing management packs to import

This is a good time to point out that you don't need to import every management pack into your environment just because you've downloaded it. In our example, we've chosen not to import the Windows Server 2003 and Windows Server 2008 Best Practice Analyzer management packs as we don't have a requirement to monitor them.

6. At this point, OpsMgr carries out a quick check to verify if any of the management packs you've chosen have been previously imported and it also checks to see if any dependencies are missing. In *Figure 5.30*, you can see there's an informational status beside the **Windows Server Operating System Library** management pack informing us that an earlier version is already imported. This is expected behavior due to the original installation importing this management pack by default so we can just hit the **Install** button to import the management packs into the database.

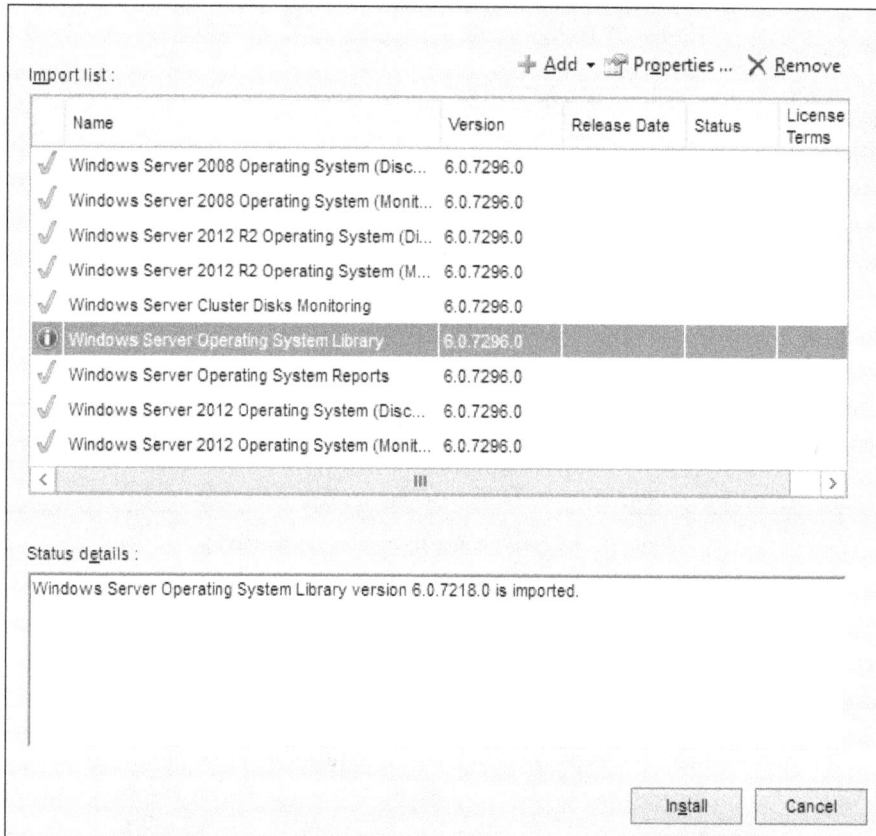

Figure 5.30: Previously imported management pack informational status

7. When the import process is complete, click on **Close** to exit the dialog box.

Creating a custom overrides management pack

When you import a new sealed management pack, its best practice to then create an associated new unsealed management pack that will be used to store overrides and customizations into.

Here's what you need to do to create an overrides management pack using the Operations console:

1. In the **Monitoring** workspace of the console, locate the folder that represents your newly imported sealed management pack and make a note of its display name – in our example, the display name we're looking for is simply **Microsoft Windows Server**.

2. Browse to the **Administration** workspace, right-click on Management Packs and then click on the **Create Management Pack** option from the resultant menu.

3. At the **Create a Management Pack** dialog box, type the display name of the sealed management pack that you noted in the first step and add **Overrides** to the end of it (using this naming convention for your override management packs makes administration easier). As you can see in *Figure 5.31*, we've named this one **Microsoft Windows Server Overrides**.

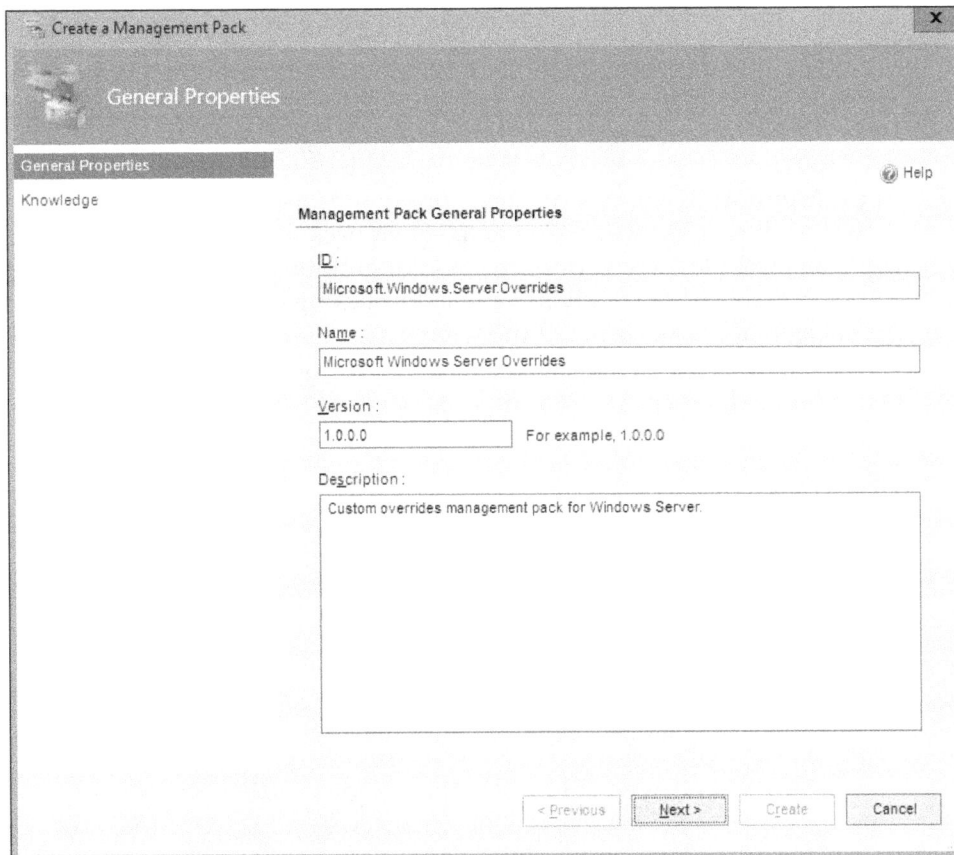

Figure 5.31: Creating your overrides management pack

4.   You can leave the version number as it is and type a description for this management pack if you wish. Click on **Next** to move on when you're ready.

5.   From the next dialog box, click on the **Create** button to finalize the management pack creation.

6.   To confirm your new overrides management pack has been created, back at the **Management Packs** view, type overrides into the **Look for** field and you should see it show up in the list similar to our example in *Figure 5.32*. This is a good example of maintaining a solid naming convention for your override management packs as it makes searching through hundreds of imported management packs easy.

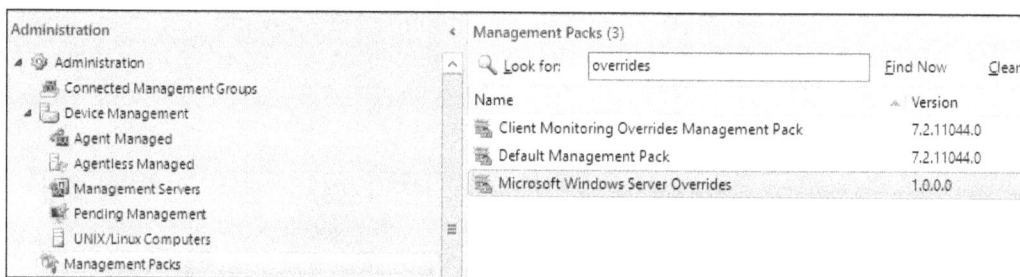

Figure 5.32: Searching for override management packs

7.   At the **Monitoring** workspace, scroll through the list of folders and you should see your new overrides management pack listed here too. Most likely, you won't want to have your override folders cluttering up the **Monitoring** workspace, so you can easily hide them by clicking on the **View** menu from the navigation bar at the top of the screen, then selecting the **Show or hide views** option. From there, you can uncheck any folders that you don't wish to display as shown in *Figure 5.33*.

Figure 5.33: Hiding management pack folders from the Monitoring workspace view

The **Show or Hide views** option here will only hide the view from the logged on user and will not give the same restricted access to it that you get when configuring role-based access control permissions. This option also does not affect other users from seeing the folder through their own console session. If you want to create override management packs with no folder view at all, you could use PowerShell to create them and Microsoft's Russ Slaten has authored a handy script that will do this for you. You can download the script from the following link: http://tinyurl.com/opsmgrpowershellmps

Management pack dependencies

From time to time, you might encounter an issue similar to *Figure 5.34* when importing management packs that have a dependency on other management packs that must be imported first.

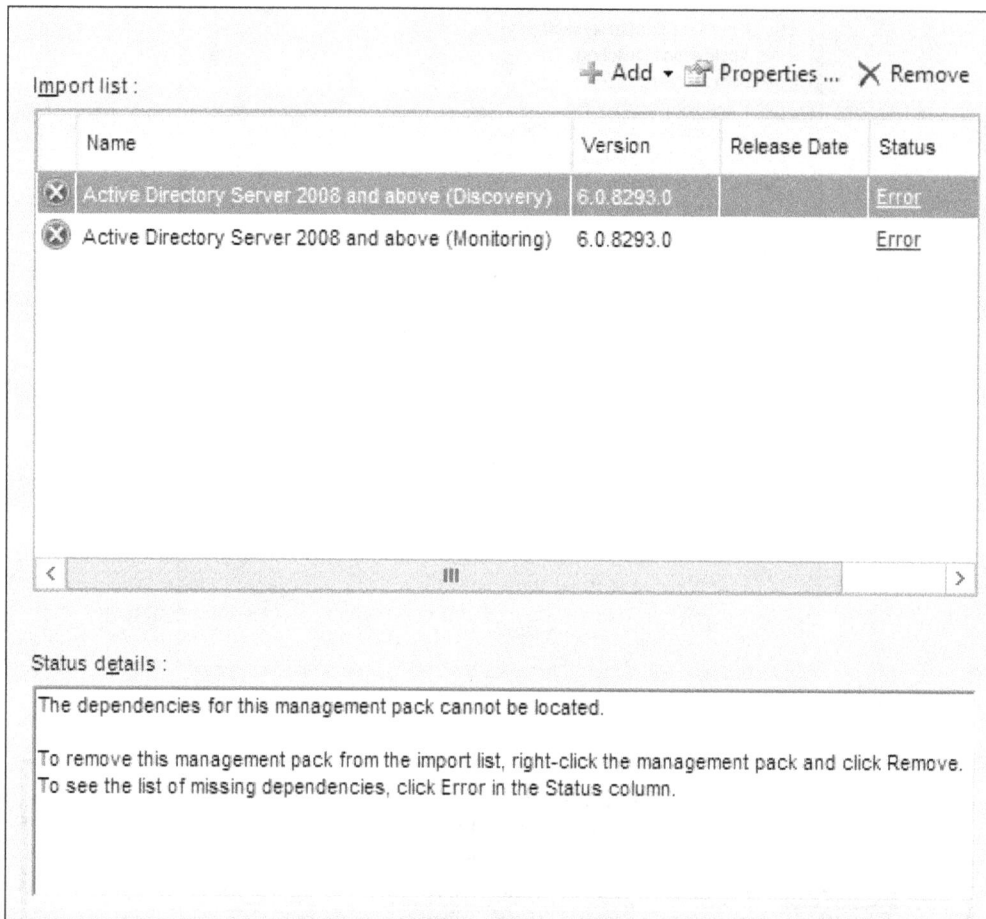

Figure 5.34: Management pack dependency check

Clicking on the **Error** link will open the **Import Management Pack Error** dialog box shown in *Figure 5.35*.

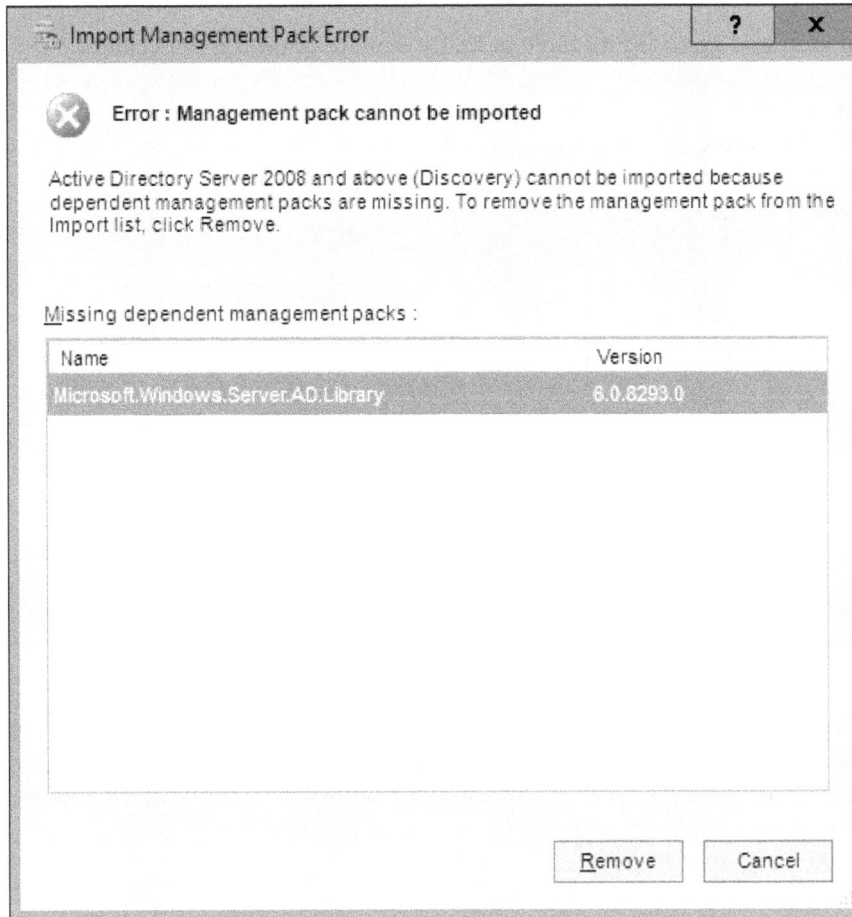

Figure 5.35: Identifying missing dependent management packs

If you only have the option to **Remove** a management pack here, then you will need to go back to the **Select Management Packs** dialog box, click on the **Add** button and search for the missing dependency on your local disk.

That's all well and good if you have actually downloaded the dependent management pack and know where to find it, but if the dependency is a Microsoft management pack, you can speed things up a little by clicking on **Yes** when you first see the **Online Catalog Connection** dialog box shown in *Figure 5.36*. You get this prompt the first time you click on the **Add from Disk** option at the **Select Management Packs** dialog box.

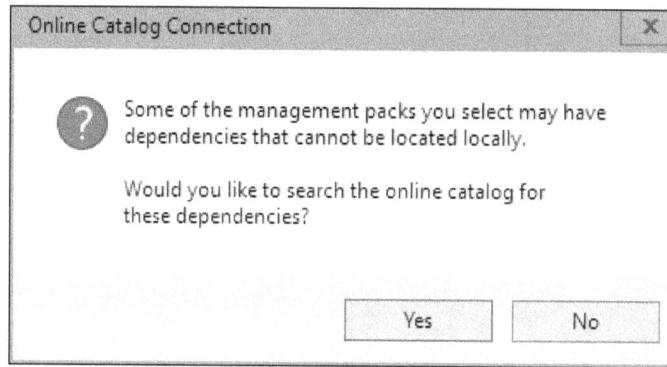

Figure 5.36: Searching the online catalog for missing dependencies

When you choose this option before importing your Microsoft management packs, the next time there's a dependency error detected, you'll be presented with an option to resolve the dependency and OpsMgr will then download the missing management pack from the catalog. *Figure 5.37* shows this in action.

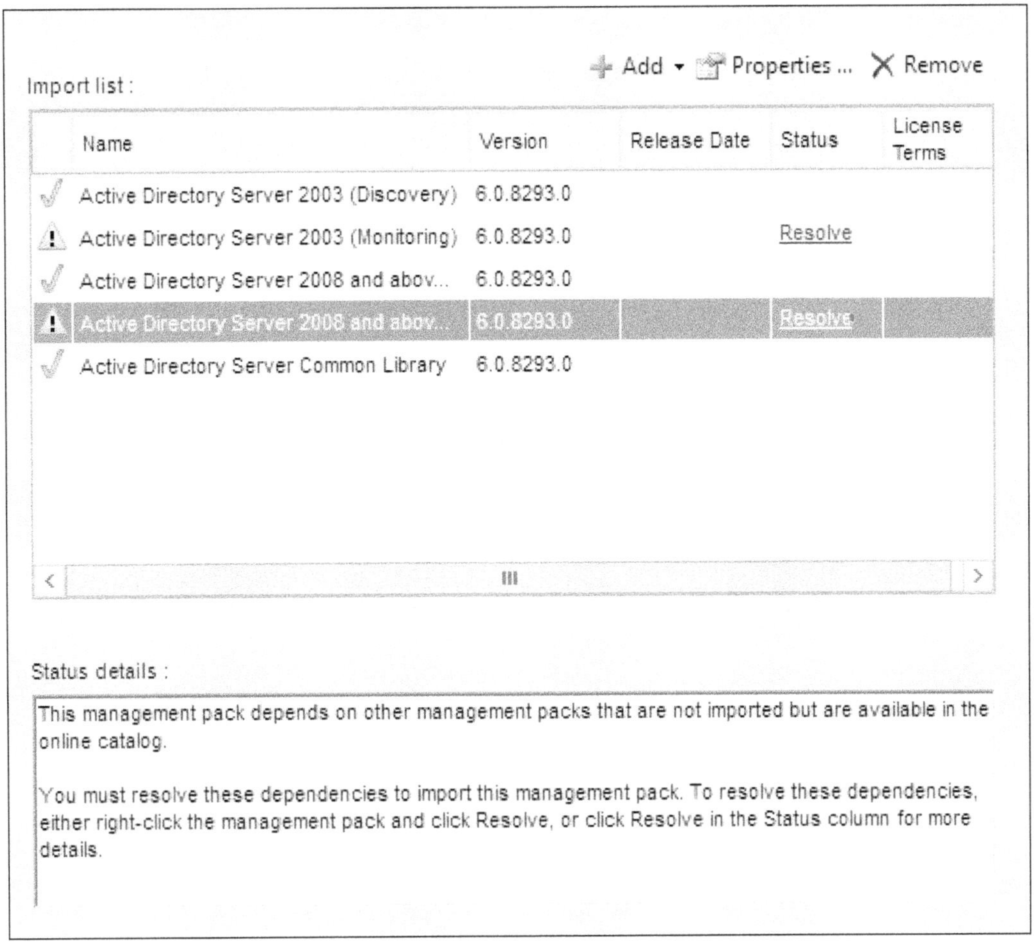

Import list :

+ Add ▾   Properties ...   ✕ Remove

	Name	Version	Release Date	Status	License Terms
✓	Active Directory Server 2003 (Discovery)	6.0.8293.0			
⚠	Active Directory Server 2003 (Monitoring)	6.0.8293.0		Resolve	
✓	Active Directory Server 2008 and abov...	6.0.8293.0			
⚠	Active Directory Server 2008 and abov...	6.0.8293.0		Resolve	
✓	Active Directory Server Common Library	6.0.8293.0			

< ❙❙❙ >

Status details :

This management pack depends on other management packs that are not imported but are available in the online catalog.

You must resolve these dependencies to import this management pack. To resolve these dependencies, either right-click the management pack and click Resolve, or click Resolve in the Status column for more details.

Figure 5.37: Resolving dependency errors

Verifying discoveries

When you've imported your management packs and created override management packs for customizations, you can check to see if the objects you want to monitor have been discovered.

To do this, open the **Monitoring** workspace, browse to the folder for your management pack and click on a state view. We'll use the **DC State** view of the **Microsoft Windows Active Directory** management pack shown in *Figure 5.38* to verify that the management pack discoveries have worked.

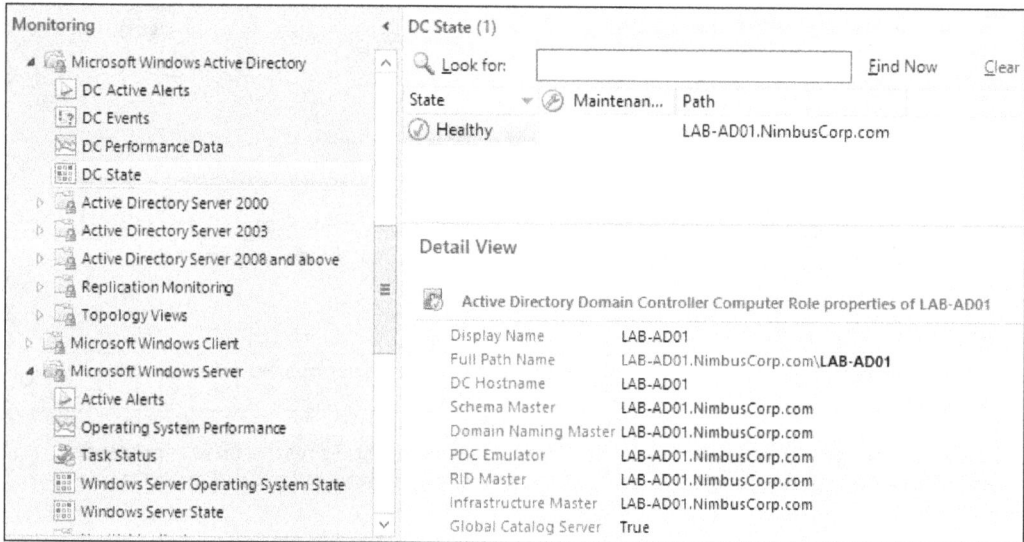

Figure 5.38: Verifying management pack discoveries

If you find that your discoveries haven't worked, make sure to revert back to the management pack guide (R.T.F.M. remember), to confirm if you need to enable a discovery rule first as some management packs have this disabled by default. Other discovery rules can take anywhere up to 24 hours to run and again, the management pack guide will confirm this for you.

Configuring Run As profiles

When imported, a lot of management packs create a new **Run As Profile** as a method of allocating scoped user account permissions to the objects the management pack monitors. Run As profiles can be managed in the **Administration** workspace under the **Run As Configuration** view. Here, you can create new Run As Accounts for both Windows and UNIX/Linux computers and then assign them to the Run As profiles for each management pack as required.

To configure the Run As Profile for the Microsoft Windows Active Directory management pack, follow these steps:

1. Browse to the **Administration** workspace, expand **Run As Configuration**, click on **Profiles** and then locate the **AD MP Account** profile shown in *Figure 5.39*.

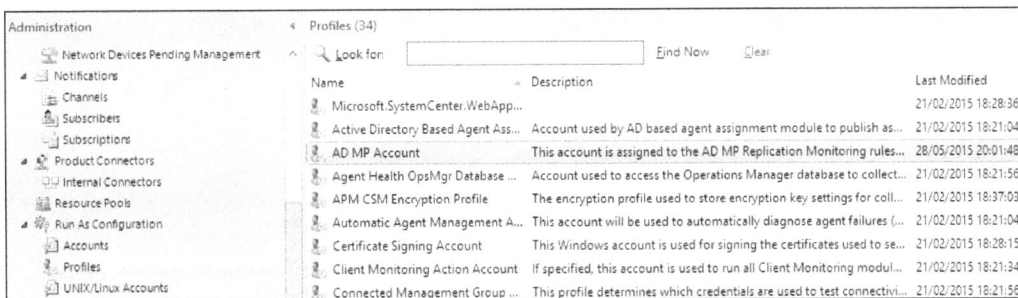

Figure 5.39: Selecting a Run As Profile to configure

2. Double-click on the profile to start the Run As Profile wizard and click on **Next** twice to bring you to the Run As Accounts dialog box.

3. Hit the **Add** button to open the **Add a Run As Account** dialog box, and then click on **New** to open the **Create Run As Account Wizard**. Click on **Next**.

4. At the **General Properties** dialog box, leave **Windows** selected as the **Run As account type**, then enter a display name and description for the new account as shown in *Figure 5.40* and click on **Next** to move on.

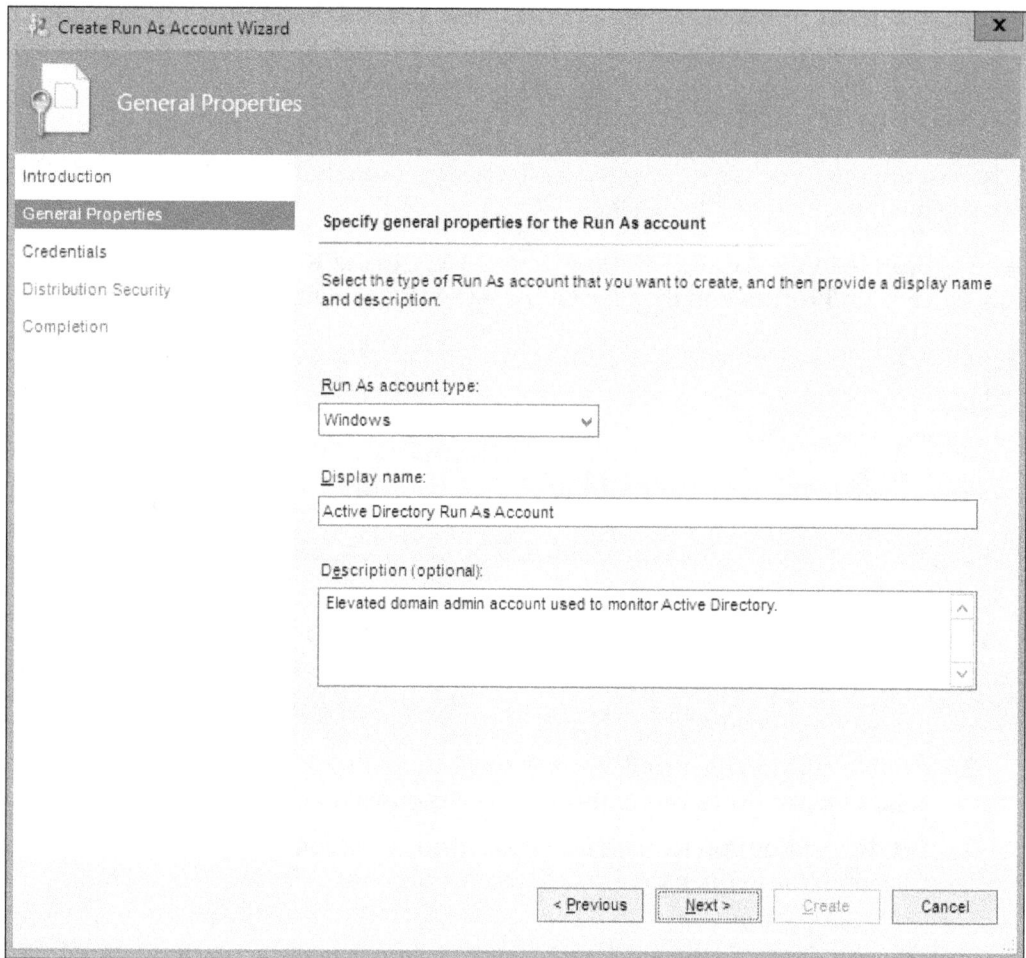

Figure 5.40: Configuring a Run As Account

5. At the **Credentials** dialog box, input a user name, password and domain for the **Run As Account** – remember, this account needs to have the relevant permissions to monitor Active Directory and in our example, we'll use the opsmgr_admin service account that we created in *Chapter 2, Installing System Center Operations Manager*. Click on **Next** to continue.

6. The **Distribution Security** dialog box presents two options for distributing the new account to – **Less Secure** and **More Secure**. Its best practice to always use the **More Secure** option here where you will be asked to manually select the monitored computers that this new Run As account will be targeted to. Click on **Create** to move on when you've made your choice, and then click on **Close** to exit the **Create Run As Account** wizard.

7. Back at the **Add a Run As Account** dialog box, you will see the **Run As account** field is now populated with your newly created Run As Account and you will now need to decide which objects this account will manage. As you can see in *Figure 5.41*, we've chosen to target our new account at the **Active Directory Domain Controller Computer Role**.

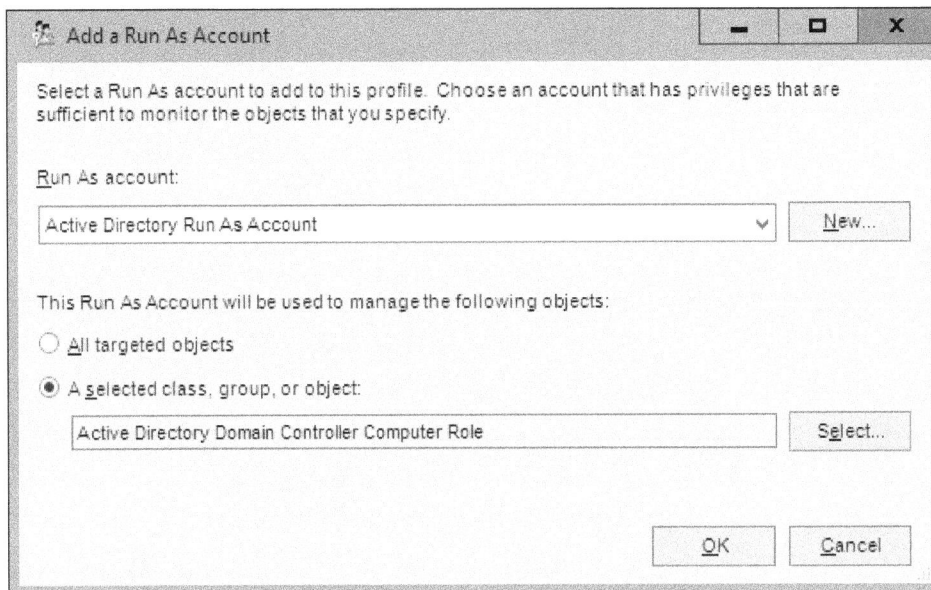

Figure 5.41: Targeting objects to monitor with your new Run As Account

8. Click on **OK** to add the Run As Account to the Run As Profile, then hit **Save**.

9. When the wizard completes successfully, you will be presented with the Completion dialog box where you can see a warning about credential distribution beside your new Run As Account shown in *Figure 5.42*.

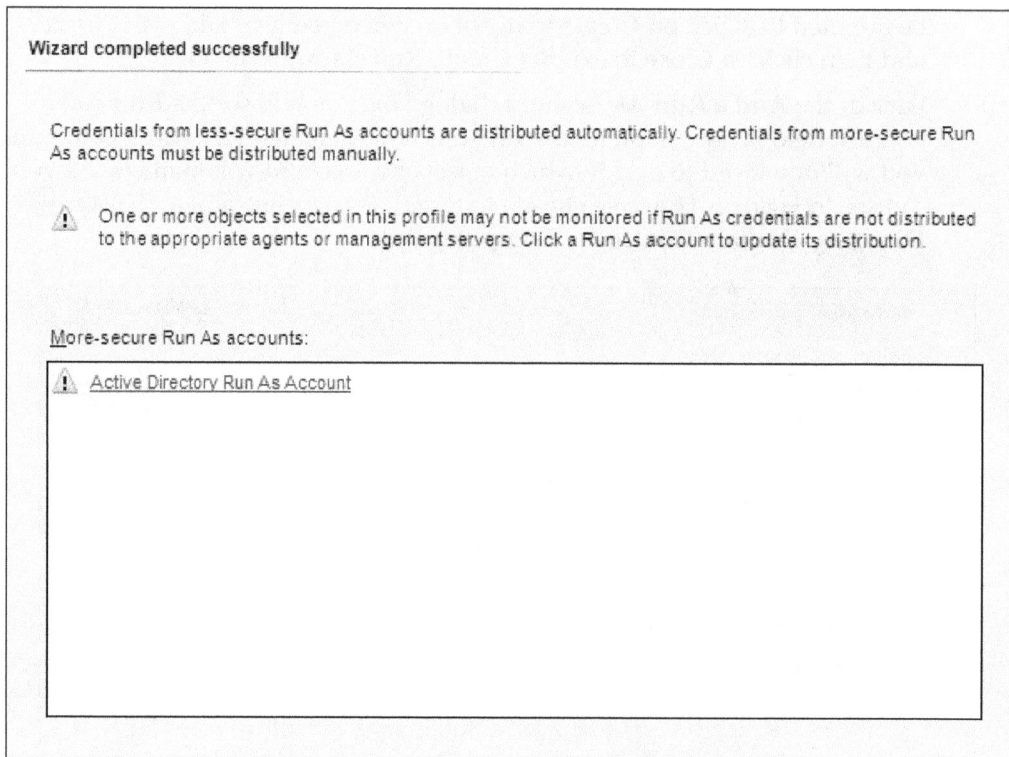

Wizard completed successfully

Credentials from less-secure Run As accounts are distributed automatically. Credentials from more-secure Run As accounts must be distributed manually.

⚠ One or more objects selected in this profile may not be monitored if Run As credentials are not distributed to the appropriate agents or management servers. Click a Run As account to update its distribution.

More-secure Run As accounts:

⚠ Active Directory Run As Account

Figure 5.42: Run As Account credential warning

10. Click on the Run As Account to open its properties and at the **Distribution** tab; you'll see the **More Secure** option you selected previously with no computers listed for distribution. Click on the **Add** button here to open the **Computer Search** dialog box where we can search for computers to distribute this new account to.

11. Search for the computers you want to distribute the account to (in this case we want to distribute to only Active Directory domain controllers), add them, and then click on **Close** to return to the **Distribution** tab. In *Figure 5.43* you can see the new account distributed to a domain controller using the **More Secure** option.

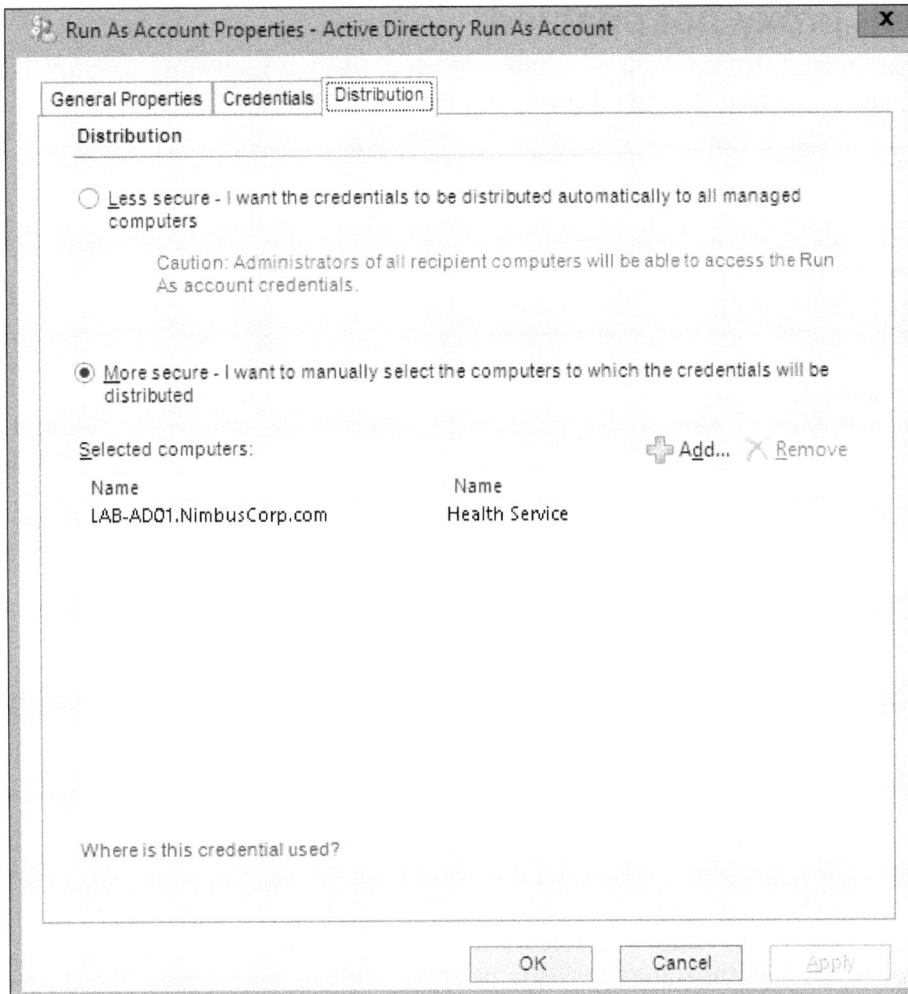

Figure 5.43: Configure the More Secure distribution option

12. Click on **OK** and hit the **Close** button to complete the Run As Profile configuration process.

Agent proxy not enabled

A common alert that you will see in the console soon after importing certain management packs is the **Agent proxy not enabled** one shown in *Figure 5.44*.

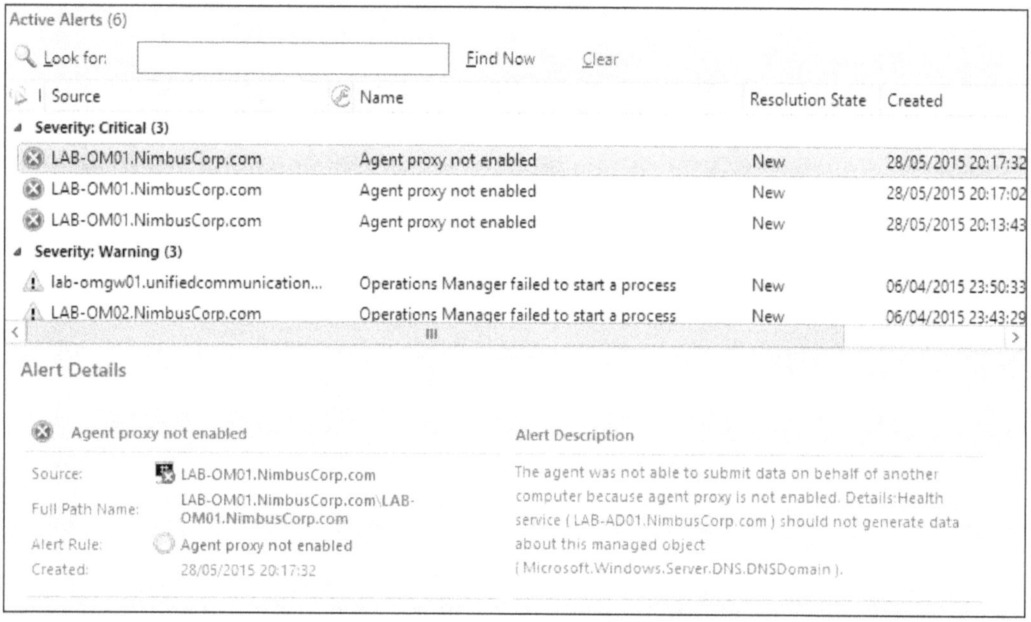

Figure 5.44: Agent Proxy Not Enabled alert

This alert indicates that the agent attempted to discover or generate data about an object but the Agent Proxy setting on the agent hasn't been enabled to allow this. Double-clicking on this alert and selecting the **Product Knowledge** tab will give you a detailed **Summary**, **Cause** and **Resolution** for it. The management pack guide will also indicate if this setting needs to be enabled on agents for monitoring the objects it's targeted at.

Here's what you need to do to enable Agent proxy for any agents that generate this alert:

1. In the alert description, note the name of the Health Service (agent) that generated the alert.

2. Browse to the Administration workspace, locate the agent in the **Agent Managed** view, double-click on it to open the agent properties, and then select the **Security** tab.

3. Check the box beside **Allow this agent to act as a proxy and discover managed objects on other computers** as shown in *Figure 5.45*.

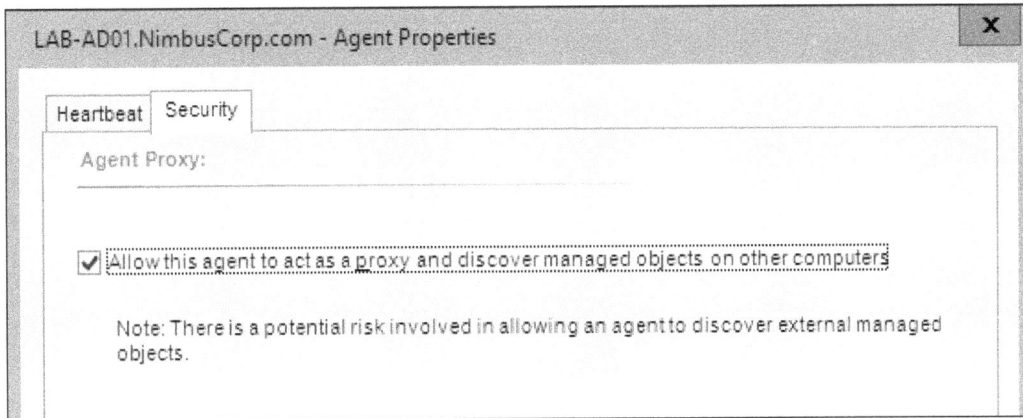

Figure 5.45: Enabling Agent Proxy

4. Click on **OK** to close the dialog box and close the **Agent proxy not enabled** alert in the **Monitoring** workspace (this was generated by a rule and won't close automatically).

5. After a short while, the objects that require this setting will start to be monitored.

Exporting unsealed management packs

Every now and again, you will need to export an unsealed management pack from OpsMgr (sealed management packs can only be deleted from the console and not exported) and the process to do so is simple and given as follows:

1. In the **Administration** workspace of the **Operation Console**, browse to the **Management Packs** view and locate the management pack that you wish to export (use the **Find** action from the toolbar for this if you've a large number of management packs deployed already).

2. Right-click on the management pack, then choose the **Export Management Pack** action as shown in *Figure 5.46*.

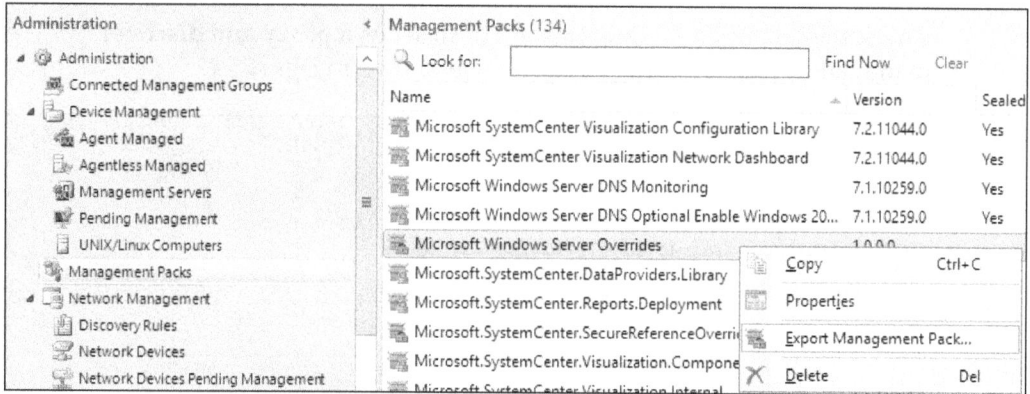

Figure 5.46: Exporting an unsealed management pack

3. At the **Browse for Folder** dialog box, select a location to store the exported management pack and click on **OK** twice to complete the export.

Deleting management packs

When you wish to delete a management pack, there's a couple of things to keep in mind. Firstly, if you need to re-import a management pack that you delete at a later stage, ensure you have either exported it (if it's unsealed) or you have a copy of the original sealed management pack downloaded and stored in a library. Secondly, ensure the management pack you want to delete has no outstanding dependencies on other management packs as this will block you from deleting until the dependent management packs are removed first.

Here's how to delete a management pack:

1. In the **Administration** workspace of the **Operation Console**, browse to the **Management Packs** view and locate the management pack that you wish to delete (use the **Find** action from the toolbar for this if you've a large number of management packs deployed already).

2. Right-click on the management pack, then choose the **Delete** action as shown in *Figure 5.47*.

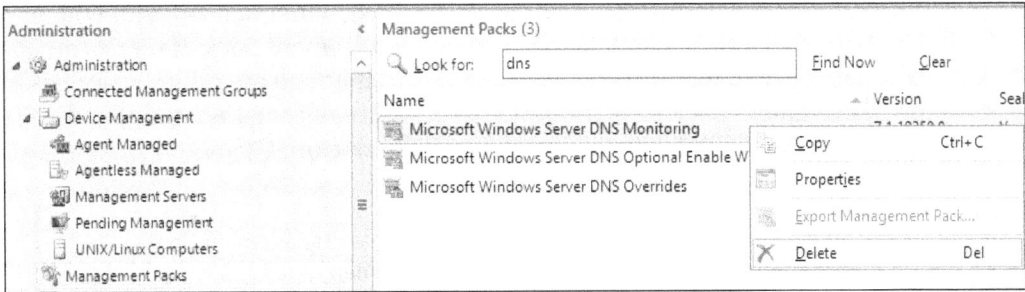

Figure 5.47: Deleting a management pack

3. If the management pack has any dependencies, you'll be presented with the **Dependent Management Packs** dialog box shown in *Figure 5.48*.

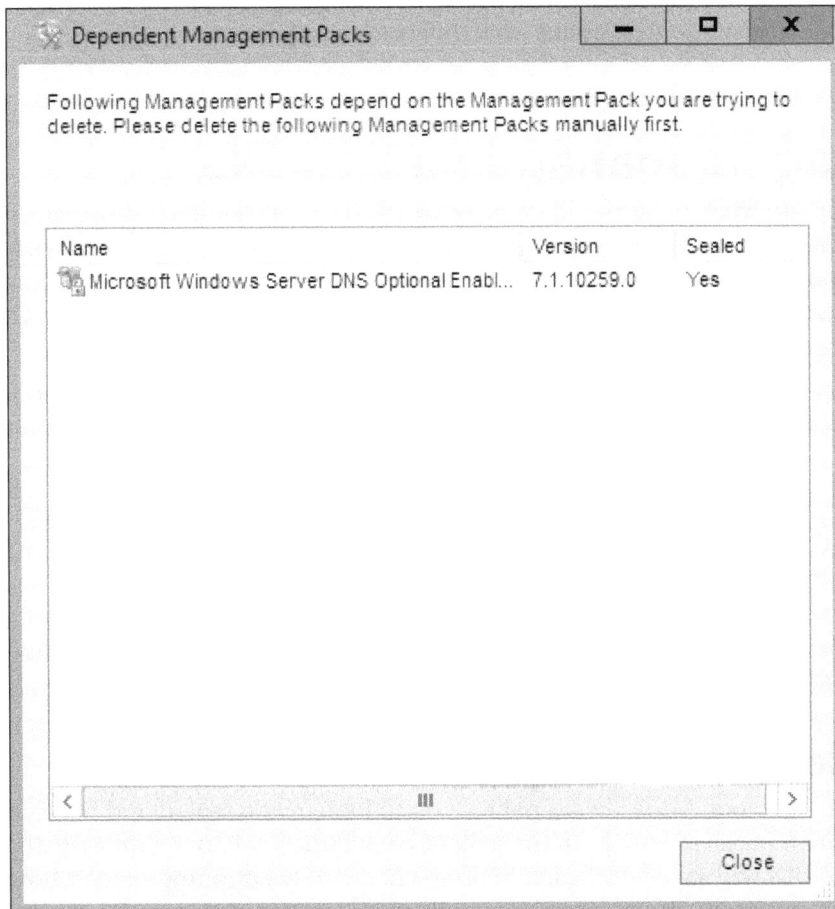

Figure 5.48: Dependent Management Packs dialog box

4. When all dependent management packs have been first deleted, you will then have the option to delete the original management pack. If there's no dependency, you will be prompted to confirm that you are happy to delete the management pack (this prompt is your final safety-net warning) and clicking on **Yes** will delete the management pack from OpsMgr.

> When you use the Operation Console to delete management packs, you are limited to only deleting one management pack at a time. In most cases, this won't be a problem, but if you wanted to delete multiple management packs at the same time, then you'll need to call on some PowerShell 'Kung-Fu' to help you out. The Remove-SCOMManagementPack cmdlet allows you to bulk-remove management packs. Cameron Fuller (System Center MVP) has written a very informative blog post with some great examples of how to use it at http://tinyurl.com/opsmgrbulkmpdelete.

Managing management packs

When you are working with management packs in OpsMgr, it's important to have the right tools and tricks to help simplify managing them. A few years back, I wrote a blog post (http://tinyurl.com/kgessentialtools) about some essential community management packs, tools and scripts to enhance your OpsMgr deployments and in this section we'll discuss some of these in more detail.

Boris's OpsMgr tools

Boris Yanushpolsky (Principal Program Manager, Microsoft) originally developed a set of tools to make the lives of OpsMgr 2007 administrators easier and a few years later, Daniele Muscetta (Senior Program Manager, Microsoft) gave those tools an update to ensure they could work with newer versions of OpsMgr.

You can download each of the tools explained in the following sections from http://tinyurl.com/opsmgrtools.

MP Viewer

A really useful tool, MP Viewer enables you to look inside sealed and unsealed management packs as well as management pack bundles. Having an easy and quick way to do this will save you heaps of time when you need to understand how a particular management pack has been authored. You can also save the results to an Excel or HTML file for further analysis. *Figure 5.49* shows the MP Viewer tool analyzing the Active Directory management pack.

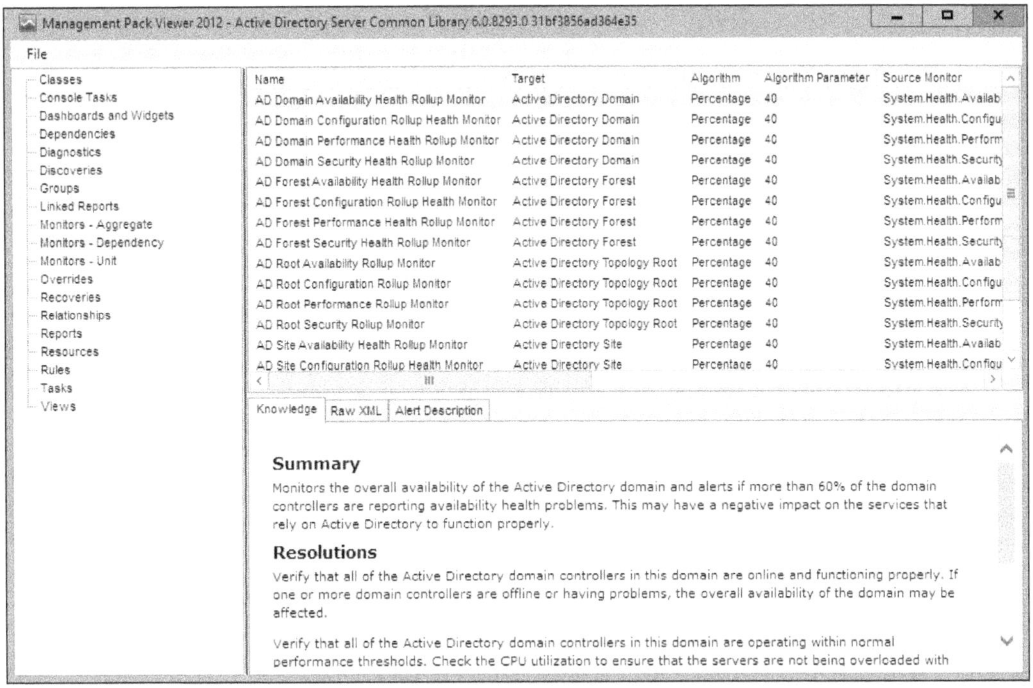

Figure 5.49: MP Viewer tool in action

> You can use the **Unseal/Unpack Management Pack** option from the MP Viewer **File** menu to quickly unseal a sealed management pack as a **.XML** file to a folder location of your choice for editing or reviewing.

Override Explorer

With this utility, you can connect to your Operations Manager environment and view all of the overrides contained in both sealed and unsealed MPs. An excellent feature of this tool is that you can quite easily move overrides between MPs – very useful if you've saved an override to the wrong location. It can also be used to change the target for your overrides or just delete them with the click of a mouse.

You can view overrides with a type-based view or a computers-based view. If you need to export any overrides, Override Explorer can easily export them to Excel or XML format. In *Figure 5.50* we can see the option to move an override to a different management pack using the **Move to different MP** action.

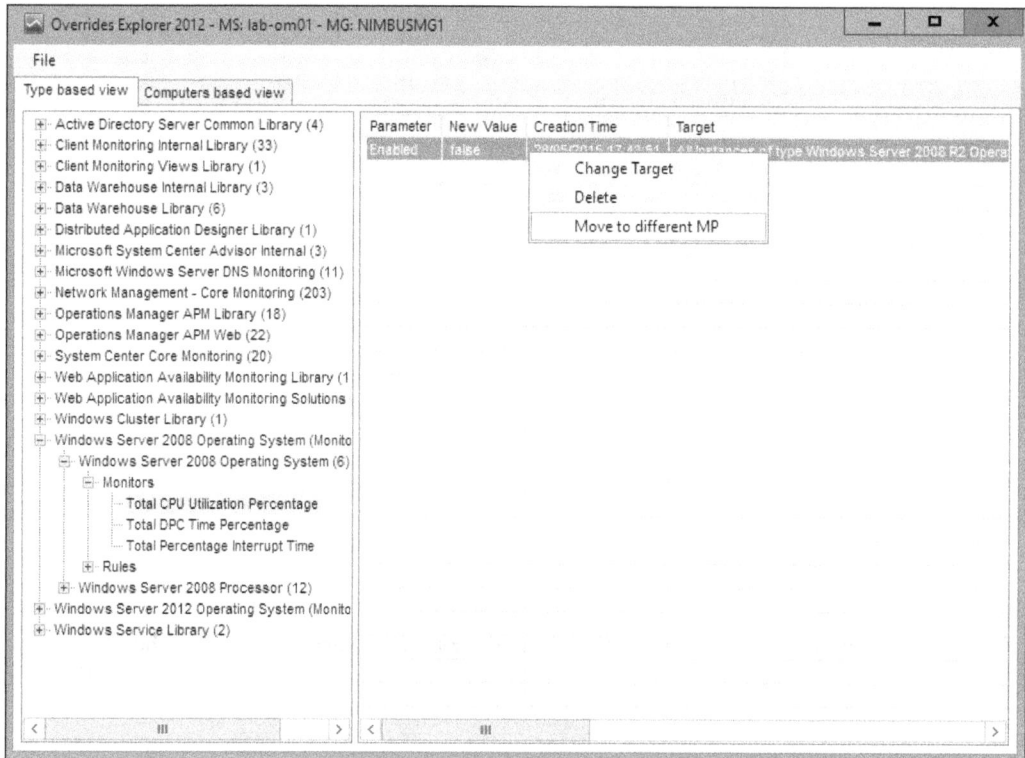

Figure 5.50: Moving overrides between management packs with Override Explorer

Proxy Settings

Another tool that I use regularly, Proxy Settings enables you to browse through all the groups within your Operations Manager environment and to easily bulk-enable or disable the Agent Proxy setting on the agents that you want. As we demonstrated in the *Importing management packs* section earlier, this setting can only be changed one agent at a time through the console and in an environment where you've deployed a lot of agents, this will be your go to tool.

In *Figure 5.51* we've targeted the All Windows Computers group where we can see that a number of our agents don't have the Agent Proxy setting enabled. All we have to do is highlight and right-click on all the agents with a Proxying Enabled setting of **False**, and choose the **Enable proxying** option.

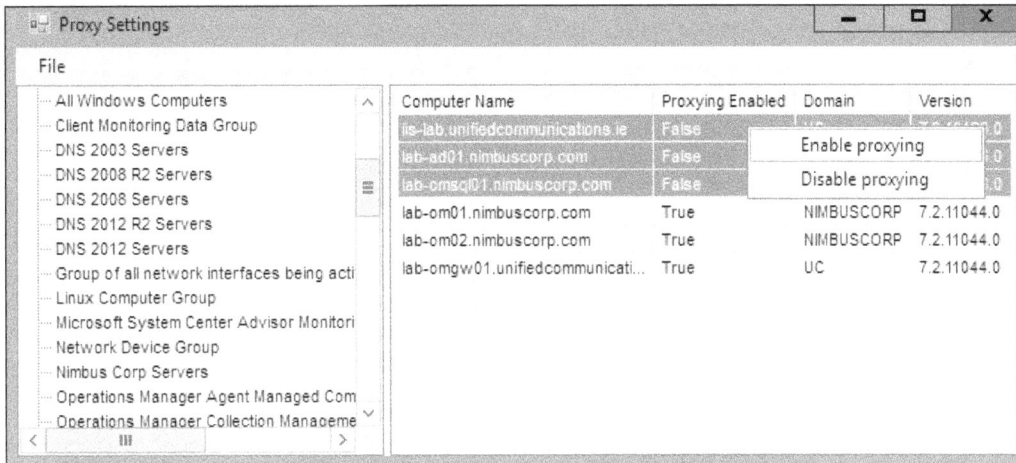

Figure 5.51: Bulk-enabling the Agent Proxy setting

> The Agent Proxy setting can also be configured for all agents with a setting of False using this one line of PowerShell (assuming you're using the Operations Manager Shell): Get-SCOMAgent | where {$_.ProxyingEnabled -match "False"} | Enable-SCOMAgentProxy

Override Creator

If you ever have a requirement to bulk-enable or disable rules, monitors or discoveries at the same time, then Override Creator will certainly come in handy.

A few years back, the old DHCP management pack was so badly written that to properly deploy it, you needed to disable over thirty rules and monitors before it went into production! Without this tool, that would have been an arduous task to take on and thankfully it made things a lot easier.

As you can see in *Figure 5.52*, you have the option to apply your overrides to all instances, a particular group or a single instance and you can also choose the unsealed overrides management pack they will be stored in.

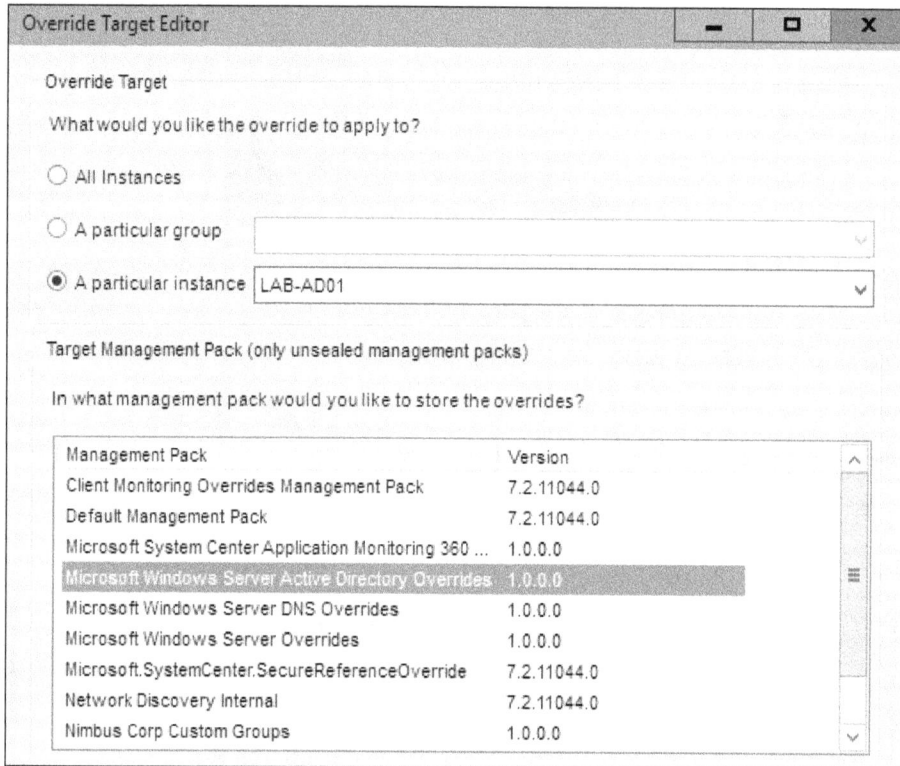

Figure 5.52: Bulk-managing overrides with Override Creator

Editing and authoring tools

As you become more familiar with management packs, you'll have the confidence to start editing existing ones and maybe even authoring your own. To do this though, you'll need the right tools to help you out. These are some of my favorites:

Notepad++

One of the best free XML editors around, Notepad++ is an invaluable tool when working with unsealed MPs in OpsMgr. The way it presents XML content makes it so much easier to read and work with in comparison to basic text editors such as the built-in Microsoft Notepad. This is one of the first tools I download for my OpsMgr deployments and you can get the latest version at `https://notepad-plus-plus.org/`

Silect MP Author

You can create new management packs through the Authoring workspace in the Operation Console but, unless you have a deep knowledge of management pack authoring, you'll find that functionality is basic at best. This is where Silect's MP Author tool can fill the gap.

With an intuitive user interface driven by wizards and some handy built-in templates for authoring management packs, it's no surprise that a large percentage of community management packs have been authored using this tool. No developer skills are required either and it's available as a free download at `http://www.silect.com/mp-author`

Visual Studio Authoring Extensions

If the thoughts of Visual Studio sends shudders down your spine, then the **Visual Studio Authoring Extensions** (**VSAE**) are not for you! If, on the other hand, you feel comfortable using Visual Studio (one of the most popular tools in the developer world), then VSAE will be right up your street.

VSAE is an add-in for Visual Studio that replaces the functionality of the no longer supported OpsMgr 2007 Authoring Console (not to be confused with the Authoring workspace within the normal Operations console) and the legacy OpsMgr 2007 Resource Kit tools.

You'll definitely need to ramp up some basic developer skills to become proficient in VSAE but when you do, you'll find that creating complex sealed and unsealed management packs becomes much easier than using other authoring tools.

The latest version of VSAE is available from the following link `http://www.microsoft.com/en-ie/download/details.aspx?id=30169`.

> If you're interested in authoring your own management packs using any of the tools mentioned in this chapter, first check out System Center Management Pack Authoring Guide for a deep-dive into everything you need to know. The guide is available as a TechNet Wiki page at `http://tinyurl.com/opsmgrmpauthorguide`.

Summary

In this chapter, we discussed the differences between sealed and unsealed management packs and explored their various elements. We also discussed the best places to locate and download Microsoft, third-party vendor, and community management packs. You learnt how to import, export, and delete management packs from within the Operation Console and we gave you the lowdown on the tools you need to manage, edit, and author.

In the next chapter, you will learn how to bring your network devices under monitoring using both SNMP and ICMP discoveries, along with gaining an understanding of the various dashboards and reports available to you for network monitoring.

6
Managing Network Devices

Network devices play a key role in our IT environments. Without them, we wouldn't have interconnectivity between our servers, clients, and applications and it goes without saying that their availability and performance should be monitored with OpsMgr.

Here, we will discuss the out-of-the-box network monitoring capability of OpsMgr and also learn how to discover and manage network devices using the **Simple Network Management Protocol (SNMP)** and **Internet Control Message Protocol (ICMP)**.

At the start of the chapter, we introduce the different vendors, devices, and protocol support available for network monitoring along with some requirements and considerations to get it up and running smoothly. After discovering some devices, we will demonstrate how to best use the different network monitoring dashboards to deliver purposeful visualizations based on performance and availability.

We'll finish the chapter with a rundown on the network monitoring reports available to you with this feature.

Here's what you will learn:

- Network monitoring overview
- Discovering network devices
- Managing network devices
- Working with dashboards
- Network monitoring reports

Network monitoring overview

The out-of-the-box network monitoring capability has been around since the original OpsMgr 2012 release and not much has changed since then. You have the ability to perform advanced monitoring of your network devices using **SNMP** or basic discovery and availability monitoring using **ICMP** (Ping).

If you use SNMP, you can get detailed monitoring of ports, interfaces, hardware, **virtual local area networks (VLAN's)**, and even **Hot Standby Router Protocol (HSRP)** groups. With ICMP, all you get is an indication that the IP address of the network device is responding to Ping requests with very little information about the underlying components or interfaces.

Although the network monitoring feature of OpsMgr won't have network administrators throwing out the specialist tools they use from the likes of Cisco, for the IT administrator and IT pro, it's still very useful when used in the overall context of IT service monitoring. This is because, regardless of the method used to discover and monitor your network devices, if it has an IP address, you can at least get an overview of its availability in OpsMgr and then visualize it as a part of your IT service models, reports, and dashboards.

Multi-vendor support

OpsMgr network monitoring works with any device that supports SNMP and also provides extended monitoring for devices that implement the management information base **(MIB) RFC 2863** and **MIB-II RFC 1213** standards.

Microsoft has published an Excel spreadsheet containing a list of nearly 850 devices from various vendors that are supported for extended monitoring in OpsMgr. If you need a reference for supported vendors, you can download the spreadsheet from the following link:

`http://tinyurl.com/opsmgrnetworkdevicelist`

This spreadsheet details the **SNMP Object ID (OID)** device type, vendor name, model, and the components that are supported for extended monitoring.

If a vendor's network device is supported for extended SNMP monitoring, then it will be discovered as a certified device in OpsMgr. A certified device can show monitoring information for components such as processor, memory, fans, and chassis.

A non-certified device discovered using SNMP will be registered as a generic device in OpsMgr. This means that you won't see advanced information on hardware components, but you'll still get interface and availability monitoring, which is more than you'd get from an ICMP monitoring.

Multi-device support

Some of the network device types that OpsMgr can monitor include switches, firewalls, load balancers, air-conditioning units, and UPS devices, basically anything that supports SNMP or ICMP. It's having this flexibility to bring all of the fabric components in your datacenter under monitoring that sets OpsMgr apart from other monitoring solutions.

Multi-protocol support

Three different versions of SNMP are supported for network device monitoring — SNMP v1, SNMP v2c, and SNMP v3. The first two versions are the most common and require an SNMP community string as a passphrase for the monitoring connection to be completed, whereas the newer SNMP v3 requires a unique username and password to be configured before you can monitor devices that support it.

For ICMP, the network devices are discovered and monitored using **Internet Protocol version 4 (IPv4)**; OpsMgr also provides support for **Internet Protocol version 6 (IPv6)** when running a recursive discovery on your network.

Additional SNMP monitoring options

If you find that your network devices are discovered as non-certified (generic) and you need to get more monitoring information from them, consider some of these options:

- Check with the device vendor to see if they have authored a management pack of their own to light up extra capabilities for their hardware.

- Author your own SNMP monitoring management pack. Admittedly, this is a big suggestion to make in a beginners guide book but if you're willing to give it a go, then System Center MVP Daniele Grandini has put together an excellent series of blog posts that will walk you through this process from start to finish. You can check out the series at `http://tinyurl.com/opsmgrsnmpauthoring`.

- If you've deployed OpsMgr 2016, then the new Network Monitoring Management Pack Generator tool (`http://tinyurl.com/opsmgrmpgenerator`) will help you author a custom SNMP management pack in no time. This tool (`NetMonMPGenerator.exe`) is located in the `\Server` directory of the OpsMgr 2016 install location and with it you can create a management pack that monitors network device components, such as Memory, Processors, Fans, Sensors, and Power Supplies. You can download the full user guide for this tool from `http://tinyurl.com/mpgeneratorguide`.

Requirements and considerations

There are a number of things that you'll need to consider before you dive in to monitor your network devices, such as resource pool design, firewall rules to be configured, management packs to be deployed, and user role requirements.

Resource pools

In the *Deploying UNIX/Linux agents* section of *Chapter 4, Deploying Agents* we showed you how to create a resource pool for cross-platform monitoring. You'll need to create additional resource pools when designing a network monitoring architecture for your OpsMgr environments, to ensure optimal performance and scalability.

For example, if you have a large number of network devices to be monitored, it's recommended that you assign a resource pool that includes management or gateway servers that will be specifically responsible for monitoring those devices. In this way, you can control the OpsMgr servers that are to be used to monitor agents and the ones that are exclusively monitoring your network devices.

The OpsMgr Sizing Helper tool provides guidance on how to design resource pools for network monitoring.

Firewall rules

The firewall rules between the OpsMgr servers listed in the network monitoring resource pool and the network devices that are being monitored need to be configured to allow bi-directional communication on ports 161 (UDP) and 162 (UDP) in order to support SNMP. Bi-directional ICMP traffic communication is also required to support devices that won't be monitored using SNMP. If the Windows Firewall is configured on your OpsMgr servers, then you will need to make the changes there too, to ensure that network monitoring communication is successful.

Management packs

All core management packs required for network monitoring are deployed automatically as a part of the original OpsMgr installation and these are listed as follows:

- SNMP Library
- Network Device Library
- Network Discovery Internal
- Network Management – Core Monitoring
- Network Management Library
- Network Management Reports
- Network Management Templates
- Windows Server Network Discovery
- Windows Client Network Discovery

The last two additional management packs in this list are needed to discover the network adapters of Windows server and client computers. It's also recommended to deploy the latest versions of core Microsoft operating system management packs to ensure that the network adapters on your agent-managed computers get monitored properly.

User roles

The user account that you use to create the network discovery rules must be a member of the **Operations Manager Administrators** user role, which is configurable in the User Roles section of the Administration workspace.

Understanding network discovery

The first step that you need to take to monitor and manage your network devices is to create a discovery for them. You will need to decide if you will use SNMP, ICMP, or both for discovery and then create a discovery rule to go out and find the network devices that you wish to monitor. The following sections will help you understand the process of network monitoring discovery in OpsMgr.

Discovery rules

A network discovery rule is created using the Computer and Device Management wizard from the Administration workspace of the OpsMgr console, and only one discovery rule can be assigned to each management server or gateway server. For this very reason, you will need to think about resource pool design and the placement of your management and gateway servers to ensure that they communicate with the network devices that they will be assigned to monitor.

Discovery rules can be configured to run automatically on a schedule or manually on-demand when you need to. The advantage for large organizations, of running a discovery rule on a schedule, is that you can ensure that any new network devices that have been brought online can be captured for monitoring with little effort (assuming all security requirements have been met) and any network devices that have been retired will be removed from monitoring automatically.

Discovery types

There are two types of discovery rules that you can configure – **Explicit** and **Recursive**. Here's an explanation of both.

Explicit discoveries

An explicit network discovery rule will only attempt to discover the network devices that you explicitly specify in the wizard by IP address or FQDN. Once all the prerequisites for discovery have been met and a device has been successfully accessed, monitoring will be enabled for it and any devices that cannot be successfully accessed will be placed in the Network Devices Pending Management view for review.

An explicit discovery rule can be configured to discover and access devices using SNMP, ICMP, or a combination of them both.

Recursive discoveries

With a recursive discovery, you can first explicitly specify one or more network devices and after they are discovered OpsMgr will perform a scan to discover any other connected network devices using the **Address Routing Protocol (ARP)** table, IP address table, or topology MIB of the initially discovered devices. This type of discovery grows the network map and presents all the applicable devices to you for monitoring.

Similar to the explicit discovery rule, recursive discovery can also be configured to discover and access devices using SNMP, ICMP, or both. IPv6 addresses can also be identified, however; the initial discovered device must use an IPv4 address.

With recursive discovery, you can also create a filter by using properties, such as the device type, name, and **object identifier (OID)** to give more control over what is or isn't discovered.

DNS resolution of network devices

When planning your network monitoring designs, pay careful attention to the DNS resolution of your network devices. A common mistake people make when bringing their network devices under monitoring is to just use IP addresses to identify them and as a result, when OpsMgr is finished discovering the devices, they will display within the console as a list of IP addresses instead of a descriptive DNS name.

When discovering devices, OpsMgr uses a naming algorithm where it attempts DNS resolution from the following sources – where the first one in the list to succeed becomes the name of the device:

- Loopback IP
- sysName
- Public IP
- Private IP
- SNMP Agent IP

To ensure your network devices are discovered with useful DNS names, you will need to put in some work either on your corporate DNS servers by creating 'A' records for each network device or by creating custom entries on the local 'hosts' file for each OpsMgr server that will discover and manage your network devices.

> If you decide to use custom entries in your local 'hosts' file to support DNS name resolution of your monitored network devices, remember to update the hosts file on each management and gateway server that are members of the network monitoring resource pools. If you don't do this, then there's a possibility that some network devices will only be discovered with their IP address.

Run as accounts

For network device discovery to be successful, a Run As account needs to be configured in OpsMgr with credentials that match the relevant access and security policies of the device to be monitored.

For SNMP v1 and SNMPv2 devices, a passphrase in the form of a community string is required and for SNMPv3, access credentials in the form of a username and password are needed. Read-only or read-write permissions can be configured on network devices to control how much interaction OpsMgr has with them and in nearly all cases, read-only will be sufficient.

The community string or access credentials must first be configured on the network device by someone with the relevant permissions to do so. It's useful to discuss this requirement with network administrators before you deploy OpsMgr as this step has the potential to become a time-consuming task if there's a lot of network devices to be configured.

Run as profiles

During installation, two new network monitoring Run As profiles are automatically created. These profiles are used specifically for SNMP discoveries and are defined in the following table:

Profile Name	Description
SNMP Monitoring Account	Used for SNMPv1 and SNMPv2 monitoring.
SNMPv3 Monitoring Account	Used for SNMPv3 monitoring.

The Run As accounts that you create or specify for network device discovery are automatically assigned to the appropriate SNMP Monitoring Run As profile.

Discovery stages

When a discovery rule kicks off, it will run through the following three stages:

Probing

This is the first discovery stage; here, the management server attempts to contact a device using the specified protocol (SNMP, ICMP or both) and uses the methods outlined in the following table:

Type	Description
SNMP Only	Successful discovery if an SNMP GET message is processed.
ICMP Only	Successful discovery if it can Ping the network device.
SNMP and ICMP	Successful discovery only if both protocols are processed.

Processing

When the Probing stage is completed, OpsMgr processes all the information returned from the device and maps out its components, such as ports and interfaces, memory, processors, VLAN membership, and HSRP groups.

Post-processing

At the final post-processing stage, OpsMgr correlates the network device ports to the servers that the ports are connected to. It inserts all relevant items into the Operational database and associates Run As accounts to each network device.

After the three discovery stages are complete, the resource pool that you've specified for network monitoring in the discovery rule configuration will begin to monitor the discovered network devices.

Discovering network devices

Now that you have an understanding of the discovery process, it's time to monitor some network devices and this section will walk you through the process. Before you begin though, ensure that all the previously discussed requirements are in place and confirm that the IP addresses or DNS names of your network devices are correct.

> If you're working through the steps in this book in your lab and you don't have any network devices to monitor, then take a read through Cameron Fuller's blog post on using the free and very useful Xian SNMP Device Simulator tool from Jalasoft. This tool gives you the ability to simulate network devices using SNMP v1, v2c and v3 authentication. http://tinyurl.com/snmpsimulator.

Here's what you need to do to begin monitoring your network devices:

1. From the **Administration** workspace in the OpsMgr console, expand the **Network Management** view.

2. Right-click on **Network Management**, then click **Discovery Wizard** as shown in *Figure 6.1* (you can also choose to click on the **Discovery Wizard...** link located above the Wunderbar).

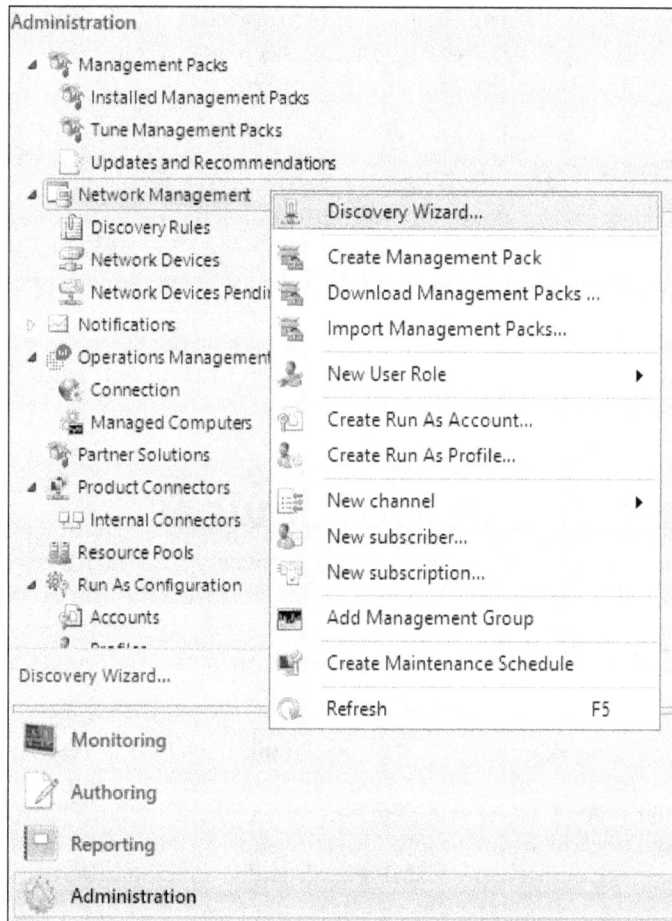

Figure 6.1: Opening the Discovery Wizard

3. From the Computer and Device Management Wizard, select the **Network Devices** option as shown in *Figure 6.2*, then click **Next** to continue.

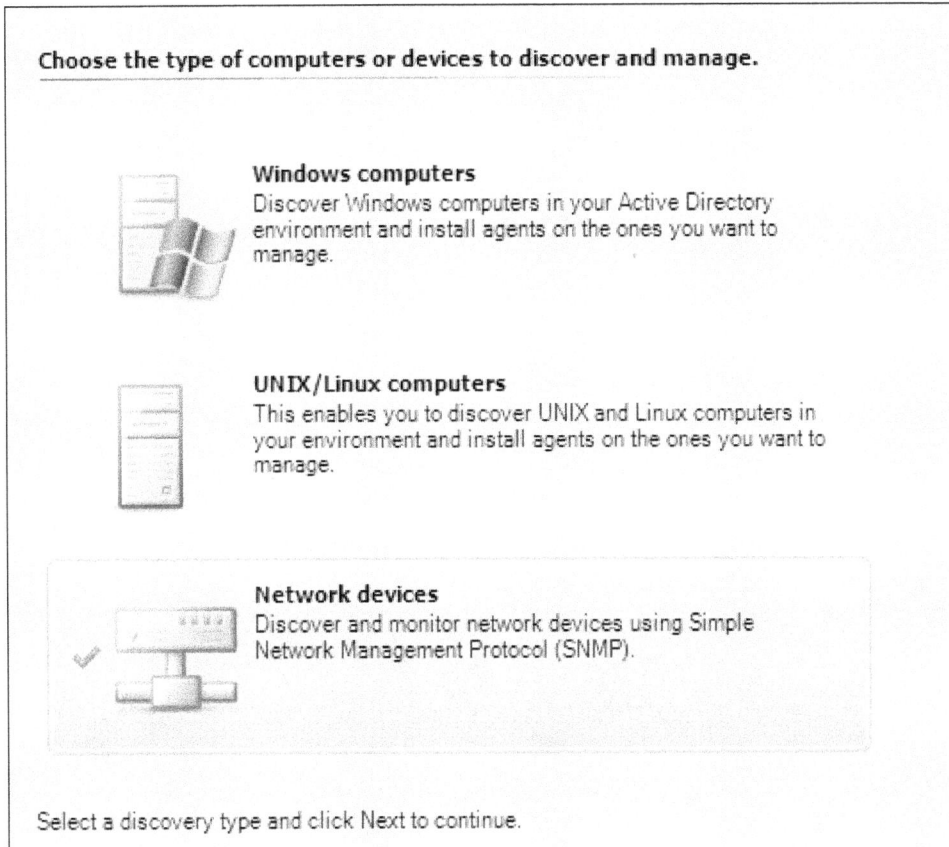

Figure 6.2: Choosing the Network Devices wizard

4. At the **General Properties** dialog box, enter a name and a description for the discovery rule, select the management server or gateway server that will run the discovery and then choose a resource pool created specifically for network monitoring as shown in *Figure 6.3*. Click **Next** to move on.

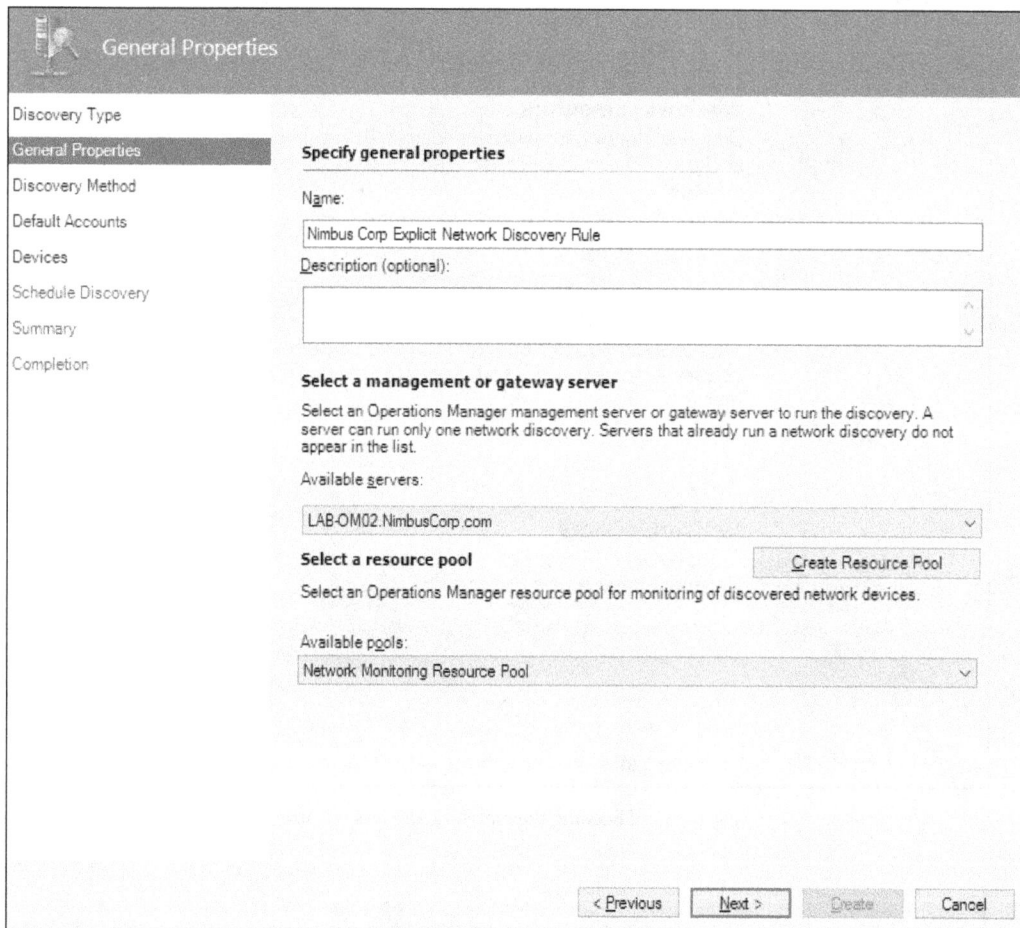

Figure 6.3: Configuring the discovery rule

5. From the **Discovery Method** dialog box, select the discovery type you want to use, as shown in *Figure 6.4*, we'll choose the **Explicit discovery** option, then click **Next** to continue.

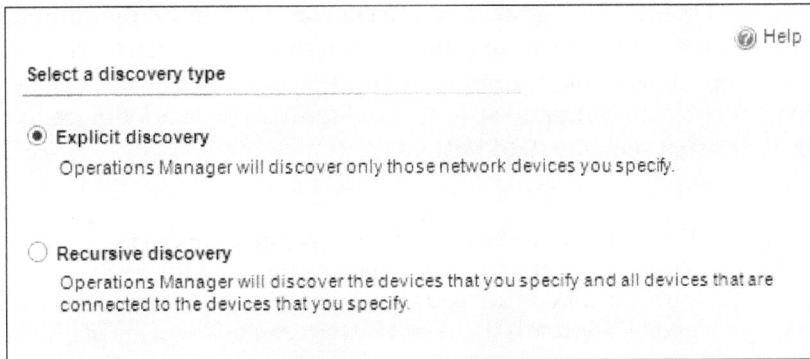

Figure 6.4: Choosing a discovery type

6. In the **Discovery Settings** dialog box, you can create a new SNMP v1/ v2c **Run As** account or use an existing one. If you use different SNMP community strings on different network devices, then you'll need to create separate Run As accounts for each device. *Figure 6.5* shows an example of multiple Run As accounts being selected for a network discovery. Click **Next** to continue.

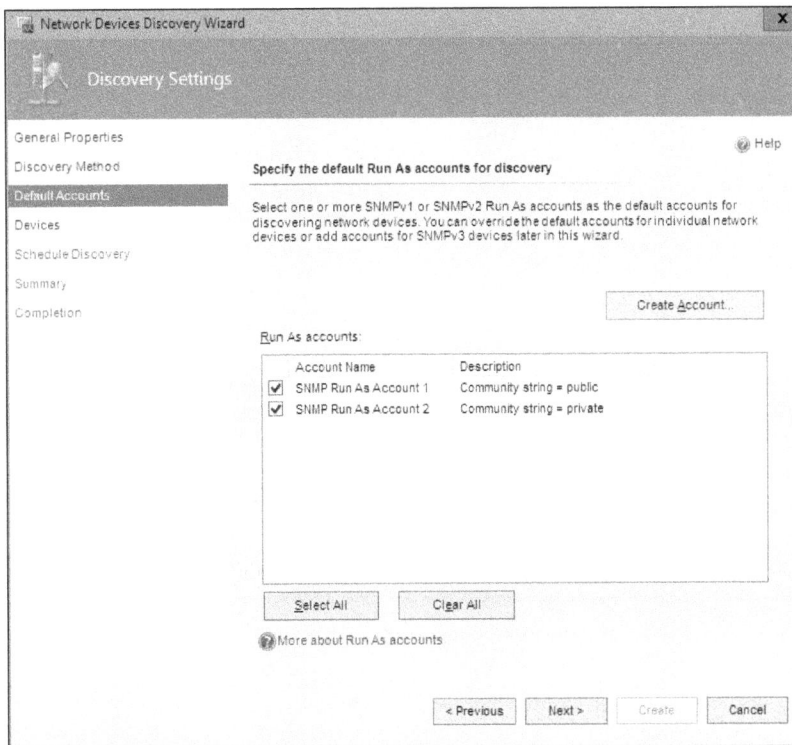

Figure 6.5: Specifying Run As accounts

7. From the **Devices** dialog box you can choose to either hit the **Import** button to import a text file containing the IP addresses of your network devices (very useful when you have more than a few devices to monitor), or you can click the **Add** button to specify an individual network device. For this example, we'll click the **Add** button.

> If you choose the **Import** option here, then you can use a simple .txt or .csv file containing the IP addresses of each network device you wish to monitor. Make sure that each IP address is listed in its own separate line in the file.

8. In the **Add a Device** dialog box, input an IP address or DNS name for your network device, choose which access mode you wish to use (SNMP, ICMP or both), select the SNMP version you wish to use (you can configure an SNMP v3 account at this point if you wish), then leave the **Use selected default accounts** option enabled, as shown in *Figure 6.6* and hit **OK**.

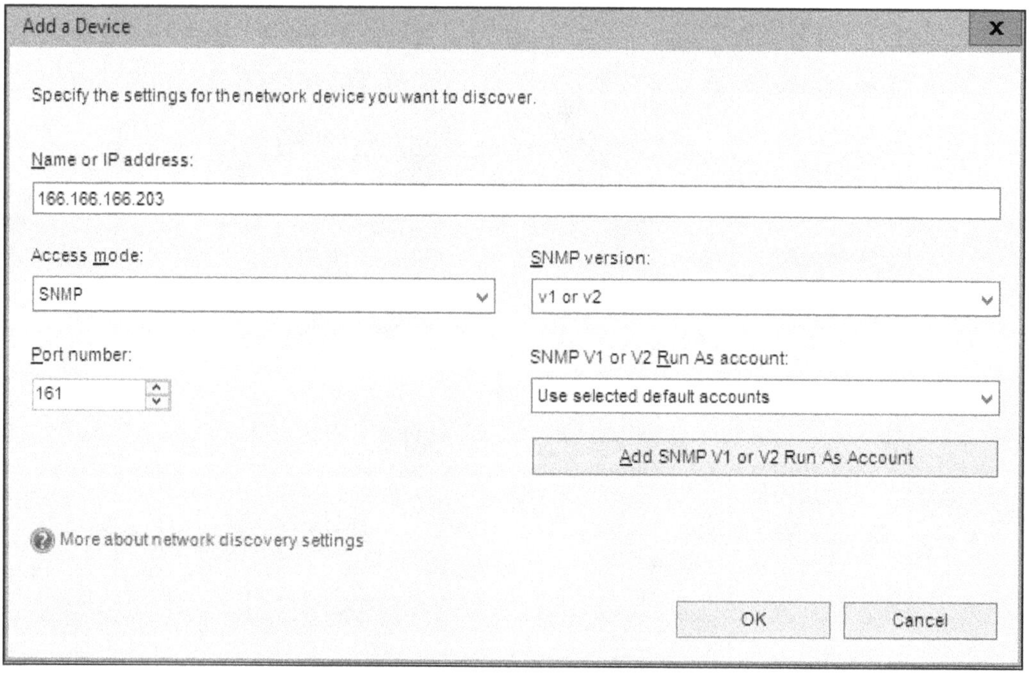

Figure 6.6: Configuring discovery settings

> When configuring the Access Mode setting for a device, be aware that if you leave it as the default ICMP and SNMP option, then both access types must succeed before proceeding. This means that if ICMP can't Ping the device or SNMP can't connect, then the discovery fails. This is useful to know in case you have an internal firewall policy that blocks ICMP (Ping) traffic. In most cases, it's best to choose either one or the other and not both here.

9. In *Figure 6.7* you can see some network devices specified and if you want to modify the number of retries and timeout thresholds, you can click the **Advanced Discovery Settings** button now. When you're happy enough to move on, click **Next**.

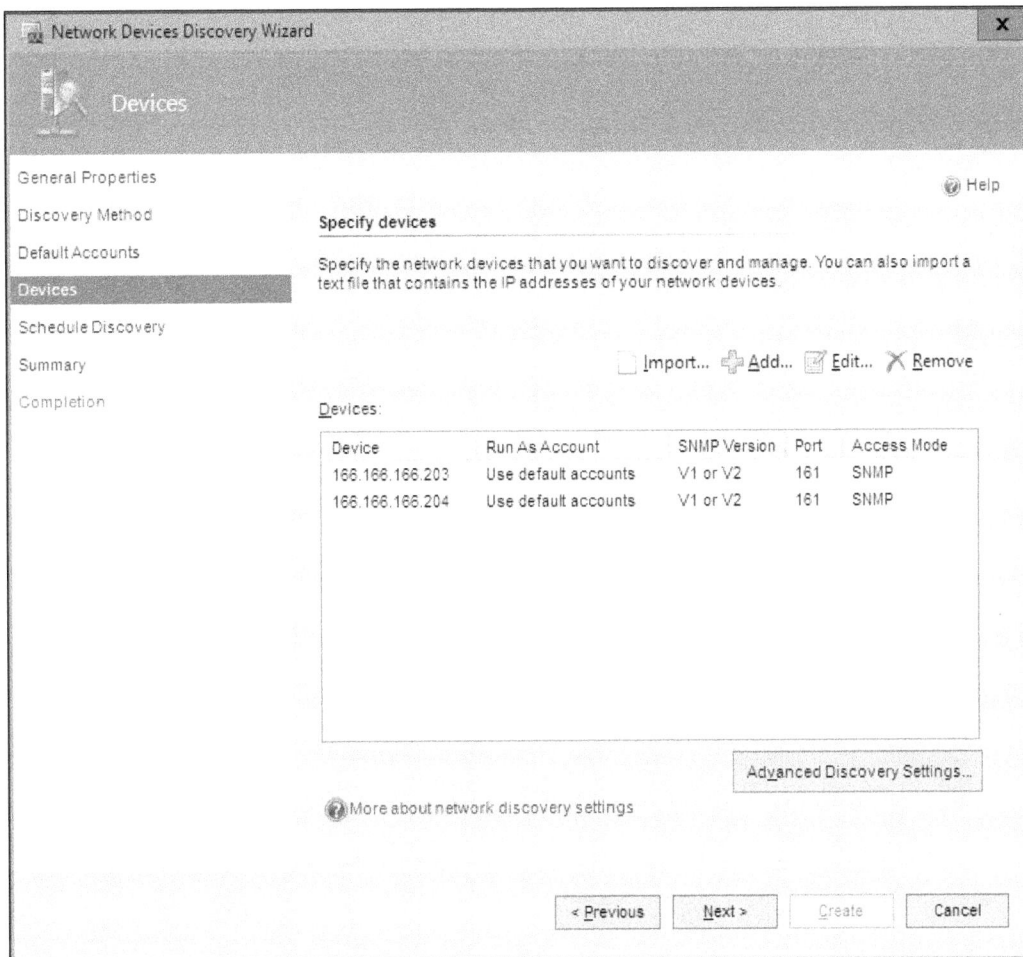

Figure 6.7: Configuring discovery settings

10. In the **Schedule Discovery** dialog box, choose to run the discovery rule on a schedule, or to just run it manually. Running the discovery rule on a schedule can be useful if you work in an environment where network devices are added and removed on a regular basis or it can also be helpful if you want to minimize discovery traffic during office hours. As shown in *Figure 6.8*, we'll choose to run our discovery rule manually.

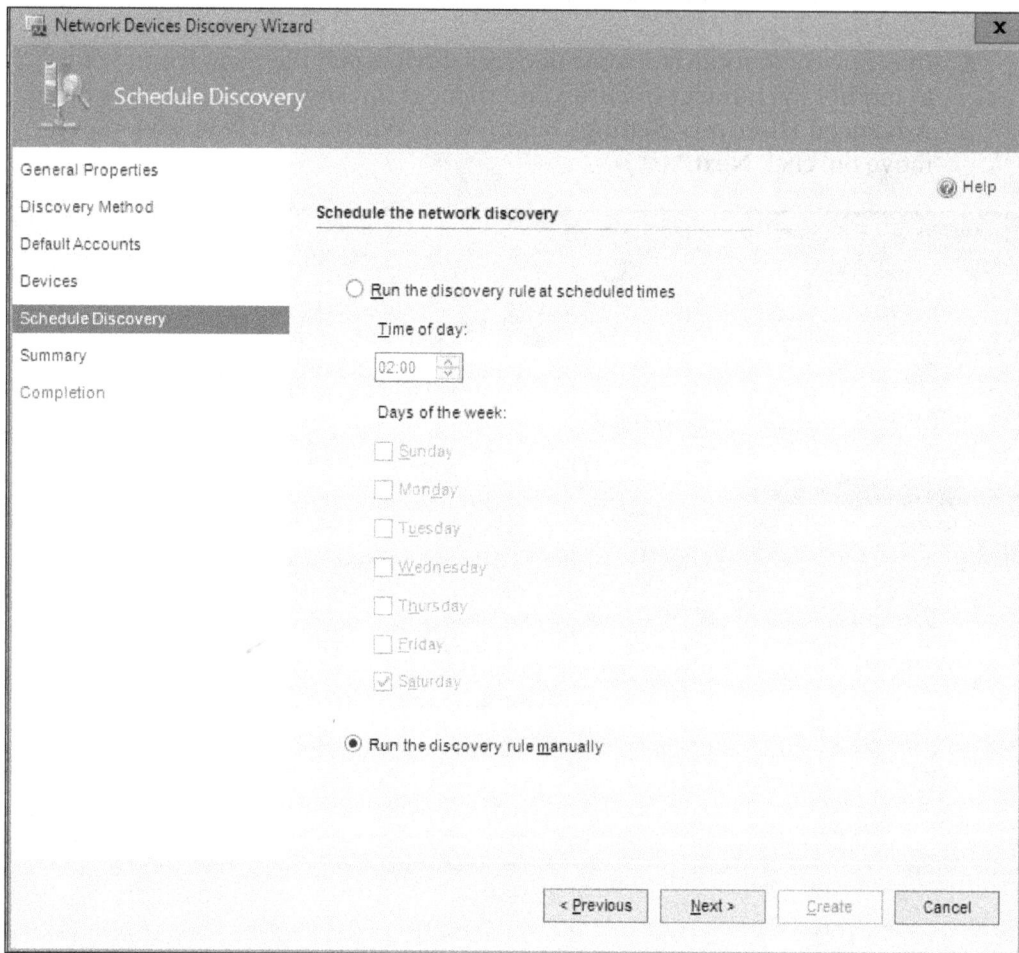

Figure 6.8: Choosing when to run the discovery rule

11. Click **Next** to move on; at the **Summary** dialog box, hit the **Create** button to create your new discovery rule.

12. If you see a warning pop up indicating that you need to distribute the new Run As accounts to the management server, click **Yes** to do so before clicking on the **Close** button to close the wizard and run the discovery rule automatically.

13. When the discovery rule is finished processing, you should be able to see the number of network devices you specified show up in the **Last Discovered** column as shown in *Figure 6.9*.

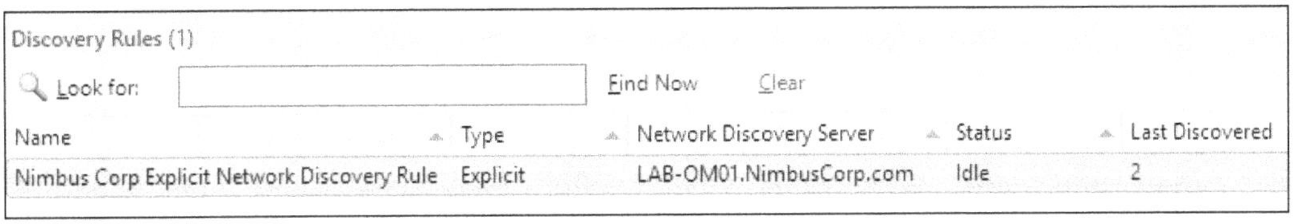

Discovery Rules (1)				
Name ▲	Type ▲	Network Discovery Server ▲	Status ▲	Last Discovered ▲
Nimbus Corp Explicit Network Discovery Rule	Explicit	LAB-OM01.NimbusCorp.com	Idle	2

Figure 6.9: Successful processing of a discovery rule

Network Device Discovery Failure

From time to time, it's not uncommon to have a device (or a number of devices) fail to be discovered. This can be a problem if you don't know where to find a list of these failed devices. In this instance, the failed device or devices will be listed in the **Network Devices Pending Management** view from within the Network Devices section of the Administration workspace.

Once you've located the failed devices, you can use one of these options to try to rediscover them again:

- Right-click on the failed device from within the **Network Devices Pending Management** view and then click **Submit Rediscovery**.

- Rerun the discovery rule by right-clicking on the rule and selecting the **Run** option.

Managing network monitoring

When network devices have been discovered, you can see a list of them from the Network Devices view under **Network Management** in the **Administration** workspace as shown in *Figure 6.10*.

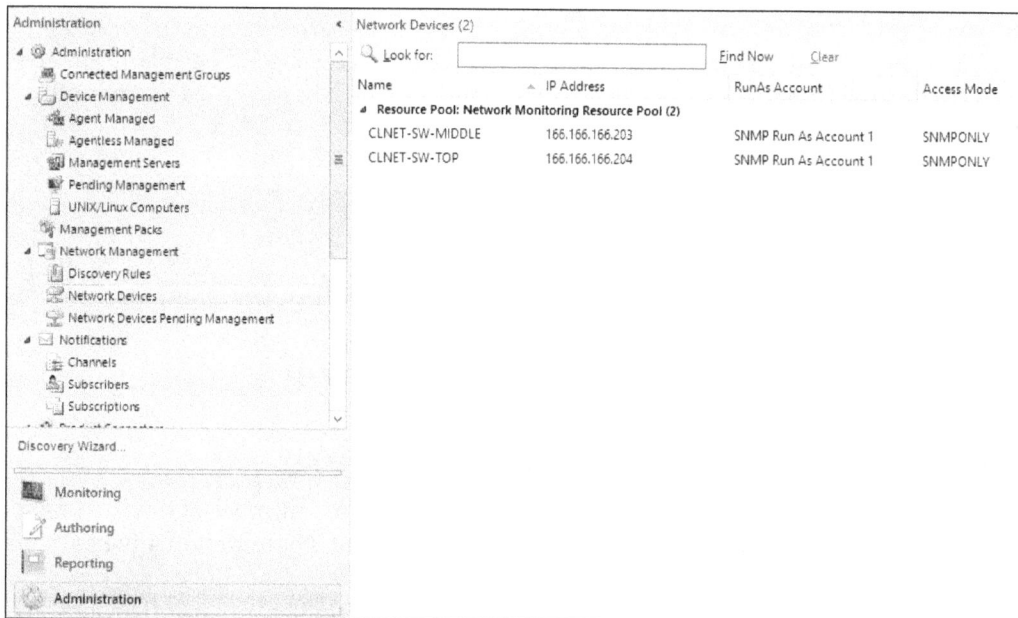

Figure 6.10: Viewing a list of discovered network devices

If you've configured the DNS resolution for your network devices, you'll see a DNS name listed alongside the IP address, the Run As account, and access mode used by the discovery rule. Although this information is useful, managing network devices from here is quite limited compared to what you can do from within the **Network Monitoring** folder located in the **Monitoring** workspace of the console.

> You can delete a monitored network device from OpsMgr by right-clicking on the discovered device from the **Network Devices** view of the Administration workspace and then clicking on the **Delete** option.

Network monitoring folder

The **Network Monitoring** folder is available from within the **Monitoring** workspace as soon as you install OpsMgr (it's a component of one of the management packs we listed earlier in the *Requirements and considerations* section) and as you can see from *Figure 6.11*, it contains alert views, state views, performance views, and dashboards to help you manage your devices.

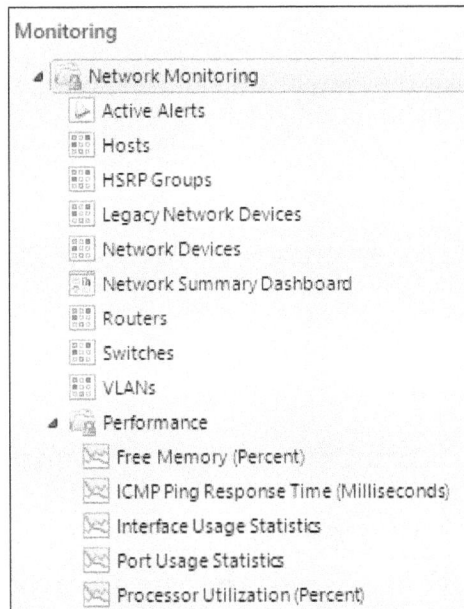

Figure 6.11: Network Monitoring folder

The following steps will show you how easy it is to obtain information about a particular network device that OpsMgr is monitoring:

1. Expand the **Network Monitoring** folder from the **Monitoring** workspace and click the **Network Devices** view.

2. Select a network device from the central **Network Devices** state-view pane to get a detailed view of information on the device as shown in *Figure 6.12*. Notice this device has been discovered as **Certified**, meaning we have extended monitoring of it when using SNMP.

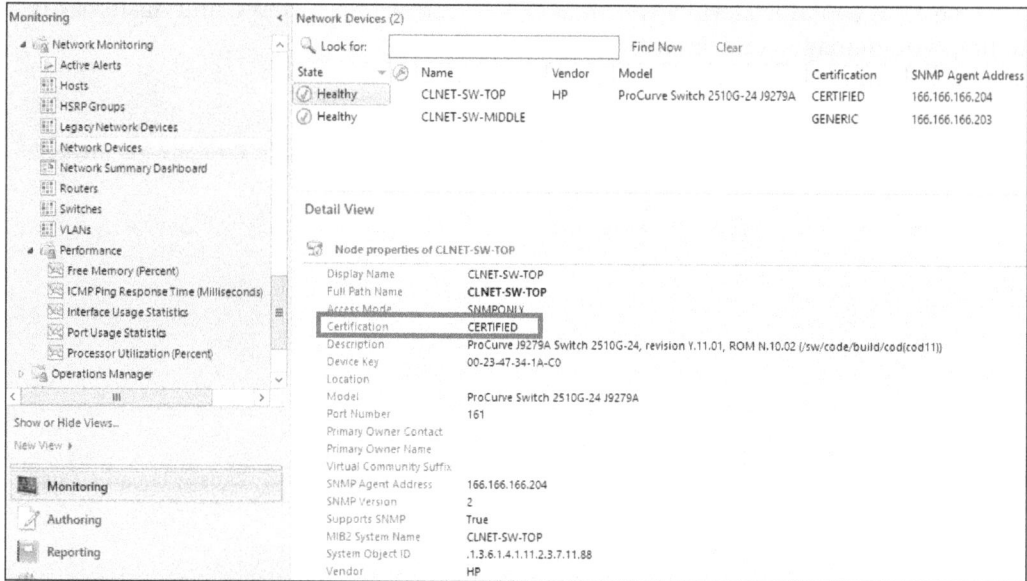

Figure 6.12: Detailed information and state view

3. Now, right-click the device, select **Open** from the context menu, then click **Diagram View** and click down a level in the diagram to get a visual of some of the components that are being monitored. *Figure 6.13* gives an example of what can be monitored on a certified device managed by SNMP.

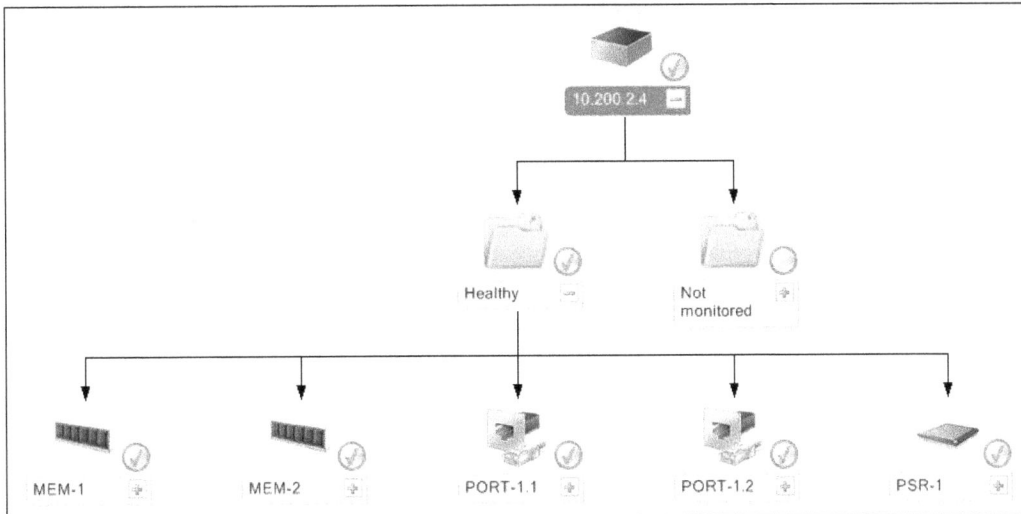

Figure 6.13: Diagram view of a certified network device

4. With the top-level network device selected from within the diagram view, click the **Performance View** option from the tasks pane on the right to pivot to a scoped view of performance counters for that particular device as shown in *Figure 6.14*.

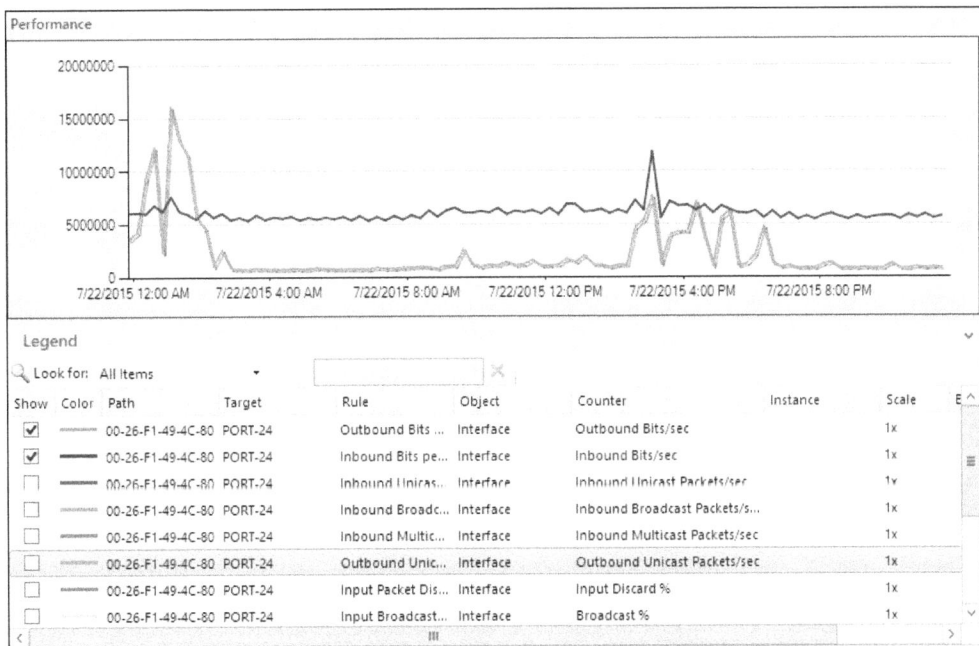

Figure 6.14: Network device performance view

5. Close the performance view to return to the Network Devices state view that you started from.

Working with node tasks

When you click on a network device from a view within the OpsMgr console, you should notice the **Node Tasks** menu appear within the **Tasks** pane on the right as shown in *Figure 6.15*.

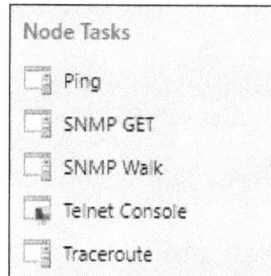

Figure 6.15: Node tasks in the console for network monitoring

These tasks can be very useful when you're looking to pinpoint a connectivity issue or check configuration on your network devices. The following sections will explain what each task does:

Ping

This task performs a simple ICMP command (using `ping.exe`) against a selected network device. It will run the ping from the OpsMgr server that's responsible for managing the network device. *Figure 6.16* shows an output window from the Ping task that successfully confirms connectivity to a network device.

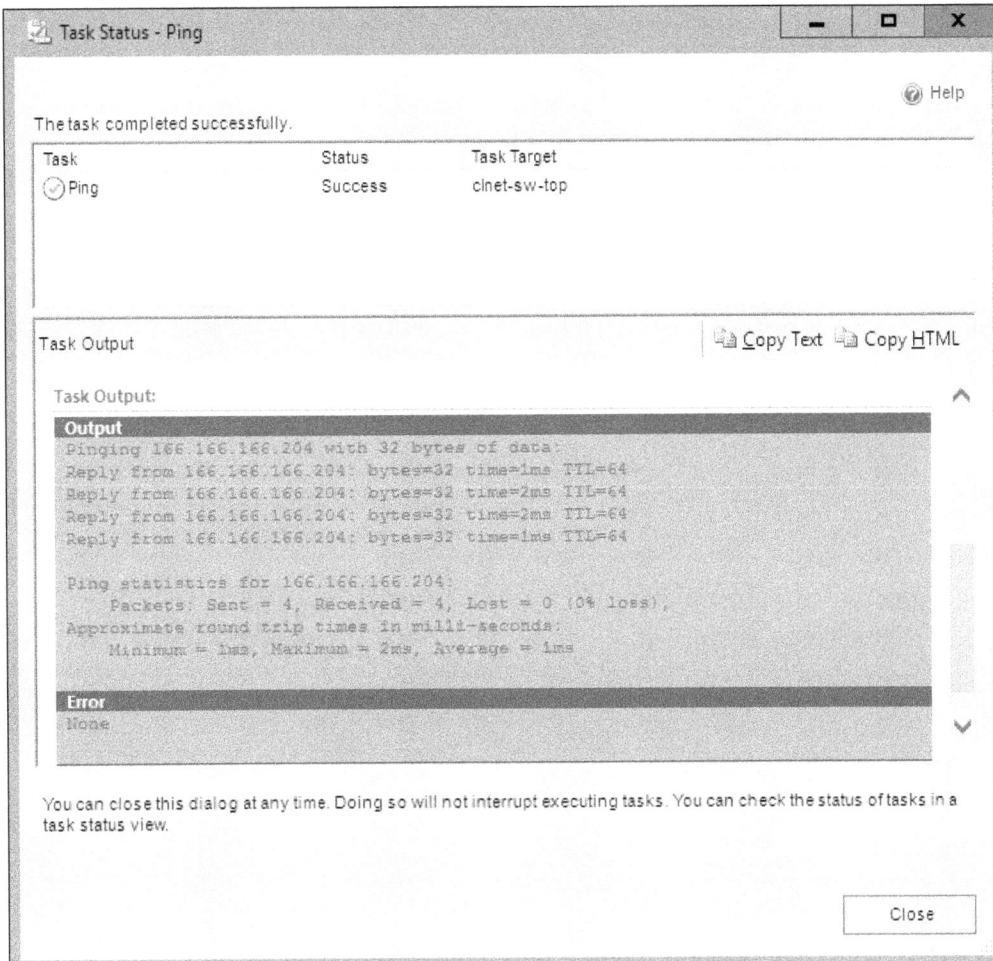

Figure 6.16: Ping task output

SNMP Get

This task retrieves a value for the **Object Identifier (OID)** from the network device using an SNMP GET request.

SNMP Walk

This task can be used to troubleshoot behavior and verify the configuration of SNMP devices. It uses SNMP GETNEXT requests to retrieve a MIB subtree and output the results to the console and it specifies an OID of .1.3.6.1.2.1 as part of its network monitoring context. In *Figure 6.17*, you can see the task has run successfully and you can also see that the task has created a file containing the output of the SNMP Walk on the C:\ drive of the OpsMgr server that manages the network device.

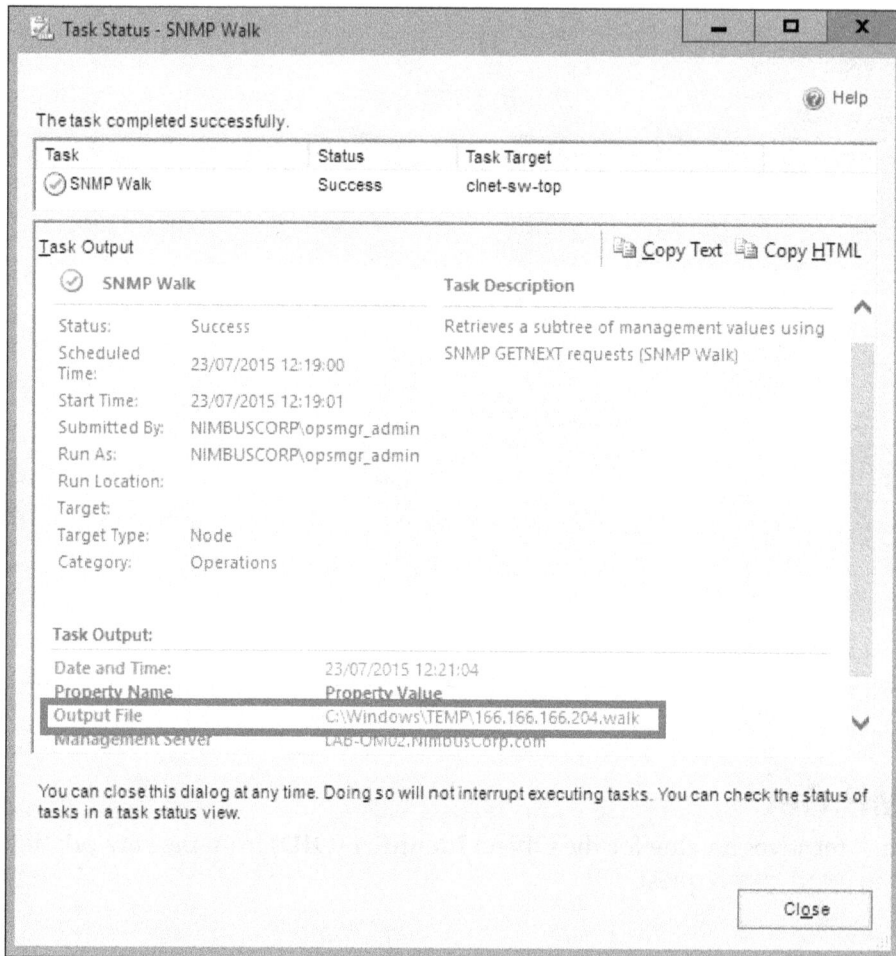

Figure 6.17: The SNMP Walk node task

If you want to view the contents of the output file, just open it using a text editor such as Notepad and you'll see an output similar to *Figure 6.18*.

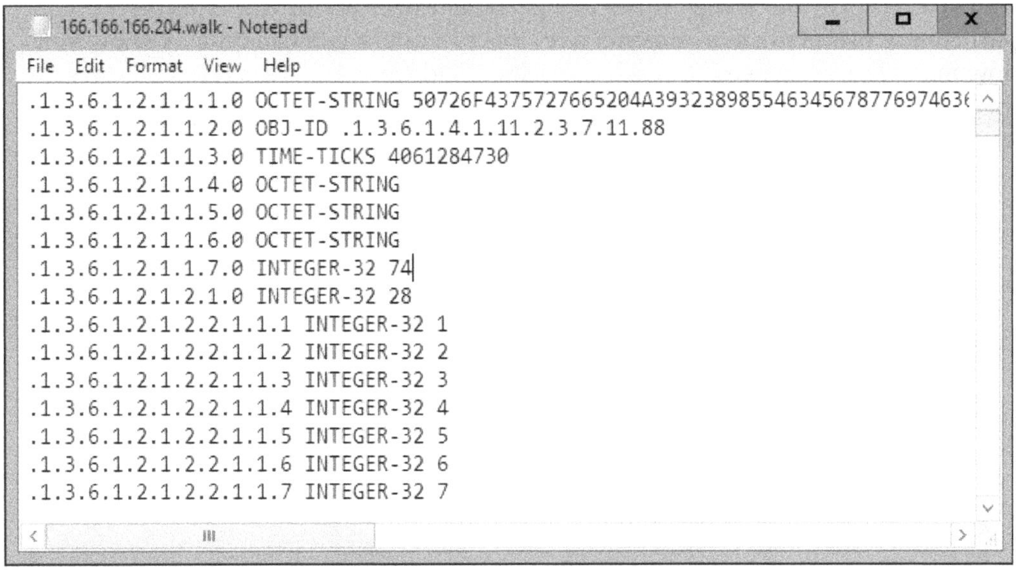

Figure 6.18: SNMP Walk output file

Telnet console

If the Telnet Client feature has been deployed on the computer that is used to launch this task, then a telnet session (using `telnet.exe`) is initiated. This task can be used as an administration tool to connect to a network device and is dependent on remote telnet administration sessions being enabled on the device.

Traceroute

This task runs an old-school diagnostic tool (`tracert.exe`) that traces the network route path (hops) and transit times to a particular network device. This can be particularly useful in environments with lots of routers as it can quickly show you how many hops you need to reach a specific IP address. In *Figure 6.19* you can see the output from this task indicating that only one hop was necessary to reach our switch.

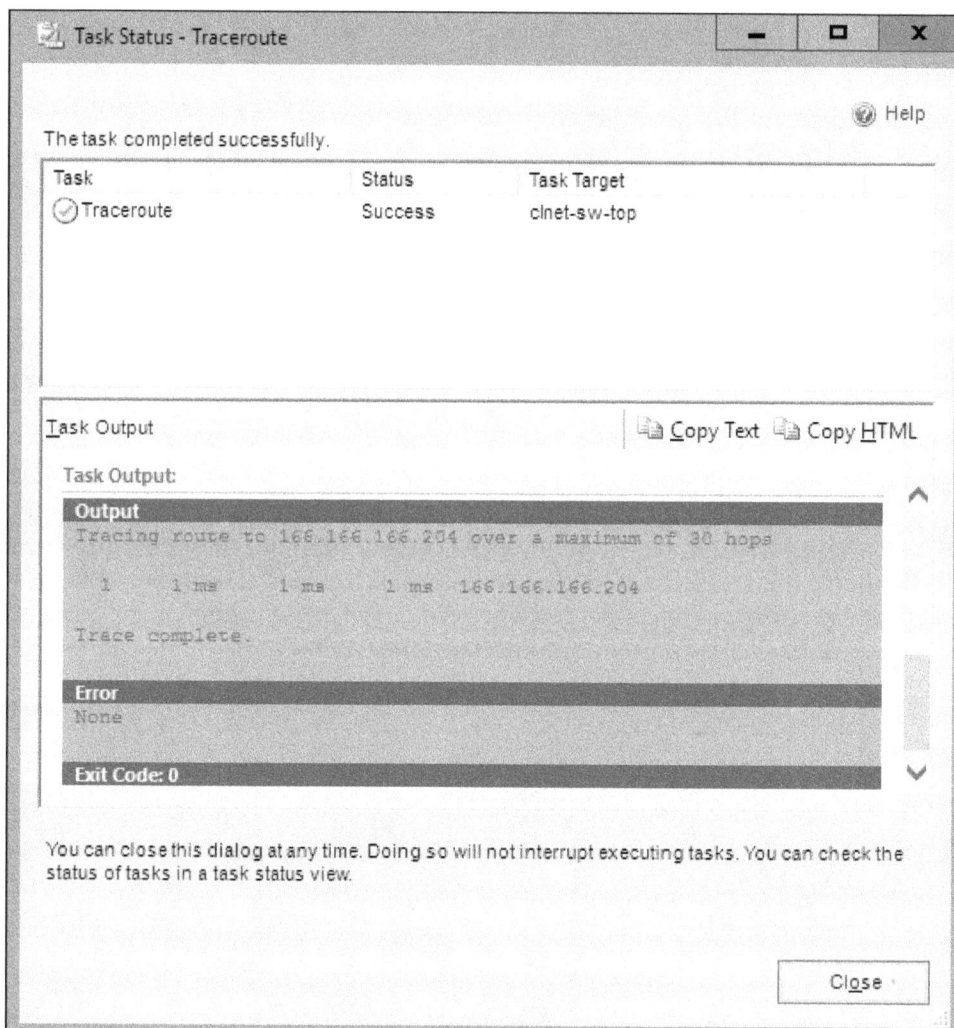

Figure 6.19: Using the Traceroute task to calculate network paths

Monitoring interfaces

An important aspect of monitoring network devices is to have visibility of the interfaces (or ports) on the devices that your servers are connected to. For example, these days network switches are fairly reliable and they rarely need to be replaced due to a hardware fault; however, it's entirely possible that someone working onsite in your datacenter might accidentally disconnect a network cable from the switch, resulting in a connectivity issue on your servers.

To ensure that you get alerted when a scenario like this occurs, OpsMgr provides the capability to monitor each individual interface on your network devices when using SNMP as part of your discoveries. Taking this into account, you might be surprised to learn that the default monitoring status for an interface that is connected to a computer is configured as not monitored! Only ports that connect to other network devices are monitored by default.

Although this might sound a little strange at first, when you think about it, this is actually the best approach to take, especially when you consider core switches configured in stacks can possibly contain hundreds of interfaces, some of which might even be connected to end-user client pc's with no monitoring required. Monitoring every interface by default would generate a huge number of false alerts and noise in the console.

Working with network adapter groups

In the **Groups** section of the **Authoring** workspace, you will find four network adapter groups that have been created as part of the OpsMgr installation. These groups are used to manage interface monitoring and are shown in *Figure 6.20*.

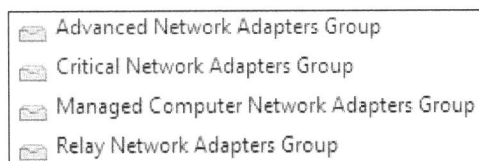

Advanced Network Adapters Group

Critical Network Adapters Group

Managed Computer Network Adapters Group

Relay Network Adapters Group

Figure 6.20: Default network adapter groups

The following sections explain what each group does:

Advanced network adapters group

This group is used for interfaces that require an advanced level of monitoring. The elevated monitoring assigned to it involves running advanced performance counters, such as **Cisco Collision** packets. If these types of performance counters and metrics are of interest to you, then manually add your interface to this group to enable them. Be aware though, the counters that apply to this group are often a duplication of performance counters already collected and might just contribute to alert noise instead of being useful.

Critical network adapters group

If for some reason your critical server interfaces were not being monitored as a part of the Managed Computer Network Adapters group, then adding them here will give you visibility of them. No interfaces are added to this group automatically, you must manually populate it with members if required.

Managed computer network adapters group

If you have the OpsMgr agent deployed to a computer with a supported operating system, then the network adapter for that agent will automatically populate within this group during the post-processing discovery stage.

Relay network adapters group

When you run a full discovery and add a device that's connected to another device, the connecting interface for the two devices gets monitored automatically. This is default behavior and requires no additional administrative effort from you.

Interface stitching

During the discovery of network devices, OpsMgr automatically maps interfaces on network devices to the agent-managed servers that they are connected to. This process is known as **Interface Stitching**. For interface stitching to be successful, you need to ensure you've deployed management packs for the operating systems that run on your agents – the Windows Server Core OS management packs for example. In the next section, you'll see interface stitching in action through some of the network monitoring dashboards available.

Dashboards

With each new release of OpsMgr, the dashboards on offer get better and better and although Microsoft never claim to be the best on the market for network monitoring, the visualizations you get out of the box with OpsMgr are more than effective in showing the health of your network devices and connections.

In *Chapter 9, Visualizing Your IT with Dashboards*, we'll dive into all of the dashboard options available to you with OpsMgr but for now, the following sections will give you the low-down on the four dashboards specifically targeted at network monitoring.

Network Summary Dashboard

The first dashboard that we will look at is the **Network Summary Dashboard**. Accessed from the **Network Monitoring** folder in the **Monitoring** workspace, this dashboard contains seven widgets/views that include information on nodes with the slowest response time, nodes with the highest CPU usage, interfaces with the highest utilization, send/receive errors, and nodes with the most alerts.

As shown in *Figure 6.21*, this dashboard can be quite useful to network administrators as it's focused on the performance and throughput of network devices.

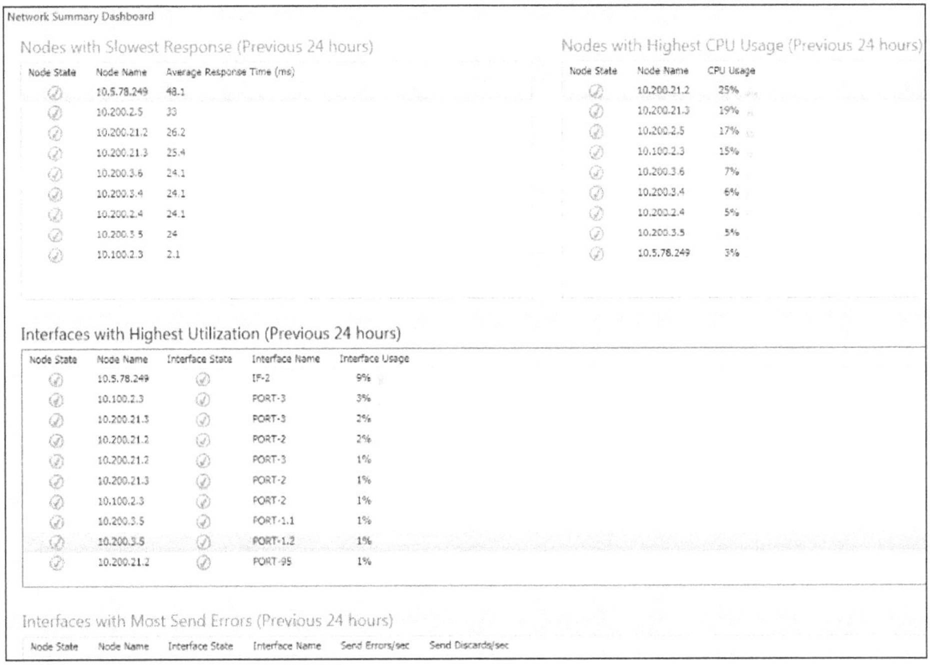

Figure 6.21: Network Summary Dashboard

Network Vicinity Dashboard

Unlike the Network Summary Dashboard, which is accessed from within the Network Monitoring folder, the Network Vicinity Dashboard is always available to open using the **Tasks** pane to the right of the Monitoring workspace. It's also available whenever you right-click on a monitored network device and choose the **Navigation** option from the context menu.

As you learnt earlier, interface stitching is when OpsMgr automatically maps network device interfaces to the agent-managed servers they're connected to and the Network Vicinity Dashboard is where you can see this in action.

When you open this dashboard initially, you'll be presented with two views – **Vicinity View** and **Instance Details**. The Vicinity View will build out a map of all the connected network devices that OpsMgr knows about which are connected to the original network device you selected when launching the Network Vicinity Dashboard in the first place.

As you can see from *Figure 6.22*, things start to get really interesting though when you click the **Show Computers** option from the Vicinity View as a new map is built using interface stitching. This map shows you all of the connections on that network device from the agent-managed computers that OpsMgr is monitoring.

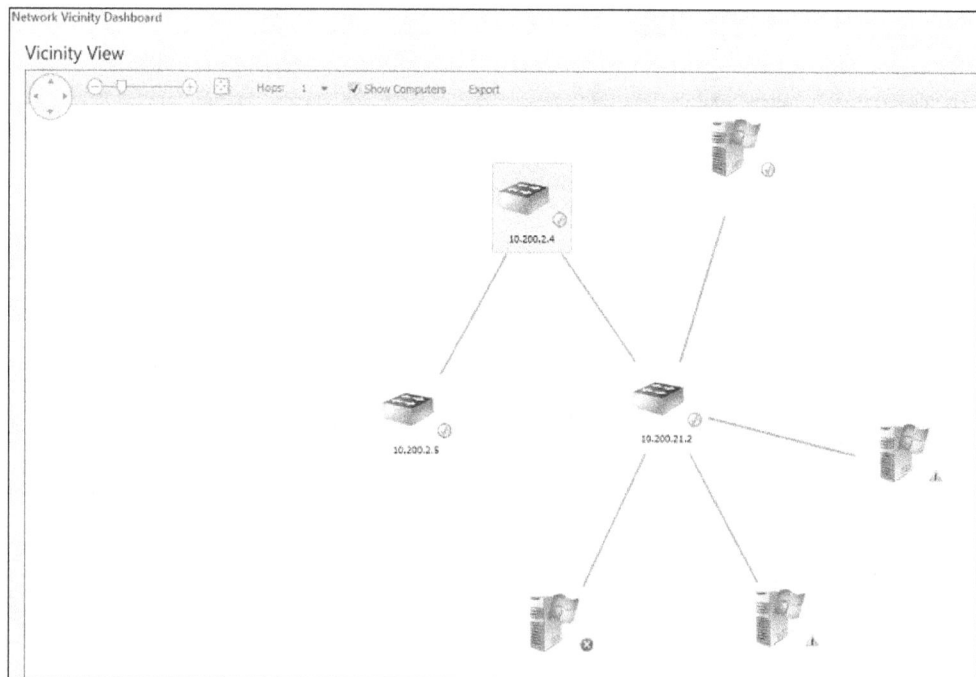

Figure 6.22: Interface Stitching in action with the Network Vicinity Dashboard

Another interesting point about this dashboard is the color of each link that connects the network devices to your agent-managed computers. Each colored line represents the live health state of that particular link. So, if the link is up, it'll be green in color and if it's down, it'll be red. You can right-click on the link to select it and open the Health Explorer, where you can get additional information about which network interface your server is connected to.

Network Node Dashboard

Launched using the **Tasks** pane or through the **Navigation** option from the right-click context menu of a monitored network device, the Network Node Dashboard brings together a number of network monitoring views. It includes a smaller version of the vicinity view along with availability, response times, processor usage, and details about your instance.

As shown in *Figure 6.23*, having the option to track the availability of a device from one day up to the previous 30 days is very useful and it's a great place to check if one of your applications has encountered reduced availability over the last month.

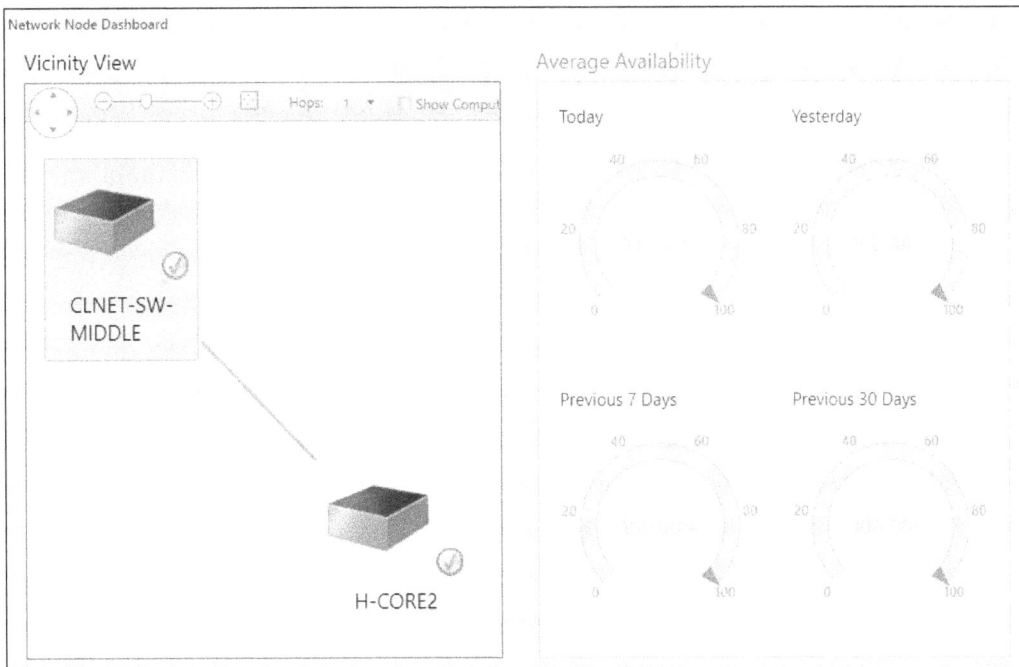

Figure 6.23: Two of the views available in the Network Node Dashboard

Another view you get within the **Network Node Dashboard** is shown in *Figure 6.24* and this view is focused on the availability of the interfaces on your network device.

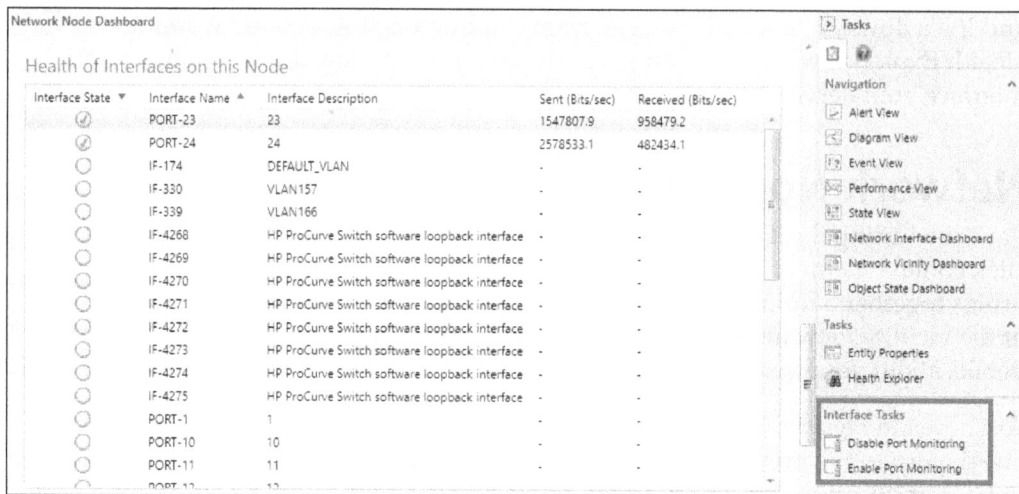

Figure 6.24: Monitoring your interfaces with the Network Node Dashboard

Here you can see the interface name, description and also statistics for sent and received data. This view is a good example of where OpsMgr only monitors interfaces that are connected to other network devices by default.

Although all interfaces on your network device are listed here, only the (important) ones that are connected to other devices are monitored. If you wish to monitor any other interface, you can do so by clicking on the **Enable Port Monitoring** task from the Tasks pane or you could also add the interface to the Critical Network Adapters Group we discussed earlier.

Network Interface Dashboard

When you click on an interface from a view within the console, you'll notice the **Network Interface Dashboard** option becomes visible from the **Tasks** pane as shown in *Figure 6.25*.

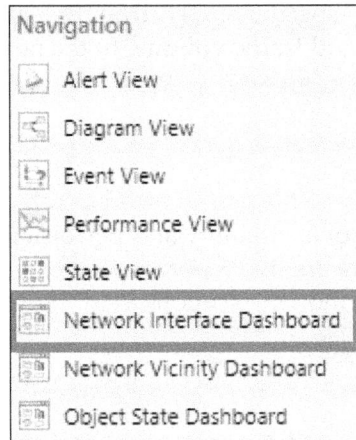

Figure 6.25: Launching the Network Interface Dashboard

Clicking this option will open the **Network Interface Dashboard** shown in *Figure 6.26*, where you can see performance graphs with information about bits sent/received, packets sent/received, errors, alerts and instance details.

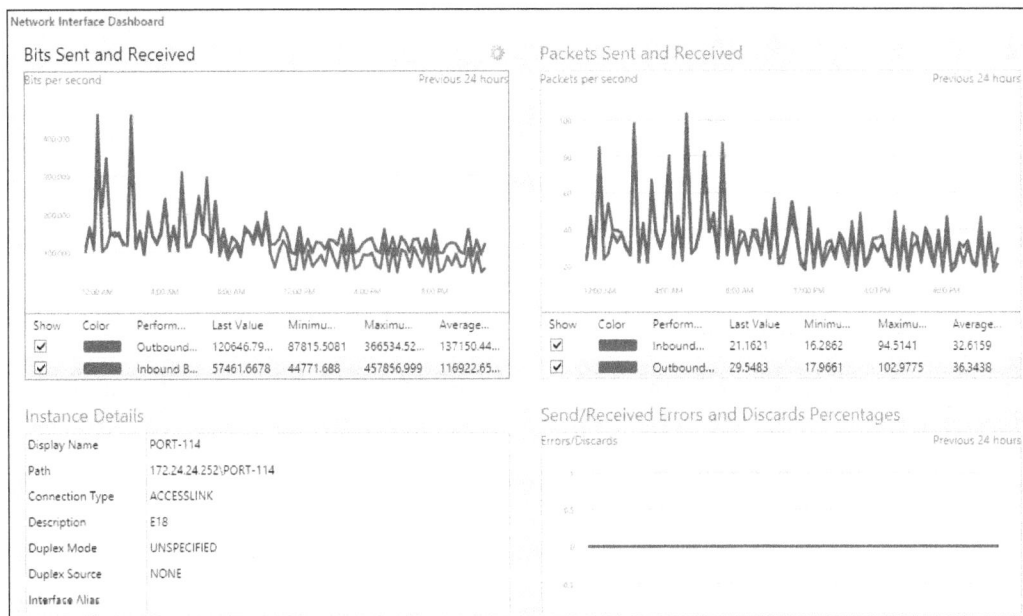

Figure 6.26: Performance graphs with the Network Interface Dashboard

You can also launch interface-specific reports from this dashboard to get detailed analysis about packet errors and traffic volume. In the next section, we'll discuss network monitoring reports.

Reports

Along with the extensive list of availability and performance reports that come out of the box with OpsMgr, there are five reports specific to network monitoring. These reports are explained in the following sections.

Device reports

If you wish to report on how much free memory or CPU utilization your network device has, then these two reports will do the job:

- Memory Utilization
- Processor Utilization

Interface reports

Given that each individual interface on a network device can be responsible for different application and fabric workloads, it's imperative that you have a reporting solution available to you that can analyse things like packets, errors and traffic volume. These self-explanatory named reports are what you need:

- Interface Error Packet Analysis
- Interface Packet Analysis
- Interface Traffic Volume

To show you how easy it is to quickly create one of these interface reports, follow these steps:

1. Expand the Network Monitoring folder from the Monitoring workspace and click the **Network Devices** view.

2. Select a network device from the central Network Devices state view, and then click on the **Network Node Dashboard** link from the Tasks pane on the right.

3. Now scroll down through this dashboard to the **Health of Interfaces on this Node** view and click on an interface that you wish to report on. The **Report Tasks** section of the **Tasks** pane should change to reflect the three network interface reports as shown in *Figure 6.27*.

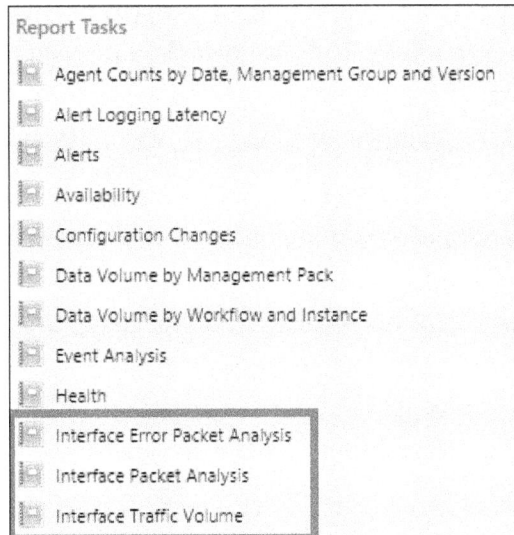

Figure 6.27: Network interface reports

4. Click the link for the **Interface Traffic Volume** report to open the report configuration window and you'll notice that the interface you wish to report on has been automatically populated in the **Objects** section.

5. Once you have your interface targeted, choose the units that you want it to be measured in (for example bits, kilobits, megabits, or gigabits) and then define the date range for the report. *Figure 6.28* shows the report parameter page populated with some interface-specific data.

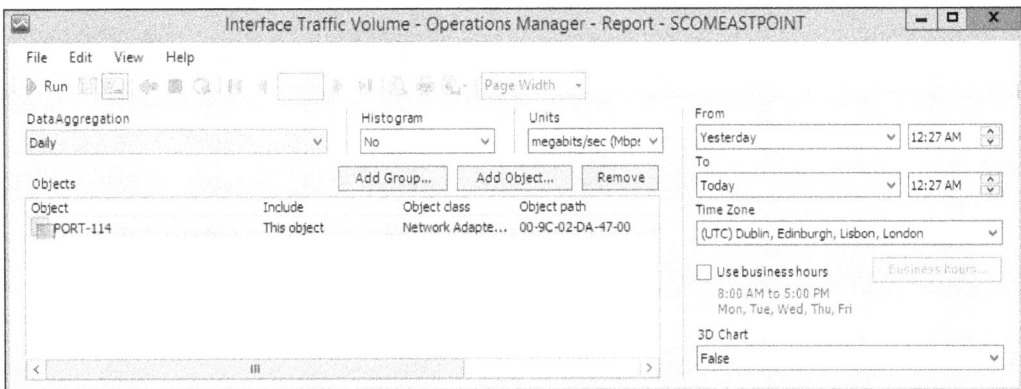

Figure 6.28: Configuring the interface report

6. When you've finished configuring your parameters, click the **Run** button to initiate the new report. *Figure 6.29* shows the easy-to-understand output of this interface report.

Report Time	: 7/26/2015 12:35 AM
Data Aggregation	: Daily
Report Duration	: From 7/19/2015 to 7/26/2015
Histogram	: No
Expressed in	: megabits/sec (Mbps)

PORT-172.24.24.252/114

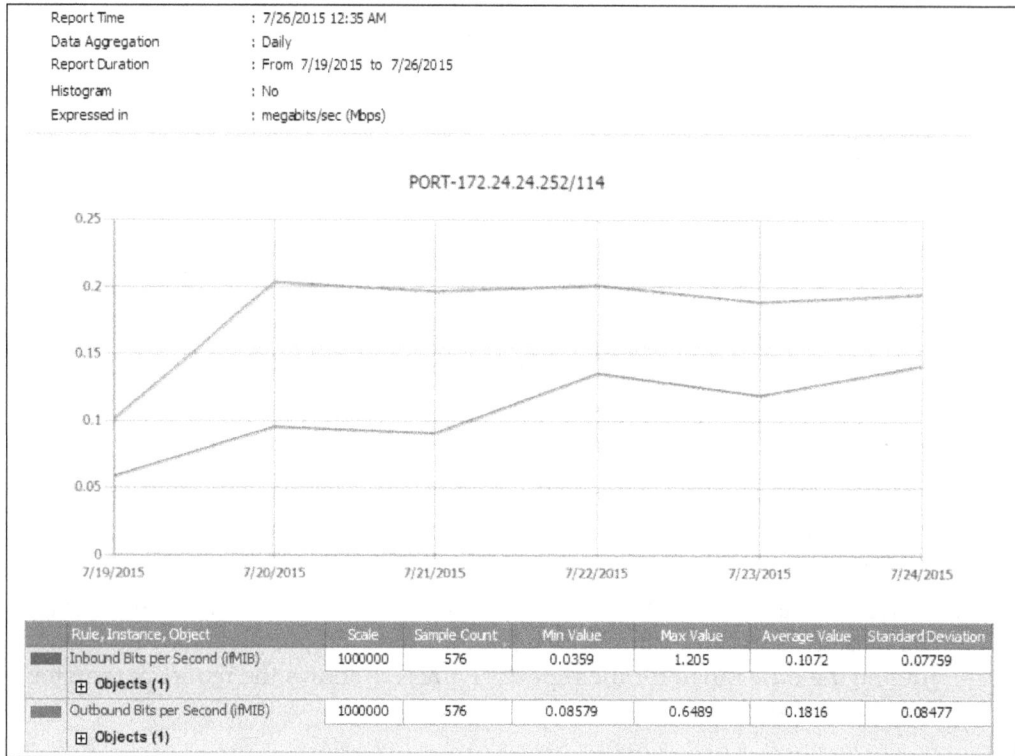

Rule, Instance, Object	Scale	Sample Count	Min Value	Max Value	Average Value	Standard Deviation
Inbound Bits per Second (ifMIB)	1000000	576	0.0359	1.205	0.1072	0.07759
⊞ Objects (1)						
Outbound Bits per Second (ifMIB)	1000000	576	0.08579	0.6489	0.1816	0.08477
⊞ Objects (1)						

Figure 6.28: Interface Traffic report

If you want to learn more about OpsMgr reporting, then towards the end of this book in *Chapter 10, Creating Alert Subscriptions and Reports,* we'll discuss it in more detail.

Summary

In this chapter, we gave you an overview of the Network Monitoring feature of OpsMgr and discussed what you need to have in place in your environment to ensure successful monitoring of your network devices.

We demonstrated how to configure a discovery rule and bring some devices under monitoring and we walked you through using the built-in tasks, dashboards and reports that are specific to this feature.

In the next chapter, you will learn how to create service models of your IT services using distributed applications in OpsMgr.

7
Configuring Service Models with Distributed Applications

One of the key benefits of OpsMgr is having the ability to bring all of the monitored components of an IT service together and model them into a single entity using the Distributed Application feature. With this capability you can easily transition from a server monitoring solution to a service monitoring solution, where you then get the full picture of what's affected within the context of the IT service when a particular alert fires.

In this chapter, we begin with an overview of distributed applications and then we discuss some of the predefined distributed application models that you get when you first deploy OpsMgr. We then switch gears and move into creating your first distributed application and along the way, we'll walk you through each of the built-in template designs that you can use to model your IT service.

We will finish the chapter by demonstrating how to create an associated **Service Level Agreement (SLA)** for your distributed application and some basic views to help manage it from within the OpsMgr consoles.

Here's a rundown of what you will learn from this chapter:

- Overview of distributed applications
- Template design models
- Creating distributed applications
- Configuring health rollup policies
- Creating SLAs

Distributed applications overview

The term **distributed application** originates from the developer world where an application would typically comprise two (client and server) or three (client, server and middleware) tiers within the service model. Using this type of distributed model, application developers gained a complete understanding of how each tier functioned and this enabled them to deliver faster development cycles for new releases.

In the operations world, IT administrators have responsibility for monitoring and managing the many disparate components that form the basis of their organizations IT service catalog. The pressure is on for them to deliver comprehensive monitoring of IT services but with a visibility that's easy to understand for both senior management and non-tech savvy employees alike. This is where Microsoft has seized their opportunity with distributed applications in OpsMgr by enabling IT administrators to map out the different components of an IT service and bring it together in one holistic view.

These components can be defined by different management packs and most likely, will be managed by different agents. Some components might even be located on the internet or in different datacenters.

In *Figure 7.1*, you can see an example of a demo IT service and its components modeled in OpsMgr using a distributed application.

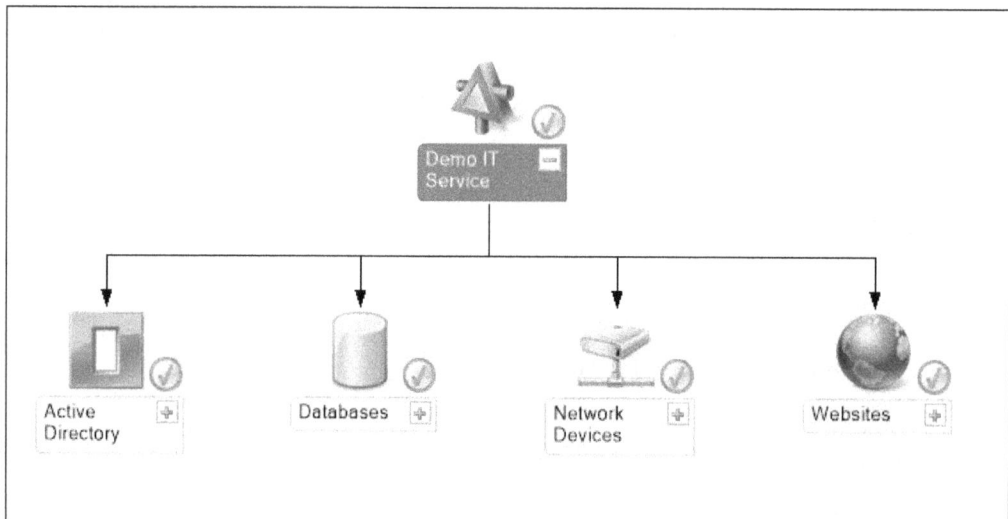

Figure 7.1: Example of an OpsMgr distributed application

The top-level health state for this IT service is determined by the rolled-up health of its child components and the health of the child components is dependent on how much high-availability and resiliency each one has. For example, losing a clustered network device or mirrored database would mean that the overall IT service stays up and just has a problem that needs to be dealt with sooner rather than later, as opposed to losing a non-clustered network device or stand-alone database, which would immediately cause the overall IT service to become unavailable.

> To properly represent an IT service in OpsMgr as a distributed application, you must work with the relevant owners of the service to ensure it is fully mapped out and documented. When you have this information, you can then go ahead and get it configured and deployed from within the Operations console.

Creating distributed applications

When you're ready to create your first distributed application, you will need to get familiar with the Distributed Application Designer. Accessed from within the Authoring workspace of the Operations console, the Distributed Application Designer is a graphical tool that enables you to model your IT service as a distributed application with relative ease.

In *Figure 7.2* you can see our demo IT service modeled within the **Distributed Application Designer**.

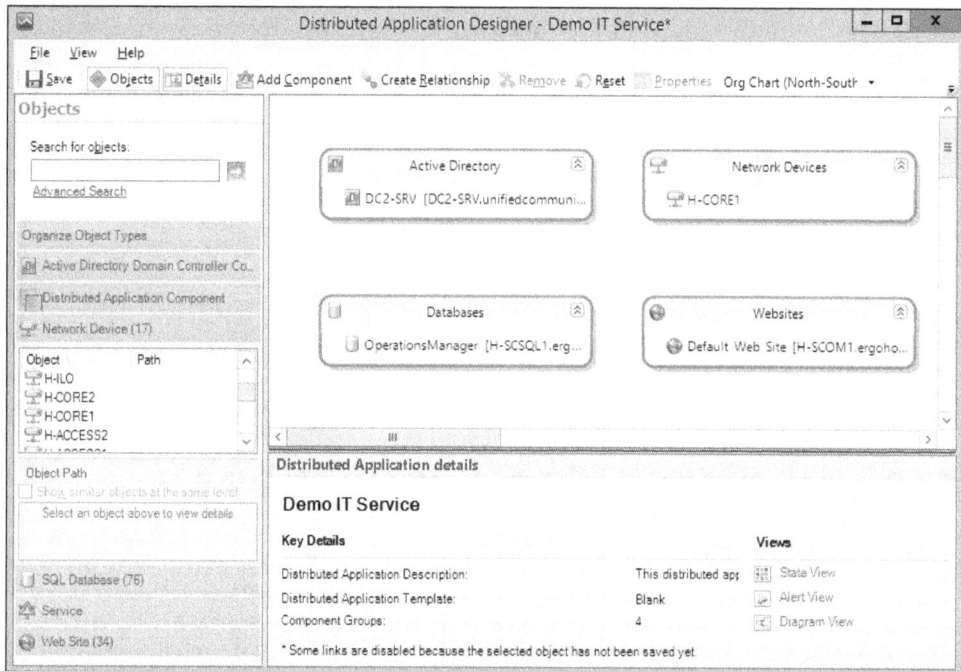

Figure 7.2: Distributed Application Designer

The **Objects** section to the left of the image allows you to search through classes for object types that will be added as components of the IT service. The boxes in the center of the designer are called **component groups** and each component group is associated with at least one object type or class.

Once you have the correct object type selected and the service already mapped out in your documentation, it's just a simple click-and-point process to add objects into a new or existing component group.

Understanding distributed application templates

When you run the Distributed Application Designer to create a distributed application, you will be presented with a number of pre-built templates to choose from. Some of these templates are targeted at specific monitoring scenarios and contain component groups mapped to classes that are relevant to those scenarios. The following sections will describe each template option available to you.

.NET 3-Tier Application template

This template contains three different application tiers:

- Presentation
- Business
- Data

It also contains a client-perspective tier that can be used to check availability using synthetic transactions. *Figure 7.3* shows an example of this template and its different component groups.

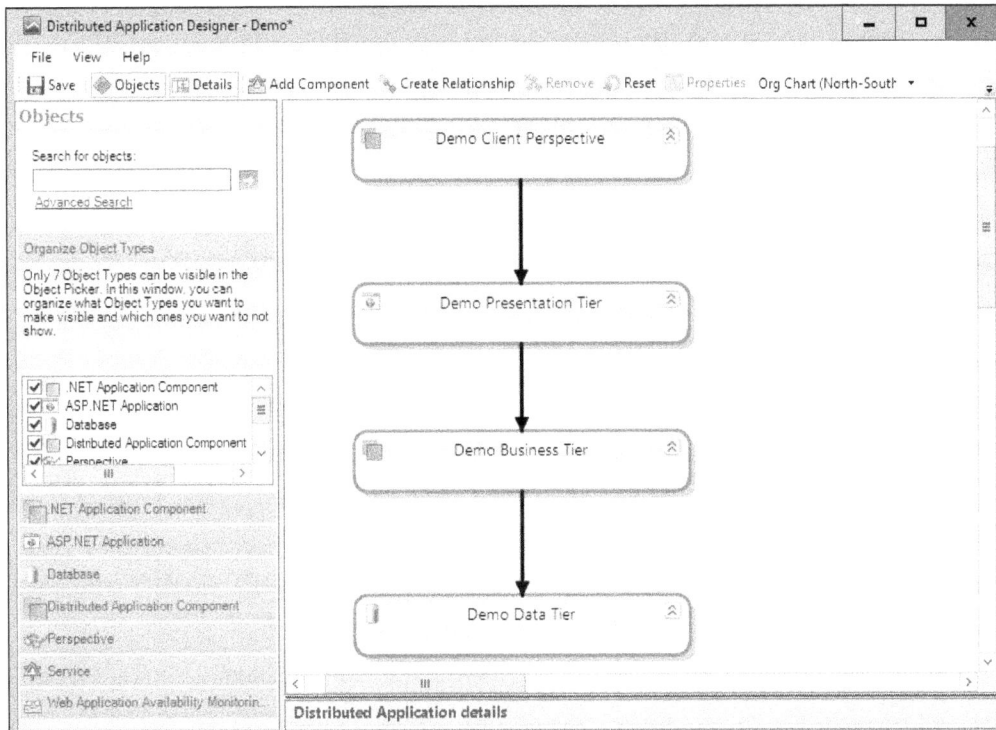

Figure 7.3: .NET 3-Tier Application template

Line of Business Web Application template

This template contains two component groups that focus on application models containing just websites and databases. It can be a useful template to use if you have a web application that requires monitoring of these objects and it's not too difficult to customize the template by adding extra component groups for things, such as client perspectives and other application layers. *Figure 7.4* shows an example of this template:

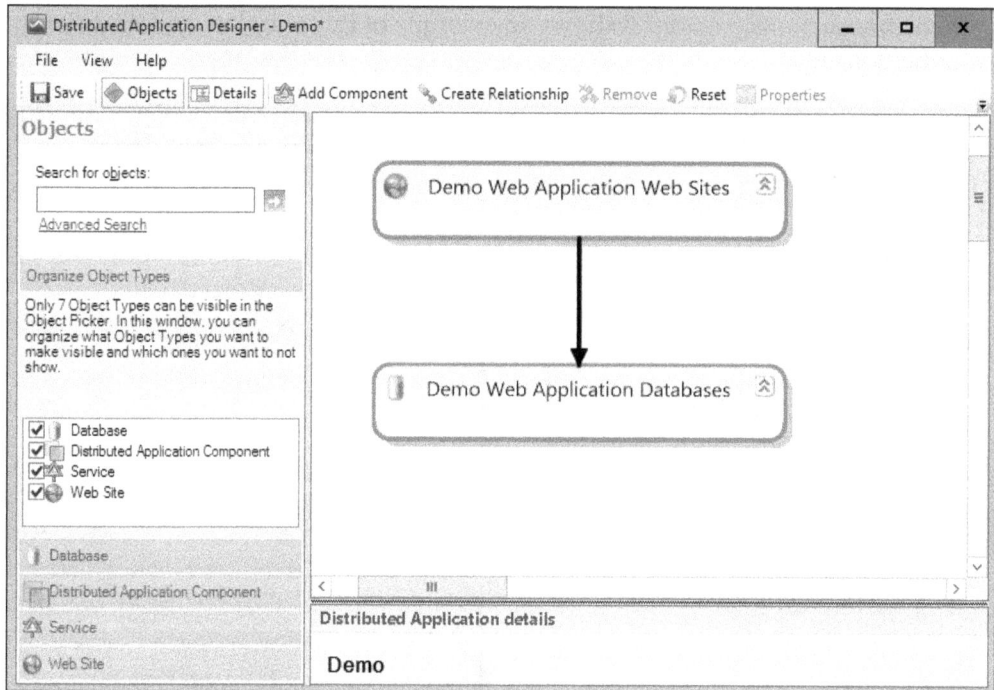

Figure 7.4: Line of Business Web Application template

Messaging template

One of the more complex distributed application templates, this one is focused on a messaging service that uses an application such as Microsoft Exchange Server. This template contains six different component groups covering things like client perspectives, Active Directory, storage and network layers – as well as the messaging application components and associated roles. *Figure 7.5* shows an example of these component groups within the template.

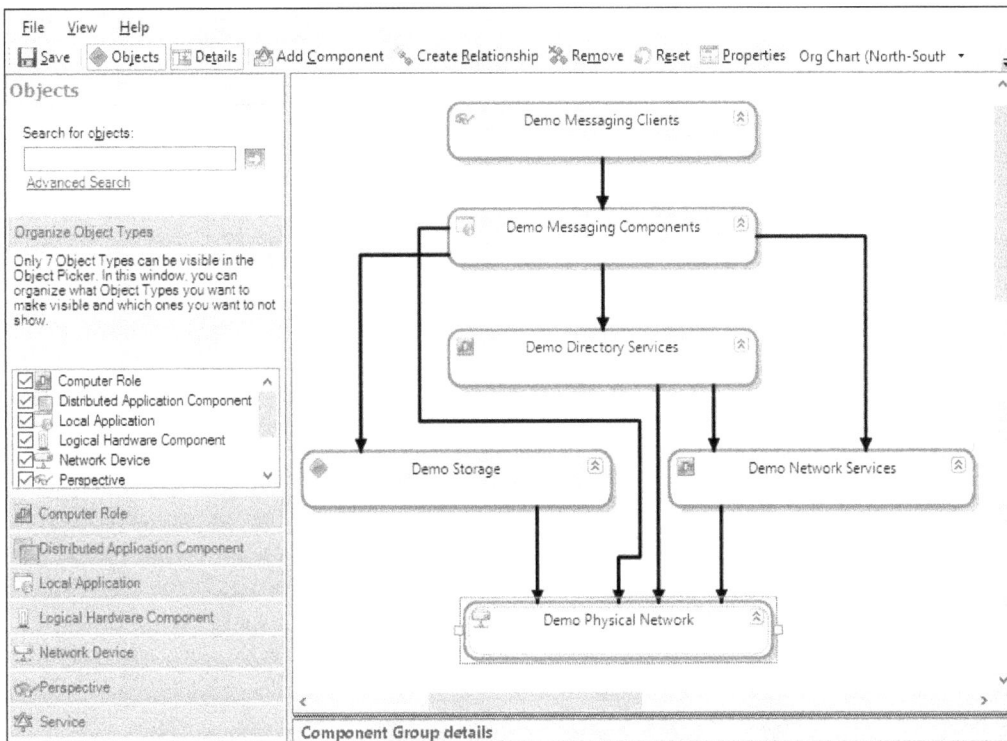

Figure 7.5: Messaging template

Blank (Advanced) template

The name of this template should be a give away to the fact that it's a clean slate (blank) template that leaves the customization to you. This will be the template that you will use the most due to its flexibility and advanced customization options. In *Figure 7.6* you can see there are no component groups pre-configured within this template.

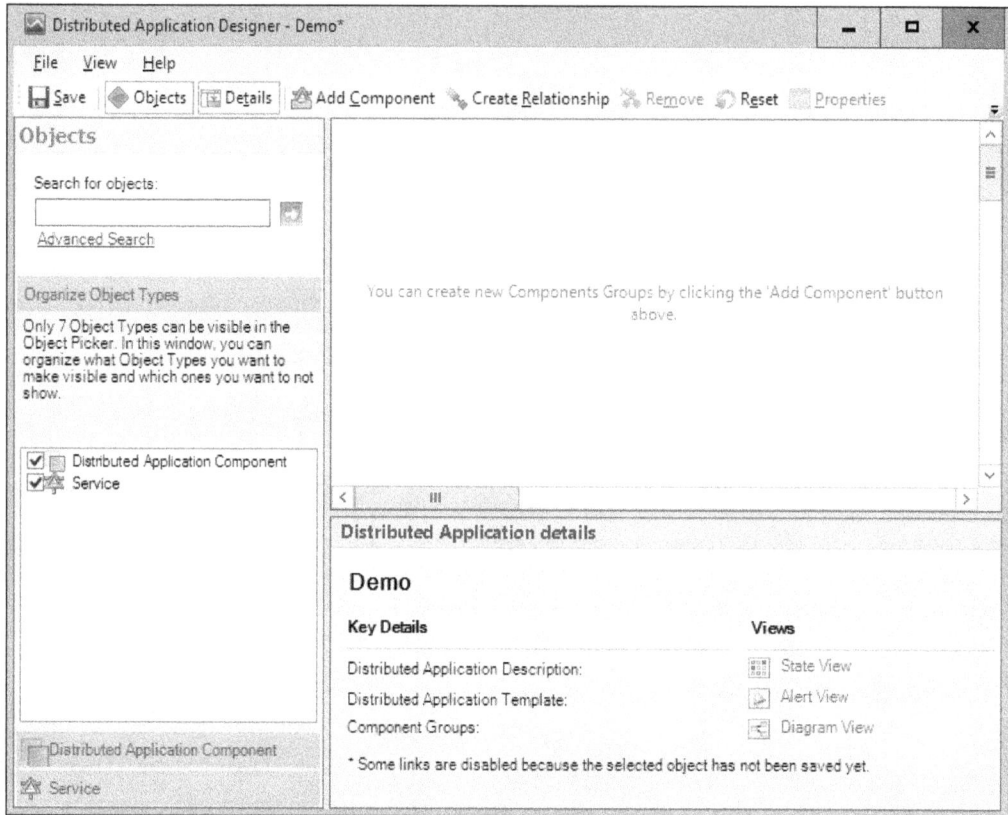

Figure 7.6: Blank (Advanced) template

Modeling your IT service

With an understanding of the Distributed Application Designer and distributed application templates, it's a good time to walk you through creating your first IT service model. In this walkthrough we'll create a distributed application based on the 'Demo IT Service' example we showed earlier in *Figure 7.1*. If you want to model a different IT service that's more aligned with your own environment, just substitute the component groups and classes where applicable.

Follow these steps to create a new distributed application model:

1. From the Authoring workspace in the OpsMgr console, click on the **Create a New Distributed Application** link from the tasks pane to open the **Distributed Application Designer**.

2. Type a name for the new distributed application along with a description and click on the **Blank (Advanced)** template as shown in *Figure 7.7*.

Figure 7.7: Creating a new distributed application

3. Before you can create a new distributed application, you need to choose an unsealed management pack to store it in.

> It's always good practice to keep your distributed applications in separate unsealed management packs.

For this reason; we'll click on the **New** button from the **Save to a Management Pack** section.

1. At the **Create a Management Pack** wizard, give the new unsealed management pack a name and type a description as shown in *Figure 7.8*, click on **Next**, and then hit the **Create** button to create the new unsealed management pack.

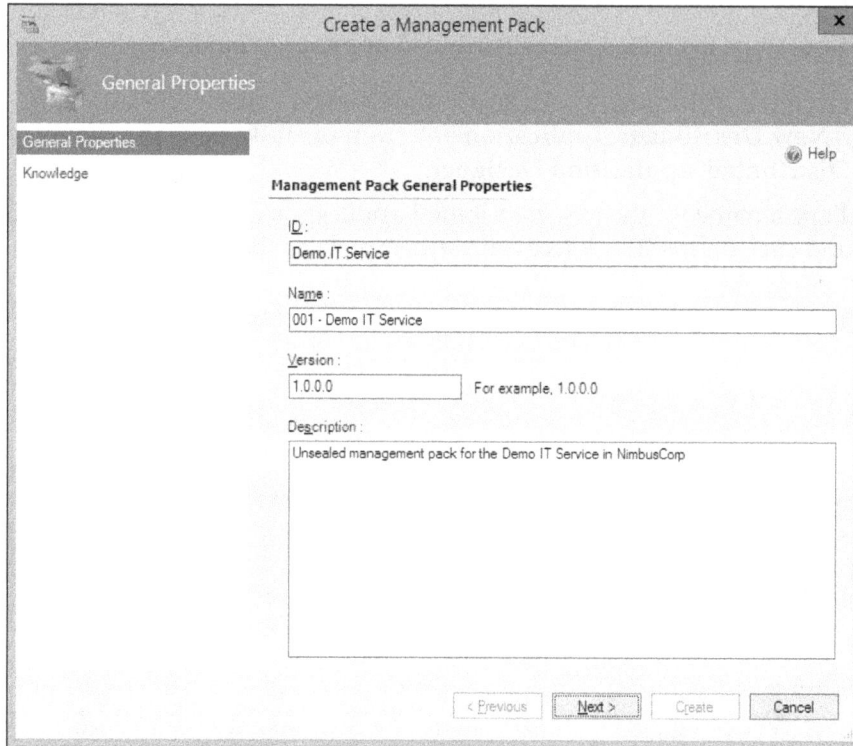

Figure 7.8: Creating an unsealed management pack

When naming the unsealed management packs that will store your distributed applications, be consistent with the naming convention and if possible, start the name with a number. For example, try something similar to **001 – Active Directory**, **002 – Email** and **003 – Payroll**. Adding a numerical value to the start of your distributed application unsealed management packs will ensure that their folder views stay together at the top of the monitoring workspace.

2. Back at the **Create a Distributed Application** dialog box, you should now have the name of your new unsealed management pack listed as the location to save the new distributed application to. Click on **OK** to continue.

3. As we've chosen the **Blank (Advanced)** template for this distributed application, there are no pre-defined component groups to use and we must specify these now. We've determined that this IT service will contain four child component groups comprising Active Directory, SQL databases, network devices and some websites. To add the first component group, click on the **Add Component** button from the ribbon at the top of the designer.

4. From the **Create New Component Group** dialog box, type a display name for your component group (we'll work on the Active Directory one first), click on the **Objects of the following type(s)** radio button, and then expand to the following object type: **Configuration Item | Logical Entity | Computer Role | Windows Computer Role | Active Directory Domain Controller Computer Role**, as shown in *Figure 7.9*. Click on **OK** to create the component group.

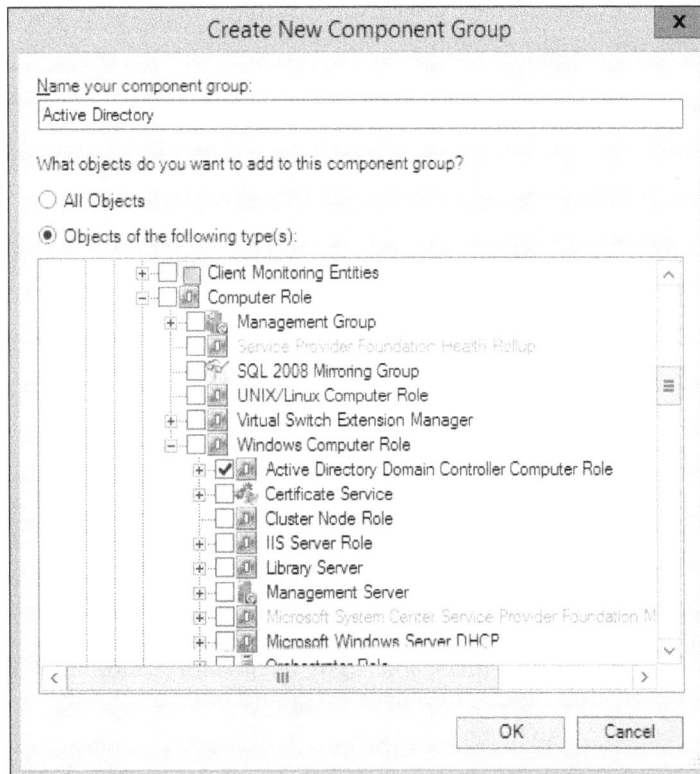

Figure 7.9: Creating a component group

5. You will now notice a new class (**Active Directory Domain Controller Computer Role**) has been added to the **Objects** pane on the left and all objects that are members of that class will be listed there. In the center of the window you will see the new empty component group that you created in the previous step. Right-click on the object that you wish to add to the distributed application, select the **Add To** option and then click on the name of the component group you just created as shown in *Figure 7.10*.

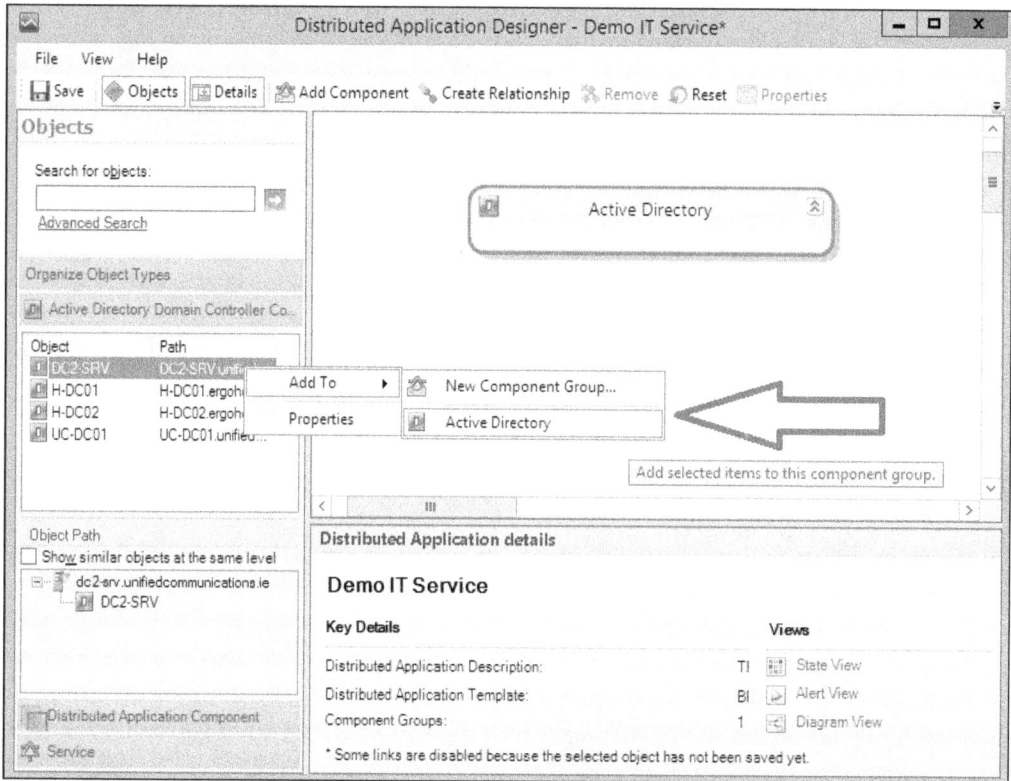

Figure 7.10: Adding an object to a component group

As an alternative to using the right-click, **Add To** option, you can simply drag and drop the object from the Objects pane onto a component group that is associated with the object class. This is a quick and handy method for adding single or multiple objects to component groups.

6. For the next component group (this time we'll create one for SQL databases), click on the **Add Component** button again, give the component group a name, select the **Objects of the following type(s)** radio button, and then navigate to the following object type: **Configuration Item | Logical Entity | Application Component | Database | SQL Database**, and click on **OK** to create the component group.

> If you're having difficulty locating the class hierarchy that your monitored object belongs to, then a good tip would be to browse to the **Monitoring** workspace and locate a state view in the management pack folder that delivers the monitoring capability for the object(s); from there, right click on the state view and click on the **Properties** option. In the **Show data related to** field of the **Criteria** tab you will see the class of the object. This is the class that you need to use for your distributed application component group.

7. With the new component group created, select the database(s) you want to use from the **SQL Database** class list on the left and right-click, select **Add To**, then choose the new databases component group you just created and you should have something that looks like *Figure 7.11*.

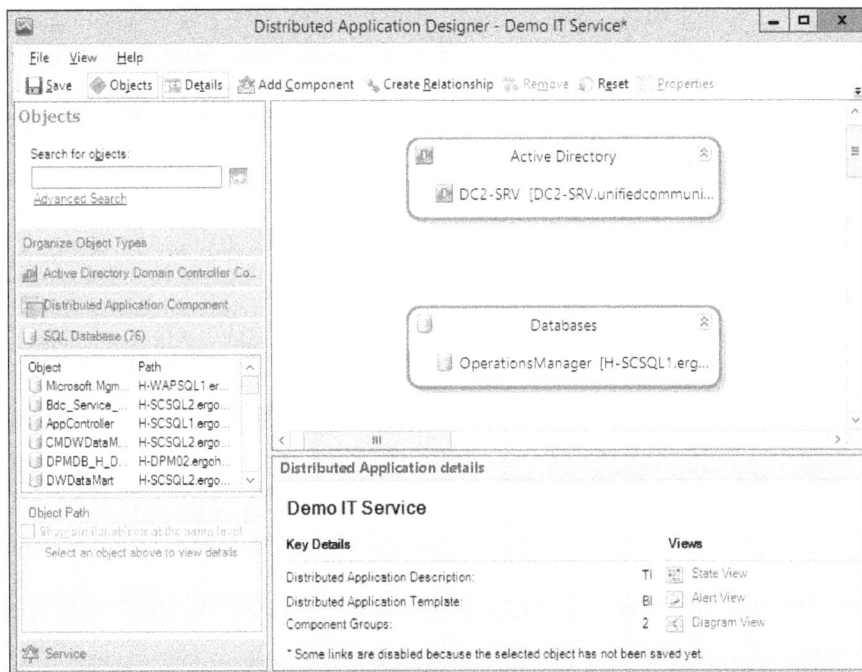

Figure 7.11: Adding more component groups

8. The next two component groups that we will create will contain network devices and websites. For these two, you can repeat the previous few steps and run through the **Add Component** button process – adding a component group named **Network Devices** and another named **Websites**.

> You may have noticed the **Create Relationship** button in the ribbon of the Distributed Application Designer and wondered what its purpose is. This is essentially just an aesthetic option that shows a dotted relationship line between component groups when the distributed application is viewed as a Diagram. It doesn't create any new monitors or extra monitoring and it's not something that is regularly or widely used within the OpsMgr community.

9. There's a little known shortcut that you can take when creating component groups that will definitely save you some time – the only caveat is that this shortcut will only work if OpsMgr has already discovered at least one object of the same class. For example, if you want to add a new component group for network devices and you already know the name or IP address of a previously discovered network device, then all you have to do is to type the name of the device into the **Search for objects** field within the **Objects** pane and then hit *Enter* on your keyboard. This will display results for all objects OpsMgr has found with the same name and when you locate the object you want, right-click on it, select **Add To** and then select the **New Component Group** option shown in *Figure 7.12*.

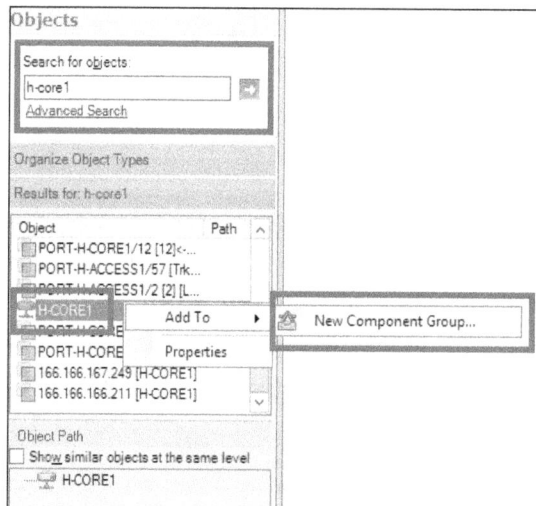

Figure 7.12: Shortcut for adding new component groups

When using the **Search for objects** field, you will find that certain object names return large numbers of results and it might be difficult to locate the exact one you want. If this is the case, then you can use the **Advanced Search** link (located below the **Search for objects** field) to help you scope your search to a specific class.

As you become more familiar with the icons that represent each class object (for example, in *Figure 7.12* the **Network Device** class displays an icon of a network device), you will find it much easier to quickly identify the objects you want without having to dig too deep.

10. After you select the **New Component Group** option, this opens up a scoped version of the **Create New Component Group** dialog box (shown in *Figure 7.13*) and all you need to do is give it a name, and then click on **OK**.

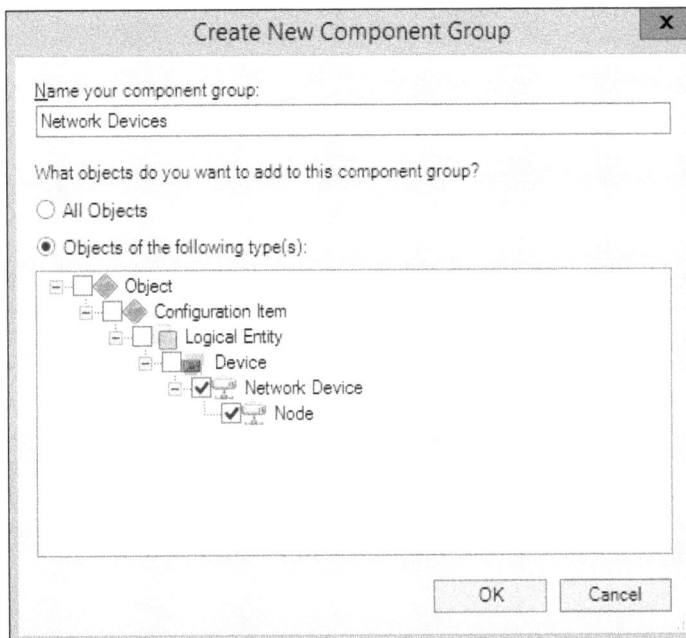

Figure 7.13: Scoped component group creation

11. Your final design should look something similar to *Figure 7.14* (add or remove other objects as you need) and when you're happy that all objects and component groups have been added to the service model, click on the **Save** button to create your new distributed application.

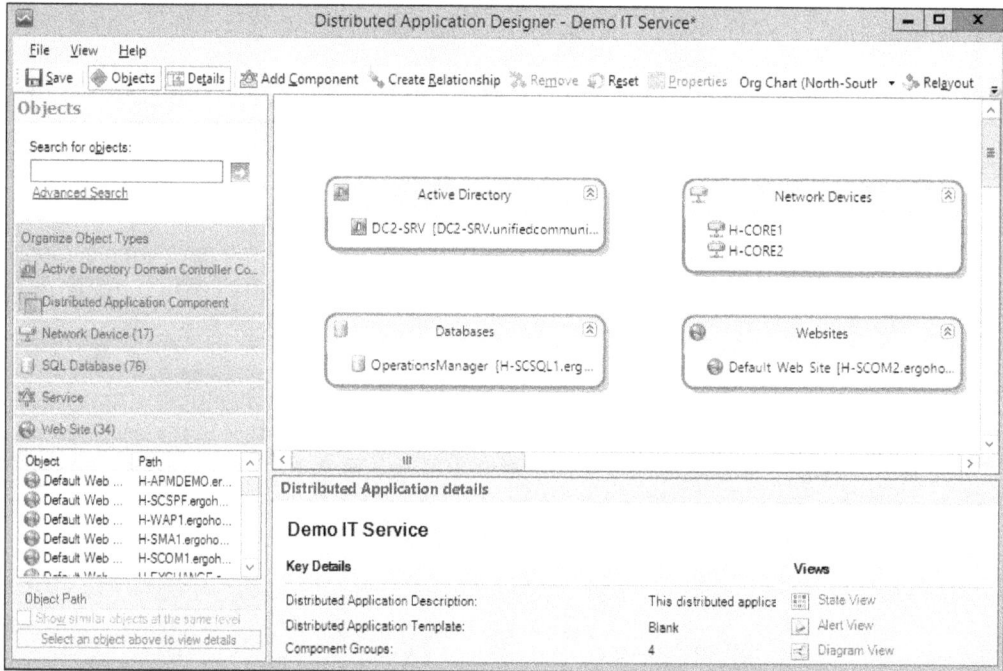

Figure 7.14: Completed distributed application model

If you've added a number of component groups to your distributed application design and you're finding it hard to view them all within the same window, just click on the **Relayout** button from the ribbon at the top of the Distributed Application Designer and OpsMgr will automatically size the component group layout for you.

Configuring health rollup policies

When your new distributed application has been saved and created, you will need to plan and configure a health rollup policy for each component group in the model. A health rollup policy is essentially a policy that determines how the cumulative health of the objects in a component group rollup to its parent. For example, if you have a component group that contains a number of highly available clustered servers, and then you could afford to lose one of those servers before the overall distributed application (IT Service) goes into a critical state. A health rollup policy will tell OpsMgr how to deal with this type of scenario.

There's a number of ways that you can configure health rollup policies in OpsMgr. One option is to click on a component group when you have the Distributed Application Designer open and then choose one of the four links from the **Health Roll-up** section of the **Component Group Details** pane as shown in *Figure 7.15*.

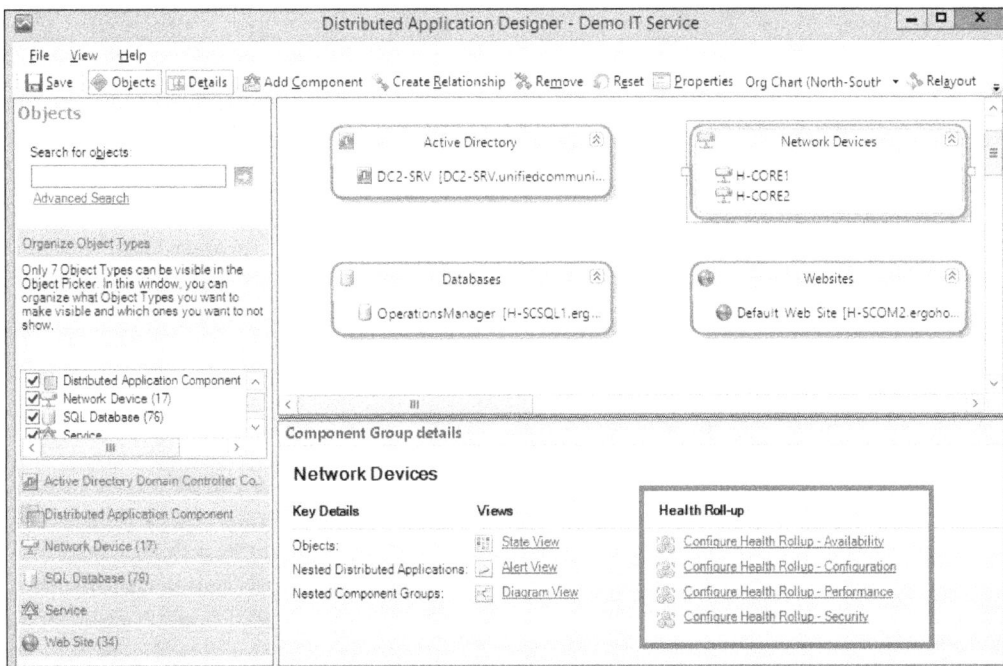

Figure 7.15: Configuring health rollups

Each of the four links allows you to configure a specific health rollup for the
Availability, Configuration, Performance or **Security** of your component group.
Clicking on one of these will open an **Override Properties** dialog box for the
Component Group Health Roll-up monitor as shown here in *Figure 7.16*.

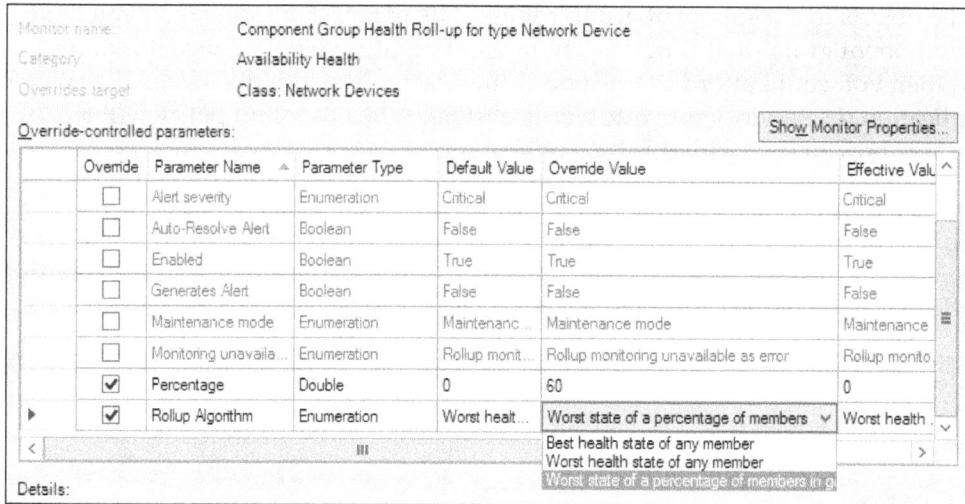

Figure 7.16: Choosing the rollup algorithm

You can configure a health rollup algorithm with three options as shown in
Figure 7.16:

- **Best health state of any member**
- **Worst health state of any member**
- **Worst state of a percentage of members in good health state**

The best and worst health state of any member options is self-explanatory, but the
final **Worst state of a percentage of members in good health state** can be a bit of a
strange one to understand. What this means is that you can specify a percentage of
component group members that OpsMgr takes into account and then it will use the
worst health state from any of those members as its rollup.

Another option for configuring health rollup is to use the Health Explorer for the
component group and gain access to the policy through the Component Group
Health Roll-up monitor properties.

These steps will walk you through the configuring health rollups using the Health Explorer option:

1. From the Distributed Applications view of the Authoring workspace in the OpsMgr console, right-click on the distributed application and choose the **View Diagram** option (you can also open a diagram view of the distributed application from the Monitoring workspace).

2. Right-click on the component group that you want to configure a health rollup policy for and select **Health Explorer** as shown in *Figure 7.17*.

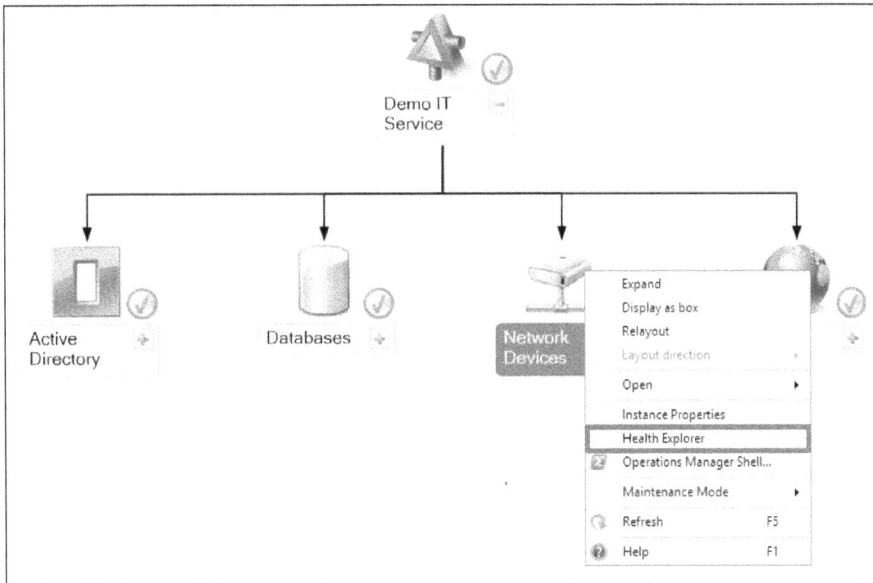

Figure 7.17: Launching Health Explorer from a component group

3. In the **Health Explorer**, deselect the **Filter Monitors** button to display all health monitors relevant to the component group.

4. Now expand the **Availability** monitor and you should see the **Component Group Health Roll-up** monitor just below it. Click to select this monitor and if you expand it one more level, you can see all the objects contained within the component group.

5. Right-click on the **Component Group Health Roll-up** monitor and select the **Monitor Properties** option as shown in *Figure 7.18*.

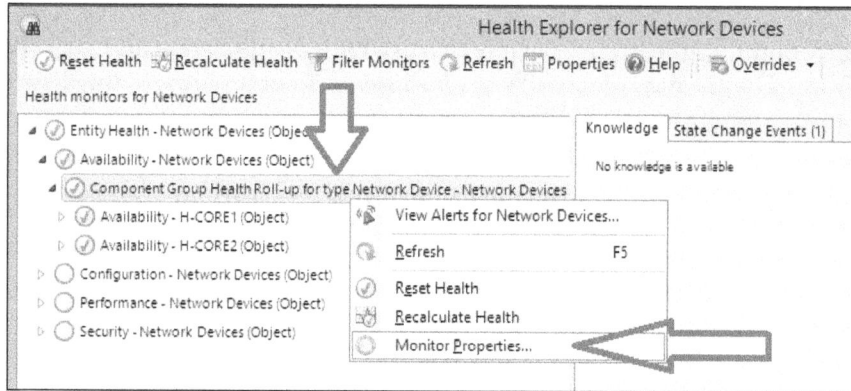

Figure 7.18: Accessing the component group health rollup monitor properties

6. When the monitor properties window opens, click on the **Health Rollup Policy** tab and choose the health rollup policy that best suits your component group.

> The benefit of using this Health Explorer method is that you get a handy example rollup diagram for each option, which is especially useful when choosing **Worst state of the specified percentage of members in good health state**. You can also decide how to rollup objects that are unmonitored or in maintenance mode here.

Figure 7.19 shows how we've configured the rollup for our Network Devices component group.

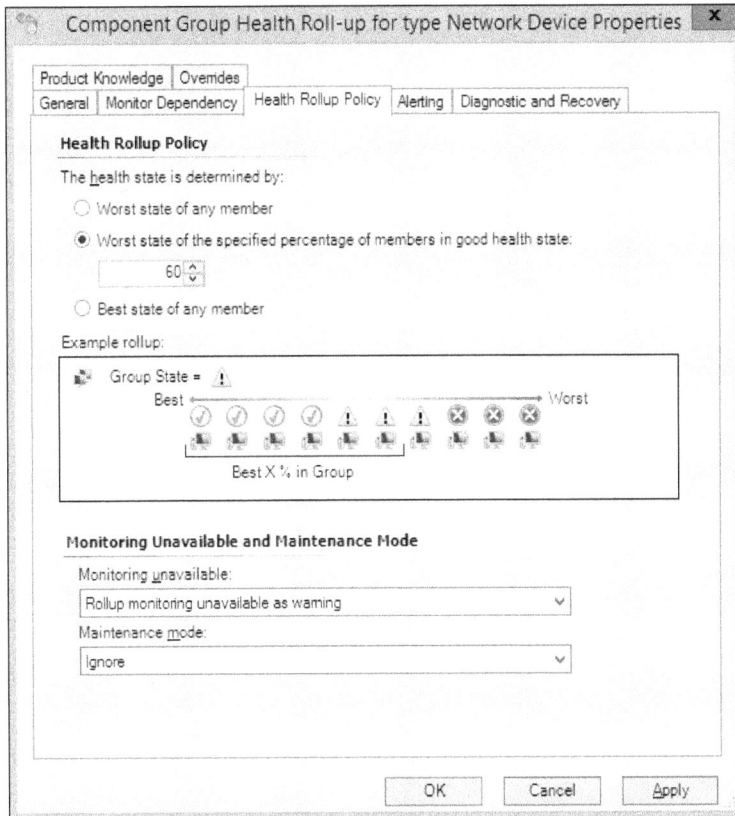

Figure 7.19: Modifying health rollup policy with example rollup diagrams

> If you find that the options within the **Health Rollup Policy**
> tab are grayed out and inaccessible, then you've opened the
> properties for the wrong monitor. It must be the **Component
> Health Group Roll-up...** monitor for this to work.

7. Click on **OK** when you're done configuring the policy to save your changes
   and then close the Health Explorer to finish the process. If you need to
   configure health rollup policies for any other component groups, just repeat
   these steps for each one.

Creating service level objectives

After you have created a distributed application and configured its health rollup policies, its good practice to create and assign some service level tracking to it. Using service level tracking in OpsMgr, you can define a **Service Level Objective (SLO)** to measure the availability/performance of a specific object – in this case the IT service/distributed application model. Using SLO's, an OpsMgr administrator can then work with the IT service owner to create a **Service Level Agreement (SLA)** that specifies how available the service should be over a given period of time.

Even if you work within an organization that doesn't implement or hasn't yet got around to mapping out SLAs for IT services, using this functionality in OpsMgr is a great way of delivering some tangible value back to higher tiers of management within the business (think CIO's and board members) in the form of SLA reporting and dashboards.

Here's what you need to do to create an SLA for the distributed application you built earlier:

1. From the **Authoring** workspace, expand **Management Pack Objects**, now right-click on **Service Level Tracking** and then choose the **Create** option as shown in *Figure 7.20*.

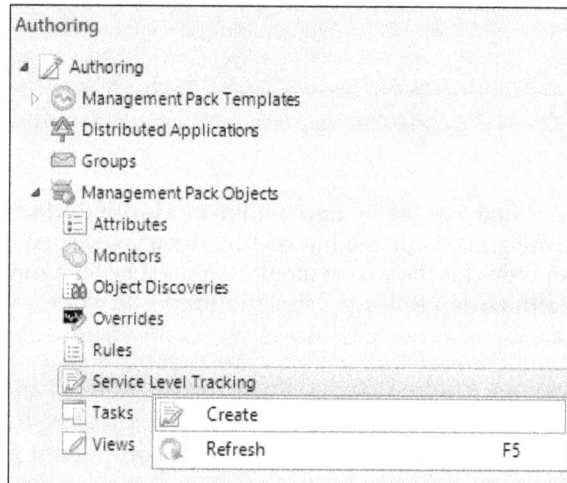

Figure 7.20: Create a new SLA

2. At the **General** dialog box in the **Service Level Tracking** wizard, type a name and description for the new SLA as shown in *Figure 7.21*, and then click on **Next** to move on.

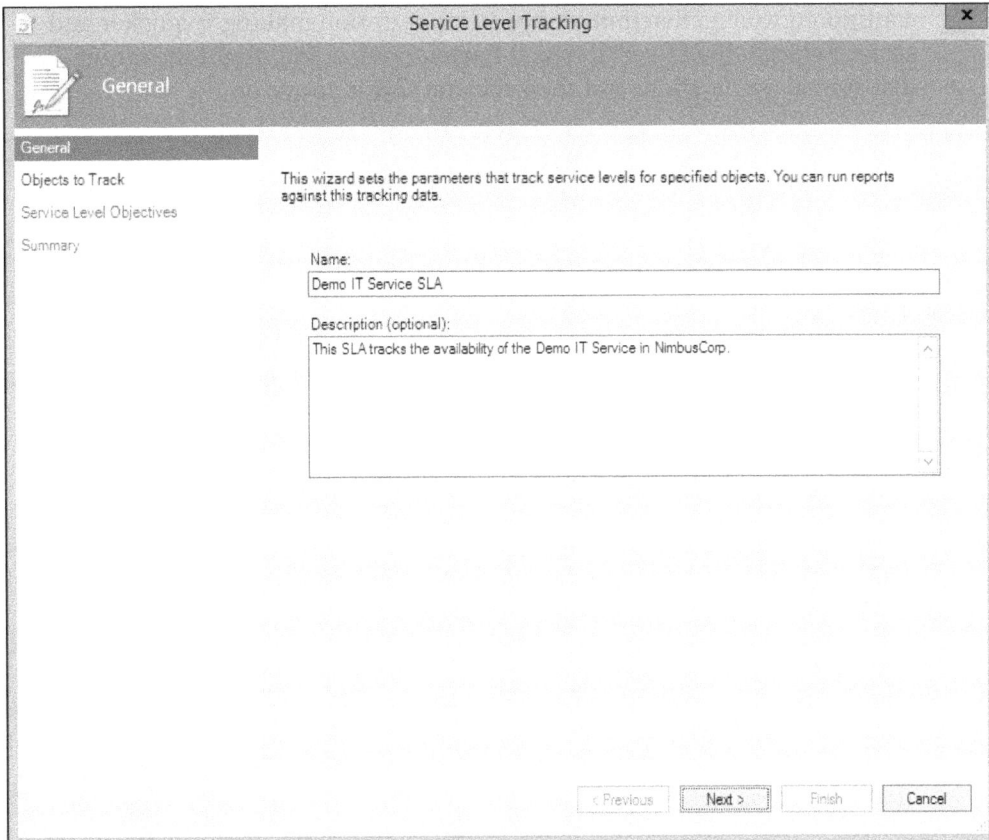

Figure 7.21: Giving your SLA a name and description

3. At the **Objects** to **Track dialog** box, you need to specify a target class that the SLA will apply to. Click on the **Select** button to open the **Select a Target Class** dialog box and type the name of your distributed application into the **Look for** field. As you can see in *Figure 7.22*, the search filter is automatically configured to the **Distributed Application** option making it quicker and easier to locate the IT services you have modeled. Highlight the target distributed application, and then click on **OK** to move on.

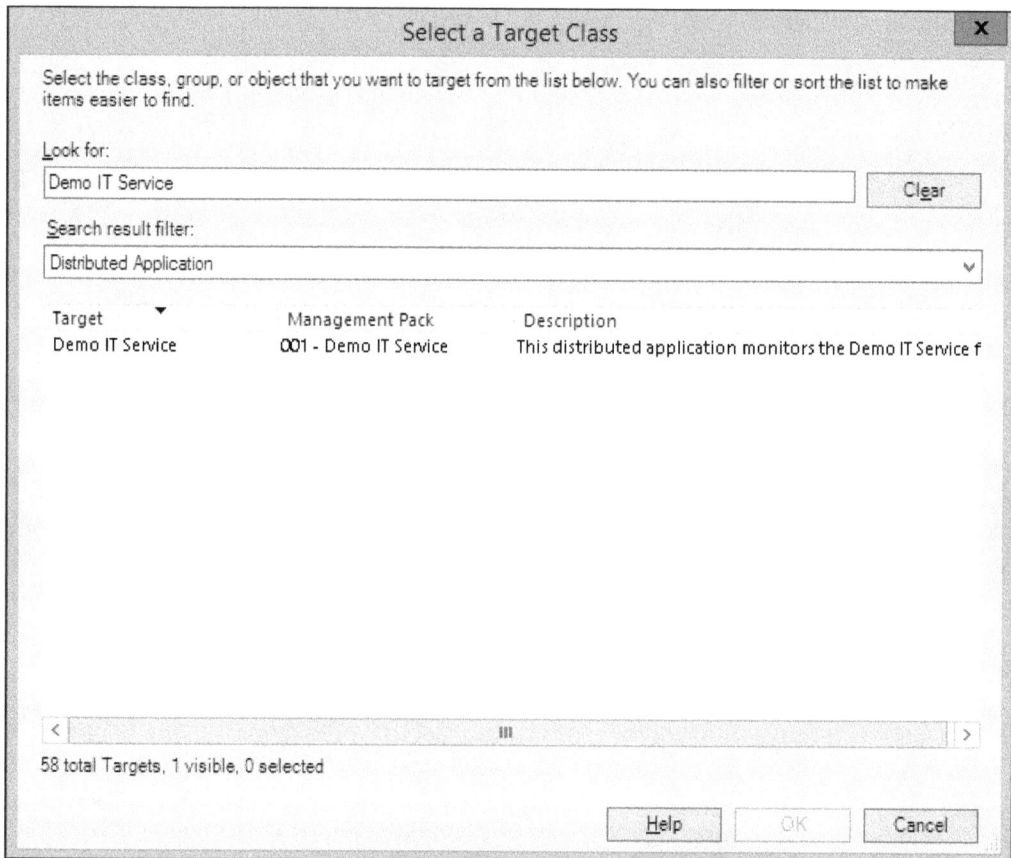

Figure 7.22: Selecting a target class for your SLA

4. Back at the **Objects** to **Track dialog** box you should see the name of your distributed application and the management pack its stored in pre-populated in their relevant fields. Click on **Next** to continue.

5. From the **Service Level Objectives** dialog box, click on the **Add** button, and then choose the **Monitor State SLO** option from the list to open the **Select a Target Class** dialog box again. Type the name of your distributed application into the **Look For** field, select the distributed application from the center pane and then click on **OK**.

6. The **Service Level Objective (Monitor State)** dialog box is where we now get to specify our availability goal and the different states that we wish to be counted as downtime with relation to this objective. In *Figure 7.23*, you can see that we've decided on an availability goal of **99.5** percent and we're only interested in a Critical health state reflecting downtime of the IT service. Click on **OK** when you're ready to move on.

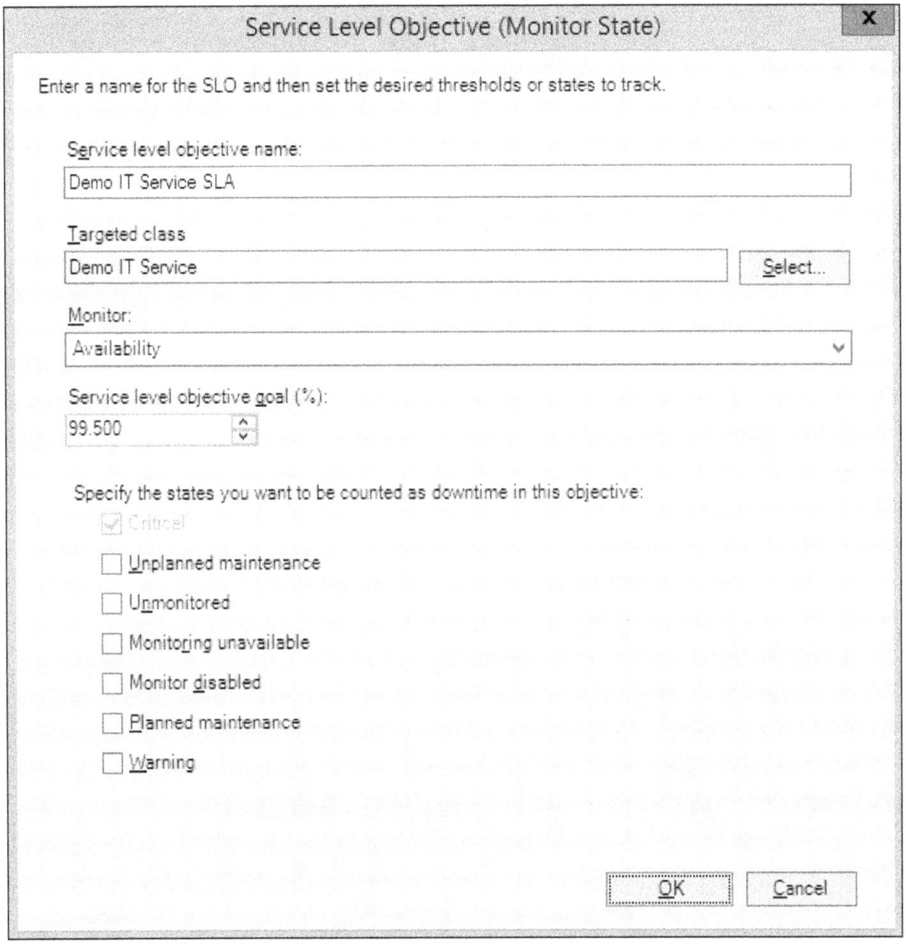

Figure 7.23: Specifying a service level objective goal percentage

7. Back again at the **Service Level Objectives** dialog box, you can choose to add another SLO for the distributed application that targets a performance collection rule or you can leave just the availability state monitor SLO that we created as shown in *Figure 7.24*.

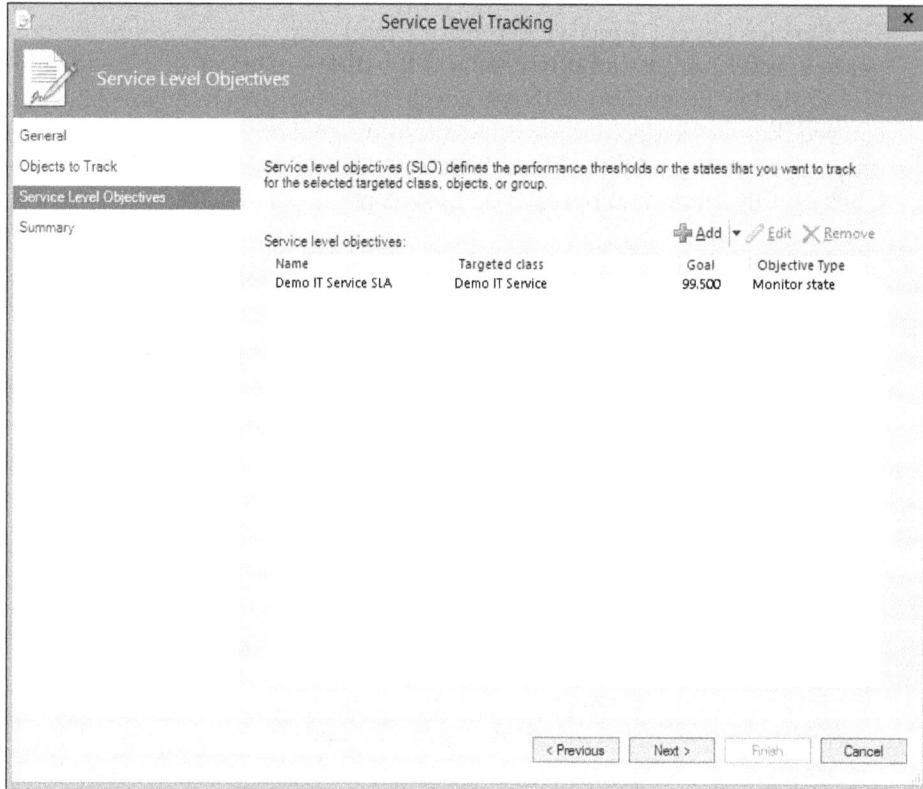

Figure 7.24: Service Level Objectives dialog box

8. Click on **Next** to move on, then review your configuration from the **Summary** dialog box and hit **Finish** when you're ready to create the new service level objective.

Editing distributed applications

A common request we get from customers after creating distributed applications is how to edit or update them. This request is often based on a requirement to enhance the service model by adding in some synthetic transactions to emulate the end-user experience of a particular application.

In the *Management Pack Templates* section of *Chapter 3*, *Exploring the Consoles* we introduced you to the different synthetic transaction options that can be created using default templates in OpsMgr. In the next exercises, we will create two new monitors with these templates – one to check the availability and performance of a corporate website hosted outside the organization and another to validate that a specific TCP port is open on an internal server. When these synthetic transactions have been created, we will add them to the service model of the Demo IT Service distributed application we previously deployed.

Building synthetic transactions for websites

Corporate websites are rarely deployed inside the infrastructure you have responsibility for and typically, they're hosted externally by a third-party service provider. Although the service provider has a responsibility to keep the website up and running, you still need to know whenever it goes down or when the performance degrades.

Follow these steps to create a synthetic transaction that reflects end-user experience when accessing a corporate website:

1. From the **Authoring** workspace, expand **Management Pack Templates**, right-click on **Web Application Transaction Monitoring** and then choose the **Add Monitoring Wizard** option as shown in *Figure 7.25*.

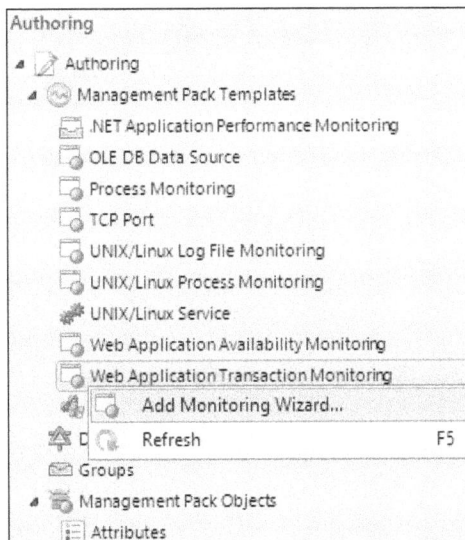

Figure 7.25: Launching the Add Monitoring Wizard

2. At the **Select Monitoring Type** dialog box shown in *Figure 7.26*, ensure the **Web Application Transaction Monitoring** template is selected then click on **Next** to move on.

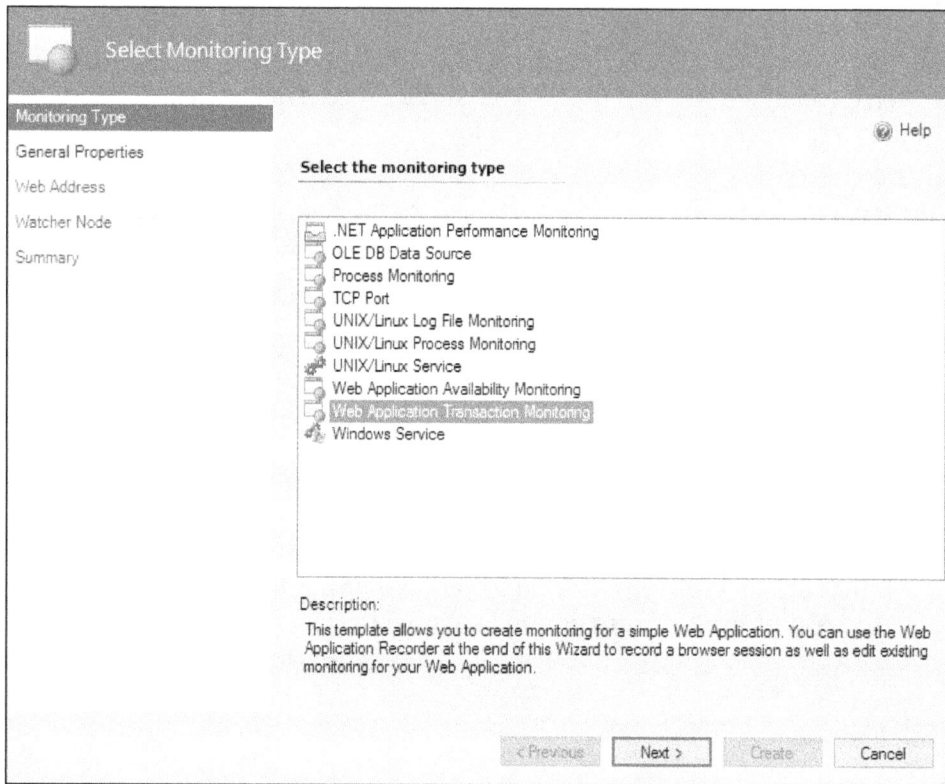

Figure 7.26: Selecting a monitoring template

3. Type a name for the synthetic transaction and select a management pack to store it in. As shown in *Figure 7.27*, we've stored this in the same management pack that we have stored the distributed application in. Click **Next** to continue.

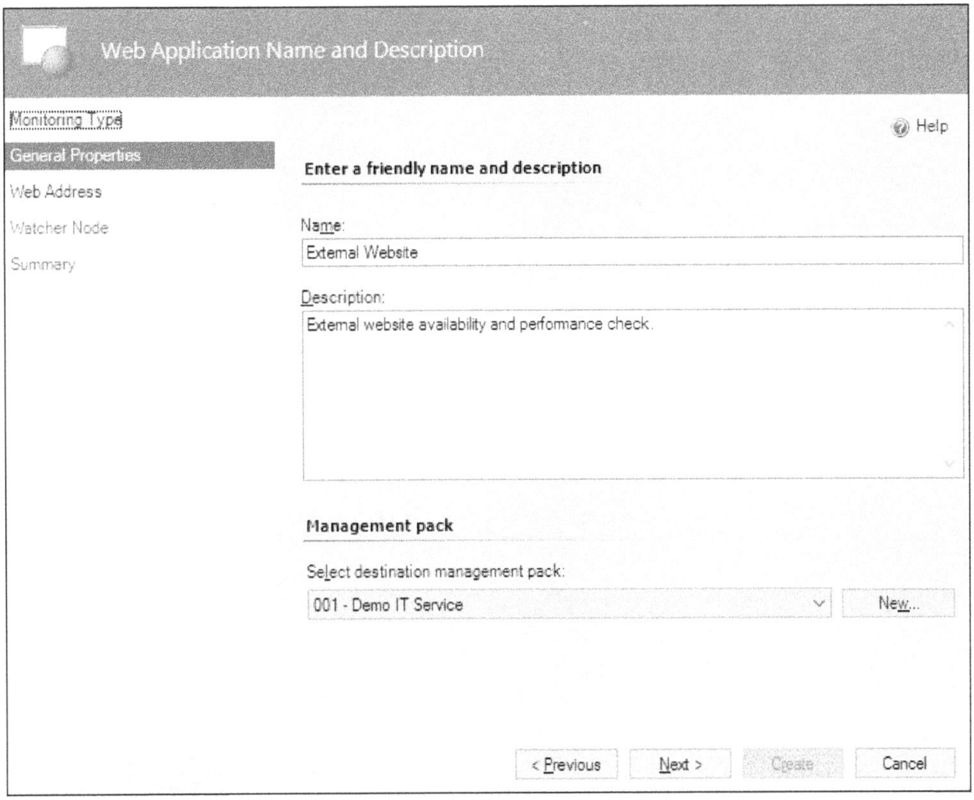

Figure 7.27: Choosing a management pack for the synthetic transaction.

4. At the **Test Web Address** dialog box shown in *Figure 7.28*, type the URL for your external website, choosing from either **http** or **https**, and click on the **Test** button to confirm the website is accessible (this test assumes you have internet connectivity from the server you are running the console from). Hit **Next** when you're ready to move on.

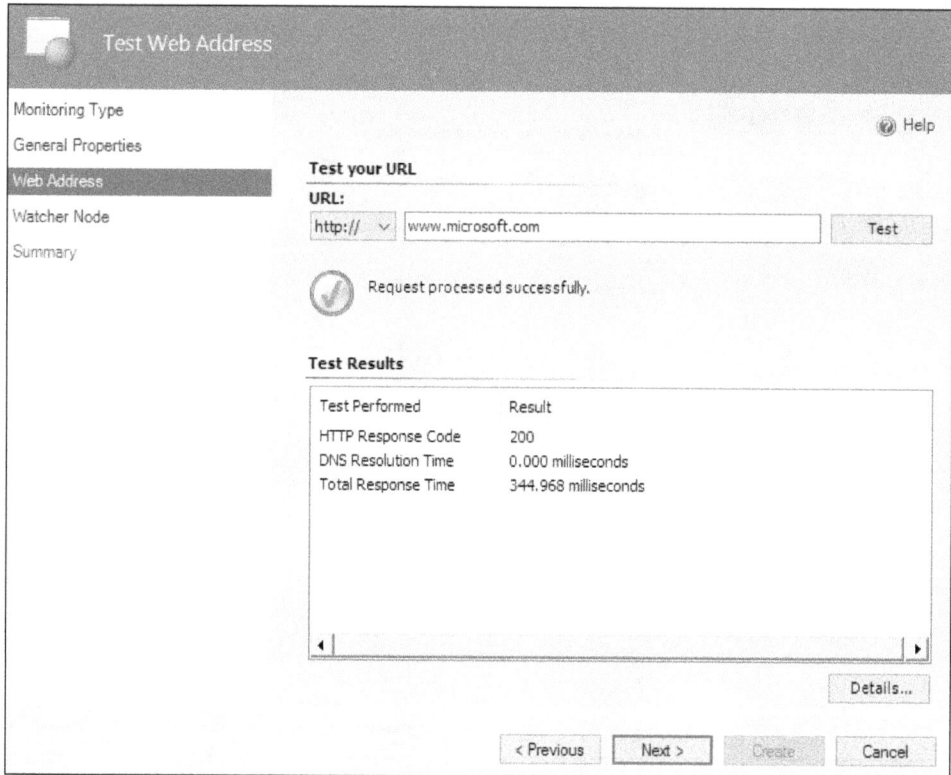

Figure 7.28: Testing the website URL request.

5. From the **Watcher Node** dialog box, select the OpsMgr agents (watcher nodes) that you would like to run the synthetic transaction checks from. More than one agent can be selected as a watcher node and this is a useful feature to have when you need to check connectivity from different locations across the business. As shown in *Figure 7.29*, we'll choose one watcher node from our local domain and the other will be located in the untrusted domain that hosts our Gateway server. Select how often you wish to run the query then click on **Next**.

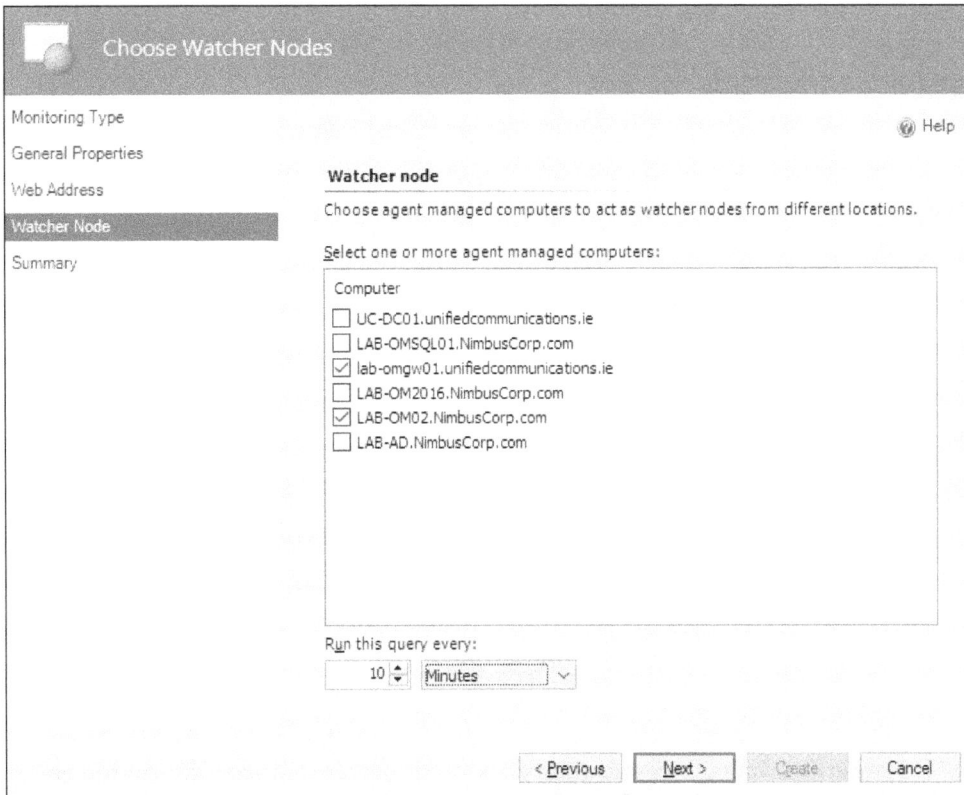

Figure 7.29: Selecting watcher nodes

6. At the **Summary** dialog box shown in *Figure 7.30*, check the box beside the **Configure Advanced Monitoring** or **Record a browser session** option then click on **Create** to build the synthetic transaction.

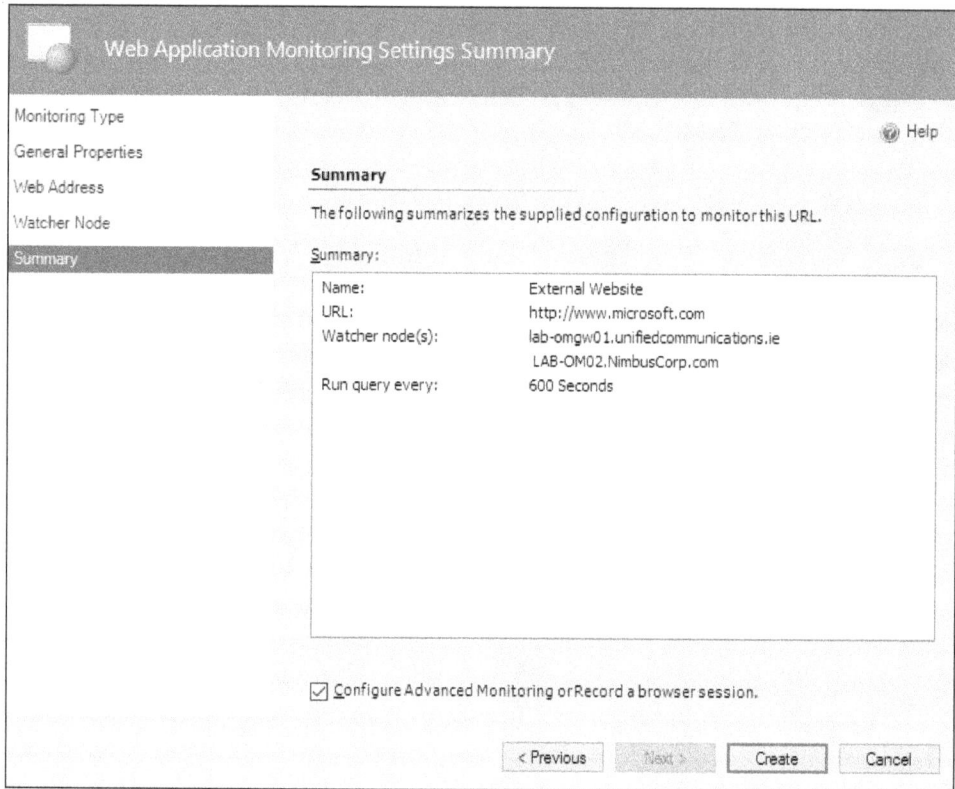

Figure 7.30: Choosing the advanced monitoring option

7. When the **Web Application Editor** opens, click on the **Configure Settings** link from the **Actions** pane on the right to launch the **Web Application Properties** dialog box and then click on the **Performance Criteria** tab and add some **Transaction Response Time** values for error and warning health status as shown in *Figure 7.31*. Click **OK** to close the dialog box.

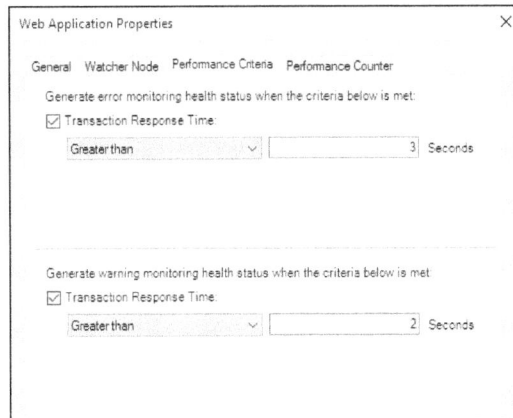

Figure 7.31: Specifying performance criteria for the website check

8. Back at the **Web Application Editor** (shown in *Figure 7.32*), you can specify additional criteria for error and warning health states – including http status code validation and content match checks. Verify your changes and click on **Apply** to commit them to the synthetic transaction.

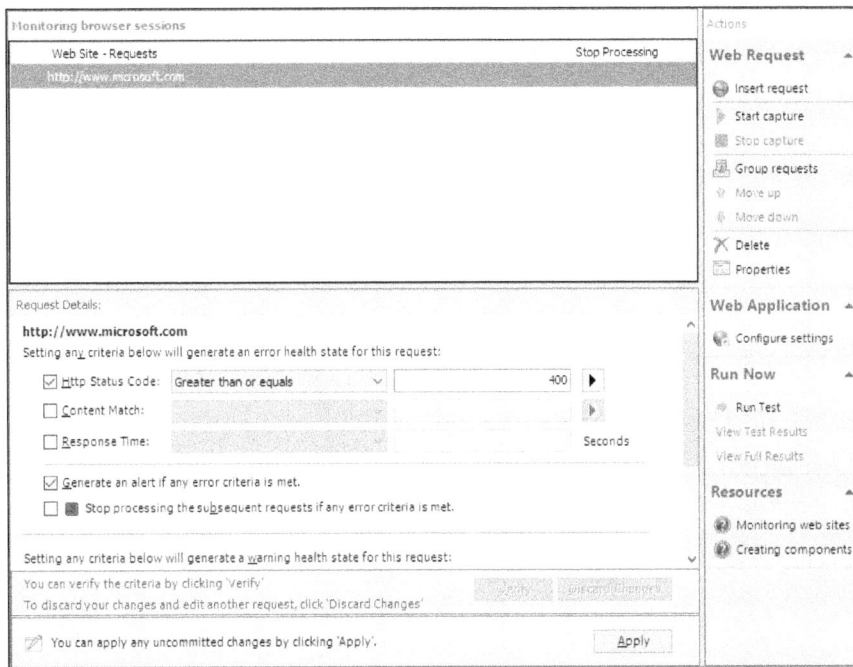

Figure 7.32: Web Application Editor

9. Close the Web Application Editor to finish the process.

Creating a TCP port monitor

In the majority of OpsMgr deployments I've worked on, there's been a requirement to monitor at least one custom TCP port that end-users interact with to gain access into a mission critical application and using the TCP Port management pack template helps us to deliver on this.

The following steps will walk you through creating a synthetic transaction that will check if a custom TCP port (54321) is open on a particular application:

1. From the **Authoring** workspace, expand **Management Pack Templates**, right-click on **TCP Port** and launch the **Add Monitoring Wizard** again.

2. At the **Select Monitoring Type** dialog box shown in *Figure 7.33*, ensure the **TCP Port** template is selected and then click on **Next** to move on.

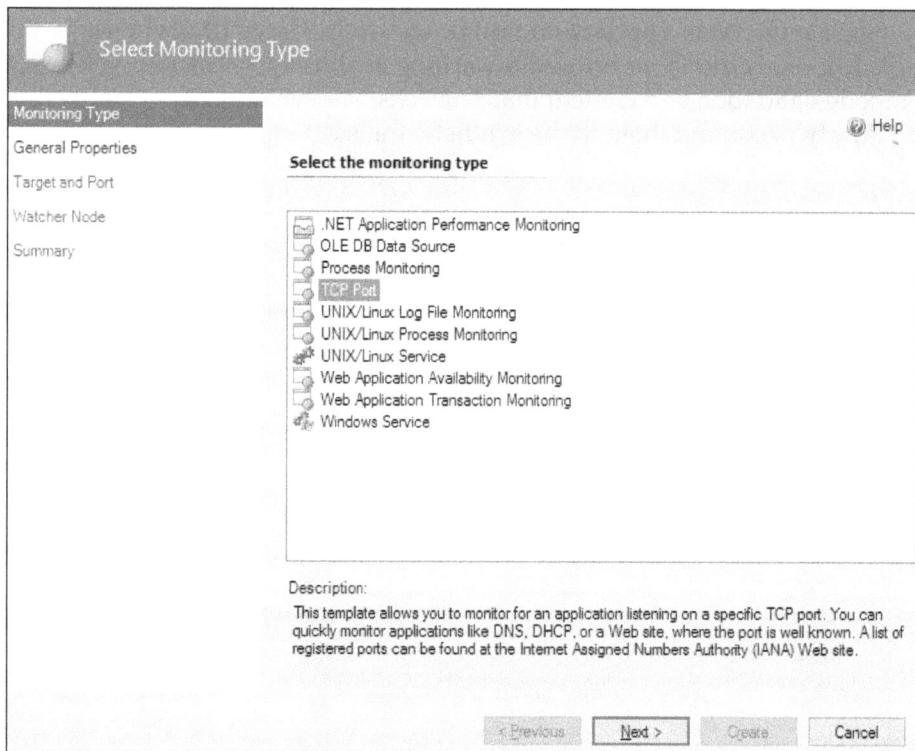

Figure 7.33: Selecting the TCP Port template.

3. Type a name for the synthetic transaction and select a management pack to store it in. As shown in *Figure 7.34*, we've stored this in the same management pack that we have stored the distributed application and other synthetic transaction in. Click **Next** to continue.

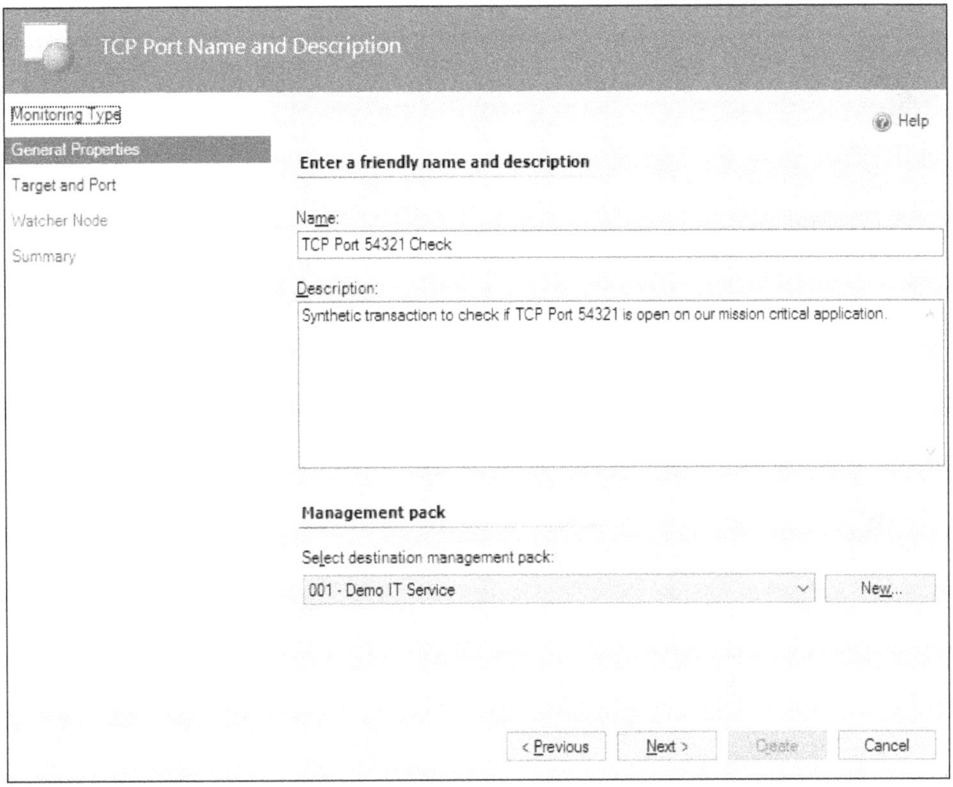

Figure 7.34: Configuring general properties for the TCP Port check.

4. At the **Target and Port** dialog box, enter an IP address or DNS name for the **Computer or device name** field (this will be where you want to check for the open port) and type the TCP port number into the **Port** field. Now click on the **Test** button and you should see a successful test as shown in *Figure 7.35*. Click **Next** to continue.

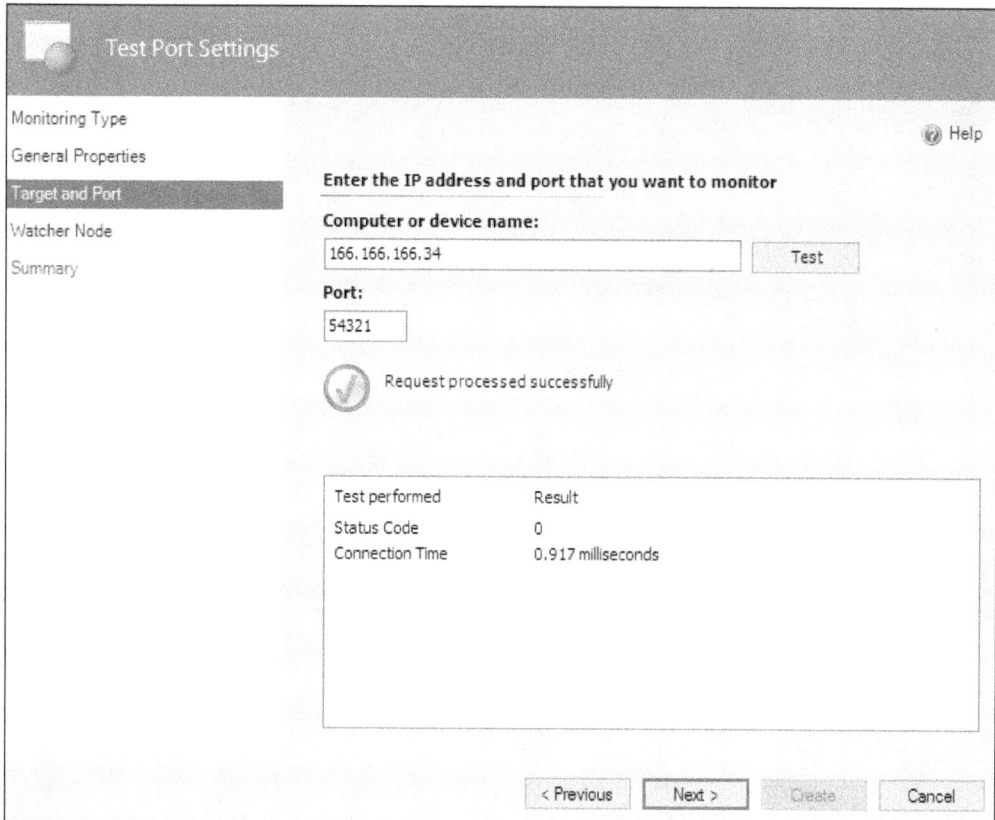

Figure 7.35: Testing the TCP Port check

5. Choose the watcher nodes to run the check from and enter how often you'd like it to run and then click on **Next**.

6. At the **Summary** dialog box, click on **Create** to finish the process and create the new TCP Port synthetic transaction check.

Updating the service model

When you have the new synthetic transactions created, you'll need to add them to the service model in your distributed application and the following steps will walk you through this process:

1. From the **Authoring** workspace, click on the **Distributed Applications** link from the navigation area on the left, right-click on the distributed application you want to modify and then select the **Edit** option from the resulting menu as shown in *Figure 7.36*.

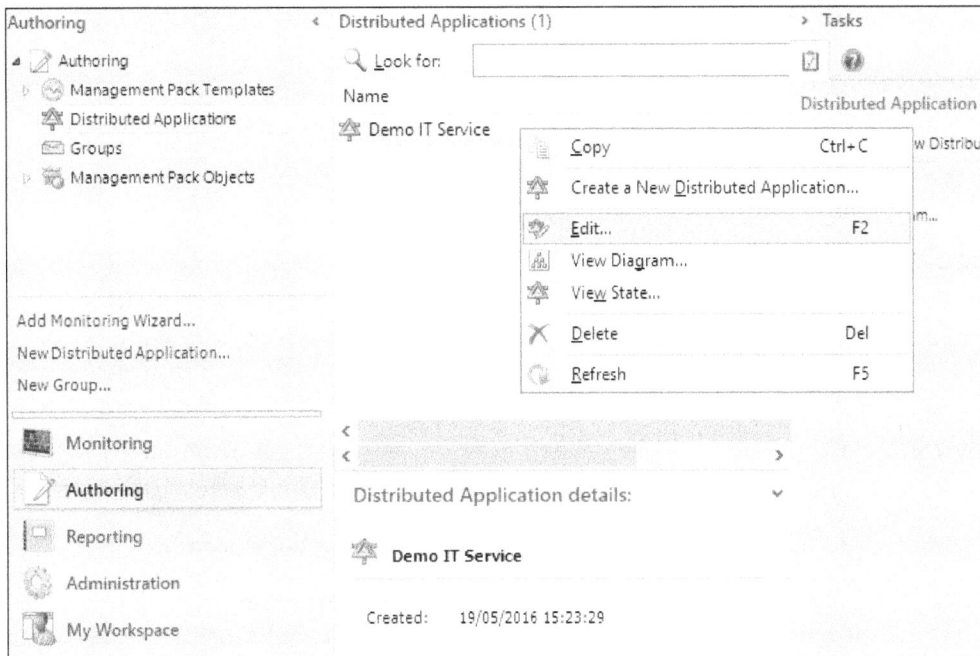

Figure 7.36: Editing an existing distributed application.

2. When the Distributed Application Designer opens, click on the **Add Component** button.

3. From the **Create New Component Group** dialog box, type a display name for your component group (we'll call this one **End User Experience**), click on the **Objects of the following type(s) radio** button, and then navigate to **Configuration Item | Logical Entity | Perspective**, as shown in *Figure 7.37*. Click on **OK** to create the component group.

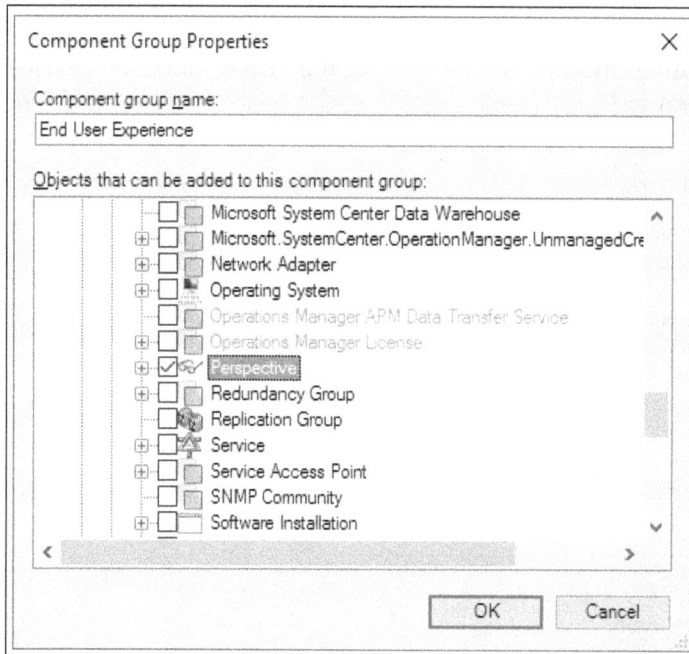

Figure 7.37: Adding a component group for synthetic transactions.

4. Using the **Perspective** class located in the navigation bar on the left, as shown in *Figure 7.38*, add the new synthetic transactions to the new component group.

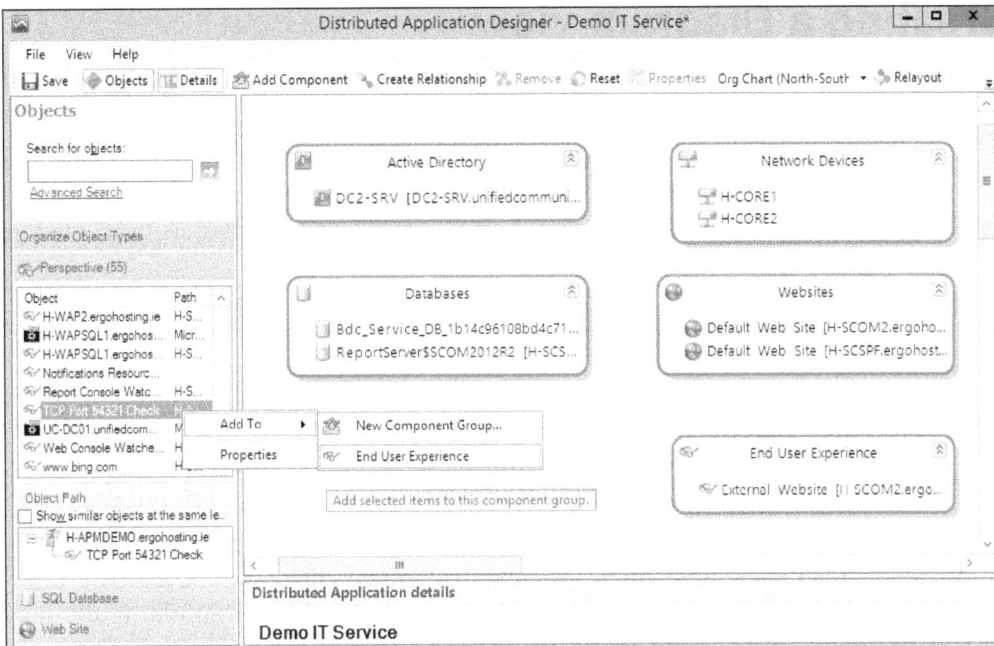

Figure 7.38: Populating the new component group.

5. Click the **Save** button to update the service model and when it's finished updating, close the designer to return to the console and complete the process.

Adding distributed application views

The final steps you need to work through when you have your distributed application and service level objectives created is to make them easily visible (and manageable) from within the Monitoring workspace. By adding a few simple views to the management pack folder that contains the distributed application, administrators and operators who plan on using the OpsMgr consoles for monitoring will reap the benefits.

It's worth pointing out before we begin that the views we create in this section are just suggestions to get you started and you can go ahead and add whatever works for you or your customer environments as applicable.

Creating a Diagram view

The first view we will create is a Diagram view so we can get a visual representation of the IT service and its child component groups.

1. In the Monitoring workspace, right-click on the location that you wish to create your new view (we'll choose the 001 – Demo IT Service management pack folder we created earlier in the *Modeling Your IT Service* section), click on **New**, and then click on **Diagram View**.

2. In the **Name** field, type a name for your distributed application diagram view – we'll choose 'Demo IT Service' as a name here.

3. Click the **Browse** button to open the **Object Search** dialog box.

4. From the **Look for** drop-down menu, choose the **Service** class and then type the name of the distributed application and hit **Search**. Now select the distributed application from the **Available Items** section, click on **Add**, and then hit **OK** to open the **Create Diagram View** dialog box.

5. Select the **Create your own template** option and click on the **Create** button to build your diagram view. The end product should look similar to the distributed application in *Figure 7.39*.

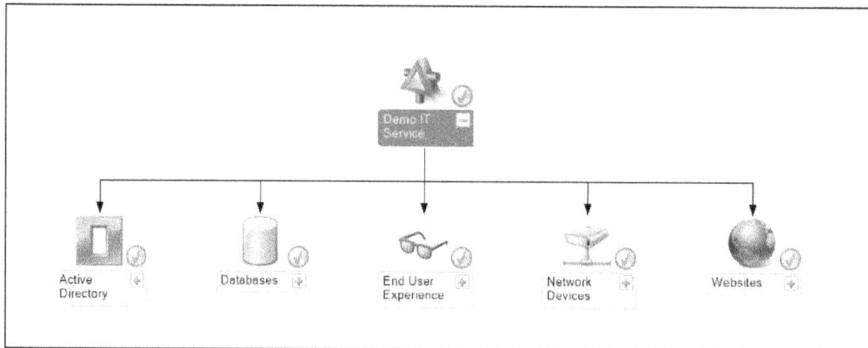

Figure 7.39: Viewing the service model diagram.

Creating an Alert view

The next view that we want to create is an alert view, which will be scoped directly at our new distributed application. Using a view like this makes it easy for IT service owners to see all alerts that are specific to the service they are responsible for.

1. In the Monitoring workspace, right-click on the folder location that contains your distributed application (this should be the same folder you used in the previous section), click on **New** and then click on **Alert View**.

2. In the **Name** field, type a name for your view – we'll use 'Demo IT Service Alerts' for our example.

3. At the **Criteria** tab, define the parameters of your alert view:

   ○ On the **Show Data Related To** box, click on the ellipsis button (**...**), select the **View All Targets** option, type the name of your distributed application into the **Look For** field, select the distributed application from the list and click on **OK**.

   ○ In the **Show Data Contained In A Specific Group** box, leave the (**All**) groups option selected.

   ○ From the **Select Conditions** area, select the check boxes for the alert criteria that you wish to show in the view; we've chosen a criterion that specifies all alerts **except** those with a resolution state of **Closed**.

4. Click the **Display** tab and as shown in *Figure 7.40*, add an additional column to display here for **Repeat Count** and change the **Group items by** option to **Descending**.

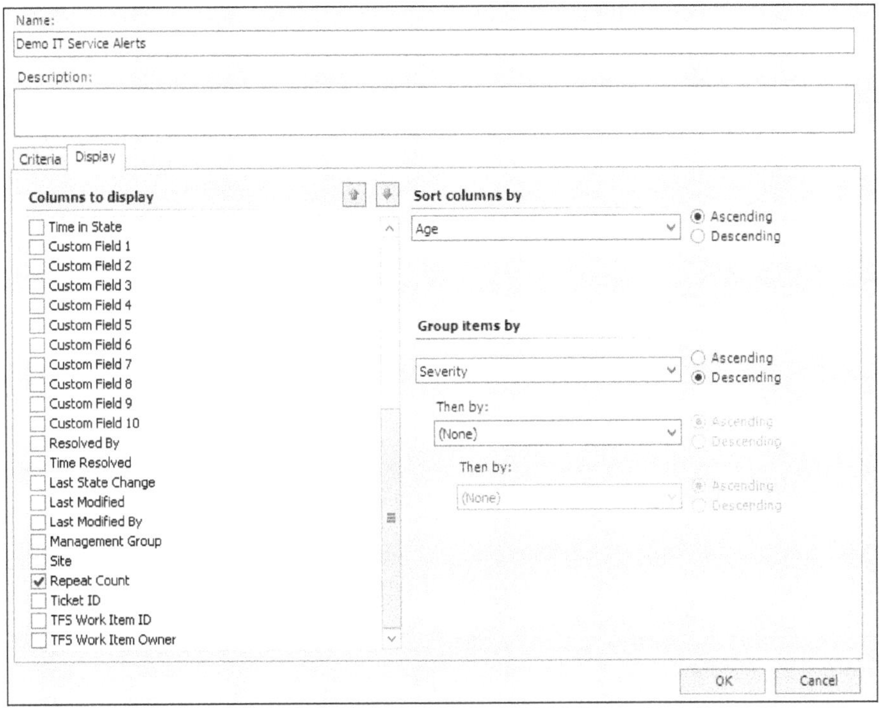

Figure 7.40: Viewing the service model diagram

5. Click **OK** when you're done to complete the Alert view.

Creating an SLA view

The last distributed application view that we will add is the SLA view. This is a dashboard template designed to show service level objectives and it can be configured to show single or multiple objectives as required.

Here's what you need to do to create an SLA view for your distributed application:

1. In the Monitoring workspace, right-click on the folder location that contains your distributed application (this should be the same folder you used in the previous sections), click on **New**, and then click on **Dashboard View**.

2. At the **New Dashboard and Widget Wizard**, select the **Service Level Dashboard** option shown in *Figure 7.41* then click on **Next** to move on.

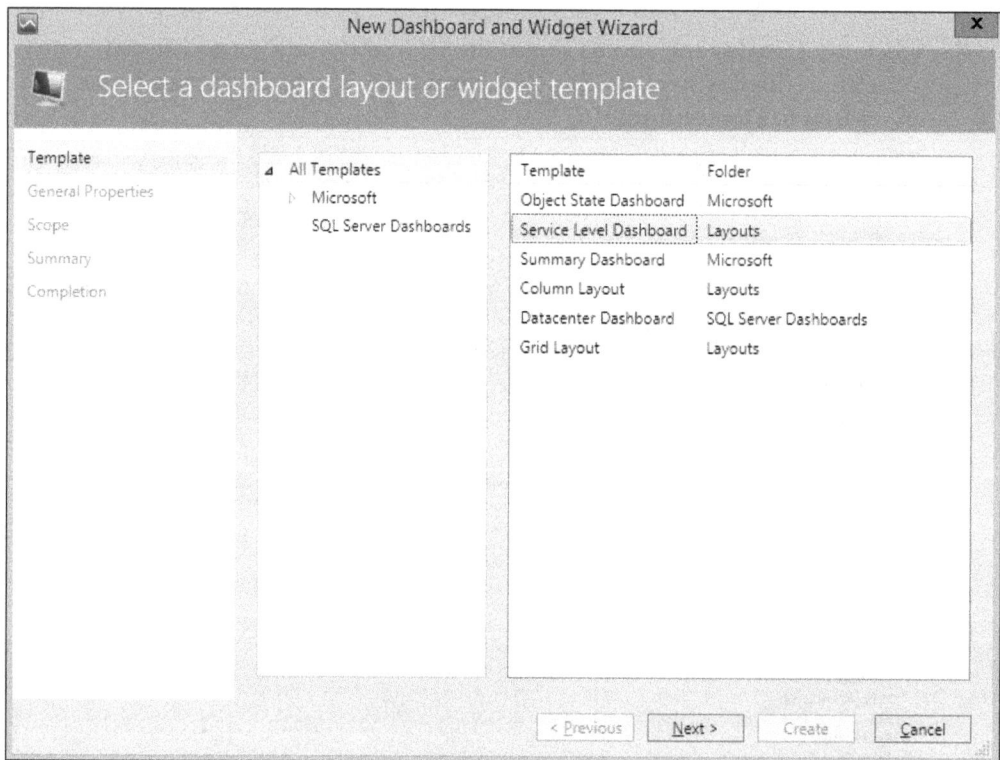

Figure 7.41: Creating a service level dashboard

3. Give the dashboard a name (we'll use 'Demo IT Service SLA' here) and click on **Next** to continue.

4. From the **Specify the Scope** dialog box, click on the **Add** button to open the **Add SLA** dialog box.

5. In the **Available Items** list, locate the SLA you created earlier in the *Creating service level objectives* section, add it to **Selected Items** and click on **OK** to close the dialog box.

6. You should now see your SLA listed in the **Specify the Scope** dialog box and here you can choose the time period that the SLA will report back on. In *Figure 7.42*, you can see that we've chosen a 24 hour period but you can select from minutes, hours, days, months and years as required.

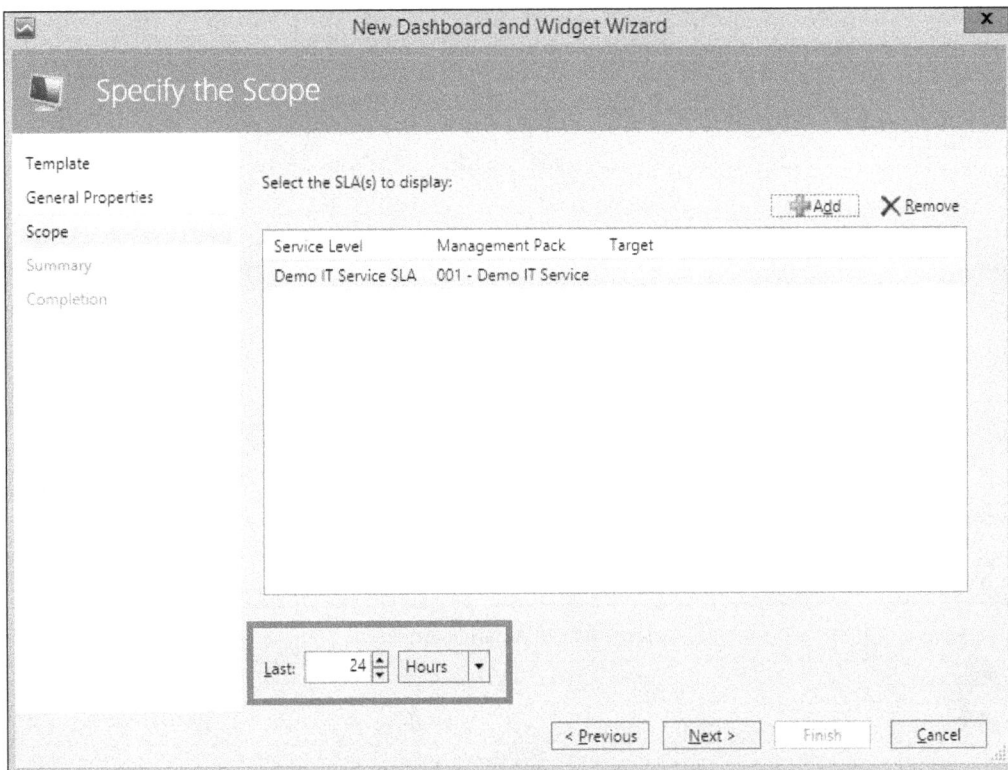

Figure 7.42: Selecting a time period for your SLA

7. When you're ready, click on **Next** to move on and then at the **Summary** dialog box, hit **Create** to complete the wizard, and you should end up with a dashboard similar to the one in *Figure 7.43*.

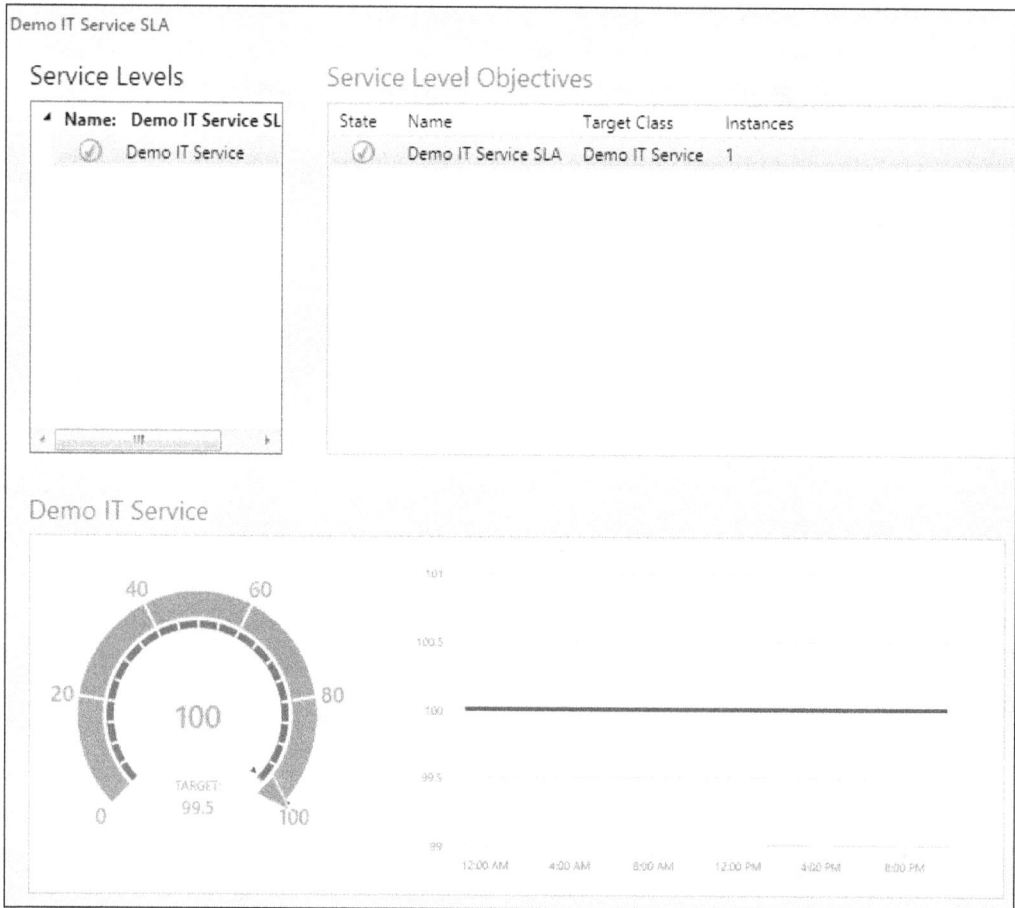

Figure 7.43: SLA dashboard view

Summary

In this chapter, we began with an overview of what a distributed application is and how it applied to OpsMgr. We then discussed the different pre-built distributed application templates that you can use before walking you through creating a new distributed application using the Blank (Advanced) template.

We also gave you an understanding of health rollup policies and how to configure them before demonstrating how to create service level objectives that mapped back to SLA's defined by the organization. At the end of the chapter, we showed you some typical examples of views that you can add to the Monitoring workspace to make it easy to manage and interact with your monitored IT services.

In the next chapter, we will show you some tips and tricks for tuning your alerts – including how to use distributed application model views to help reduce noise based on the context of your IT services.

8
Alert Tuning the Easy Way

A crucial task when managing any monitoring system is to work through the many alerts that are generated and ensure that the 'noisy' ones are filtered out and the over-zealous ones have their thresholds modified. This process is known as alert tuning and when implemented properly, it will deliver alerts that are actionable and worth knowing about.

In this chapter, we explain what alert tuning is in the context of OpsMgr and the importance of having a process-driven alert management strategy. We will discuss the different built-in alert resolution states and we'll demonstrate how to configure new custom resolution states to suit your business requirements.

Later in the chapter, we'll show you some tips and tricks using scripts, custom tasks, and built-in tools to ensure tuning alerts in your OpsMgr environments is a relatively easy and straight-forward process. We then close out the chapter with some pointers on how to manage your overrides through the authoring and reporting workspaces.

Here's an overview of what you'll learn about:

- Alert resolution states
- Working with alerts generated by monitors and rules
- Using the Health Explorer
- Creating custom tasks to tune alerts
- Managing overrides

Alert tuning overview

One of the most common complaints that I hear from customers when I ask them about their existing monitoring solutions or OpsMgr deployments is that there's too many alerts in the console and it's hard to decipher which ones are important and which should be ignored. This situation is compounded further when email alerting is configured and it's not uncommon for staff to simply create a rule in their email client that moves all emails sent from the monitoring solution into a subfolder (or direct to deleted items) and then completely ignore them.

If a monitoring solution is let get to this point, then it quickly becomes useless. With a proper alert management/tuning strategy for OpsMgr in place, you'll quickly see the true benefits of this awesome product and it will definitely save you some time when troubleshooting and resolving issues.

Alert tuning is an ongoing administration process in OpsMgr and when you modify an alert (for example, tweaking thresholds or disabling it completely), you're creating a change that's referred to as override. Overrides can only be saved in unsealed management packs and managing these override management packs through a consistent naming convention and sorting process will ensure the efforts you put into alert tuning can be easily migrated between different management groups. This can be very useful in a scenario where you have a separate management group for testing in which you can pre-tune alerts and see their impact before importing them into the production management group.

Defining an alert management process

If you're faced with a console packed full of alerts, it's tempting to just dive straight in and begin disabling or modifying them but beware, without a defined alert management process in place, you'll soon find yourself diving deep into troubleshooting mode without any real context behind how the overall IT services might be affected by your changes.

The following sections will give you some pointers to help you put together a solid alert management process.

Choose your Management Packs wisely

In *Chapter 5, Working with Management Packs* you learnt about management packs and how they give OpsMgr the knowledge it needs to monitor your infrastructure and applications. It goes without saying so, that the first thing you need to start your alert management process with is by ensuring that only management packs you actually require are imported.

It's pretty common for OpsMgr administrators to get trigger happy with the **Import Management Packs** option in the **Administration** workspace and to import the full list of management packs from the online catalog – even when they're not required! When I've come across this situation in customer environments, I've heard people say things like "I've deployed the BizTalk management pack now as there's a chance that we'll install that product next year"! This is a crazy strategy that leads to management pack sprawl, performance issues and undoubtedly alert noise as different discoveries, and rules attempt to fire against existing agents that don't host the relevant applications or hardware to be monitored.

From time to time, you might come across a management pack that offers monitoring for something that you have running in your environment and you might automatically assume that you should go ahead and import this management pack straight away. This isn't always the best course of action as some management packs will just create so much alert noise based on false-positives and non-actionable problems that you'd be better off without them! The Windows Server 2003/2008 Group Policy management pack is a perfect example of this - far too much noise and not worth the hassle of deploying as there's very little alerts that IT administrators care to action.

> Be careful and always evaluate before you deploy and make sure to import only management packs that will deliver monitoring value to your organization right now, not in the future.

Read the Management Pack guides

It's very important to always read the management pack guides before deploying and working with new management packs. Most guides are packed full with information on what gets monitored by default and they'll also give you pointers on the overrides you might want to make depending on the type of environment you're monitoring.

These guides also come in handy time and time again as a reference for when someone within the organization (an IT service owner or manager for example) wants to know exactly what type of monitoring they'll get from a particular management pack. Although some of the management pack guides might be just a few pages in length, others, such as the SQL Server management pack guide are sometimes closer to 100 pages!

Staying with the SQL Server management pack guide as an example, consider you have a customer that wants to know why the SQL Server management pack you've deployed into their OpsMgr environment isn't picking up SQL Server Agent jobs that are running for a longer-than-expected timeframe. A quick check of the guide will tell you the particular monitor for that scenario is disabled by default as this has the potential to be a noisy alert in certain environments. This is a great example of using management pack guides to assist with your alert management process.

Work with the infrastructure and IT service owners

If you want to ensure your alert management process runs smoothly, then it's always a good idea to involve the infrastructure and IT service owners that will ultimately have responsibility for taking action on the alerts that fire into the console.

Working with the relevant teams in your organization will help you understand which alerts are important, which ones need to be tuned, and which ones can be disabled. An agreement should be put in place with each team that only actionable alerts are relevant and these alerts should be either forwarded to each team using an email alert subscription or routed directly to the service desk ticketing system.

Another piece of advice would be to analyze the different monitors and thresholds that have been applied to any existing monitoring solutions that are currently being used by the infrastructure and IT service owners. Using this information can be useful as you plan a smooth transition to OpsMgr as a replacement monitoring platform.

> Prior to kicking off an OpsMgr deployment, you may have a requirement to gather performance metrics and benchmarks for some of your primary Microsoft workloads, such as Active Directory, SQL, Exchange, and IIS. Using the free **PAL (Performance Analysis of Logs)** tool will assist you with this gathering of information and it's a good place to start when agreeing thresholds for monitors in OpsMgr with the relevant IT service owners. You can download the PAL tool from `https://pal.codeplex.com/`

Alert resolution states

With alert resolution states, you have the option to classify alerts with a specific state, depending on their status and your business requirements. You can manage alert resolution states from the **Settings** view of the **Administration** workspace and in *Figure 8.1*; you can see the seven different states that are configured by default.

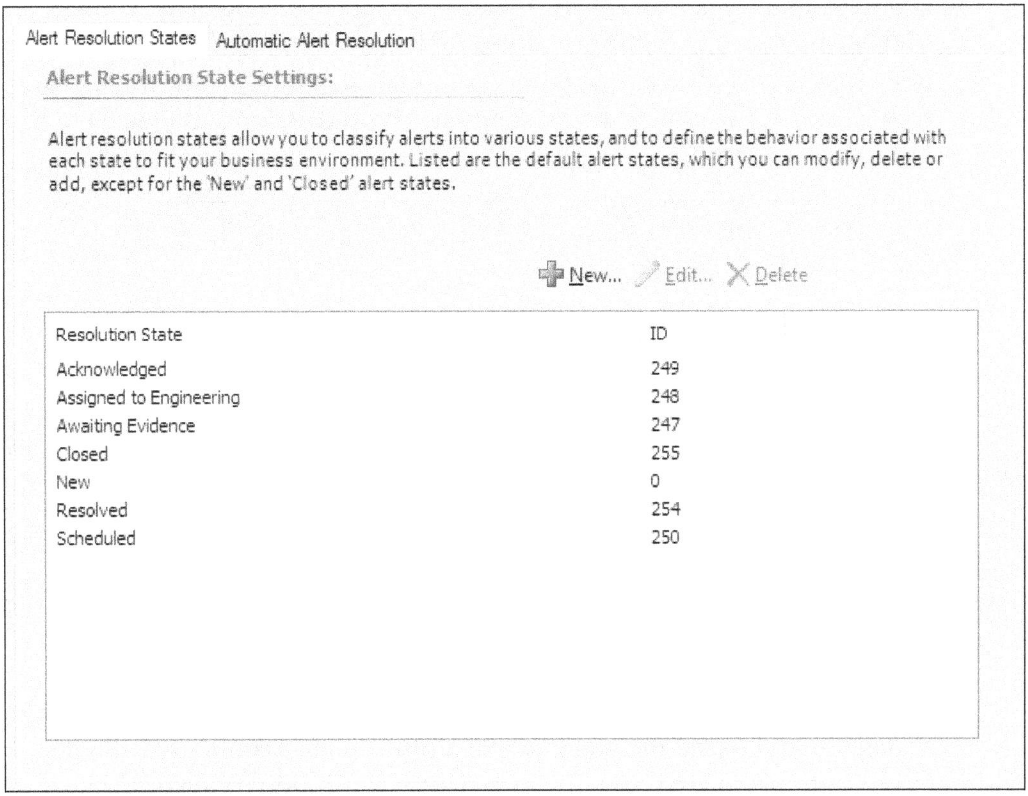

Alert Resolution States   Automatic Alert Resolution

Alert Resolution State Settings:

Alert resolution states allow you to classify alerts into various states, and to define the behavior associated with each state to fit your business environment. Listed are the default alert states, which you can modify, delete or add, except for the 'New' and 'Closed' alert states.

➕ <u>N</u>ew...   ✏ <u>E</u>dit...   ✖ <u>D</u>elete

Resolution State	ID
Acknowledged	249
Assigned to Engineering	248
Awaiting Evidence	247
Closed	255
New	0
Resolved	254
Scheduled	250

Figure 8.1: Default alert resolution states

From the figure, you'll notice there's an ID value alongside the resolution state name. You cannot edit or delete any of these default resolution states but you can however, create new resolution states to suit your needs.

Creating a custom resolution state

A total of 255 alert resolution states can be used in OpsMgr and excluding the default states that cannot be modified; you can create up to a maximum of 247 more. Follow these steps to create a new custom alert resolution state:

1. From the **Administration** workspace in the OpsMgr console, select **Settings** and then double-click on **Alerts** from the central pane to open the **Global Management Group Settings – Alerts** dialog box.

2. Now click on the **New** button to open the **Alert Resolution State** dialog box, type a name for your new alert resolution state and assign a unique ID to it as shown in *Figure 8.2*.

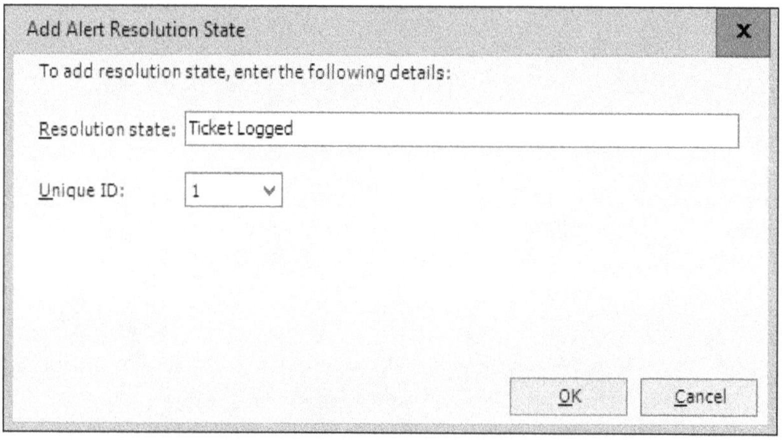

Figure 8.2: Adding a custom alert resolution state

3. Click on **OK** to return to the **Global Management Group Settings – Alerts** dialog box and repeat the previous step until you have configured all your additional custom alert resolution steps. In *Figure 8.3*, we've highlighted some examples of common custom alert resolution states that we've configured in our environment.

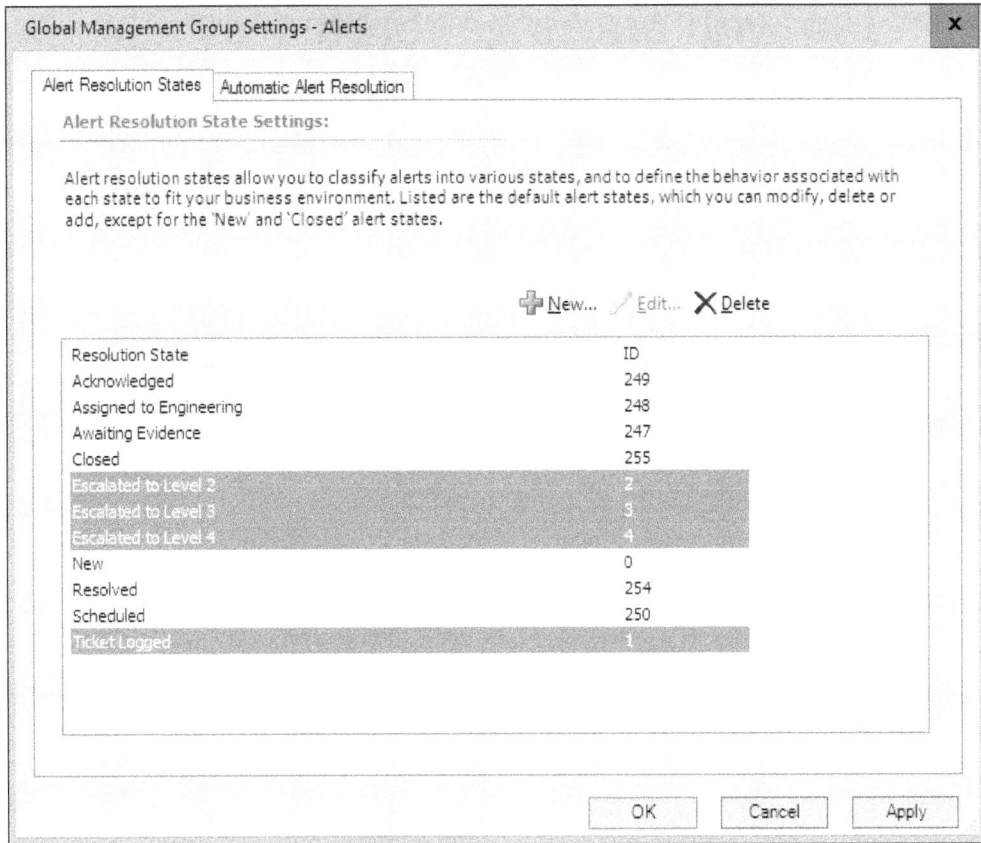

Figure 8.3: Custom alert resolution state examples

4. Click on **OK** to finish the process.

> An alternative method for creating custom alert resolution states is to use the `Add-SCOMAlertResolutionState` cmdlet from the OpsMgr PowerShell module. You can get more information on this cmdlet and its syntax from `http://tinyurl.com/opsmgralertresolution`.

Working with alerts generated by monitors

In *Chapter 5, Working with Management Packs*, we discussed the difference between monitors and rules and in the context of alert tuning, it's important to have the ability to easily identify when an alert is generated by one or the other.

A quick way to identify if an alert was generated by a monitor is to click on the alert from within the console and check either the **Alert Details** or **Alert Actions** pane to see if they refer to a monitor as shown in *Figure 8.4*.

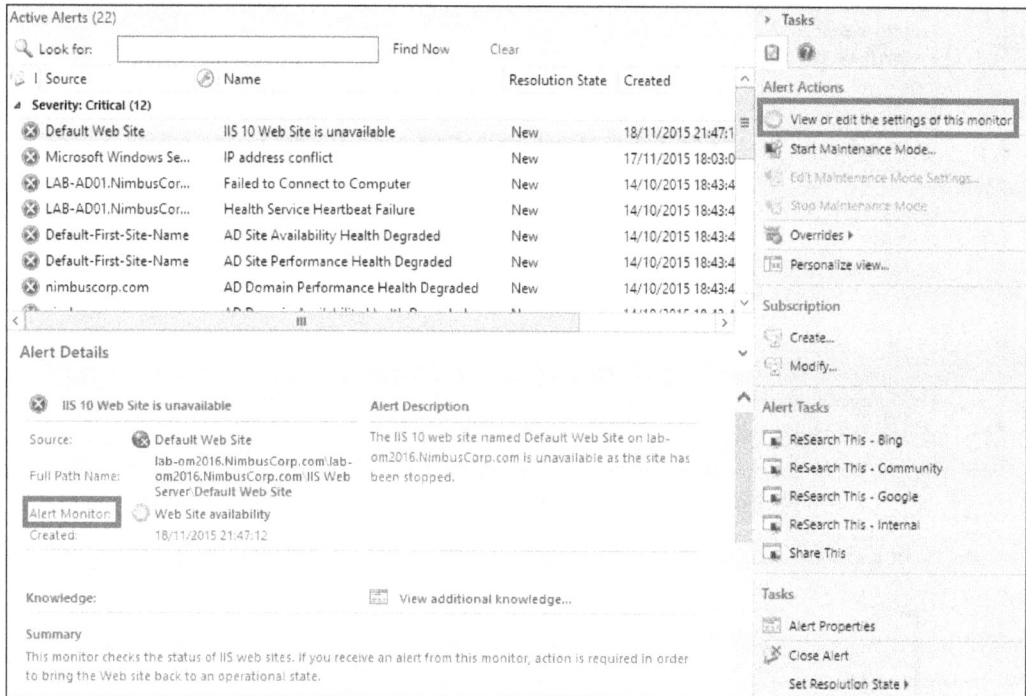

Figure 8.4: Identifying an alert generated by a monitor

Alerts generated by monitors tend to behave differently and have a lot more options that can be configured with overrides than alerts generated by rules.

Overriding monitor generated alerts

If you need to change how an alert generated by a monitor behaves, then you'll need to configure an override for that alert. Overrides can be configured within the console using the Monitoring, My Workspace or Authoring workspaces.

The following steps will walk you through creating an override from the Monitoring workspace for an alert generated by a monitor:

1. From an alert view in the console, right-click on the alert, choose **Override the Monitor**, and then select an option to target the override at from the list as shown in *Figure 8.5*.

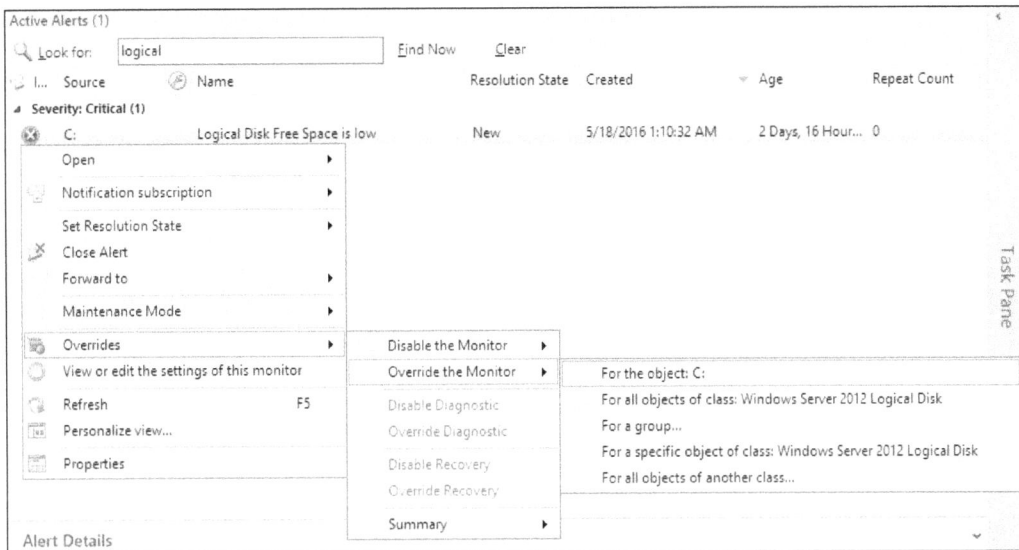

Figure 8.5: Overriding a monitor

When creating an override, you will be presented with five options for which you have to target the override. The first option at the top of the list (**For the object:**) will always target the override of the actual object which raised the alert, and the second option (**For all objects of class:**) will target the override of all objects of that same class.

If you wish to target an override at a group, then choose the third option (**For a group:**) and the fourth option (**For a specific object of class:**) targets a different object of the same class that generated the original alert. The fifth option in the list (**For all objects of another class:**) is the least used option when overriding alerts and it enables you to target objects from another class to the one that raised the alert in the first place.

2. From the **Override Properties** dialog box, you can control how the alert fires by modifying the value of each of the parameters within the monitor. The **Override** column shows you the parameters that have been modified and as you can see from *Figure 8.6*, it's easy to distinguish between **Default**, **Override** and **Effective** values. It's good practice to always add a comment into the description field for each override you're making (just click on the **Edit...** link) as this can be helpful when trying to understand the reason someone made an override in the first place.

Monitor name:	Windows 2012 Logical Disk Free Space Monitor				
Category:	Availability Health				
Overrides target:	Object: C:				

Override-controlled parameters:

	Override	Parameter Name	Parameter Type	Default Value	Override Value	Effective Value
	☐	Alert severity	Enumeration	Match monit...	Match monito...	Match monito...
	☐	Auto-Resolve Alert	Boolean	True	True	True
	☐	Debug Flag	Boolean	False	False	False
	☐	Enabled	Boolean	True	True	True
▶	☑	Error % Threshold for Non-System Drives	Double	5	10	5
	☐	Error % Threshold for System Drives	Double	5	5	5
	☑	Error Mbytes Threshold for Non-System Drives	Double	1000	2048	1000
	☐	Error MBytes Threshold for System Drives	Double	300	300	300
	☐	Generates Alert	Boolean	True	True	True
	☐	Interval Seconds	Integer	3600	3600	3600

Details:

Error % Threshold for Non-System Drives   Description   Edit...

The new custom override will be created in the 'Microsoft Windows Server Overrides'.Click apply to view the new effective value for this parameter.

Parameter Description:
Error % Threshold for Non-System Drives

KG - Modifying thresholds for Non-System Drives as per customer requirements.

Management pack

Select destination management pack:

Microsoft Windows Server Overrides   New...

Figure 8.6: Changing the monitor parameters through overrides

3. When you're finished configuring each override value, at the **Select destination management pack** section, choose an associated unsealed management pack to store the override into, and then click on **OK** to save the changes.

> This is probably a good time to point out a golden rule in OpsMgr when creating overrides. You should always choose an unsealed management pack that references the sealed management pack from which you can make the override to and **never** save any overrides into the **Default Management Pack**.
>
> The reason for this is that it can cause dependency issues at a later stage when you want to upgrade or remove other management packs and you'll need to break out your XML editing skills to fix those issues, which are never fun!

Closing versus disabling alerts generated by monitors

Should you come across a console full of alerts, the temptation to just select everything, right-click and hit the **Close Alert** option is something that might be appealing to you, but in the case of alerts generated by monitors, this isn't the wisest thing to do!

An alert generated by a monitor impacts the health state of a monitored object and when the issue that initially caused the alert is resolved then the monitor will self-heal and automatically close the alert. If you decide to manually close an alert generated by a monitor without the condition that originally caused the alert to fire being resolved, then you will end up with a closed alert but a still unhealthy object that can appear hidden unless you're looking at a state view or using the Health Explorer to view that object.

When you find that a particular monitor is generating unnecessary and noisy alerts on a regular basis, then instead of constantly just closing the alert, you should either create an override to modify the thresholds of how the alert fires or simply disable it.

Here's one way to properly disable an alert generated by a monitor:

1. From an alert view in the Monitoring workspace, right-click on the alert, select **Overrides** and then click on **Disable the Monitor** as shown in *Figure 8.7*.

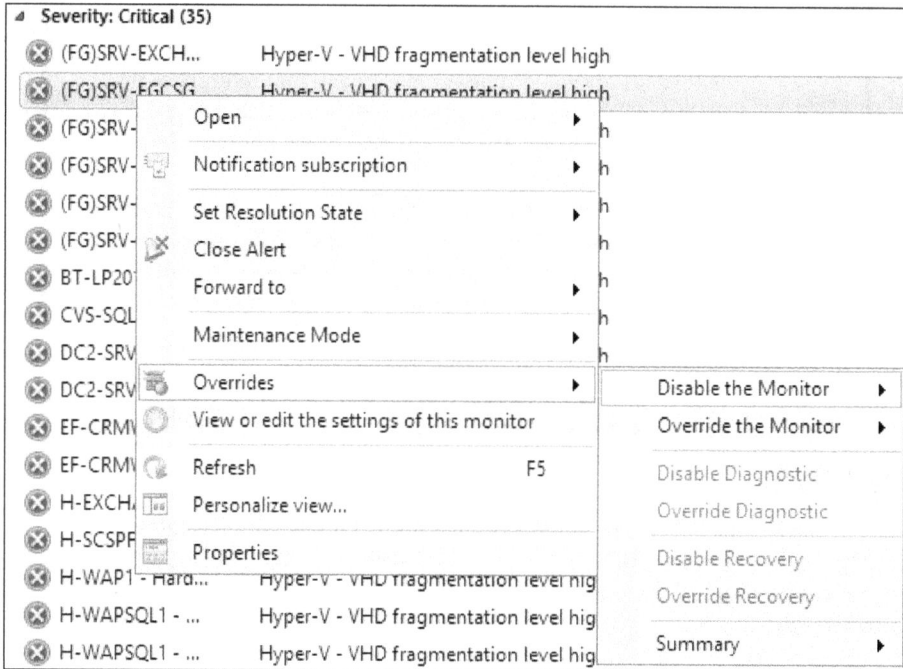

Figure 8.7: Disabling an alert generated by a monitor

2. Choose a target for the override from one of the five options that the pop-out menu suggests; we'll choose the **For all objects of class** option, as we want to disable this alert completely for all objects of the same class.

3. Now, because you selected the **Disable the Monitor** option in the first step, you should see the **Enabled** parameter has a check in the **Override** box and the **Override Value** parameter has been changed to **False** for you – as shown in *Figure 8.8*.

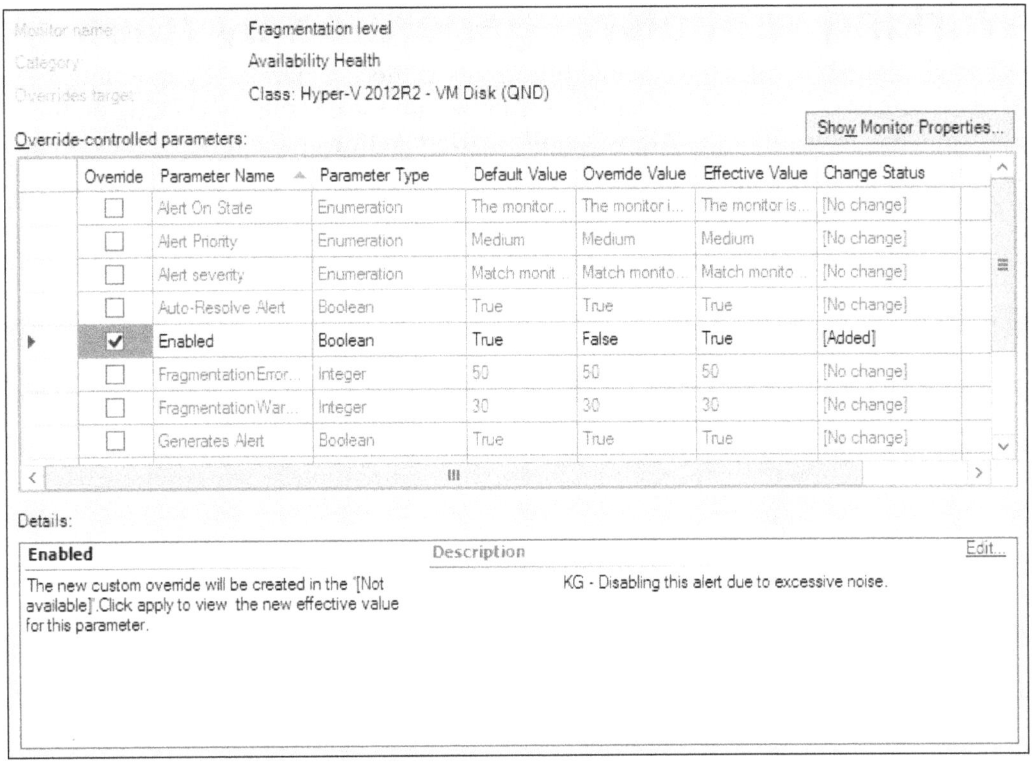

Figure 8.8: A monitor with its Enabled value automatically set to False

4. Select an unsealed management pack to save the override to, add a comment to the **Description** section, and then click on **OK** to save your changes.

5. This will now disable the original monitor and in turn, the alert that was generated by that monitor will automatically close itself from within the console.

Disabling an alert in the Monitoring workspace like this is an easy way to disable the monitor for a specific object, class or group without having to go through additional steps from within the Authoring workspace.

Working with alerts generated by rules

Alerts generated by rules have a few differences to those generated by monitors. These rule-based alerts can be identified from within the console by clicking on the alert and checking either the **Alert Details** or **Alert Actions** pane to see if they refer to a rule as shown in *Figure 8.9*.

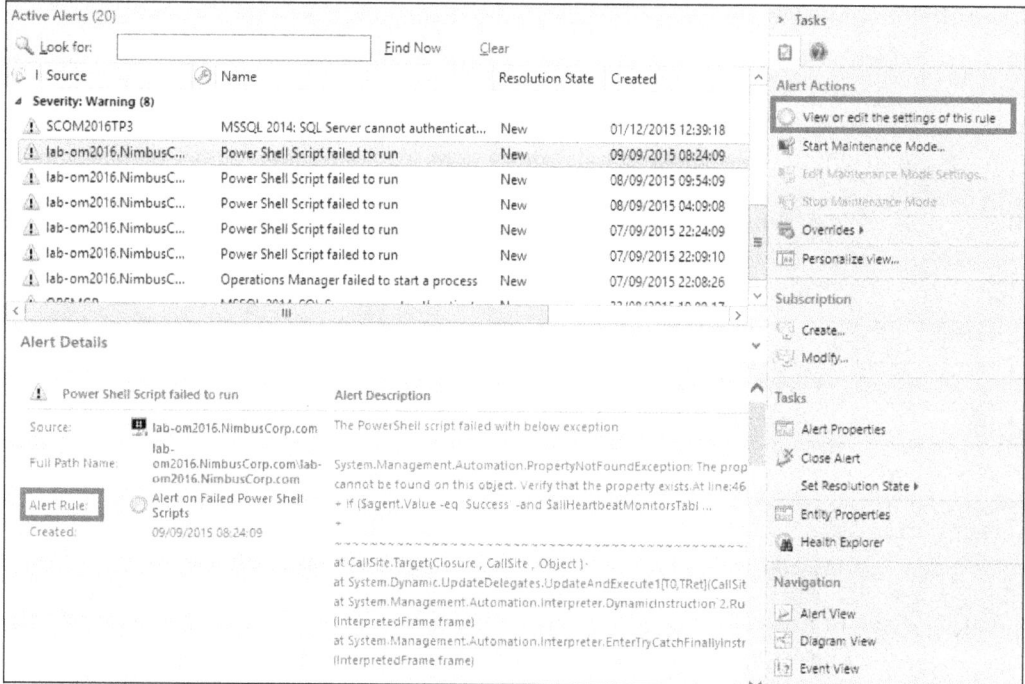

Figure 8.9: Identifying an alert generated by a rule

Overriding rule generated alerts

When you want to override an alert that's generated by a rule, the initial process is similar to that of overriding a monitor and you can manage them from within the console using the Monitoring, My Workspace or Authoring workspaces. Once you get into the override properties area of the rule however, you'll notice there's a lot less parameters to override when compared to a monitor.

The following steps will walk you through creating an override from the Monitoring workspace for an alert generated by a rule:

1. From an alert view in the console, right-click on the alert, choose **Override the Rule**, and then select an option to target the override at from the list as shown in *Figure 8.10*.

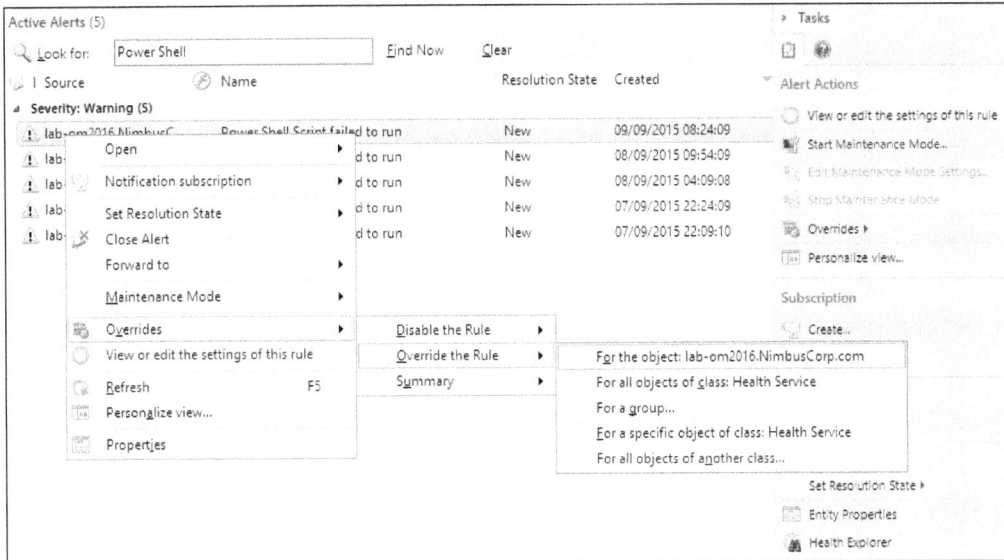

Figure 8.10: Overriding a rule-generated alert

2. From the **Override Properties** dialog box shown in *Figure 8.11*, you can see a rule only has a very small number of override parameter options to choose from. These parameters typically allow you to enable or disable the rule, to change its priority or modify the severity (Critical, Warning or Information) of the alert.

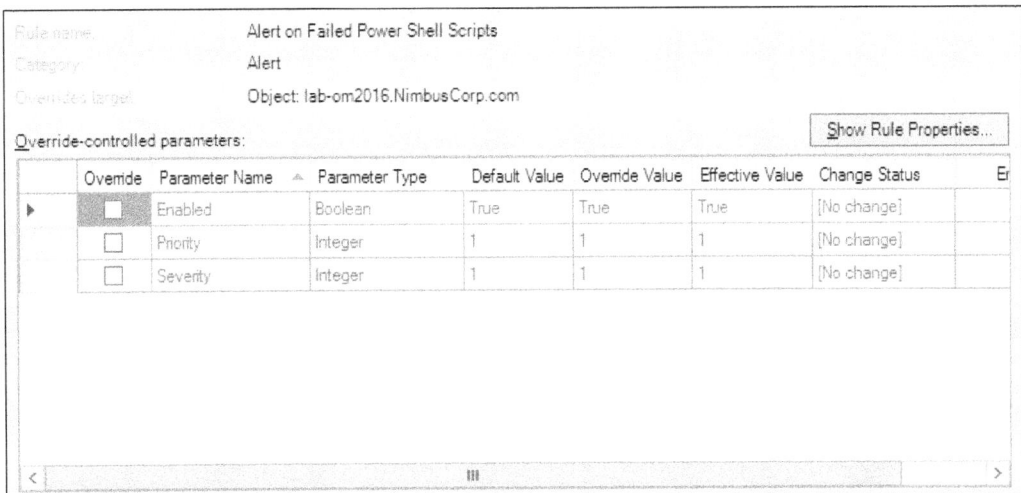

Figure 8.11: Override properties of a rule

> When you need to change the severity of an alert generated by a rule, you'll usually be presented with a confusing numeric integer value for the Severity parameter – instead of the more familiar Enumeration value of Critical, Warning and Information. The integer values for Severity are represented as 0 – Information, 1 – Warning and 2 – Critical. Similarly, for the Priority parameter, the integer values are 0 – Low, 1 – Medium and 2 – High.

3. In this example, we will override the severity parameter of the alert that's firing and we want to change it from its current severity of Warning (identified by a default integer value of 1) to Informational, which has an integer value of 0. This override is shown in *Figure 8.12*.

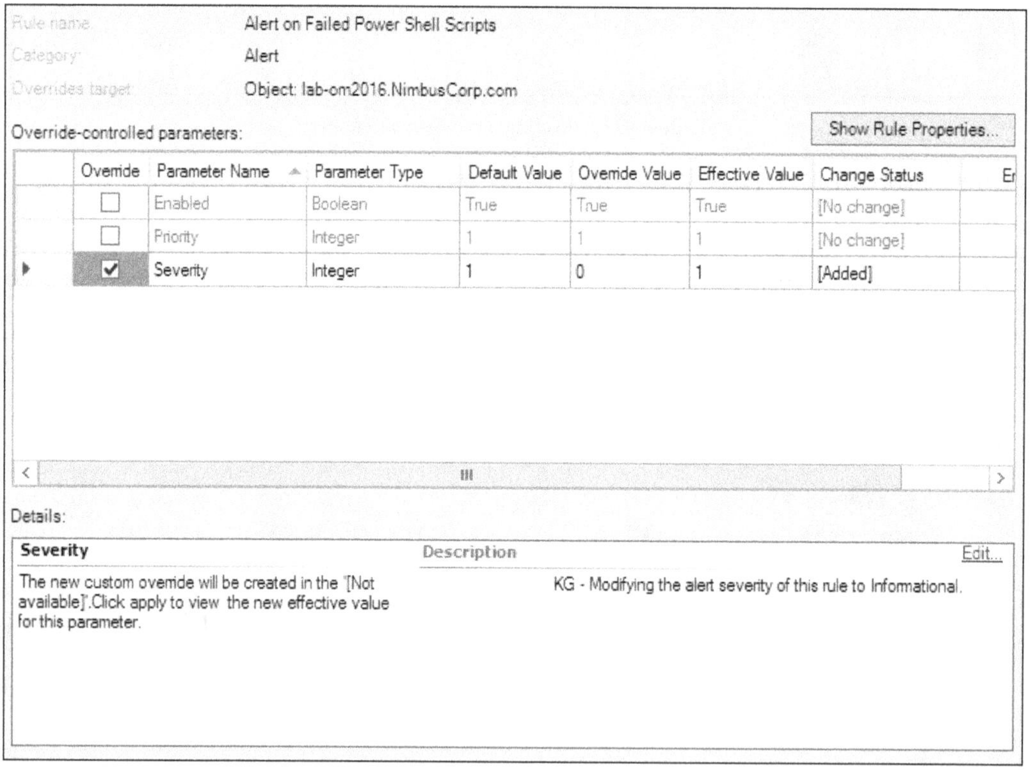

	Rule name:		Alert on Failed Power Shell Scripts				
	Category:		Alert				
	Overrides target:		Object: lab-om2016.NimbusCorp.com				

Override-controlled parameters: **Show Rule Properties...**

	Override	Parameter Name ▲	Parameter Type	Default Value	Override Value	Effective Value	Change Status	Er
	☐	Enabled	Boolean	True	True	True	[No change]	
	☐	Priority	Integer	1	1	1	[No change]	
▶	☑	Severity	Integer	1	0	1	[Added]	

Details:

Severity	Description	Edit...
The new custom override will be created in the '[Not available]'.Click apply to view the new effective value for this parameter.	KG - Modifying the alert severity of this rule to Informational.	

Figure 8.12: Modifying the Severity parameter of a rule

4. While you're working with overrides for either rules or monitors, you might notice the **Enforced** option shown in *Figure 8.13*. When selected, this attribute ensures that the override you've just created takes precedence over all other overrides of the same type and context that don't have the **Enforced** option enabled.

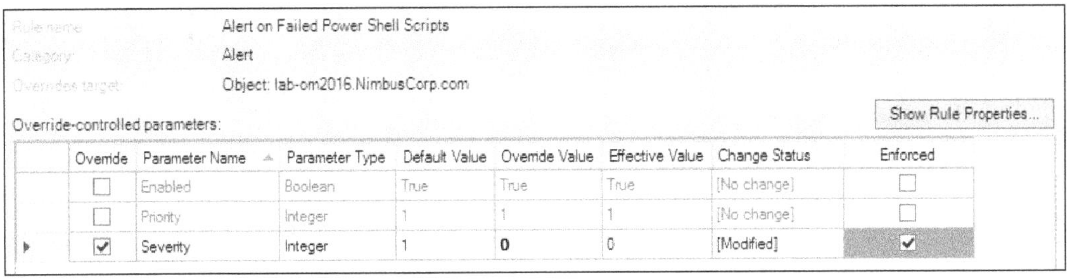

	Override	Parameter Name	Parameter Type	Default Value	Override Value	Effective Value	Change Status	Enforced
	☐	Enabled	Boolean	True	True	True	[No change]	☐
	☐	Priority	Integer	1	1	1	[No change]	☐
▶	☑	Severity	Integer	1	0	0	[Modified]	☑

Rule name: Alert on Failed Power Shell Scripts
Category: Alert
Override target: Object: lab-om2016.NimbusCorp.com

Show Rule Properties...

Override-controlled parameters:

Figure 8.13: Setting the Enforced parameter for overrides

> Depending on your requirements (and ultimately how many different OpsMgr administrators you have creating overrides in your organization), configuring the Enforced option for your overrides can be a good or a bad thing. When you plan your overrides properly, this shouldn't be a setting you need to consider using as it can create confusion when alerts that should have a particular override setting configured don't seem to be applied.

5. In the **Select destination management pack** section, choose an associated unsealed management pack to store the override into, and then click on **OK** to save the changes.

Closing versus disabling alerts generated by rules

Unlike alerts that are generated by monitors, rule-based alerts don't automatically close and will stay in the console until you manually close them. If you close an alert generated by a rule and the conditions that made the rule fire in the first place occur again, then the rule will appear back in the console until you either resolve the issue or disable the alert completely.

If you don't close a rule-based alert and it's configured to run on a regular schedule, then instead of getting hundreds (or even thousands) of alerts for the same rule landing in the console, you will notice the repeat count value for the alert incremented by one each time it fires. This repeat count value is shown in *Figure 8.14*.

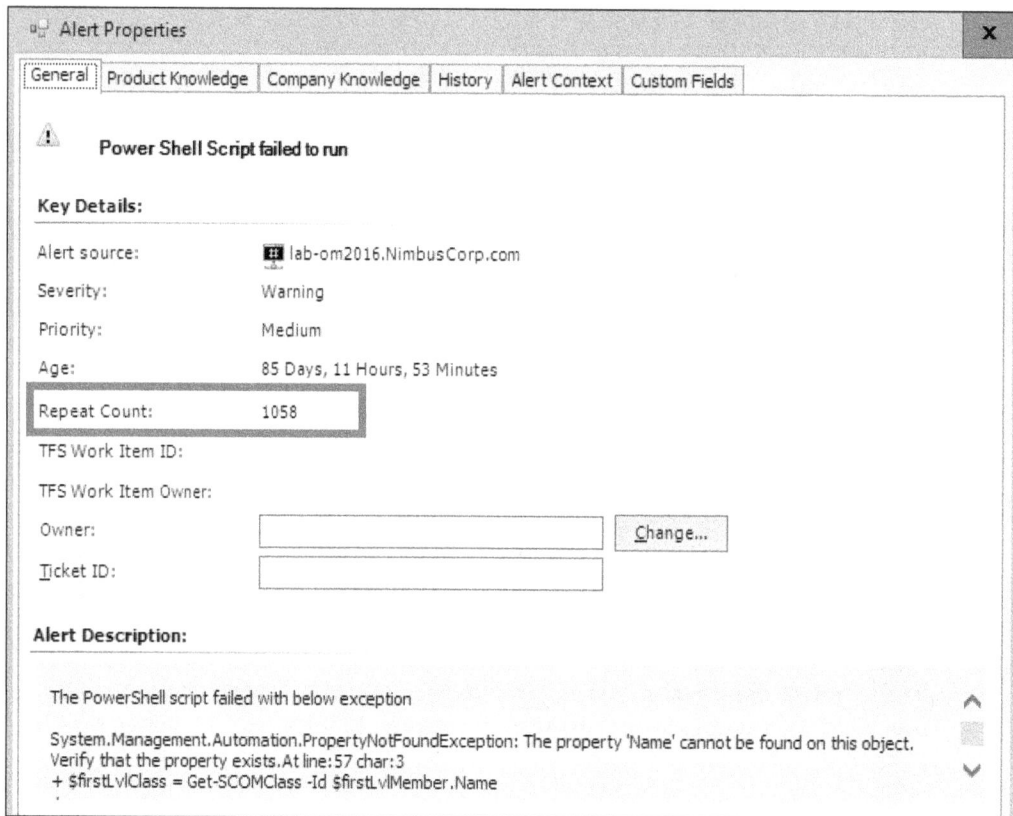

Figure 8.14: Example of an incremented Repeat Count value for a rule

When you want to disable a rule-based alert, you can do so by following the same steps as those to disable an alert generated by a monitor.

Sky Blue to the rescue!

One of the best things about working with OpsMgr is the amazing amount of free resources made available by the System Center community. The excellent 'Sky Blue' management pack from Charles Champion (Premier Field Engineer at Microsoft) is an example of one of these community resources and this is a management pack you definitely want to deploy to help you with your alert tuning and management processes.

As you learnt earlier in the *Working with alerts generated by monitors* section, it's a bad idea to close alerts generated by monitors without resolving the original problem or creating an override for it. The reason for this is that the health state of the monitor stays unhealthy and the alert that notified you of the change in state is now missing from the console. This is a common scenario that we come across on customer sites and one that the Sky Blue management pack will quickly remediate.

This basic (but very useful) management pack protects against accidental alert closures by re-opening manually closed alerts where the monitor is in an unhealthy state. A single rule runs a PowerShell script from within this management pack every five minutes that looks for all closed alerts that were generated by a monitor, checks the health state of those monitors, and then re-opens any alert where the monitor state is not healthy and not in maintenance mode with an assigned resolution state of New (value 0).

Figure 8.15 shows the single rule contained within the Sky Blue management pack along with an example of a manually closed alert being re-opened and its alert history updated to reflect the change. The text displayed in the **Alert History** tab can be modified as required to suit your organization.

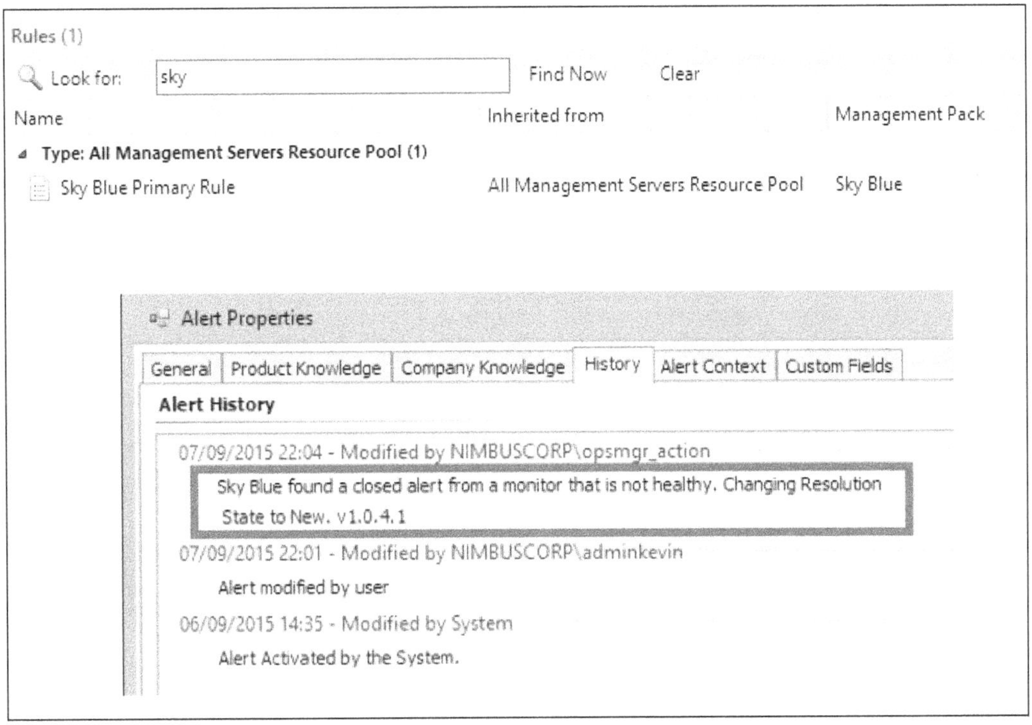

Figure 8.15: Sky Blue management pack

You can get more information about this management pack from Charles Champion's blog post at `http://tinyurl.com/skybluemp` and you can download the latest version of it from GitHub from `https://github.com/cchamp-msft/SkyBlue`.

Using the alert widget

In the *Working with Views* section of *Chapter 3*, *Exploring the Consoles* we walked you through creating an Alert view and highlighted the benefit of configuring the Repeat Count column to help you quickly identify alerts generated by rules that had a high repeat count. Although this view can be useful for identifying alerts generated by rules, it's not as easy to identify alerts generated by monitors as a small number of monitors can also potentially have a repeat count value (where those monitors have their AutoResolve value set to False).

The Alert Widget is a view that you can use within a dashboard layout to clearly identify which alerts were generated by monitors.

The following steps will help you first create an empty dashboard layout from where you will then create the Alert Widget view:

1. In the **Monitoring** workspace, right-click where you want to create the new view, click on **New**, and then click on **Dashboard View**.

2. Choose a dashboard layout style from the **Select a dashboard layout or widget template** dialog box. We'll choose the **Grid Layout** as shown in *Figure 8.16*. Click on **Next** to continue.

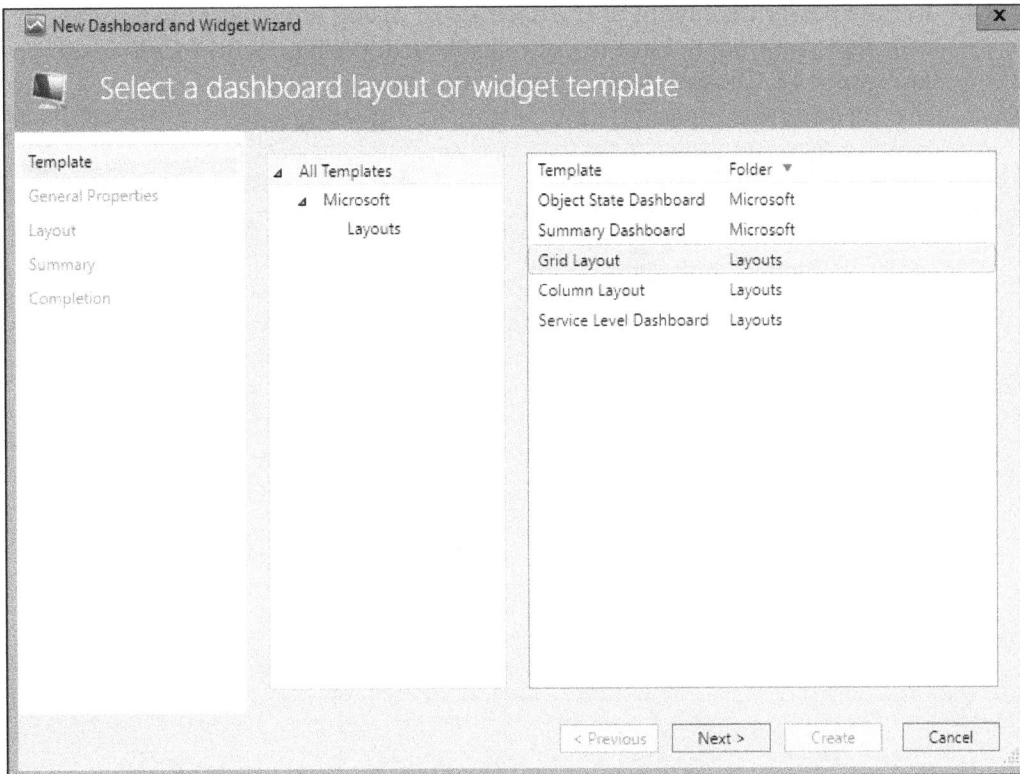

Figure 8.16: Choosing the Grid Layout dashboard

3. In the **Name** field, type a name to identify the view – we'll use 'Tuning Assistance Dashboard' for our example.

4. In the **Specify the layout of the dashboard** dialog box, select the number of cells that you wish to have in your dashboard. We'll go with **1 Cell** as shown in *Figure 8.17*. Click on **Next** to move on.

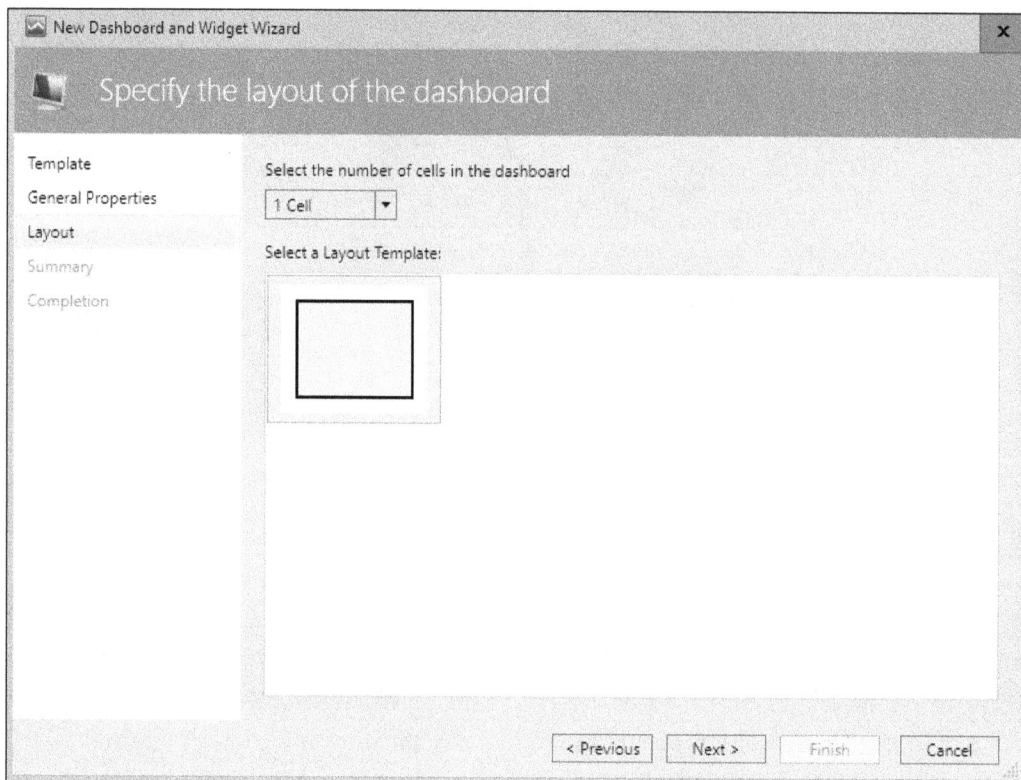

Figure 8.17: Choosing a single-cell layout

5. Confirm your settings at the **Summary** dialog box, and then hit the **Create** button to create the new dashboard layout. Click on the **Close** button to complete the creation of the dashboard layout.

Now that you have your dashboard layout created, the following steps will walk you through adding a new Alert Widget:

1. From the single-cell grid dashboard layout that you've just created, select the link titled **Click to add widget...** and here, you'll be presented with the **New Dashboard and Widget Wizard** shown in *Figure 8.18*. Choose the **Alert Widget**, and then click on **Next** to move on.

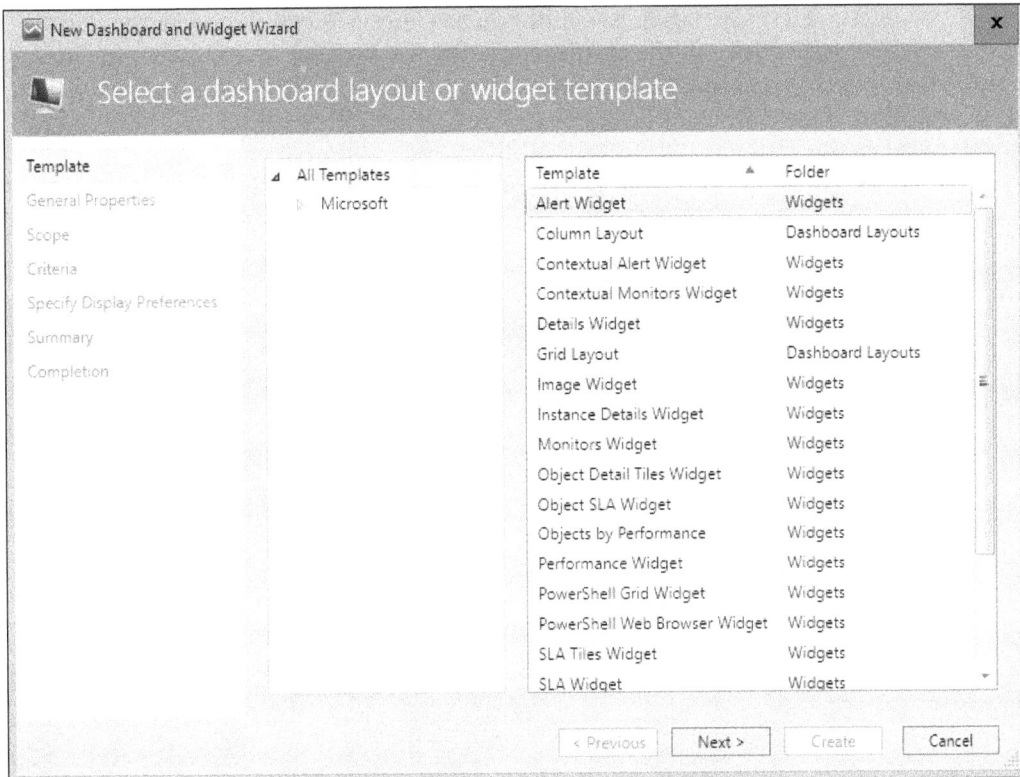

Figure 8.18: Selecting the Alert Widget

2. In the **Name** field, type a name to identify the widget and click on **Next** to continue.

3. In the **Specify the Scope** dialog box, leave the default scope set to (All) and hit **Next** to move on.

4. From the **Specify the Criteria** dialog box, you can optionally scope the alerts by priority, severity or resolution state, and then click on **Next** when you're ready to continue.

5. Now, the **Display** dialog box that you see here is where the 'secret sauce' lives for this view. In the **Columns to display** section, you will see an optional column titled **Is Monitor Alert**. This column is only available as an option when you use the Alert Widget from within a dashboard and *Figure 8.19* shows how we've configured this for our example (you can use the blue arrow buttons to move the **Is Monitor Alert** column up the list so it's easier to view later).

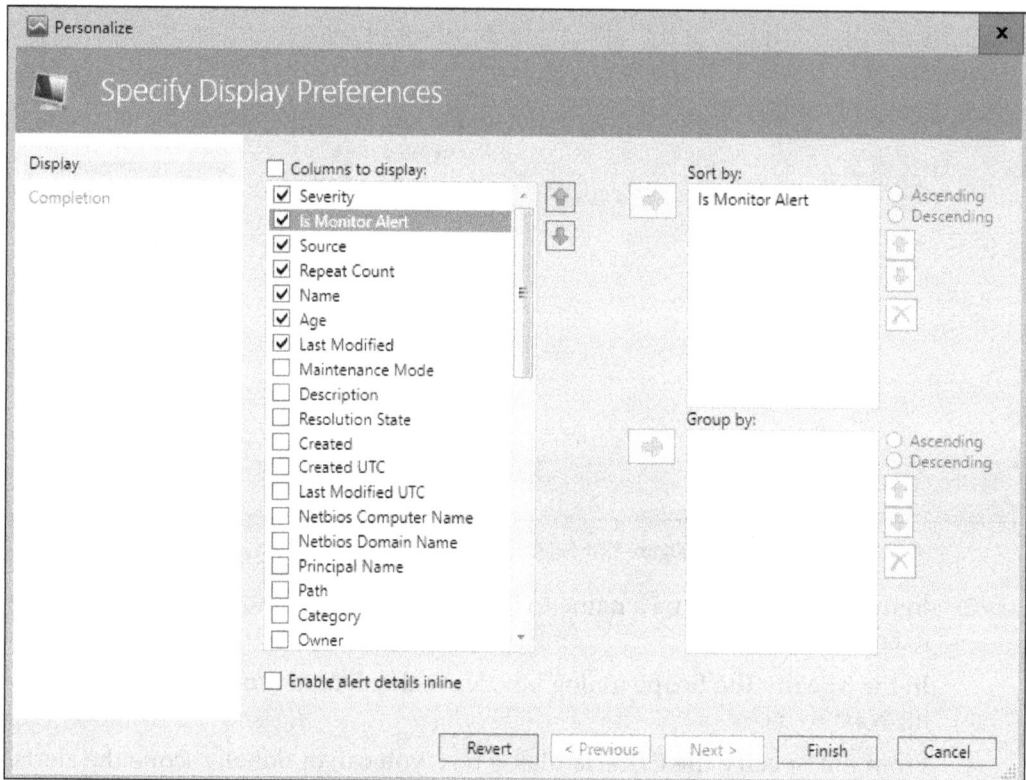

Figure 8.19: Enabling the 'Is Monitor Alert' column

6. Click on **Next** to move on, and then hit the **Create** button to create the new view. With the new Alert Widget view created, you should be presented with a view similar to our example shown in *Figure 8.20*.

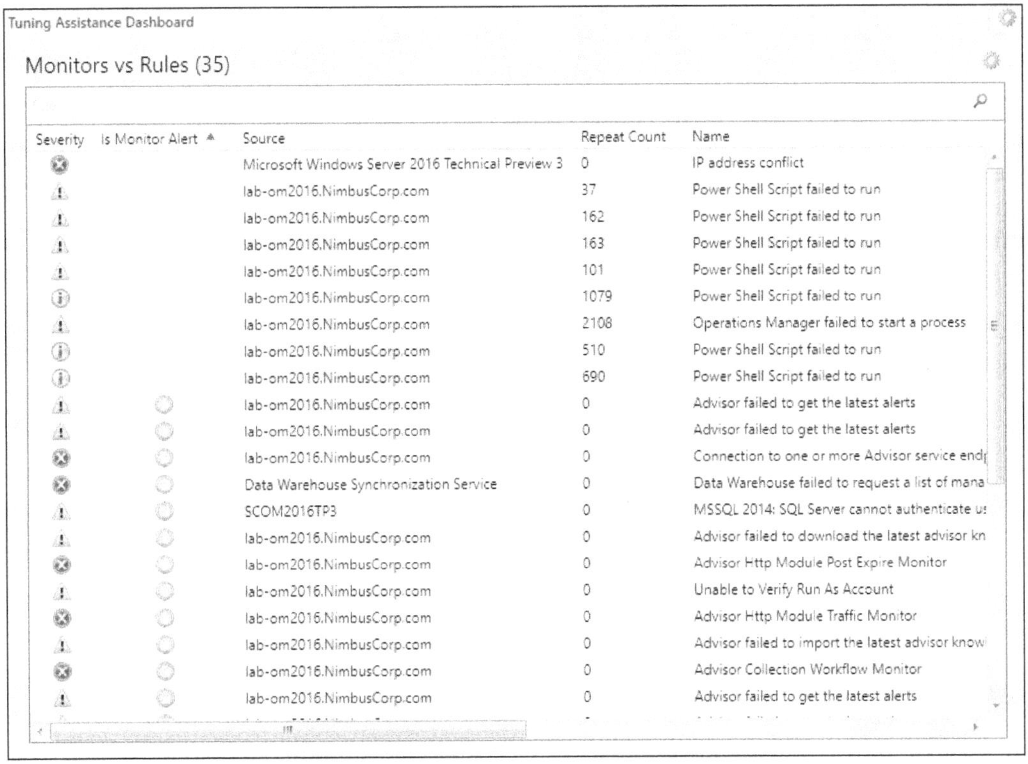

Figure 8.20: Viewing alerts generated by monitors

7. In this view, you can see that any alerts generated by a monitor are listed in the **Is Monitor Alert** column with a blue circle icon beside them. Any alerts with no blue icon beside them in this column have been generated by rules and they have an associated repeat count value beside them. Optionally, you can click on any column name to sort it in ascending or descending order to show your monitors or rules at the top or bottom of the view.

This type of view can come in very handy when you have a large number of alerts in your console and you want to get a quick overview of which alerts have been generated by monitors and which ones have been generated by rules.

One script to 'Rule' them all

A downside of alerts generated by rules is that even after the condition that fired the alert is resolved, the rule stays in the console until such time as you manually close it or alert age grooming kicks in, which by default is configured for 30 days through the **General: Alerts** setting in the settings area of the Administration workspace. In environments where there are a large number of monitored agents generating alerts on a regular basis, you'll quickly find your Active Alerts view has thousands of alerts waiting to be dealt with.

To combat this administrative headache, another great community resource is available, this time from Bob Cornelissen (Cloud and Datacenter Management MVP). Using PowerShell, Bob wrote a simple script that can be run on a schedule to automatically close any alerts generated by rules that are older than a specified number of hours (96 hours is the default value and can be modified to suit your needs). You can edit the script to add your own comment to alerts that get closed using the script and you can modify the resolution state value to suit your needs too.

As a good starting point, you could use the built-in Task Scheduler in Windows to create a custom schedule for this script that runs once or twice a week to keep your alert views neat, tidy and current. Bob has made the script available through the TechNet Gallery and you can download it from `http://tinyurl.com/omrulescript`.

Get the full picture with Health Explorer

An essential built-in tool for tuning alerts in OpsMgr, the Health Explorer can be used to view state changes, investigate problems, and understand which monitor is alerting you to a problem. Available through the Operations console and the Web console, you can launch the Health Explorer from most views within the Monitoring workspace and it gives you a live overview of the health of any monitored object in OpsMgr.

Follow these steps to start getting familiar with using the Health Explorer:

1. From an Alert view in the Monitoring workspace, right-click on an alert, select **Open**, and then click on **Health Explorer** as shown in *Figure 8.21* (you can also launch it using the Health Explorer task from the **Tasks** pane on the right).

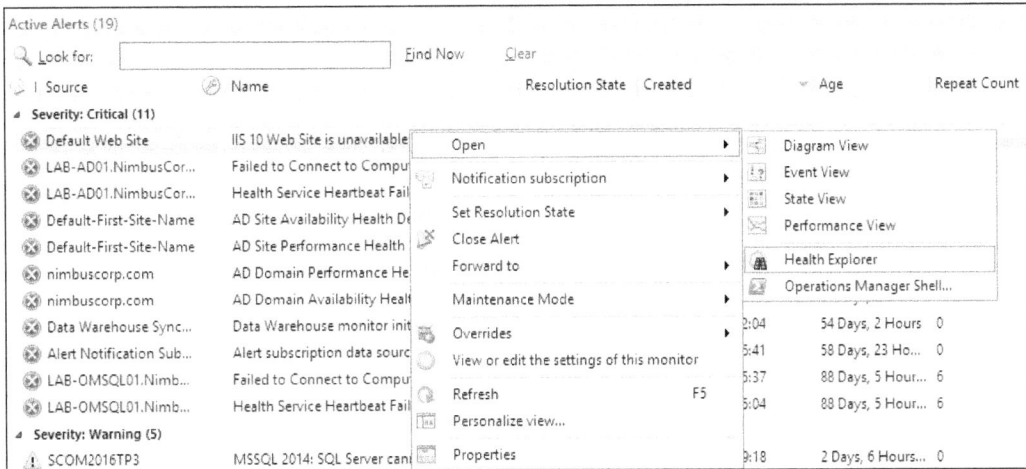

Figure 8.21: Launching the Health Explorer from an alert

2. When it launches, you'll be presented with a scoped view of any unhealthy child monitors related to the managed object that generated the alert, along with the **Knowledge** and **State Change Events** tab as shown in *Figure 8.22*.

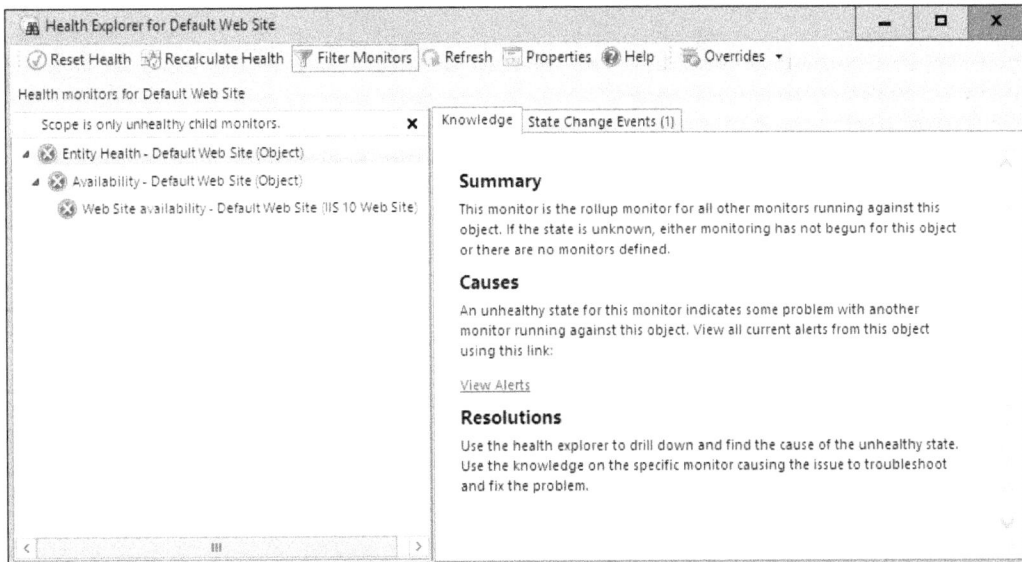

Figure 8.22: Health Explorer scoped by default to unhealthy monitors

3. From the image in our example, we can see that the Health Explorer has scoped the view to show only unhealthy monitors and there's a monitor in the Availability category titled 'Web Site availability' that has changed to a critical state for a website on one of our IIS servers.

4. Clicking the **Filter Monitors** button from the navigation bar at the top will remove the scoped filter and you can then see all monitors that are currently targeted at the managed object defined into four categories (**Availability, Configuration, Performance** and **Security**) as shown in *Figure 8.23*.

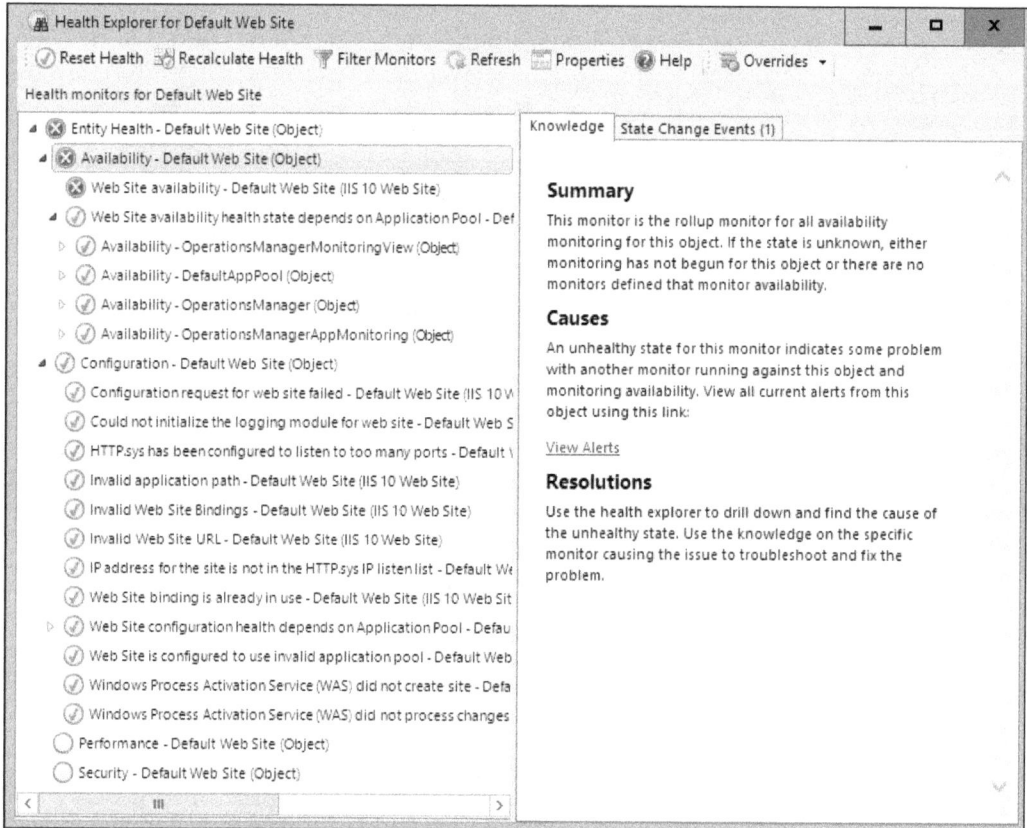

Figure 8.23: Viewing the Health Explorer without filters

5. When you click on a monitor that's in an unhealthy state, you'll notice the **Knowledge** tab changes to display useful information about the cause of the problem along with some suggestions on how to resolve it. As you can see in *Figure 8.24*, the **Knowledge** tab also contains a link to a task that will attempt to fix the problem – in this case, it's a task that will attempt to restart the failed IIS website.

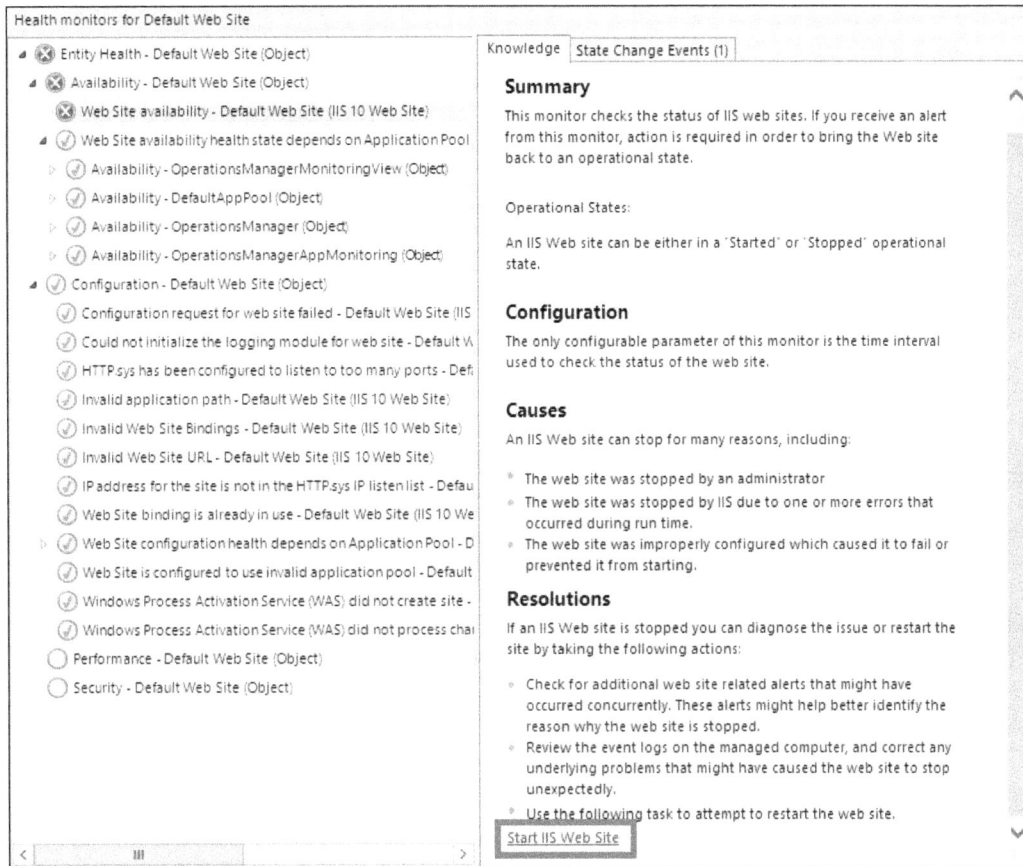

Figure 8.24: Using tasks and information in the Knowledge tab to resolve problems

6. When we click on this particular task, it restarts the IIS website that was offline and after a few minutes, the Health Explorer will update all monitors to a healthy state as shown in *Figure 8.25*.

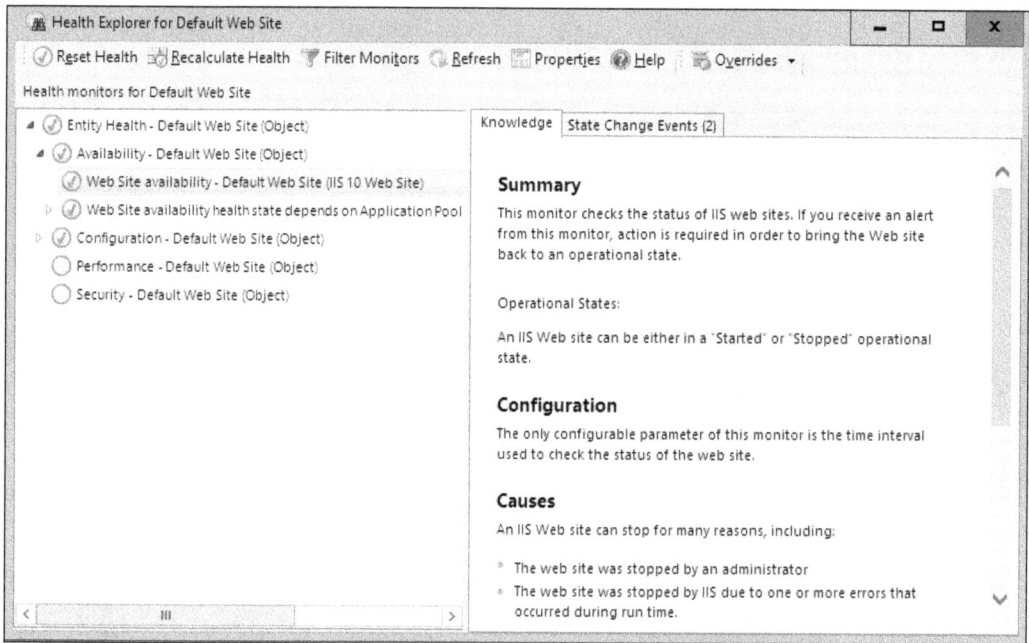

Figure 8.25: All monitors healthy after resolving the problem

The **State Change Events** tab shown in *Figure 8.26* is another useful view within the Health Explorer that can help you to identify dates and times for when a monitor changed its operational state. You can get an overview of the context of a state change event when that data is available.

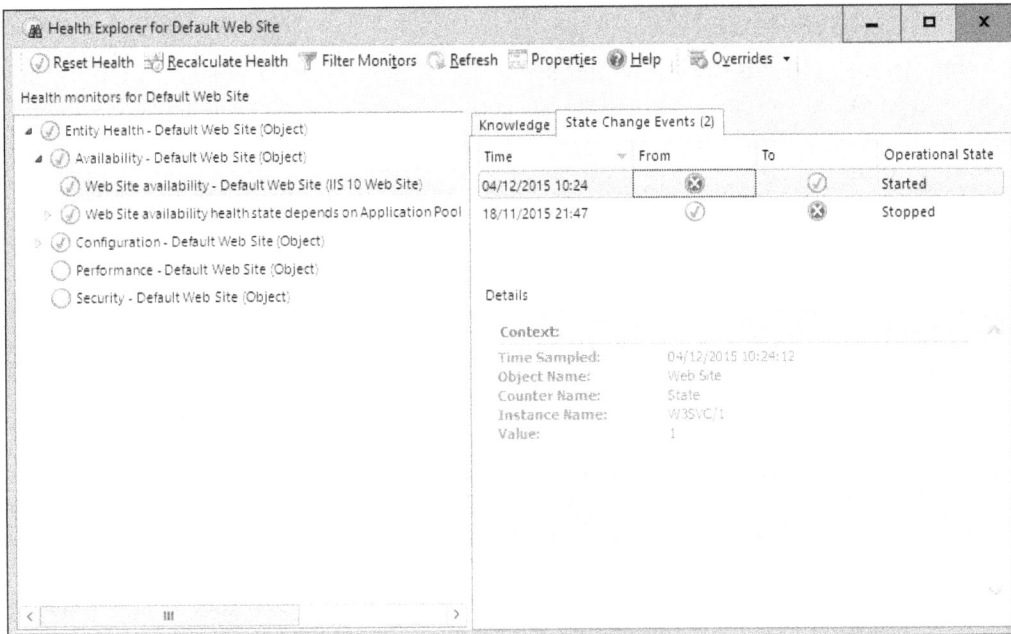

Figure 8.26: Viewing the State Change Events tab

Using the Health Explorer navigation bar

The navigation bar at the top of the **Health Explorer** window (shown in *Figure 8.27*) has some useful options to help you when tuning alerts.

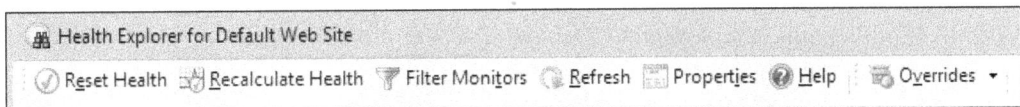

Figure 8.27: The Health Explorer navigation bar

We've already discussed the **Filter Monitors** button and here's some information on what the remaining buttons are used for:

Reset Health

When you click on the **Reset Health** button, you can force a quick reset of the health of a monitor to a healthy state. If an issue is still present, the monitor will go back into an unhealthy state again within a short space of time. This is a common option to use when creating or testing overrides.

Recalculate Health

On the surface of it, this option would seem like a logical one to have as it was designed to initiate a real-time recalculation of the state of a monitor to save you waiting on your override changes to kick in. In reality though, the **Recalculate Health** button will only work with monitors that use a feature called **On Demand Detection** and unfortunately only a very small percentage of monitors use this. As a result, this option is practically useless and a waste of your time.

Refresh

This button simply refreshes the Health Explorer view that you have open. Identical to hitting the *F5* button to perform refresh.

Properties

Selecting a monitor from the Health Explorer and clicking on the **Properties** button will open the properties window for that specific monitor. In *Figure 8.28*, you can see the properties of the **Web Site availability** monitor where you have a number of different tabs that enable you to effectively configure and manage that monitor.

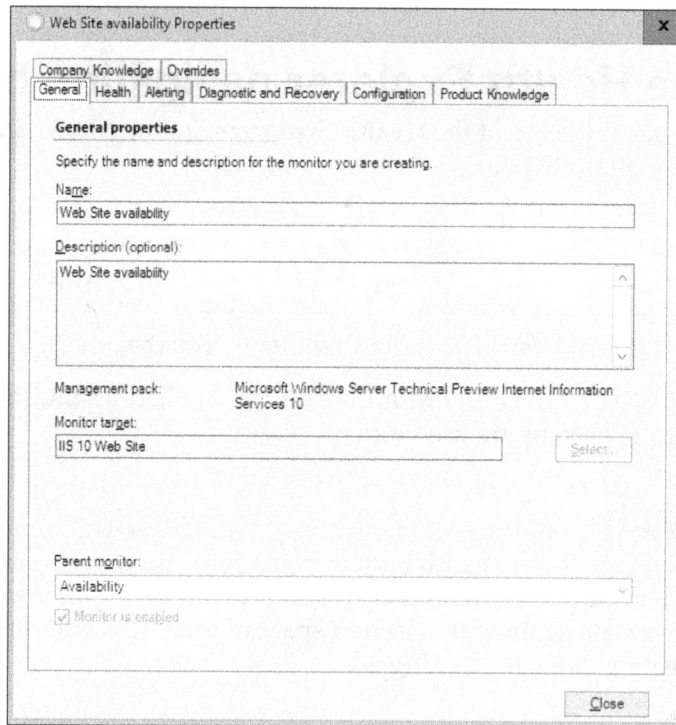

Figure 8.28: Viewing the properties of a monitor

The **Management Pack** and **Monitor Target** sections in the **General** tab of the monitor properties window are always a useful reference to help you understand the management pack the monitor is stored in and what it's targeting.

Help

Similar to most products from Microsoft, when you click on the **Help** button the built-in help documentation will launch and will be contextually targeted at whatever section you opened the help from in the first place.

Overrides

Another commonly used button, clicking on **Overrides** will give you the same override option that you have when working from the Monitoring workspace where you can disable or enable overrides for a specific monitor. From this button, you can also view a summary of overrides that have been applied to the monitor, the object or the class. In *Figure 8.29*, we can see an overrides summary telling us that the monitor is disabled for a specific object and this can be very useful when troubleshooting overrides and alert tuning.

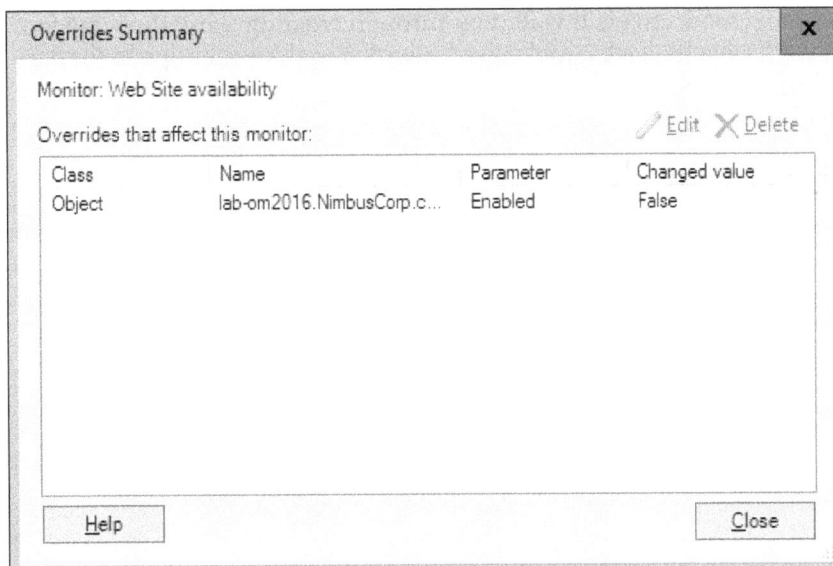

Figure 8.29: Checking the summary of an override

Using custom tasks to tune alerts

In *Chapter 5*, *Working with Management Packs* we discussed the different types of tasks available in OpsMgr and with the help of some customized console tasks, you will simplify your alert tuning process, quickly identify the root cause of problems and implement resolutions with ease.

Three custom tasks that I always deploy with OpsMgr are—**Google It!**, **Run Remote Desktop**, and **Run PuTTY**. Using these tasks (shown in *Figure 8.30*), I can lookup information about an alert on the Internet and then pivot to remotely log on to the computer or device to manage it and resolve the issue if required.

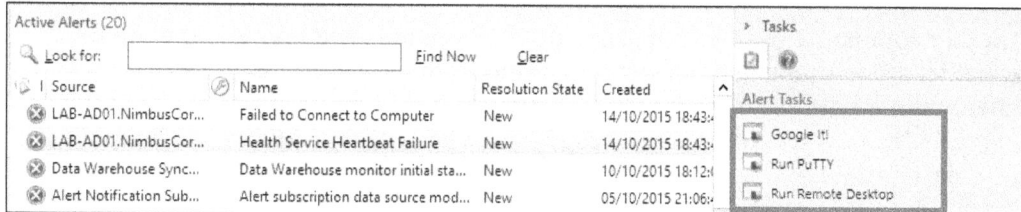

Figure 8.30: Custom console tasks for alert tuning

In the following sections, we'll walk you through creating these three custom console tasks and we'll save the tasks into a new unsealed management pack for easy management.

Creating the 'Google It!' task

This task gives us the ability to click on an alert from the console and then open a Google search with the display name of the alert appended into the search. Using this task, you can quickly get more information about an alert from the Internet when you find that the built-in knowledge from the monitor or rule isn't as comprehensive as it should be.

Follow these steps to get your first custom task deployed:

1. From the Authoring workspace, expand **Management Pack Objects**, right-click on **Tasks**, and then click on **Create a New Task** as shown in *Figure 8.31*.

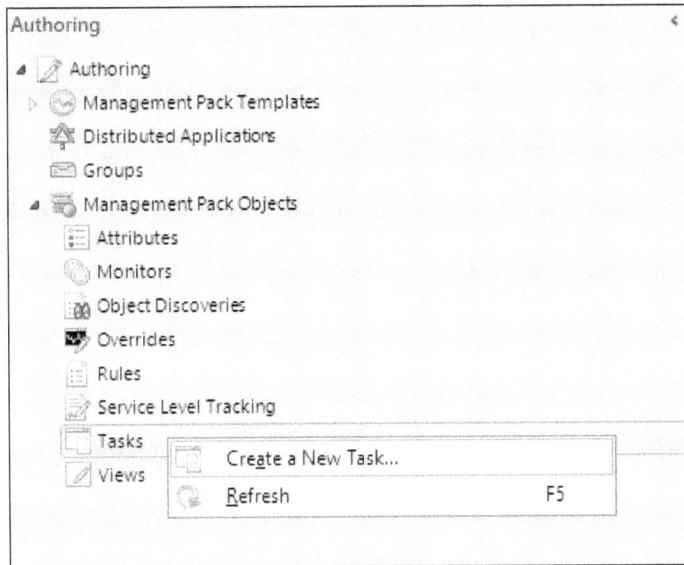

Figure 8.31: Creating a new custom task

2. When the **Create Task Wizard** launches, as shown in *Figure 8.32*, choose the **Alert command line** option from the Console Tasks section and select a management pack to store the new custom task into (you can use the **New** button here to create a new unsealed management pack if required). Click on **Next** to continue.

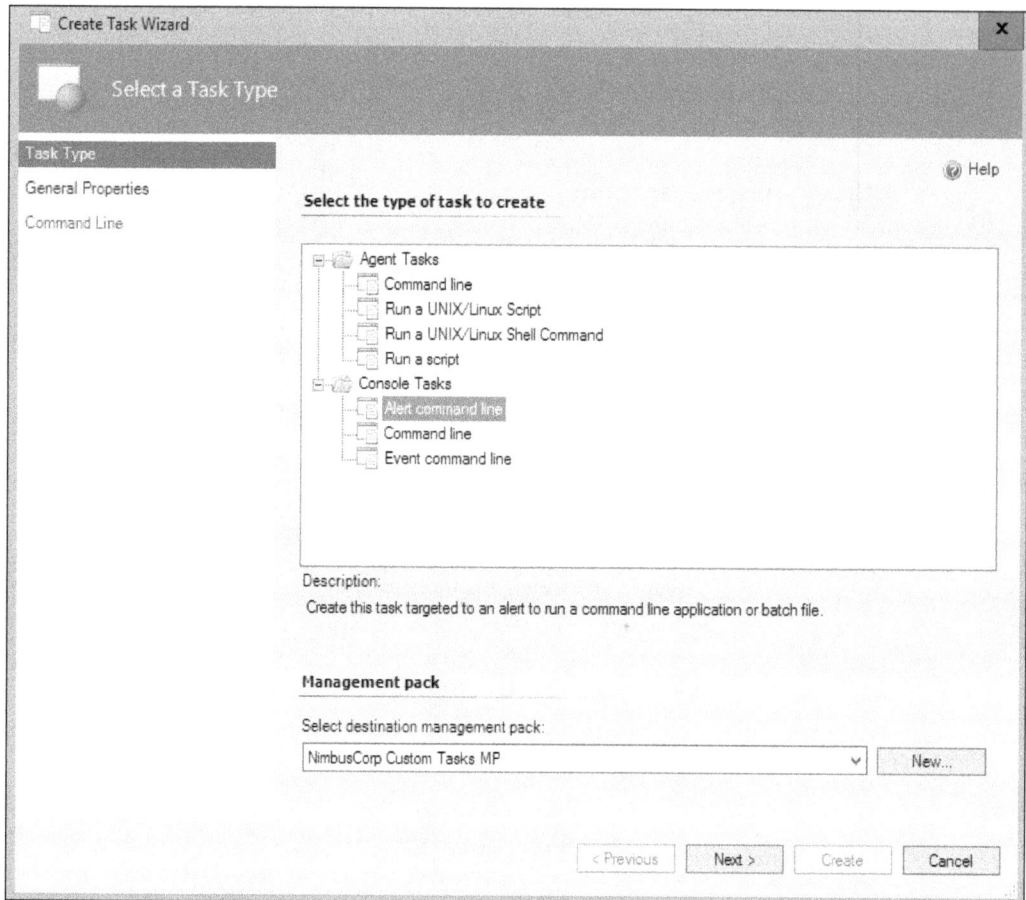

Figure 8.32: Choosing a console task

It's important to understand at this point that when you're creating any Console Task, these tasks will only be presented to the Operations console (the Web console can't see them) and the computer that you run the console from must have the ability to run the task from a command line.

A couple of other things to be mindful of are proxy settings and user account permissions. If you're running a task that needs to open an Internet or remote desktop session, then the user account you're using to launch the task must have the relevant permissions in the first place to connect to the Internet or run a remote desktop or PuTTY instance.

3. In the **General Properties** dialog box shown in *Figure 8.33*, type a name for the task and add a description about what it will do. Click on **Next** to move on.

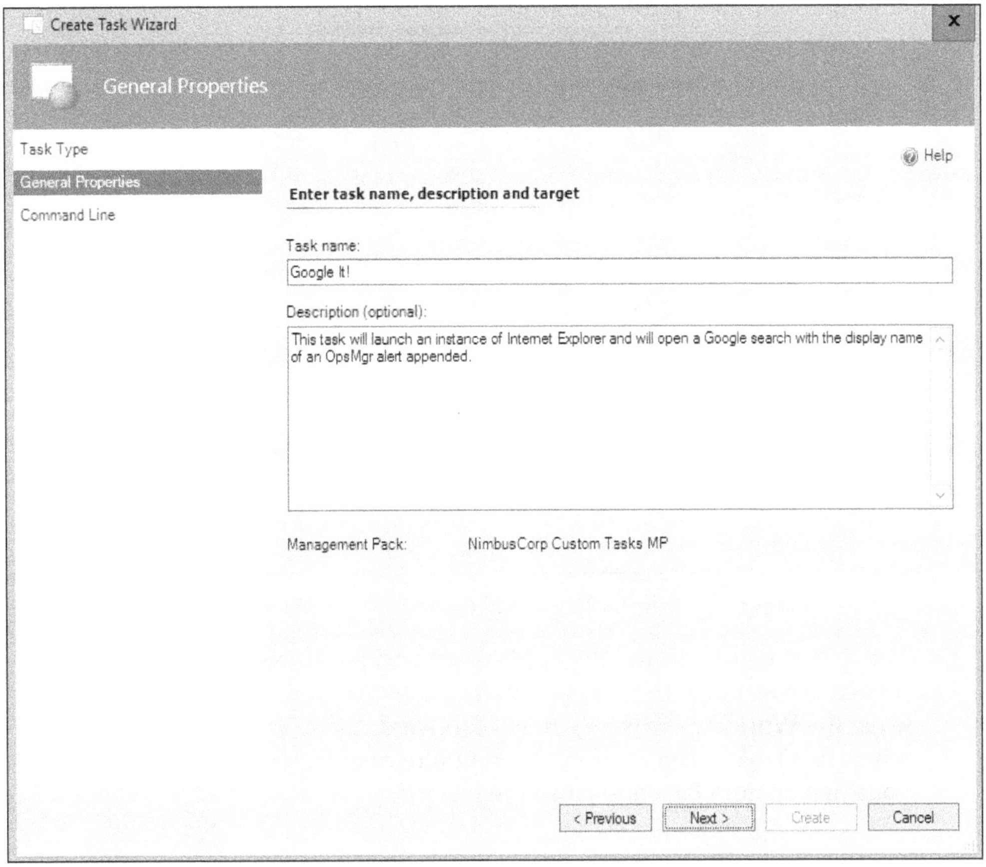

Figure 8.33: Naming your new task

4. From the **Command Line** dialog box, copy the full path to the executable of your favorite web browser (we'll use Internet Explorer here) into the **Application** field and then copy `http://www.google.com/#hl=com&source=hp&q=$Name$` into the **Parameters** field as shown in *Figure 8.34*.

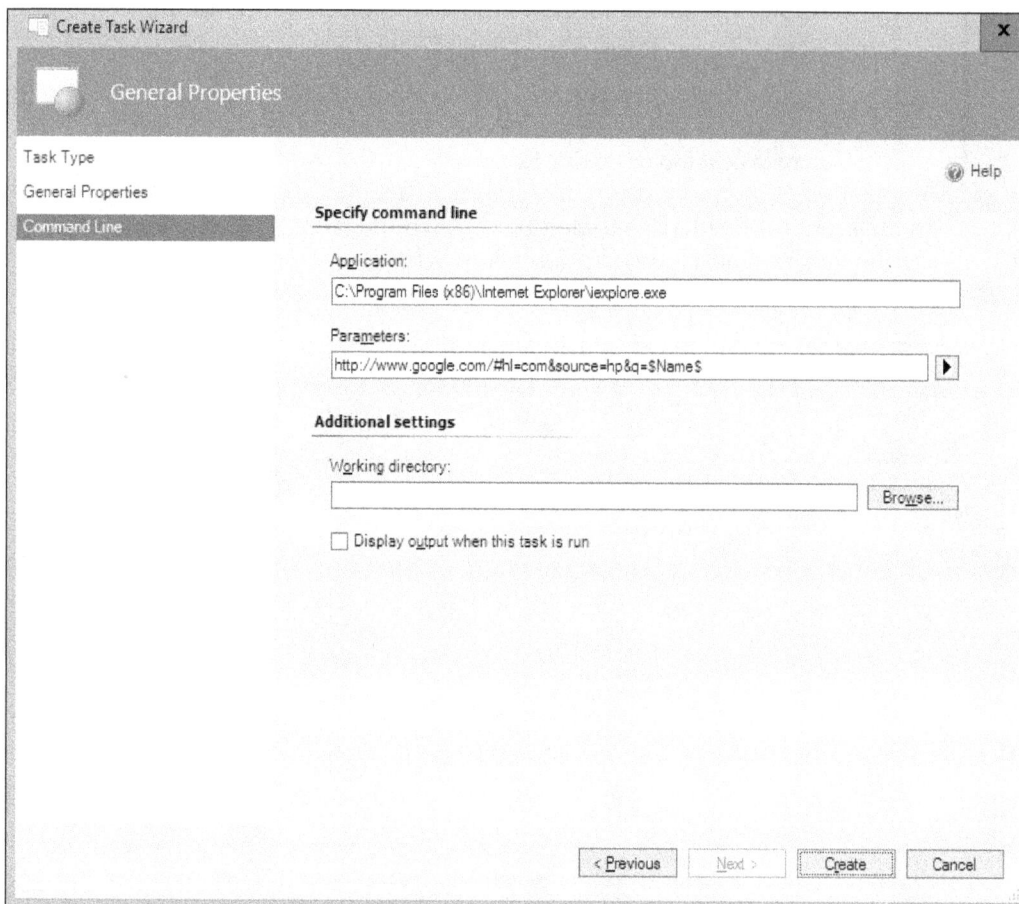

Figure 8.34: Specifying the path and parameters for your custom task

5. Verify that you've added the application and parameter values exactly as shown in the image (if you get either of these wrong, the task won't run), leave the **Working Directory** field blank and uncheck the **Display output when this task is run** option. When you're ready, click on **Create** to create your first custom task and close the wizard.

Creating the 'Run Remote Desktop Connection' task

When you've configured this task, you can use it to create a **remote desktop protocol (RDP)** connection directly from the computer you launch the task from to the Windows computer that's firing alerts into the console.

Here's what you need to do to get it configured:

1. From the Authoring workspace, expand **Management Pack Objects**, right-click on **Tasks** and then click on **Create a New Task**.

2. When the **Create Task** wizard launches, choose the **Alert command line** option again and select the same management pack you used earlier to store the other custom task. Click on **Next** to move on.

3. In the **General Properties** dialog box, type a name for the task (we'll use `Run Remote Desktop` for the name) and add a description. Click on **Next** to move on.

4. From the **Command Line** dialog box, type the full path to the RDP executable, located at `%windir%\system32\mstsc.exe` on Windows computers into the **Application** field.

5. Now copy `/v: $NetbiosComputerName$` into the **Parameters** field, make sure that you type this exactly as shown in *Figure 8.35*.

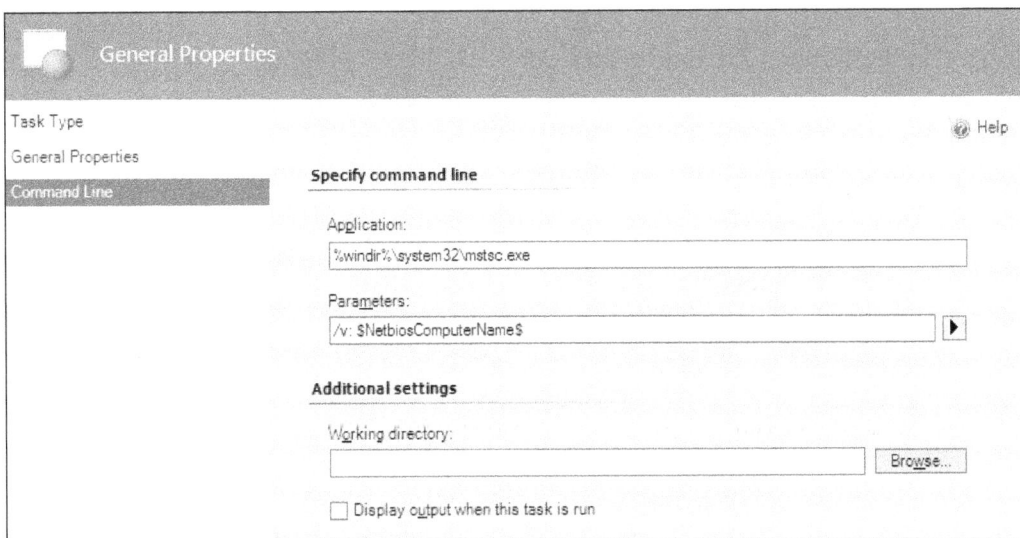

Figure 8.35: Specifying the path and parameters for your custom task

6. Leave the **Working Directory** field blank, clear the checkbox for **Display output when this task is run** and hit the **Create** button to close the wizard.

Creating the 'Run PuTTY' task

This is the final custom task that we'll create here and when you have this configured, it will give operators the ability to launch a PuTTY session to help manage UNIX/Linux computers, network devices, SAN's and other devices remotely. PuTTY is an open source terminal emulator and you will need to first download the Windows installer (not the stand-alone executable) from the following website: `http://tinyurl.com/puttydownload`.

When using custom console tasks, OpsMgr needs to have a consistent location for the application path and as such, for this task to work properly, it's imperative that you use the Windows installer version of PuTTY to deploy it as a fixed path application on the computer you've deployed your OpsMgr console to.

When you've downloaded and deployed the PuTTY installer, follow these steps to get the custom task created:

1. From the Authoring workspace, expand **Management Pack Objects**, right-click on **Tasks** and then click on **Create a New Task**.

2. Similar to the previous tasks, choose the **Alert command line** option and select the same management pack you used earlier to store the other task to and then click on **Next** to continue.

3. In the **General Properties** dialog box, type a name for the task and add a description. Click on **Next** to move on.

4. From the **Command Line** dialog box, type the full path to the PuTTY executable, located at `C:\Program Files (x86)\PuTTY\putty.exe` into the **Application** field.

5. Now copy `$NetbiosComputerName$` into the **Parameters** field and make sure that you type this exactly as shown in *Figure 8.36*.

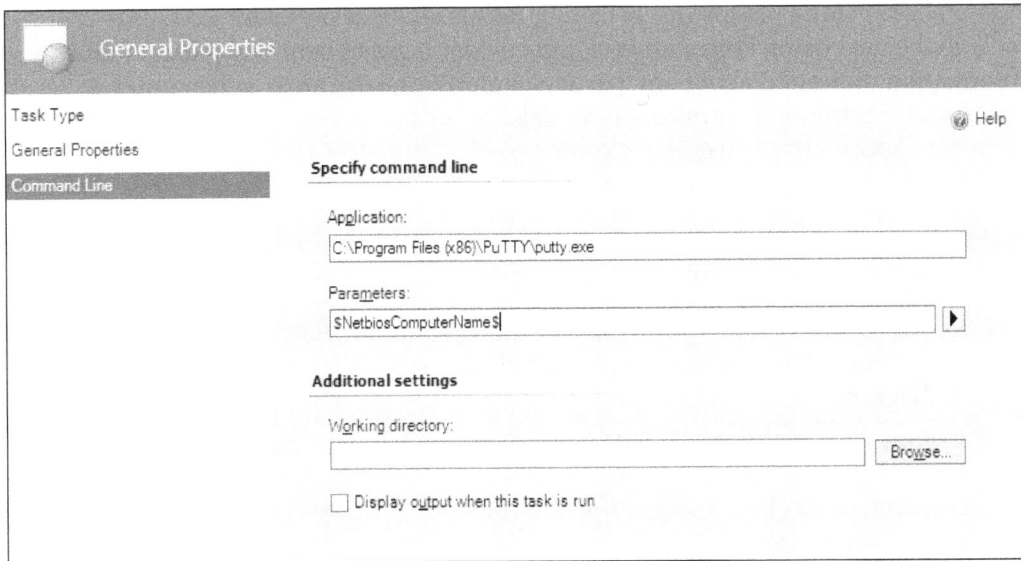

Figure 8.36: Configuring the PuTTY custom task

6. Leave the **Working Directory** field blank, clear the checkbox for **Display output when this task is run** and hit the **Create** button to close the wizard.

Now that you've learnt how to create custom console tasks, you can experiment with creating additional tasks that might be more specific to your own IT environment. In the next section, we'll put the three tasks we've just created to good use when we perform some alert tuning using distributed applications.

Contextual Tuning with distributed applications

When using traditional monitoring systems, administrators can find that after an alert is received, all too often it's difficult to understand the overall impact of what systems and services are affected. Having the ability to quickly gather as much information as possible about the issue and to then have the tools on hand to implement a solution and get things back up and running is another challenge they might encounter.

An excellent feature of OpsMgr is having the ability to easily pivot from one view to the next using both standard and custom tasks to help you glean as much information as needed about any particular alert or health state. When you've configured Distributed Application models for your IT services and then this pivot capability becomes very useful for tuning alerts within the context of the IT service they are affecting.

Follow these steps as an example on how to use custom tasks and distributed applications to solve problems and tune alerts:

1. From the Monitoring workspace, open a diagram view of an unhealthy distributed application model and click to select the top-level object in the diagram.

2. Now click the **Problem Path** button located between the **Layout** direction and **Filter by health** buttons, as shown in *Figure 8.37*. This button will map a path through your distributed application directly to the object that's in an unhealthy state.

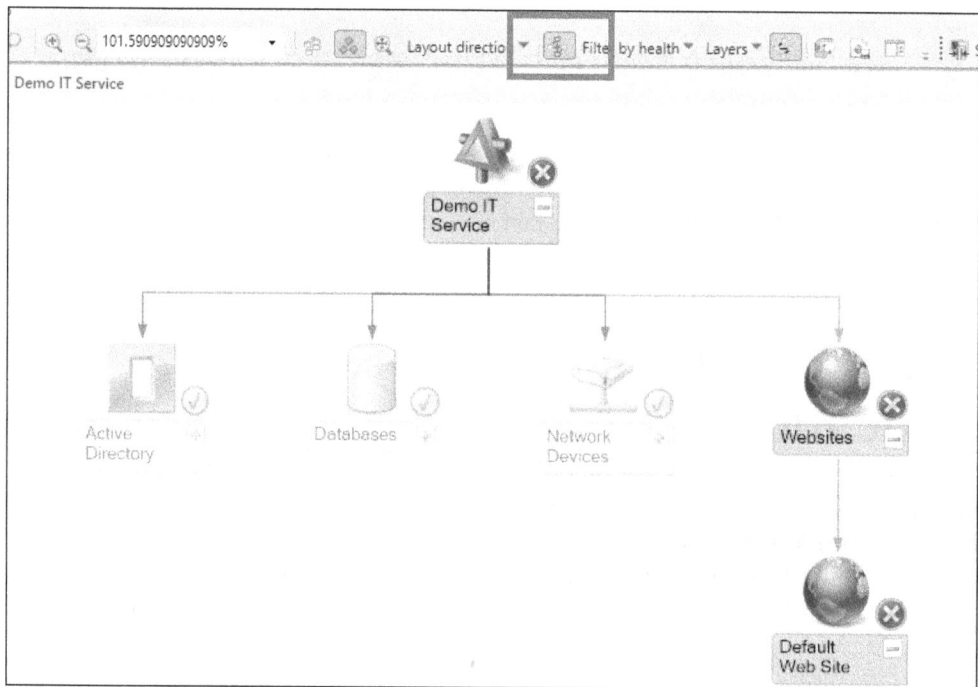

Figure 8.37: Using the Problem Path button

3. Select the unhealthy object, as shown in *Figure 8.38*, click on the **Alert View** link from the **Tasks** pane on the right to pivot to a scoped alert view of any open alerts associated with the object.

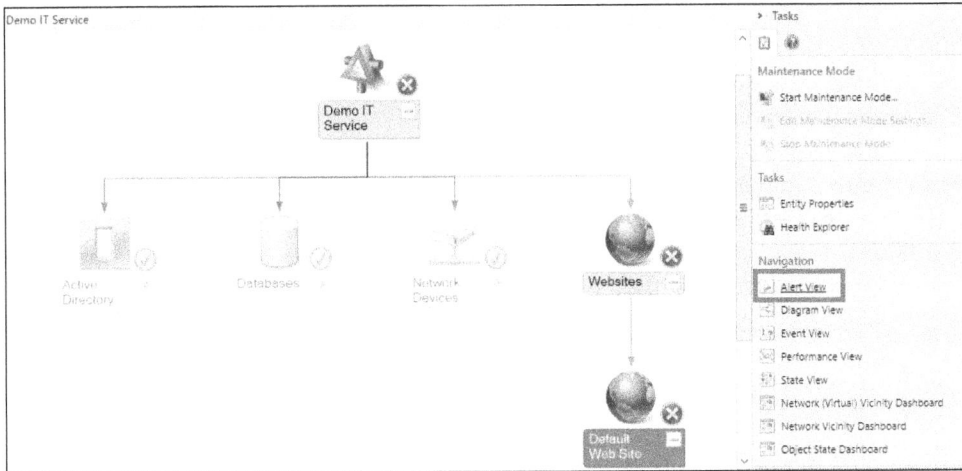

Figure 8.38: Opening a contextual alert view from a distributed application

4. When the alert view opens, you will see all open alerts that are relevant to the object that you launched the Alert View link from Tasks pane. If after checking the alert description and reading the **Product Knowledge** information, you find you still need to gather more information about the alert, you can now click on **Google It!** console task from the **Tasks** pane as shown in *Figure 8.39*.

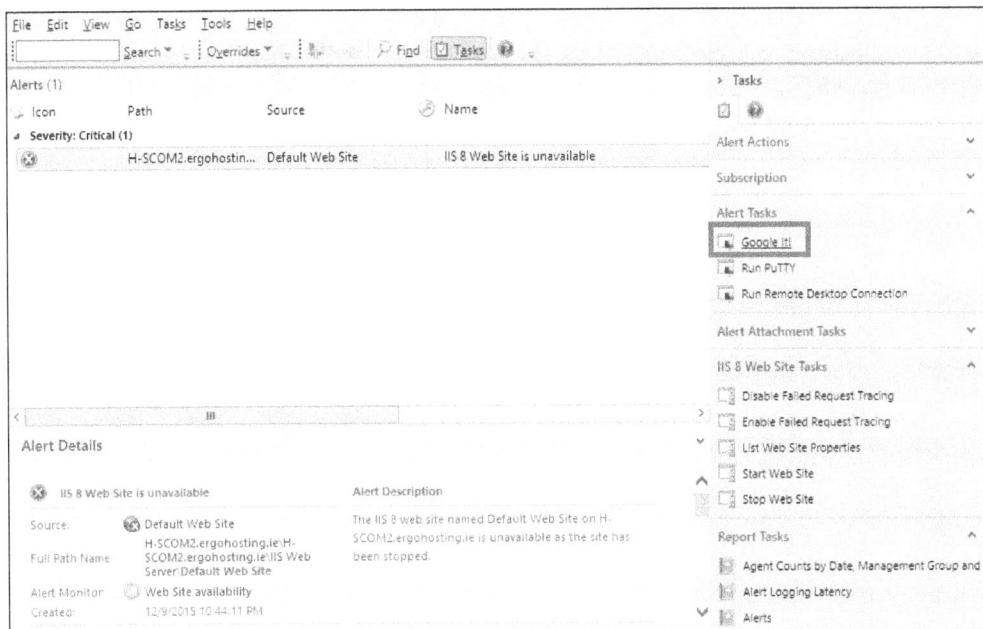

Figure 8.39: Gathering more information using custom tasks

5. After you've gathered the information you need to resolve the problem from the web, you can then choose another task from the **Tasks** pane to help you remedy the problem. If there's an associated task specific to the management pack that generated the alert and will solve the problem, then use that. The **Start Web Site** task in our example would be enough here. If there's no obvious management pack task to use, then you can pivot to either the Run Remote Desktop Connection task (if it's a Windows computer) or the Run PuTTY task (if it's a UNIX/Linux computer or other device) to remotely connect and resolve the issue.

> You can also use this pivoting technique from within a distributed application to help you tune large numbers of alerts through the scoped alert view for each component group. This will give you the context that you need to understand when you want to override or just disable a bunch of alerts.

Tuning with the Alert Data Management feature

If you're running OpsMgr 2016, then you've probably noticed the **Alert Data Management** feature located in the **Administration** workspace (under **Management Packs**) and shown in *Figure 8.40*. This feature is a welcome addition to OpsMgr and it's clear that Microsoft have listened to their customer's feedback about the ongoing administrative overhead of alert tuning.

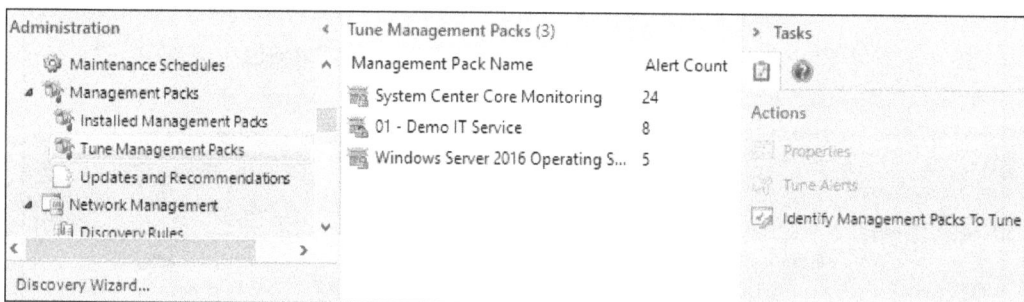

Figure 8.40: The Tune Management Packs feature in OpsMgr 2016

If you've only recently deployed management packs to your environment and are monitoring a small number of agents and devices, it's most likely that that when you click on the **Tune Management Packs** link in the **Administration** workspace, you'll be presented with an empty pane in the middle of the screen with no suggested management packs to tune.

To get going, click on the **Identify Management Packs To Tune** action from the **Tasks** pane on the right and you'll be presented with a dialog box similar to *Figure 8.41*. Here you can specify a date range to display alerts from and to populate the feature with suggested alerts, modify the minimum number of alerts to display with a lower number and hit **OK**.

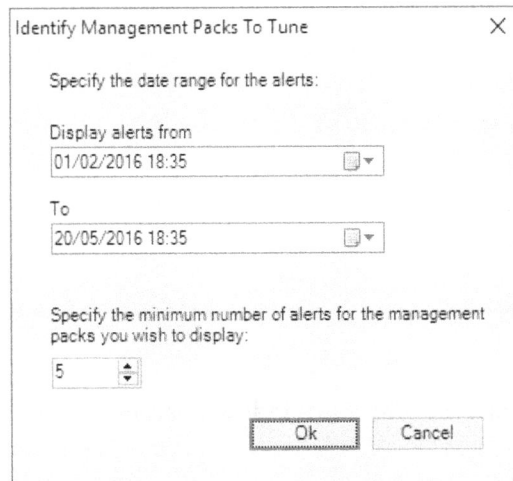

Figure 8.41: Specifying a date range and minimum number of alerts to display

This should now display a number of suggested management packs for you to tune and when you select one of them, the **Tasks** pane presents two new actions to work with (**Properties** and **Tune Alerts**) as shown in *Figure 8.42*.

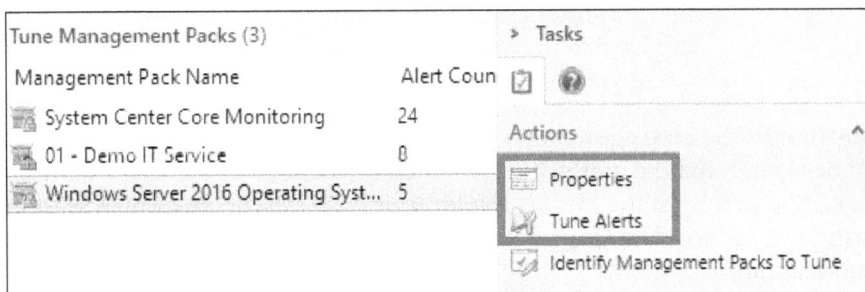

Figure 8.42: Enabling the new management pack tuning actions

Clicking on the **Properties** action displays details about the management pack and its dependencies and clicking on **Tune Alerts** launches a new window (shown in *Figure 8.43*) designed specifically to help you tune alerts that have been raised by the selected management pack during the period specified.

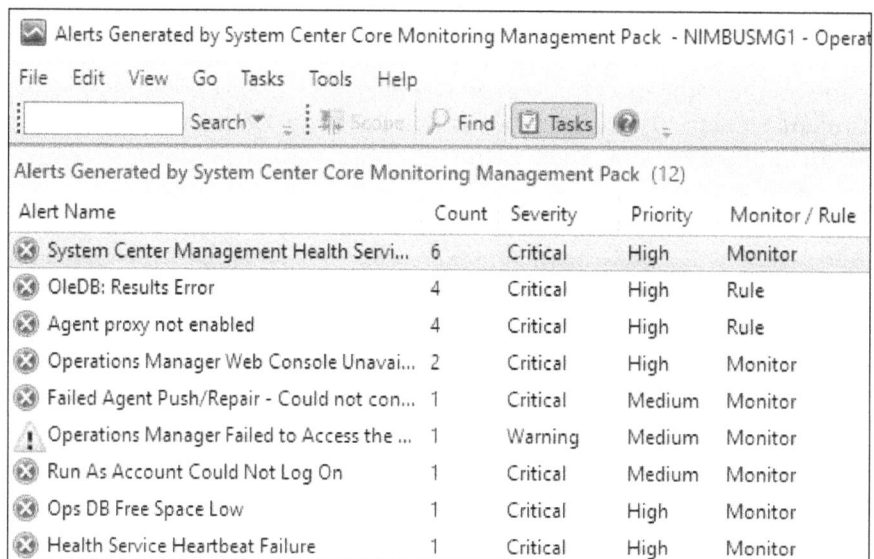

Alerts Generated by System Center Core Monitoring Management Pack (12)				
Alert Name	Count	Severity	Priority	Monitor / Rule
System Center Management Health Servi...	6	Critical	High	Monitor
OleDB: Results Error	4	Critical	High	Rule
Agent proxy not enabled	4	Critical	High	Rule
Operations Manager Web Console Unavai...	2	Critical	High	Monitor
Failed Agent Push/Repair - Could not con...	1	Critical	Medium	Monitor
Operations Manager Failed to Access the ...	1	Warning	Medium	Monitor
Run As Account Could Not Log On	1	Critical	Medium	Monitor
Ops DB Free Space Low	1	Critical	High	Monitor
Health Service Heartbeat Failure	1	Critical	High	Monitor

Figure 8.43: Scoped alert tuning

You can right-click on any alert in this window to access the actions menu shown in *Figure 8.44*.

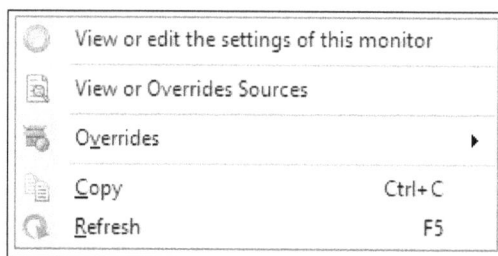

View or edit the settings of this monitor	
View or Overrides Sources	
Overrides	▶
Copy	Ctrl+C
Refresh	F5

Figure 8.44: Actions menu for tuning alerts

The **View or edit the settings** action in the list opens the properties of the monitor or rule that has generated the alerts and the **Overrides** option is the exact same action that you can launch from the Health Explorer or by right-clicking on an alert in the Monitoring workspace. The **Copy** action will copy the text from the selected alert fields and columns.

Clicking the **View or Overrides Sources** action launches the **View Sources** dialog box shown in *Figure 8.45*.

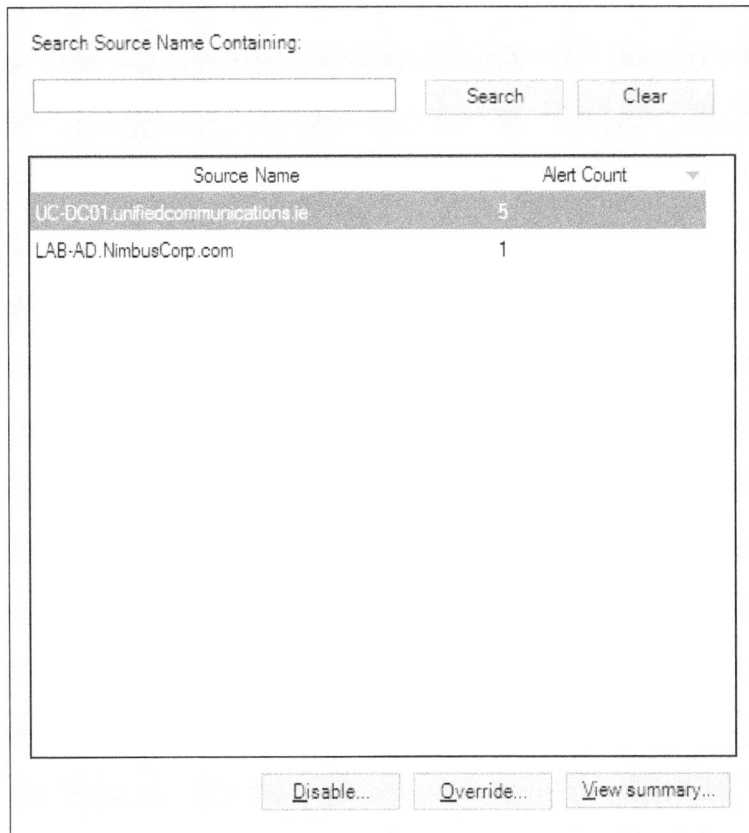

Figure 8.45: Viewing alert sources

This dialog box will show you the sources of the targeted management pack class that generated the alert – along with a repeat count of the number of alerts that particular source has generated. You can use the **Disable**, **Override** and **View Summary** buttons here to tune your alerts and view a summary of where else they might be applied.

Managing overrides

An important skill of tuning alerts in OpsMgr is to know where to go and what tools to use when you need to have a more granular experience of managing your overrides.

In the *Managing management packs* section of *Chapter 5, Working with Management Packs* you learnt about the excellent community tools from Microsoft's Boris Yanushpolsky and one of those tools that comes in handy when managing your overrides is the Override Explorer. Using this tool, you can connect to an OpsMgr management group and view all the overrides in your environment along with having the options to change the override target, delete the override or simply move it to another management pack. With Override Explorer, you also have the option to export your overrides to an Excel or XML file for later reference.

Working with the Overrides view

Back in the OpsMgr console, you can manage all the active overrides in your environment from the Authoring workspace as demonstrated in the following steps:

1. In the **Authoring** workspace, expand **Management Pack Objects** and click on the **Overrides** view as shown in *Figure 8.46*.

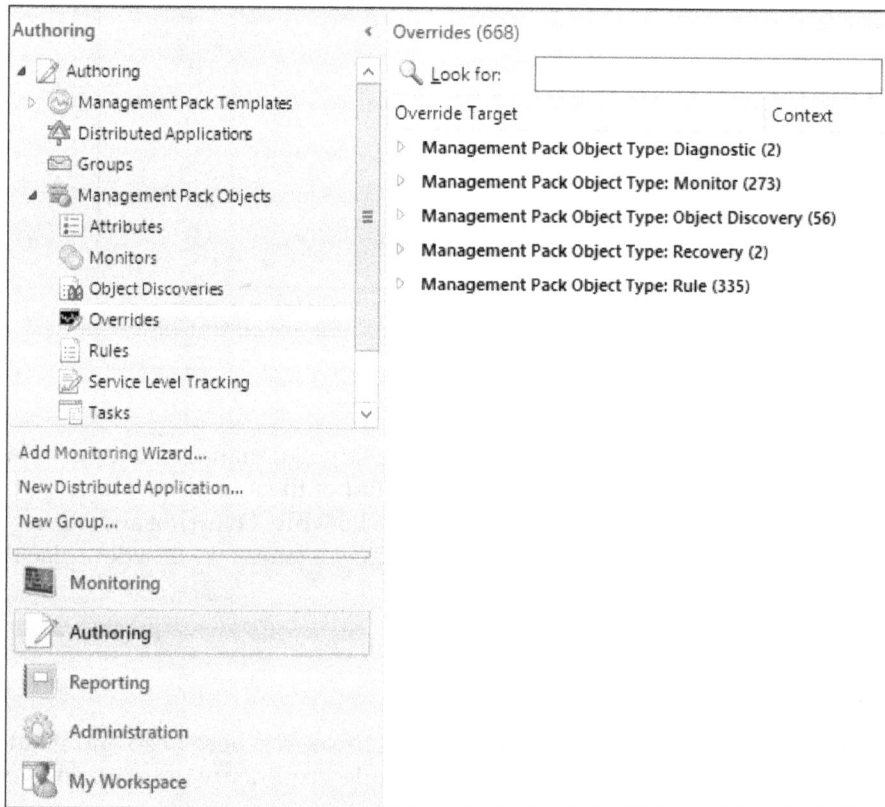

Figure 8.46: Viewing overrides from the Authoring workspace

2. The Overrides view groups your overrides by **Management Pack Object Type** and you can use the **Look for** field to search for your override by using the name or a keyword contained in the name of the rule or monitor as shown in *Figure 8.47*.

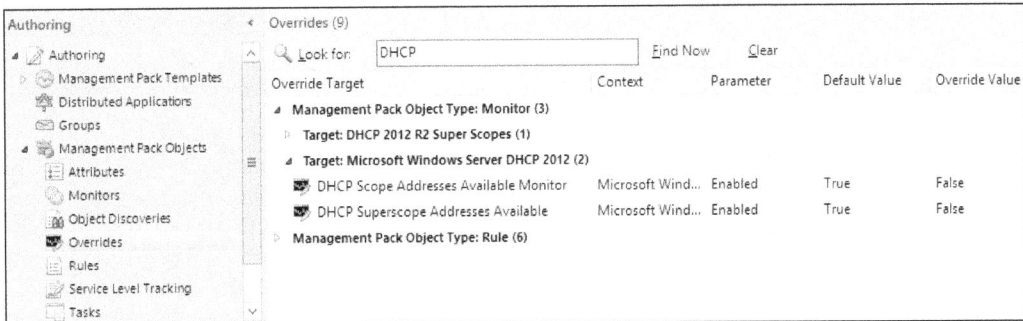

Figure 8.47: Searching for overrides

3. If you're not sure of the name of the rule or monitor and there's too many overrides to choose from, you can scope the view by clicking on the **Scope** button from the navigation bar. As you can see in *Figure 8.48*, this will allow you to select a class, group or object to target the view at and narrow down your search.

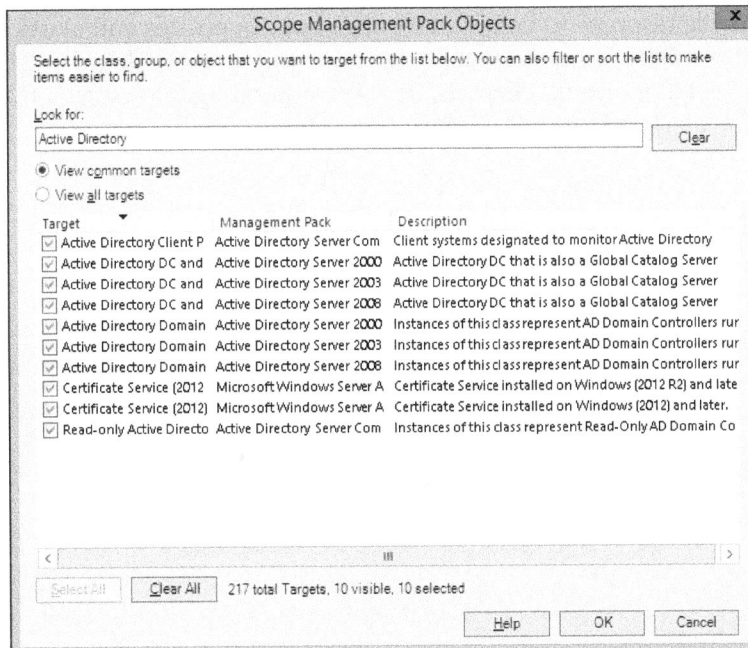

Figure 8.48: Scoping your Overrides view

4. When you find the override you're looking for, you can manage it by right-clicking on the override and choosing an option from the resultant context menu shown in *Figure 8.49*.

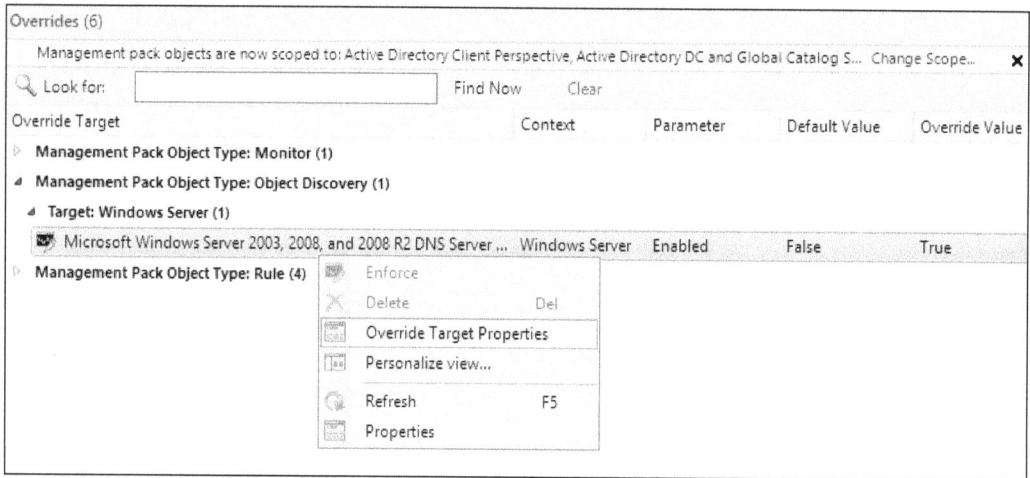

Figure 8.49: Managing an override from a scoped view

Using reports to manage alerts and overrides

Another valuable resource to help you manage your overrides and alerts is the Reporting workspace. Although we'll cover reporting in more detail in *Chapter 10, Creating Alert Subscriptions and Reports,* now is a good time to walk you through some of the common alert and override-focused reports.

A standard deployment of OpsMgr that includes the Reporting role will give you a number of useful reports that can help you get a better picture of common alerts, events and overrides. Most of these reports are stored in the **Microsoft Generic Report Library** as shown in *Figure 8.44*.

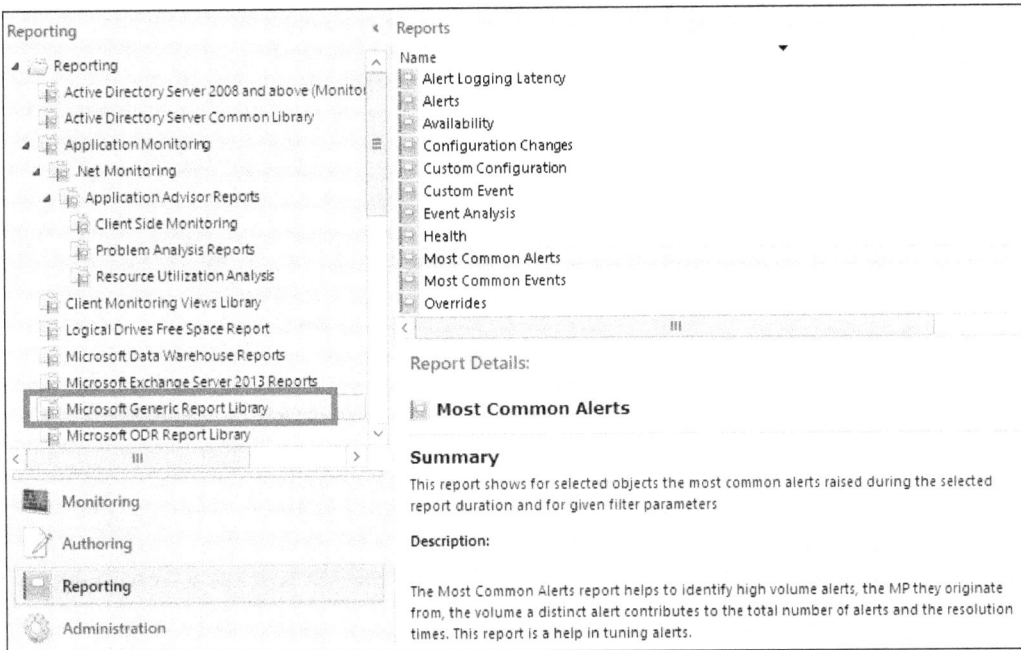

Figure 8.50: Using reports for alert management

The **Most Common Alerts** report is one of the more popular reports to use when you want to get an understanding of the noisiest alerts and the management packs those alerts originate from. You can see the output of this report in *Figure 8.51*.

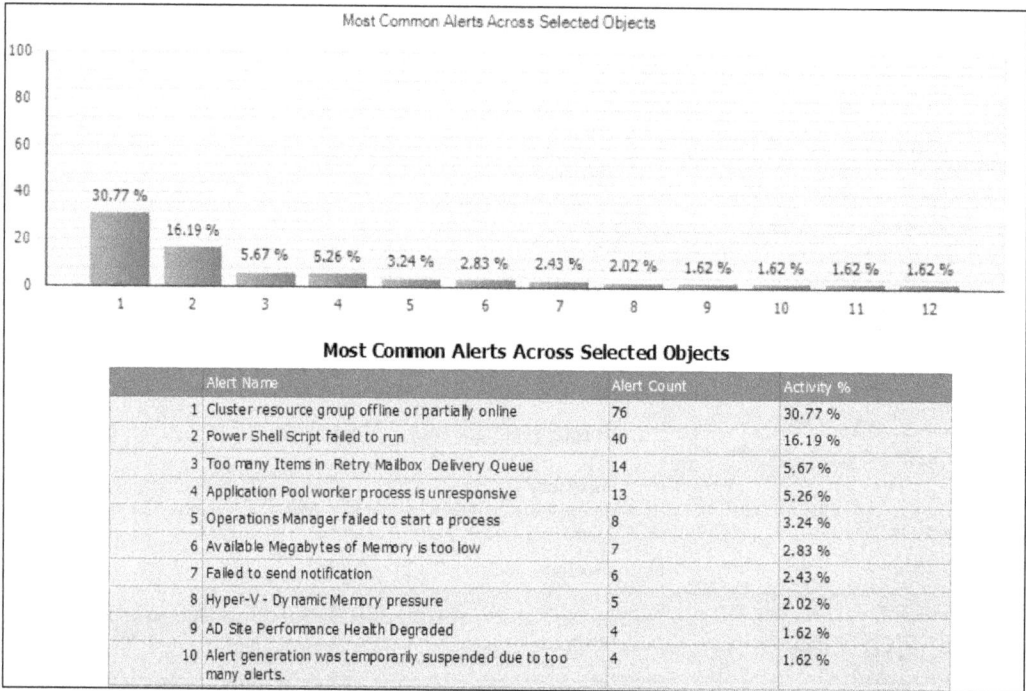

Figure 8.51: Most Common Alerts report

If you wish to have a report that contains all the overrides in your environment, then the **Overrides** report is what you need. This report can be scoped to contain overrides for every management pack you've deployed, or you can just scope it to look at the overrides contained in selected management packs. An example of this report is shown in *Figure 8.52*.

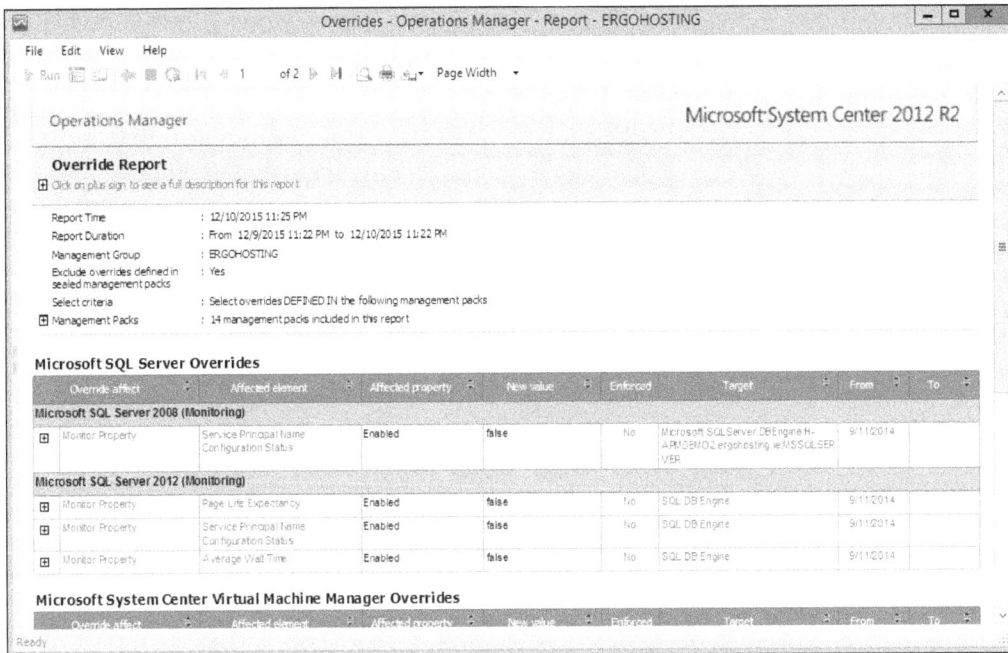

Figure 8.52: Most Common Alerts report

Summary

In this chapter, we discussed how to define an efficient alert management process and we talked about the different alert resolution states that you get by default with OpsMgr, along with how to create your own custom resolution states.

We gave you an understanding of the difference between working with alerts generated by monitors and alerts generated by rules. You learnt about when and how to use the Health Explorer for alert tuning and we demonstrated how to create some custom console tasks that can be used with distributed applications to manage alerts within the context of an IT service. We ended the chapter with information about working with overrides through the Authoring and Reporting workspaces.

In the next chapter, we will be working with some of the built-in OpsMgr dashboard and visualization templates along with introducing you to some additional community dashboard solutions and resources.

9
Visualizing Your IT with Dashboards

One of the most important deliverables of a monitoring solution is how you visualize the data and present it back to your customers and end users. With OpsMgr, there's a wide variety of options to choose from that enable you to create dashboards containing meaningful information. You can take advantage of pre-built dashboard layouts that can be populated with different visualization widgets to help display your monitoring data – or you can get inspiration from some of the free dashboard solutions that have been made available by the general OpsMgr community.

We will start this chapter with an introduction to all the built-in dashboard layouts and templates that OpsMgr has to offer before walking you through some of the most popular widgets that you can use to light up your displays and impress the boss!

Towards the end of the chapter we'll point you in the direction of some recommended community dashboard resources and we'll also give you some information on third-party vendor add-ons that you can use to really take those visualizations to the next level.

Here's what you'll learn by the end of the chapter:

- Dashboard layouts and templates
- Working with widgets
- Using Visio to create dashboard views
- Community dashboard resources
- Third-party vendor solutions

Exploring dashboard layouts and templates

In the *Working with Views* section of *Chapter 3, Exploring the Consoles*, we introduced the Dashboard View and walked you through creating a new dashboard using the Grid Layout with four different widgets. Here, we'll take a look at each of the other dashboard layouts and templates that you can work with in OpsMgr and we'll also show you how to unlock a hidden Datacenter Dashboard template that contains some unique options for visualizing the health and performance of your monitored objects.

In *Figure 9.1*, you can see a list of all the available dashboard layouts and templates that you get with a default installation of OpsMgr. These options can be accessed when you create a new dashboard view in the **Monitoring** workspace.

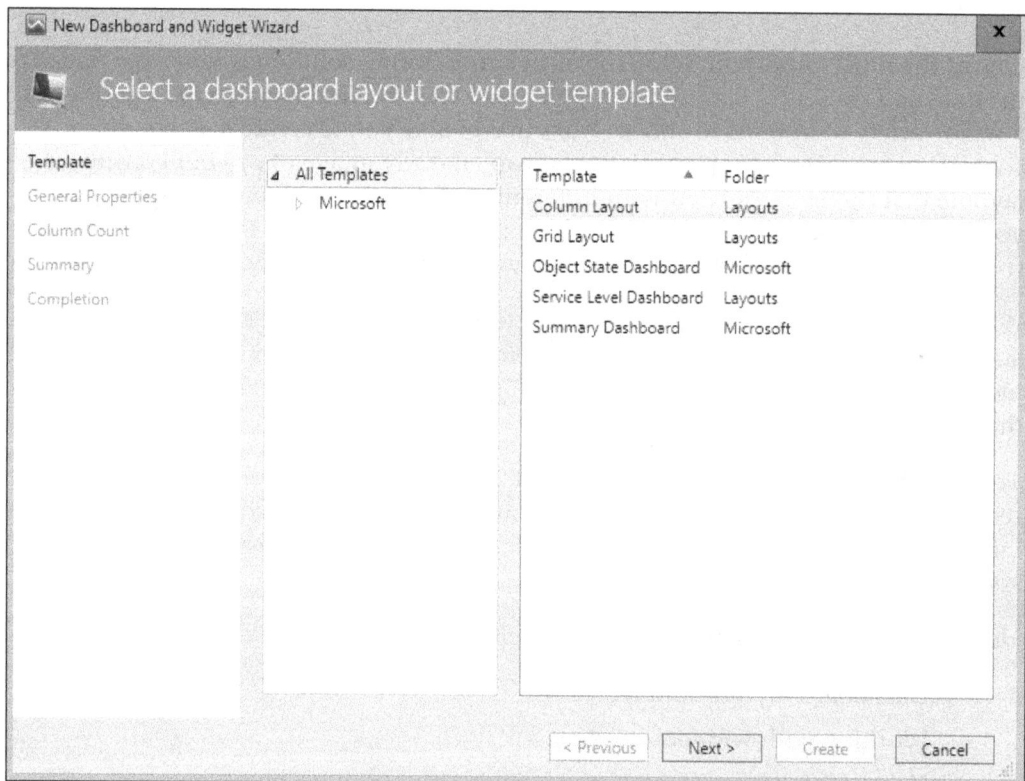

Figure 9.1: Default dashboard layouts and templates

Column Layout

When configuring this layout, you can choose up to a maximum of five empty columns/cells to add to a dashboard. Each column can be populated with a different widget type and you can add extra cells by clicking the gear icon at the top right of the dashboard and selecting **Add Cell**.

Follow these steps to create an empty dashboard with a Column Layout (we'll revisit this dashboard later and populate the cells with some widgets):

1. In the **Monitoring** workspace, right-click on the location that you wish to create the new dashboard, click on **New**, and then click on **Dashboard View**.

2. Choose a dashboard layout style from the **Select a Dashboard Layout or Widget Template** dialog box, we'll choose the **Column Layout** here, and then click on **Next** to continue.

3. In the **Name** field, type a name to identify the dashboard – we'll use 'Nimbus Corp Column Dashboard' as an example. Optionally, you can type a description of the view into the **Description** field, and then click on **Next**.

4. At the **Specify the Number of the Columns** dialog box, select the number of columns that you wish to have in your dashboard (we'll pick two columns here but you can go up to a maximum of five), and then click on **Next** to move on.

5. Click on **Create** to deploy the new dashboard layout and close the wizard.

Object State Dashboard template

This dashboard template is deployed by default with five widgets designed to show detailed information about a particular group or object.

Follow these steps to create an Object State Dashboard:

1. From the Monitoring workspace, right-click on the location that you wish to create the new dashboard, click on **New**, and then click on **Dashboard View**.

2. Now choose the **Object State Dashboard** option and click on **Next** to continue.

3. Type a name for the dashboard – we'll use 'Nimbus Corp Object State Dashboard' as an example. Optionally, type a description of the view and click on **Next** to move on.

4. At the **Specify the Object** dialog box, choose a group or monitored object (we've chosen one of our Hyper-V nodes) and then click on **Next** to move on.

5. Select any criteria that you want to apply to this dashboard and then click on **Next** and hit **Create** to close the wizard.

6. As each of the five widgets come already configured with this dashboard template, clicking on the dashboard will give you an instantly populated view similar to that in *Figure 9.2*.

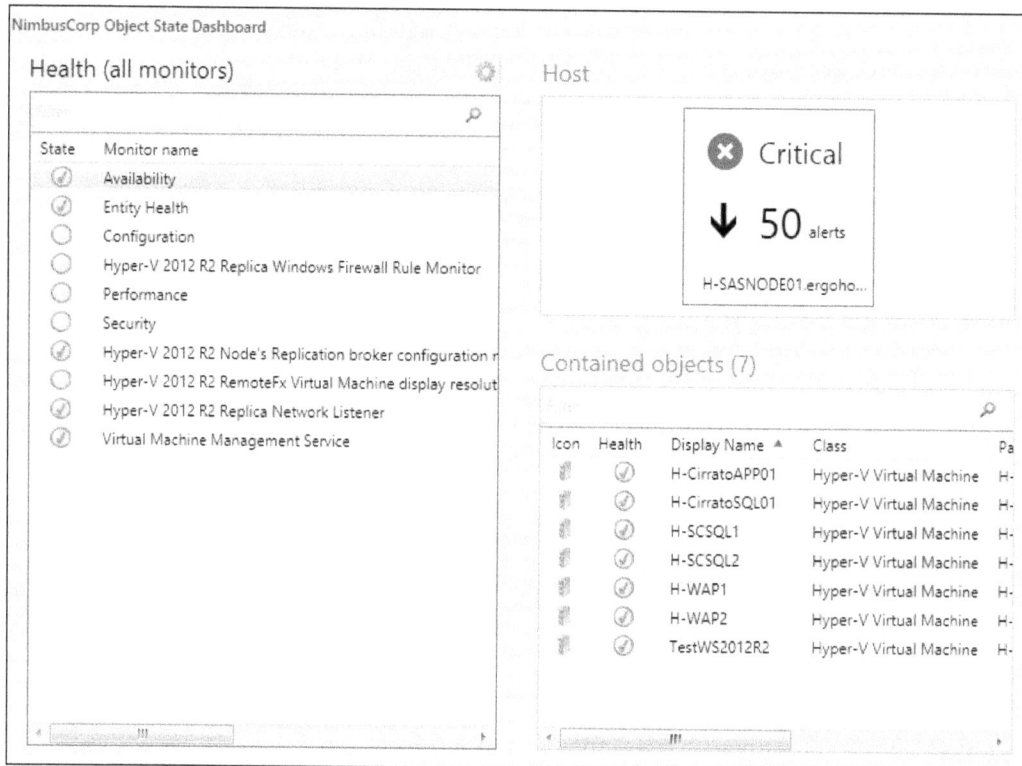

Figure 9.2: Object State Dashboard

Service Level Dashboard layout

A favorite with senior management staff, this dashboard displays selected service level objectives that have been created in OpsMgr – we've covered this topic in detail in the *Creating service level objectives* section of *Chapter 7, Configuring Service Models with Distributed Applications*.

Here's what you need to do to configure a new Service Level Dashboard:

1. From the **Monitoring** workspace, right-click on the location that you wish to create the new dashboard, click on **New**, and then click on **Dashboard View**.

2. Now choose the **Service Level Dashboard** option and click on **Next** to continue.

3. Type a name for the dashboard – we'll use 'Nimbus Corp Service Level Dashboard' as an example. Optionally, type a description of the view and click on **Next** to move on.

4. At the **Specify the Object** dialog box, click on the **Add** button and then choose the service level objective(s) that you want to add to the dashboard. Choose a value for the Last section to determine how far back the SLA is measured.

5. Click on **Next** to continue, and then hit **Create** to close the wizard.

6. In *Figure 9.3*, you can see the different **Service Levels** that have been added to this dashboard and there's a nice visual in the bottom pane that clearly defines if the SLA has been met or not.

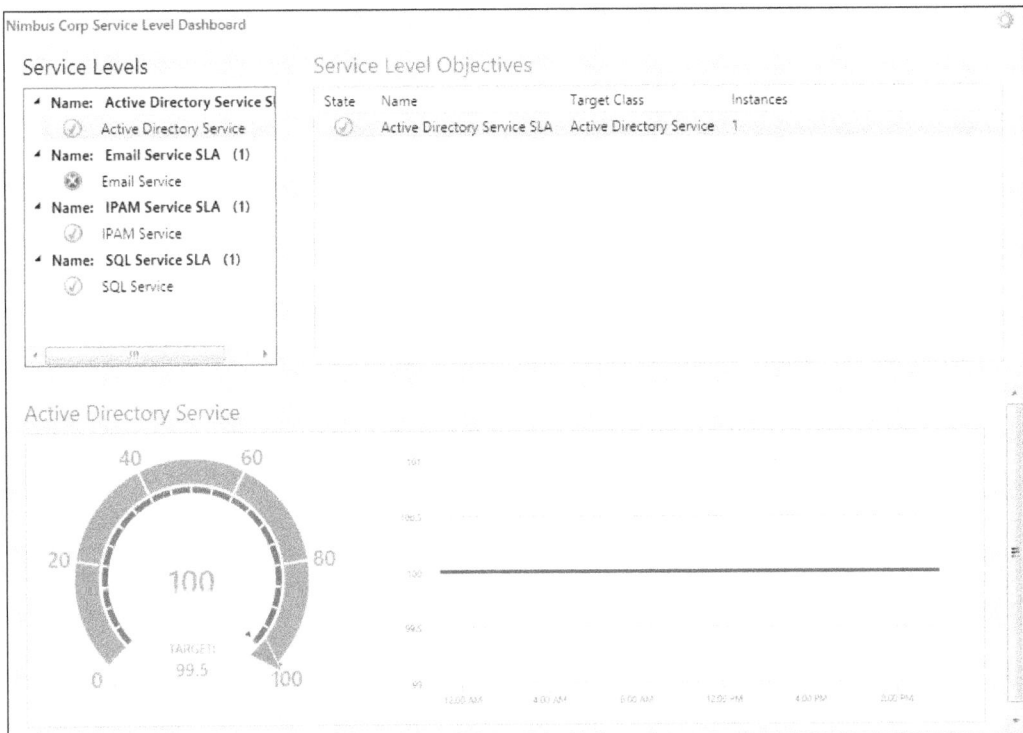

Figure 9.3: Service Level Dashboard

Summary Dashboard template

When you deploy this template, you get a four-cell dashboard that's pre-populated with the following widgets: Objects by Performance, Performance, State, and Alerts. None of the widgets in this dashboard have been scoped to monitored objects so that's something you need to do after you create it.

Follow these steps to create this dashboard:

1. From the Monitoring workspace, right-click on the location that you wish to create the new dashboard, click on **New**, and then click on **Dashboard View**.

2. Now choose the **Summary Dashboard** option and click on **Next** to continue.

3. Type a name for the dashboard – we'll use 'Nimbus Corp Summary Dashboard' as an example. Optionally, type a description of the view and click on **Next** to move on.

4. Click on **Create** to close the wizard and create the new dashboard.

5. Using the gear icon beside each widget to help you populate the cells with data, you should end up with a dashboard similar to *Figure 9.4*.

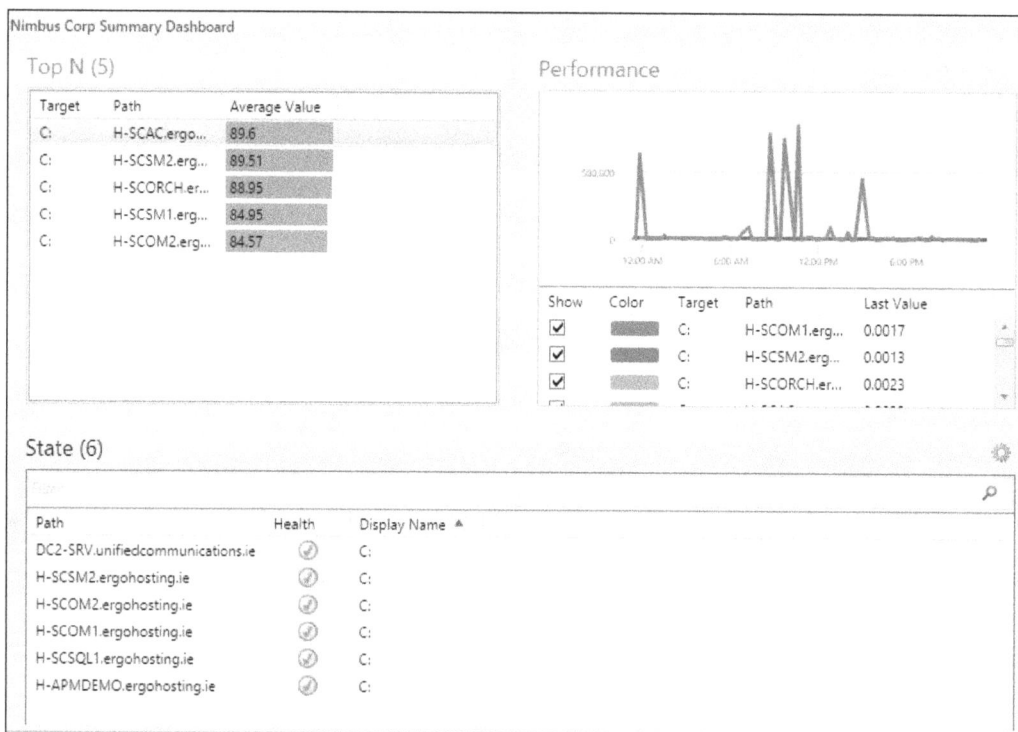

Figure 9.4: Populated Summary Dashboard

Widgets

As you learned earlier, the built-in dashboards in OpsMgr come as either a template or a layout. The templates tend to be already pre-populated with cells and these give you a limited choice of customization. With layouts however, you have the option to customize your dashboards by choosing from a list of widgets that will define and display data from your monitored objects.

Once you have your dashboard layout configured, choosing widgets to populate the dashboard is easy. All you need to do is select the **Click to add widget...** link from an empty dashboard cell as shown in *Figure 9.5*.

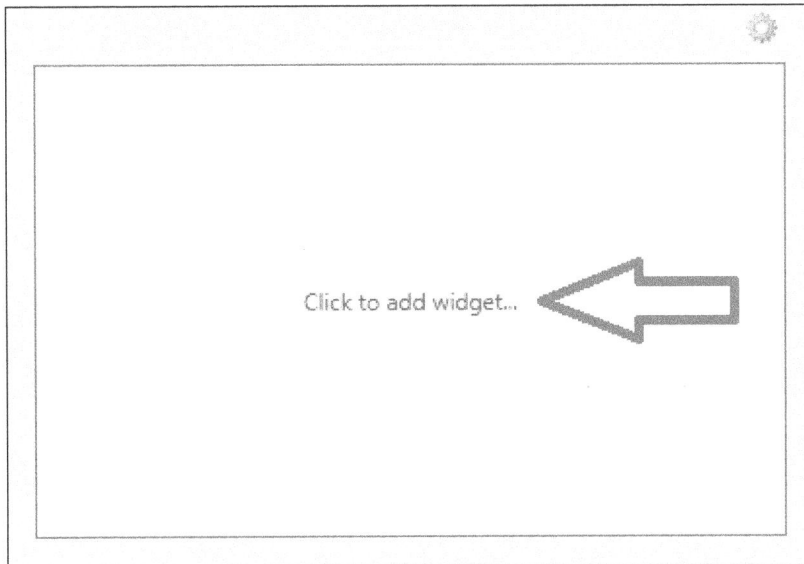

Figure 9.5: Adding widgets

This will then open the **New Dashboard and Widget Wizard** and as shown in *Figure 9.6*, you'll be presented with a long list of widgets that you can use to bring your dashboards to life.

All Templates	Template ▲	Folder
◢ Microsoft	Alert Widget	Widgets
Dashboard Layouts	Contextual Alert Widget	Widgets
Widgets	Contextual Health Widget	Widgets
	Details Widget	Widgets
	Image Widget	Widgets
	Instance Details Widget	Widgets
	Object Detail Tiles Widget	Widgets
	Object Health Widget	Widgets
	Object SLA Widget	Widgets
	Objects by Performance	Widgets
	Performance Widget	Widgets
	Powershell Grid Widget	Widgets
	Powershell Web Browser Widget	Widgets
	SLA Tiles Widget	Widgets
	SLA Widget	Widgets
	State Tiles Widget	Widgets
	State Widget	Widgets
	Topology Widget	Widgets
	Web Browser Widget	Widgets

Figure 9.6: Selecting a widget

In the *Using the alert widget* section from *Chapter 8, Alert Tuning the Easy Way*, we discussed how to create a new dashboard with the alert widget to help you tune your alerts and in the next few sections, we will discuss and demonstrate how to configure some of OpsMgr's most popular dashboard widgets.

State Tiles widget

The State Tiles widget shows you a health state and number of alerts summary tile for one or more monitored objects. The up or down arrow in a tile indicates a higher or lower alert count than the previous value. This widget is shown in *Figure 9.7*.

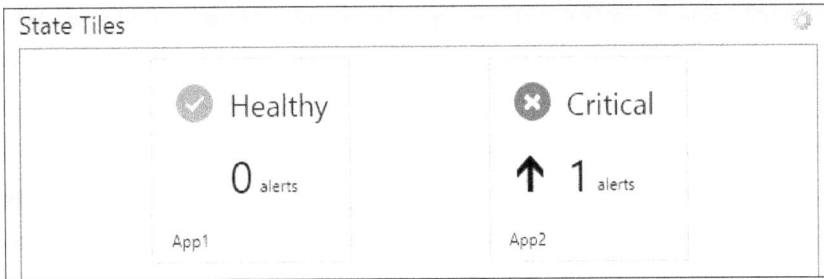

Figure 9.7: State Tiles widget

Contextual widgets

The contextual alert and contextual health widgets show the same type of data as the standard alert and health widgets with one exception. These contextual widgets don't light up any data until you click on an object from another widget, which then targets the alerts or health states in context with the object you've clicked on. These widgets are very useful in multi-cell dashboards that operators need to interact with.

To demonstrate the capability of contextual widgets, we'll return to the empty Column Layout that we created earlier in *Exploring dashboard layouts and templates*. From this layout, follow these steps to add a new State Tiles and Contextual Alert widget:

1. From the Monitoring workspace, locate the Nimbus Corp Column Dashboard and hit the **Click to add widget...** link from the empty cell on the left.

2. Now from the **New Dashboard and Widget Wizard**, select the **State Tiles Widget** option and click on **Next** to continue.

3. Give the widget a name — we'll use 'Critical Servers'. For our example, add an optional description and then click on **Next**.

4. Hit the **Add** button at the **Specify the Objects** dialog box, select the **Groups and Objects** option and then search for and add some monitored servers. Click on **Next** to move on.

5. At the next dialog box, select any alert criteria that you want to scope the widget to and then click on **Finish** to close the wizard and create the view.

6. For the second empty cell on the right, select the **Click to add widget...** link and choose the **Contextual Alert Widget** option as shown in *Figure 9.8*. Click on **Next** to continue.

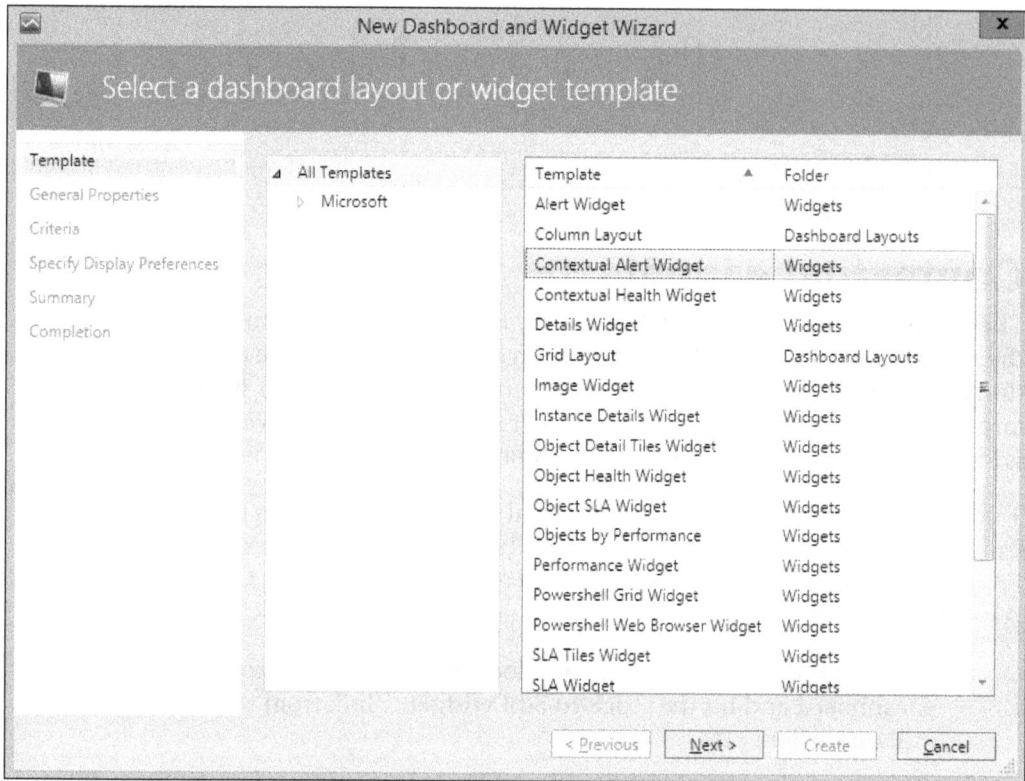

Figure 9.8: Adding a Contextual Alert Widget

7. Enter a name and optional description, and then click on **Next** through the **Criteria and Specify Display Preferences** dialog boxes making changes as you need before clicking the **Finish** button to close the wizard.

8. In *Figure 9.9*, you can see the completed column layout dashboard with a **State Tiles and Contextual Alert** widget. Now when you click on one of the state tiles on the left, you see only alerts that relate to the context of the object in the widget on the right.

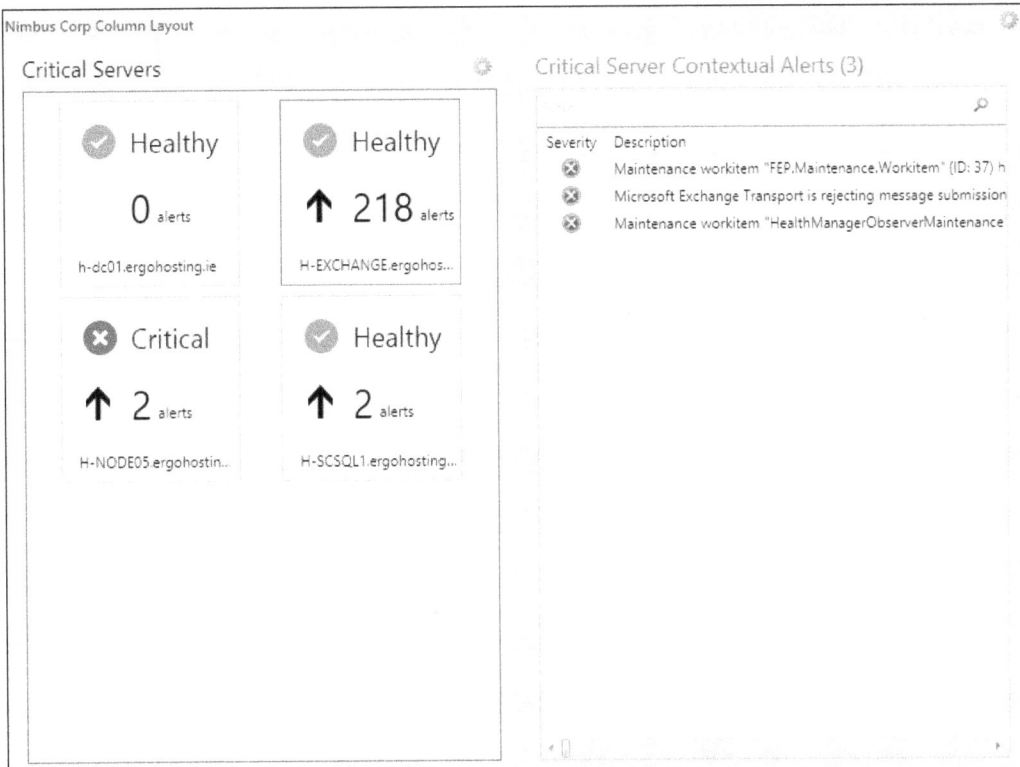

Figure 9.9: Adding a Contextual Alert Widget

Performance widgets

To help you visualize your performance data and metrics, you can use either the Objects by Performance Widget or the Performance Widget. Examples of both these widgets can be found in the **Summary Dashboard Template** (shown earlier in *Figure 9.4*) and each has their own specific use case.

The **Objects by Performance Widget** is handy when you need to show a 'Top N' or 'Bottom N' view of a specific performance counter across a number of monitored objects. With this widget, you could perhaps create a Top 10 Servers % Free Disk Space view to highlight available disk space across all your Windows servers or you might want to show a number of servers with the lowest Disk I/O.

The Performance Widget is closer to your more traditional performance counter views where a simple graph is created to show the highs and lows of specific performance counters over a given period of time.

Detail widgets

There are two widgets that serve the sole purpose of providing you with details about a specific monitored group or object – the **Details Widget** and the **Instance Details Widget**.

Similar to the Contextual Alert Widget, the Details Widget is context sensitive and it will display text information about an object that you've clicked on from another widget. To try this widget out, create a dashboard layout that has two cells and add a State Tiles Widget to one cell and a Details Widget to the other cell. When you've both cells configured, click on a state tile and you will see the Details Widget change to reflect the contextual details of the object you've just clicked on as shown in *Figure 9.10*.

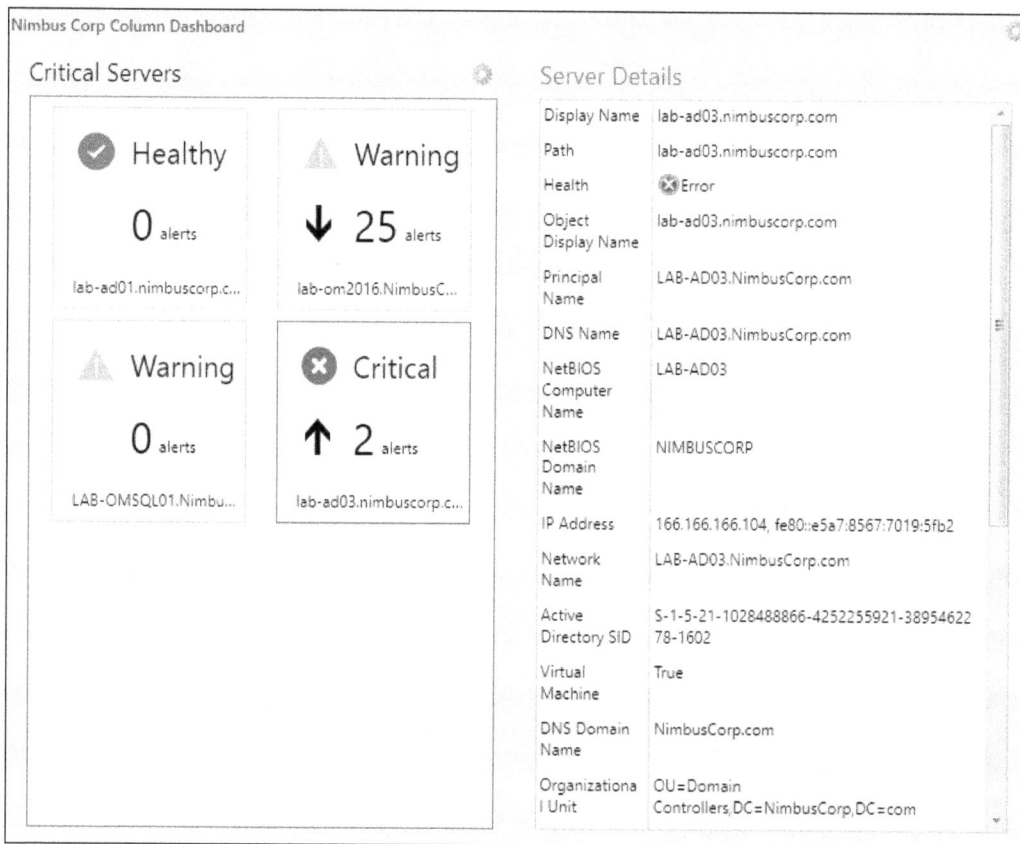

Figure 9.10: Displaying contextual information with the Details Widget

The Instance Details Widget differs from the Details Widget due to the fact that it's not contextual and you need to scope the group or object that it will show details about during initial configuration of the widget. Once this widget is created, it will always show details about the same group or object and the only way to change this is to delete its contents and reconfigure it again.

Image widget

This is a simple but very useful widget when you combine it into a dashboard layout that has a number of different widgets. It gives you the ability to upload an image file in one of three formats: *.bmp, *.png, or *.jpg.

The benefit of being able to add an image to your dashboard with the Image Widget is that you can then place a company logo into one of the cells to personalize the dashboard and make people take notice easier. In *Figure 9.11*, you can see that we've added a company logo to an Image Widget within a four-cell grid dashboard.

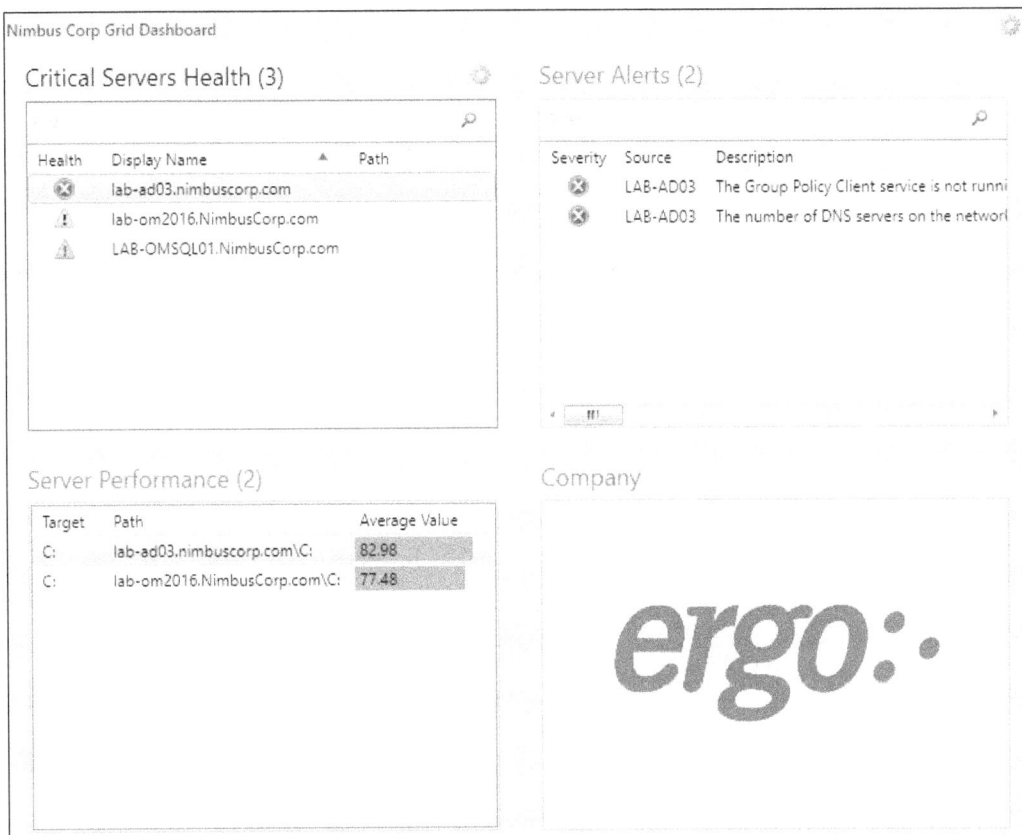

Figure 9.11: Using the Image Widget to display company logos

SLA widgets

If you've created and assigned some SLA's to your monitored environment (see *Creating service level objectives* in *Chapter 7, Configuring Service Models with Distributed Applications* for a walkthrough), then you can choose from the SLA Widget, the Object SLA Widget or the SLA Tile Widget.

The **SLA Widget** shown in *Figure 9.12* is pretty basic and can be scoped to display one or more pre-configured SLA's over a given period of time.

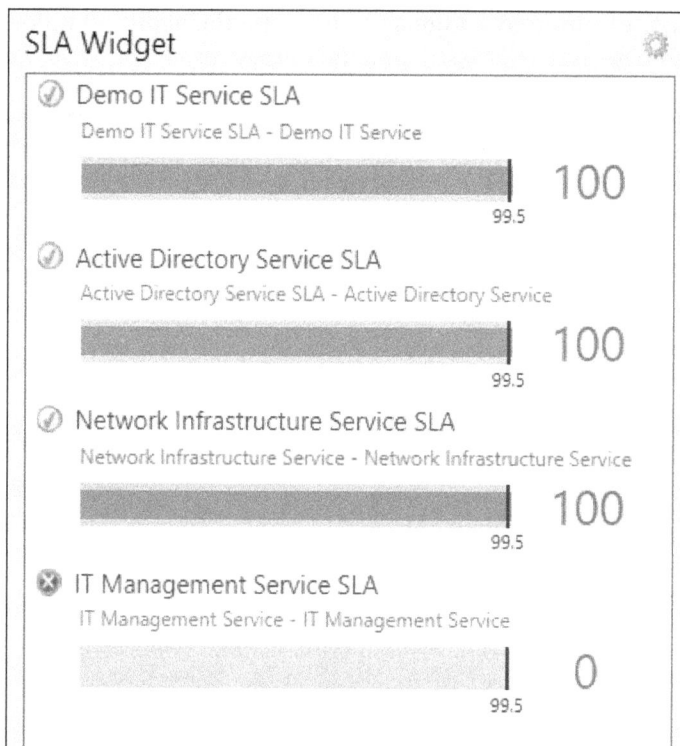

Figure 9.12: The SLA Widget

A word of warning with the SLA Widget is that it doesn't scale too well when you add a lot of SLA's and as a result, you'll find that it's slow to load and will randomly generate errors. If you have a lot of SLA's that you want to display, then we recommend you choose from one of the other SLA widgets instead.

The **Object SLA** widget shown in *Figure 9.13* looks very similar to the SLA widget but this one can be used to scope an SLA assigned to a group or a single object. This widget graphically displays the last measured value of each SLA and can be configured to show data over periods of hours or days.

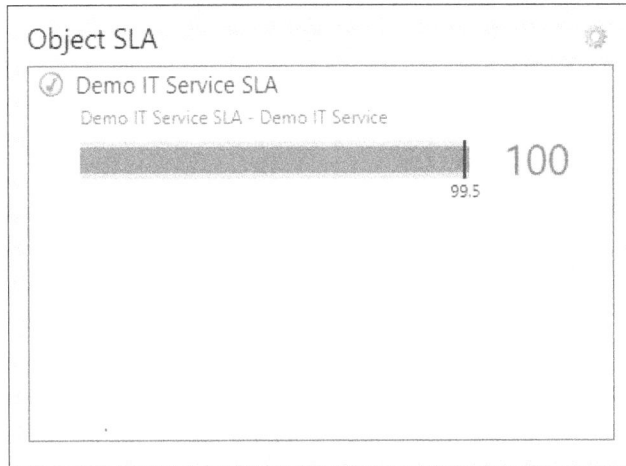

Figure 9.13: The Object SLA widget

With the **SLA Tiles** widget, you can see a summary of how each of your SLA's are doing and if they have passed or failed their configured values. An example of this widget is shown in *Figure 9.14* and this can be configured to display SLA's from minutes to years where required.

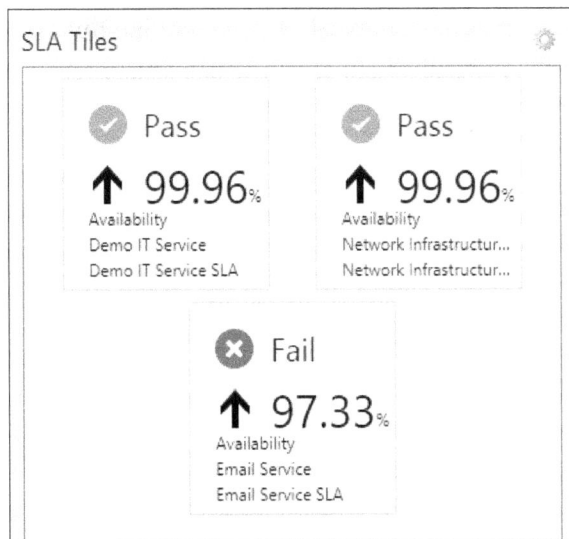

Figure 9.14: Monitoring multiple SLA's with the SLA Tiles widget

> When working with SLA dashboards, you might encounter a strange issue where the friendly display name of your SLA (e.g. Email Service) is replaced with an OpsMgr assigned name in the format of `MOMUIGeneratedSLAxxxxxx`. If this happens to your SLA's, then follow the information in this post: `http://tinyurl.com/opsmgrsladashfix` or this post `http://tinyurl.com/OpsMgrSLAFix` to resolve the issue.

PowerShell widgets

Often when working with pre-built dashboard templates and widgets, you'll encounter limitations to how much you can customize them and that's when you need to turn to some creative scripting. To help accommodate this, Microsoft has added two PowerShell widgets to OpsMgr giving you much more possibilities to visualize your data.

The **PowerShell Grid widget** enables you to run a PowerShell script and display the results of that script in a dashboard. Now, on the surface of it, you might think that this widget will only show you the text output of your script but with some clever scripting, you can create some seriously cool dashboards. An example of one of these dashboards is the Google Maps integration dashboard that System Center MVP Tao Yang created a while back: `http://tinyurl.com/tyangdashboard`. If that isn't cool enough for you, then check out the concept Jukebox dashboard that System Center MVP Stefan Roth created here: `http://tinyurl.com/srothdashboard`

The **PowerShell Web Browser widget** displays the output of a webpage retrieved by a script and displays it as a dashboard. If you combine this widget with the PowerShell Grid widget you can create dashboards similar to the one in *Figure 9.15* to help with OpsMgr administration tasks.

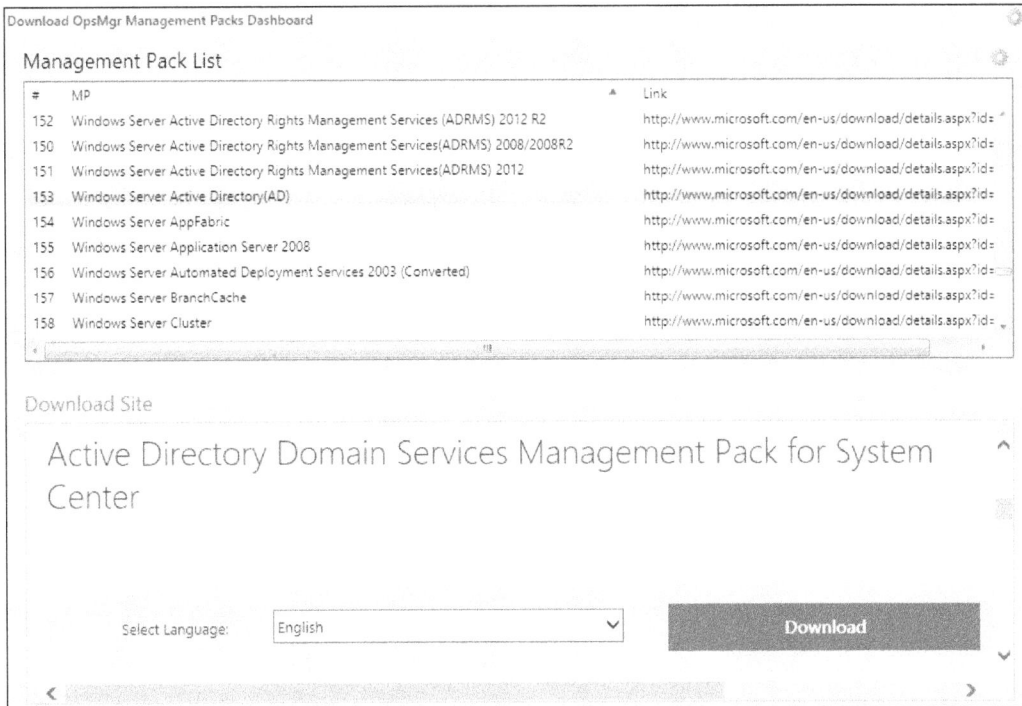

Figure 9.15: Combining the PowerShell widgets to create useful dashboards

The dashboard in this example was created using two scripts from Stefan Roth and you can download the scripts and get more information on this solution from his blog post here: `http://tinyurl.com/srothdownloadmps`.

Impressing your boss with the Topology Widget

One of the most underestimated dashboard widgets in OpsMgr is the **Topology Widget**. This is the one widget that I deploy in every customer engagement I work on. Dashboards created with it are generally the ones that make the most impact for end users and senior management when we display them on a big screen.

Firstly, don't be fooled by its name. You would be forgiven for thinking that this dashboard was some kind of add-on for Active Directory or a similar service that requires topology mapping but actually, you should think of this as your blank canvas for creativity!

Essentially this widget enables you to upload a background image (which can be in *.png, *.bmp or *.jpg format) and then add any monitored objects that you wish from OpsMgr over the top of the image to create a live dashboard similar to the sample IT Services Dashboard shown in *Figure 9.16*.

Figure 9.16: Topology widget dashboard example

The IT Services Dashboard background image in our example was created using Microsoft Visio and then saved as a static *.png file to be uploaded to the Topology Widget. When it was uploaded, we added a list of monitored IT services, which were modelled as distributed applications and then simply dragged the health state icon for each one to the relevant location on the background image.

The following sections will show you how to create a similar style dashboard image using Visio and how to add that image into OpsMgr where you can then light it up with live health states of your monitored objects.

Creating a dashboard image with Microsoft Visio

Although the Topology Widget can import an image created with any application that is saved in *.png, *.bmp or *.jpg format, I find that using Microsoft Visio to create the image delivers the most flexibility for customization. There's also an abundance of free Visio resources available on the Internet to help you design the image you want.

Follow these steps to create a new dashboard image for the Topology Widget with Microsoft Visio:

1. If you have Microsoft Visio already installed on your computer, open it. If you don't have a copy of it, then head over to the Microsoft Evaluation Center and download a trial version of it from here: https://www.microsoft.com/en-us/evalcenter/.

2. Your Visio designs are only as good as the stencils and icons you have at your disposal and a while back, I created some custom Visio stencils (some of these are shown in *Figure 9.17*) for System Center that can be downloaded from here: http://kevingreeneitblog.blogspot.ie/2013/11/new-scom-2012-r2-infrastructure-visio.html.

Figure 9.17: Custom Visio stencils for System Center

3. Now get to work on designing an image that suits the monitoring requirements for your organization.

> Keep in mind here that, although you can add any monitored
> object from OpsMgr, it's a good idea to start with a dashboard
> image that will represent a high-level overview of your IT
> services and critical infrastructure components.

In *Figure 9.18*, you can see an example of a dashboard image we've created
with Visio to help represent the branch office sites and IT services for an
organization based in the UK and Ireland. For this image, we've used a
combination of basic Visio shapes, my custom Visio stencils and some
random icons that we've downloaded.

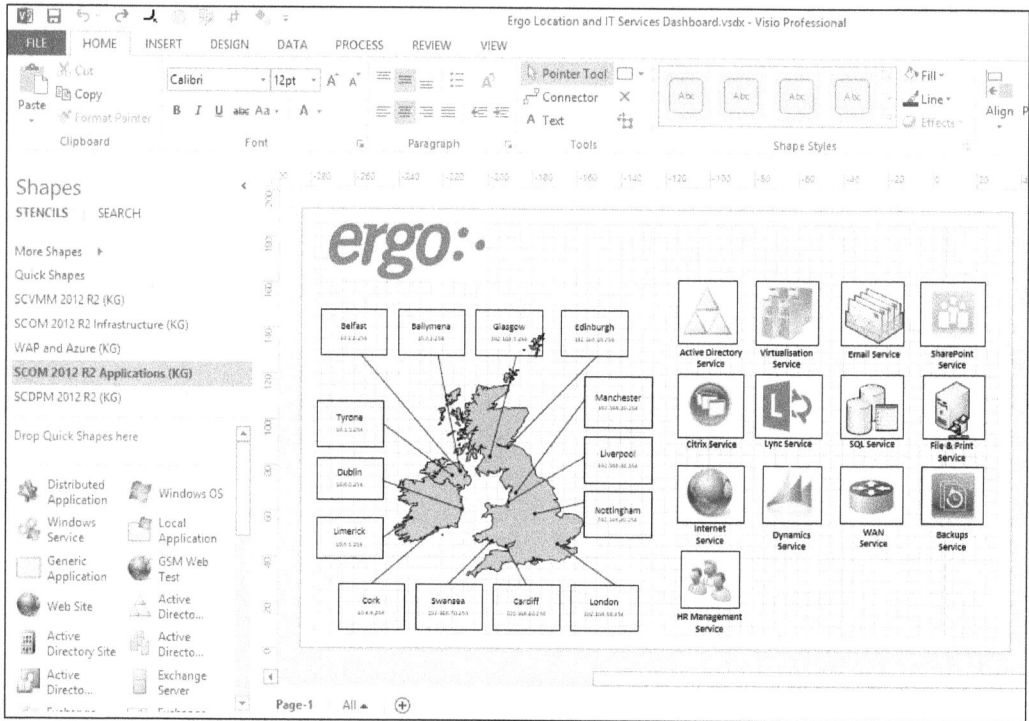

Figure 9.18: Creating the Visio dashboard image

> If you're finding a hard time locating icons and images to properly
> represent your IT services, then check out the Icon Archive at
> http://www.iconarchive.com/. Here you can choose from
> thousands of icons to help enhance your OpsMgr dashboards.

4. When you've finished designing your dashboard image in Visio, it's time to save the image in a format that can be used by the Topology Widget. To do this, first select the **Design** tab in Visio, click on the **Size** button from the **Navigation** bar and then select the **Fit to Drawing** option as shown in *Figure 9.19*. This is an important step as it helps to scale the image properly before you export it.

Figure 9.19: Scaling your dashboard image in Visio

5. Now click on **File** from the Visio navigation bar, select **Save As** and choose a location to save the image to. From the **Save As** dialog box, give your dashboard image a name and select the **Portable Network Graphics (*.png)** option from the **Save as Type** menu as shown in *Figure 9.20*.

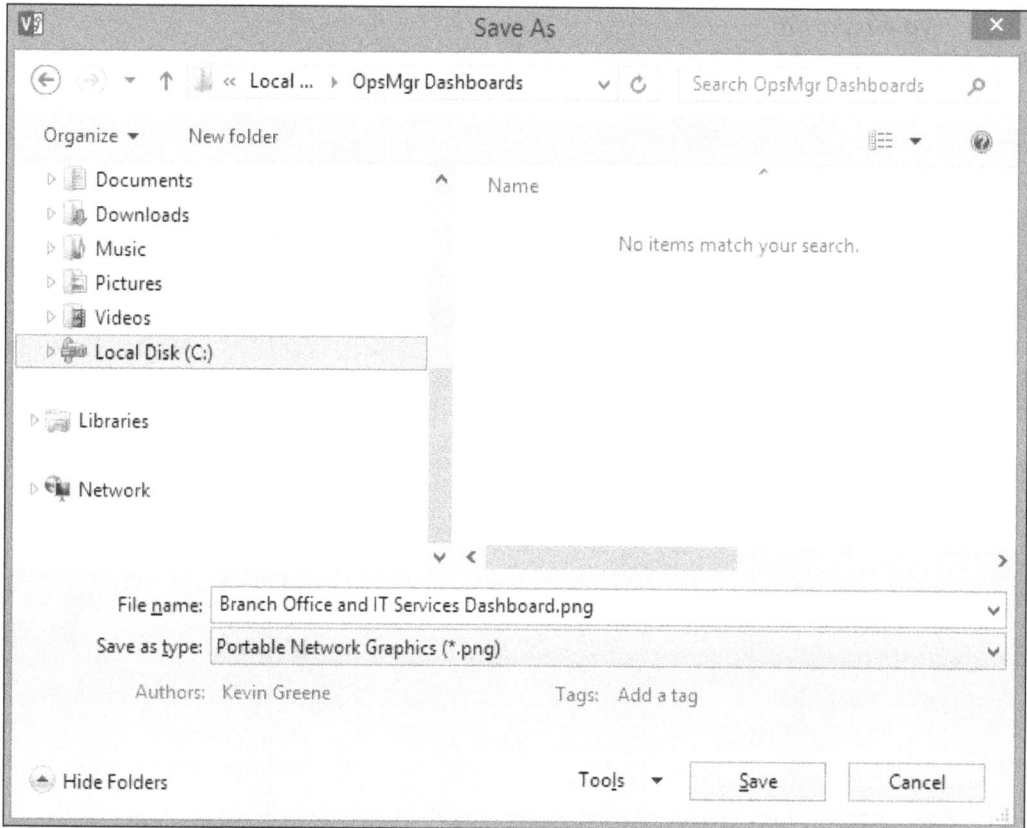

Figure 9.20: Saving the Visio image as a PNG file

6. Click on the **Save** button to save the image, accept the defaults and hit the **OK** button at the **PNG Output Options** dialog box to complete the image creation.

> There's no limit to the type of dashboard images you can create with Visio and if you need a little more inspiration, then take a look at some of the examples in this post: http://www.culham.net/scom/scom-dashboards-examples/.

It's also a good idea to check with the various infrastructure and application teams within the organization to see if they have any previously created Visio diagrams of server racks and network topologies. If you have any photographs that you want to use, these will work too – just as long as they've been saved in an acceptable format.

With your dashboard image now created and ready to go, here's a step-by-step guide for creating a custom single-cell Grid Layout dashboard containing a Topology Widget:

1. In the **Monitoring** workspace, right-click where you want to create the new view, click on **New**, and then click on **Dashboard View**.

2. Choose **Grid Layout** from the **Select a Dashboard Layout or Widget Template** dialog box and click on **Next** to continue.

3. In the **Name** field, type a name for your dashboard – we'll use 'Nimbus Corp Sites and Services' for our example.

4. At the **Specify the Layout of the Dashboard** dialog box, select the **1 Cell** option, click on **Next** and then hit the **Create** button. When the dashboard layout has been created, click on **Close** and you should be presented with a view similar to *Figure 9.21*.

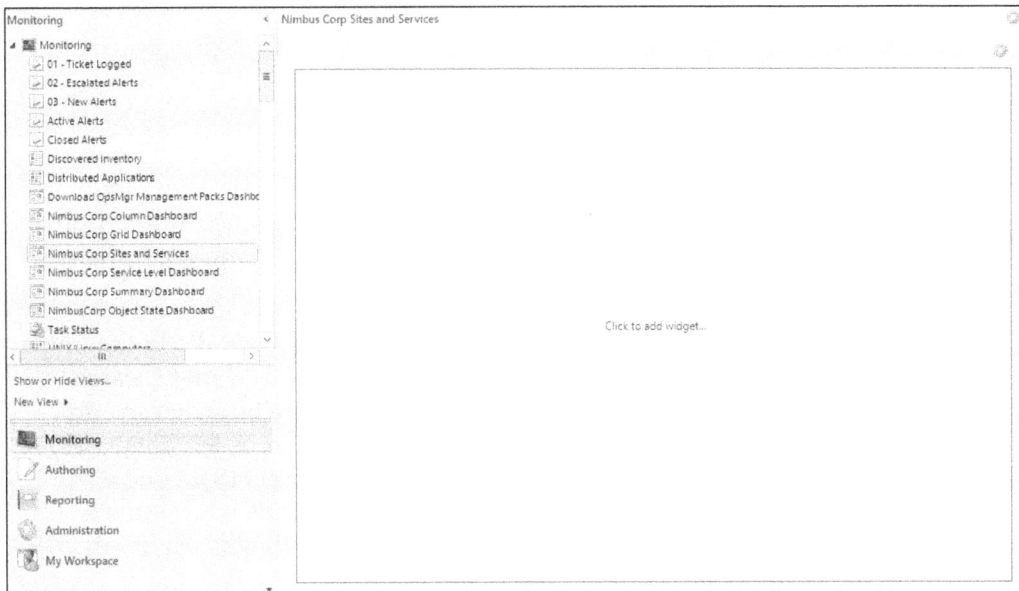

Figure 9.21: Creating a new Sites and Services dashboard

5. From here, select the **Click to add widget...** link to open the **New Dashboard and Widget Wizard** and choose the **Topology Widget** as shown in *Figure 9.22* then click on **Next** to move on.

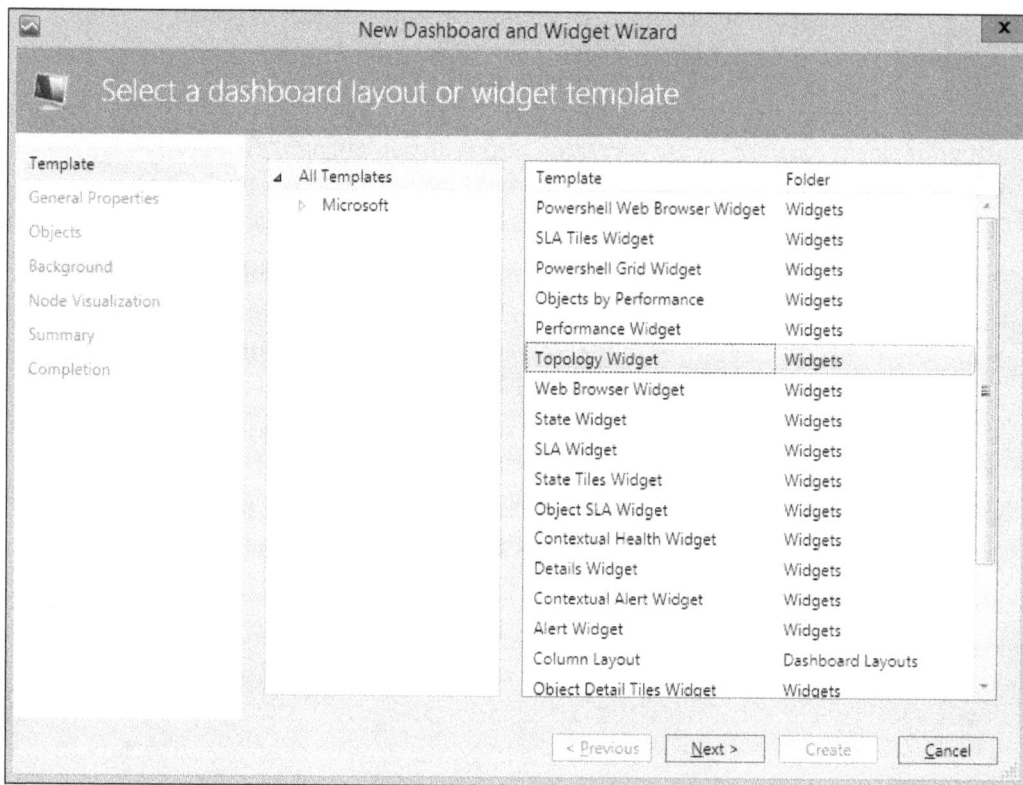

Figure 9.22: Choosing the Topology Widget

6. In the **Name** field, type a name for the widget and click on **Next** to continue.

7. At the **Specify the Objects** dialog box, click on the **Add** button to open the **Select Objects** dialog box.

8. As shown in *Figure 9.23*, click on the **Groups and Objects** radio button, type the full or partial name of the monitored objects that you want to search for, we'll use the names of our distributed applications here but you can add anything that you want (for example individual servers, roles, databases, network devices, and so on). Click on **Add** for each object that you've selected in the **Available items** window, and then hit **OK** when you've added everything you need.

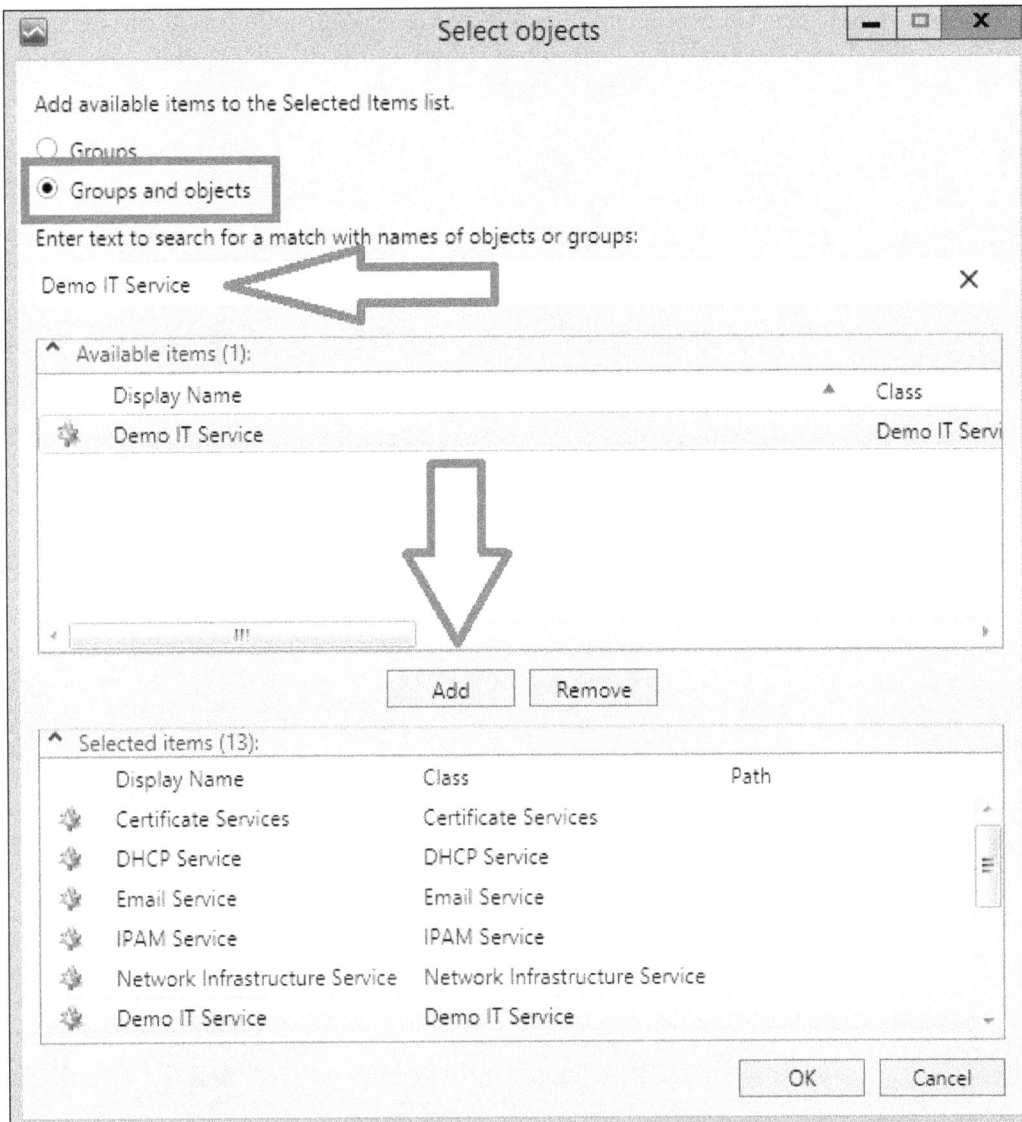

Figure 9.23: Adding monitored objects to your Topology Widget

9. Back at the **Specify the Objects** dialog box, verify all of the monitored objects you wish to add to the dashboard are listed and click on **Next** to move on.

10. Copy the saved dashboard image file that you created earlier with Visio to the computer that you're running the Operations Console from and at the **Background** dialog box, click on the **Add Image** button.

11. Browse to the location you've saved the image file to and double-click on it to upload it to the **Topology Widget** as shown in *Figure 9.24*. With the uploaded image selected, click on **Next** to continue.

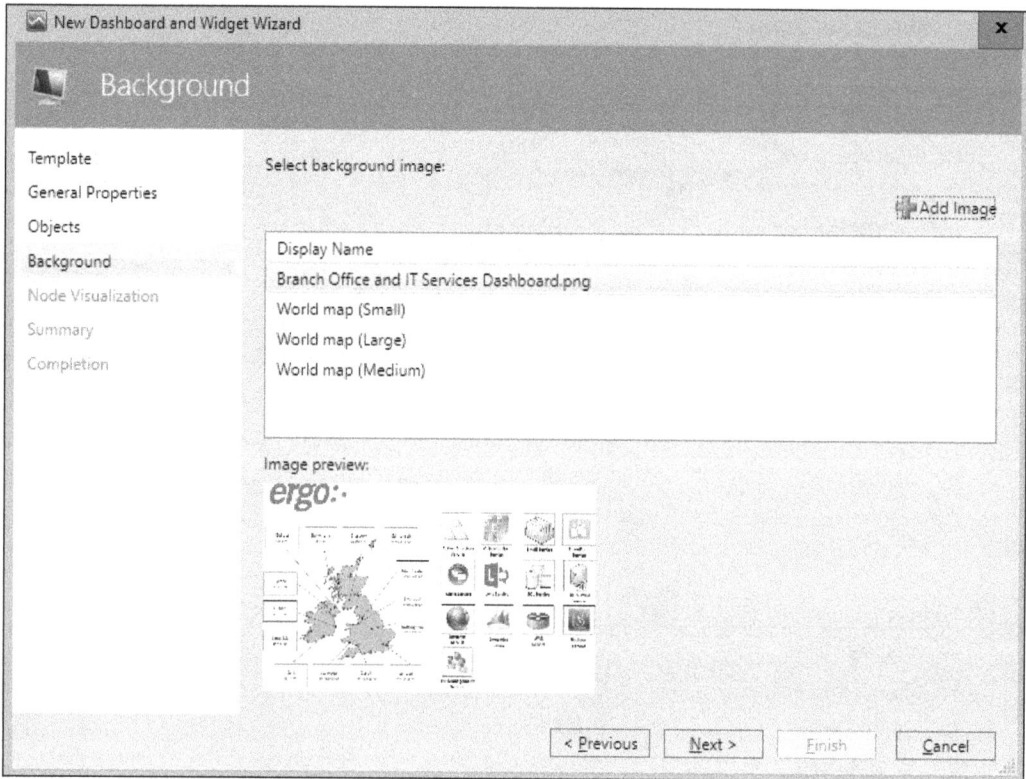

Figure 9.24: Uploading the custom dashboard image

You might notice that, although you can add new background images here, there's no option to remove any images that you no longer need. If this is something that you wish to do, then take a read over Cameron Fuller's post here - http://tinyurl.com/cfullerquicktrickwidgets - but be warned, this workaround will also remove any images you have previously used in dashboards that contain Image Widgets.

12. From the **Node Visualization** dialog box you have two options to choose
from – **Vicinity Node** (which displays the standard diagram view icon for
each monitored object) or **Default Node** (this displays the standard health
state icon for each monitored object). We'll select the **Default Node** option as
shown in *Figure 9.25*. Click on **Next** to move on, hit **Create** and then click on
Close to finish the wizard.

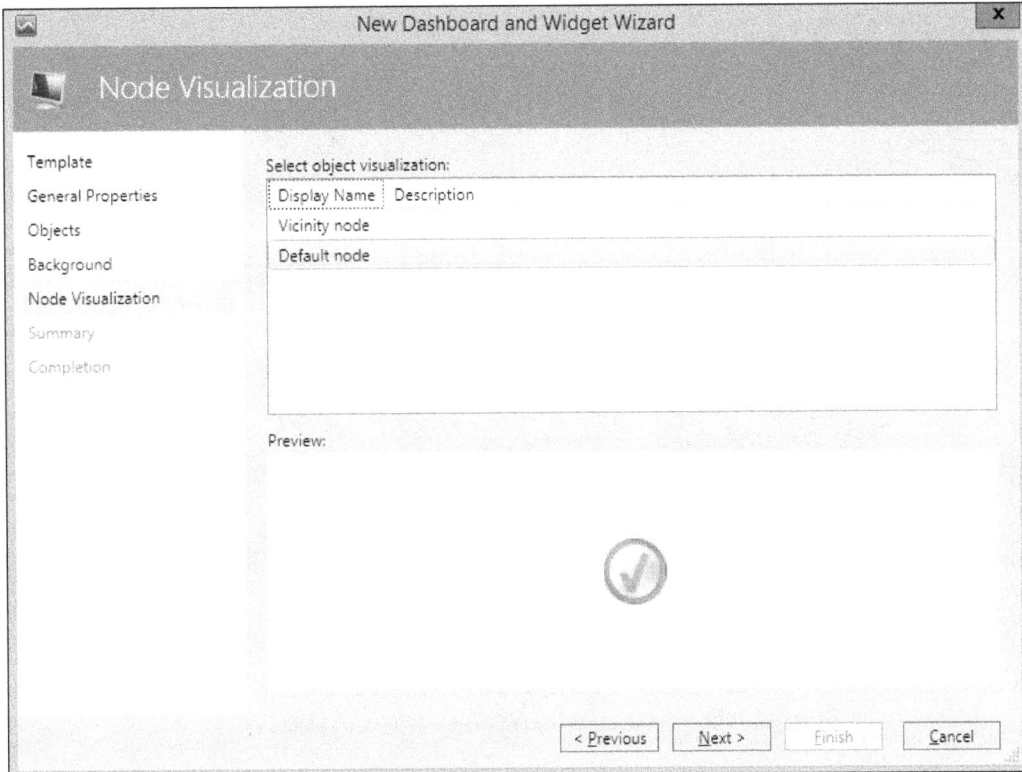

Figure 9.25: Choosing an object visualization option

13. When you first see your new dashboard, you'll notice that all the health state icons for your monitored objects are located in the center of the image. This is by design and if you hover your mouse pointer over the top health state icon, you'll see the display name pop up similar to *Figure 9.26*.

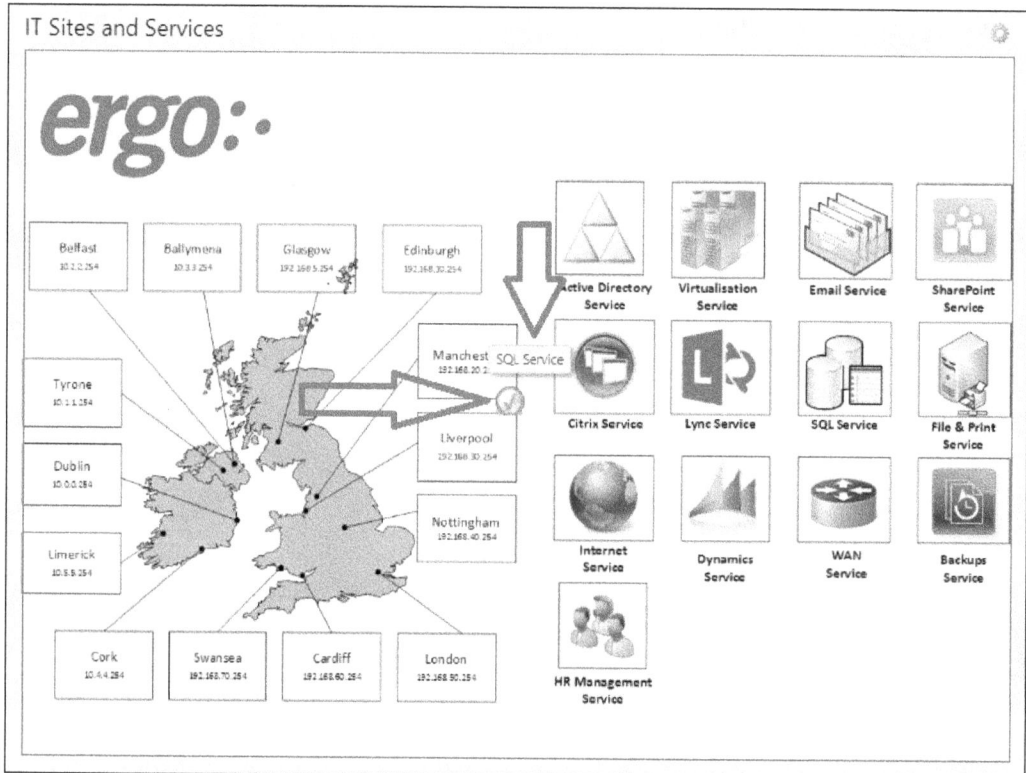

Figure 9.26: Identifying the monitored object health state icon

14. All you need to do now is to click on on the health state icon that you've identified and then drag and drop the icon to the location on the background image where you want it to be placed. Repeat this process for each monitored object until you have fully populated your dashboard similar to *Figure 9.27*.

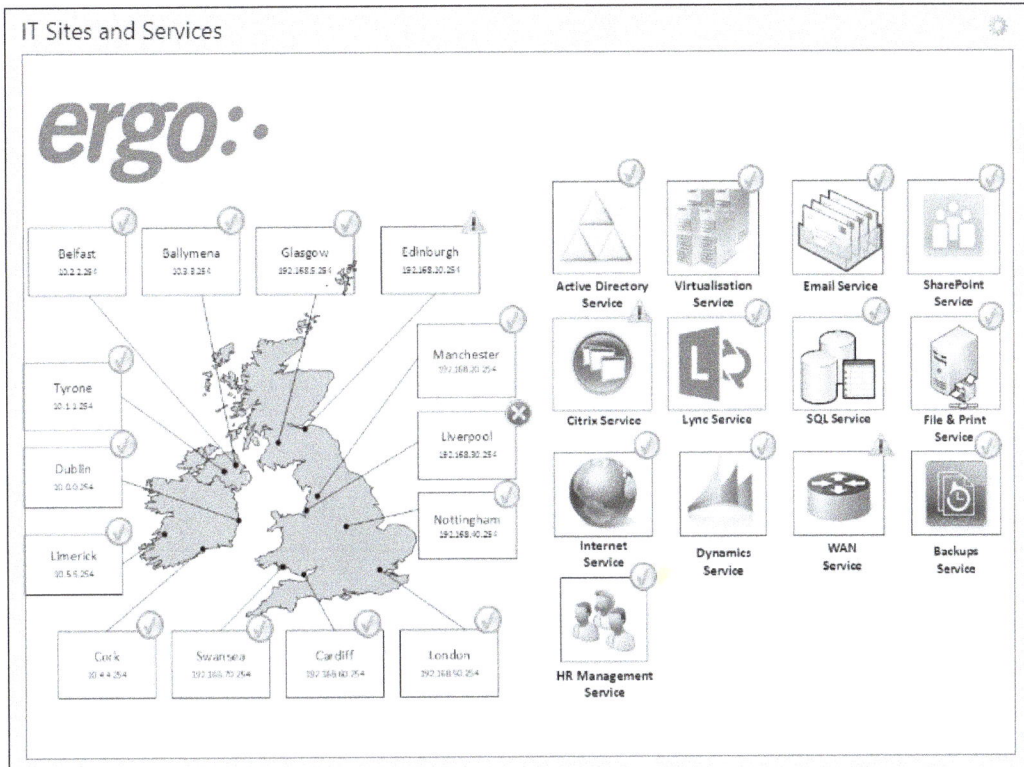

Figure 9.27: Fully populated dashboard using the Topology Widget

These is just one example of what you can do with the Topology Widget and we recommend you have some fun experimenting with different combinations of dashboard layouts and widgets to see what you can come up with.

Microsoft workload dashboards

For more ideas on the type of dashboards that you can deploy in OpsMgr, take a look at some of the built-in dashboards that come with a number of the Microsoft workload management packs. For example, if you've deployed the Exchange Server 2013 management pack, you'll see how Microsoft combine different layouts and widgets to monitor Exchange Server workloads. *Figure 9.28* shows an example of the **Organization Summary** dashboard.

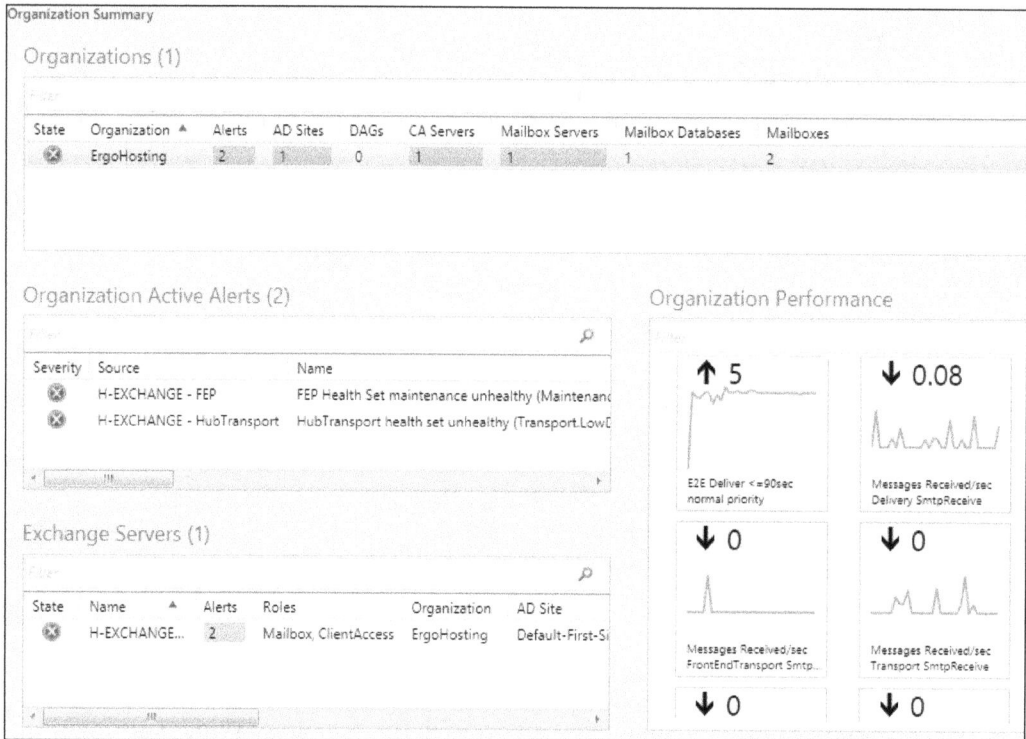

Figure 9.28: Exchange Server 2013 Organization Summary dashboard

If you've deployed **System Center Virtual Machine Manager (SCVMM)** management pack and then you can see dashboards similar to the **Virtual Machine Dashboard** shown in *Figure 9.29*, which provides health and performance information for your virtual machines.

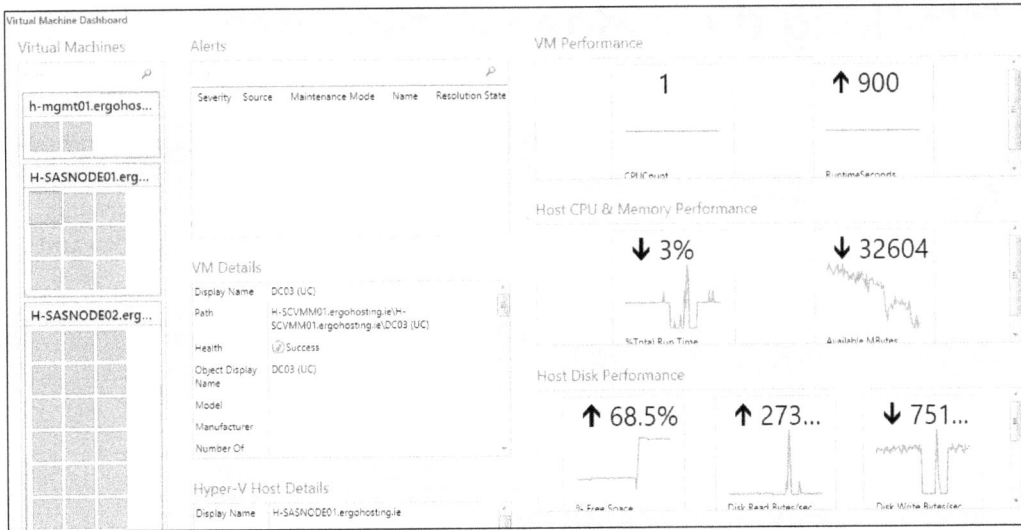

Figure 9.29: SCVMM Virtual Machine Dashboard

The same management pack also has a very useful dashboard for monitoring your virtual hosts and this can be seen in *Figure 9.30*.

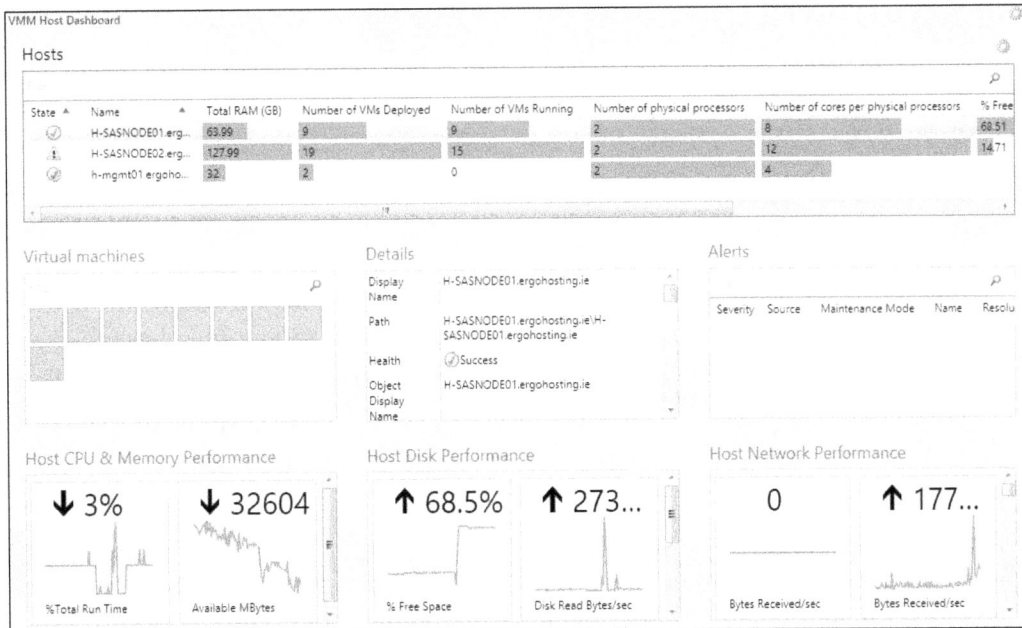

Figure 9.30: SCVMM Host Dashboard

Unlocking the hidden datacenter dashboard template

Staying with dashboards that help monitor Microsoft workloads, the SQL team have created something quite different to the other management packs that Microsoft have to offer. Their SQL summary dashboard (shown in *Figure 9.31*) introduces us to a new dashboard template style that uses color-coded tiles to display health and performance data for your SQL environments.

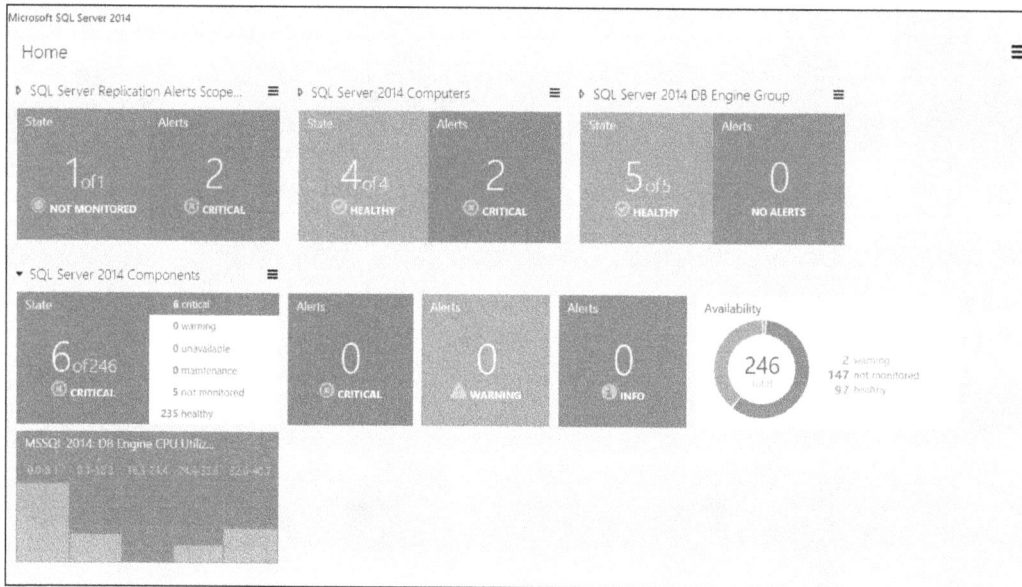

Figure 9.31: SQL Database Summary Dashboard

Now this dashboard is all well and good when you want to monitor SQL, but wouldn't it be great if you could use this template for other monitored objects? Thankfully, that's exactly what the SQL team have given us the option to do – you just need to know how to access and configure it.

Follow these steps to configure this dashboard solution to monitor your Windows servers:

1. The first thing you need to do is to download and import the latest version of the SQL management pack (version 6.6.4.0 or higher is required). Head over to the OpsMgr Management Pack Wiki to find the latest version: http://tinyurl.com/opsmgrmpwiki.

2. Don't worry if you don't have any SQL workloads to monitor, you will still need to at least import the dashboards, presentation, visualization and library management packs as shown in *Figure 9.32*.

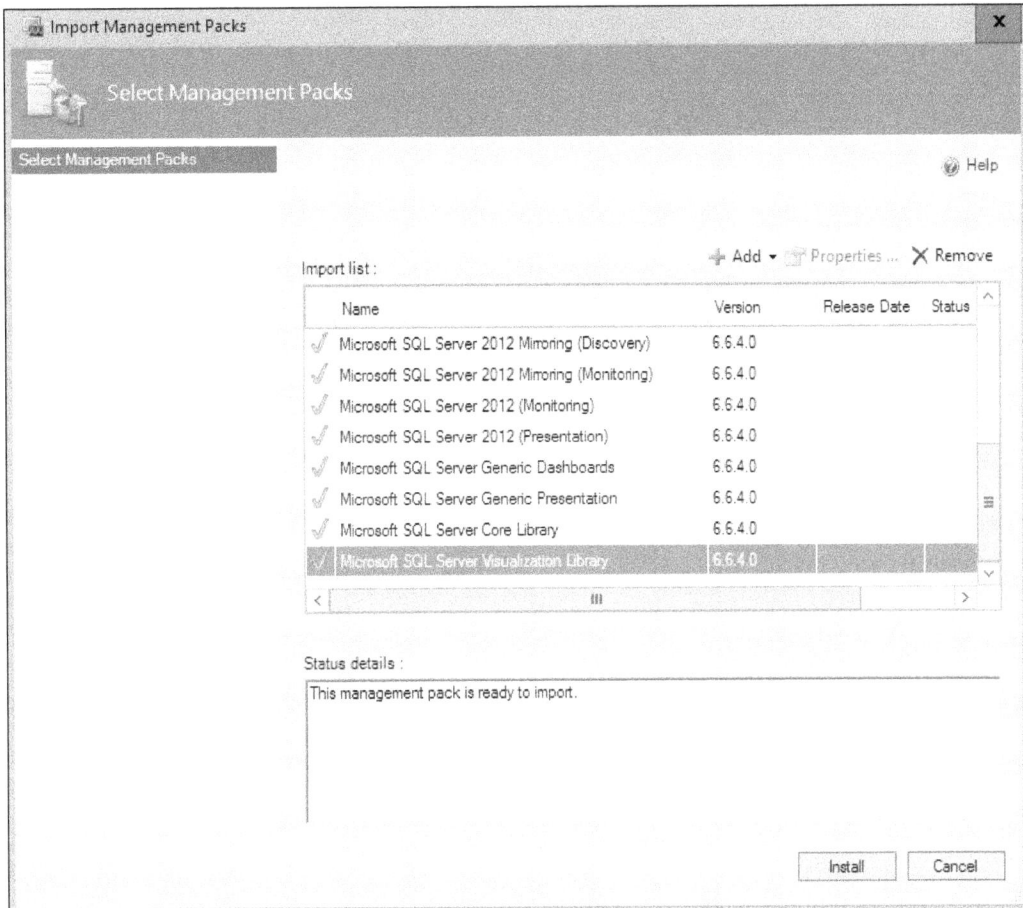

Figure 9.32: Importing the SQL management packs

3. Once the SQL management packs have been imported, browse back to the **Monitoring** workspace, right-click on a location where you want to create the dashboard, click on **New** and then select **Dashboard View**.

4. This time you should have a new dashboard template selection available titled **SQL Server Dashboards** and when you select this option you will be presented with the **Datacenter Dashboard** template as shown in *Figure 9.33*. Click on **Next** to move on.

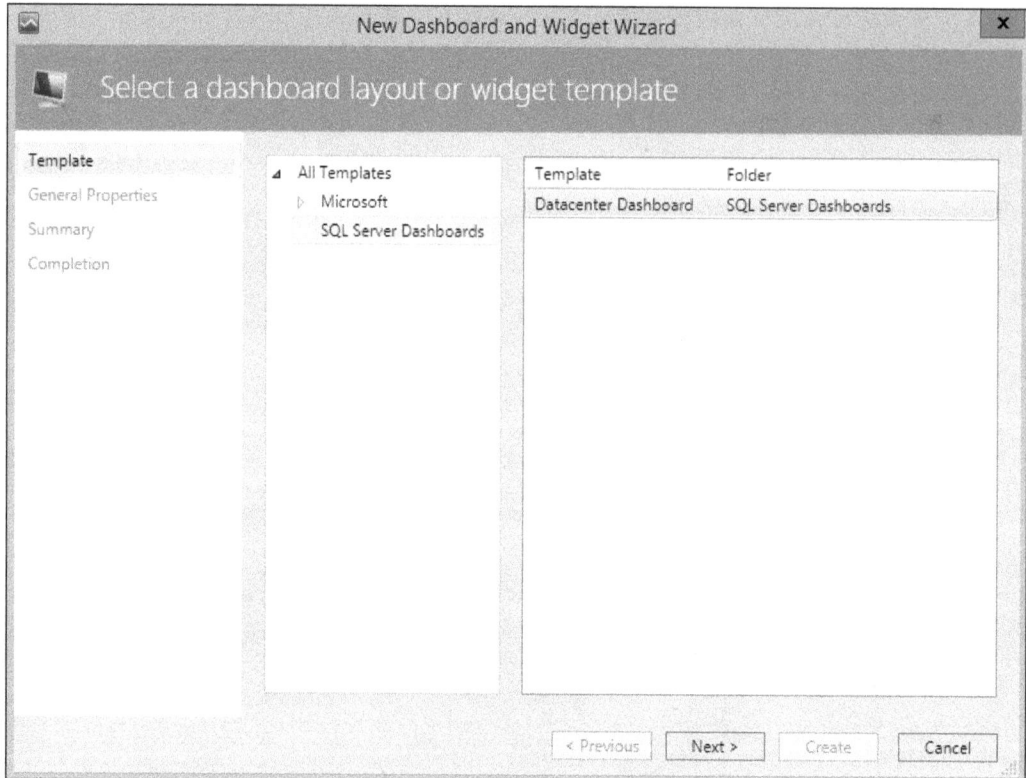

Figure 9.33: Selecting the new dashboard template

5. Type a name for your dashboard – we'll use `Nimbus Corp Server Summary` – then click through the final two dialog boxes to complete the wizard.

6. Back in the **Monitoring** workspace, you will be presented with a new dashboard where you'll need to define a group to monitor. To do this, click on the icon in the corner that we've highlighted in *Figure 9.34* and select **Add Group** from the context menu as shown.

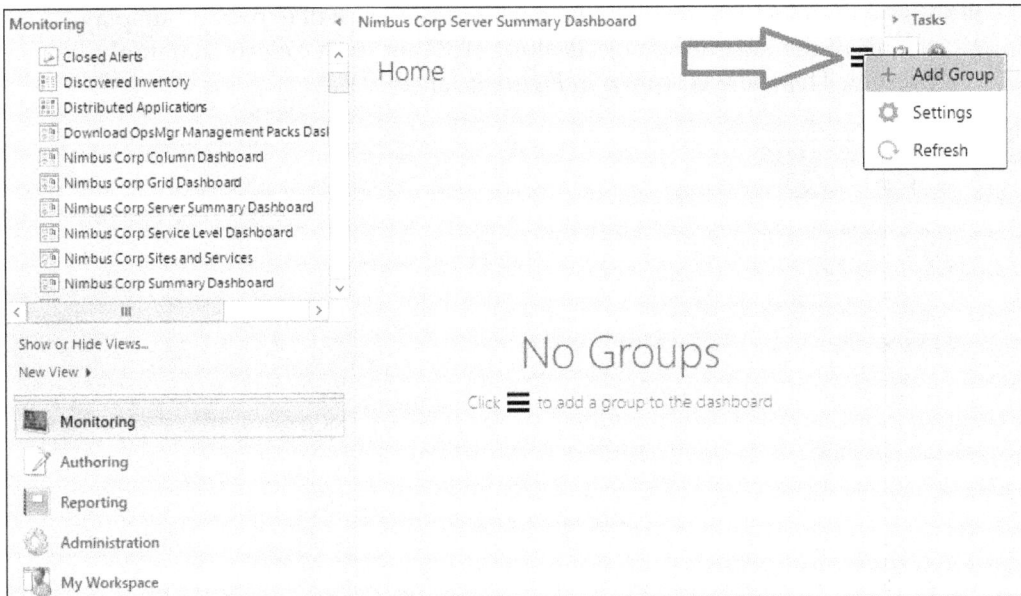

Figure 9.34: Adding a group to the new dashboard

7. From the **Add Group** dialog box, we'll specify the **All Windows Servers** group but this can be any OpsMgr group that you wish. Optionally, you can modify the display name of your group and when you're ready, click on **OK** to save the changes and populate the dashboard.

8. At the **Home** screen for the new dashboard, you should see some tiles appear representing health state and alerts for the group that you specified in the previous step. Click on the arrow beside the display name of your group and the tiles will expand out to show you something similar to *Figure 9.35*.

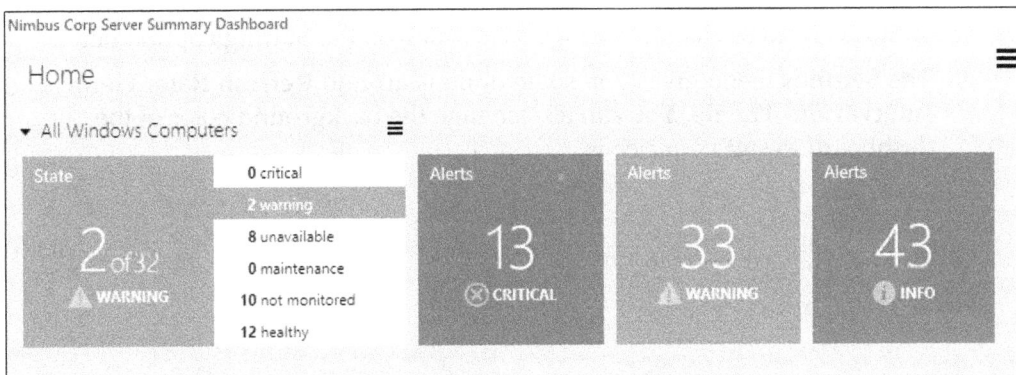

Figure 9.35: Viewing group health state from the new dashboard template

9. If you double-click on a tile, the dashboard view will expand to display details of the unhealthy objects along with any active alerts that might be present. This view is shown in *Figure 9.36*:

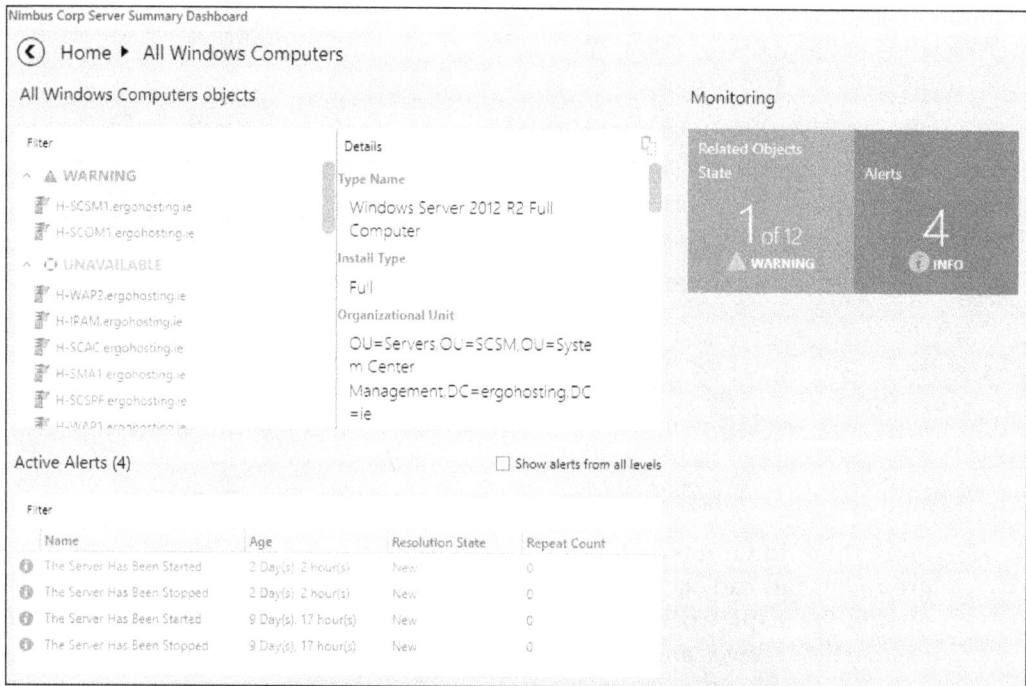

Figure 9.36: Diving into the dashboard tiles for more information

10. You can navigate back to the default dashboard view at any stage by clicking the left arrow beside **Home**. From there, you can click on the menu button (represented by three black lines) located in the top right corner to add another group or change settings. We'll click on the **Settings** option here.

11. The **Settings** menu gives you some options around **Refresh Rate, Time Interval** and **Theme**. You can also change the background color of the dashboard to suit your needs.

Community dashboard resources

Given the large community that surround and contribute free solutions for OpsMgr, it's no surprise that there's a fair amount of resources available to get you up and running quickly with some custom dashboards. One of these resources to check out is the Operations Manager Dashboards repository on the TechNet Gallery:
`http://aka.ms/scomdashboards`

Here you can download some free sample dashboards with new heat-map widgets, scripts and templates. *Figure 9.37* shows this repository and its well worth a visit.

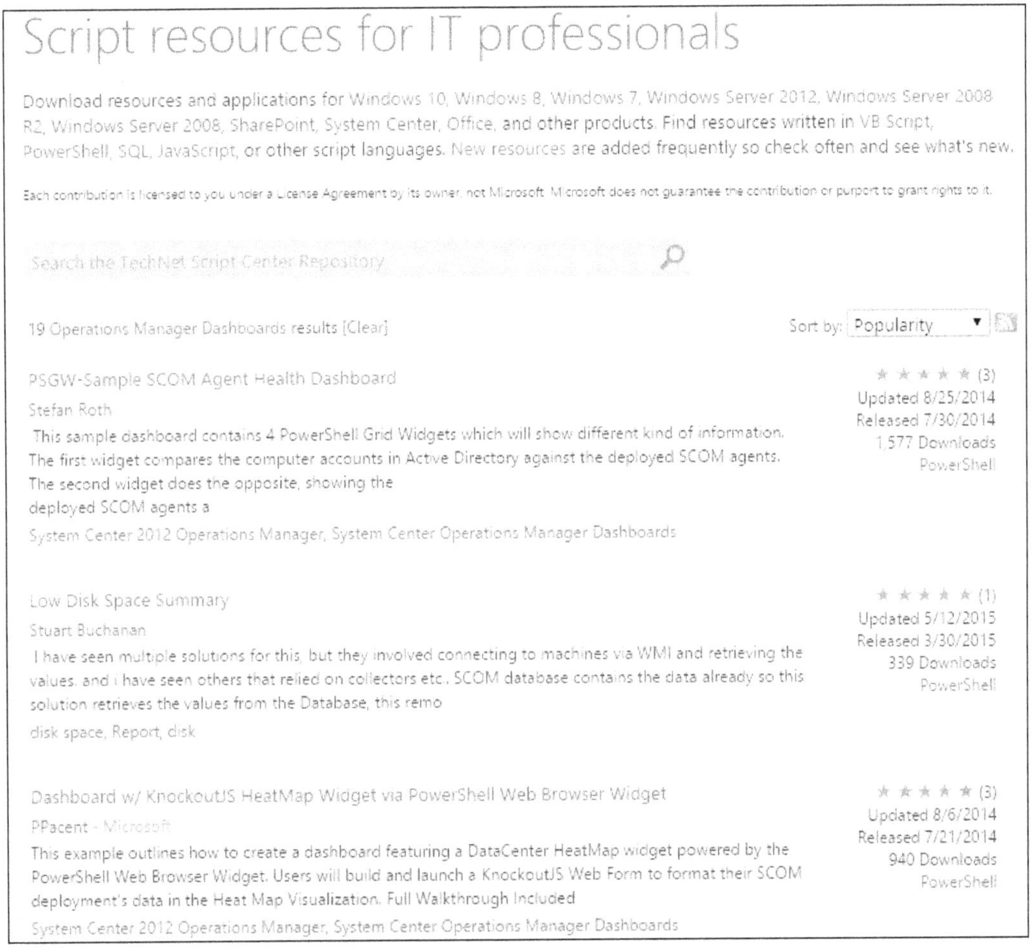

Figure 9.37: The OpsMgr Dashboards repository

We also recommend visiting the blog of Microsoft's Wei H. Lim at `http://blogs.msdn.com/b/wei_out_there_with_system_center/`. For the past few years, Wei has been releasing his own custom PowerShell scripts and sample dashboards for OpsMgr and some of the ideas he comes up with for visualizations are really useful. As an example of some of the dashboards he has made available, take a look at the 'Sample Object Health Dashboard with Rainbow Bar Columns' shown in *Figure 9.38*.

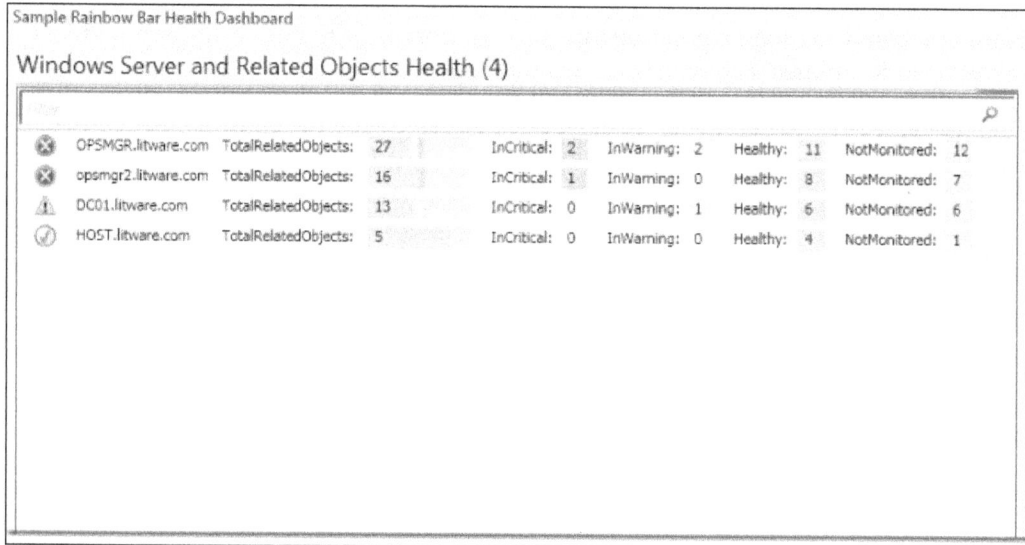

Sample Rainbow Bar Health Dashboard

Windows Server and Related Objects Health (4)

⊗ OPSMGR.litware.com	TotalRelatedObjects: 27	InCritical: 2	InWarning: 2	Healthy: 11	NotMonitored: 12
⊗ opsmgr2.litware.com	TotalRelatedObjects: 16	InCritical: 1	InWarning: 0	Healthy: 8	NotMonitored: 7
⚠ DC01.litware.com	TotalRelatedObjects: 13	InCritical: 0	InWarning: 1	Healthy: 6	NotMonitored: 6
⊘ HOST.litware.com	TotalRelatedObjects: 5	InCritical: 0	InWarning: 0	Healthy: 4	NotMonitored: 1

Figure 9.38: Sample Object Health dashboard from Wei H. Lim

Another handy dashboard view he has created is the 'Sample Speedometer Gauge Dashboard' shown in *Figure 9.39*. This dashboard can be used as an alternative way to measure performance metrics.

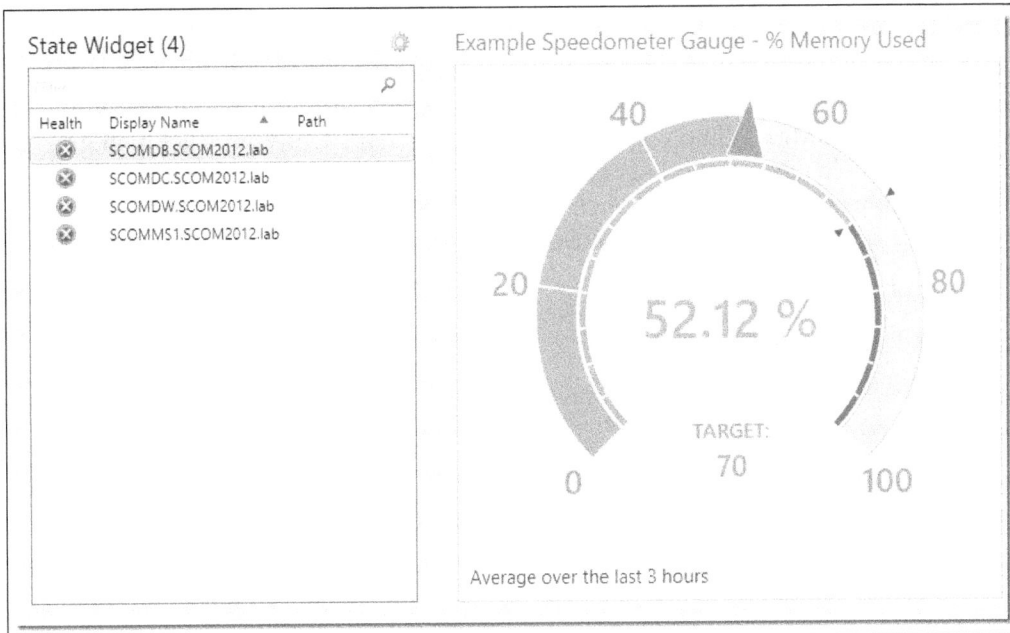

Figure 9.39: Sample Speedometer Gauge dashboard from Wei H. Lim

As is the case with all dashboard solutions, be sure to read the deployment guide first as most of the community ones are driven by PowerShell and may need some initial tweaking to get them up and running.

Third-party dashboard solutions

If you feel you need more than what you can get out of the box and you really want to enhance your dashboards to bring your visualizations to the next level, then there are a number of third-party vendors that can offer you some excellent alternatives for a reasonable fee. Here's a run-down of three of our favorite third-party dashboard solutions:

Savision

The team in Savision (www.savision.com) has been around for a long time and are synonymous with delivering enterprise-grade business service management solutions for OpsMgr. When you deploy their Live Maps Unity product, you get access to a whole new method of creating and publishing your dashboards. You can choose from pre-built templates, such as the **Services Dashboard** shown in *Figure 9.40* or you can use the authoring console to create a new dashboard from scratch.

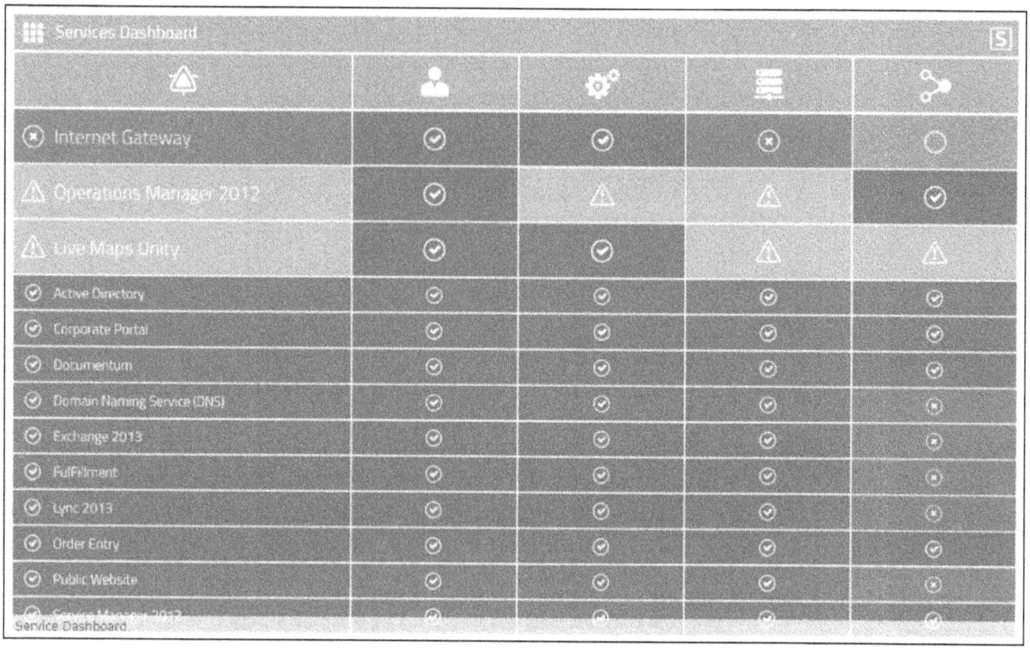

Figure 9.40: Savision Live Maps Unity in action

SquaredUp

Based in the UK, the guys over at SquaredUp (`www.squaredup.com`) have focused their development efforts on designing a slick HTML5 presentation layer console for OpsMgr that can be used to author and display dashboards on any device with a web browser. This is an excellent alternative to the OpsMgr Web Console, which is built on the Silverlight platform and limited to working only on Microsoft devices that support it. In *Figure 9.41*, you can see the SquaredUp console in action with a 360 degree application dashboard.

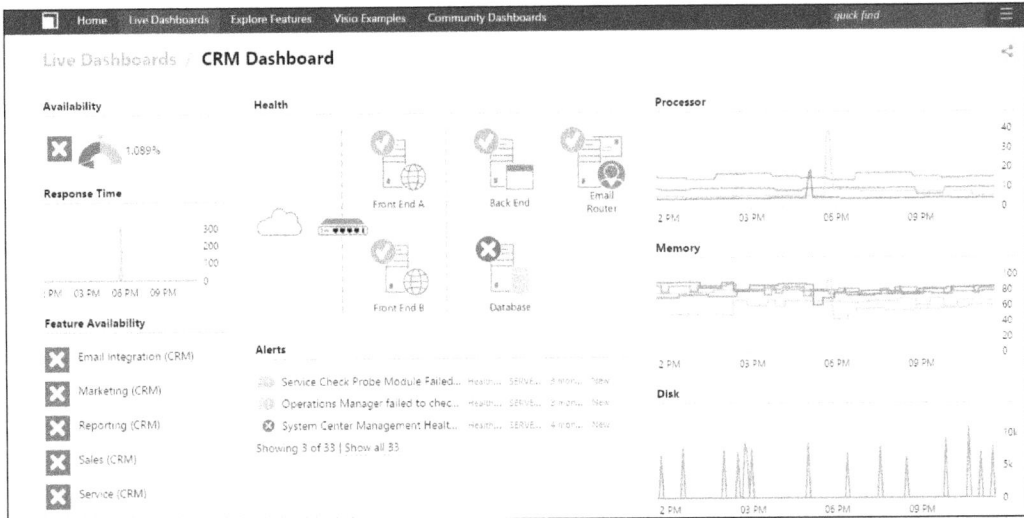

Figure 9.41: Displaying a dashboard in the SquaredUp console

OpsLogix

A well-known organization within the System Center community, OpsLogix (www.opslogix.com) have developed a HTML5 platform named ProView that integrates with OpsMgr and Microsoft Visio to deliver a seamless design and publishing solution for your dashboards. Priced competitively, ProView is another option to use as a replacement for the Silverlight based Web Console that comes out of the box with OpsMgr. In *Figure 9.42*, you can see how this solution integrates as an add-on to Visio to help author your dashboards on the fly.

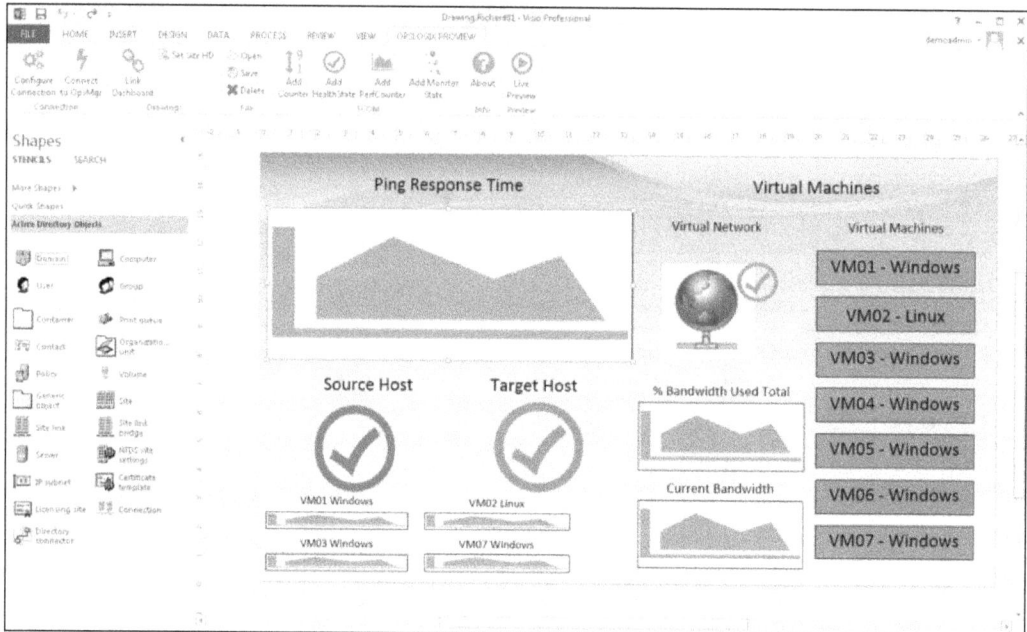

Figure 9.42: Authoring dashboards with ProView

If you would like to try out any of these third-party dashboard solutions, then we'd recommend giving each of them a test drive to see which one suits your needs and budget. All of these vendors offer free fully functional trials of their products and deploying them is pretty easy too.

Summary

In this chapter, we discussed the different dashboard layout and template options you have at your disposal and we also walked you through some of the most popular widgets that you can add to your dashboards.

You learnt about the visual impact that you experience when you use the Topology Widget with Microsoft Visio and we also showed you how to make use of a new Datacenter Dashboard template that was hidden within the SQL visualization management packs.

Towards the end of the chapter we discussed some of the free community dashboard resources that are available and we also gave you a brief introduction to some of the best third-party vendor solutions in the market.

In the next chapter, we will focus on creating and customizing alert subscriptions along with giving you an introduction to working with reports in OpsMgr.

10
Creating Alert Subscriptions and Reports

Outside of the OpsMgr administrators and key operators, the first introduction most other IT team members and management have to the monitoring solution is through alerting and reports. When the team responsible for managing OpsMgr has completed their initial alert tuning exercises, an agreed process is typically put in place to send alerts with specific criteria to the relevant people across the business. These alerts can be forwarded through transport mediums, such as e-mail, SMS texts, Instant Messaging, and custom scripting.

Detailed reports containing useful health, performance and availability data can also be scheduled to ensure an analytic and pro-active approach is taken to ensure systems are maintained at optimal levels. Reports are an excellent way to keep senior management in the loop about what's happening with the infrastructure and to provide information on whether or not agreed SLA's have been met.

In this chapter we will help you to understand how best to make the most of your OpsMgr alerts by creating targeted subscriptions that will forward them to the right people within the organization. From a reporting perspective, we'll walk you through the best ways to create, manage and schedule reports that will deliver better visibility of current and historical monitoring data.

Here's an overview of what you will learn:

- Understanding and configuring alert notification channels
- Creating subscribers and alert subscriptions
- Configuring SQL reporting
- Role-based access control for Reporting
- Creating and scheduling reports

Alert notifications overview

When working with any monitoring system, it's impractical for most people to constantly watch the console for new alerts or to keep an eye on a dashboard day and night waiting for it to change state. For these reasons, alert notifications have become the de facto standard for giving IT teams a heads up on what's happening within their infrastructures and applications.

OpsMgr has a number of different methods available to ensure alerts are forwarded to you and the process of delivering them involves three high-level steps – configuring notification channels, creating subscribers and scheduling subscriptions. The notification channels specify the transport medium, the subscriber is the person (or people) that alerts are sent to and the subscription defines criteria for the type of alerts that will be sent.

Working with alert notification channels

Alert notification channels are configured through the Administration workspace under the Notifications section. These channels act as the mode of transport for sending alerts and you can choose from **E-mail**, **Instant Messaging**, **SMS Text Message** or a custom **Command** option.

By default, no notification channels are created when you initially deploy OpsMgr so it's up to you to decide which type best suits your requirements. The following sections detail each channel and give some examples on how to configure them.

E-mail (SMTP)

By far the most popular method of transporting alert notifications, the E-mail (SMTP) channel communicates with an SMTP-capable server (such as Microsoft Exchange), and can be configured to send e-mail alerts either anonymously or with Windows Integrated authentication.

Follow these steps to configure an E-Mail (SMTP) channel:

1. From the **Administration** workspace, expand the **Notifications** section and right-click on **Channels**. Now select **New channel** from the context menu and click on the **E-Mail (SMTP)** option as shown in *Figure 10.1*.

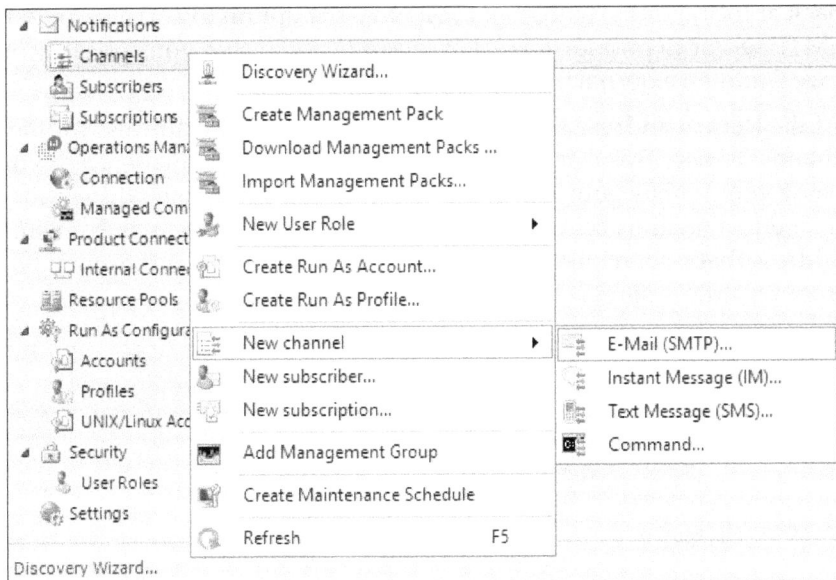

Figure 10.1: Creating a new channel

2. At the **Description** dialog box of the **E-Mail Notification Channel** wizard, type a name and description for your new channel, then click on **Next** to continue.

3. Click on the **Add** button from the **Settings** screen to open the **Add SMTP Server** dialog box, enter the FQDN and port number to use for your SMTP server and select an authentication method. In *Figure 10.2* you can see we've chosen the **Windows Integrated** option for authentication. This is because the Exchange Server we're using doesn't allow anonymous access and later we'll need to configure a Run As Account to authenticate. If your SMTP server allows anonymous authentication, then you can just select that option here. Click on **OK** when you're ready to move on.

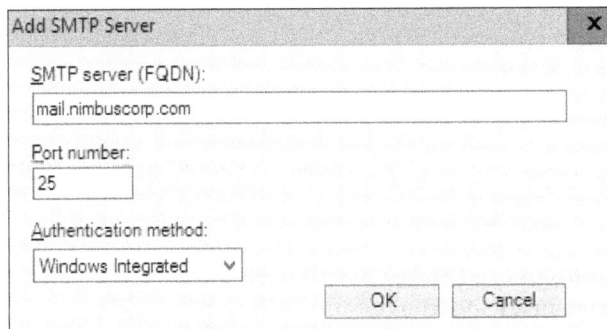

Figure 10.2: Adding an SMTP server

4. Back at the Settings dialog box, you have the option to add a secondary SMTP server to provide a level of redundancy in case your primary one fails – we'll add an external SMTP server here as a fail-safe.

5. At the **Return address** field you need to type an email address for the SMTP channel to use. This can be an address that you've just made up (if you're using anonymous authentication) or it can be a real email address that is linked to a mailbox on the SMTP server. We recommend using an email address that's descriptive enough to inform the recipient the email has come from OpsMgr – similar to the one shown in *Figure 10.3*.

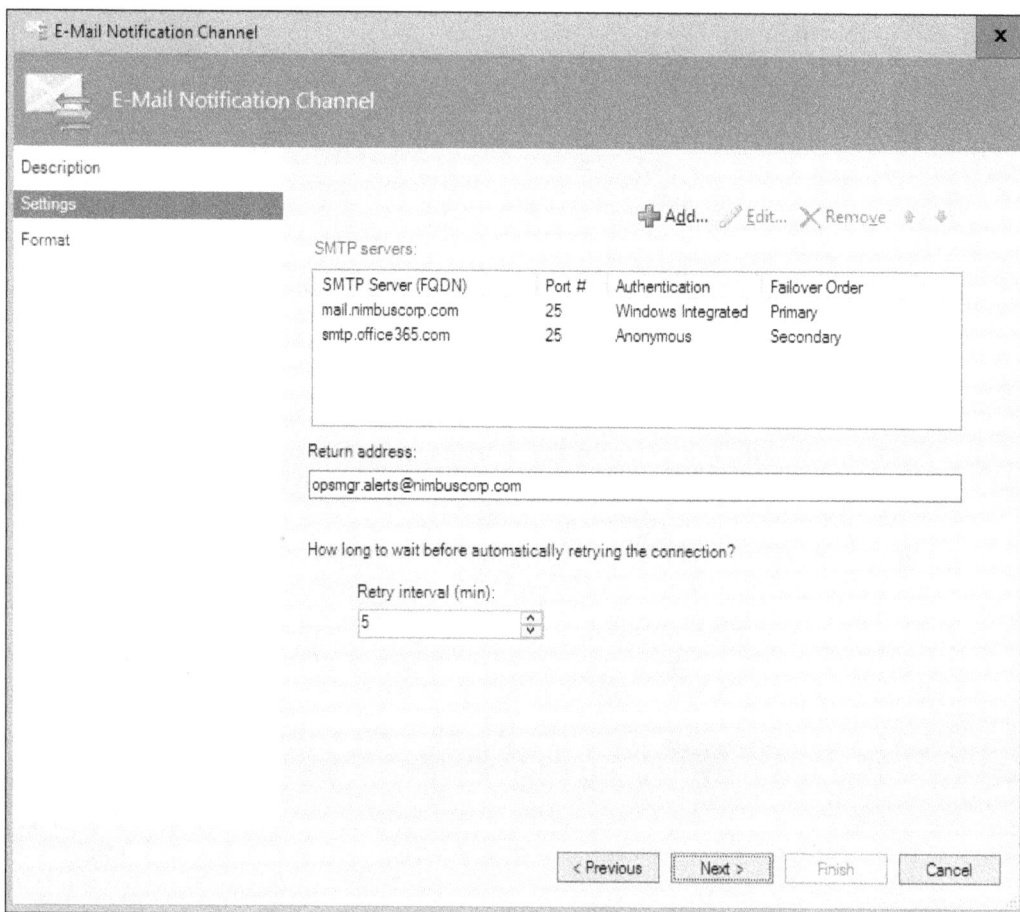

Figure 10.3: Configuring settings for the SMTP channel

6. Specify the amount of time to wait before the channel automatically retries the connection (or just leave the default value), then click on **Next** to move on.

7. When you arrive at the **Format** dialog box, pay special attention to the **E-mail subject** and **E-mail message** fields. These fields are mostly pre-populated with values that will automatically insert alert information from OpsMgr but it's a good idea here to modify the beginning of the e-mail subject line with a reference to the fact that it's an OpsMgr alert. In *Figure 10.4* you can see how we've modified the subject line.

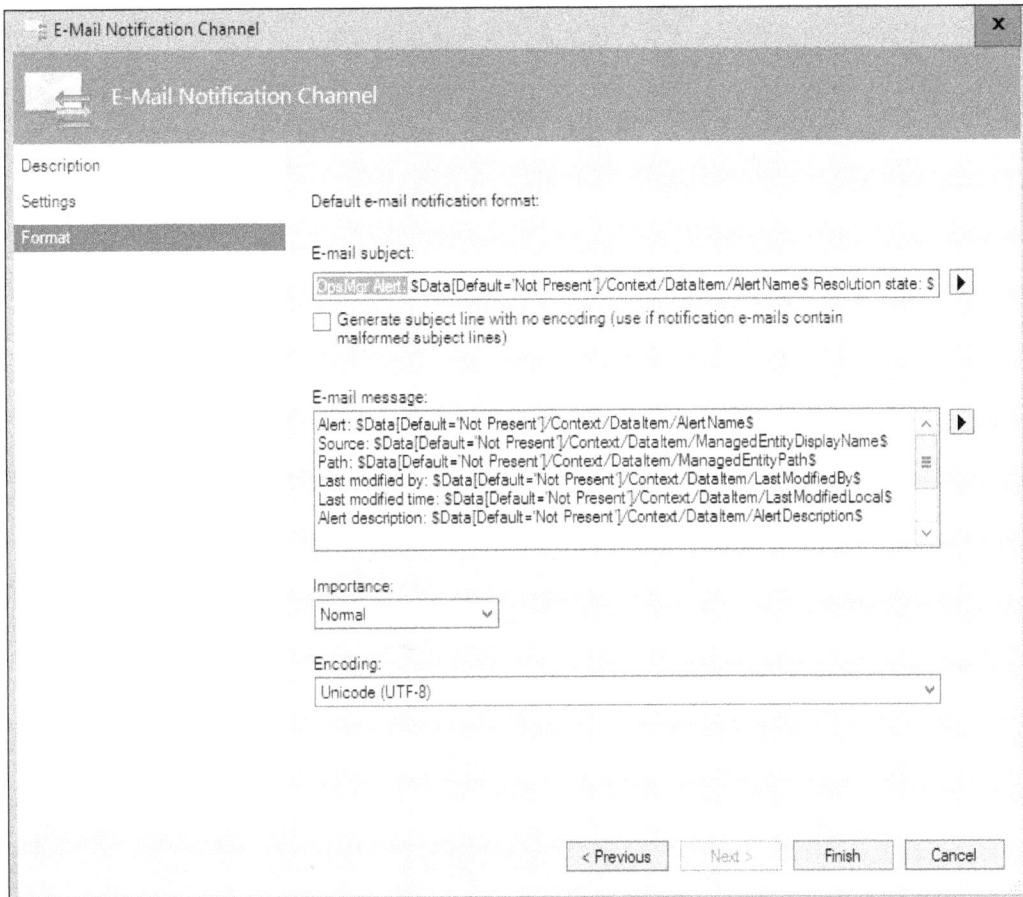

Figure 10.4: Formatting the email notification content

8. Use the **Importance** drop-down menu to select the level of importance that you want the email to be delivered as. This is very useful when you want to highlight critical alerts, such as outages to your recipients. Choose your **Encoding** preference, click on **Finish**, then hit the **Close** button to exit the wizard and create the new channel.

Configuring the Windows Integrated Authentication Account

If you've chosen the Windows Integrated authentication method when creating your E-Mail (SMTP) channel, then you will need to create and assign a Run As Account to the **Notification Account Run As Profile**. In our example, this account will be used to authenticate with our Exchange Server.

When the Notification Account profile isn't configured and Windows Integrated authentication is enabled, OpsMgr attempts to authenticate using the Management Server Action Account that most likely won't have the relevant permissions. This will result in a "Failed to send a notification" or "Failed to send a notification using a server/device" alert appearing in the console and no e-mail notifications being sent.

To configure this Run As account and profile, follow these steps:

1. Browse to the **Administration** workspace, expand **Run As Configuration**, click on **Profiles** and then locate the **Notification Account** profile shown in *Figure 10.5*.

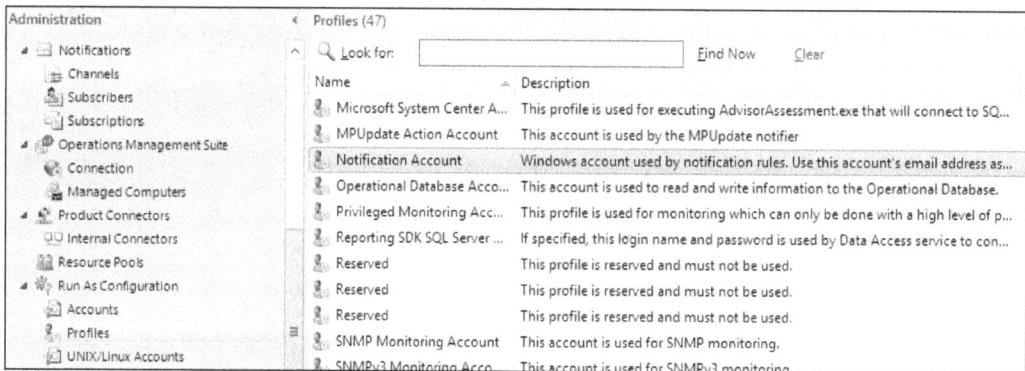

Figure 10.5: Configuring the Notification Account profile

2. Double-click on the profile to start the **Run As Profile** wizard and click on **Next** twice to bring you to the Run As Accounts dialog box.

3. Hit the **Add** button to open the **Add a Run As Account** dialog box, and then click on **New** to open the **Create Run As Account Wizard**. Click on **Next**.

4. At the **General Properties** dialog box, leave **Windows** selected as the Run As account type, then enter a display name and description for the new account and click on **Next** to move on.

5. At the **Credentials** dialog box shown in *Figure 10.6*, input a user name, password and domain for an account that has permissions to authenticate and send e-mails through your mail server. Click on **Next** to continue.

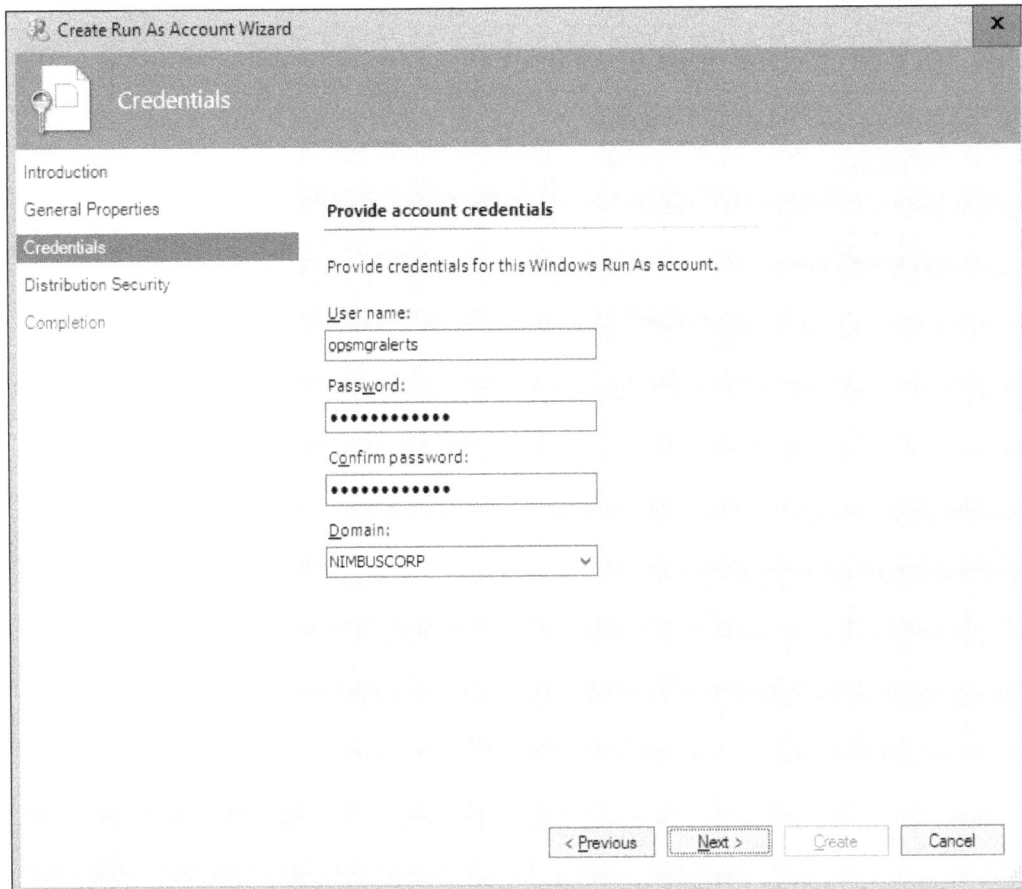

Figure 10.6: Specifying credentials for the notification account

6. At the Distribution Security dialog box, select the **More Secure** option and click on **Create**, then click on **Close** to exit the wizard.

7. Back at the **Add a Run As Account** dialog box, you will see the **Run As Account** field is now populated with your newly created Notification Account. Leave the **All targeted objects** option selected and click on **OK**.

8. Hit the **Save** button to complete the wizard and from the **More-secure Run As Accounts** section, click on the name of your notification account, which should open the **Distribution** tab of the account properties as shown in *Figure 10.7*.

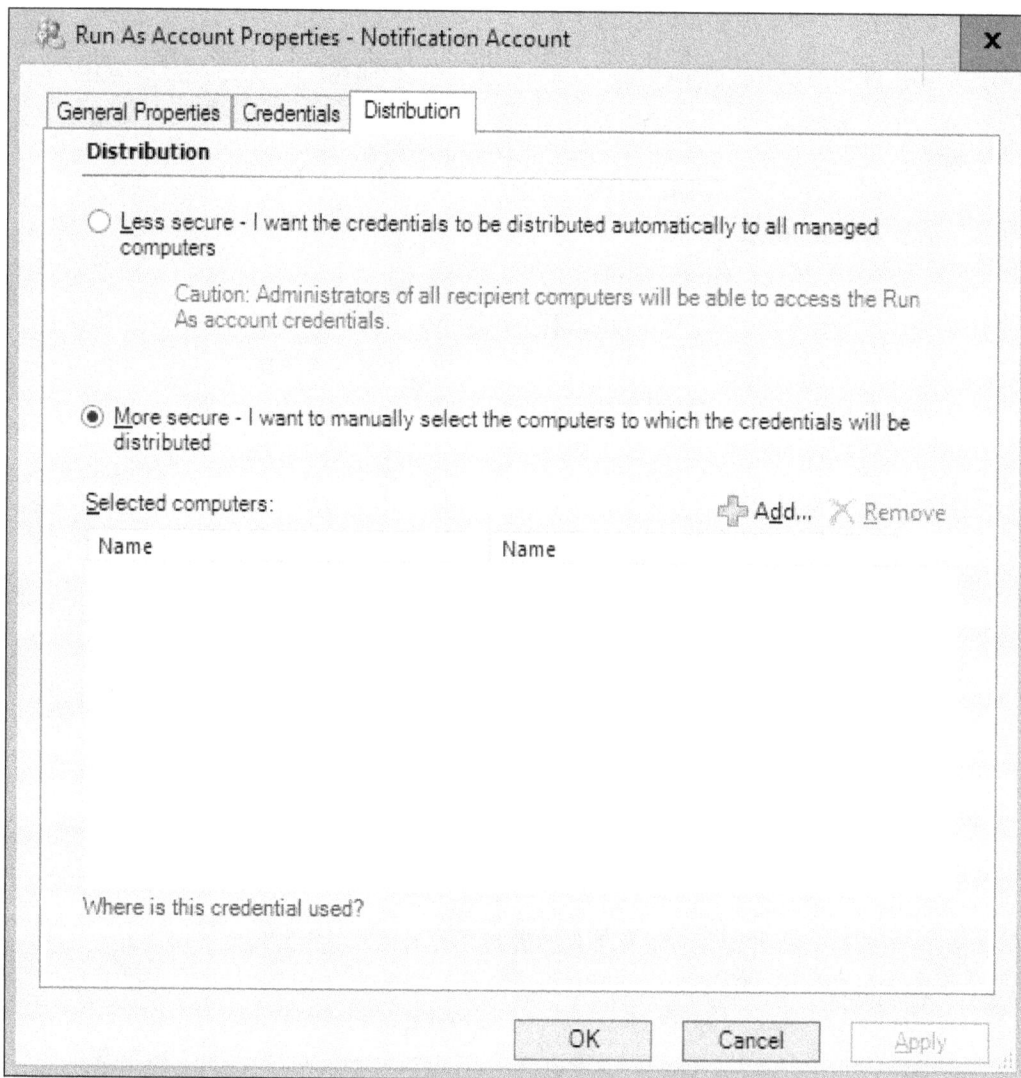

Figure 10.7: Distributing the notification account

9. Click on the **Add** button to open the **Computer Search** dialog box and from the **Option** menu, select the **Search by resource pool name** option. Now click on the **Search** button to list all of the available resource pools in your management group. Choose the **Notifications Resource Pool** as shown in *Figure 10.8* and click on **OK** to move on.

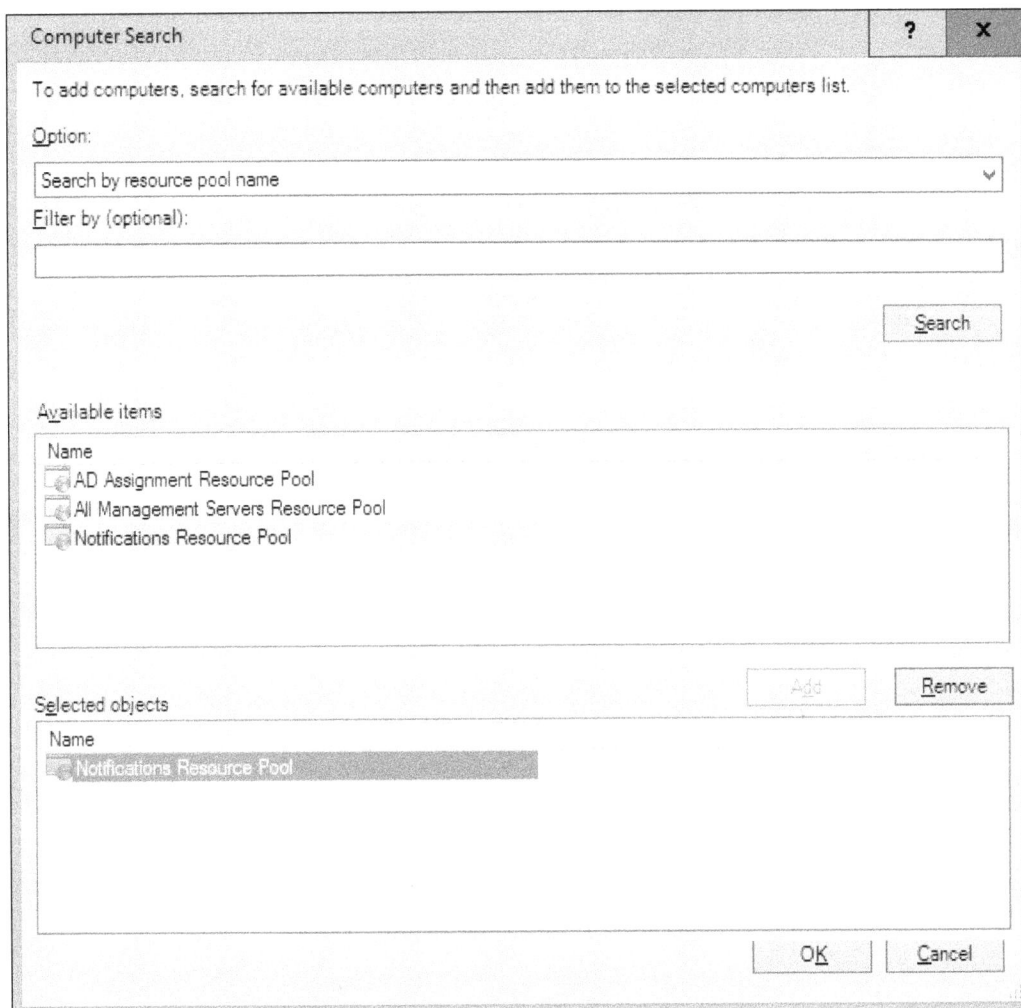

Figure 10.8: Selecting the Notifications Resource Pool

10. As you can see from *Figure 10.9*, the **Distribution** tab of the Notification Run As Account should now specify the **Notifications Resource Pool** for the more secure distribution option.

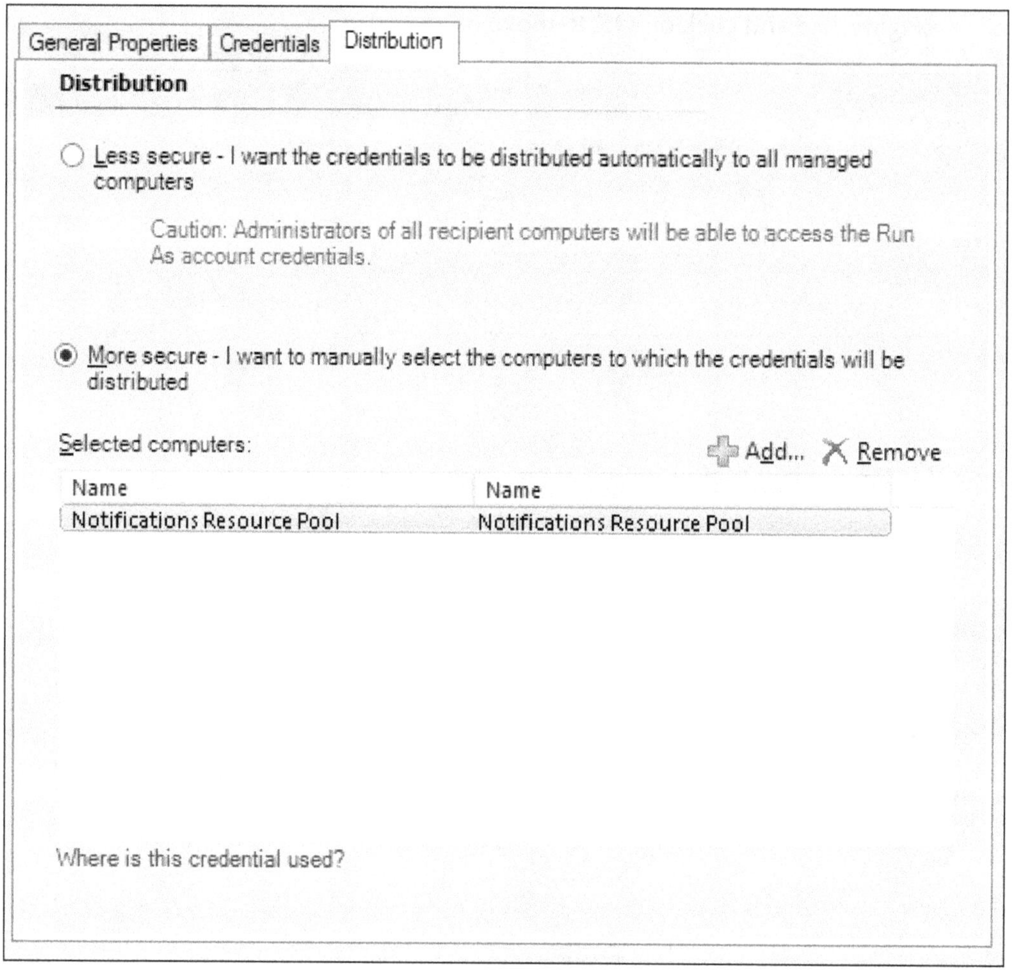

Figure 10.9: Distributing the account to the Notifications Resource Pool

11. Click on the **OK** button followed by **Close** to complete the notification account creation and profile assignment.

> As we've chosen the Notifications Resource pool to distribute the notification account to, in the event of the current management server being offline, another management server will automatically take over responsibility for authenticating channels and you won't miss any important e-mail alerts.

Instant Message (IM)

If you've deployed Microsoft Lync or Skype for Business in your organization, then the **Instant Message** (**IM**) channel might be something of interest to you. With this channel you have the option to integrate OpsMgr with an IM-capable platform to deliver alert notifications as instant messages.

It goes without saying that using a channel such as this for notifications means that an instant messaging application needs to be constantly running on a subscriber's computer, tablet or phone to ensure the alert is seen. This could be useful for quickly alerting users working in 24/7 **Network Operations Center** (**NOC**) environments when high-priority incidents like server outages occur.

Assuming you or a colleague has administrative access to Lync or Skype for Business, the process of configuring this channel is relatively straight-forward. Follow these steps to get it up and running:

1. Download and install the Microsoft **Unified Communications Managed API (UCMA)** onto every Management Server that will be a member of the Notification Resource Pool. The version of UCMA to deploy will depend on the version of Lync or Skype for Business you're running and the latest UCMA installer (at the time of writing) can be found at http://tinyurl.com/msftucma

2. From the **Administration** workspace, expand **Notifications**, right-click on **Channels**, select **New channel,** and then click on the **Instant Message (IM)** option.

3. Type a name and description for the channel, and then click on **Next**.

4. At the **Settings** screen, type the FQDN of the Front End server role for Lync or Skype for Business into the **IM server** field. In the **Return Address** field, enter the SIP address for an account that is enabled for Instant Messaging and leave the default settings for the protocol, authentication and IM port options as shown in *Figure 10.10*. Click on **Next** to continue.

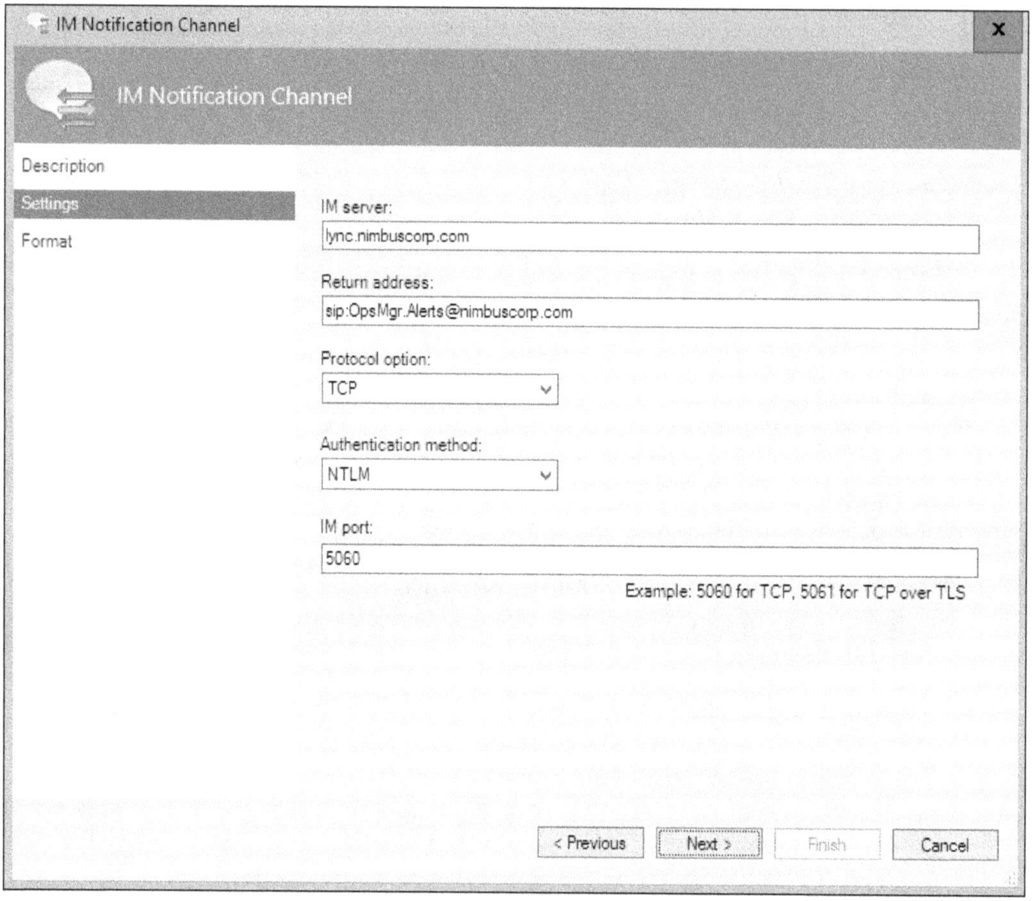

Figure 10.10: Creating an Instant Message (IM) channel

5. From the **Format** section shown in *Figure 10.11*, make any changes you need in the **IM message** field – it's a good idea here to add some descriptive text to the start of the message to help advertise the instant message as coming from OpsMgr – and leave the encoding format set to Unicode (UTF-8).

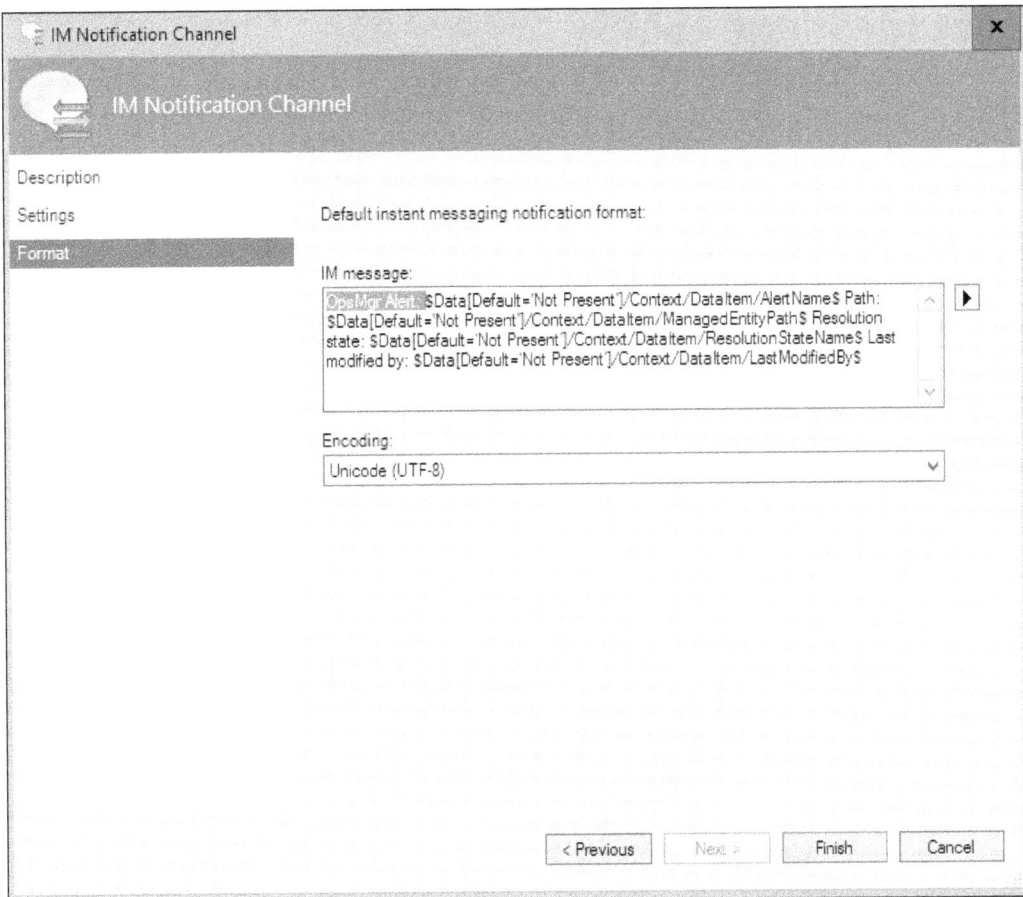

Figure 10.11: Formatting the IM message

6. Click on the **Finish** button to close the wizard and create the notification channel.

> If you don't have access to Lync or Skype for Business and would like to test out the **Instant Message (IM)** channel with just a personal Skype account, then check out this solution from Tao Yang (Cloud and Datacenter MVP) using PowerShell and the official Skype API here - `http://tinyurl.com/tyangskypealerts`. Tao has kindly included the scripts you need along with a step-by-step guide to help get you up and running in no time.

Text message (SMS)

Although most organizations will choose the E-Mail (SMTP) channel as a delivery mechanism for their alerts, there's a chance that at some point, the Internet or e-mail server connection to and from your OpsMgr servers will fail – leaving no way for SMTP alerts to reach the outside world. This is where SMS text alerting becomes a great secondary notification option. All you need is an SMS-capable modem (MultiTech have some reasonably priced ones available from `www.multitech.com`) and a properly configured channel.

Before you create the channel, ensure that at least one OpsMgr Management Server that is a member of the Notifications Resource Pool is connected to and can communicate with your SMS-capable modem. Using a physical server for this role is easiest as most modems will have a USB or serial cable for direct connection but if you're using a virtual OpsMgr server, you'll need to use Serial-Over-IP software (which is usually supplied with the modem) for communication.

> Marnix Wolf has a useful blog post that shows a schematic drawing of how you can connect an SMS modem to a virtual OpsMgr server – `http://tinyurl.com/mwolfsmsalerting`. You can also get additional information on this topic from `http://tinyurl.com/opsmgrsms`

With the modem connected up, here's how you configure the Text Message (SMS) channel:

1. From the **Administration** workspace, expand **Notifications**, right-click on **Channels**, select **New channel** from the context menu and click on the **Text Message (SMS)** option.

2. Type a name and description for the channel, and then click on **Next**.

3. At the Settings dialog box shown in *Figure 10.12*, modify the start of the **Text Message** field to inform the recipient the SMS message is coming from OpsMgr.

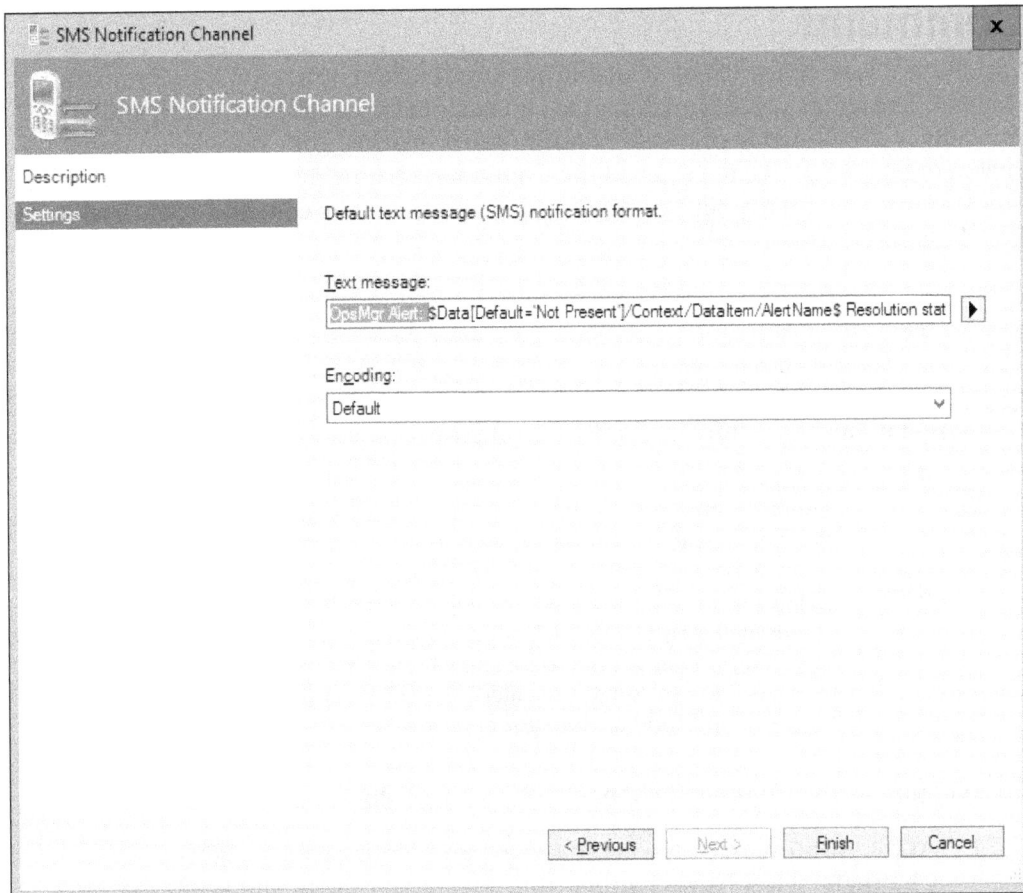

Figure 10.12: Configuring the SMS notification channel

4. Modify the **Encoding** option (or just leave it as Default), then click on the **Finish** and **Close** buttons to complete the wizard and create the channel.

Command

Last but not least in the list of available alert notification options is the Command channel. This gives you a launch pad to run custom executables and scripts that can deliver a wide range of flexible notification scenarios. For example, on previous customer engagements, we've used the Command channel to forward alerts from OpsMgr into third-party service desk systems with relative ease and some basic PowerShell scripting.

If you find that the E-Mail (SMTP) channel is limited in how you can present e-mails to your users, then download Tao Yang's excellent *Enhanced E-Mail Notification Script* - `http://tinyurl.com/opsmgrenhancedemails`, which is a great example on how to use the Command channel to create nicely formatted HTML alert notifications that combine standard alert information with company knowledge articles.

> Another community example of leveraging the flexibility of this channel to extend SMS alerting while also adding MMS and even voice phone call notifications is available at `http://tinyurl.com/opsmgrchannelalerts`. This solution launches a PowerShell script from the Command channel that forwards alerts to a 'middle-man' service at `https://www.twilio.com/`. From there, Twilio can convert the alert to an SMS message or a robotic voice call and forward it to your end-users!

To configure a new Command channel, follow these steps:

1. At the **Administration** workspace, expand **Notifications**, right-click on **Channels**, select **New channel** from the context menu and select the **Command** option.

2. Type a name and description for the channel, and then click on **Next**.

3. At the Settings dialog box, specify the full path to your executable along with the required parameters and startup folder. In *Figure 10.13*, we've configured our channel to work with Tao Yang's *Enhanced E-Mail Notification Script*.

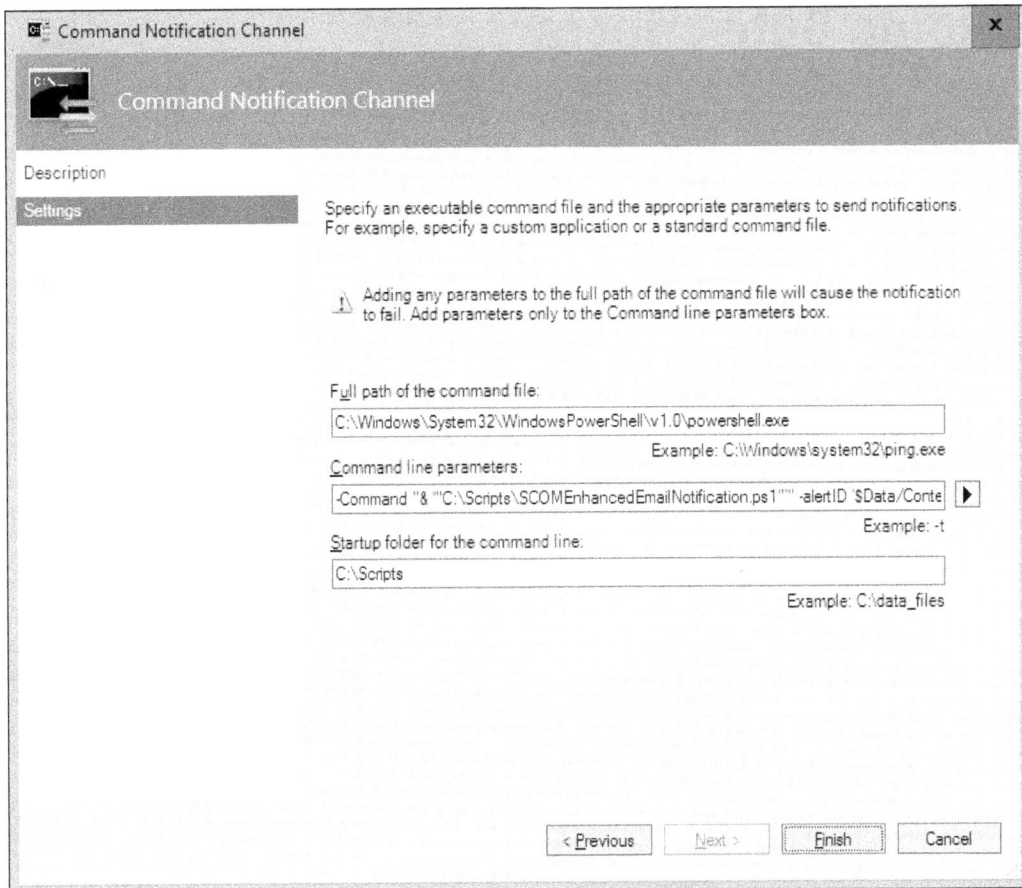

Figure 10.13: Customizing the Command channel

4. Hit the **Finish** button to complete the wizard and create the channel.

> You can use the Add-SCOMNotificationChannel cmdlet to create channels in PowerShell. For a full syntax of this cmdlet, check out this link on TechNet - http://tinyurl.com/opsmgraddchannel

Adding Subscribers

After you've created your alert notification channels, you'll need to add some subscribers to send the alerts to. When you configure a subscriber in OpsMgr, you have the option to define a number of different delivery addresses for that subscriber (in the format of e-mail, IM or text message) along with a schedule of when to forward alerts to particular addresses. As an example, you could choose to send only e-mail and instant message alerts during normal working hours and then use SMS text alerting for any out-of-hours alerts.

Follow these steps to get your first subscriber configured:

1. From the **Administration** workspace, expand **Notifications**, right-click on Subscribers and select **New subscriber** from the context menu to open the Notification Subscriber Wizard.

2. The **Description** dialog box (shown in *Figure 10.14*) will attempt to automatically populate the **Subscriber Name** field with the name of the user account that is running the wizard so if the new subscriber is anyone other than yourself, you'll need to either type in the correct name or you can click on the ellipses button to browse Active Directory and add the user from there. Click on **Next** when you're ready to continue.

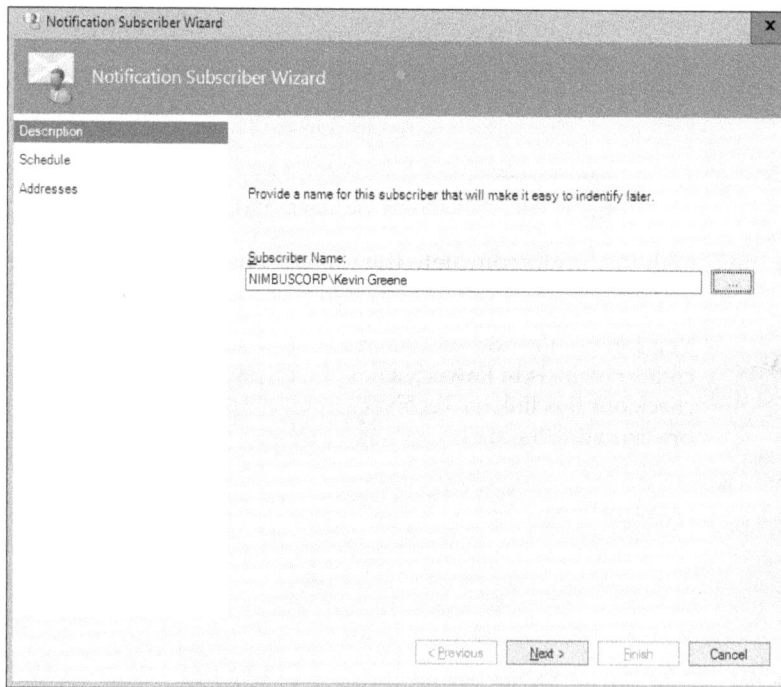

Figure 10.14: Adding a new subscriber

3. At the **Schedule** dialog box you can configure a master schedule for when alert notifications will be sent to this subscriber. Leave the default option of **Always send notifications** configured here (we can create a more granular schedule for each notification address later) and click on Next.

4. The **Addresses** dialog box is where you can choose the type of notification delivery addresses that you want to apply to this particular subscriber. Click on the **Add** button to start the **Subscriber Address** wizard.

5. Type a name for the subscriber address that you're about to configure and make sure it's descriptive enough to help you differentiate from multiple address types assigned to the same subscriber. You could use examples like 'Work E-mail', 'Mobile Phone Number' or 'Lync Address' here. Click on **Next** to continue.

6. From the Channel dialog box, choose the channel type and enter a delivery address associated with the subscriber for the selected channel. In *Figure 10.15*, we've configured the E-Mail (SMTP) channel and an e-mail address for delivery. Hit **Next** when you're ready to move on.

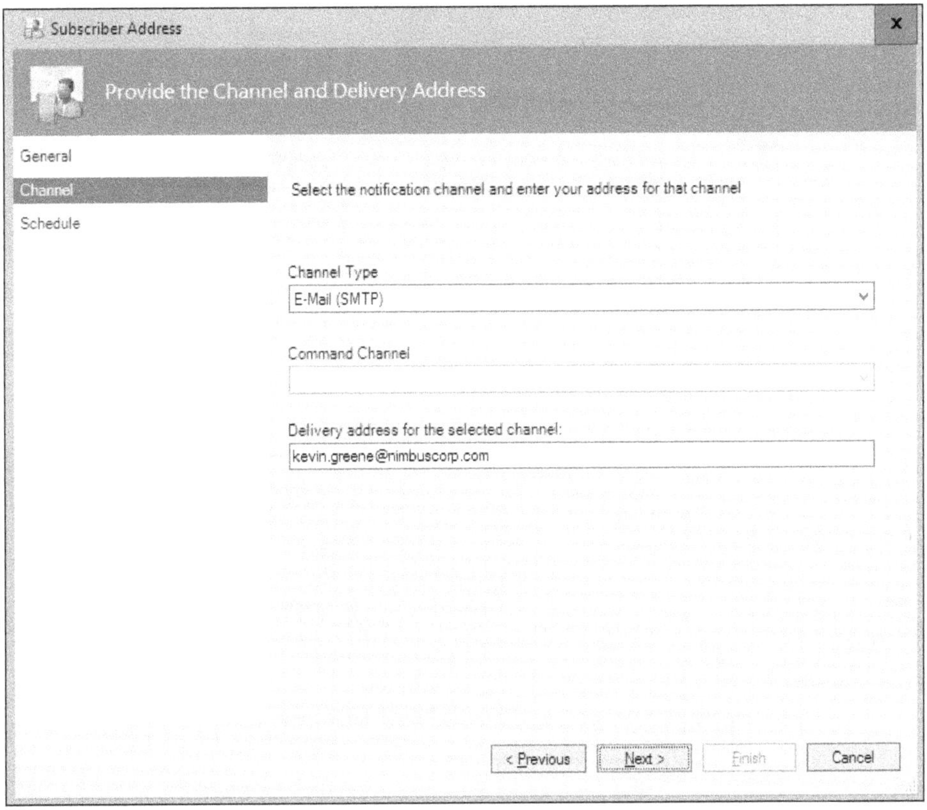

Figure 10.15: Configuring the channel and delivery address of a subscriber

> Distribution list e-mail addresses can also be used for subscribers when you need to deliver notifications to multiple users within the organization.

7. At the **Schedule** dialog box you can configure specific times for when alert notifications are sent to the delivery address. For e-mail addresses you'll probably be happy to use the **Always send notifications** option but for text messages to your phone, you might only want to receive them outside of normal working hours. If you want the latter option, then click on the **Only send notification during the specified times** radio button and then click on **Add** to open the Specify Schedule dialog box.

8. In *Figure 10.16* you can see how we've configured a notification schedule for a delivery address to send alerts every day of the week - but with an exclusion setting to ensure they're only sent outside of work hours.

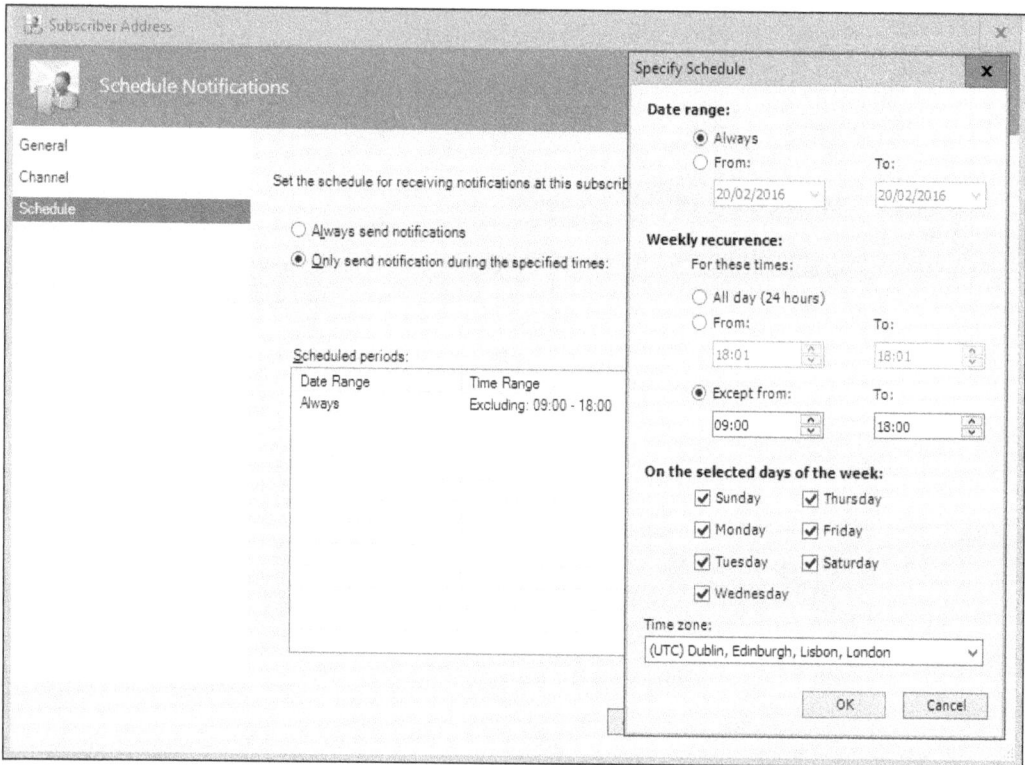

Figure 10.16: Scheduling a date and time range for notifications

9. Click on the **Finish** button to close the Subscriber Address wizard and back at the **Notification Subscriber Wizard**, add more subscriber addresses if required, then click on **Finish** again to close the wizard and create the subscriber.

> PowerShell is your friend if you want the quickest method of creating subscribers and the following line will create a new subscriber with an e-mail, SMS and IM delivery address - `Add-SCOMNotificationSubscriber -Name "Kevin Greene" -DeviceList "kevin.greene@nimbuscorp.com","sms:+35 3871234567","sip:Kevin.Greene"`.
>
> To add a schedule to a subscriber, use the `Add-SCOMSubscriberSchedule` cmdlet detailed here - `http://tinyurl.com/opsmgraddsubscriber`

Configuring Subscriptions

If you want your subscribers to receive alert notifications for specific alerts over a given notification channel, then you'll need to configure a subscription to tie all of the notification components together.

The process of creating custom subscriptions is very similar to the wizard-driven process of creating rules in Microsoft Outlook to determine how e-mails are handled when they're received. Criteria conditions are specified within the subscription to determine if and when alerts will be sent to specific subscribers. Using the console, you can create a new custom subscription from scratch through the Administration workspace or you can create a targeted subscription direct from an alert within the Monitoring workspace.

Creating Subscriptions from the Administration workspace

When configuring new alert subscriptions, it's a good idea to plan the types of alerts that you wish to send to subscribers. For example, you might decide to only send alerts with a resolution state of New and a severity of Critical to operators working outside normal business hours. This type of subscription will ensure that the on-call team don't get woken up during the night for alerts that may not be too important and it will help to increase confidence in the monitoring solution for everyone involved in managing the IT estate.

To create a new subscription from the Administration workspace, follow these steps:

1. Expand **Notifications**, right-click on Subscriptions and select **New subscription** from the context menu to open the **Notification Subscription Wizard**.

2. As shown in *Figure 10.17*, type a name for the subscription and enter some detailed information into the description field about what exactly the subscription does – this description comes in handy when you're managing a large number of subscriptions and need to quickly identify what each one does. Click on **Next** to continue.

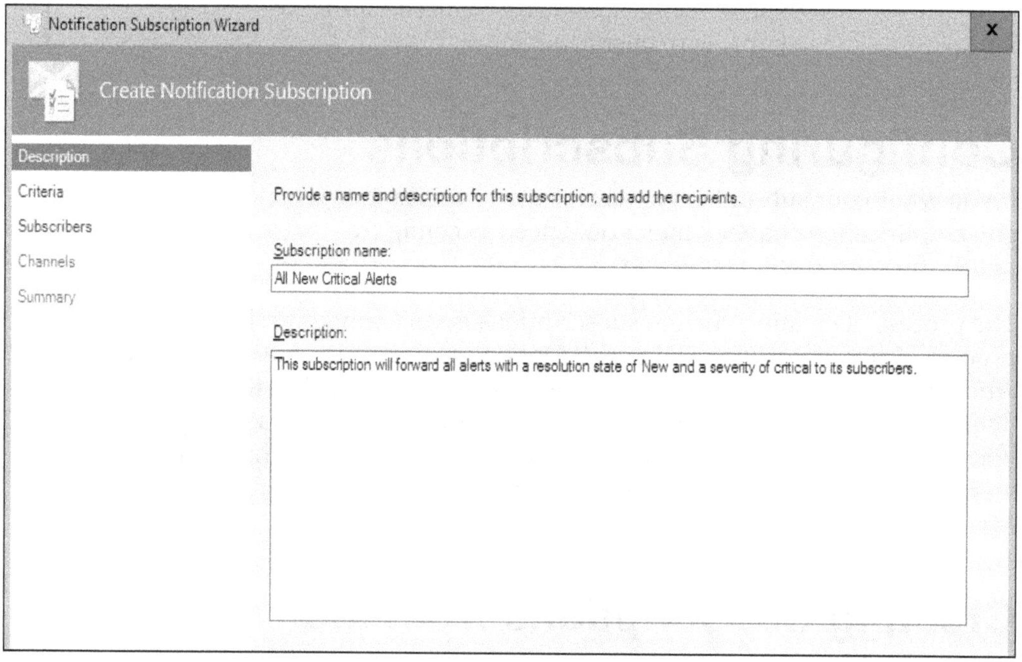

Figure 10.17: Creating a new notification subscription

3. At the **Criteria** dialog box, select the conditions that you want to apply to alerts that will be forwarded with this subscription. You can apply multiple conditions to the same subscription and the majority of them are self-explanatory. For this example, we'll select the **of a specific severity** and **with a specific resolution state** conditions. We populate these conditions by clicking on the blue links in the **Criteria Description** field and choosing the **Critical** and **New** criteria as shown in *Figure 10.18*. When you've made all your criteria selections click on **Next** to move on.

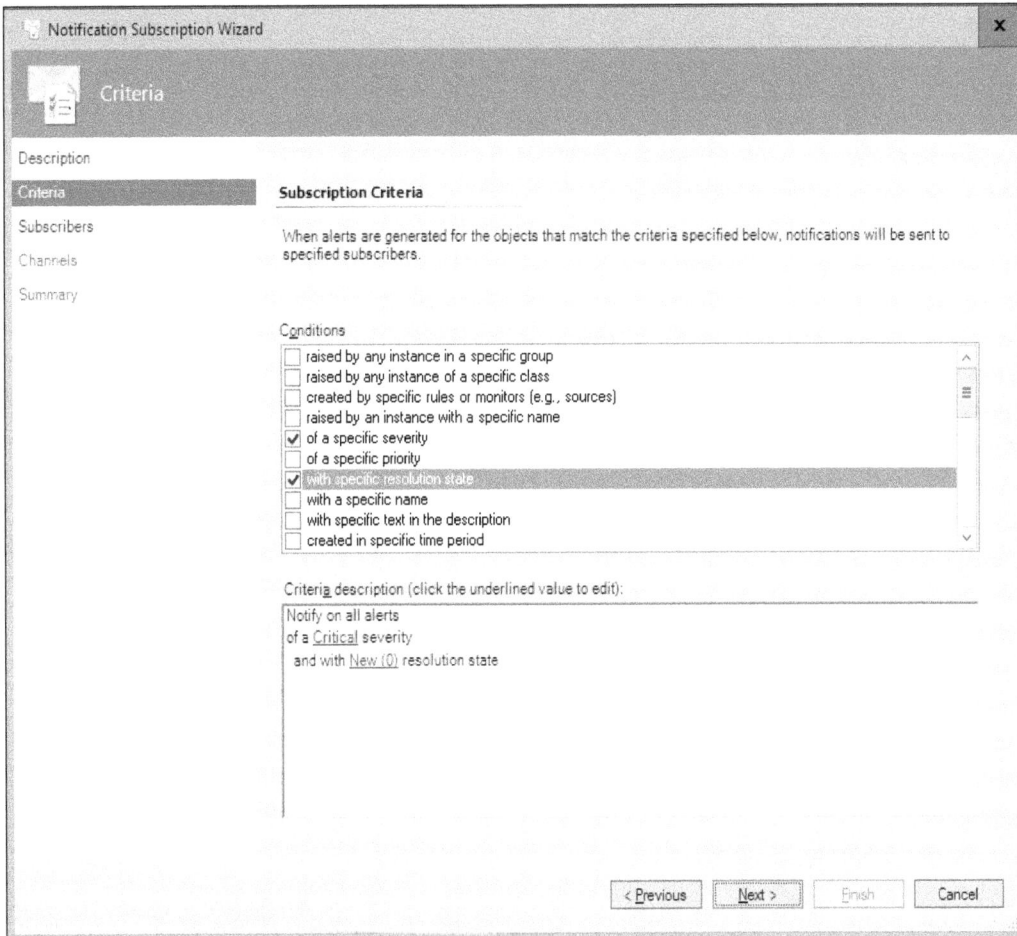

Figure 10.18: Specifying the subscription criteria

4. From the Subscribers dialog box, hit the **Add** button to open the **Subscriber Search** dialog box shown in *Figure 10.19*. Click on the **Search** button and you'll be presented with a list of all available subscribers. If you've a large number of subscribers already created, you can use the filter field to refine your search. When you've added the required subscribers, click on **OK** to close.

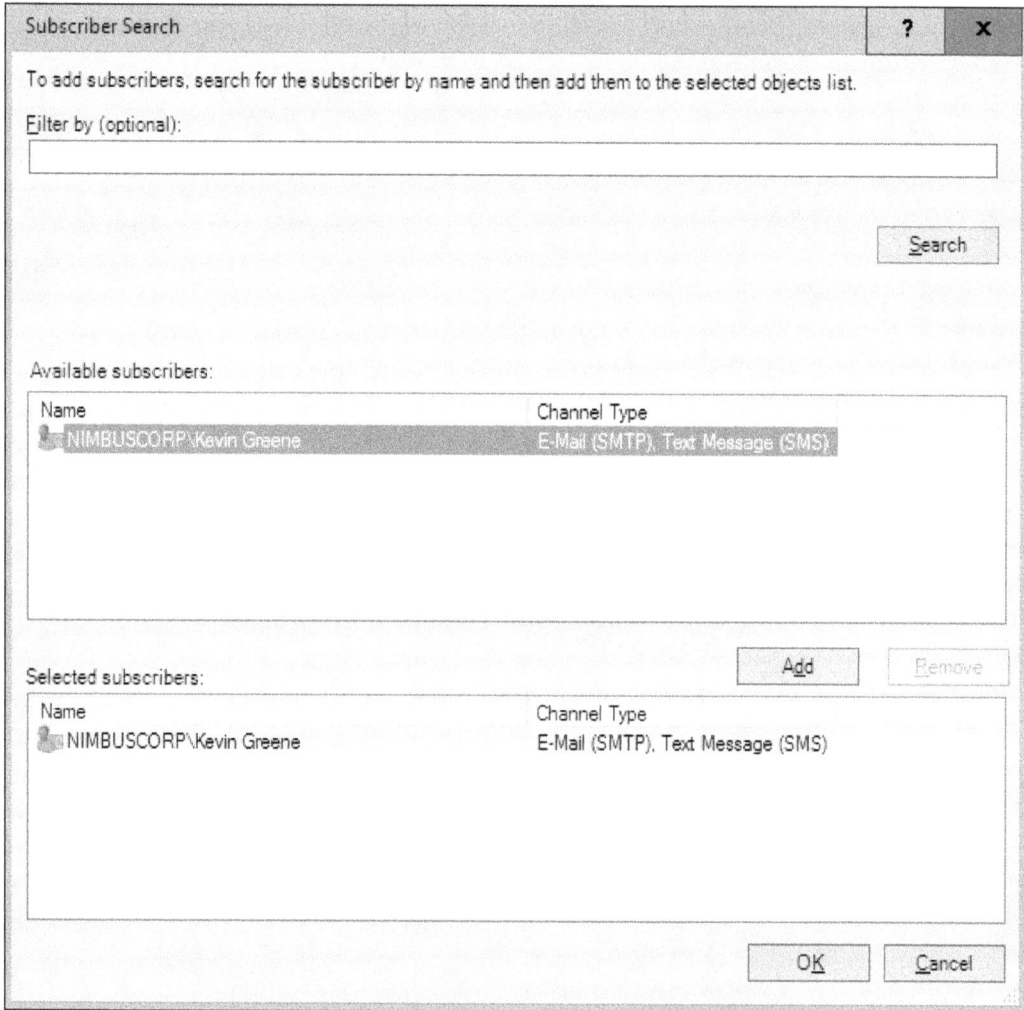

Figure 10.19: Adding a subscriber to a subscription

5. Back at the **Subscribers** dialog box, you have the option to create a new subscriber by clicking the **New** button, which is an alternative way of launching the Notification Subscriber Wizard we discussed earlier. Hit **Next** when you're ready to move on.

6. The Channels dialog box shown in *Figure 10.20* is where you specify the channel type(s) that will apply to the subscription. If you added subscribers with multiple delivery addresses (e-mail and SMS for example), then you can use the **Add** button to add multiple channels here to ensure alert notifications are forwarded over all transport mediums. You can also use the **New** button to launch the wizard for creating new channels and this button will also allow you to create a customized copy of an existing channel.

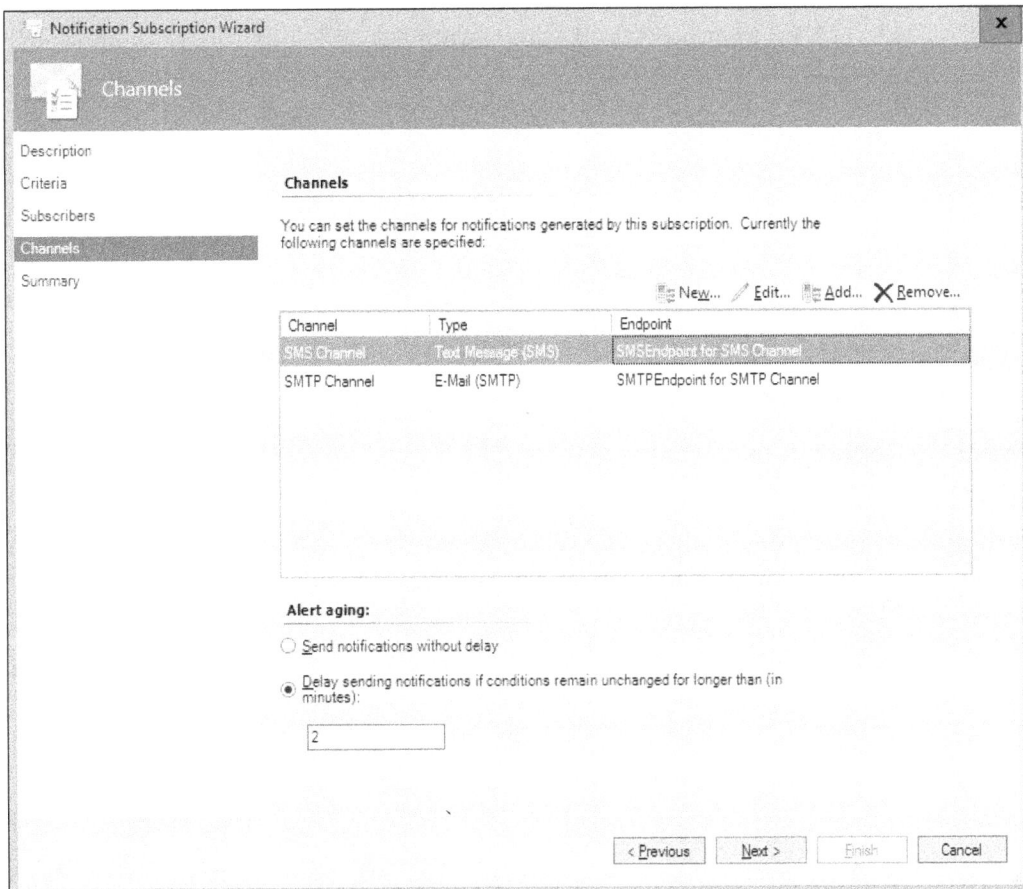

Figure 10.20: Selecting channels to use with your subscription

7. Use the **Alert aging** section of the **Channels** dialog box to specify how long OpsMgr will wait before sending alert notifications. This is a very useful feature and by simply specifying a value of one or two minutes here, you'll stop noisy alerts that might be briefly flipping state (Memory and CPU usage are two examples) from healthy to critical and then back to healthy. Anything that helps avoid situations where your call operators consistently get woken from their beds to deal with a critical alert only to see that everything is healthy by the time they logon to check can only be a good thing!

8. Click on **Next** to move on and at the **Summary** dialog box, leave the **Enable this notification subscription** box checked (unless you don't want to immediately enable the subscription) and hit **Finish** to close the wizard and create the subscription.

> If you want to roll out your PowerShell Kung-Fu again, you can use the `Add-SCOMNotificationSubscription` cmdlet to create new subscriptions. You can find all the syntax information and some sample scripts here - `http://tinyurl.com/opsmgraddsubscription`

Scoping Subscriptions from the Monitoring workspace

An easy way of creating notification subscriptions for specific alerts is to open an alert view in the Monitoring workspace, right-click on the alert and select the **Notification subscription** option from the menu as shown in *Figure 10.21*.

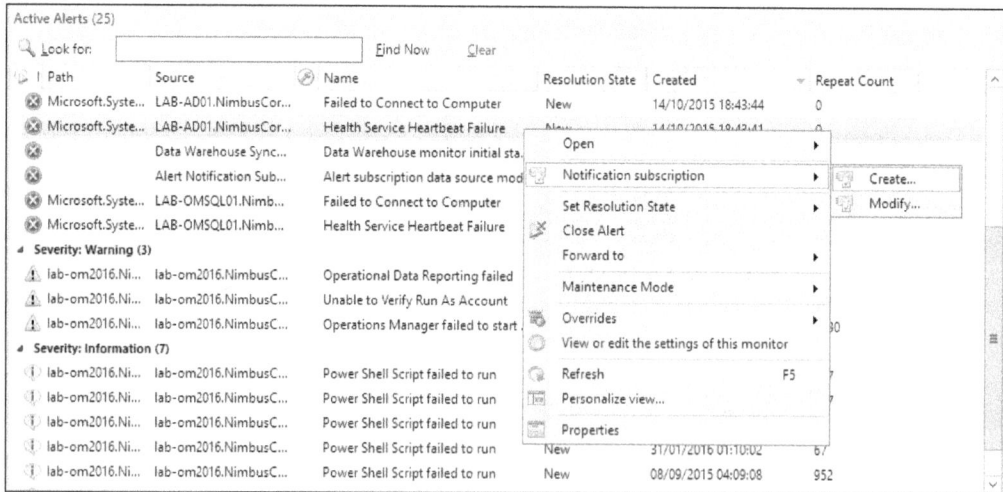

Figure 10.21: Creating a scoped subscription from an alert view

The **Create** option from the menu launches the Notification Subscription Wizard and will pre-populate a name, description and the **created by specific rules or monitors** subscription criteria similar to *Figure 10.22*.

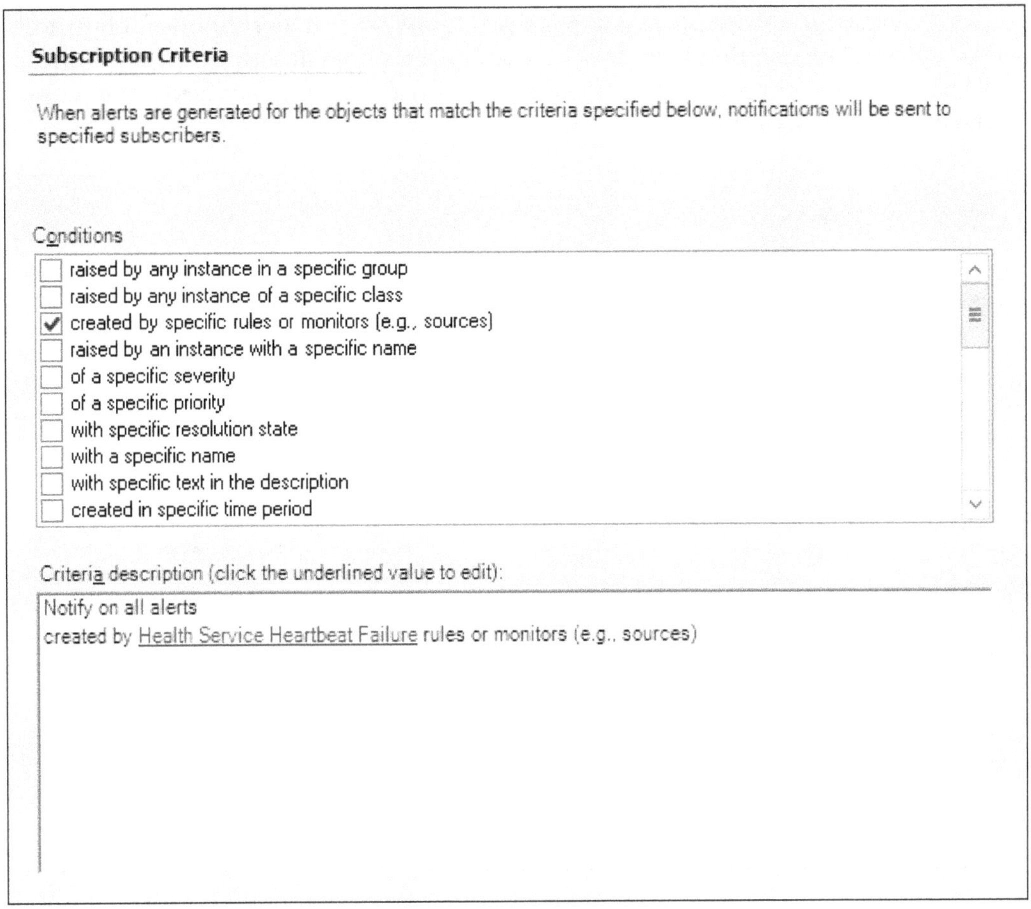

Subscription Criteria

When alerts are generated for the objects that match the criteria specified below, notifications will be sent to specified subscribers.

Conditions

- [ ] raised by any instance in a specific group
- [ ] raised by any instance of a specific class
- [x] created by specific rules or monitors (e.g., sources)
- [ ] raised by an instance with a specific name
- [ ] of a specific severity
- [ ] of a specific priority
- [ ] with specific resolution state
- [ ] with a specific name
- [ ] with specific text in the description
- [ ] created in specific time period

Criteria description (click the underlined value to edit):

Notify on all alerts
created by <u>Health Service Heartbeat Failure</u> rules or monitors (e.g., sources)

Figure 10.22: Pre-populated criteria from a scoped subscription

> When creating scoped subscriptions from the Monitoring workspace, be aware that the default pre-populated criteria doesn't add a resolution state criteria. This means that you will be notified on all alerts – including those with a resolution state of **Closed**. This can generate unnecessary notification noise for your operators and it's a good idea to specify the **New** resolution state criteria here.

Subscribers and channels are not pre-populated when you create a scoped subscription so you'll need to add these as you work through the remaining steps in the wizard.

If you've already created some scoped alert notification subscriptions that target specific alerts, you can use the **Modify** option from the **Notification subscription** menu after you right-click on an alert in the console. Selecting this option will present you with the **Select Subscription** dialog box shown in *Figure 10.23*. Here, you can choose the subscription you wish to add the scoped alert notification to and as you select a subscription from the list, the informational description at the bottom will change to explain if your modification will broaden or restrict the overall scope of the original subscription.

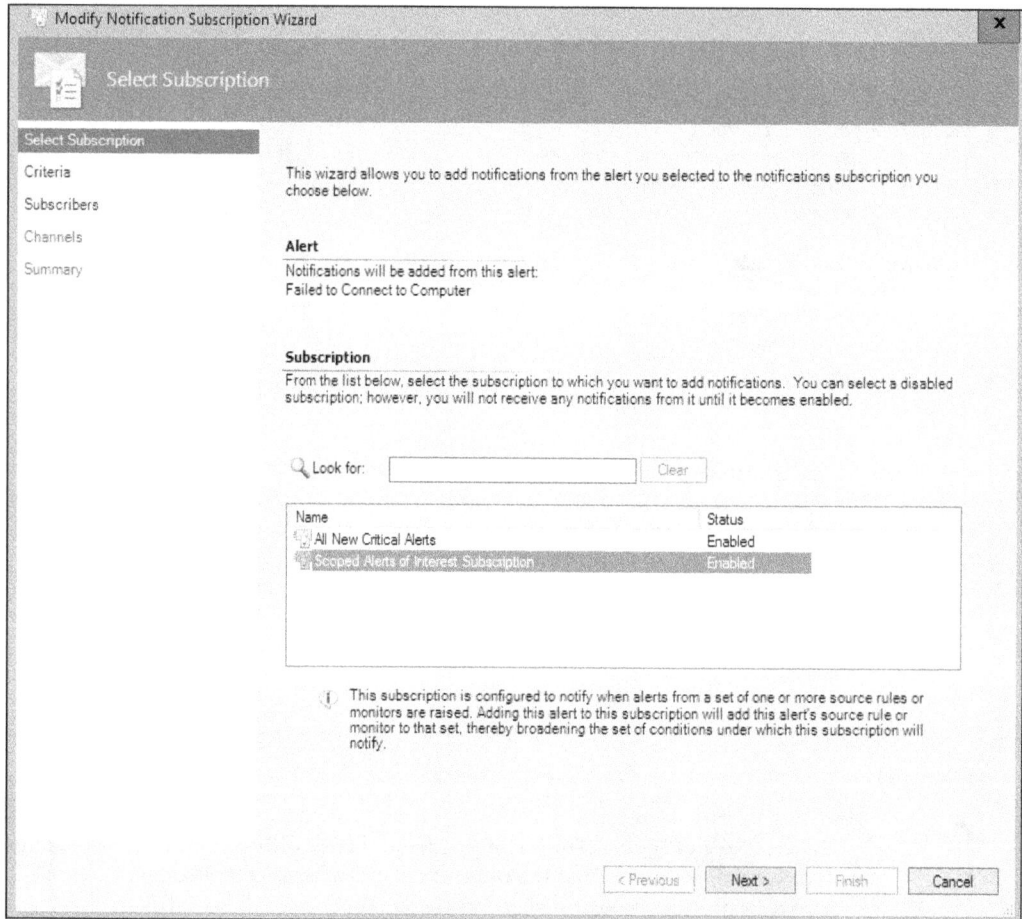

Figure 10.23: Using the Modify option to change a scoped subscription

Testing Subscriptions

With your channels, subscribers and subscriptions all created, the next step is to give them a test run to ensure they're working as expected. E-mail alerting is by far the most popular method of alert notification and in most environments configuring a test subscriber with an internal or external (Gmail or Outlook.com) e-mail address is all that's required to see how the subscriptions are working.

However, if you're working in an environment that has a fairly locked down SMTP server (or maybe even no SMTP server if you're running a home-lab for testing), then you might be interested in giving a handy little tool called Papercut a try. Papercut is a free desktop e-mail receiver utility designed specifically to test e-mails from an application. Available on GitHub (`https://github.com/jaben/papercut`), it can be configured to run on startup or on-demand and sits in the system tray of your computer as shown in *Figure 10.24*. You can configure Papercut to listen on a designated IP address and port. To get it working with OpsMgr, all you need to do is point an E-Mail (SMTP) channel at the IP address and port, link a subscription to the channel and run your tests. For a step-by-step walkthrough on getting this up and running with OpsMgr, check out this blog post from a community on `http://tinyurl.com/opsmgrpapercut`

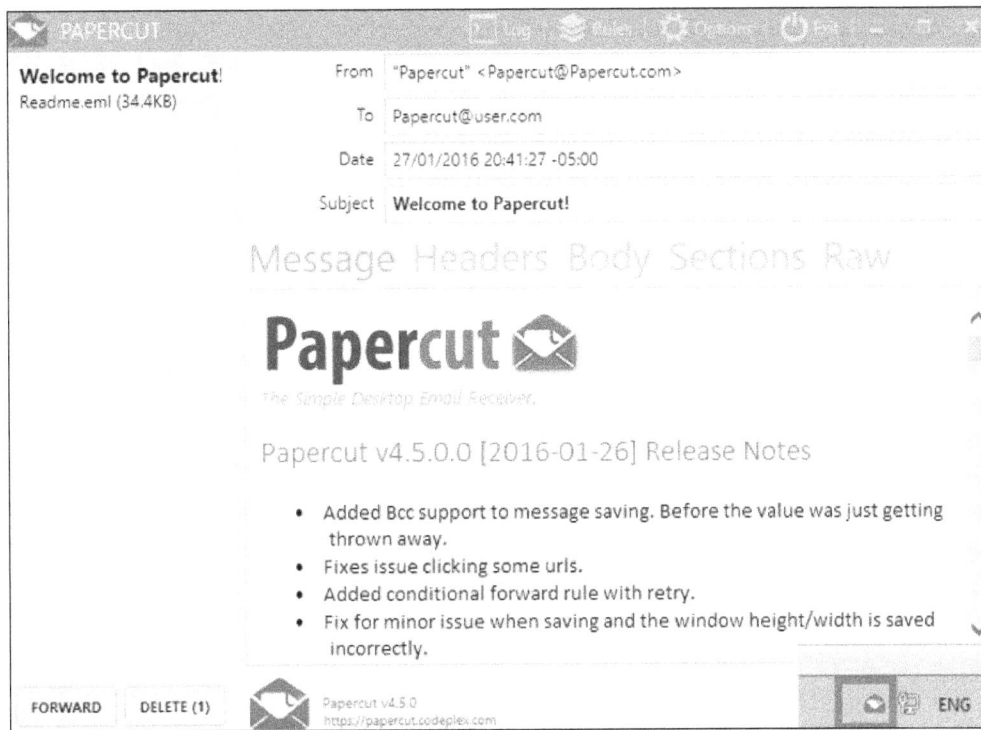

Figure 10.24: Testing e-mail notifications with Papercut

Managing Subscriptions

The more notification subscriptions you configure, the more management overhead challenges you'll have. Management tasks can range from simply needing to enable or disable all subscriptions for maintenance and patching cycles, to having the ability to create multiple copies of existing subscriptions so as to support tiered recipient support groups. In the next few sections we'll describe some of the options available to you for overcoming these challenges.

Enabling and disabling Subscriptions

From time-to-time you will have a requirement to enable or disable your subscriptions and you can do this from the Administration workspace in the console. To disable a subscription all you need to do is to right-click on it and select the **Disable** option as shown in *Figure 10.25*.

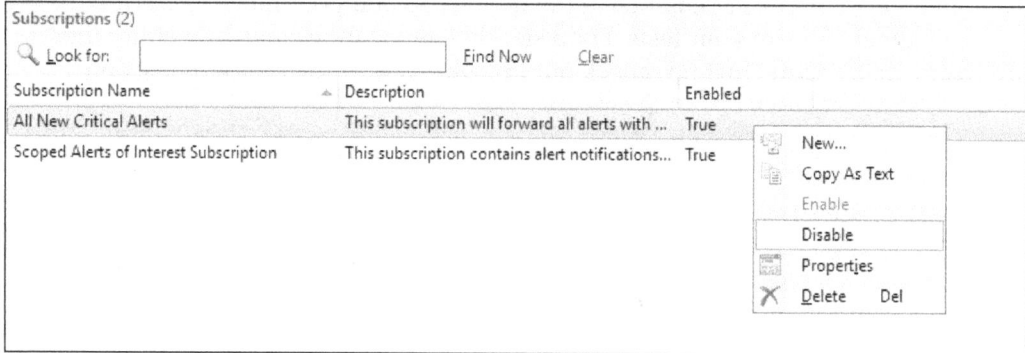

Figure 10.25: Disabling a subscription from the console

Right-click and select the **Enable** option if you wish to enable the subscription again. The problem with using the console for these tasks is the fact that you can only enable or disable subscriptions one at a time – not in bulk. This obviously becomes an administrative pain the more subscriptions you have. Thankfully, PowerShell comes to the rescue again!

> The following scripts make use of special cmdlets that come bundled with the Operations Manager Shell so make sure you're using this to launch them. If you're using a normal PowerShell window, then you'll need to first import the OpsMgr PowerShell module by typing `Import-Module OperationsManager`.

To disable all notification subscriptions at the same time, use this:

```
Get-SCOMNotificationSubscription | Disable-
SCOMNotificationSubscription
```

To re-enable them all again this is what you need:

```
Get-SCOMNotificationSubscription | Enable-
SCOMNotificationSubscription
```

You might have a requirement to only disable subscriptions that contain certain text in their name, if so, then this will work (replace *TestSubscription* with the relevant text):

```
Get-SCOMNotificationSubscription | where {$_.displayname -like
"*TestSubscription*"} | Disable-SCOMNotificationSubscription
```

Stefan Roth's MAS Tool

If you'd prefer to use a GUI-based utility to manage your subscriptions in bulk, then Stefan Roth (Cloud and Datacenter MVP) has just what you're looking for. His MAS (Modify Alert and Subscription) Tool will present you with a list of all the subscriptions in your OpsMgr environment where you can then select individual ones or the whole lot in bulk and enable or disable them as required. Shown in *Figure 10.26*, you can download the MAS Tool from Stefan's blog here - `http://tinyurl.com/srothmastool`, and as an added bonus, this free utility has the capability to bulk close alerts and assign specific resolution states to them all in one go.

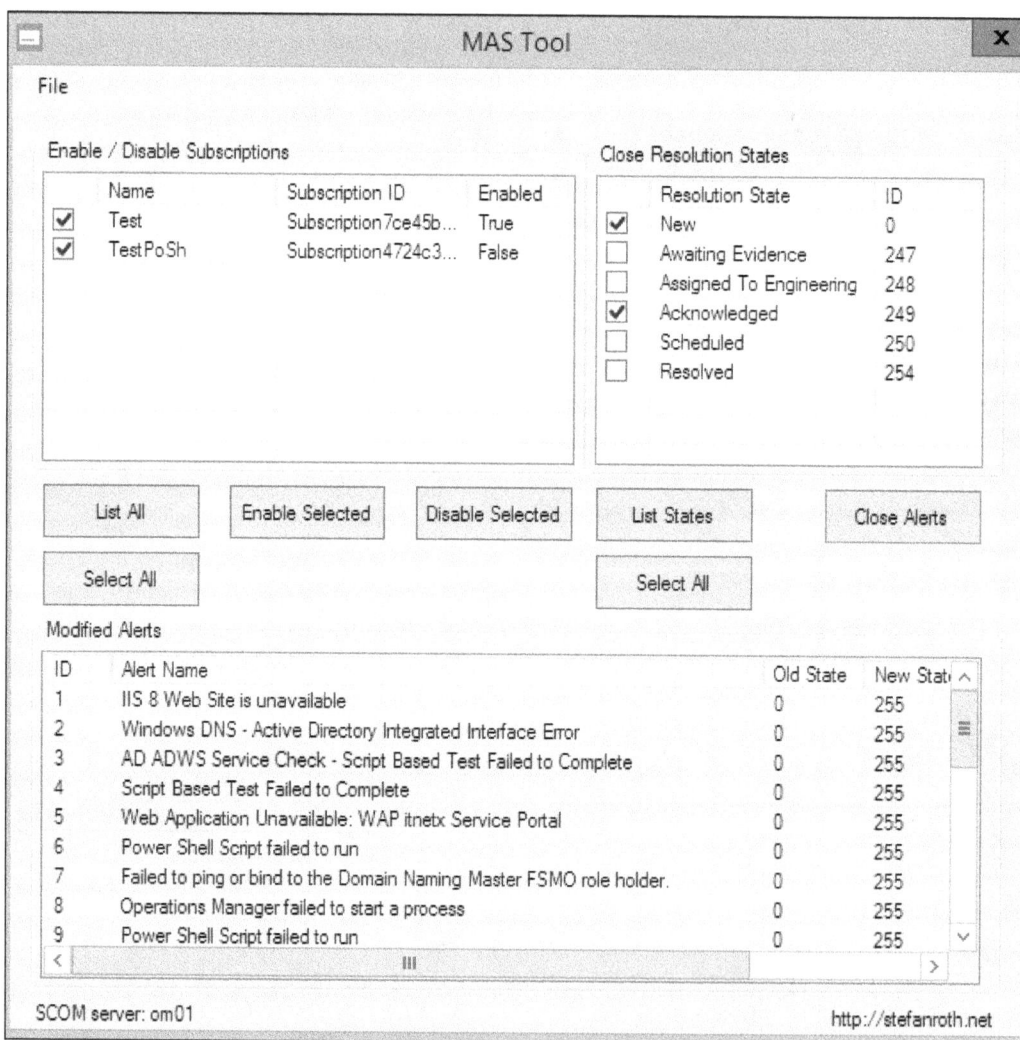

Figure 10.26: Stefan Roth's MAS Tool

Copying subscriptions

Out-of-the-box you have no option to make a copy of an existing notification subscription. You might need this functionality in situations where you have different levels of support groups that you want to send similar alert notifications to (Level 1, Level 2, or Escalation for example). Without the ability to easily copy a subscription, the long way would mean that you'd have to open an existing one, make note of how it's been configured (description, criteria and so on.) and then manually create a new subscription using the Notification Subscription Wizard.

To save you the hassle, Tim McFadden (*Premier Field Engineer at Microsoft*) has created the excellent Subscription Copier tool that does exactly what it says on the tin! As you can see in *Figure 10.27*, this tool connects to your Management Server, lists all existing subscriptions, gives you the option to select how many copies you want and also has a handy re-alert option that will create copies of the same subscription with alert aging set to the number of minutes you specify.

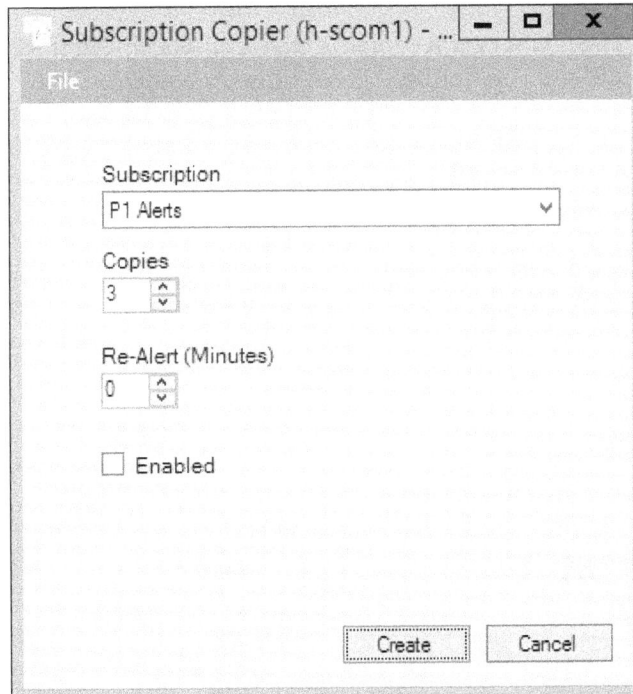

Figure 10.27: Subscription Copier tool from Tim McFadden

You can get more information on this tool and download it for free from Tim's blog here - `http://www.scom2k7.com/subscription-copier/`.

> If you'd prefer to create copies of your subscriptions using PowerShell, then check out the sample Cloning Notification Subscriptions script from Pete Zerger `http://tinyurl.com/opsmgrclonesubscriptions`

Reporting overview

In *Chapter 9, Visualizing Your IT with Dashboards* we discussed how to present real-time data back to the business through the use of dashboards. These are all well and good for the here-and-now picture but what if you need to show historical information about the health or performance of your environment? This is where the Reporting feature of OpsMgr stands out.

Built on Microsoft's **SQL Server Reporting Services (SSRS)** platform, this feature can be both fantastic and frustrating – depending on what you're trying to achieve with it! Some of the benefits OpsMgr reporting brings to the table are things like historical trending of health and performance, detailed information about configuration, capacity planning assistance and the ability to deliver monitoring and SLA information to people outside of the IT team.

With potentially hundreds of pre-built reports to choose from (depending on the management packs that you've deployed), you can be up and running in no time with the data you require being delivered on a scheduled basis in popular formats , such as PDF, Excel, and Word to name a few.

On the down-side, if you want to create a new report from an empty template, you might run into problems where the report runs blank due to incorrect targeting or parameters. In the next few sections we'll detail how to properly configure the Reporting role with SSRS and we'll discuss the best ways to avoid getting those dreaded blank reports.

Configuring SQL Reporting Services

If you've been working through the steps in this book, then you should have the Reporting Server role already deployed – this topic was covered in *Chapter 2, Installing System Center Operations Manager*. What we didn't dive into in that chapter however, was how to best configure the back-end SQL Server Reporting Services instance. Without an understanding of this, you won't be able to schedule OpsMgr reports by e-mail and you will also encounter problems when trying to restore or move the Reporting role to another server.

Here's a step-by-step walkthrough of what you need to configure:

1. Log on to the server that you're running the OpsMgr SSRS instance from, open SQL Server **Reporting Services Configuration Manager**, choose the correct server and instance name, then click on **Connect** as shown in *Figure 10.28*.

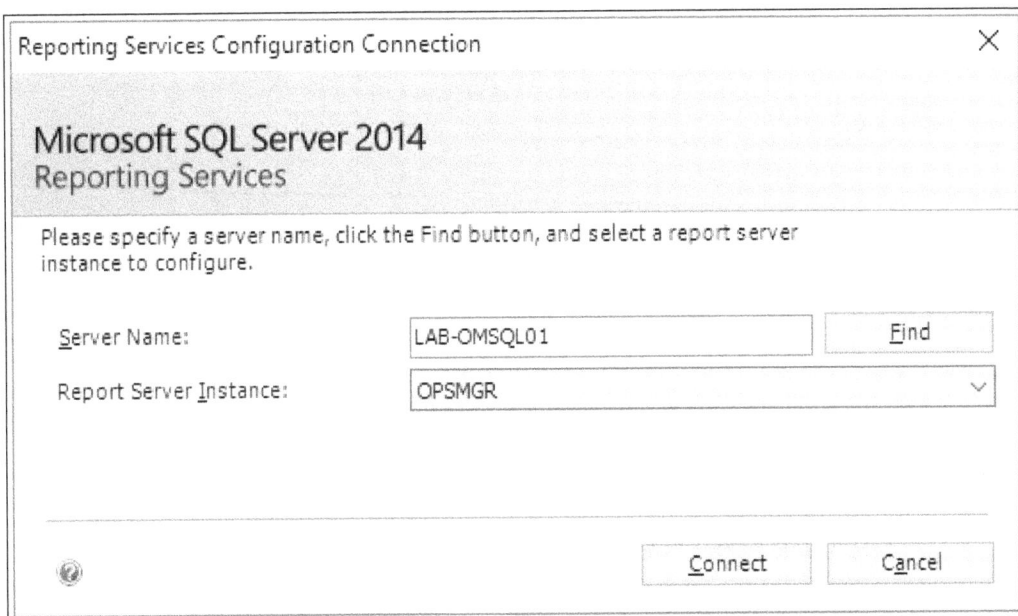

Figure 10.28: Connecting to the SSRS instance

2. The majority of settings in the **Reporting Services Configuration Manager** will have been pre-populated during the installation of the OpsMgr Reporting role and if you click on the **Report Manager URL** section from the navigation bar, you'll be presented with a URL reference similar to the one highlighted in *Figure 10.29*. This URL can be used as an alternative option for remotely managing your reports outside of the normal OpsMgr console. Make a note of this URL as we'll be using it later when scoping the Report Operators role.

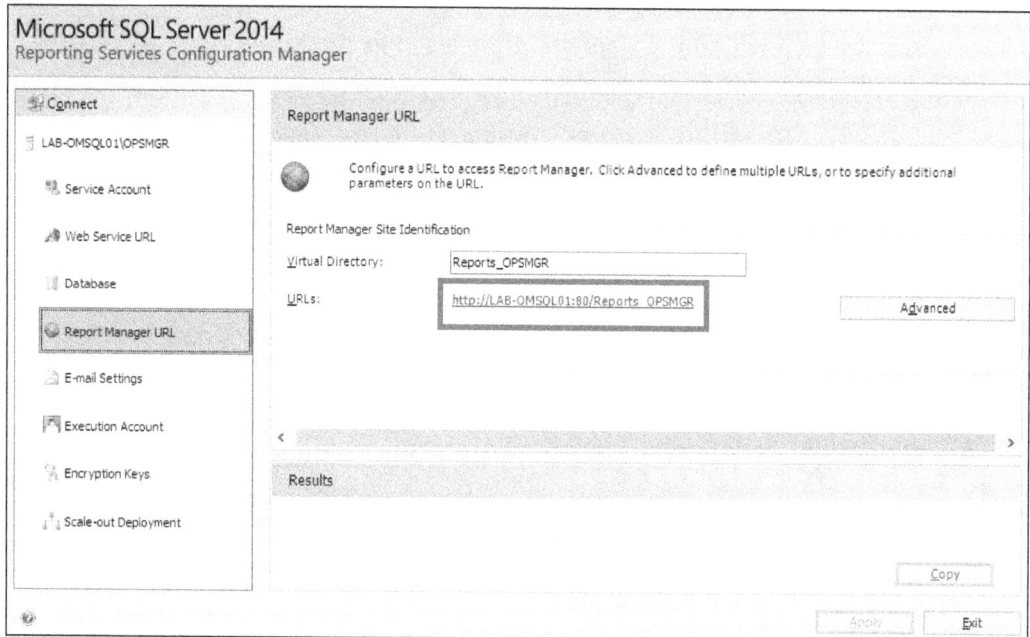

Figure 10.29: Viewing the Report Manager URL in SSRS

3. Now for the most important SSRS configuration item that you need to update. Click on the **E-Mail Settings** link from the navigation bar and you'll be presented with an empty SMTP settings section. If you leave the fields in this section empty, then you will not see the E-Mail option to schedule reports in OpsMgr! In *Figure 10.30* you can see that we've typed the address of the same SMTP server we used in our E-Mail (SMTP) notification channel earlier and we'll give it a sender address that references where the reports will be coming from too. Click on **Apply** to save the changes.

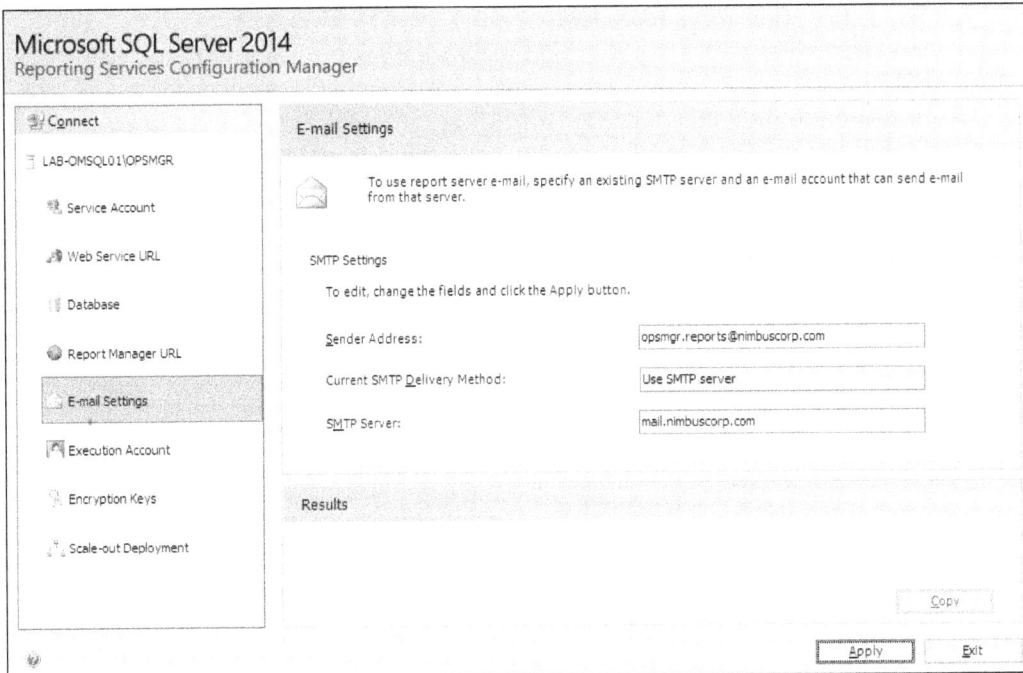

Figure 10.30: Updating the Reporting Services e-mail settings

Remember to ensure that your SMTP server is configured with
relay permissions to allow the IP address of your SSRS server
to send e-mails through it. This will nearly always be a separate
server to your OpsMgr Management Servers and it's easy to
forget about adding a rule to allow relaying with the end result
being that your scheduled reports fail delivery.

4. The **Encryption Keys** section shown in *Figure 10.31* is where you manage the encryption keys for your SSRS instance. It's important that you use the **Backup** button to create a backup of the key as this is needed when you need to restore or move the OpsMgr reporting role. Make sure you store a copy of this key in a location that's separate to the original SSRS server and keep a note of the password that you've assigned to the backup too.

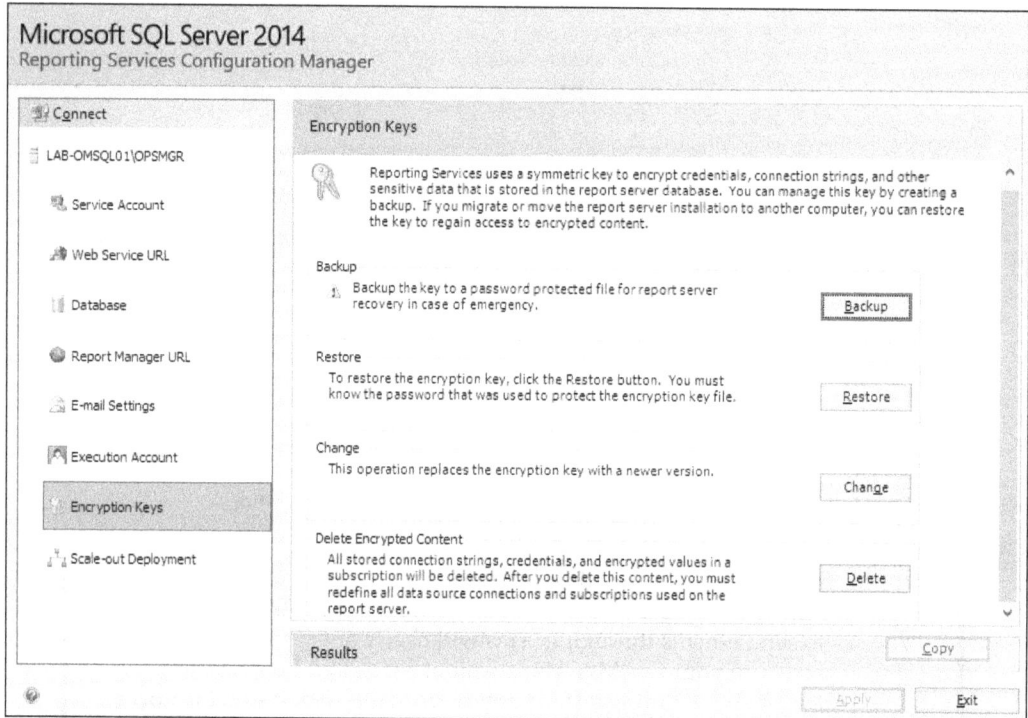

Figure 10.31: Managing the SSRS encryption key

5. Hit the **Exit** button when you're finished managing SSRS.

Scoping the Report Operators role

You can control which users have access to your OpsMgr reports by scoping a custom Report Operators role in the Administration workspace. This role gives users the ability to view reports based on their configured security scope. The catch here though is that after you add users or groups to the custom Report Operators role, you then need to modify security role assignments in SSRS.

Here's what you need to do to create a new custom User Role:

1. In the **Administration** workspace, right-click on **User Roles**, then click on **New User Role** and choose **Report Operator** from the menu.

2. Type a name and description to identify the new user role and as shown in *Figure 10.32*, click on the **Add** button and specify the user account (or security group) that you wish to scope this role to, then click on **Next** to continue.

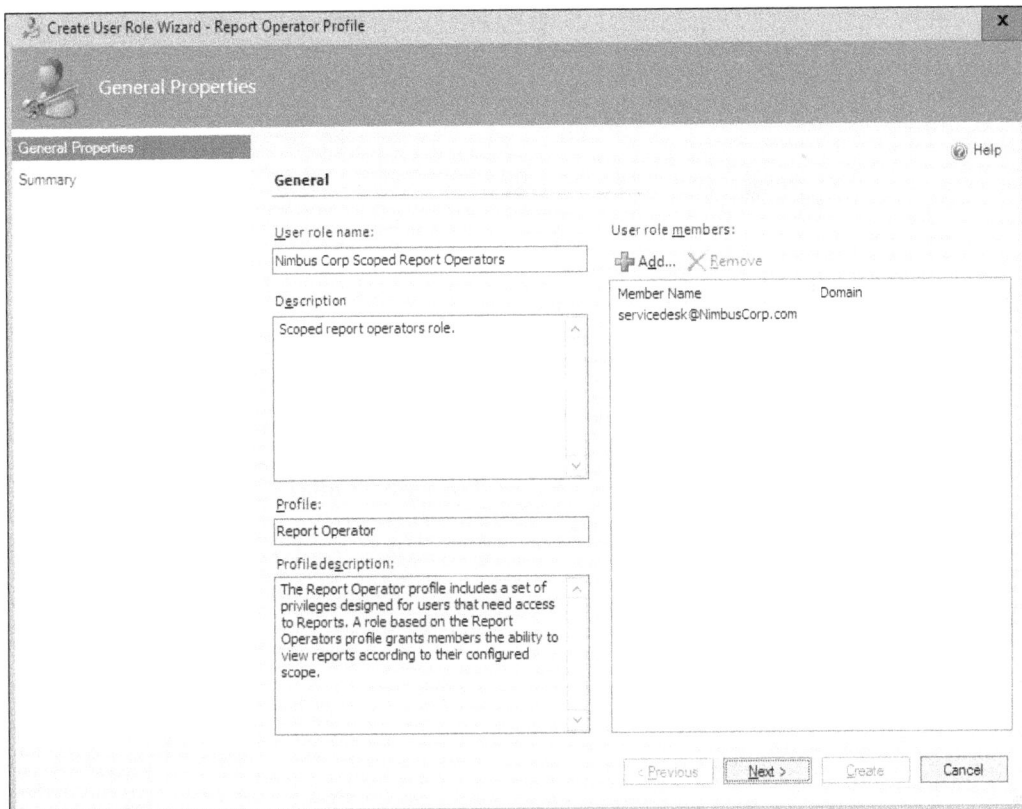

Figure 10.32: Creating a new scoped Report Operators role

3. At **Summary** dialog box click on **Create** to close the wizard and create the new role.

4. Now double-click on the newly created Report Operators role, open the **Identity** tab shown in *Figure 10.33* and click on the **Copy** button to copy the Unique Identifier for the role.

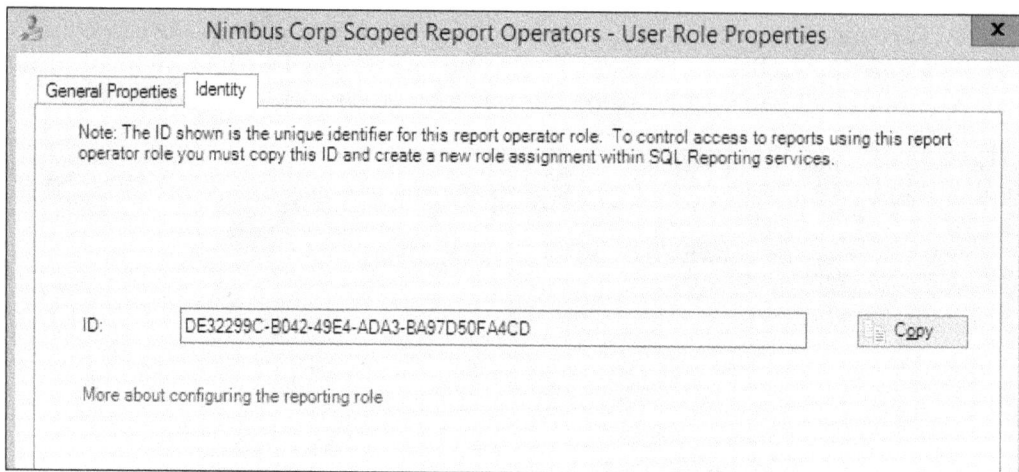

Figure 10.33: Copying the unique identifier for the new Report Operators role

5. With the Unique Identifier copied, open a web browser and browse to the Report Manager URL that you noted when configuring SQL Reporting Services. You should be presented with a view similar to *Figure 10.34*.

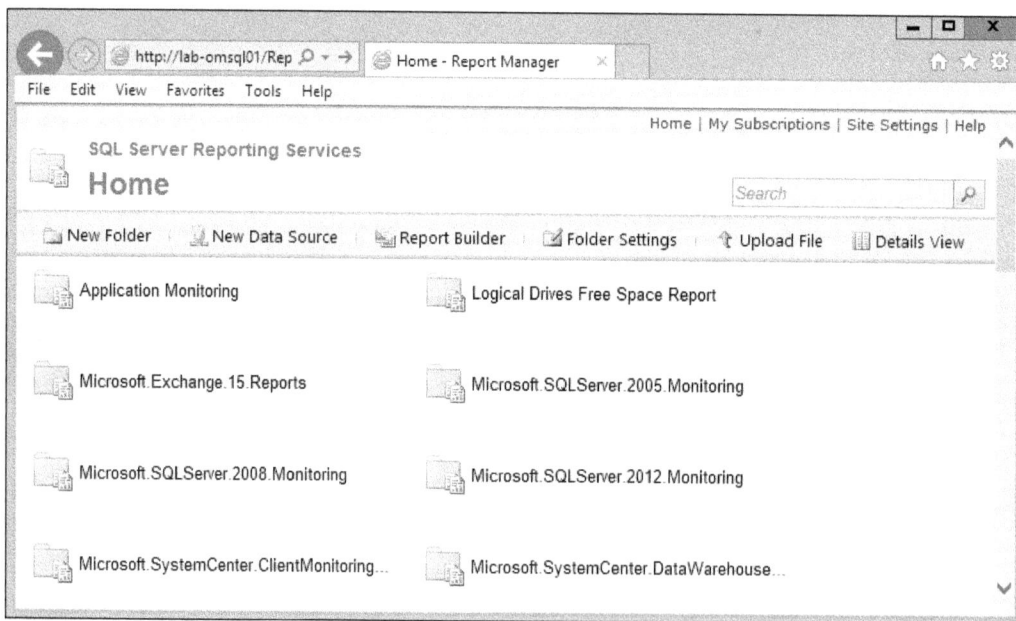

Figure 10.34: Accessing reports through the Report Manager URL

6. Click on the **Folder Settings** link from the navigation bar and then click on the **New Role Assignment** link from the **Security** section.

7. At the **New Role Assignment** window, copy the Unique Identifier from the custom Report Operators role into the **Group or user name** field as shown in *Figure 10.35* and select the checkbox for **Browser** and **My Reports**. This will define a role that can only view reports and not author or edit their definitions. Click on **OK** to close the window and create the role assignment.

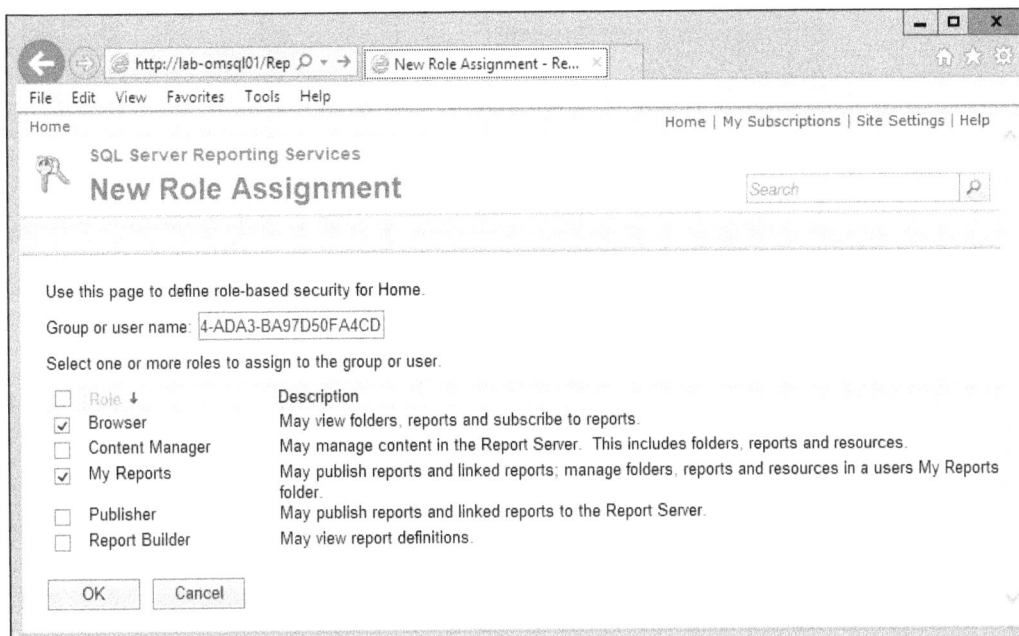

Figure 10.35: Creating a new system role assignment in SSRS

8. Now click on the **Home** link at the top-right of the screen and this will bring you back to a list of folders that contain all your OpsMgr reports. If you wish to restrict access to certain folders, then you'll need to click on the folder containing the report and then choose the **Folder Settings** link from the navigation bar.

9. Inside the reports folder settings, you need to click on the **Security** link to see a list of groups and users that currently have access to the folder (the unique identifier that you assigned to the user role earlier should be visible here). You can then hit the **Edit Item Security** link and you will be prompted to click on **OK** on the message shown in *Figure 10.36* that asks if you want to apply different security settings to the folder than those of its parent.

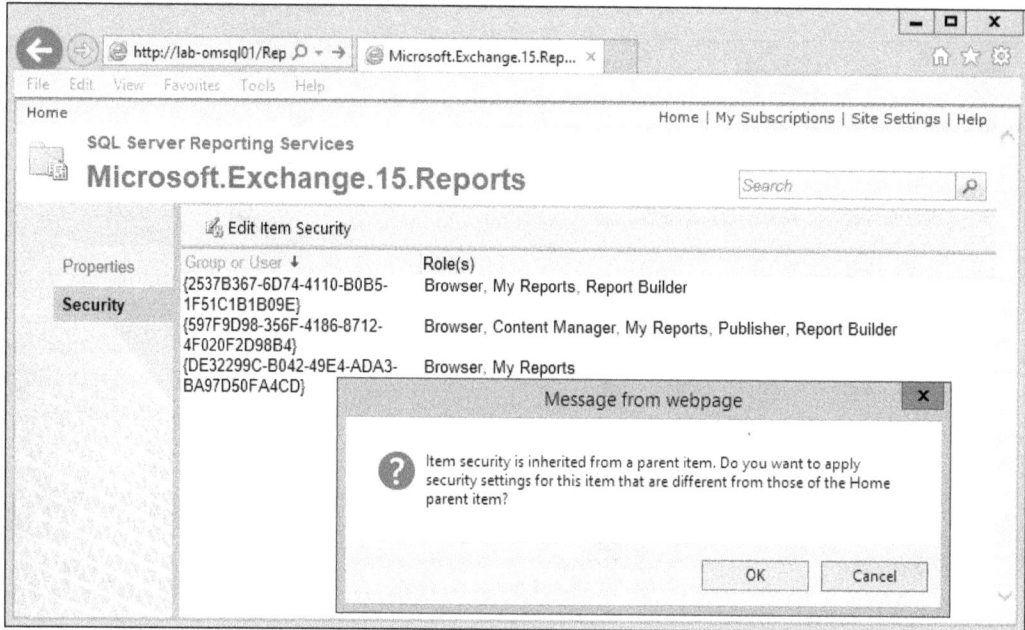

Figure 10.36: Editing security on a report folder

10. Now you can select the group or user that you want to remove permissions for (this should be the one that references the unique identifier for your Report Operators role) and hit the **Delete** option. Click on **OK** on the confirmation prompt shown in *Figure 10.37* to confirm the change and remove permission to the folder.

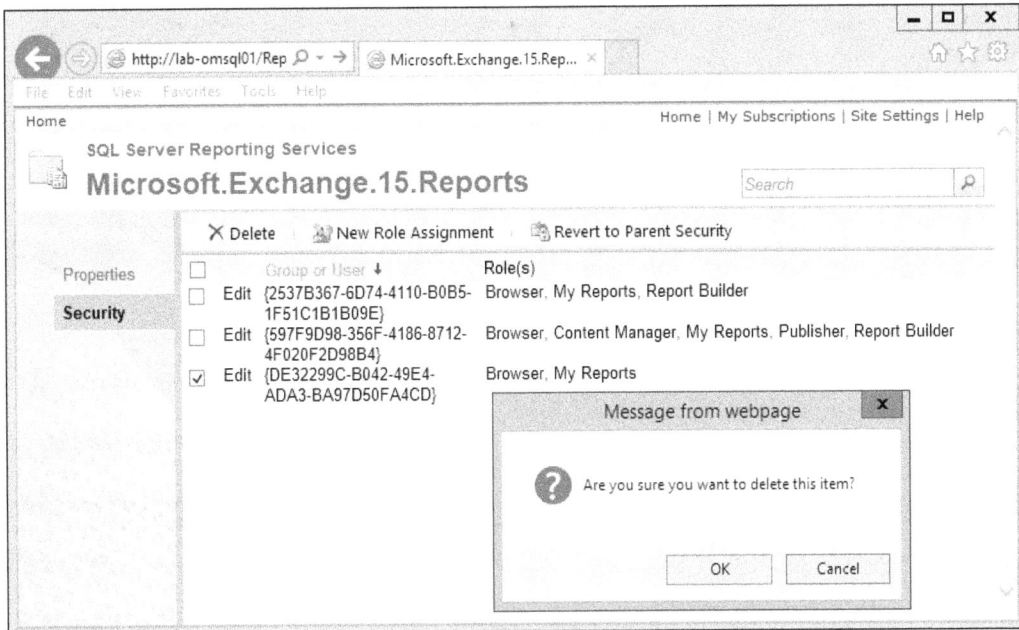

Figure 10.37: Removing permissions from a report folder

When editing report permissions, you can use the **Revert to Parent Security** option at any time to force the folder or report to go back to inheriting permissions from its parent. Think of this as a 'get-out-of-jail-free' card in case you mess things up!

11. Repeat the process of removing permissions for each folder (or individual report) that you wish to restrict and when the user next logs on to OpsMgr, they will be presented with a custom scoped view in the **Reporting** workspace. We've used this process to scope only reports relevant to Windows Server for our custom Report Operators role as shown in *Figure 10.38*.

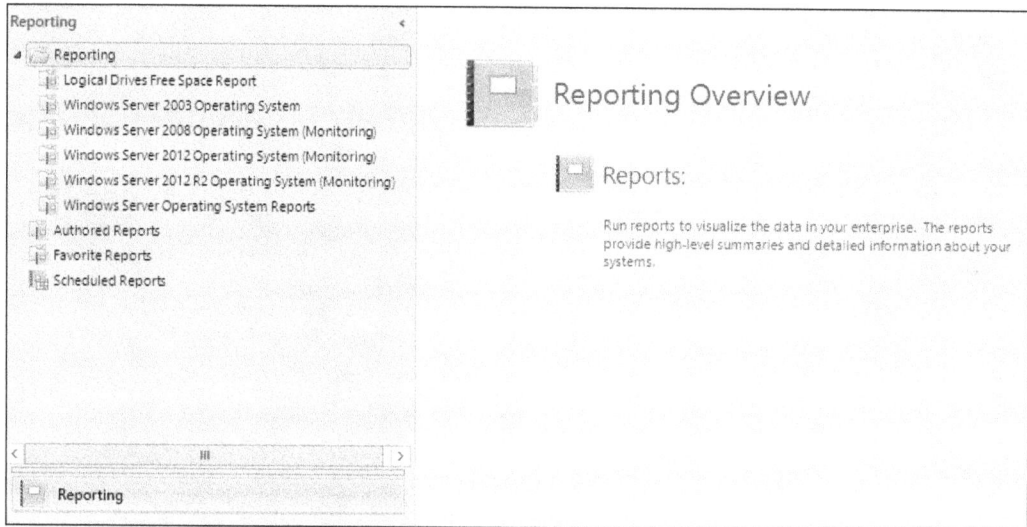

Figure 10.38: Reports scoped to a custom Report Operators role

Working with reports

Reports can be run directly from SSRS or within the OpsMgr console from the Reporting and Administration workspaces. Using the console to run reports should be the preferred option for most people as it adds a more user-friendly graphical layer on top of the SSRS Report Manager.

For example, clicking on the name of a report from within the Reporting workspace will present you with a **Report Details** pane (shown in *Figure 10.39*) giving you information on what the report can do and for more complicated reports, it gives details on how to actually run them.

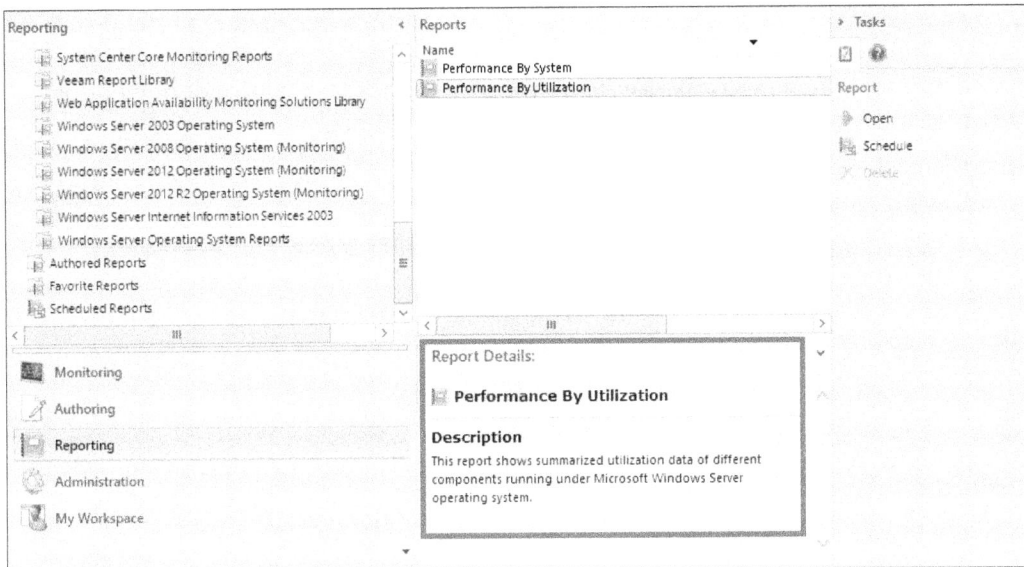

Figure 10.39: Viewing details about a selected report

Having this detailed information to hand is really useful when you're trying to understand which report is best suited to your requirements and to save time troubleshooting, we recommend reading through the Report Details section of every report before you run it.

Running reports

Blank reports is the most common problem you'll encounter when working with the Reporting feature in OpsMgr. The solution to this problem is understanding the type of objects and classes that the report is configured to return data on and some reports are easier than others to get right on the first attempt thanks to some built-in help from the vendors that created the original report definition.

An example of easy to run reports are the ones that come bundled with the Windows Server Operating System management pack. Follow these steps to run a report on operating system performance (this process assumes that you've deployed the Windows Server Core Operating System management packs):

1. Open the **Reporting** workspace, click on the **Windows Server 2012 R2 Operating System (Monitoring)** folder from the navigation bar, as shown in *Figure 10.40*, select the **Windows Server 2012 R2 Operating System Performance** report, read the information in the Report Details pane and then click on **Open** from the **Tasks** menu on the right.

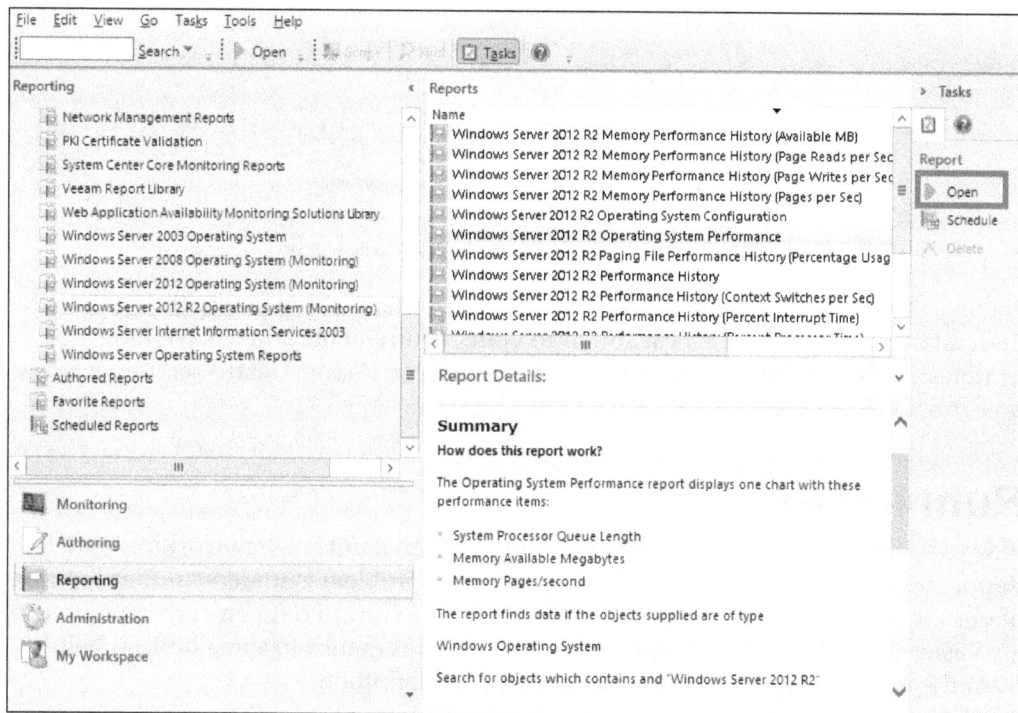

Figure 10.40: Selecting a report to open

2. With the report open, click on the **Add Object** button to open the dialog box and notice the **Filter Options have been applied** warning message here. This is a useful feature that indicates the object search has been filtered to include objects of a specific class. Clicking the **Options** button will show you the type of class that's been filtered – shown for this report in *Figure 10.41*. Click on **OK** to go back to the **Add Object** dialog box.

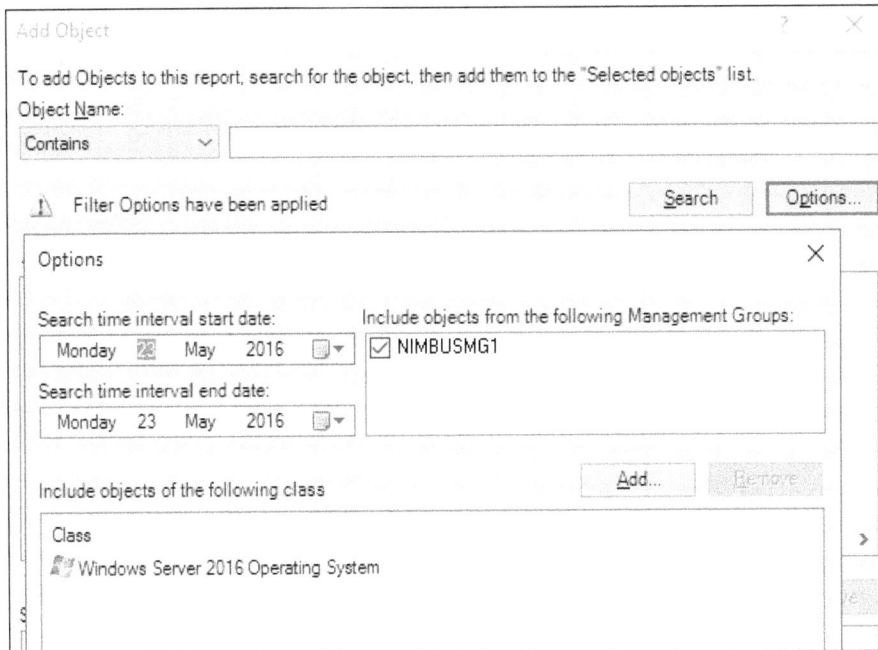

Figure 10.41: Displaying filter options for a report

3. At the **Object Name** field, click on the **Search** button to display all monitored Windows Server class instances, add a server (or servers) to the **Selected Objects** section using the **Add** button and click on **OK** to close the dialog box and return to the main report parameter area.

4. Similar to *Figure 10.42*, choose a timeframe for the report duration by changing the **From** and **To** fields on the left - we've used the **Advanced** option to offset the number of days with a minus value of 5 days.

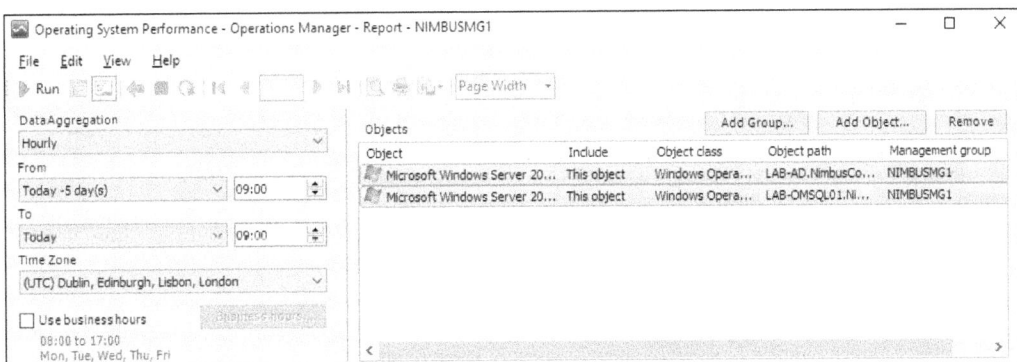

Figure 10.42: Configuring the report duration and other parameters

5. Click on **Run** to render the report and you should be presented with something similar to the one shown in *Figure 10.43*.

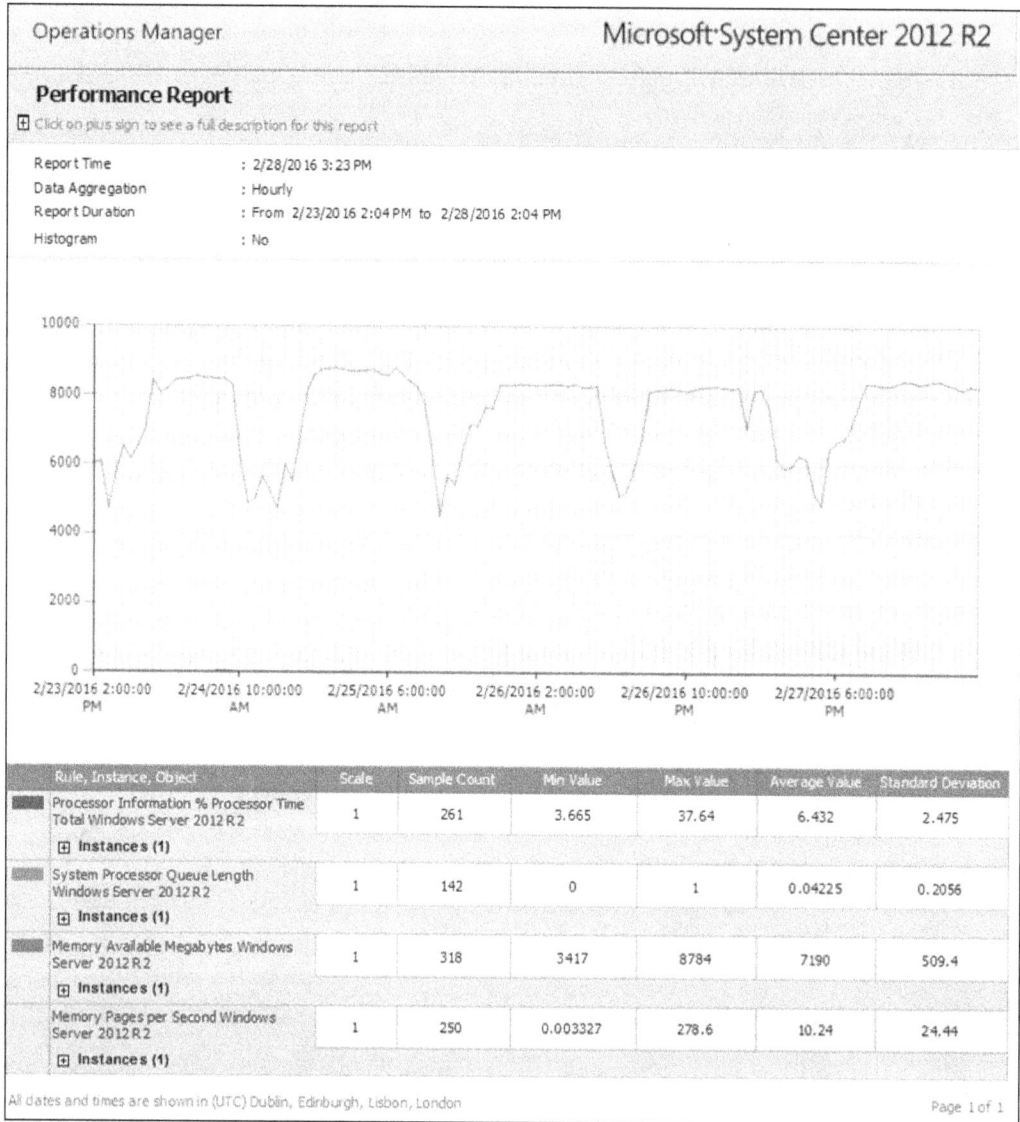

Figure 10.43: Viewing the report.

Linked reports and views

The great thing about using the console to run and view reports is that you can quickly pivot from one report to another to help you dive deeper for your analysis requirements. With some reports, you can also navigate to scoped console views relevant to the contents of the report and these views enable you to see the current performance and availability data (as opposed to historic data from the report) of your monitored objects.

To identify a linked report, hover your mouse pointer over the blue text link (usually this will be the name of a rule, instance or object) in the original report and the mouse pointer should change to an icon of a hand. If it does, just click on this link to open the new report.

In *Figure 10.44* you can see the **Memory Available Megabytes Windows Server 2012 R2** linked report that we launched from our original Windows Server 2012 R2 Operating System Performance report simply by clicking on the name of the performance rule – which is colored with blue text and located in the Rule, Instance, or Object column.

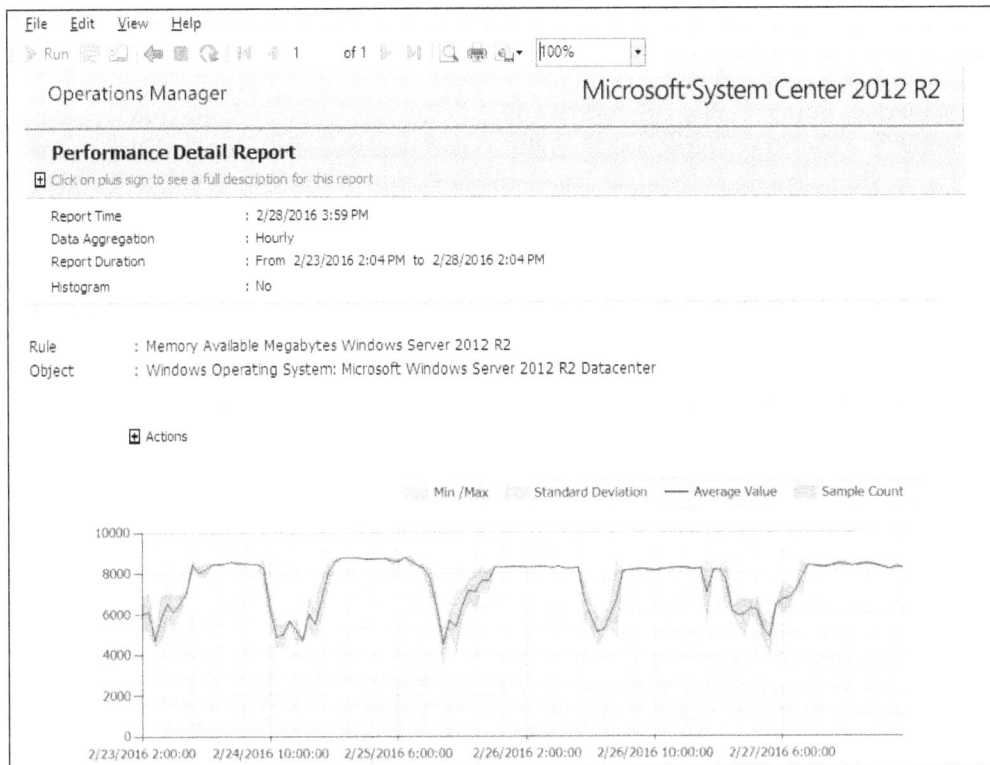

Figure 10.44: Pivoting to a linked report

If the report you are viewing has an **Actions** section, click on the plus symbol to expand and see the additional reports and console views that are available to you as shown in *Figure 10.45*.

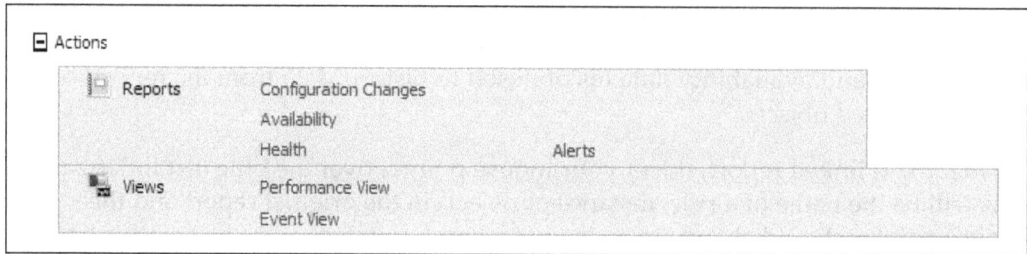

⊟ Actions			
Reports	Configuration Changes		
	Availability		
	Health	Alerts	
Views	Performance View		
	Event View		

Figure 10.45: Viewing available Actions from a report

Try clicking on any of the links the **Actions** section presents to you and you'll see how you can drill down even further for additional 'here and now' monitoring data from linked reports and views.

Use targeting to save time

A good tip to avoid blank reports is to run reports from the Monitoring workspace. Just like when views and tasks change to reflect the type of object you've selected from the Monitoring workspace, you will find that a number of contextual reports will appear in the **Tasks** pane on the right. When you run these reports, they will automatically populate with the class and object that you have selected – therefore ensuring you get valid data returned in the report.

Here's how you can run a targeted Windows Server Operating System report from the Monitoring workspace:

1. Open the Monitoring workspace, browse to and expand the **Microsoft Windows Server** management pack folder on the left, click on the **Windows Server Operating System State** view and select a monitored server from the central pane. As you can see in *Figure 10.46*, the list of reports presented changes to reflect some reports relevant to the class of the object you've selected – in our case the Windows Server Operating System class. Click on the **Windows Server 2012 R2 Operating System Performance** report to open the parameters for it.

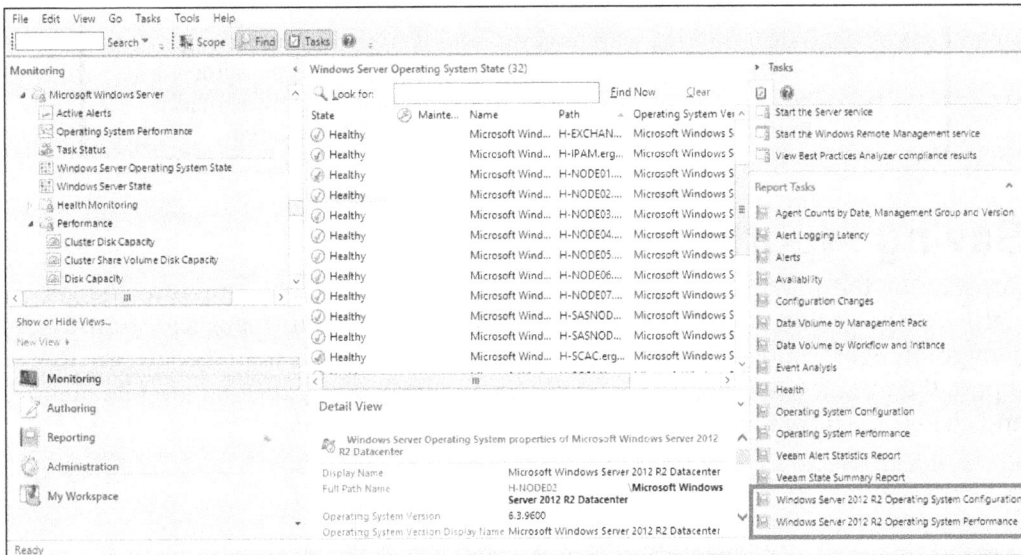

Figure 10.46: Targeted reports from the Monitoring workspace

2. Now when the report parameters section in *Figure 10.47* opens, you'll notice that the object you selected from the previous state view is automatically populated into the **Objects** pane with the correct class for the report.

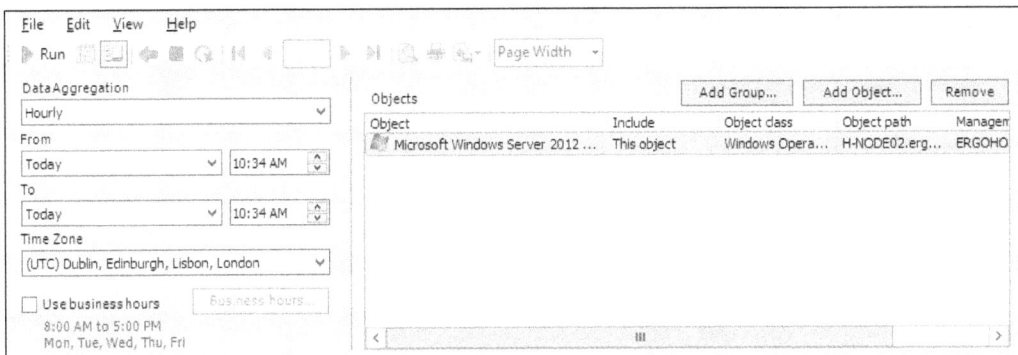

Figure 10.47: Automatically populated Objects pane from a targeted report.

3. Once here, you can modify the time range and other parameters for the report before running it. When the report runs it will then be presented in the same way as if you ran the report directly from the Reporting workspace. The only difference is that you've saved yourself a few steps by not needing to manually add objects and change filter options.

> When working with targeted reports from the Monitoring workspace, you can select multiple objects from the same view before clicking the report and this will then add those objects to the Objects pane within the report parameters area.

Saving reports

Considering the amount of time some reports might take you to configure and get right, it's a good thing that there's a handy option to save your reports for future configuration or testing. All you have to do to save a report is to first configure the report, then run it from the console. After the report has run, click on the **File** menu and choose the **Save to favorites** option as shown in *Figure 10.48*.

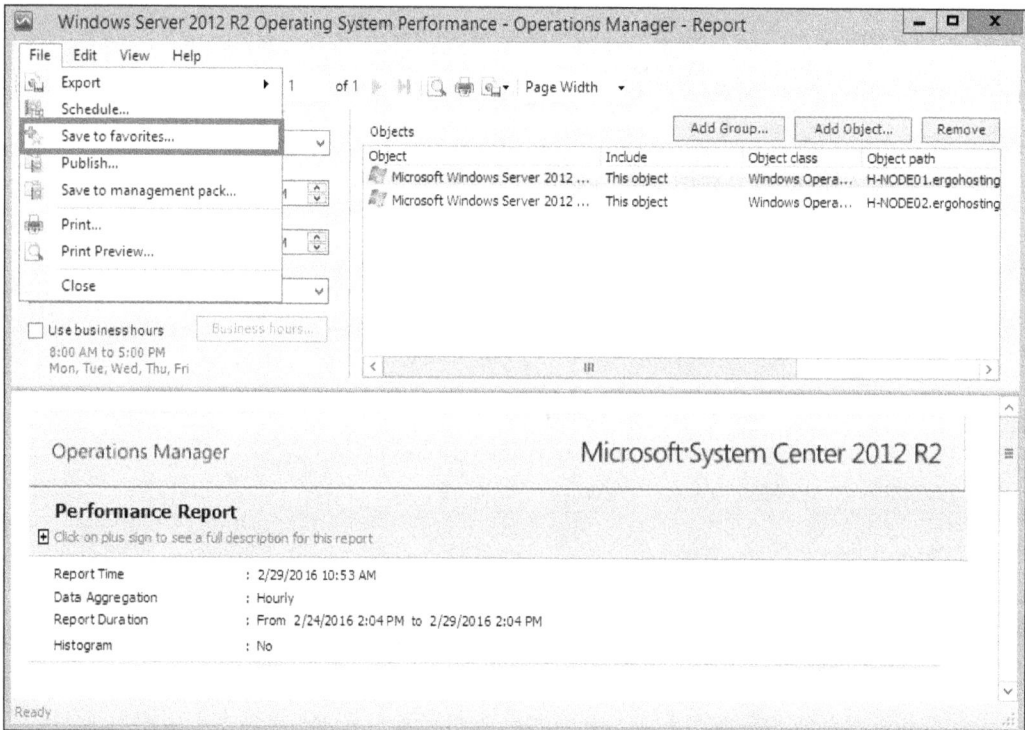

Figure 10.48: Saving a report

The saved report can now be viewed and managed from the **Favorite Reports** folder – which is located in the **Reporting** workspace and shown in *Figure 10.49*.

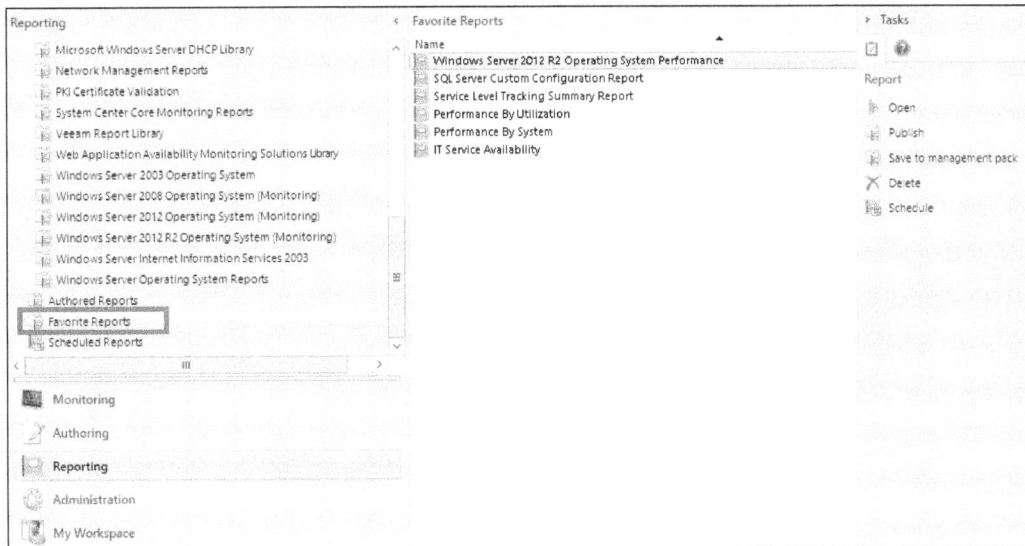

Figure 10.49: Accessing the Favorite Reports folder

> Reports saved to the Favorite Reports folder are accessible only by the user account that was used to save them there. If you wish to make a report accessible to other users, you will need to either schedule the report for delivery to them or you can publish the report to the Authored Reports folder.

Accessing reports from the Web console

A query that comes up quite a bit on the OpsMgr TechNet forums is how to access the Reporting workspace from the OpsMgr Web console. The short answer is you can't access this workspace with the Web console – even with an OpsMgr administrator account.

There is a workaround however. If you save reports to your Favorite Reports folder in the full console, the next time you open the Web console, you will find those saved reports in the **My Workspace** area under the **Favorite Reports** view similar to *Figure 10.50*.

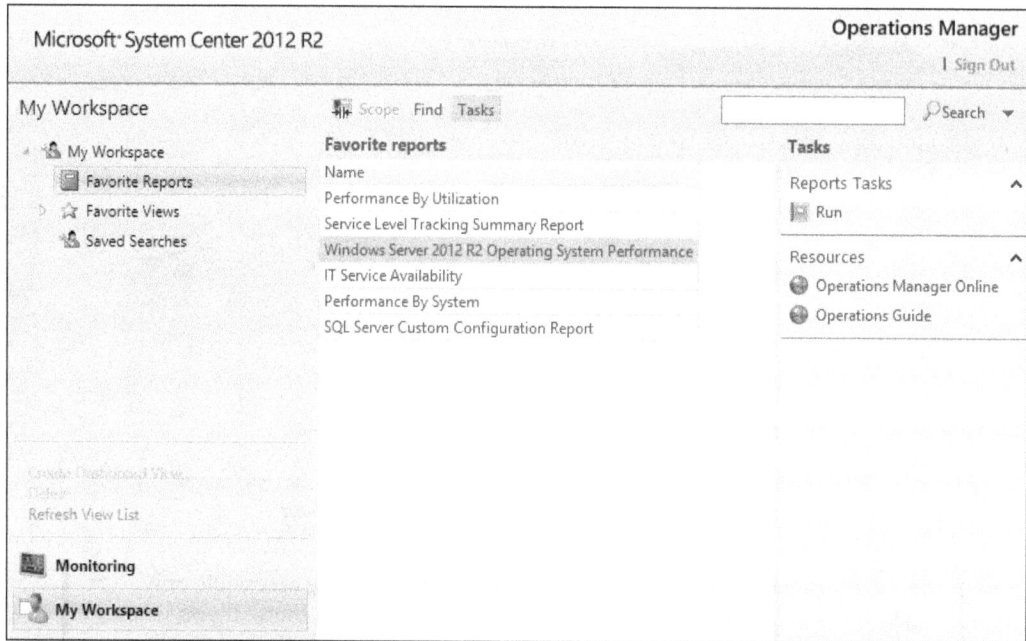

Figure 10.50: Accessing reports from the Web console

From here, you can simply select a saved report and hit the **Run** link on the right to open it. Working with reports through the Web console is limited though and you won't have the option to modify any report parameters like the Report Duration times. These changes still need to be made through the full console and saved again for them to reflect back in the Web console.

Exporting reports

When you have created the report you need and want to view it in a format other than that of the OpsMgr console, you can use the **Export** option from the **File** menu. In *Figure 10.51*, you can see the different report formats available to you and when you choose a format, you will be presented with a Save As dialog box – where you can give the exported report a name and choose a location to save it to.

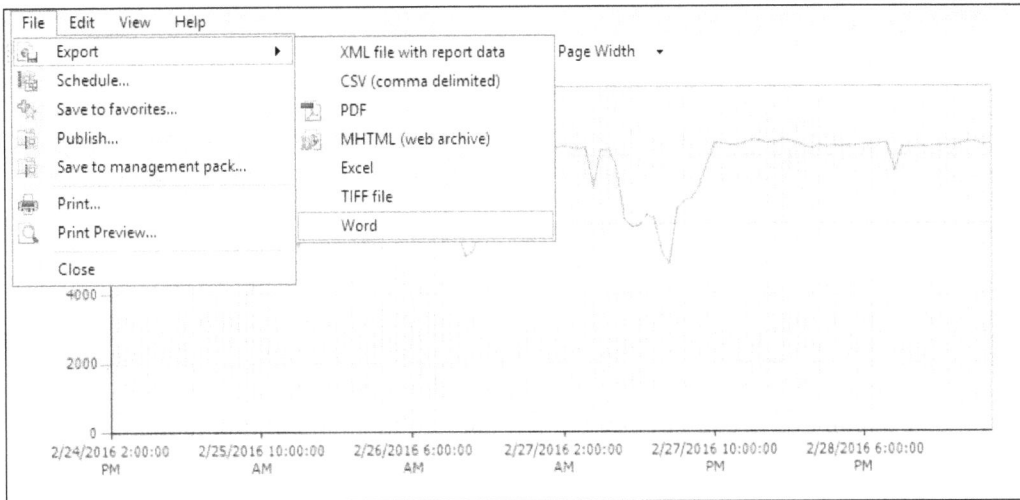

Figure 10.51: Exporting a report to a different format

> Using the Export option is a great way to get an understanding of how a report will look before you schedule it to be delivered to users via e-mail. This has proven to be a good validation point for us in the past as the PDF format doesn't always present reports the way you'd expect them to look and we can then check what it looks like as a Word or Excel file instead.

If you're using the Web console to view your saved reports, you can also export to different formats there by clicking on the **Export** button shown in *Figure 10.52*.

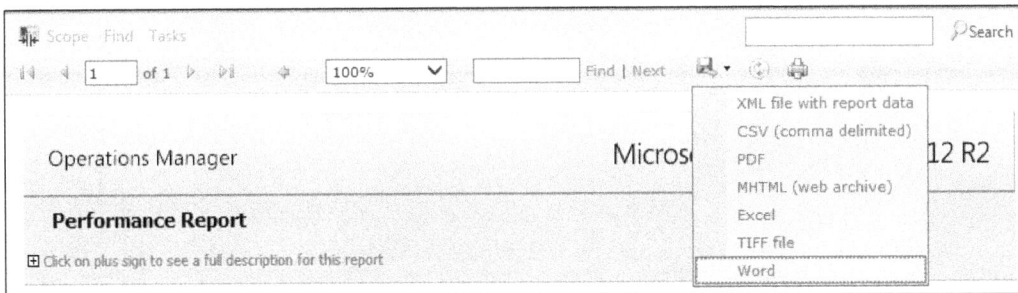

Figure 10.52: Exporting from the Web console

Scheduling reports

The advantage of using the Reporting capability of OpsMgr is that you don't need to give everyone access to the consoles so they can get a view of how the IT infrastructure is behaving. Instead we can create reports with the relevant information and then schedule them for delivery to go out to all concerned parties for consumption.

Here's all you need to do to schedule a report for delivery:

1. Run the report from the Reporting workspace in the console and ensure that it's returning the type of information that you want your users to see. When you're happy with the content of the report, click on **File** and select the **Schedule** option from the drop-down menu to launch the **Subscribe to a Report** wizard.

2. At the **Delivery Settings** dialog box (shown in *Figure 10.53*), type a name for the report into the **Description** field and select **E-Mail** from the **Delivery method** drop-down menu. For the e-mail settings, enter the e-mail addresses that should receive the report and change the other options as required. Click on **Next** to move on.

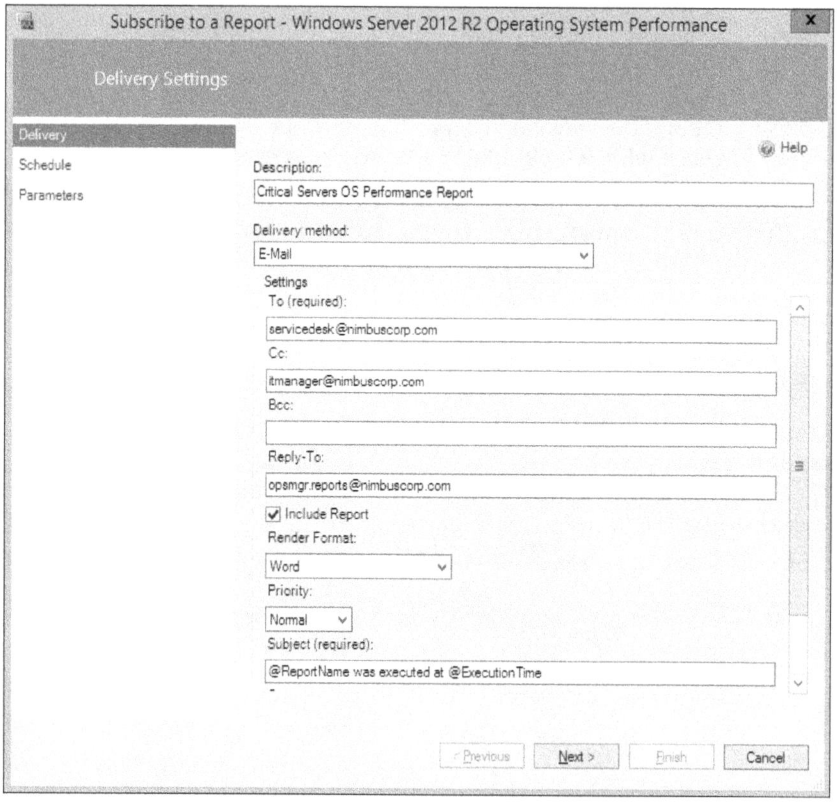

Figure 10.53: Scheduling a report

> If you don't see the **E-Mail** option from the Delivery Method menu at this point, then you'll need to go back and review the *Configuring SQL reporting services* section of this chapter and enter your e-mail settings as required.

3. At the **Schedule** dialog box, choose a schedule (once-off, hourly, daily, weekly or monthly) and an effective beginning time to use with this report subscription, then click on **Next** to continue.

4. The **Report Parameters** dialog box shown in *Figure 10.54* presents the original parameters that you specified when running the report initially and you have a choice to leave these as they are or modify them to your needs.

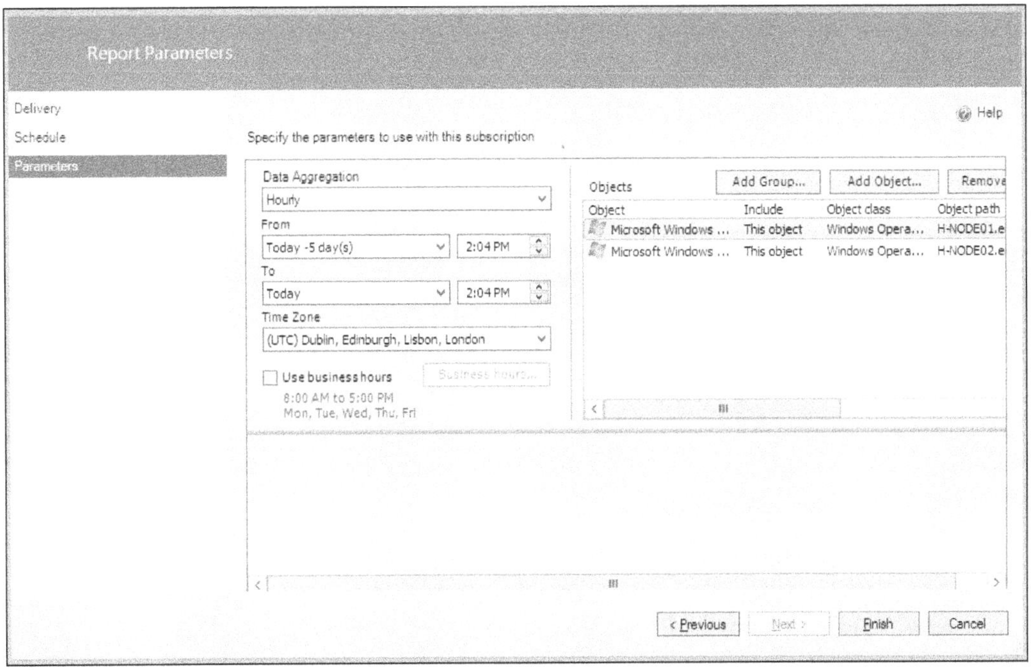

Figure 10.54: Modifying parameters for the scheduled report

5. Click on **Finish** to create the new report subscription and browse to the **Scheduled Reports** folder in the Reporting workspace to confirm the report is ready to go. In *Figure 10.55* you can see the report we've just scheduled and when you click on the report, the **Report Subscription Details** pane will give you details about the schedule and execution status. This information is useful when troubleshooting non-delivery of scheduled reports.

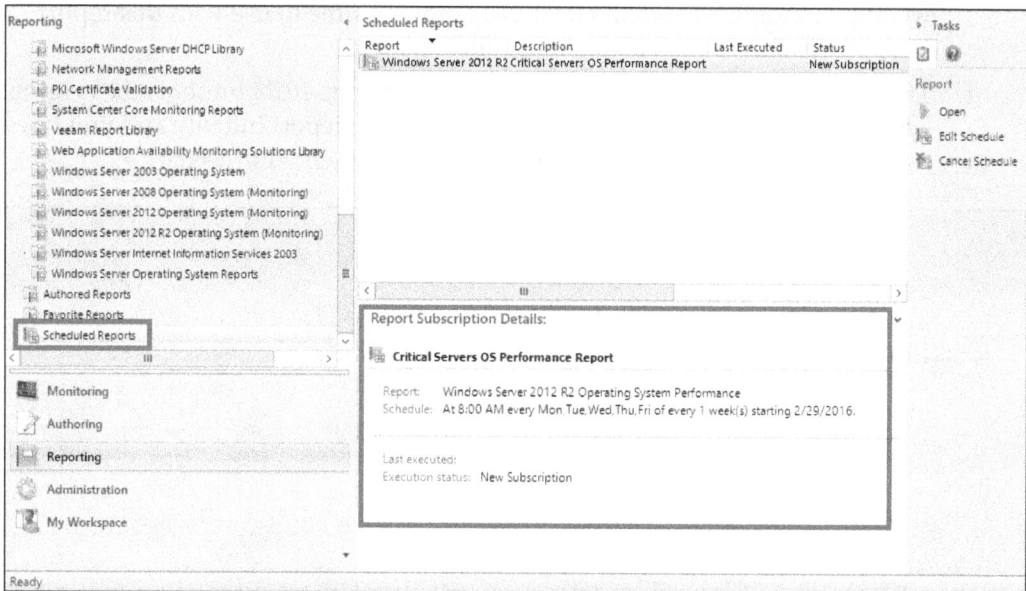

Figure 10.55: Reviewing the scheduled report subscription details

Publishing reports

If you create or modify a report in the Reporting workspace and want to make that report available to other users then there is an option to publish the report to SQL Reporting Services where you can then make it visible to everyone else.

Here's what you need to do:

1. Run the report from the Reporting workspace in the console and ensure that it's returning the type of information that you want your users to see. When you're happy with the content of the report, click on **File** and select the **Publish** option from the drop-down menu.

2. Enter a name and description for the published report and click on **OK**.

3. Browse to the **Authored Reports** folder and confirm that your published report is listed as shown in *Figure 10.56*.

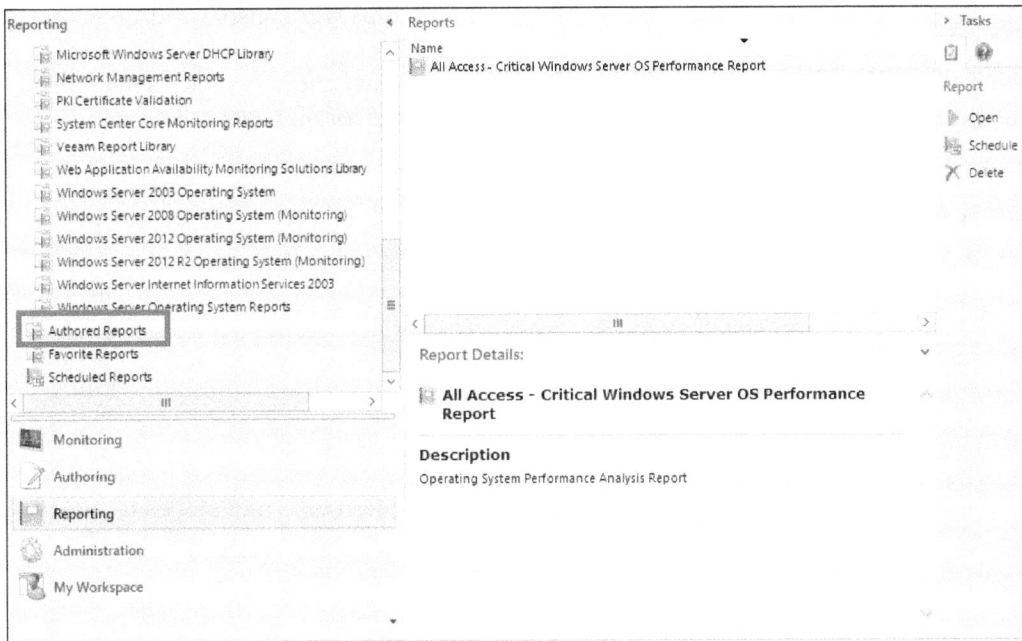

Figure 10.56: Authored reports in the console

4. Now open a web browser, browse to your SSRS Report Manager URL and from the home page, use the **New Folder** button to create a new folder named OpsMgr Authored Reports.

5. Back at the Home page, click on the **My Reports** folder to open it and you should see the report that you published earlier in OpsMgr similar to *Figure 10.57*.

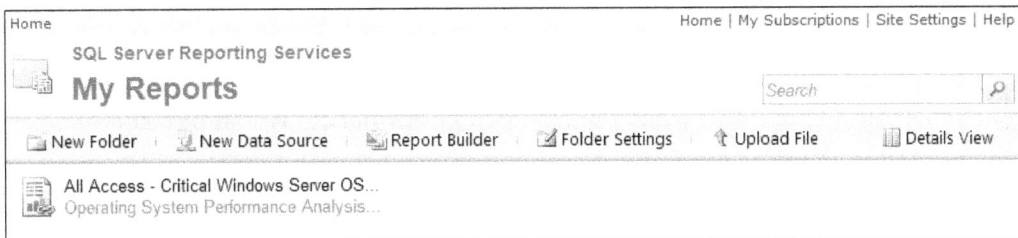

Figure 10.57: Viewing your published report in SSRS

6. Move your mouse pointer over the report and then click on the arrow to show the drop-down menu. From there, select the **Move** option, choose the newly created **OpsMgr Authored Reports** folder as the move location and click on **OK** to move the published report.

7. Open the **Reporting** workspace again in the OpsMgr console and hit *F5* on your keyboard to refresh the list of report folders. You should now see the new **OpsMgr Authored Reports** folder in the list and when you select this folder, you'll see the published report available for all users as shown in *Figure 10.58*.

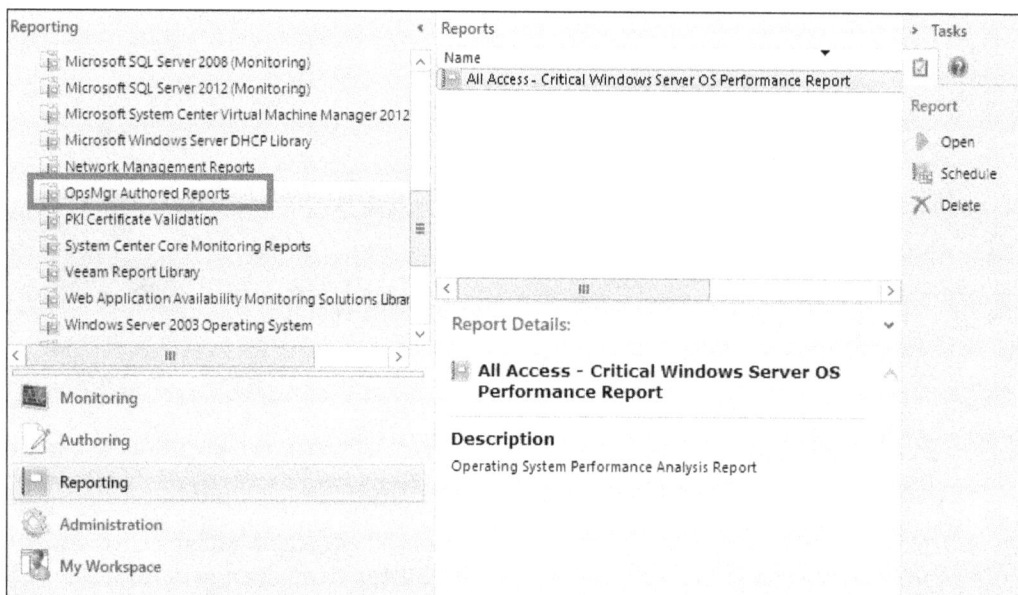

Figure 10.58: Making authored reports available to all users

Useful Microsoft reports

Understanding the right report for the job makes all the difference when you're under pressure from the business to produce historical information about the systems you monitor and in this section we discuss some standard Microsoft reports that you should find useful when reporting on performance, availability and SLA's.

Windows Server Operating System Reports

When you deploy the Windows Server Core OS management packs, you get a large number of pre-built reports that are designed to return information on things like Memory, Disk, CPU and operating system configuration.

The parent report we ran earlier in the *Running reports* section of this chapter is just one example of these type of reports but if you're looking for something with more of a visual summary, then it's worth checking out the **Performance By System** and **Performance By Utilization** reports shown in *Figure 10.59*.

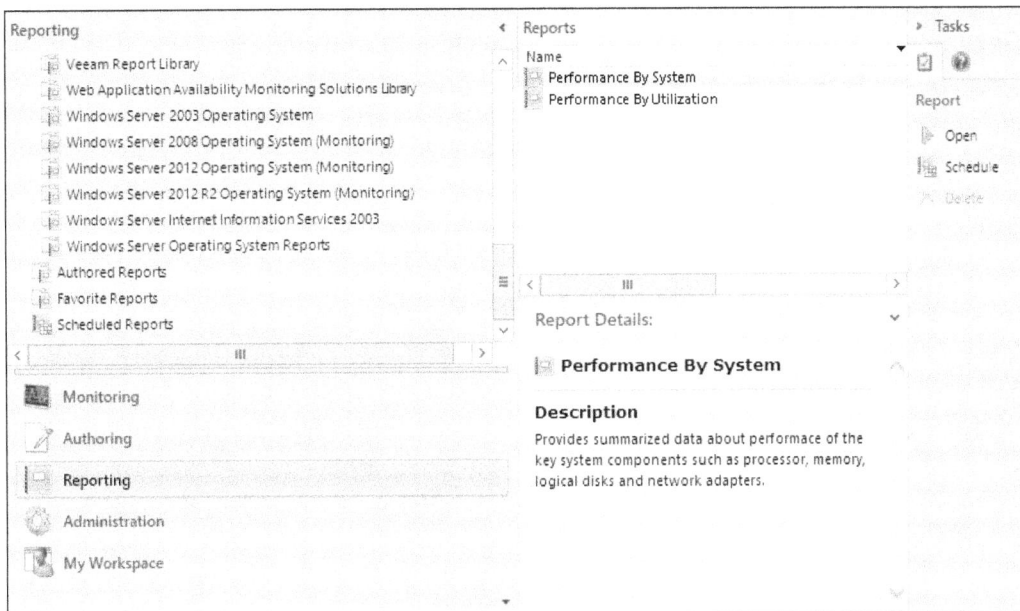

Figure 10.59: Windows Server performance reports

The Performance by System report shown in *Figure 10.60* allows you to see performance data based on key performance indicator resources for individual or multiple servers.

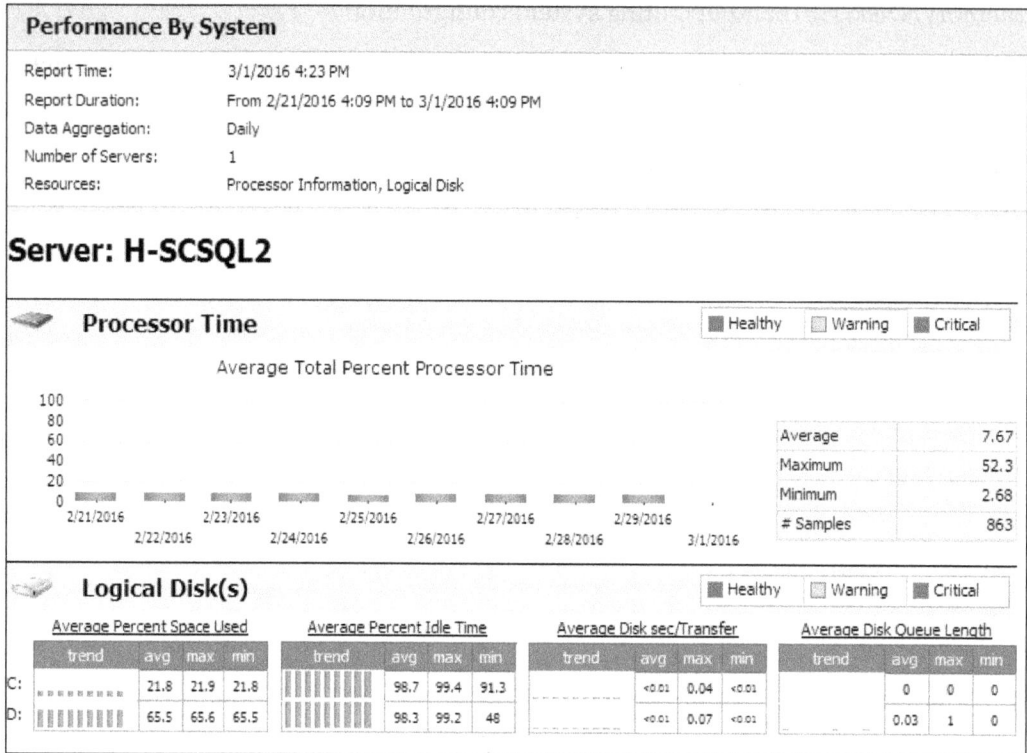

Performance By System

Report Time:	3/1/2016 4:23 PM
Report Duration:	From 2/21/2016 4:09 PM to 3/1/2016 4:09 PM
Data Aggregation:	Daily
Number of Servers:	1
Resources:	Processor Information, Logical Disk

Server: H-SCSQL2

Processor Time   ■ Healthy ☐ Warning ■ Critical

Average Total Percent Processor Time

Average	7.67
Maximum	52.3
Minimum	2.68
# Samples	863

2/21/2016 2/22/2016 2/23/2016 2/24/2016 2/25/2016 2/26/2016 2/27/2016 2/28/2016 2/29/2016 3/1/2016

Logical Disk(s)   ■ Healthy ☐ Warning ■ Critical

	Average Percent Space Used				Average Percent Idle Time				Average Disk sec/Transfer				Average Disk Queue Length			
	trend	avg	max	min	trend	avg	max	min	trend	avg	max	min	trend	avg	max	min
C:		21.8	21.9	21.8		98.7	99.4	91.3		<0.01	0.04	<0.01		0	0	0
D:		65.5	65.6	65.5		98.3	99.2	48		<0.01	0.07	<0.01		0.03	1	0

Figure 10.60: Performance by System report

If you want an overall summary of the top performing (or underperforming) servers in your environment, then the **Performance By Utilization** report shown in *Figure 10.61* should do the trick.

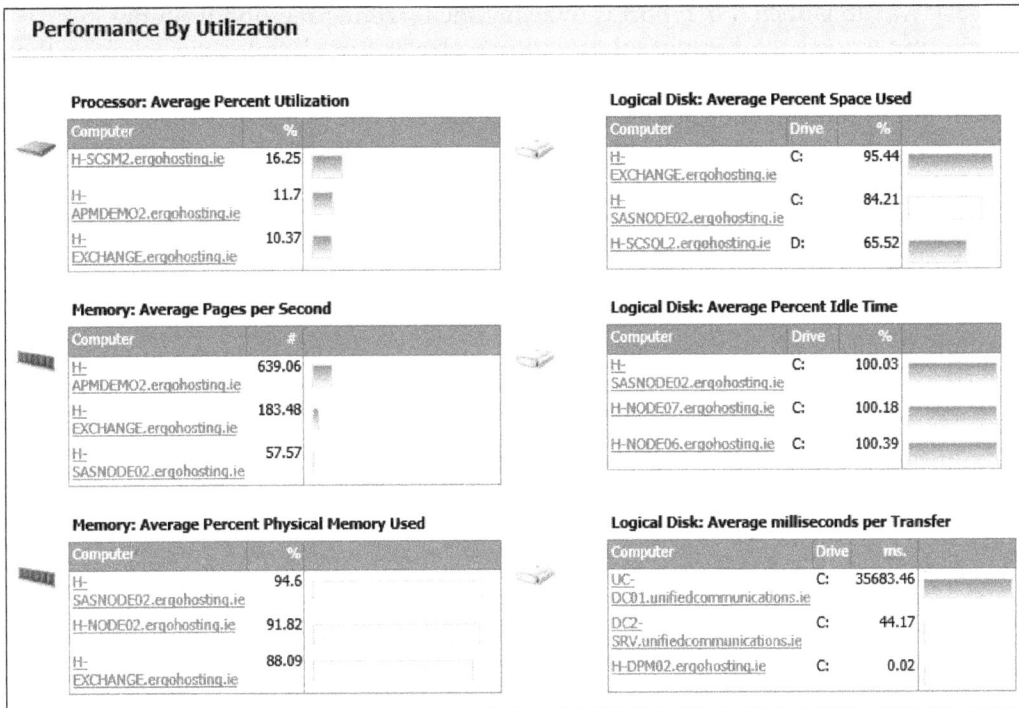

Figure 10.61: Performance by Utilization report

Availability reports

One of the most simplistic and top requested reports that OpsMgr has to offer is the Availability report. This report does exactly what it says on the tin – it reports on the availability of monitored objects.

An easy way to launch this report is by using the targeting method from the Monitoring workspace. Simply select multiple objects from a state view, click on the **Availability** link from the Report Tasks pane, configure a timeframe and run the report. The end result should look something like the one in *Figure 10.62*.

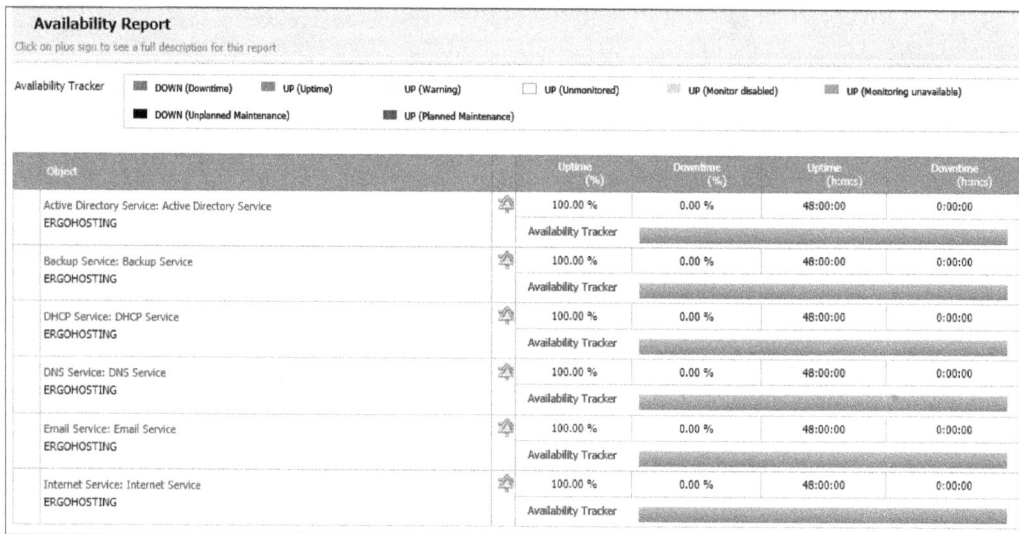

Figure 10.62: Availability report

SLA reports

In the *Creating service level objectives* section of *Chapter 7, Configuring Service Models with Distributed Applications* you learnt how to create SLA's and associate them with monitored objects. If you need to report on these SLA's, then the **Service Level Tracking Summary** report will meet this requirement. You can find this report in the Reporting workspace under the **Microsoft Service Level Report Library** folder and when targeted at multiple SLA's, it should look similar to the example in *Figure 10.63*.

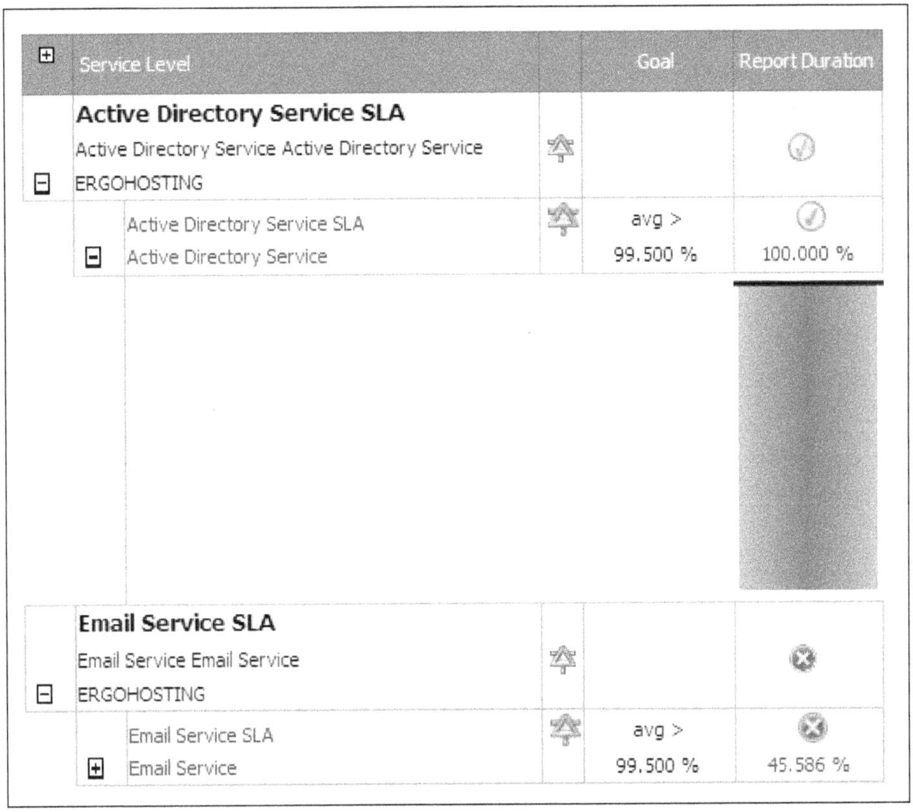

Figure 10.63: Service Level Tracking report

Community reports

If you find that the reports that come out of the box with OpsMgr and the Microsoft management packs are lacking in what you need, then you only need to look to the community for some handy free reports to add to your arsenal. In this section we'll point you in the direction of these community resources to help enhance your reporting experience.

Veeam report library for System Center

The first free community reports example that you can check out is the Veeam Report Library for System Center (`https://www.veeam.com/report-library-system-center.html`). This library of reports extends the idea of the built-in Generic Report Library and contains report templates for alerting, performance and health state. *Figure 10.64* shows the **Alert History** report that's been targeted at the All Windows Computer group in our environment.

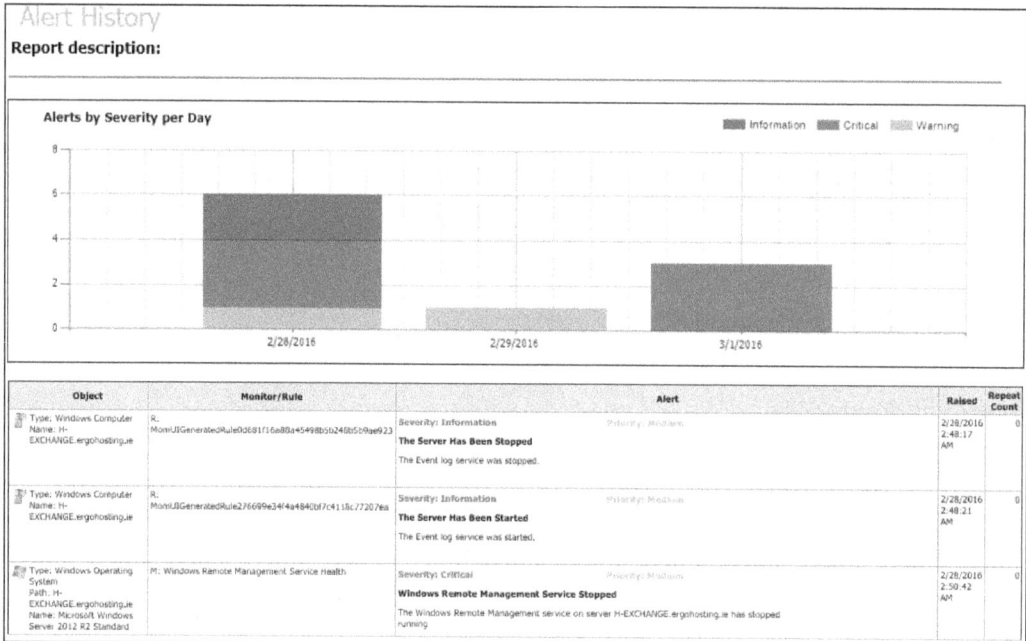

Figure 10.64: Veeam Alert History report

SCOM Health Check Reports V3

A few years back two well-known community contributors and OpsMgr ninja's (Oskar Landman and Pete Zerger) released a set of reports that gave you the ability to perform health checks of your OpsMgr environment and their latest V3 update now contains over twenty-five of them to choose from (shown in *Figure 10.65*).

Figure 10.65: List of reports available in the Health Check Reports library

We totally recommend deploying these reports to your management group and you can get a detailed explanation of these reports along with a download link from System Center Central at `http://www.systemcentercentral.com/scom-health-check-reports-v3`.

Summary

In this chapter, we covered a lot of content about alerting and reporting in OpsMgr. At the start, we discussed how to configure the various channel options for notifications and then demonstrated how to create new subscribers and subscriptions to forward alerts to.

We also showed you some options on testing your subscriptions along with demonstrating some handy tools to help manage those subscriptions on an ongoing basis.

The second half of the chapter discussed the Reporting feature and we walked you through how to run a basic report as well as giving you some tips and tricks on targeting to minimize troublesome blank reports.

You learnt how to save, export, schedule and publish reports and we demonstrated a little-known method of accessing saved reports through the Web console. We closed out the chapter by discussing some useful Microsoft and community reports that should give you even more options for gathering historical and health check data.

In the next chapter, we will discuss how to best backup, maintain and troubleshoot your OpsMgr environment.

11
Backing Up, Maintenance and Troubleshooting

If you are going to invest a lot of time into designing, deploying and administering OpsMgr, then understanding how to back it up, perform general maintenance tasks and troubleshoot when you have a problem are important skills to learn.

Backing up the OpsMgr SQL databases will form the backbone of any backup plan you implement but ensuring you have the option to easily backup and restore your unsealed management packs and **SQL Server Reporting Services** (**SSRS**) instances is something you will really appreciate in times of trouble.

When carrying out maintenance on your monitored agents, you will need to gain an understanding of how to initiate and manage the Maintenance Mode feature in OpsMgr and for the management servers; you'll also want to ensure the backend SQL databases are groomed and running optimally.

Successfully troubleshooting problems, knowing how to work with SQL queries, console views, reports, events, and even some support tools from the installation media become essential to your overall administration role.

In this chapter, we'll walk you through these different scenarios starting with some examples on how to backup and recover your OpsMgr environment. We'll then give you some pointers for performing maintenance on your agents and management servers. Towards the end of the chapter, you'll learn some tips and tricks on how to troubleshoot some common problems should they arise.

Here's a high-level overview of what you will learn:

- Backing up OpsMgr
- Enabling Maintenance Mode for agents
- Performing maintenance tasks on management servers
- Troubleshooting common problems

Backing up and recovering OpsMgr

Before you dive straight in backing up OpsMgr, you will need to create a plan that lists the components you wish to backup along with a schedule of when you need to execute those backup jobs.

Depending on the organization, your backup plan may also need to include detailed information on which teams have responsibility for backing up the relevant OpsMgr components along with documentation about the applications used to perform the backups. For example, in large organizations, responsibility for backing up the databases may lie with a dedicated SQL team; while backing up the unsealed management packs and virtual machines might be a job for a dedicated backup team. In smaller environments, the OpsMgr administrator will most likely have responsibility for backing up the entire environment and the backup plan will become less defined.

On customer projects, we typically use information from the following table to help design a backup plan and schedule for the OpsMgr databases:

Component to Backup	Data Description	Backup Frequency
Operational database (OperationsManager)	The most important database in the OpsMgr infrastructure. If you lose this database, you will need to reinstall the entire management group.	Daily
Data warehouse database (OperationsManagerDW)	Contains all your long-term reporting data. Losing this would result in the loss of all your historical reports and operational data but the management group would still be available.	Daily

Component to Backup	Data Description	Backup Frequency
Reporting database (ReportServer)	This database contains your report definitions and report subscription information. If you lost this, then you would need to manually reimport your reports and recreate the subscriptions. The overall management group will still be available if this goes down.	Daily or weekly. This frequency can be reviewed depending on how many times you modify or add reports to OpsMgr.
Audit database (OperationsManagerAC)	This database will only be available if you've deployed the **Audit Collection Services (ACS)** feature and if you lose it, then ACS will not be available but the management group will remain available.	Daily
Master database (Master)	Important system database for the SQL instance that OpsMgr runs in. Contains system information data specific to the SQL instance.	Daily
Msdb database (Msdb)	Important system database for the SQL instance that OpsMgr runs in. Contains data on all scheduled SQL jobs for the specific instance.	Daily or weekly. This frequency can be reviewed depending on how many times you modify or add scheduled SQL jobs to the SQL instance.

While working out the best time of day or night to run backups on your OpsMgr SQL databases, keep in mind that OpsMgr performs its own partitioning and grooming task at 12:00 am every night and its best to ensure your backups aren't running at this time. You can read more about this task in the *Database grooming and maintenance* section of this chapter.

For the management pack library, important files and virtual machines, we normally refer to this table as part of our backup plan:

Component to Backup	Data Description	Backup Frequency
Unsealed management packs	These unsealed management packs contain all the customizations that you've made in the management group. Having these backed up regularly will enable you to perform granular restores of specific management packs instead of having to recover the entire Operational database.	Daily
Sealed management packs and other important files	Having a backup of the sealed management packs that you've imported into OpsMgr is useful when you need to roll back to an earlier version or when you want to migrate to another management group. You can also include the SSRS encryption key and any other important files that you might need here.	Weekly or monthly. These files won't change much and you can review the frequency of this backup depending on your requirements.
OpsMgr virtual machines	If OpsMgr is running on a virtual platform (Hyper-V or VMware for example), then having a regular host-level backup of these virtual machines in their entirety will massively expedite recovery in the event of a disaster.	Daily or weekly. This frequency can be reviewed depending on the **recovery point objective** (**RPO**) and **recovery time objectives** (**RTO**) required by the organization.

Backing up the databases with SQL

Although most enterprise organizations will use a dedicated backup application, such as System Center **Data Protection Manager** (**DPM**), Commvault or Tivoli, an alternative and easy method for smaller businesses to back up the OpsMgr databases is to use the built-in backup feature of SQL.

Understanding how to use SQL to backup your databases is a useful skill as there may be times when you need to make some changes and you want to quickly carry out a full backup without having to mess around with the corporate backup application.

Here's what you need to do to backup your OpsMgr databases using SQL:

1. Launch SQL Management Studio and using an account with sysadmin, db_ owner or db_backupoperator permissions, connect to the instance that hosts your OpsMgr databases.

2. Expand the **Databases** view, right-click on the **OperationsManager** database, select **Tasks**, then click on the **Back Up...** option as shown in *Figure 11.1*.

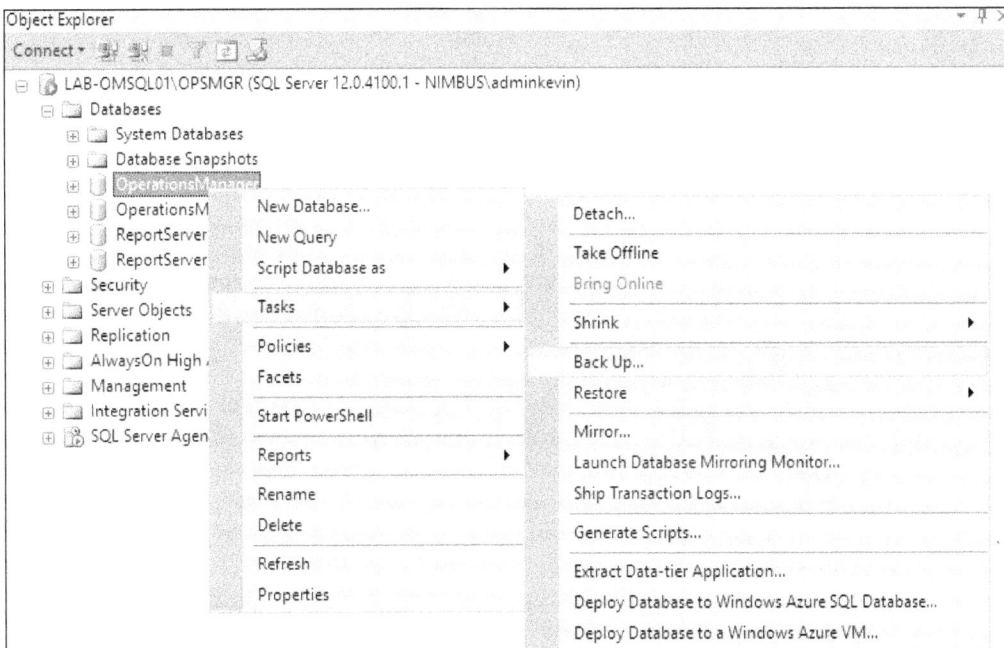

Figure 11.1: Backing up a database with SQL Backup

3. When the **Backup Database** dialog box opens, you'll notice that the backup type is set to **Full** by default. This type of backup means that the database file is backed up in its entirety every time the backup job runs – as opposed to just incrementally backing up changes in the database since the last job. This type of backup job also ignores truncating any transaction logs when the database recovery model is not set to **Simple**. At the **Destination** section you can choose from either a **Disk** or **Tape** option as the location to store the backup (the **Tape** option will only be available if the SQL server can see an attached tape backup device). Select the **Disk** option for this example and click on the **Add** button to specify a backup destination for the files.

> After you install OpsMgr, the default Recovery Model for the databases will always be set to Simple. With a Simple recovery model, database restores are much easier as transactions aren't logged and recoveries are only applicable from the last full backup. In scenarios where you're using a high availability solution, such as SQL AlwaysOn for your OpsMgr databases, the recovery model will be configured as Full. With this type of recovery model, you should be mindful when configuring your backup applications as you will need to choose a job type that will back up the transaction logs as well as the databases – otherwise you'll find yourself quickly running out of disk space due to the transaction logs not being truncated.

4. At the **Select Backup Destination** dialog box you'll be presented with a default path that will be a sub-folder of the directory where the OpsMgr instance is stored. Here, you'll need to click on the ellipses (**...**) button to open the **Locate Database Files** dialog box where you then have an option to either stick with the suggested path or choose another location to store the files. Wherever you decide to store the files (we've selected a custom location of D:\SQL Backups), you must specify a name for the new backup file in the **File name** field. As shown in *Figure 11.2*, this file name must end with a .bak extension.

Figure 11.2: Naming the SQL backup file

5. Click on **OK** twice to close the two dialog boxes and return to the **Back Up Database** dialog box. From here, select the **Media Options** link from the navigation bar and choose your options. We'll select the **Overwrite all existing backup sets** option and leave the rest at their default settings as shown in *Figure 11.3*.

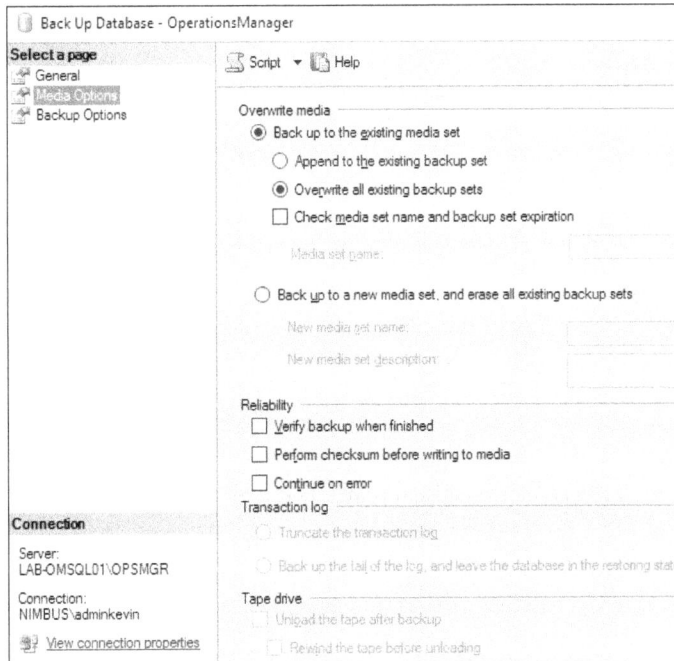

Figure 11.3: Selecting backup options

6. Now click on the drop-down arrow beside the **Script** button and select the **Script Action to Job** option as shown in *Figure 11.4*.

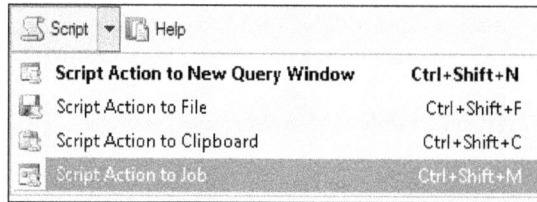

Figure 11.4: Scripting the backup as a SQL Agent job

7. At the **New Job** dialog box, give the backup job a name and description then click on the **Schedules** link from the navigation bar.

8. Hit the **New** button to open the **New Job Schedule** dialog box shown in *Figure 11.5* and configure the schedule settings for this backup job - we'll select a daily backup schedule kicking off at 04:00 AM to avoid any unnecessary performance hits. Click on **OK** when you're finished configuring the schedule.

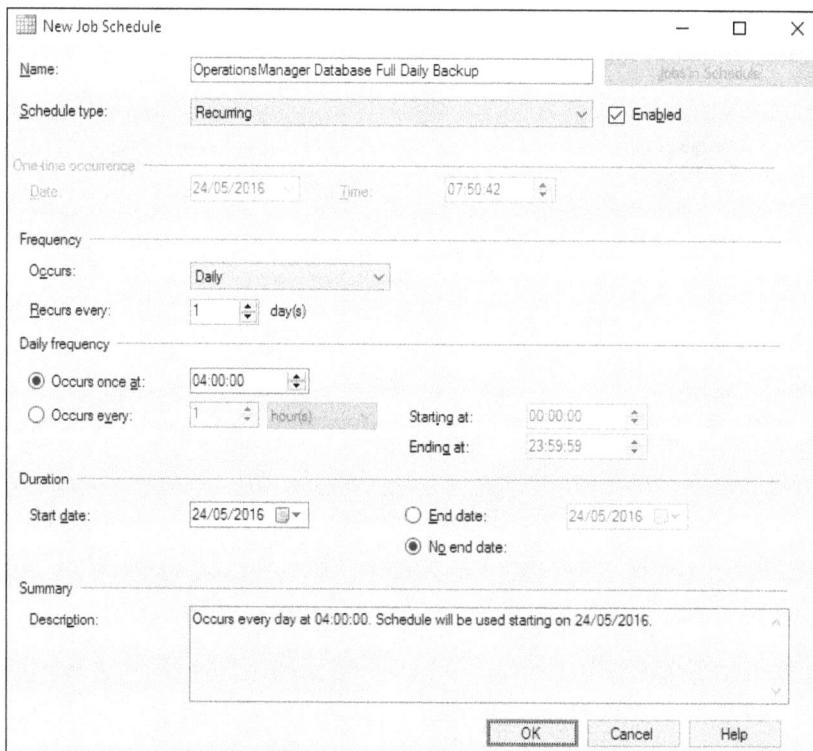

Figure 11.5: Creating the SQL backup job schedule

9. At the **New Job** dialog box you have an option to send notifications based on failed or successful backup jobs and when you're ready to finalize the backup job creation, click on **OK** to close.

10. From the **Back Up Database** dialog box, click on **OK** once more and the backup job will run using the settings you've configured. You'll be presented with a pop-up message when the backup job completes successfully.

11. Repeat this process for the other OpsMgr databases that you've included in your backup plan and if you need to modify or delete any of these jobs in the future, then you can access them from the **Jobs** folder under the **SQL Server Agent** view shown in *Figure 11.6*.

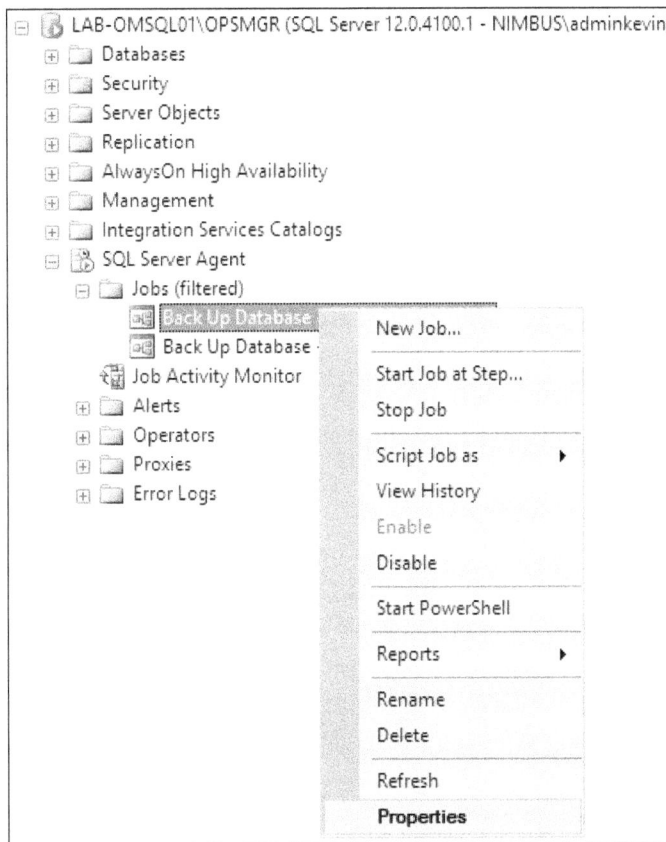

Figure 11.6: Viewing or modifying SQL Server Agent backup jobs

Backing up unsealed management packs

As you learned in *Chapter 5, Working with Management Packs*, unsealed management packs contain all of the overrides, dashboards, rules, monitors and other customizations that have been applied to the OpsMgr management group. After the SQL databases, these management packs should take priority as the next most-important components to backup.

If you've followed best practice recommendations and created an unsealed management pack to store overrides in for every sealed management pack that you've deployed, then you're ultimately going to end up with a large number of files to manage as part of your unsealed management pack backup plan. Also, as each unsealed management pack is stored within the Operational database, you'll need to work out how best to export all of them to a central location in .XML file format, which can then be backed up using your backup application.

Having the unsealed management packs available individually will avoid the need to restore the whole database when you need to roll back to an earlier version of overrides or customizations. The caveat is however, that exporting them from the database every day (either individually or with PowerShell) is an administration task that you could do without and having a solution that will do this automatically for you will make things much easier in the long run.

One option to meet this requirement is the free Unsealed MP Backup for OpsMgr management pack that has been authored by some well-known System Center community members and can be downloaded here - `http://tinyurl.com/ opsmgrbackupmp`

After importing this management pack, you will find a new rule (disabled by default) that's targeted at the Root Management Server Emulator role and as you can see in *Figure 11.7*, there are a few options to modify - including things like backup location, number of days to retain copies and frequency.

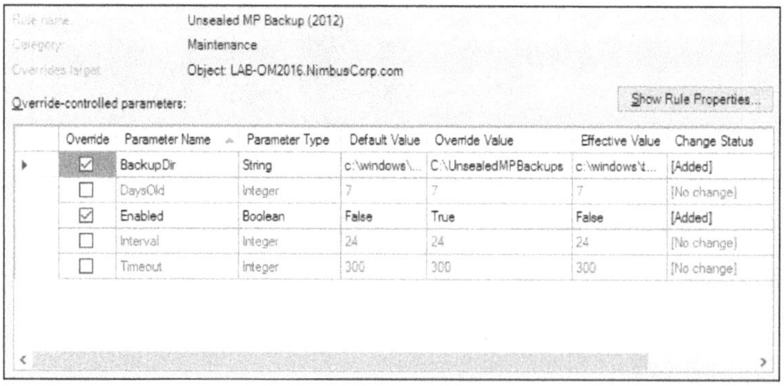

Figure 11.7: Configuring the Unsealed MP Backup management pack

As is always the case, make sure to read the associated management pack guide and follow the instructions to configure the Run As Profile with an account that has the Operations Manager Administrators role assigned to it.

> If you don't configure the Run As Profile for the Unsealed MP Backup management pack, the export won't work and you'll end up with empty folders and no exported management packs.

When this rule runs each day, you can then point your corporate backup application at the directory that contains the exported unsealed management packs and include it in your daily backup plan.

Backing up other important OpsMgr files

Along with the databases and unsealed management packs, you'll need to periodically backup the SSRS encryption key and also your sealed management pack library to ensure you have everything you require should you ever need to perform a restore or migration of OpsMgr.

In the **Configuring SQL Reporting Services** section of *Chapter 10, Creating Alert Subscriptions and Reports* we discussed how to backup the SSRS encryption key and the location you've saved this key to will need to be added to your corporate backup application sets along with the central storage location for your sealed management pack library (as mentioned in *Chapter 5, Working with Management Packs*).

Recovering the OpsMgr databases

In the rare event that you might lose one or both of your OpsMgr databases (possibly due to corruption) and assuming the SQL server instance is still up and running, the recovery process is pretty straight-forward. The backup application you used to back up the databases should be the same application that you use to recover them.

As we used SQL in our earlier example to back up the databases, we'll now use it to perform a recovery. Here's what you need to do:

1. Logon to each of your management servers, close all open console connections and then stop the System Center Data Access Service to ensure nothing attempts to write to the database.

2. Now launch SQL Management Studio using an account with sysadmin, db_owner or db_backupoperator permissions and connect to the instance that hosts your OpsMgr databases.

3. Before you can perform a recovery, you need to delete the existing corrupt database and to do this, right-click on the database and click on **Delete**. This will open the **Delete Object** dialog box and you'll need to uncheck the **Delete backup and restore history information for databases** option as shown in *Figure 11.8*. When you've unchecked the option, click on **OK** to delete the database.

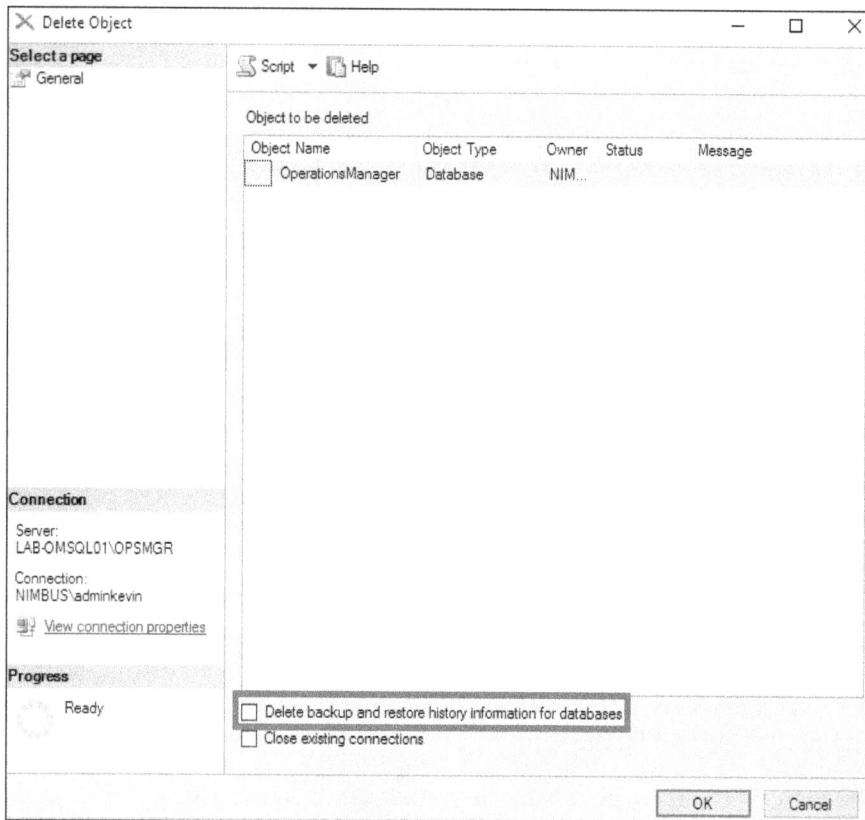

Figure 11.8: Deleting the original database before a restore

4. When the dialog box closes you will be returned to the object explorer for your SQL instance and here you need to right-click on the **Databases** folder and choose the **Restore Database** option from the resulting menu.

5. At the **Restore Database** dialog box shown in *Figure 11.9*, choose **Database** as the source, select the name of the database you wish to restore from the drop-down menu and use the **Timeline** button to choose the date and time of the backup you wish to restore. Click on **OK** to begin the restore.

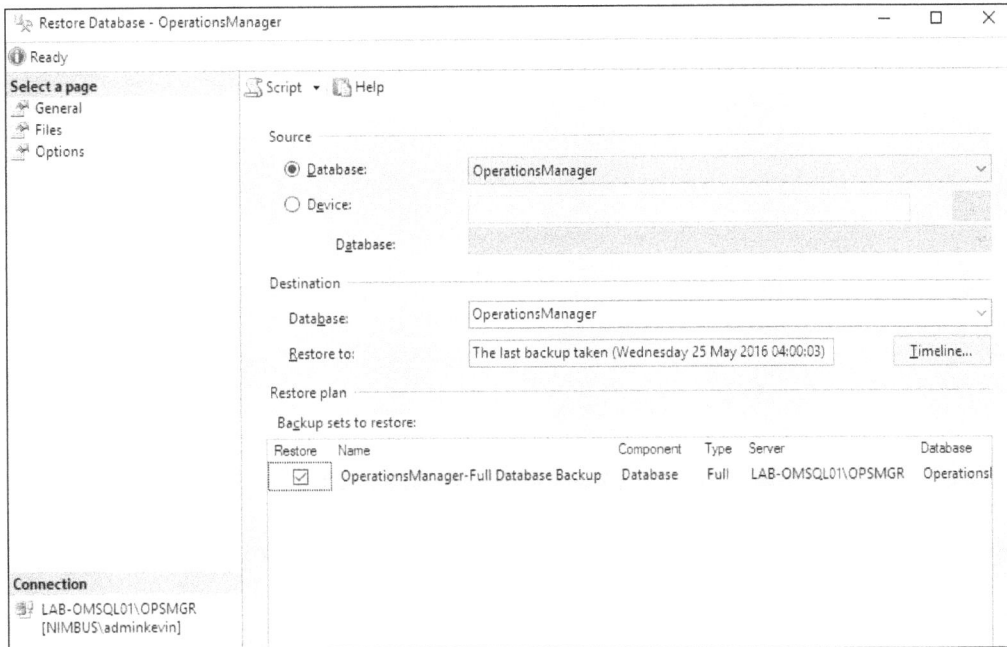

Figure 11.9: Restoring a database using SQL

6. When the database restore is complete, log back on to your management servers and restart the **System Center Data Access Service**. Once the service has restarted, open the console and ensure the management group comes back online and that everything is in working order again.

> Where possible, it's always a good idea to restore both the Operational database and the Data Warehouse database so as to ensure there are no data synchronization issues as a result of one database being older than the other.

If you find that using SQL is a little convoluted and you'd like something a bit more seamless, then other SQL-aware backup applications, such as System Center

DPM have easy-to-follow recovery wizards that will get you back up and running in no time. *Figure 11.10* has an example of some of the database recovery options you get when using DPM - including options to recover the database to its original SQL instance by overwriting the existing database or to recover to a different SQL server instead.

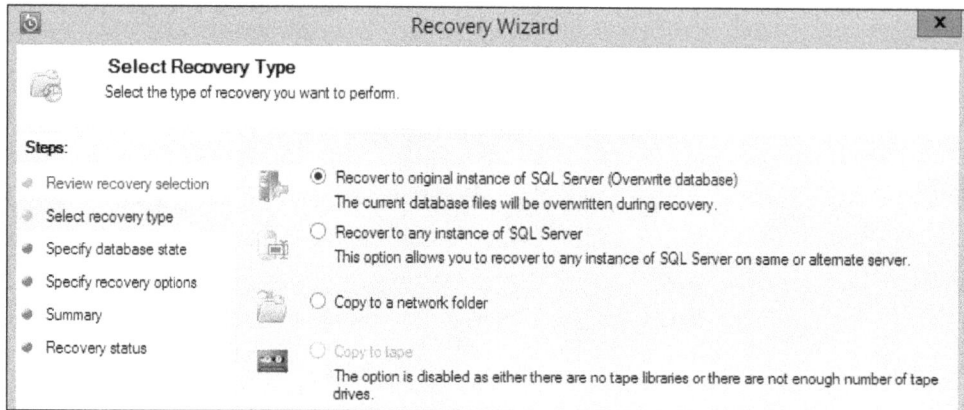

Figure 11.10: Using System Center DPM to recover a SQL database

If you find yourself in a situation where you need to recover or migrate the OpsMgr databases to a different server or SQL instance, then there's a good bit more involved and you can get a full walkthrough of the process for the Operational database here - `http://tinyurl.com/opsmgrdbmove`. To recover or migrate the Data Warehouse database, then check out the information in this link - `http://tinyurl.com/opsmgrdwmove`

Working with Maintenance Mode

Most organizations put some time aside each week, month, or quarter to carry out essential patching and maintenance on their servers to help avoid outages or unauthorized entry. Inevitably, those servers will need to be rebooted at the end of each maintenance cycle before coming back into production. To reduce unnecessary alert noise from monitored servers during these maintenance windows, OpsMgr has a handy feature called Maintenance Mode that you can enable.

When Maintenance Mode is enabled on an agent, all monitoring is disabled for a specified amount of time, thus alleviating noisy alerts related to patching and reboots. The agent will then automatically bring itself out of Maintenance Mode once the specified time is reached.

The Maintenance Mode feature isn't just exclusive to agents and it can actually be enabled against any monitored object that OpsMgr knows about. As an example, you might have a Hyper-V host or physical switch with a faulty network interface that keeps firing false-positive alerts into OpsMgr. You want to stop monitoring the interface until it has been replaced but you don't want to stop monitoring the entire host or switch. All you need to do is enable Maintenance Mode on that specific interface and you won't receive any more alerts until you're ready to bring it back online again.

> It's never recommended to place your management servers into Maintenance Mode. The reason for this is that there's a chance the workflow responsible for bringing the server out of maintenance won't fire and that server will then just stay in Maintenance Mode until you manually remove it!

Manually enabling Maintenance Mode

Working with Maintenance Mode is pretty simple and here's how you can manually enable it using the console:

1. From the Monitoring workspace, open the **Windows Computers** state view, right-click on the name of a computer, select **Maintenance Mode** from the menu, and click on the **Start Maintenance Mode...** option as shown in *Figure 11.11*.

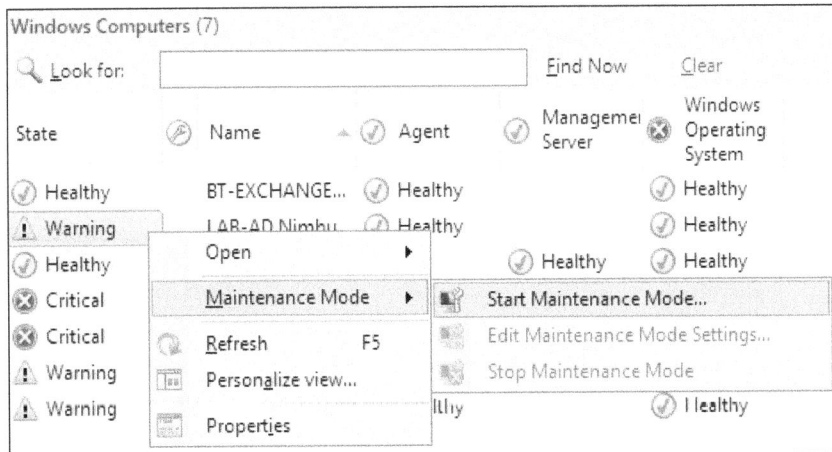

Figure 11.11: Starting Maintenance Mode on a monitored object

> A diagram view is another good place to launch Maintenance Mode from as you get a hierarchical overview of all the components a monitored object contains and this visual makes it easier to understand what exactly goes into a 'Not monitored' state.

2. At the **Maintenance Mode Settings** dialog box, first choose whether or not you want to put the selected object on its own or the selected object and all its contained objects under maintenance. Choose a category and type a comment before then selecting the duration in minutes or a specific end date and time for your maintenance window as shown in *Figure 11.12*. Click on **OK** to save the settings and enable Maintenance Mode.

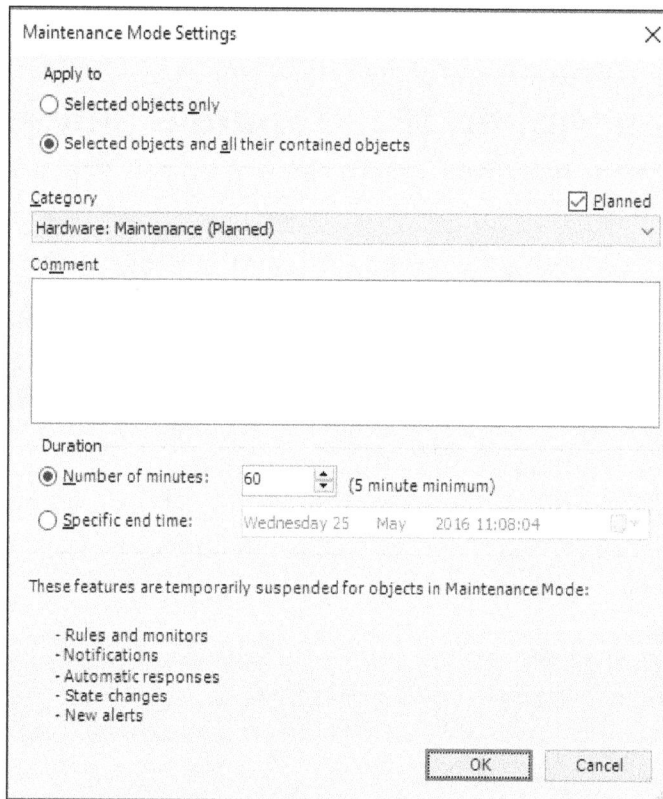

Maintenance Mode Settings   ✕

Apply to

○ Selected objects <u>o</u>nly

◉ Selected objects and <u>a</u>ll their contained objects

<u>C</u>ategory   ☑ <u>P</u>lanned

Hardware: Maintenance (Planned)   ⌄

Co<u>m</u>ment

Duration

◉ <u>N</u>umber of minutes: 60   ⬍   (5 minute minimum)

○ <u>Sp</u>ecific end time: Wednesday 25   May   2016 11:08:04

These features are temporarily suspended for objects in Maintenance Mode:

- Rules and monitors
- Notifications
- Automatic responses
- State changes
- New alerts

               OK   Cancel

Figure 11.12: Configuring maintenance mode settings

3. When Maintenance Mode has been enabled on an object, similar to *Figure 11.13*, you'll see it goes into a **Not monitored** state and a wrench icon appears alongside its name. The Details pane will also contain information about the Maintenance Mode start and end times.

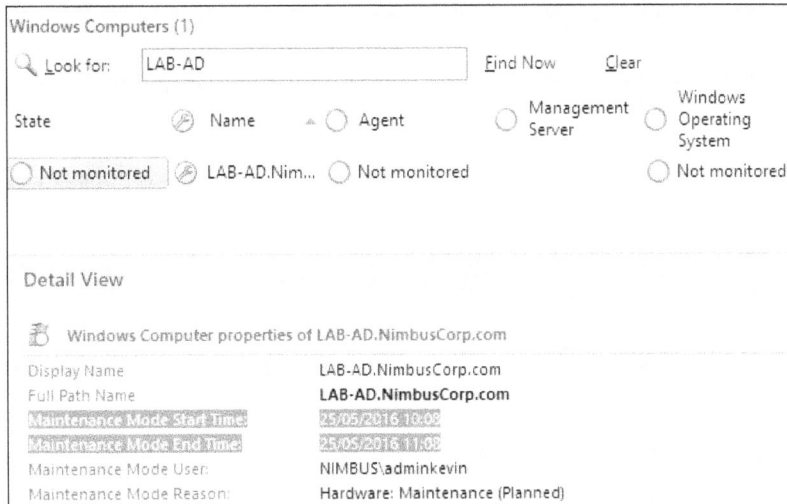

Figure 11.13: Viewing an object in maintenance mode

> If you'd prefer to use PowerShell to enable Maintenance Mode on your monitored objects, then you can use the `Start-SCOMMaintenanceMode` cmdlet. You can find some syntax examples and more information on this from the following link - `https://technet.microsoft.com/en-us/library/hh918505(v=sc.30).aspx`

Scheduling Maintenance Mode with OpsMgr 2012 R2

While manually enabling Maintenance Mode is a fairly straight-forward process, it's not really much use to you if you have automatic patching and reboot cycles on your servers that kick in late at night while you're at home or on vacation! It makes sense so, that you have an option to schedule the Maintenance Mode feature in OpsMgr to kick in whenever your organizations agreed maintenance windows are in place.

If you're using OpsMgr 2012 R2, then you won't find an option within the console to create and manage Maintenance Mode schedules. Although this is something that you'd think would be standard in any enterprise monitoring solution, for some strange reason, Microsoft decided to leave it out. Instead, you'll have to use a combination of custom OpsMgr groups, PowerShell, and Windows Task Scheduler to meet your requirements.

Far from this being an over-complicated scenario to achieve, two well-known community contributors (Pete Zerger and Matthew Long) have provided a complete PowerShell script that can target a group of objects in OpsMgr and place its members into maintenance mode for a given period of time. All you have to do is to create a scheduled task using Windows Task Scheduler that will execute the script at times that correspond to your maintenance windows.

This is one of my favorite solutions for scheduling Maintenance Mode in OpsMgr 2012 R2 and you can download the script directly from the following link - `http://tinyurl.com/opsmgrmmschedule`

> Cameron Fuller has written a post - `http://tinyurl.com/opsmgrmmremove` - where he demonstrates a single line of PowerShell to remove all objects from Maintenance Mode. This can be useful when the amount of time allocated to your maintenance windows changes and you need to bring everything back under monitoring sooner rather than later.

Scheduled Maintenance Mode in OpsMgr 2016

If you've deployed OpsMgr 2016 then Microsoft has thankfully given us an option to manage scheduled Maintenance Mode plans either through the console or with some new PowerShell cmdlets.

Follow these steps to create a new maintenance schedule with the OpsMgr 2016 console:

1. Open the **Administration** workspace, right-click on **Maintenance Schedules** and select **Create Maintenance Schedule** from the resulting menu as shown in *Figure 11.14*.

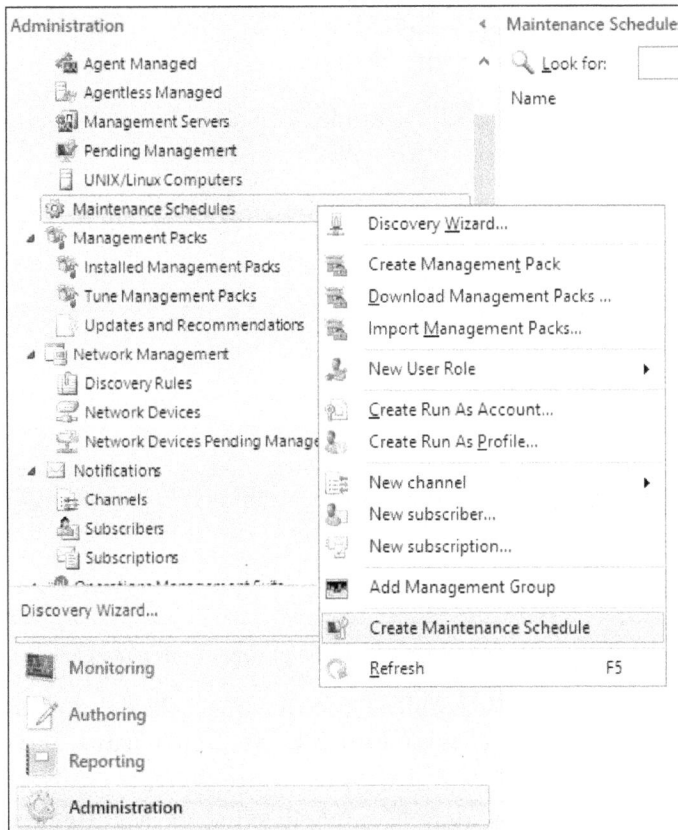

Figure 11.14: Creating a maintenance schedule in OpsMgr 2016

2. At the **Create Maintenance Schedule** wizard, select an option for the **Apply to** section, and then click on the **Add/Remove objects** button.

3. The **Object Search** dialog box will populate the Computer class into the **Search for** menu by default and you can change this class to help you search for another monitored object or just leave it as-is. Search for and add the object(s) you wish to include in the maintenance schedule and click on **OK** to close the dialog box. Click on the **Next** button to move on.

4. Configure your required maintenance schedule similar to *Figure 11.15*, then hit **Next** to continue.

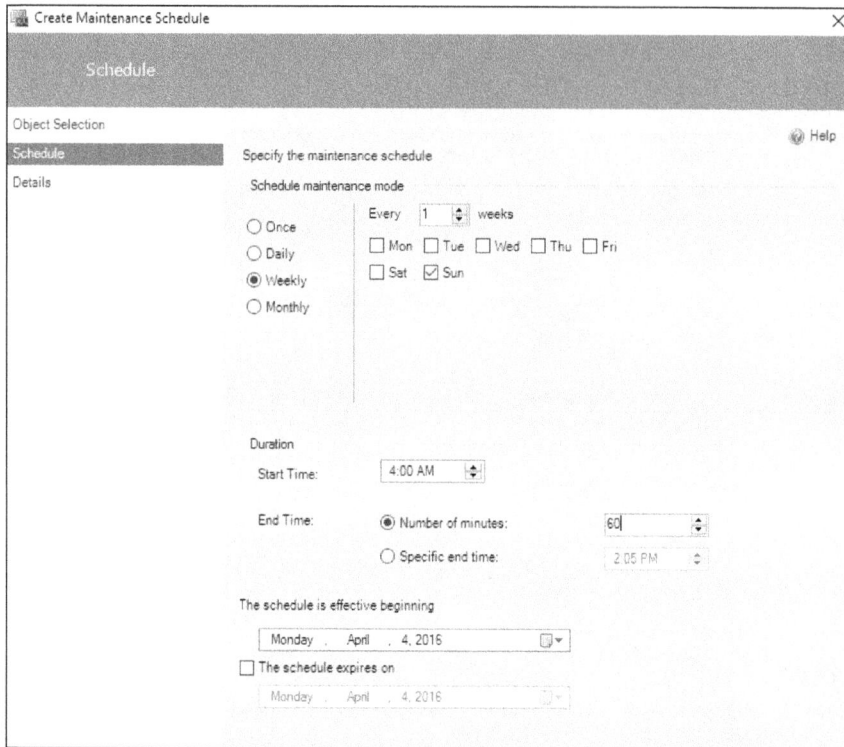

Figure 11.15: Configuring a schedule for your maintenance plan

5. At the **Schedule Details** window, type a name, select a category and add a comment before clicking **Finish** to close the wizard, and create the new schedule.

6. You should now see the new schedule listed in the **Maintenance Schedules** section of the Administration workspace as shown in *Figure 11.16*.

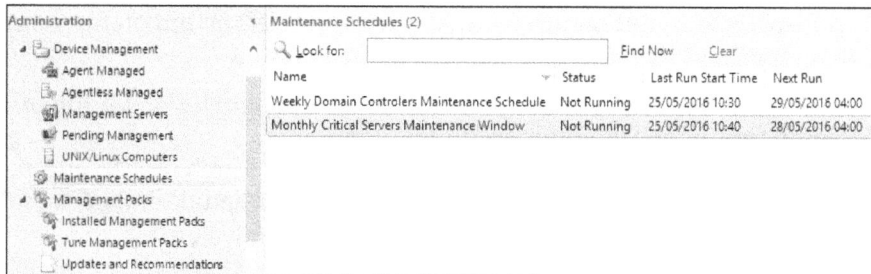

Figure 11.16: Configuring a schedule for your maintenance plan

7. You can disable, edit or delete schedules by using the relevant actions from the **Tasks** pane on the right.

> To create a new maintenance mode schedule with PowerShell, you can use the `New-SCOMMaintenanceSchedule` cmdlet (`http://tinyurl.com/opsmgrnewmmschedule`). If you need to manage an existing schedule, then use `Edit-SCOMMaintenanceSchedule` (`http://tinyurl.com/opsmgreditmmschedule`)

Using SQL queries for maintenance

One of the most visited blog posts related to OpsMgr on the internet has to be Kevin Holman's 'Useful Operations Manager SQL Queries' post - `http://tinyurl.com/kholmansqlqueries`. Originally written for OpsMgr 2007 but still fully relevant for later releases, this blog post contains a goldmine of SQL queries that you can use to carry out maintenance and troubleshooting tasks in your environment.

Over the years, I've probably used every one of those SQL queries but these are the ones I tend to re-use on a regular basis:

- Large table query
- Top 20 alerts in an Operational database, by repeat count
- Top 20 performance insertions by perf object and counter name
- State changes per day
- Noisiest monitors changing state in the database in the last 7 days
- Find the rules collecting the most performance signature data in the database
- Find all groups for a given computer/object
- Set an individual agent back to Remotely Manageable
- Find a computer name from a Health Service ID

Make sure to bookmark the link to this excellent post in your favorites as the more familiar you get with OpsMgr administration and maintenance, the more you'll find yourself returning to it as a reference.

The Self Maintenance Management Pack

Like any well-oiled system, you should carry out regular maintenance tasks to ensure everything runs smoothly and for OpsMgr, Tao Yang (System Center MVP) has created the perfect management pack to ease the burden of maintaining your management servers. His OpsMgr Self Maintenance Management Pack has evolved through a number of iterations since its original release in 2013.

If you haven't heard of this management pack before (or if it's not yet imported it into your management group), then take a few minutes to download the latest version from Tao's website here - `http://blog.tyang.org/`. At the time of writing, version 2.5.0.1 is the most up to date release of the management pack and the amount of time and effort Tao has put into developing this free community resource is nothing short of remarkable.

In *Figure 11.17* you can see an example of some of the useful maintenance tasks included in this management pack, one of which is the **Backup Management Packs** task. This could be used an alternative to the Unsealed MP Backup for OpsMgr solution we mentioned earlier in this chapter.

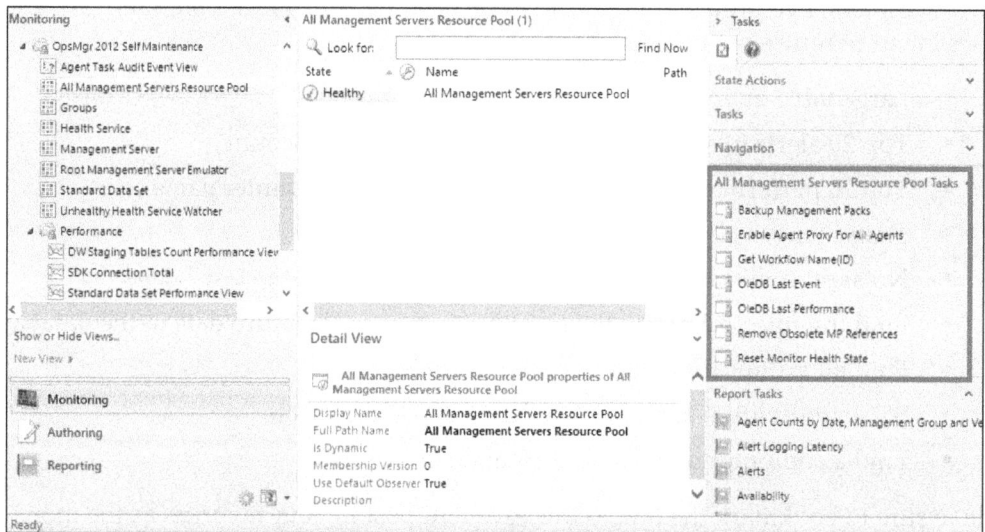

Figure 11.17: Using Tao Yang's OpsMgr Self-Maintenance management pack

If you've been busy deploying agents into your management group, then the Enable Agent Proxy for All Agents task is another maintenance solution that might come in handy as a quick way to bulk-enable the Agent Proxy setting on all new agents at once.

There are workflows and tasks to help you check data warehouse retention values, view current Update Rollup patch levels for OpsMgr components, configure group health rollup monitors and even check heartbeats to your cloud-based **Operations Management Suite (OMS)** environments.

These are just some examples of how you can use this management pack to help maintain OpsMgr and with the accompanying documentation covering nearly 70 pages, you get a full overview of all the rules, monitors, discoveries, tasks, and views that it has to offer. If you want to get the best out of this management pack, then it's important that you take the time to read through the guide from front to back so you learn how to configure all the various maintenance options at your disposal.

Database grooming and maintenance

A key maintenance task for OpsMgr environments is ensuring the size of the databases is kept under control. This requirement can be achieved through understanding how data retention is configured and managed for both the Operational database and the Data Warehouse database. Data retention settings are defined to let OpsMgr know how long each database should hold onto information related to the different monitoring datasets. These settings will also have a direct effect on the size of your backup jobs and ongoing storage requirements.

Operational database free space requirements

Microsoft recommends that the Operational database should always have at least 50% free space available to support growth and indexing. This requirement refers to the amount of free space inside the database file itself and not on the volume that hosts the database.

A nice visual way to check the free space of a database is to launch the **Disk Usage** report from the SQL Management Studio tool as shown in *Figure 11.18*.

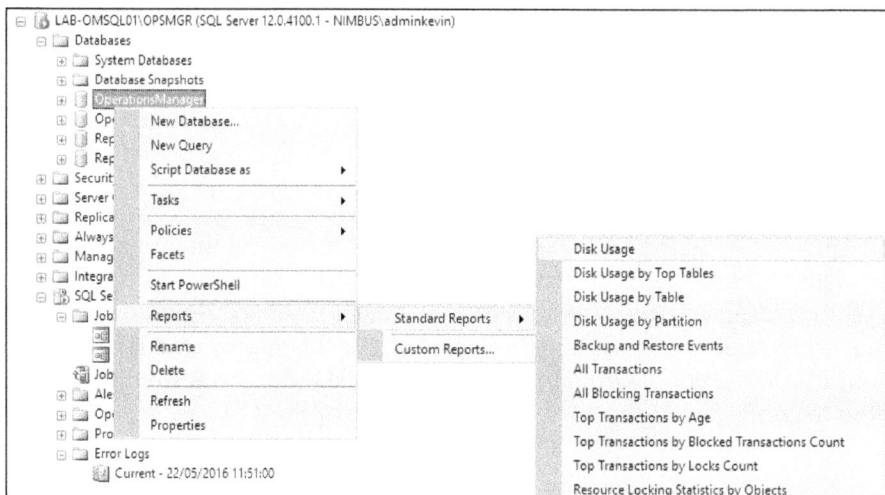

Figure 11.18: Launching the SQL Disk Usage report on a database

When the report launches, you'll be presented with a view similar to *Figure 11.19* where you can see an exact breakdown of how disk space inside the data files and transaction logs is distributed.

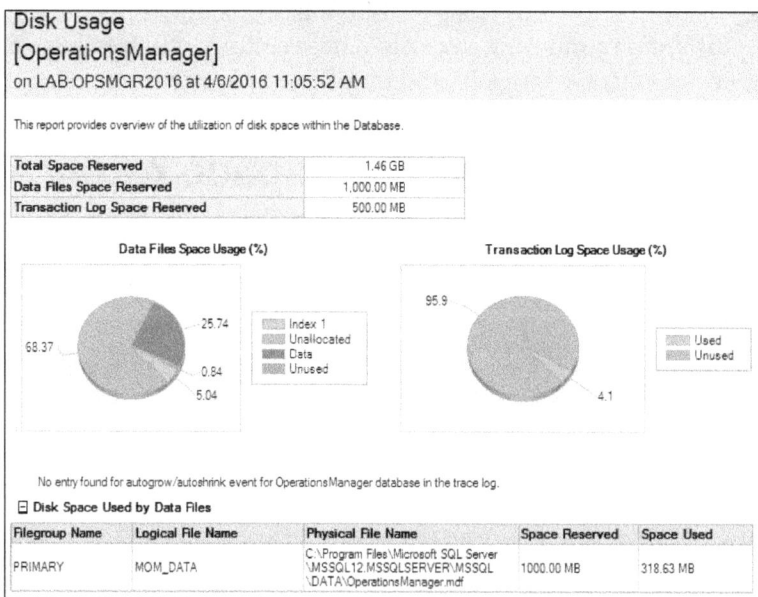

Figure 11.19: Viewing the Disk Usage report on a database

If the free space inside the Operational database drops below 40%, the self-monitoring **Operational Database Space Free (**%**)** monitor will automatically kick-in to alert you that the database is running out of space. This alert is shown in *Figure 11.20* and it will detail the amount of free space currently available along with some information about how to resolve the issue.

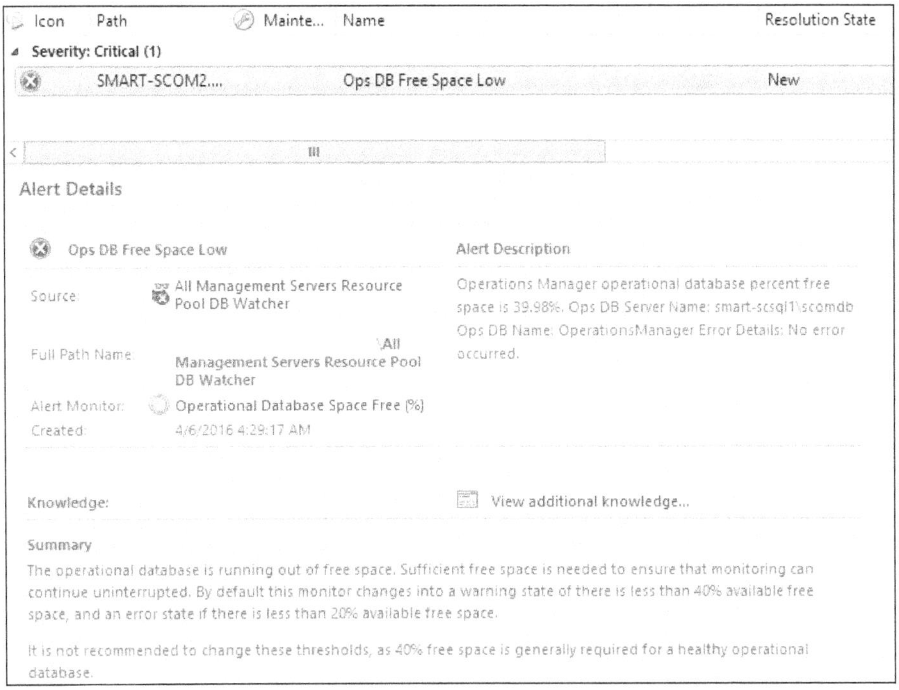

Figure 11.20: Self-monitoring alert for Operational database free space

A common cause of the Operational database disk space getting used up quickly is if you've under-sized it initially during installation and then later add a large number of new agents or management packs. When you see this alert you have two options – either increase the size of the database or perform some database grooming to remove unnecessary monitoring data and reduce the size.

Unless you've sized the database incorrectly to begin with – remember to always use the OpsMgr Sizing Helper tool discussed in *Chapter 1, Introduction to System Center Operations Manager* - then we do not recommend increasing the size of the Operational database and instead prefer the database grooming method discussed in the next section to regain control of the space.

In SQL, there's a feature called **Autogrow** that can be enabled or disabled on every database and the Operational database has this feature disabled by default. This setting should always remain disabled for the Operational database - ignore any DBA that tells you otherwise!

The reason for this is that in the event of a large amount of data being passed to the database, with Autogrow enabled, the Operational database will continue to grow at a rapid pace until your logical disk is full and OpsMgr stops working.

Grooming the Operational database

The process of configuring data retention settings is known as **Database Grooming** and for the Operational database; this can be configured from within the Administration workspace of the console.

Here's how to configure Operational database grooming:

1. Open the Administration workspace; select **Settings** from the navigation pane, then double-click on **Database Grooming** as shown in *Figure 11.21*.

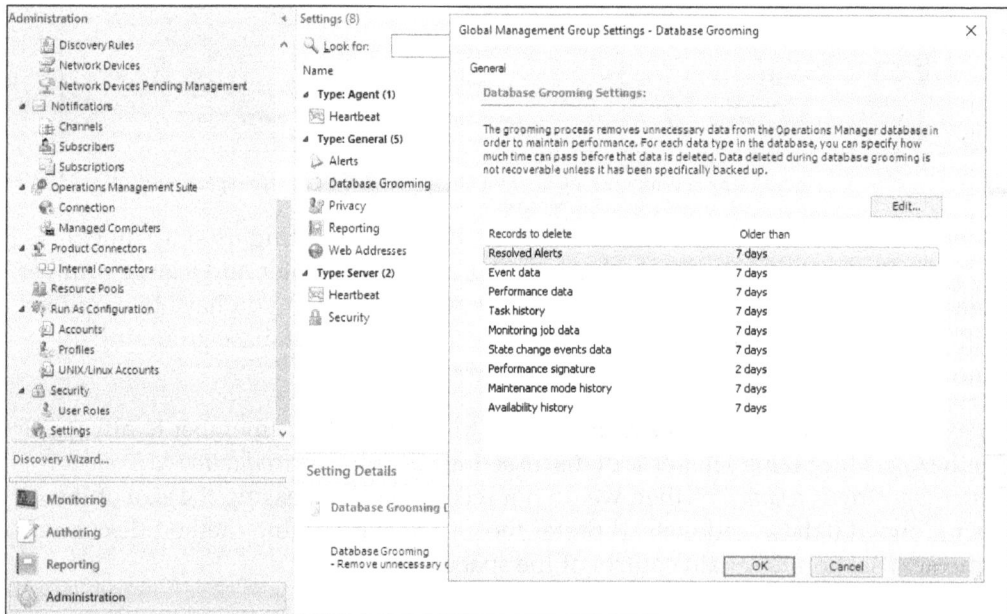

Figure 11.21: Configuring grooming on the Operational database

2. By default, all datasets are configured with a data retention setting of 7 days – the only exception being Performance signature, which has a setting of 2 days. Select a dataset that you want to edit from the **Records to delete** column and click on the **Edit** button.

3. Modify the number of days for the **Older than** value and click on **OK** to close the dialog box. Repeat this step for any additional datasets that you want to modify and when you're done, click on **OK** to close the **Database Grooming** dialog box.

> To maintain optimal performance within the console and keep disk space usage for SQL to a minimum, it's not recommended to extend the data retention value of any of the Operational database datasets beyond the default 7 days. You should only use this grooming process for reducing the retention days of datasets that are less important to your organization.

The new database grooming settings you configure in the Administration workspace will be applied automatically at 12:00 AM every day when the **Partitioning and Grooming** rule kicks in. Shown in *Figure 11.22*, this rule is targeted at the **All Management Servers Resource Pool** class and it runs a workflow that sets the retention values you've previously specified.

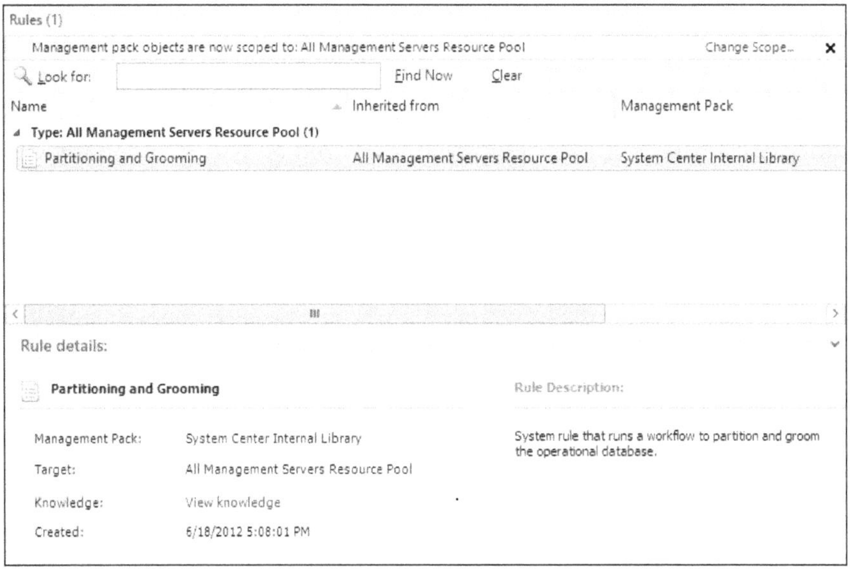

Figure 11.22: Built-in partitioning and grooming rule

> Microsoft's Kevin Holman has written an excellent deep-dive post on how the **Partitioning and Grooming** rule works including a very handy tip on how to quickly reduce the size of the Operational database using the `EXEC p_PartitioningAndGrooming` stored procedure. For more information, check it out here - `http://tinyurl.com/opsmgrdbgrooming`

Grooming the Data Warehouse database

The Data Warehouse database will likely be one of the largest SQL databases that most organizations will have to manage – mainly due to the fact that by default, it retains data related to every monitored object for up to 400 days! This monitoring information is stored in a number of different datasets and depending on the management packs deployed; each OpsMgr environment could have a different list of datasets. To add to the complexity, some of the datasets retain different aggregations (raw, daily and hourly) for the same type of data.

In the majority of cases, not all datasets and aggregations need to be configured with such long-term retention values and typically, engaging with your colleagues or customers in a discussion about their actual reporting requirements is a good way of understanding what needs to be retained short-term and long-term.

There's no option in the console to configure database grooming on the Data Warehouse database – instead you'll need to get familiar with the **Data Warehouse Data Retention Policy** (`dwdatarp.exe`) command line tool. Although some people might not be comfortable working with a command line tool, this is a much better improvement on earlier releases of OpsMgr – where you had to manually edit SQL tables to configure grooming and aggregation settings.

The `dwdatarp.exe` tool doesn't come bundled with the OpsMgr installation media and you'll need to download it from Microsoft's website here - `http://tinyurl.com/opsmgrdwdatarp`.

There's no installation required for this tool and these steps will walk you through grooming the data warehouse with it:

1. Copy the `dwdatarp.exe` tool to the SQL server hosting the OpsMgr data warehouse, launch a command prompt with administrative permissions and browse to the folder that you've copied the tool over to.

2. At the command prompt, type the following line (substituting it with your SQL server and instance names):

    ```
    dwdatarp.exe -s SQLSERVER\SQLINSTANCE -d OperationsManagerDW > c:\
    dwoutput.txt
    ```

3. As shown in *Figure 11.23*, a newly generated text file outputting the current retention settings should now be available at the path you specified.

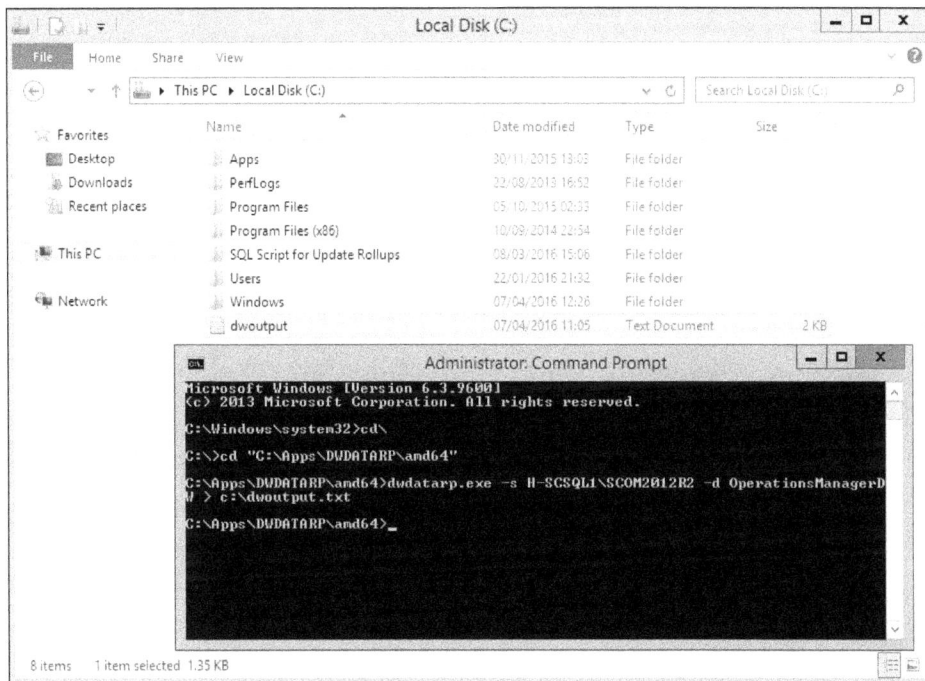

Figure 11.23: Creating a data retention and aggregation output file

4. When you open the output file you'll be presented with a list of datasets along with their aggregation type, maximum retention age and current size within the database. In *Figure 11.24* you can see the output settings of the common datasets in our data warehouse database - notice the **Hourly Aggregations** for Performance and State data are the two largest datasets in the database.

```
                                     dwoutput - Notepad                    _  □  X

File   Edit   Format   View   Help

Dataset name                  Aggregation name      Max Age    Current Size, Kb
----------------------------  --------------------  -------    --------------------
Alert data set                Raw data                 400        29,744 (  0%)
Client Monitoring data set    Raw data                  30             0 (  0%)
Client Monitoring data set    Daily aggregations       400            32 (  0%)
Configuration dataset         Raw data                 400       371,800 (  1%)
Event data set                Raw data                 100     3,786,288 ( 14%)
Performance data set          Raw data                  10       737,696 (  3%)
Performance data set          Hourly aggregations      400    10,191,152 ( 38%)
Performance data set          Daily aggregations       400       455,520 (  2%)
State data set                Raw data                 180        72,080 (  0%)
State data set                Hourly aggregations      400    10,583,904 ( 40%)
State data set                Daily aggregations       400       398,608 (  1%)
```

Figure 11.24: Viewing retention and aggregation settings

5. At this point you should be having a conversation with your customer or colleagues to discuss the best retention policy for each of these datasets. When you have an agreement on the number of days to retain data for each set, return to the command prompt again and browse to the folder that the dwdatarp.exe tool is located.

6. Armed with the information from your discussion about how long to retain each dataset, type the following command (you will need to update the server and dataset name along with defining a numeric value for the agreed number of days you wish to retain the data for):

    ```
    dwdatarp.exe -s SQLSERVER\SQLINSTANCE -d OperationsManagerDW -ds
    "Performance data set" -a "Hourly aggregations" -m 90
    ```

7. Repeat this step for each dataset that you wish to modify the retention for and when you're finished, it's a good idea to create a new output file a day or two later so you can compare the values and ensure the dataset sizes have reduced.

> For a deeper dive into using the Data Warehouse Data Retention Policy tool, check out Kevin Holman's post here - `http://tinyurl.com/kholmandwgrooming`

Deploying update rollups

A common ongoing maintenance task you will have responsibility for is deploying the latest update rollups that Microsoft release for OpsMgr. Update rollups comprise bug fixes, enhancements to existing features and sometimes they even introduce new features and capabilities. Usually, Microsoft releases a new update rollup three or four times a year and it's definitely a good idea to keep your management group updated on a reasonably regular basis.

The process for deploying update rollups to OpsMgr has stayed the same for the past few years and you have a choice of using Windows Update for automatic download and installation or you can just manually download the update and install it yourself. Although you might be tempted to just use the Windows Update option, you'll need to be aware that once the update bits have been deployed to the various OpsMgr roles, you still need to manually complete additional steps (run some SQL scripts and import new management packs) to complete the process.

It's our preference to usually wait a few weeks after the initial release of an update rollup before putting it into production as this lets the rest of the world test it out first and avoids any nasty bug surprises. When we're happy the update rollup is stable, we then take a read through the online documentation for the update before heading over to Kevin Holman's blog (`https://blogs.technet.microsoft.com/kevinholman/`) and manually deploying the new rollup following his detailed step-by-step blog posts. He always has the inside track on anything that might catch you out when deploying these updates and you can't go wrong if you follow his advice every time a new update rollup becomes available.

Troubleshooting common OpsMgr issues

With the best will in the world and no matter how well you manage your OpsMgr environment, there's inevitably going to be times when you run into problems. In the following sections we'll show you some management packs, tools and reports that can be used to aid troubleshooting and we'll also cover a few of the more common issues that you might encounter.

Working with the Operations Manager management pack

A lot of people working with OpsMgr tend to underestimate the usefulness of one of the very first management packs that gets deployed into their management groups during installation – the Operations Manager management pack.

This management pack is an excellent starting point to go to when you're having problems with any of your management servers, gateways, agents and even network devices. In *Figure 11.25* you can see the abundance of views and dashboards it offers to help gain a better understanding of the health and performance of your monitoring environment.

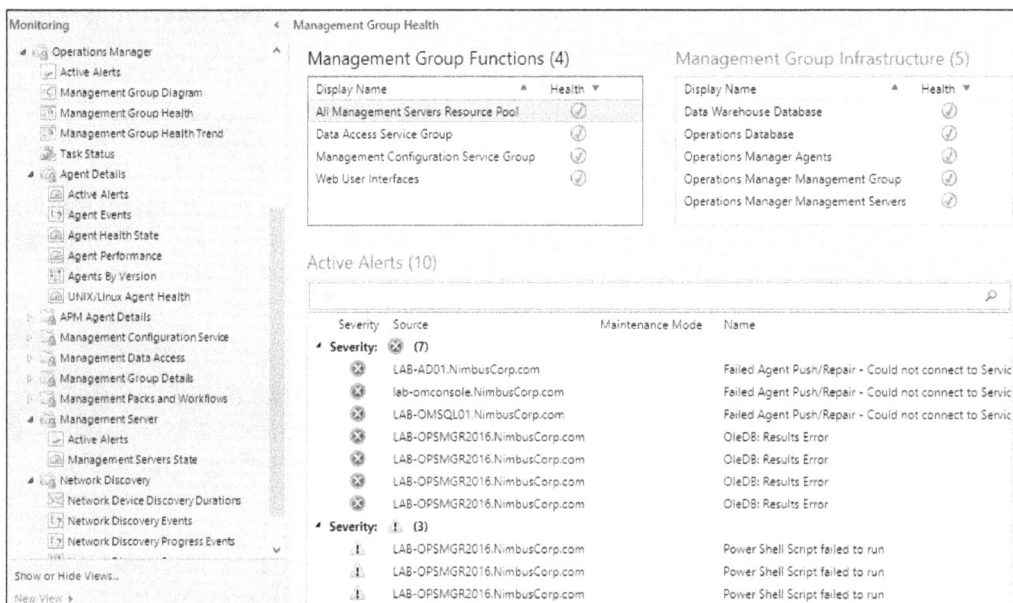

Figure 11.25: The Operations Manager management pack

Introducing System Center Internal Task Library

If you've ever encountered the problem of incorrect health states on roll-up monitors when using the Health Explorer or a diagram view, then you'll appreciate what the System Center Internal Task Library management pack can do for you.

An incorrect health state for a roll-up monitor typically means that the parent roll-up monitor shows an unhealthy state but the child monitors are all healthy – similar to the roll-up monitor shown in *Figure 11.26*.

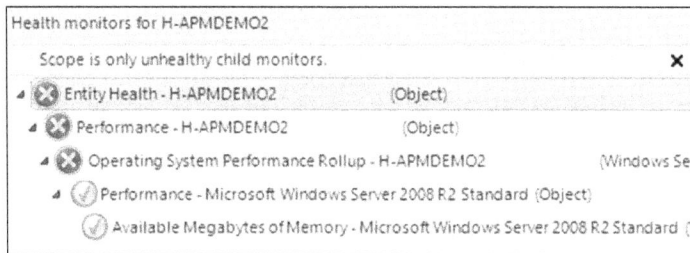

Figure 11.26: Incorrect roll-up monitor health state

Putting the object into Maintenance Mode for a few minutes is a workaround that normally resolves this problem. However, if you import the System Center Internal Task Library management pack from the `SupportTools` directory on your OpsMgr installation media (shown in *Figure 11.27*), then you'll have access to some new tasks in the console, one of which will help you resolve the incorrect roll-up monitor problem without using Maintenance Mode as a workaround.

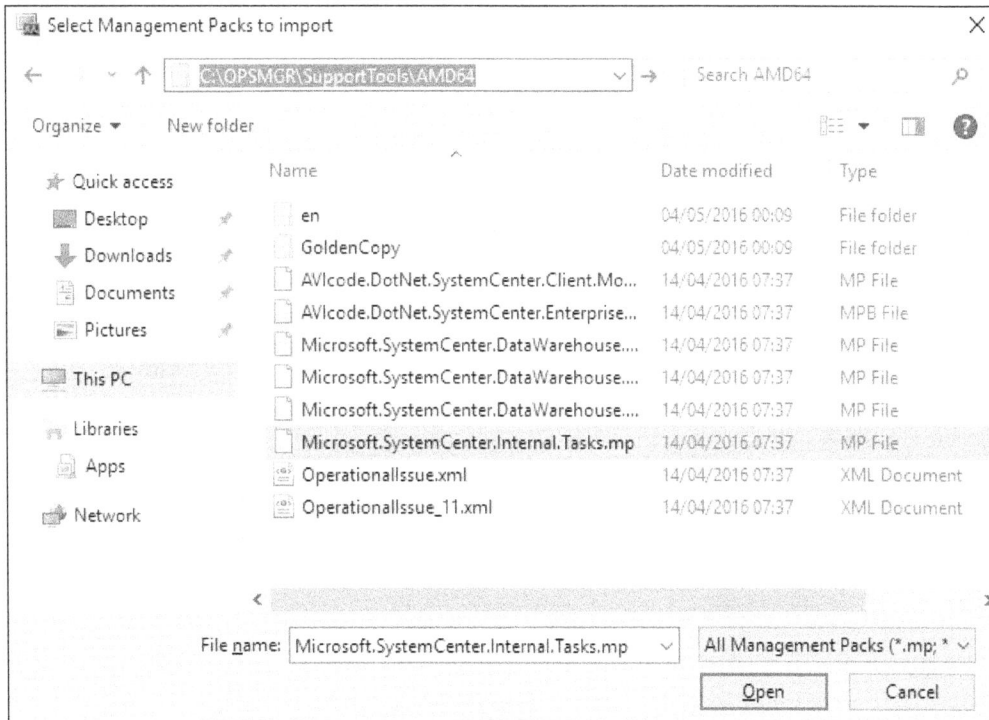

Figure 11.27: Importing the Internal Task Library management pack

In *Figure 11.28* you can see the four new tasks this management pack has to offer and the highlighted **Resubmit local cache state change events** task can be run against the entity that contains the incorrect roll-up monitor, which should then force a recalculation of its health state and return the monitor to its proper state.

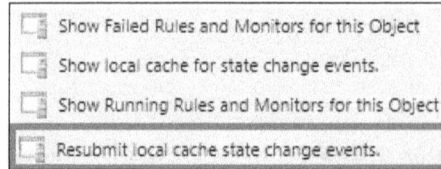

Figure 11.28: Tasks in the Internal Task Library management pack

Microsoft's Daniel Mueller wrote a detailed post on this management pack a few years back that contains additional information and examples for the other three tasks. Check it out here - `http://tinyurl.com/opsmgrfixrollup`

Agent troubleshooting

Agents are the lifeblood of your monitoring environment as they tirelessly work behind the scenes – constantly querying monitored computers and passing all that useful data back to the management servers so it can be easily consumed as alerts and dashboards in the console. If an agent stops communicating with OpsMgr (and the monitored computer is still online), you'll need to understand where to go to get it back online sooner rather than later.

Gray health states

When an agent stops communicating with OpsMgr you will usually see from the console that it has changed to a gray health state with the icon and health display name also showing its last known state before the communication problem (shown here in *Figure 11.29*).

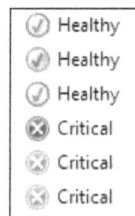

Figure 11.29: Gray state agents showing their last known health

The first and most obvious thing that you'll want to check when you notice a gray state agent is to confirm that the computer is actually powered up and contactable across the network (a quick Ping check will do for this). You should also confirm that the Microsoft Monitoring Agent (`healthservice.exe`) is still installed on the computer and that the agent control panel applet is present and has the correct references for your management group.

If the agent is still installed, open the Operations Manager log in Windows Event Viewer on the computer and then restart the Microsoft Monitoring Agent service. This should generate a number of events in the log that might point you to a reason why communications are down.

You should also check to confirm that TCP port 5723 is still contactable on the management server from the agent. Use a **telnet** command to check this port is open and also verify there are no firewall devices blocking communication of this port.

Clearing the agent cache

When you've worked through all of the obvious steps to try and get the agent to communicate again but it still remains in a gray state, it's time to clear the agent cache and force it to request a new configuration in the same way it would after the agent has been installed initially.

Here's how you can clear the agent cache:

1. Logon to the server that has the gray state agent, launch the `services.msc` snap-in and stop the Microsoft Monitoring Agent service (HealthService).

2. Now use Windows Explorer and browse to `C:\Program Files\Microsoft Monitoring Agent\Agent\Health Service State` and delete the `Health Service Store` folder, as shown in *Figure 11.30*.

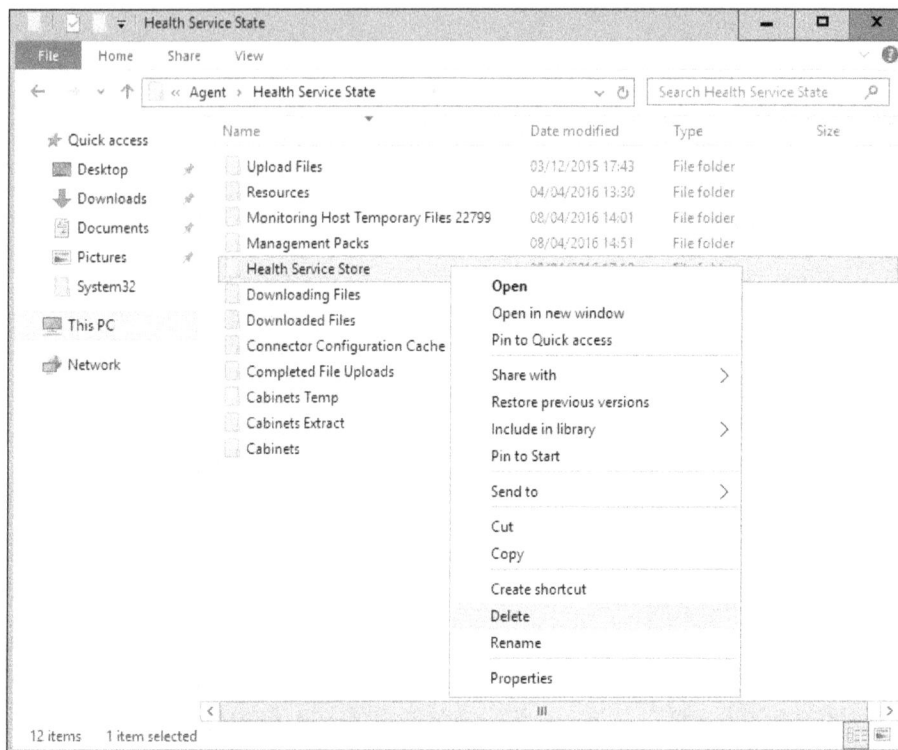

Figure 11.30: Clearing the agent health cache

3. When you've deleted the folder, restart the Microsoft Monitoring Agent service again and the Health Service Store folder will be recreated with newly requested configuration. Check the Operations Manager event log again as the agent is restarting and you should see events indicating the gray agent come back to life and has started to communicate.

> Microsoft has put together a very useful article for troubleshooting gray health states on agents with a number of different scenarios and solutions to work from. You can get more information from this link - `https://support.microsoft.com/en-us/kb/2288515`

Using the HSLockdown tool

From time to time we come across agent communication problems when the Microsoft Monitoring Agent is deployed to domain controllers and even after working through all of the steps we've previously mentioned, the agent still remains in a gray state.

A common reason we've found for this is related to the Local System account that the OpsMgr agent normally uses for monitoring the domain controller. This account can sometimes be denied access (depending on security hardening policies) and to resolve the issue we need to use the **Health Service Lockdown** (**HSLockdown**) tool that comes bundled as part of the agent installation.

You can use the HSLockdown tool to check if the local system account is blocked or not and if it is, then you can also use it to enable access again so the agent can continue monitoring. Follow these steps to verify access has been blocked:

1. On the domain controller with the gray agent state, launch a command prompt with an account that has administrative access and browse to `C:\ Program Files\Microsoft Monitoring Agent\Agent`.

2. Type `hslockdown /L` and hit *Enter* on your keyboard to get a list of all the accounts that are allowed and denied. As you can see in *Figure 11.31*, the **NT AUTHORITY\SYSTEM** account is denied access and this is what's causing our gray agent state.

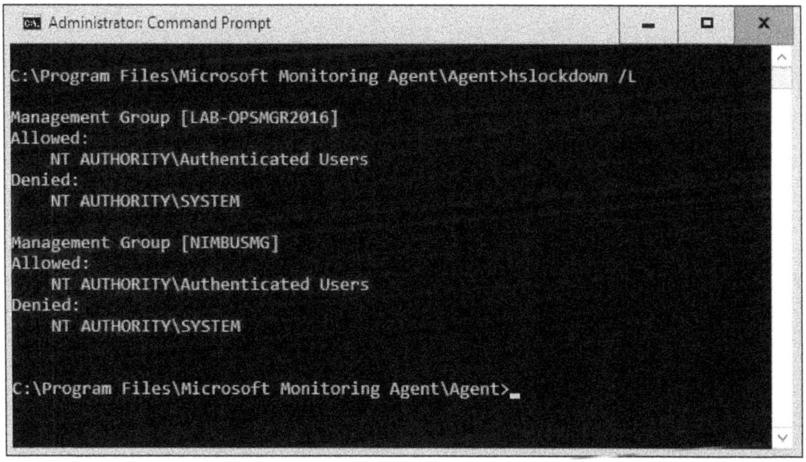

Figure 11.31: Using the HSLockdown tool to view permissions

3. To grant this account permission for monitoring, type `hslockdown /A "NT Authority\System"` and hit *Enter*. In *Figure 11.32* you can see that this account is now granted permissions to communicate and you are prompted to restart the health service to apply the changes.

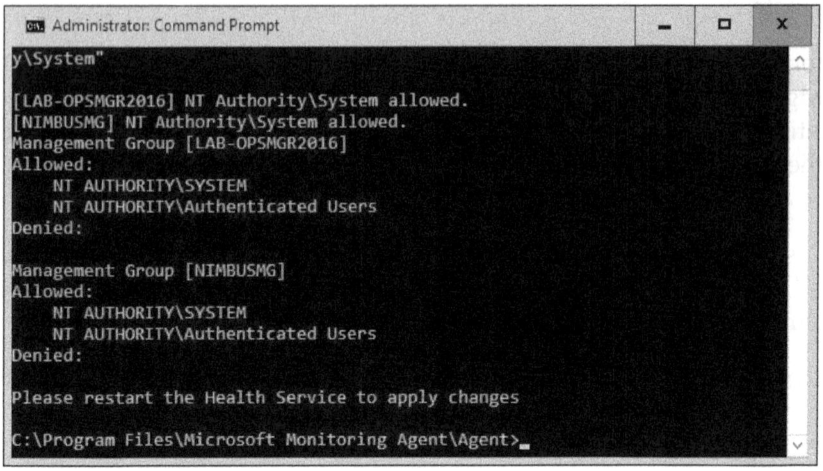

Figure 11.32: Granting permissions with HSLockdown

4. When the agent restarts it should come out of a gray state and return to normal (you may need to refresh your console view to see the new health state).

Useful troubleshooting reports

When troubleshooting issues with your OpsMgr infrastructure, it's useful to have a look over some of the default reports in the Reporting workspace, which target the management group, databases and agents - as they can contain a lot of useful information that might otherwise take you a while to track down manually.

Some examples of useful database troubleshooting reports can be found in the **Microsoft Data Warehouse Reports** folder shown in *Figure 11.33*.

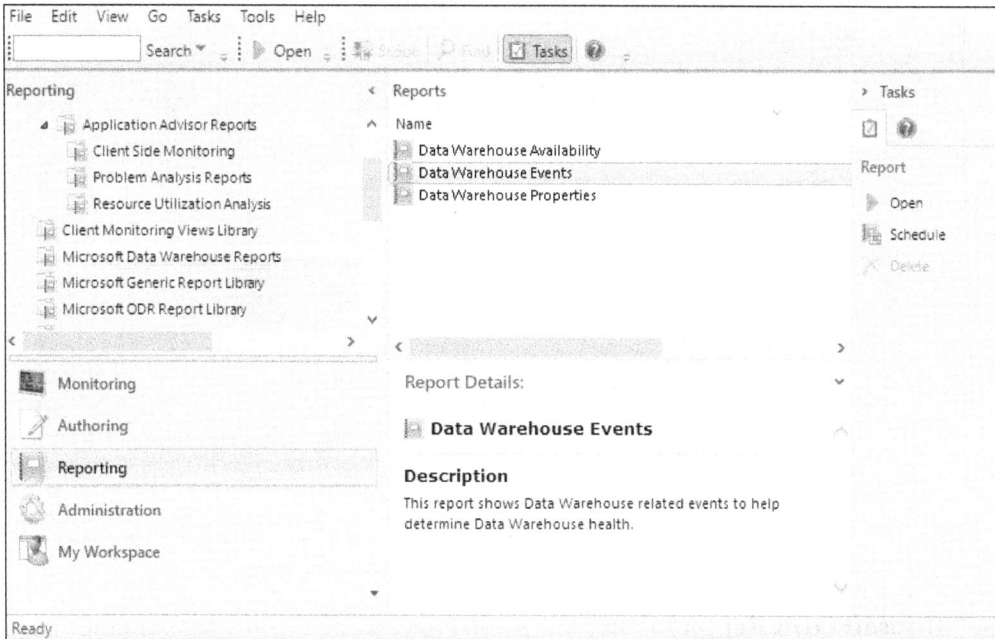

Figure 11.33: Data warehouse reports

The availability and events reports are self-explanatory and provide information that can be used to assist with outages and performance problems. The **Data Warehouse Properties Report** shown in *Figure 11.34* gives you a handy breakdown of the various datasets hosted within the database.

These are the same datasets we worked with earlier when grooming the data warehouse with the `dwdatarp.exe` tool.

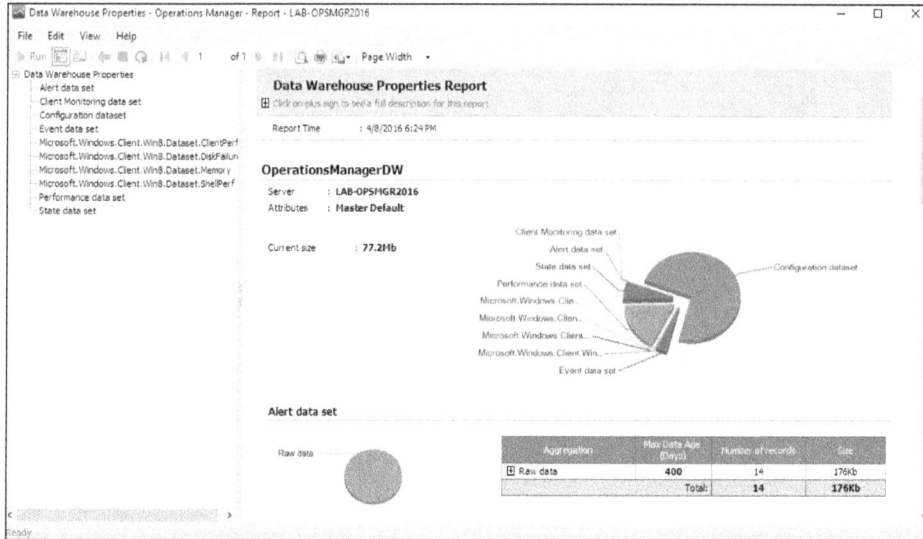

Figure 11.34: Viewing the Data Warehouse Properties report

The **Microsoft ODR Report Library** shown in *Figure 11.35* contains some other useful reports based around alerts, management pack versions, overrides and management group information.

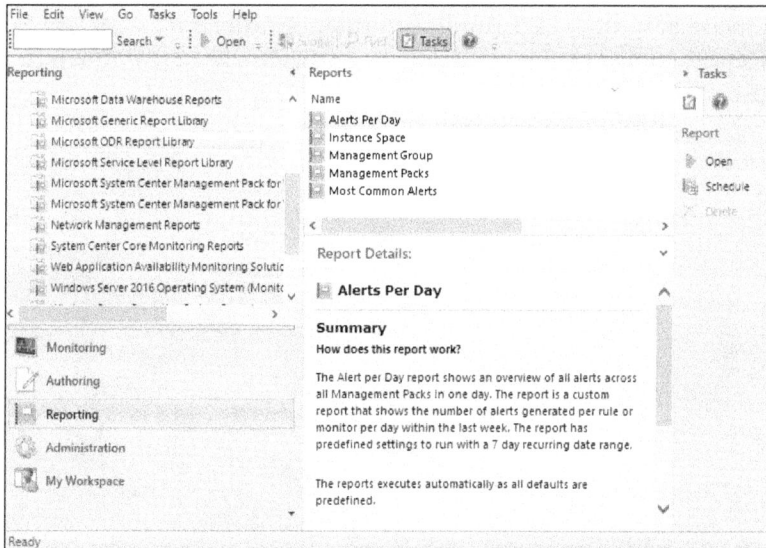

Figure 11.35: Microsoft ODR Report Library

Finally, the **System Center Core Monitoring Reports** library shown in *Figure 11.36* is where you can go to get information about agent count and health states, management pack data volumes and the amount of data generated by workflows and instances.

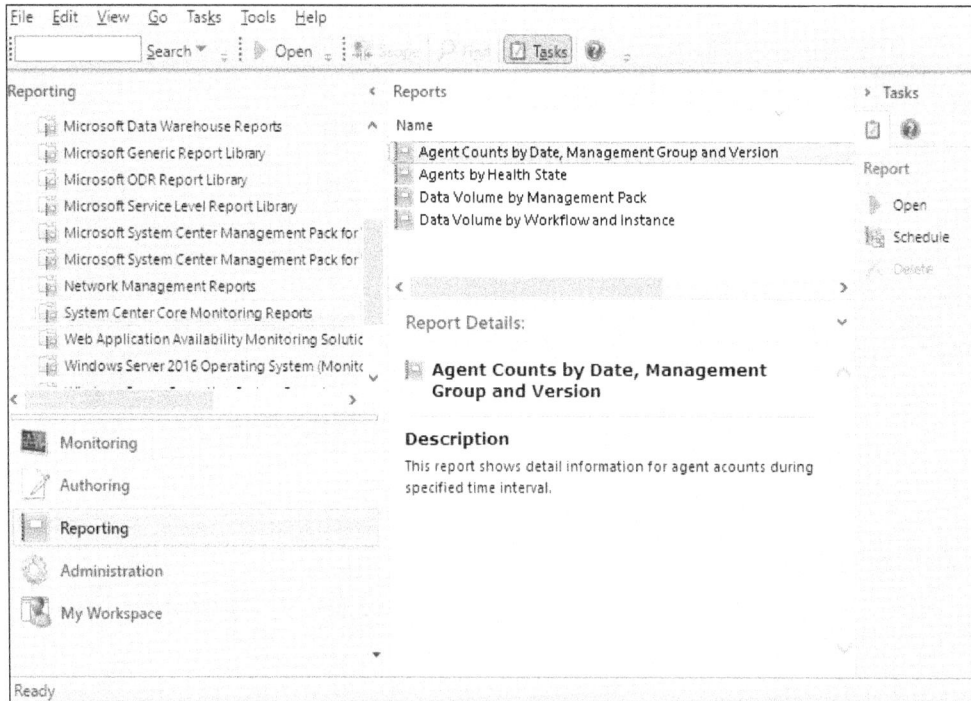

Figure 11.36: System Center Core Monitoring Reports library

The **Agent Counts by Date, Management Group and Version** report shown in *Figure 11.37* is beneficial in larger organizations when you're trying to get a handle on the number of agents that are running an older version and which could ultimately cause communication problems.

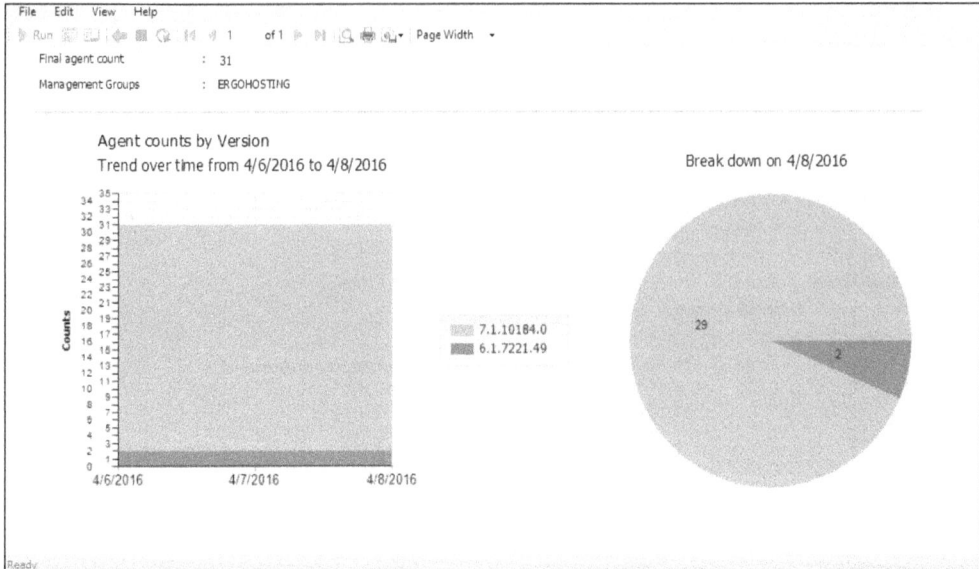

Figure 11.37: Agent Counts by Date, Management Group and Version report

Summary

At the beginning of this chapter, you learnt how to back up the OpsMgr databases, unsealed management packs and other important files. We then demonstrated how to perform a database recovery from backup due to an existing corrupt database.

We gave you an understanding of how Maintenance Mode works and walked through what you need to know for configuring maintenance schedules in both OpsMgr 2012 R2 and OpsMgr 2016.

You learnt how to configure data retention settings for the Operational database using the console and the Data Warehouse database using the Data Warehouse Retention Policy tool.

Towards the end of the chapter, we discussed some useful management packs, tools and reports that can be used to aid troubleshooting and we also walked you through resolving some common issues that you might encounter.

Index